Theory and Practice
of the Social Studies

EARL S. JOHNSON

PROFESSOR OF THE SOCIAL SCIENCES

THE UNIVERSITY OF CHICAGO

NEW YORK *The Macmillan Company*

© *The Macmillan Company 1956*

Printed in the United States of America

First Printing

Library of Congress catalog card number: 56-7312

To Esther

ACKNOWLEDGMENTS

To Louis Wirth, whose untimely death cut short the career of a brilliant and dedicated scholar and left me bereft of a dear friend and wise counselor, I owe the encouragement to undertake the writing of this book.

To my former dean, Morton Grodzins, through whose kindness I was relieved of administrative and teaching duties, I acknowledge my gratitude. These duties were assumed by my colleagues, Kermit Eby and Maynard Krueger, to whom my thanks are gratefully given.

To John R. Seeley, my former student and severest critic, I owe thanks for his critical reading of Chapters I and II. I have also to thank my colleague Benjamin Bloom and Maynard Krueger for helpful suggestions on Chapters XVII and XXV, respectively.

To my colleagues in The College of the University of Chicago I am indebted for permission to quote from their study, *Teaching by Discussion in the College Program*. I wish also to thank my colleague, Joseph J. Schwab, for his kindness in permitting me to quote from his unpublished paper, "Eros and Education: A Discussion of Discussion."

To my sister, Mrs. Homer Livergood, I owe thanks for helpful suggestions on the literary form of many chapters.

To the students in my course on the teaching of the social studies over the past fifteen years I wish to express my sincere appreciation for their criticism and forbearance. I also wish to express thanks to many teachers of the social studies in the public high schools and junior colleges of the city of Chicago, as well as to those at the Francis W. Parker School of Chicago and several of the public high schools of the Chicago metropolitan area, for their loyal co-operation in the role of critic teachers of my student apprentices. My association with these teachers has taught me many things.

To the following publishers and authors I gratefully acknowledge my thanks for their permission to reprint:

The American Council on Education for use of Albert W. Levi, *General Education in the Social Studies* (copyright 1948).

The American Sociological Society for use of Herbert Blumer, "Moulding of Mass Behavior Through the Motion Pictures," in *Human Problems of Social Planning* (copyright 1935).

The *Atlantic Monthly* for use of Sir Richard Livingstone's "The Road Ahead," November, 1948.

Gateway Books for use of John Dewey, *The Public and Its Problems* (copyright by John Dewey 1946).

Harcourt, Brace and Company for use of Frank H. Knight, "Fact and Value in the Social Sciences," in *Science and Man*, edited by Ruth Anshen (copyright 1942).

Harper & Brothers for use of Frank H. Knight, *The Ethics of Competition* (copyright 1936).

Harper's Magazine for use of Bertrand Russell, "The Function of the Teacher," June, 1940.

Harvard University Press for use of Margaret Mead, *The School in American Culture* (copyright 1951).

Henry Holt and Company for use of William James, *Talks to Teachers* (copyright 1910); John Dewey, *Human Nature and Conduct* (copyright 1921); and John Dewey, *Reconstruction in Philosophy* (copyright 1937).

Alfred A. Knopf, Incorporated for use of Walter Bagehot, *Physics and Politics* (copyright 1948).

The Macmillan Company for use of Alfred N. Whitehead, *The Aims of Education* (copyright 1929) and John Dewey, *Democracy and Education* (copyright 1916).

The National Council for the Social Studies for use of Robert Redfield, "Research in the Social Sciences: Its Significance for General Education," in *Social Education*, December, 1941.

W. W. Norton and Company, Incorporated for use of Bertrand Russell, *The Scientific Outlook* (copyright by Bertrand Russell 1931; published by The Free Press, Glencoe, Illinois, under license from W. W. Norton and Company, Incorporated).

Oxford University Press of London, England, for use of Sir Fred Clarke, *Foundations of History-Teaching* (copyright 1929).

Rinehart and Company, Incorporated for use of Erich Fromm, *Man for Himself* (copyright 1947) and *Escape from Freedom* (copyright 1941).

Rutgers University Press for use of Lawrence K. Frank, *Society as the Patient* (copyright 1948).

The Saturday Review for use of Wallace Stegner, "A Lens on Life," April 22, 1950.

Charles Scribner's Sons for use of Charles H. Cooley, *Human Nature and the Social Order* (copyright 1902), and *Social Organization* (copyright 1923); Report of the Commission on the Social Studies, *Conclusions and Recommendations* (copyright 1934); and Peter Finley Dunne, *Mr. Dooley at His Best* (copyright 1938).

The University of Chicago Press for use of Charles E. Merriam, *What Is Democracy?* (copyright 1941); George H. Mead, *Mind, Self and Society* (copyright 1934) and *The Philosophy of the Act* (copyright 1938); Frank H. Knight,

"Socio-Economic Organization," in *Second-Year Course in the Study of Contemporary Society, Syllabus and Selected Readings* (copyright 1934); Charles Newcomb, "Graphic Study of Urban Population," in *Second-Year Course in the Study of Contemporary Society* (Social Science II), *Syllabus and Selected Readings, 7th Edition* (copyright 1938); and "The Distribution of Some Selected Social Phenomena," *Third-Year Course in the Study of Contemporary Society* (Social Science 3, formerly Social Science II) (copyright 1942).

The estate of H. G. Wells for use of H. G. Wells, *The Undying Fire*, published by The Macmillan Company, Limited of London, England (copyright 1919).

Yale University Press for use of Gilbert Lewis, *The Anatomy of Science* (copyright 1926).

INTRODUCTION

An image of goodness and wisdom. I have approached the writing of this book with what I trust is true humility but not without some fear. My humility, about which I ought not to write too much lest it be suspect, springs from the great obligation which such a task entails and the limitations of my own knowledge. The fear has two origins. It springs first from "the austerity of print" and second from the nature of our time, in whose darkened air the images I hold of both teacher and student as persons of goodness and wisdom can hardly be seen with the clarity and boldness they deserve. Nevertheless, I am not daunted for I believe they are images of human beings possessed of the great virtue of critical loyalty to the democratic faith.

Furthermore, I should prefer to speak in your presence in order to be stimulated by it and to afford you the opportunity to speak back to me. But because this is impossible, I must trust what I have to say to the printed page.

The sociological approach. My approach is that for which my education as a sociologist and teacher in the social sciences has prepared me, however limited be my ability to apply my education and experience to the task which I have assigned myself. The political, economic, and cultural problems of our time fit into no watertight compartments. No bulkheads separate man's social experience. I take what I trust is pardonable pride in the belief that sociology, of all the social science disciplines, is uniquely fitted to approach these "synthetic problems."

Knowledge, theory, and art. This suggests the perspective taken in this book. I have sought to combine both substantive knowledge and theory in the social studies with the art of the teaching of them. In that, I have undertaken to offer something akin to a garment for the teacher to wear, the fabric for which is woven on the loom of science and art.

The separation of the science of social things from the art of teaching them, in the education of teachers of the social studies, confronts our pro-

fession with a long-time and grievous problem. Without substantive knowledge we have no reliable warrant for what we know, and without an acquaintance with the method of inquiry and social theory we have no guide
for teaching except routine born only of trial and error. I trust that my attempt, throughout this book, to show the indispensably mutual relation
between theory and practice has been done with balance, good sense, and
to the profit of all those who may read and use it.

Not only task-oriented.   Furthermore, as teachers, we can never know
as much as we ought to, but it is my belief that the scope, relatedness, and
richness of our knowledge should and can be greater than that which we
teach. In this view, I believe that an education for teachers must be more
than a merely task-oriented one. This is not to say that we need less education in the practice of our art. Rather, I mean to stress the interdependence of theory and practice, or the science and art of our field. The fact
that I name certain of these terms first does not mean that they are more
important than those I name second. The great need is for both, in whatever order they are named.

A context of general education.   Hence, I have undertaken to offer something in the nature of a general education in the social sciences and, within
that context, to deal with the teaching of the social studies. This means
that nothing I have written here is taken by me to be extraneous to the education of prospective teachers, those now teaching, curriculum directors,
administrators, and any layman who may wish to read one man's view of
what the social studies are and what he believes is involved in the teaching-
learning of them. I have cast my net wide.

I should now like to share with you the logic of the sequence of the
twenty-eight chapters into which my work is divided. Each group of chapters and, to some degree each chapter, may be treated as an independent
unity. Both the groups and the individual chapters may, however, be viewed
in terms of a continuity. Thus both the division and the unity of labor in
the art of teaching-learning in the social studies is identified.

My attempts to show the transition between chapters and their many
interrelations will, I trust, find their rewards in helping you see the book
in terms of both its parts and the ways in which they are related. I should
have no quarrel with anyone who wished to change the order in which the
chapters are used.

Student, teacher, and the "climate" for teaching-learning.   Chapters I
through IV treat the student and teacher as coagents and the climate of
teaching-learning. Chapter I seeks to set before you a conception of the
kind of human being fit for and able to contribute to the making of a demo-

cratic society, both of which are good and wise; Chapter II deals with what I have called "the therapeutic climate" for teaching-learning; Chapter III treats the facts of permanence (continuity) and change (discontinuity) in human affairs and in the lives of individuals; and Chapter IV discusses what is perhaps the most difficult and vexing problem which faces the teacher of the social studies. Chapters III and IV also provide the context for conceiving the teacher of the social studies in the dual role of priest and prophet.

Modern society: how and how well it works. Chapters V through VII are concerned with a description, analysis, and appraisal of modern society of which every local community is not only a part but, in many respects, a *counterpart*. Chapters V and VI treat the contemporary community—descriptively and analytically—from various aspects while Chapter VII undertakes an ex parte appraisal of how well our society works.

The social studies and general education. Chapters VIII and IX discuss general education. Chapter VIII focuses on the problem of the integration or articulation of the various phases of social knowledge and offers a kind of case study of one of the most serious gaps in secondary education, namely that between "liberal" and "vocational" curricula. Chapter IX seeks to show the relation between the social, humane, and "natural" studies.

Attitudes—their nature, place, and change. Chapters X and XI deal with the formation and change of attitudes and their place in the experience of learning. Chapter X conceives of them as the ultimate focus of all the social studies, while Chapter XI shows the "middle position" of attitudes (taken as synonymous with the making of valuations) between perception and conduct.

The method of inquiry. Chapters XII and XIII describe the method of inquiry and the relation of science to moral matters. Chapter XII defines inquiry and gives three illustrations of its use. Chapter XIII discusses the relation of the method of intelligence to the making of moral decisions.

Teaching-learning—its psychology, structure, aims, and evaluation. Chapters XIV through XVII treat the psychology and the structure of the teaching-learning act, a philosophy of aims, and the task of testing and evaluating. Chapter XIV, shows the relation of the method of inquiry to the psychology of teaching-learning, while Chapter XV shows the limitations of the stimulus-response psychology, how the psychology of "the dynamic self" gives structure to the teaching-learning act, and describes the cycle of romance, precision, and romance. Chapter XVI treats the concept and importance of "student needs" and seeks to offer a general philosophy of aims. Chapter XVII focuses not only on what students learn but also on how well they are taught. A distinction is made between testing and evaluating and the technique and the philosophy of each are treated.

Communication, discussion, and transfer of learning. Chapters XVIII through XX are concerned with three phases of teaching-learning which are common to the entire range of inquiries into human affairs. Chapter XVIII deals with what is commonly referred to as "semantics," although that word is not used in the discussion, and with the person-to-person phase of communication. Chapter XIX identifies discussion as the most difficult form of communication and offers both a theory and a plan for conducting discussion. Chapter XX deals, through a wide range of illustrations, with what is usually referred to as "the transfer of learning." It takes account of the problem of "individual differences" (as do other chapters) and distinguishes between the *affective* and *effective* phases of learning, with which Chapter XIX also deals.

The social process approach. Chapter XXI provides a common matrix or frame of reference for relating the needs of individuals and the needs of society and serves as a preface to the next five chapters.

Five perspectives on human affairs. Chapters XXII through XXVI offer and develop, with many illustrations, five perspectives on human affairs. Chapter XXII focuses on the teaching of United States history, world history, and the study of comparative cultures. Chapter XXIII discusses social problems as problems of social policy which, by their nature, involve a conflict of values, and provides a comprehensive outline for teaching about that conflict. Chapter XXIV provides both a general framework for and many illustrations of the teaching of Civics. The Constitution, civil liberties, and the civic phase of students' group associations are given special emphasis. Chapter XXV sets forth the limitations of economic theory for teaching in the secondary school, and offers an outline for the teaching of the economic approach to human affairs which is adaptable to several grade levels. Chapter XXVI undertakes to bring the geographic and ecological approaches together and illustrates how they may be used in community study.

Understanding the Community. Chapter XXVII discusses how students may go out into the community by means of field trips and how some important symbols of community life may be brought into the classroom. Among these are motion pictures, the radio, and the newspaper. These symbols are conceived as instances of mass media and are treated, not only as "aids to instruction," but as cultural objects worthy to be known in their own right. Current events and propaganda analysis are also treated.

The New Disciplines. Chapter XXVIII brings the book, full circle, back to a consideration of the democratic character through a discussion of the nature of the disciplines of imagination, precision, appreciation, and synthesis.

The high school and junior college. Although the book takes account chiefly of the high school and junior college levels of instruction, a great deal of it has immediate relevance and usefulness for the elementary and intermediate grades. If you will take appropriate account of the selective process which tends to winnow out the less able and ready learners as the levels of instruction advance, especially from the high school to the junior college, you will be able to make distinctions in your use of the book which I have not undertaken to deal with specifically.

A "summit conception." Furthermore, in discussing various aspects of teaching-learning in somewhat ideal terms, I am fully aware that ideal conditions seldom—if ever—exist. Again, in this respect, I have confidence in your ability to allow for exceptions. My choice lay between something approaching a "summit conception" of teaching-learning and trying to deal with the many exceptions to it. Here, again, I am confident that you will discover the degree to which such a conception requires modification in your day-to-day tasks. "Art is long and time is fleeting." Classes are often too large, individual differences confront and baffle us daily, and problems in instruction and "discipline" continually present new faces. These facts, among many others, require the modification of theory which is not, nor was ever intended to be, a composite of practice. Of such things I am fully aware but, despite their presence and weight, have offered nothing in the way of "recipes." My faith lies in your dedication to a task and the practice of *good* common sense.

Quotations and footnotes. Finally, a brief comment on my use of quotations and footnotes, of which there are a considerable number. In defense of my citing the sayings of social scientists and philosophers I call Emerson as my witness: "Some men's words I remember so well that I must often use them to express my thought. . . . I perceive that we have heard the same truth, but that they have heard it better." The footnotes serve two purposes: (i) to credit those whom I quote or to whose writings I owe ideas and insights, and (ii) to cite readings and make practical suggestions which I believe are appropriate and helpful. I have noted only those sources with which I am personally acquainted and none of the footnotes are added as academic adornments.

EARL S. JOHNSON

Homewood, Illinois

CONTENTS

*Theory and Practice
of the Social Studies*

CHAPTER I

The Democratic Character

The supreme end of education. The supreme end of education in a democracy is the making of the democratic character. My use of the term "making" intends, however, to give no comfort to an "assembly line" conception of education. It is not a matter of technique in which a teacher, conceived of as an active agent, "does something to" a student conceived of as a passive agent. It presumes that there are democratic characters in our society who wish to see the preservation of democracy and who wish to give an opportunity for other democratic characters to arise who will, in turn, make for the further preservation of democracy, and so on through all the generations of time.

A character theme. The great definitions of education which have come out of western social thought have a character theme.

It was Pestalozzi, child of the Enlightenment and precursor of the philosophy of pragmatism, who wrote:

> The material with which the educator works . . . is man himself, the masterpiece of Creation. It is man whom the educator must understand—man in his full scope and power. . . . The Teacher must be capable of watching man's development, whatever direction it may take, whatever the circumstances. No profession of earth calls for a deeper understanding of human nature, nor for greater skill in guiding it properly.

In the nineteenth century, John Ruskin and Ralph Waldo Emerson expressed much the same view of education. Ruskin's view was:

> You do not educate a man by telling him what he knows not, but by making him what he was not. Education is a moral experience and so teaching is a moral act. The entire object of a true education is to make people not merely do the right thing, but enjoy the right thing; not merely industrious but to love indus-

1

try; not merely learned but to love knowledge; not merely pure but to love purity; not merely just, but to hunger and thirst after justice.

Emerson believed:

The great object of education should be commensurate with the object of life. It should be a moral one: to teach self trust; to inspire the youthful man with an interest in himself; with a curiosity touching his own nature; to acquaint him with the resources of his mind, and to teach him that there is all his strength, and to inflame him with a piety toward the Grand Mind in which he lives.

From the great and noble-minded of our own time I choose Alfred North Whitehead and Albert Schweitzer. For Whitehead the purpose of education "is to stimulate and guide self-development," and for *le grand docteur* it is to engender "a reverence for life." In the light of these definitions, how mean and petty is the view that education is for personal power, for popularity, for something called success, or for wealth.

The image of goodness and wisdom. In these definitions and many others from minds as perceptive and dedicated, I find a dominating image. This is the image of goodness and wisdom. In that image the democratic character is made. Making it is the task of education in a democracy. It is that image of the self which the teacher must glorify. To that image this book is dedicated.

But about the self we hear very little. We hear much about my car, my house, my investment and, from students, my grades. It is tragic that much teaching is concerned more with what is around us than with what is within us—with what we hold title to rather than with what we are. The tragedy is that the inner environment is more immediately available and more intimately knowable, for we now have ways of following Plato's injunction to "know thyself" which did not exist in his time. Your task as teacher will be to help the student effect a *transaction* between an inner and an outer environment. You may help him effect this transaction by teaching him how to settle some issue, relieve some anxiety, fulfill some desire, or satisfy some curiosity. In its largest dimensions teaching is helping young people to inquire into the nature of their own mind and purpose which is discovered by their learning what is good and wise *to mind* and *to purpose*.

From these two related aspects of man's nature—goodness and wisdom —teaching in a democracy takes its instructions. These require that the teacher help young people translate knowledge into right conduct, which is the product of goodness and wisdom. The thing to do with an idea, said

Whitehead, is "to prove it—that is, prove its worth." Knowledge is not given by the teacher to be given back. It is given to be lived by.

Man's dual capacity. This dual capacity of man to love and to think is not a fault in him. It is the true account of his bivalent nature. He is capable of being passionate and he is capable of being reasonable. He may treat of matters of sentiment and matters of fact: things *possible* and things *actual,* with what might or should be and with what is.[1] If you deal with only one of these capacities you will deal with but half-men.

It is not required that either passion *or* reason dominate man's life. What is required is something akin to the rule of goodness under the regency of wisdom in which the passions are instructed and disciplined by reason and reason is informed by passion. In a world which is disposed to overvalue science there is much fear of the unthinking man. I should be equally fearful of the unfeeling man.

Loving and thinking. The goodness of the democratic character is revealed in its capacity to love a set of ideals, the Great Oughts of the democratic faith. Its wisdom is revealed in its capacity to think how these ideals may be protected and advanced. These two capacities are combined in *homo sapiens,* man wise, and *homo faber,* man maker—that is, maker after the image of the productive, the creative, and the working character. Thus the democratic character is the product of the interplay of loving and thinking, believing and reasoning. In these terms I speak of the teacher's image of the student as one which combines goodness and wisdom.

Character and individuality. My conception of the democratic character is moral and intellectual individuality. If I understand him rightly, it is akin to Jefferson's conception of equality. He wrote that all men "are created equal," not that they *are* equal. I understand him to mean that they are, by virtue of being human, eligible for equal *opportunity* of *access* to moral and intellectual individuality. I do not mean, and I am sure that Jefferson did not mean, that equality or individuality could be had without the help of others. If that were his thought I do not understand his concern to establish a government dedicated to the provision of the democratic climate.

But Jefferson's equality, or my individuality if you will permit me, has undergone a degradation. In the process it has come to mean the interchangeability of every man for every other. This is a denial of individuality which is equated with *difference,* not with indifference. If every man were

---

[1] See Ernst Cassirer, *An Essay on Man: An Introduction to a Philosophy of Human Culture* (Garden City, N.Y.: Doubleday & Company, Inc., 1953), "Facts and Ideals," pp. 79-86.

interchangeable with every other man it would make no difference to him whether he were himself or someone else. In that event he would be indifferent to his character. Indeed, he would be without character.[2]

The individuality of which I speak and which I take to be the moral and intellectual goal of teaching not only permits but requires that each of us be peculiarly and uniquely ourselves; that is, it demands a somewhat distinctive and unique interpretation and expression of a common fund of knowledge and ideals. Lately, however, to be peculiar, unique, or distinctive has come to be taken as synonymous with being *dangerous* because each of us does not respond to the economic, political, and cultural symbols of our way of life in the *same* way—dangerous, if we seek to be not blindly loyal, but critically loyal to those symbols. In being critically loyal we run the risk of being called subversive.

Characters that are decently different. The thing which I fear most about our time is the view that we ought to be monotonously alike. This is contrary to my understanding of the democratic character which not only permits but expects each of us to be decently different. My image of the teacher is one who seeks to help young people become, not monotonously alike, but decently different. But, in doing that, you must heed Emerson's injunction: "Don't make the student another you, one's enough." As I understand equality or individuality, then, they do not denote that kind of mathematical or physical identity of either goodness or wisdom any one element of which may be substituted for any other. They denote, rather, an effective regard for whatever is distinctive and unique in each of us, irrespective of physical or psychological inequalities.[3]

The components of the democratic character—goodness and wisdom— interact to give it the characteristics of being a working, a productive, and a creative one. This is, I suppose, what Aristotle had in mind when he spoke of "a working of the soul in a way of excellence." [4] It was likewise in Carlyle's thought that "a man perfects himself by working."

What character is. I wish now to examine what we mean by character, and leave—for the time—the discussion of the productive, the working, and

[2] Two essays by John Dewey have had much to do with shaping my thinking in these matters. They are "Mediocrity and Individuality" and "Individuality, Equality, and Superiority," in *Character and Events*, Vol. II (New York: Henry Holt & Co., Inc., 1929).

[3] See John Dewey, *The Public and Its Problems* (Chicago: Gateway Books, 1946), p. 151.

[4] Aristotle speaks of two excellencies, the intellectual and the moral: "pure science, intelligence, and practical wisdom" and "liberality and perfected wisdom" (*Ethics*, 1103a). In order to escape the dualism of Aristotle's thought, I choose to combine them into a single image of the self.

the creative type. In his *Talks to Teachers,* William James wrote, "your task is to build up a *character* in your students; and a character . . . consists in an organized set of habits of reaction." These, in turn, consist "of tendencies to act characteristically when certain ideas possess us, and refrain characteristically when possessed by other ideas." [5] As I understand him, James meant that if we do not act characteristically, that is, on the basis of an organized set of habits of reaction, we act whimsically, capriciously, unreliably. He also seems to mean that habits discipline us *not* to act, as well as to act. Thus they permit us to discriminate between inappropriate or wrong behavior and appropriate or right behavior. They permit us to "hold fast to an idea" which, James said, is the essence of the moral act.

James's discussion of habit is in his chapter on "The Will." Dewey's discussion of habit appears in chapters entitled "The Place of Habit in Conduct" and "Habits and Will." [6] But neither James nor Dewey is speaking of habit as reflex but rather as attitude or disposition to act. Dewey makes this explicit when he writes that for habit we may "also use the words attitude and disposition." For him "character is the interpenetration of habits" or attitudes, an interpenetration which is, however, never total. The term "habit," disposition, or attitude refers to that kind of human activity which is influenced by prior activity, hence acquired or learned; which is a system of minor elements of action; which is projective, dynamic, and ready for overt manifestation and which operates in a subdued or covert form when it is not obviously dominating action. [7]

From this view we know that character is amenable to change: how much, in what specific characteristics, and by what exact methods for *this* person we still know darkly. Here lies the great frontier in teaching, in social work, in politics, in law, in employer-employee relations—indeed in the whole round of human affairs. Our faith lies in this fact: man is not only a creature of instinct. (Temperamental factors and differences in innate capacity are not to be denied as quite stable factors). Man is motivated, as well as "instinctivated." We know that we can reconstruct, reorder, and reorient the human character by both formal and informal methods of education into and through the adult years.

Erich Fromm's view of character types. But we need a more analytical

---

[5] New York: Henry Holt & Co., Inc., Copyright 1909, p. 184.
[6] *Human Nature and Conduct* (New York: Henry Holt & Co., Inc., Copyright 1921), pp. 14-74, are concerned with various aspects of habit. On page 44, Dewey writes of will as "something practical and moving" which "understands the body of habits, of active dispositions which makes a man do what he does."
[7] See Dewey, *op. cit.,* pp. 40-41.

and diagnostic, withal more descriptive, image of character. For this I turn to Erich Fromm whose book, *Man for Himself: An Inquiry into the Psychology of Ethics,* is one of the most perceptive pieces of writing we have on character formation and re-formation.[8]

In general agreement with the theories of James and Dewey, Fromm tells us that character is a complex or syndrome of traits which determines how one feels, perceives, and is disposed toward things and persons, including himself. The individual relates himself to persons through "socialization," a process with which we shall deal at length in later chapters.

Fromm identifies two kinds of character orientation: the nonproductive and the productive. I shall present a composite of each, based on Fromm's analysis.[9]

The *nonproductive* orientations:

(a) the receptive orientation: wishes to *be* loved but not *to* love; insists on rights with little disposition to be responsible; is very sensitive to any withdrawal or rebuff from one whose love is being sought; listens more than speaks; wants to be *given* information rather than work for it; finds it hard to say "No" because is caught between conflicting loyalties and promises; suffers paralysis of critical ability which disposes such a person readily to accept authority; is lost and helpless when alone; is generally friendly and optimistic as long as his "source of supply" of affection is adequate but becomes anxious when it is threatened.

(b) the exploitative orientation: is much like the receptive type but much more aggressive; takes things from others; will steal another's ideas; exploits others by using them as means to advance his own welfare; may even use force and cunning to do it.

(c) the hoarding orientation: is essentially different from (a) and (b) in that one has little faith in anything obtained from the outside world; finds security in hoarding and saving; tries to get love by possessing the loved one; tends to say "No" to the world; fears intimacy since, through it, something may be lost; is suspicious.

(d) the marketing orientation: puts emphasis on buying-and-selling or in "making a deal"; drives a hard bargain; is a "personality for sale"; is success-

[8] New York: Rinehart & Co., Inc., Copyright 1947.
[9] See pp. 62-107. I take full responsibility for the interpretation and digest which follows. Fromm is careful and precise in his remark that these character orientations are "by no means as separate from one another as may appear from this sketch . . . all orientations are part of the human equipment and the dominance of any specific [one] depends to a large extent on the peculiarity of the culture in which the individual lives" (p. 78). He remarks further that the four nonproductive orientations do not, necessarily, have the negative qualities ascribed to them (p. 77). He makes the necessary corrections by showing (pp. 112-117) that the different kinds of nonproductive orientations and the productive orientation are, in reality, blends rather than complete and separate entities. "In reality, we always deal with blends" (p. 112). Fromm is dealing with ideal-type constructs with which I shall also deal in later chapters. See Chapter III for a brief definition of an ideal type.

oriented, hence, is concerned with how "nice a package" one can make of himself; wants to be in demand, hence, gets his cues for morality from the outside; believes himself to be valuable if he is "successful," if not, believes he is worthless. This orientation makes for great insecurity since one's value is not due to his own human qualities but to his "saleability"; depends on others' appraisals, not his own; judges others, as well as himself, in terms of saleability; is willing to be interchangeable with others, hence suffers a loss of the feeling of uniqueness; this makes for superficial relations and induces a loneliness which cannot be cured by individual love; gets as much factual information as he can, not for its intrinsic value, but just to possess it; views others as he views himself, as commodities; plays a false role; is respectable if respectability is the "market demand."

In contrast with these nonproductive orientations, Fromm presents the *productive* orientation of character. Its characteristics are these:

. . . is spontaneous, rather than compulsive; is capable of creative productivity unless mentally and emotionally crippled; realizes his own power is not power *over* others in the possessive or exploitative sense, but power to break through the wall of the self—not the power of domination but of potency which is the power to be productive; has depth of perception; is capable of relating himself to others in a secure, genuine, and satisfying way; is able to appreciate and share himself fully with others; through genuinely productive thinking he seeks to get real understanding and in that attempt, he uses the methods of science.[10]

We now inquire, following Fromm, how loving and thinking are related in persons with a productive character orientation. Their relation may be stated as follows: the constituent elements of love are *care, responsibility,* and *respect* for persons, as well as *knowledge* of them.[11] This loving-thinking orientation may be held toward value objects other than persons, e.g., truth, justice, brotherliness—all the Great Oughts of the democratic faith. Indeed, the objectivity which science demands, requires that the user of it be motivated by a genuine interest in and affection for what he studies and that he genuinely care for it. Thus he will be disposed to perceive it as it is, rather than as he wishes it to be.

The task of character change is a difficult and involved one. More is involved in it than can be told in this place or indeed in this entire book. What it entails must, to a large degree, be left implicit. One thing we do know, however, and that is that the student cannot start from scratch. Learning is quite as much unlearning and relearning as it is learning afresh.

---

[10] See Max Wertheimer, *Productive Thinking* (New York: Harper & Brothers, 1945).
[11] "To respect a person is not possible without knowing him; care and responsibility would be blind if they were not guided by the knowledge of the person's individuality," Fromm, op. cit., p. 101.

The "nerve of failure." Your attempt at identifying wrong learning, getting your students to unlearn and relearn may result not only in great disappointment but even in failure. Because this is true, you must be realistic enough to cultivate what David Riesman calls the "nerve of failure." What this may steel you against was told by Plato in the Fable of the Cave.

In the account, Socrates is talking with Glaucon, or rather *to* him, as was Socrates' wont. He is telling of men chained from their childhood so they could see only the shadows cast by things; they could not see the things themselves. He is telling how one was released and permitted to stand up and turn his face to the light and toward real things, rather than their shadows. At this point he asks Glaucon,

> What answer would you expect him to make if someone were to tell him that in those days [when he was chained] he was watching foolish phantoms, but that now he is somewhat nearer to reality and is turned toward things more real and seen more correctly. . . . Would you expect him to be puzzled and to regard his old visions as truer than the objects now forced upon his notice?

And Glaucon answers, "Yes, much truer."

In the foregoing I have dealt with attitudes organized in the form we call the character. Although the term "habit" was used by both James and Dewey, neither meant by it reflex behavior; rather dispositions or attitudes. Character is the relatively permanent, yet changeable, way in which these dispositions are organized. It is, in sum, what Lasswell calls "the self-system of the person." [12]

Character change is not simple. But change in character cannot be properly conceived as simple, direct or swift. Change in character involves (a) change in *cognitive structure*, new ways of perceiving and hence new knowledge, (b) change in *valuation*, new dispositions or attitudes, and (c) change in *motor behavior*, new conduct. I shall discuss these changes and the experiences which they involve in Chapter XI.[13]

Commitment to the conception of teaching which I have set forth will confront you with the reality that the school is not an "action institution." By this I mean that it does not provide students with an opportunity, *under its auspices*, to experiment with changes in their character by participating in programs of social action. While there are minor exceptions to this principle, such as helping to "get out the vote," petitioning local

[12] See "Democratic Character" in *The Political Writings of Harold D. Lasswell* (Glencoe, Ill., The Free Press, 1951).
[13] See Kurt Lewin, *Resolving Social Conflicts*, Edited by Gertrud W. Lewin (New York: Harper & Brothers, 1948), pp. 56-68, "Conduct, Knowledge and Acceptance of New Values."

governmental bodies and voluntary organizations, and publicizing "Clean-up Week," you must be content to take changes in your students' conduct pretty much on the faith which is grounded on the evidence you may be able to get that their attitudes have changed. Attitudes, in being dynamic and projective, are the energy source and motivation for conduct.

Irrational and rational faith. It is my deepest conviction that the most significant and lasting aspect of change in character will be in the quality of your students' faith. Of it there are two kinds: irrational and rational. Irrational faith is faith in a symbol, person, or idea which does not result or flow from one's own experience of thought and feeling. It is based on submission to irrational authority, far beyond one's power to control.

Rational faith, on the contrary, provides the dynamics for creative thinking because it is faith in reason and a "rational vision." It is anchored in one's own experience and in confidence in one's own powers of observation, thought and judgment. It is the faith that an hypothesis may lead to a truer picture of reality, both personal and social, than we now possess. It is the faith that growth and maturity of character come from productive activity. It is faith in the method of intelligence.[14]

[14] Fromm, *op. cit.*, "Faith as a Character Trait," pp. 197-210. See also James Harvey Robinson, *The Mind in the Making* (New York: Harper & Brothers, 1921), pp. 14-29.

CHAPTER II

The Teacher as Therapist

The therapeutic climate. The teacher is one of the most important factors in the provision of what I think of as the therapeutic climate. This is a warm personal atmosphere in which students feel secure and free to express themselves according to their normal drives and impulses. It conduces to the expression of their real character. In the role of therapist, you will practice a layman's interpretation of a psychiatric theory of interpersonal relations, the purpose of which is to put your students in better relations with themselves through improving their relations with others, and equally or more, putting them in better relations with others by improving their relations with themselves.[1]

For the creation of such a climate I suggest quite modest and nontechnical means. You may use them almost "bare-handed" or, in the idiom of early adolescence, after the manner of "Look, Ma, no hands!"—but not without head and heart.

The need for it. The need for such a climate is great and immediate. There is abundant evidence that modern youth is deeply troubled. Probably never before have so many young people faced the task of making and maintaining a character under such adverse circumstances. The security which youth once got from the family and the neighborhood must now

[1] I choose the term "therapist" rather than "mental hygienist" because the former term connotes the role and influence of one who is kind and skillful, not only in allowing people to "be themselves" but also better selves. See Lawrence K. Frank, "The Historian as Therapist" in *Society as the Patient* (New Brunswick: Rutgers University Press, Copyright 1948). See also Harry Stack Sullivan, *Conceptions of Modern Psychiatry* (Washington, D.C., The William A. White Psychiatric Foundation, 1947), in which he makes clear that, in his view, psychiatry is not concerned with something called the "absolute personality" for "a personality can never be isolated from the complex of interpersonal relations in which the person has his being," *ibid.*, p. 5.

come, in large part, from their own efforts and the other than familial institutions and associations in which they live much of their life.

A recent study in an industrial-urban county in Ohio estimates that one in every five elementary school children showed evidence of poor mental health of some degree of seriousness and that large numbers were maladjusted to a degree so serious as to be in grave need of special guidance. Caroline Ware has told us that whenever the articulate and inquiring young people of New York's East Side expressed themselves, it was to stress the confusion rather than the order in their lives.

We know that knowledge without emotional balance will not only fail to grow into wisdom but will give power to impulses that may bring corruption and sorrow, destruction and defeat. We know that our students cannot be socially minded as long as they are mentally insecure and emotionally immature and hostile. We also know that intellectual difficulties often arise in emotional disturbances. Love alone or knowledge alone will not suffice. It will be your task to create the social climate in which feeling and thinking may interact.

In the following discussion I shall try to avoid using the term "the" teacher and "the" student, likewise "the" classroom and "the" school. Such references constitute what Whitehead called "misplaced concreteness." Each is a statistical fiction. When I use them I shall be making a general reference in which "the" stands for a kind of distillate of many different elements. This should not obscure the fact that the process of education is, basically, a process of communciation which takes place on student-to-student as well as teacher-to-student axes. It is a reciprocal process which involves everybody in the class, taken singly and collectively.[2]

The social studies class as a social system. Every social studies class is, *sui generis,* a social system. That is, it is a pattern and process of many statuses and roles. By status I mean the rights and obligations which both teacher and students have at any given time as person-student and person-teacher. By role I mean the manner in which a status is acted out. Role is the dynamic aspect of status. Insofar as a student's statuses and roles in the community of the classroom are fairly stable they may be said to dramatize his self-conception, or at least the one he manifests in a given class. This self-conception is always a mixture of his ascribed and achieved statuses. It gives him his place or position in the social system of a given classroom. This is manifest in who defers to him, to whom he defers, the esteem or prestige or lack of either with which he is held by his peers; his

2 See Nathaniel Cantor, *The Teaching-Learning Process* (New York: The Dryden Press., Inc., 1953), and *The Dynamics of Learning* (Buffalo: Foster and Stewart, 1948).

rights, prerogatives, obligations, and responsibilities. Insofar as a status is ascribed, it is assigned or given, whether warranted or not. Insofar as a status is achieved, it is earned, whether by genuine or false behavior. Each is, to some degree, always a mixture of his preoccupation as *person*, and his occupation as *student*. These two conceptions of the self may cause considerable conflict in the student, or they may get along well together.

Ascribed and achieved status. However much ascribed and achieved status are mixed, they tend to combine in such roles as the athletic hero or the second-team scrub, the *bon vivant*, the "guy who drives a hot rod," the grind, the bookworm, the lady-killer, the flirt, the arguer, the "sweater girl," the shy miss, teacher's pet, the "good fellow," the leader, and so on.[3]

As I have suggested, a student is always a student in terms of the way in which his ascribed and achieved status interact, whether to the end of agreement or conflict. The "individual differences" about which we hear so much are, in important ways, differences in character which the interaction of these two kinds of status produces. They are not, as some suppose, only differences in IQ, learning rate, or any phase of studentship, per se. Your success as a teacher will rest heavily on awareness of the way in which your students' ascribed and achieved status affect each other.

An imaginary class. Let us now look at a given class, a supposed one. It is made up of the following person-students: those from the "wrong side of the tracks" and those from "Elm Street" or "The Hill"; those whose fathers support the family by the use of their hands and those who support it by the use of their heads; the sons and daughters of those who borrow and those who lend; those who come from life circumstances with little or no margins of moral or material security and those whose parents, whether by chance, chicanery, inheritance, or honest effort have an abundance of moral and material surpluses; those with only a blurred picture of their career and those with a clear one; those who view the school as something only to be endured until they can get out of it and those who

[3] Ascribed and achieved status are capable of being treated separately only on a conceptual basis; they are *ideal types* which do not exist in reality. The ideal type is a standard heuristic device of the scientist, i.e., an arbitrary construct useful in analysis. Certain elements of reality are in it but it is not itself real. It is ideal in the logical, not the ethical sense. Such terms as "urban" and "rural," "layman" and "expert," "priest" and "prophet," "economic man," "man-in-the-street," "go-getter," and the like are ideal-type constructs. They help us distinguish between certain specific phases of reality. All ideal-type constructs are fictions, although very useful ones. I shall use them throughout this book. See Robert Redfield, "The Folk Society," *American Journal of Sociology,* LII, No. 4 (January, 1947), for an excellent treatment of the ideal-type construct. For an exhaustive treatment of ascribed and achieved status see *Human Society* by Kingsley Davis (New York: The Macmillan Co., 1949), pp. 83-119.

genuinely love and respect it; those who have a distaste for, or at best an attitude of sufferance toward the teacher and those who respect both the person and the role of teacher; those who are "dull" and those who are "bright"; those who are "hand-minded" and those who are "head-minded."

Individual differences and an invitation to learning. When they come to school, no matter which type, they bring the character orientations of themselves and their families with them—their selves and their culture. It is this assembly which you will confront and which will confront you. It constitutes the raw materials for the social system which evolves in every classroom. Occupation as student and preoccupation as person interact in a myriad of ways. In confronting such an assembly, you will also confront what I think of as the "homogeneity of social knowledge" and the "heterogeneity of person-students." In this context you must devise a genuine *invitation to learning* which will make the homogeneity of social knowledge less, if it is to appeal to the heterogeneity of the person-students whom you are to teach. You must remember that each is involved in the maintenance of a self which is often highly resistant to your wish and attempt to get him to examine and change it. Teaching may, indeed, be thought of as instructing students in more satisfactory ways of *managing their tensions*.[4]

General lower- and middle-class orientations and some individual differences. Having looked at an imaginary class, let us now examine briefly the general orientations of lower- and middle-class families in American culture. The picture which it gives of the way in which children in these two class orders are brought up may help you better to understand the bearing of differential social class backgrounds in your role as teacher.[5]

---

[4] See Lawrence K. Frank, "The Management of Tensions," *Society as the Patient*, pp. 115-142.

[5] "American Culture: Generalized Orientations and Class Patterns," by Clyde Kluckhohn and Florence R. Kluckhohn, *Conflicts of Power in Modern Culture: A Symposium* (Edited by Lyman Bryson, Louis Finkelstein, and R. M. MacIver [Distributed by Harper & Brothers, 1947]), pp. 106-128. The concept of class is an ambiguous one. To a large degree the class-order in our society is defined by social science analysis rather than by the persons and families who are thus classified. All so-called "advanced" societies manifest certain persistent social differences. These we call classes. In a democratic society such as ours the class system is a relatively open one, that is, there is a high degree of upward mobility, i.e., to social class positions "higher" than the one in which a person was born. See K. R. Popper, *The Open Society and Its Enemies* (Princeton: Princeton University Press, 1950). See also Allison Davis, *Social Class Influences on Learning*. See E. K. Wickman, *Children's Behavior and Teachers' Attitudes* (New York: Commonwealth Fund, 1928) for a comparison of the attitudes of "average teachers" and "mental hygienists" toward various types of students' "misdemeanors." I take full responsibility for the following digest.

MIDDLE CLASS   **LOWER CLASS**

(Some examples of patterned behavior and attitudes
which are related to the "training" of children)

1. Encouraged to save pennies and other coins, and to have a bank account. The child accumulates and takes care of his possessions; is urged to have systematic hobbies.

2. Specific patterns for reaching specific goals relating to "good" standing in the community are such as these: early taboo on manifestation of interest in sexual matters; child hears little or no talk about sex and does not witness the sexual activities of his parents; the need for "sex education" is verbally admitted. Emphasis on washing hands, regular bowel movements, wearing clean clothes, keeping room in order, and eating neatly, etc. As respects emotional control the following patterns exist: child is prohibited from hitting other children—control of aggression is channeled through words, not fists. Child is told to "stand up for himself" and to "be brave" when hurt. Taught to control his temper. Achievement is important but the child is expected to restrain expressions of pride. Is expected to conform to the "rules of the game"; taught to pay attention to the approval of others. Receives careful training in table manners; learns the proper forms of all letters, greetings, gifts, expressions of apology, sympathy, etc. Is not permitted to associate with "undesirable" playmates; told not to speak to strangers. Specific patterns are given for having playmates over to the house, giving parties, and exchanging birthday gifts. There are also patterns for "joining' organizations. Respect for police is instilled. Obedience to parental authority, to school rules, and to rules of other organizations is expected.

1. Stress is put on getting a job as early as possible. The child early learns responsibility in financial matters (through doing odd jobs, running errands, selling papers, etc.).

2. Specific patterns for reaching specific goals relating to "good" standing in the local neighborhood are such as these: child is left to collect companions "on his own." Social autonomy at an early age is encouraged. In their gangs, children encourage each other to fight; little or no taboo on the expression of overt aggression in the family situation. Relatively speaking there are few taboos in area of sex. The attitude of "do it and try not to get caught" is prevalent respecting the police. Fear of, rather than respect for, police and other authorities is emphasized. (This attitude seems to have "moved upward" into middle-class families.)

The lower-class child's life is much less patterned or structured. His behavior is more individualized despite the fact that his character is molded by both formal and informal parental and neighborhood influences. We may, in a way, speak of him as a more "natural" human being than the middle-class child; he is not uncultured, only left more to himself to orient his character.

MIDDLE CLASS

3. Patterns which stress ownership of property; child is taught to say "this is mine—this is yours." These patterns relate to property, school work, and other types of achievement.

4. Patterns relating to education: interest in school grades is inculcated. Stress is put on homework and is supervised by parents. Opportunities provided for attending dancing school, art classes, and for having hobbies, etc.

5. Patterns for "good marriage" are the same as those found under sex taboos and proper companions.

6. Child is taught to respect his parents as the main authority. No great respect for grandparents is required. There is discrimination among relatives because of concern for family status.

7. Patterns relating to recreation: are specific patterns for individual and organized games and sports. Training is supervised and there are rules. Parents take the children on trips. Chil-

LOWER CLASS

3. (The Kluckhohns made no comment under this heading for lower-class children. From the general climate in which they grow up we may infer that these aspects of their life are much less supervised; patterns are worked out by them rather than laid down by their parents.)

4. Patterns relating to education: parents take no daily interest in the education of the children. If the child "skips" school he is often not punished by his parents. Little attention is paid to homework and there is little supervision of home study. There is little realistic planning for long-term education or efforts to relate education to practical goals.

5. No comment was made by the Kluckhohns under this heading for lower-class families. In its place they comment about relation to the "extended family line," i.e., the aunts, uncles, grandparents with more attention paid to the mother's than to the father's relatives. Children take care of smaller brothers and sisters and help with housework—mother is often absent from home because she is employed at wages to help support the family; father is often unemployed or absent. Mother is the chief family disciplinarian. Ethnic differences introduce variations in this area of the child's life.

6. (No specific comment by the Kluckhohns under this heading; their comment under No. 5 suggests the patterns in this area.)

7. Children are allowed to spend money on recreation as they please when they have the money. Their recreation is not highly supervised by the parents.

dren are told what movies they may
and may not see and are warned against
going to saloons, night clubs, and
cabarets.

Major differences in methods of training between middle and lower classes respecting rewards and punishments

1. Rewards: Because of greater economic security, the middle-class parents can give the child more material rewards than the lower-class parents can. By reason of greater economic resources, the middle-class parents can and do make extensive use of long-term rewards. Hence the "pleasure principle" is more distrusted than by the lower class. Middle-class parents, more than lower-class parents, use the threat of the withdrawal of love as a means of enforcing compliance to family standards. Lower-class parents rely to a much larger degree on short-term rewards. Because long-term rewards are unrealistic, they have no reinforcing value. The lower-class child more often escapes quasi-neurotic dependence upon his mother's approval but he also tends to lack that reward as an enduring stimulus to socially useful behavior.

2. Punishments: The middle class tends to stress deprivations of things or activities, of love and affection, of praise, rather than physical punishment. Much more submissiveness is demanded than in the lower class. The lower class stresses physical punishment more than deprivation such as is practiced by middle-class parents. However, the punishment frequently has no reinforcing power because it is administered long after the wrong act has been committed. There is also considerable inconsistency of punishment.

The teacher and class bias.   These differences are significant in and of themselves respecting the attitude of students from middle- and lower-class backgrounds, not only on the academic side but fully as importantly in affecting their attitude toward the teacher who is usually a middle-class person. It has been remarked that the chief difficulty the middle-class-oriented teacher encounters is a tendency to try to enforce middle-class standards of behavior on everyone else. It is a true but regrettable fact that some teachers (with an exaggerated middle-class loyalty) react toward lower-class students as if they had been taught middle-class standards, understood them fully, and then wilfully rejected them or transgressed against them. This is due to the mote-beam error or perhaps to a difference in definition as to what is mote and what is beam.

It is evident that the lower-class student may sometimes find the climate of the classroom prejudicial to his developing a feeling of belonging, especially if the middle-class bias of the teacher is strongly re-enforced by a large percentage of students with the same orientation. But this possibility should not be exaggerated. There is, among high school and junior college students, a quality of camaraderie or at least a tolerant decency which often cancels out not only social-class but also racial differences. Everything considered, the public school in the United States is one of our most civil and tolerant institutions.[6]

Two levels of social organization in the classroom.   Aside from the similarity of orientation between middle-class students and a middle-class teacher (I do not wish to exaggerate the significance of either beyond what the facts would show) there exists, in almost every classroom, two levels or kinds of social organizations: one official and sanctioned by the teacher and the school authorities, the other unofficial and sanctioned neither by teacher nor school authorities. These are, respectively, the social system of which the teacher is the chief organizing agent and in which the teacher's authority or prestige is the chief factor making for effectiveness as a system of social control, *and* the social countersystem which "the kids" organize and run. I mean no disrespect to the school when I observe that a penitentiary has the same kind of dual social organization. In both the school and the penitentiary these two social systems are in varying degrees of conflict for power. But in the school (and the penitentiary also, within limits) this conflict may be reduced or almost eliminated if the "legitimate" system takes account of the fact that it may be so "legitimate" and "respectable" as to encourage, unwittingly, the organization of a countersystem. These qualities, "too legitimate" and "too respectable," are sometimes covered by the innocent and well-meant phrase that such-and-such a teacher (or principal) "keeps a good school," which, in practice, may mean that he keeps everybody quiet and subservient to his authority.

The teacher's obligation.   One of your constant obligations will be to understand the organization of these two social systems, what it is that keeps them apart, and what may be done to bring them together. (It is pretty certain that each will continue to exist.) The secret for such an achievement, if secret it be, lies in making your students a party to the making of classroom policy as far as that is appropriate in a public and tax-supported institution and also as conditioned by the fact that they are citizens-in-apprenticeship rather than full-fledged members of an autonomous social system.[7]

[6] Respecting the ease or difficulty with which lower-class students may feel a genuine sense of belonging, there is ample evidence which reveals the relation between the difficulty of achieving it and the tendency of students to drop out of school. Here the close interrelation between the student's *personal* and *student* status in a classroom is evident. This is not to say, however, that difficulty in "belonging" is the sole factor inducing students to drop out.

[7] See Chester I. Barnard, *Organization and Management* and *The Functions of the Executive*. Although these books deal with the social system, its organization and control in the setting of the factory and the "office," they are immediately relevant to the problem

In short, your obligation is to help effect that kind of social organization in your classes which will permit a genuine "we feeling" to exist. This is the therapeutic climate: a commonwealth of teen-agers under the regency of the teacher.

Some principles of organization.   Such a climate is a ruled and principled one, but not ruled only by you and your principles. This raises the question of the kind and amount of organization required. The first principle is that organization is not an end in itself. An organization is but the scaffolding without which we would find the "temple of human co-operation too difficult to build." Hence you will need only that kind and amount of scaffolding necessary for the building of such a "temple" in your classes.[8]

The second principle is that no one will always naturally do the democratic thing. Democratic behavior is learned just as reading is learned. The third principle is that a student is subordinate to the "official" social system of the classroom, or any other, only as long as he is not assimilated to it, when he cannot "speak its language," does not know its rules, its code of behavior, its traditions, what is expected of him or, for whatever reason, he is in conflict with these things. Every democratic social system, in the classroom, the factory, or the nation is *effective* in that it accomplishes its objectives and is *efficient* to the degree that it satisfies its individual members.[9] Beyond these principles I shall not go in this discussion. Later chapters on the logic and sociology of communication, discussion, and the structure and methods of teaching-learning will bear on it.

The problem of discipline.   This brings me to a discussion of discipline. Once upon a time, students were in the teacher's backyard when in the classroom. But that time has passed, for the good of everybody. As the humor of a great teacher has put it, "I hope the day has passed when the student's place is to stay in it." [10]

---

we are now discussing. The best single volume which deals with this problem in the school is Willard Waller's *The Sociology of Teaching* (New York: John Wiley & Sons, Inc., 1932).

[8] See G. D. H. Cole, *Social Theory* (London: Methuen & Co., 1921), p. 85.

[9] Barnard, *The Functions of the Executive*, p. 56. A ruleless society is a contradiction in terms. Rulelessness produces that condition which the French call *anomie*, for which there is no English equivalent. It refers to such a profound weakening of the sense of "we-ness" that the social structure breaks up. It is individualism rampant. Under this condition in the civil society suicide, crime, and disorder are to be expected, because individual existence is no longer rooted in a stable and integrated social atmosphere and almost all of the meaning of life is lost. See Sebastian DeGrazia, *The Political Community: A Study in Anomie* (Chicago: University of Chicago Press, 1948).

[10] Max Marshall, *Two Sides to a Teacher's Desk* (New York: The Macmillan Co., 1951), p. 217.

The context in which a discussion of discipline ought to be placed is that of the relation between freedom and authority, for the amount and quality of freedom which exist in any social system are functions of the amount and quality of the authority which exist. This is the paradox which you must understand if you are to be a master of yourself as teacher-leader. No recipe can be given for the "right" balance between freedom and authority. One thing to know is that freedom is a *complex* and not a *simple*. This is something which the doctrinaire "progressives" never learned. They confused the democratic concept of social control with "let 'em do as they please." Thus they denied the philosophy of John Dewey—from whom they thought they learned their nonsense—and gave their students a false view of human affairs. The mental hygiene perspective gives no support to their doctrine, which is still practiced and preached in some quarters.[11]

Conceptions of discipline. To many teachers, discipline means one of the following: the degree of organization or orderliness in a classroom, the devices used for establishing it, or a polite name for punishment. These have, in common, a negative and external character—something from the outside which "makes the student be good." Genuine discipline in a democratic society is, ideally, self and mutual discipline. I would think of them as informal. Such an ideal is your bench mark, notwithstanding the fact that you will, on occasion, have to resort to formal discipline. You cannot always win by depending only on the power of a therapeutic climate or the student's self-discipline. You will also find it difficult at times to distinguish between the misdemeanor and the miscreant, but the principle of elementary justice which should guide you is that you treat misbehavior in such a way as not to aggress against the person of the misbehaving. This is the difference between prosecution and persecution. Other things being equal, it is better that your students learn the consequences of their acts than that they learn you as the "punishing teacher."

Genuine discipline inheres in the student's interest in and affection for the materials under study, for the group, and for the process of enlightenment. It does not inhere in the teacher as an authoritarian figure. Indeed, militant and autocratic tactics are invariably a sign of imperfect organiza-

11 Lawrence K. Frank, *op. cit.*, "The Reorientation of Education to the Promotion of Mental Hygiene," "Mental Security," and "Mental Health in the Schools." See Ronald Lippitt, "Field Theory and Experiment in Social Psychology: Autocratic and Democratic Group Atmospheres," *American Journal of Sociology*, XLV, No. 1 (July, 1939), and Kurt Lewin, "Experiments in Social Space," *Resolving Social Conflicts* (Edited by Gertrud Lewin), New York: Harper & Brothers, 1948. See also Ray Montgomery, "The Function of the Classroom in a Democratic Society," *The Journal of General Education*, IV, No. 4 (July, 1950).

tion or an imperfect understanding of the principles of organization. Discipline is a problem of morale.[12]

Law is law whenever it is fashioned and used for purposes of social control. But it may or may not be *fair* law. Law in a democratic society arises *out* of the will of a people and takes a position *over* them, as well as *in* them. It is effective, ideally, to the degree that it is the product of agreement or to the degree that its reasonableness is clearly known. I would, however, hold that externally imposed discipline is justified fully as much on the ground that a student should not make too big a fool of himself as that he should not damage too much an enterprise of teaching-learning.

A new definition of discipline. We now need a definition of discipline as a behavior problem and some specifics of tactic. Discipline *is* a behavior problem—which is a sign that there is a discrepancy between the student's behavior and the expectations of the environment of the classroom. Note that misbehavior is a sign or a symptom; it is not the "disease." It is not due to demons. It has natural causes; it is the obligation of both you and your students to try to discover them. The expectations are revealed in the degree of consensus which has been created between teacher and students—always imperfect. The best discipline is inner discipline. Your goal should be to help to create it. To do this you must learn how to take account of your students' impulses if you are to engage their consciousness, for William James told us long ago that consciousness is, in its very nature, impulsive. Consciousness is *man alive.* You will surely come to grief if you forget that your students have bodies. "Nature," as Whitehead put it, "can be kept at bay by no pitch-fork."

Activity is of many kinds. When a student is, in the vernacular of the naïve teacher, "doing nothing," he is *doing.* Activity cannot be escaped; purposeful activity *can.* Find out what the student's preoccupation is. Maybe he has been "resting too hard." What is he resting from? Ennui, boredom, an unclear assignment, idle talk by his associates, wordmongering by the teacher, or genuine fatigue? I once made the mistake of accusing a student of disrespect because he slept through my modern European history class. Later I found out that he worked in the post office at night and got only four hours' sleep. I took counsel with myself as to the value of modern European history for him—asleep or awake—but not before I made an awkward attempt to apologize to him. Fatigue is often a result, not of work, loss of sleep, or anything of a physical nature. It may be due to low morale, which traces to the fact that the person is engaging in behavior

[12] See Elton Mayo, *The Political Problems of an Industrial Civilization* (Boston: Harvard University Graduate School, Division of Research, 1947), p. 23.

which makes no sense to him or that he is meeting with no sense-making responses.[13]

Difficulties which students face. The threatened personality, like the fatigued one, cannot meet and cope with a threatening environment. All things considered, the environment of the school may threaten many students: they cannot "make the grade" either scholastically or socially, they are timid, beset with deep anxieties or, for any number of reasons, unable to manage the environment in such a way as to manage themselves. How to manage a lesson in history is not the least of the threats that may come to a student. If you insist on rote mastery of dates and the names of kings and generals it will likely threaten some of them the more.

But there are other difficulties which students face. There is considerable evidence that many young people, like their adult contemporaries, are indifferent to themselves and the world around them. This expresses itself in defeatism or apathy. Despite our much vaunted prosperity and high standard of living, the future is neither clear nor secure for many young people. At least it is far from being as secure as it was for their grandparents whose world was more stable but, withal, a less free one than today's. Insecurity is one of the prices we pay for freedom.[14] Moreover, the teacher is, for many students, no longer a significant landmark in their lives. They are, as David Riesman had told us, "other directed" and the teacher is often not one of their "others." [15]

The indifference of many of our young people seems to say, not that "life begins at forty," but that it ends somewhere between eighteen and twenty. But one wonders if their indifference is always real indifference. There is some evidence that it is only the attitude in which they have sought refuge when they found no "solvent" for their difficulties. They are valueless to themselves because the "world" is valueless.

Besides these characteristics, there are such disturbing factors as sickness of many kinds, living in a world of fantasy—what the psychiatrist calls "autistic revery" (which is usually a way of escape from an obligation)— lack of control of temper, humorlessness, and a deformation in perspective or outlook.

Some practical "don't's." I now suggest some "don't's"; after them some

[13] This was found to be the case in a study carried on in the General Electric plant in Cicero, Ill. See "Industrial Fatigue and Group Morale" by Robert E. Park, *American Journal of Sociology*, XL, No. 3 (November, 1934).

[14] See Dorothy Canfield Fisher, *Our Young Folks* (New York: Harcourt, Brace & Co., 1943), especially pp. 3-19.

[15] See his *The Lonely Crowd* (New Haven: Yale University Press, 1950), especially "From Morality to Morale: Changes in the Agents of Character Formation," pp. 36-64.

"do's." Do not demand that the student "pay attention" or, if you do, ask yourself what you are prepared to offer him for such "paying." What will it buy him? Montaigne told us, quoting Cicero, that the authority of the teacher is generally prejudiced in favor of those who desire to learn and against those who do not so desire. (Middle-class bias may enter here.) Do not condemn the student for an interest in nonconsequential things: he is there to be delivered from such interests. Don't din "democracy" into his ears; it is a way of life, not a whip. Do not command him, for commandments anticipate only blind obedience. Do not exhort him, for exhortation takes for granted the very virtues and capacities which he does not possess: perspective, knowledge, and a trained mind. In an age like ours the function of the moralist is not to exhort men to *be* good but to set forth plainly to them what the good *is*. Genuine sanctions are the product of agreement and custom; they are ineffective when artificially constructed.[16] It may be that I overemphasize the temptation of the teacher to be a tyrant. Perhaps as many teachers aggress against their students by the use of subtleties and wiles as by various forms of tyranny.

Do not use grades as a form of punishment. You have the right, as teacher, to judge a student's deportment. The standard for such judgment is the quality of his participation in the commonwealth of his peers. Don't, except as a last resort, send him to "the office." In many instances this seals your doom because it says out loud that the student has whipped you. I do not mean that principals and others in "the office" do not have a legitimate function as officers of control, but when either they or teachers have to employ police tactics the situation is one which demands a sober review of the organization of the entire institution.[17]

Don't try the student before his peers; they constitute a class and not a jury. A system of "student government" may employ a modified "jury procedure" but its success depends on a tradition which is rarely found. Not infrequently "student government" is little more than a puppet show in which teachers and administrative officers pull the strings. The division of authority which obtains between students and teacher and officials ought to be clearly stated; neglect in this matter is the perpetration of a fraud.

Some practical "do's." The foregoing "don't's" are in the nature of curative devices; now some "do's" which are more in the nature of pre-

[16] See Walter Lippmann, *A Preface to Morals* (New York: The Macmillan Co., 1930), p. 318.

[17] You can hardly be certain about the outcome of any harsh method of effecting discipline. The code of the countersystem has much to do with the origin of discipline cases and quite as much to do with the quality of success you will have with them. No formula can cover the many situations which may arise.

ventive devices. Neither list is exhaustive and each contains little more than suggestions: insight and *good* common sense are the ground for whatever you do in the area of discipline.

Let it be admitted at once that social control of a classroom by indirect and informal means is difficult. It is far more the function of the social climate (which is a pattern of co-operation) than any rule you may impose or any role you may play other than that of decent human being. It is a rare classroom in which the expectations of the students are identical with the expectations of the teacher. Knowledge of this will alert you to the fact that, in almost every classroom, your students are disciplining you at the time you are disciplining them—subtly but really. The wise and artful teacher knows this and undertakes to beat them at their own game. It is a clever game of guessing and outguessing and can, in many ways, be made a good game—win, lose, or draw from your standpoint. In any case, good will is a better doctor than logic or propaganda.

It is my view that shock treatment—by words or other forms of domination—does more harm than good, although others hold a different view on this matter. Much depends on the severity of the shock and the quality of affection which teachers and students hold for one another.[18] How great the likelihood is one can never be certain but shock may increase the student's disposition to "misbehave" and, if anxiety lies at the base of his failure to meet the expected norms of the group, will likely drive it deeper. My colleague Kermit Eby says that "if you don't love 'em you can't 'learn' 'em." This is love without sentimentalism, and affection which does not rule out firmness. The great majority of students will respond co-operatively to a teacher who is firm but fair. Stand *by* them, not *over* them. Do not be shocked if your students sometimes display anger. It were better for them to "out with it" at times than suppress it. If you do not display anger at times, you are a rare human being. But I offer no rule as to the "proper" or "improper" time for its manifestation. Try to avoid making any student feel inferior. It will make you no more superior in his eyes; perhaps less so. Seek, however, to avoid occasion for the angry cycle of "you dast"—"you dasn't" (which Tom Sawyer and Huck Finn enacted) to start. In such a display, nobody wins. If, as Professor William E. Hocking has observed, your task is to produce not only an equal but a superseder, you cannot exact servitude from one you have begotten.

The teacher as counselor. Your function as teacher will, likely as not, involve you to some degree in the school's program in counseling and guidance. I should like to comment briefly on that phase of your work. The

[18] See Bruno Bettelheim, *Love Is Not Enough* (Glencoe, Ill.: The Free Press, 1951).

goal of mental therapy is not primarily to make the student adjust to the culture of his classroom or school life but rather, through it, to develop integrity and respect for himself. This perspective applies to your function as lay-counselor as well as teacher.

Students do not know it, but adjustment to the norms of their teen-age social world is the dominant orientation of modern youth. This is the burden of Professor Riesman's thesis of the "other-directed" character type. The days when character got its orientation from either tradition or "inner direction" appear to have gone, at least for the foreseeable future. This fact relates immediately to your guidance and counseling role. Your appeal to a student's sense of personal dignity rather than to his respect for, or fear of, authority may find you knocking at a door which he will not be disposed to open. But you are under the obligation to make that appeal.

It is not your obligation to "fix up" any student by cajoling, threatening, or begging him to conform. Rather, give him occasion to face alternatives or, if such be the case, cease from interfering with his tendency to do so. External and formal discipline will most likely deepen his hostility to it, make him a reluctant conformist to the "letter of your law," and almost certainly more of an "outlaw" than he now is. There is no royal road to learning—either of subject matter or self. It is my belief that the role of counselor or guidance person is best played when informally played. I have the feeling that the administration of secondary education has gone overboard in the direction of a formal and bureaucratic approach to guidance and counseling. My own experience of more than thirty-five years of teaching and working with young people leads me to believe that teaching and counseling are inextricably bound together and that they should continue to be so bound. Whatever success I have had as a counselor in a number of official and quasi-official roles was due to the fact that I knew most of my advisees as persons as well as students. This knowledge cannot be had by the full-time and bureau counselor or guidance person. The closest approximation is through the medium of reports, tests, and other paper and statistical evidences,—and this is not very close.[19]

The meaning of adjustment.   Your task is to understand the meaning of *adjustment*. In our society it is a working accommodation to a culture with a fast changing equilibrium, if at times it may be said to have an equilibrium. In such a working accommodation, the student's task is to develop the inner controls and insights which will permit him to make readjust-

---

[19] Whatever the size of the school, the mental hygiene approach can have a fair chance only if the entire staff—administrators, teachers, engineers, janitors, and clerks— is included in the community of the school. See "The Forest Hill Village Project" by John R. Seeley, *Understanding the Child*, XXIII, No. 4 (October, 1954).

ments. But the illusion of permanence is a tough one and not easily dispelled.

Students ought to come to know and understand how they *do* behave before you can reasonably expect them to behave differently. The guidance and counseling function ought to be guided by that principle.

I conclude my comment on this phase of your task by remarking again on the intrusion of the middle-class bias. Montaigne wrote,

We estimate [the student] not according to his worth but after the manner of counters, according to the prerogative of his rank.

To which pathetic practice he replied (quoting Plato),

Children should be placed, not according to the resources of their father, but according to the resources of their mind.

This philosophy bears, particularly, on the teacher's role as counselor and guidance person.

The therapeutic climate is informal. You will need to know how the experience of teaching-learning can be defined so as to informalize, as much as possible, the creation of the therapeutic climate. Mental hygiene is not only or primarily a new name for a course called "Human Relations" or "How to Win Friends and Influence People." It is the result of *what* is taught, *how* and by *whom*. The full account of none of these can be given here. Suffice it to say, respecting the *what*, that it must "grow out of real life situations." To do this it must begin where the student is. He is the point of departure and the point of return. It must arise in his difficulties (many of which he is not aware of) and terminate in their clarification, to the degree possible. It must teach him how to manage his needs wisely and well. In doing that he will be involved in managing the needs of his culture. The two cannot be separated. If "any man's death diminishes me," as John Donne wrote, it is just as true that any man's life increases me, "because I am involved in mankind."

Emphasis on the "growing out" phase of youth's experience. But, if social education is to grow out of "real life situations" it must emphasize more than it often does the *growing out* phase of youth's experience. The social studies are *social* exactly in the sense that they do not treat of something called the "absolute personality." They treat of personal relations which are, at one and the same time, interpersonal relations. Their task is a therapeutic one, namely that of seeking to establish that kind and quality of interpersonal relations which will make for a good and wise character and a good and wise society. This is done by teaching students how to effect the right transaction between their inner environments—their aspirations, capacities, needs—and their outer environment, which is the social system in which they live, both in the classroom and in their corner of the Great Society. This can come about only through their mastery of their own character *by way of* their mastery of the arts of relating themselves wisely and well to their associates, and vice versa.

"Locus" and "focus" of socialization. We hear a good deal about "child centered" education. To this I would subscribe, but not to "the child" in a *social* void. In being the center of instruction, the student occupies many centers. The most intimate is the center which his character constitutes, the next his family and neighborhood, next his town or city, then his region, his nation, and finally the world of all humanity. His education is the experience of *progressive socialization* through playing the roles which these concentric and ever more public areas of his life require. Thus it is that the *locus* of his study changes, but in each locus his character formation is the *focus*.

A series of thresholds. I think of this successive and progressive set of "real life situations" as a series of thresholds. Your task is to help him step over them in such a way that the transition from one to another is achieved with a minimum of distortion to his character. To put it positively, so that he may increasingly enlarge his character in order to play wisely and well more public roles. This is what we refer to when we say of a student that he "handled himself well" in a new situation.

Your task is a twofold one: to create a democratic climate and in its atmosphere set going that kind of teaching-learning experience in which the individual needs of the student will be related outward to the social groups in which he must learn to participate if his needs are to be met. The climate does not exist for itself, that is, as only a "nice place." Among some practitioners of the mental hygiene approach I find an excessive emphasis on "belonging" and "social adjustment" as ends in themselves. These, along with social knowledge, are part of the process in which character change takes place.

Learning and role-playing. A thing is really learned when it becomes a part of the student's operating or role-playing equipment. To know is, in the final analysis, to know *how*. But his knowing or wanting to know is often blocked by various kinds of anxiety: about his career, his relations to his father, his future family life, his intimate personal affairs, and maybe such things as war and international peace. He may get some release from these anxieties in the protective atmosphere of the therapeutic climate. But the climate alone cannot turn the trick of his getting in closer touch with reality concerning himself and the things which trouble him. This involves *inquiry, study,* and *thought.* He may thus come not only to know his emotions better but learn how to redirect them into constructive paths. Spinoza wrote, "In proportion as we know an emotion it is more within our control and the less the mind suffers from it." Many students whom we believe incapable of thinking are quite capable of it once they have been relieved from their anxieties and fears. What we seek in social study is a unity of character. It is had by *discipline,* not by right of birth. Anxieties and fears are often, if not always, based on obscure and false meanings and impressions. Your task is to help your students come into possession of a body of knowledge and meaning which is closer to reality than that which many of them now possess.

Doing good is doing well. I am not content to settle for the fact that Miss Smith or Mr. Brown is "a swell guy." I would not wish them to be anything else. Their capacity to be "swell guys" may contribute to the student's goodness, but it cannot, alone, contribute to his wisdom. I find it quite impossible, however, clearly and sharply to separate goodness and wisdom, for in order to do something *good* the student must know how to do something *well.* The notion is widespread that knowledge alone will suffice to protect us from false and unscrupulous leaders and enable us to discriminate between the honest, creative types and those dishonest and destructive. But such a view is too rational. We need to *feel right* as well as *think straight.*[20] Susceptibility to evil leaders is far greater when the emotional life of a people is starved than when it is well fed. We must honestly admit the power of emotions to do good or evil. When William James said that the test of an educated man is his ability to tell a good man when he sees one, I am sure that he was thinking of the education of the "heart" as well as of the "head."

Two kinds of knowledge. Not only is your task twofold but the kind of knowledge you need is always twofold: knowledge of your subject and knowledge of your students. If this twofold knowledge cannot influence desires, if it cannot help your students determine what is of value and what is not, then the future of social education is indeed depressing. The only alternatives are brute force and propaganda. We must never forget that all effective behavior has its *affective* side.

School and life are different cadres. Another aspect of the therapeutic climate must claim attention before we turn to the *who* aspect, the teacher. It is important to note that the democratic climate of the classroom is often limited to a few teachers in a few subjects. But whether

[20] See Lawrence K. Frank, *op. cit.,* "Dilemma of Leadership," pp. 308-338.

under few or many teachers and subjects, it is not a lasting thing. The commonwealth of teen-agers is not coterminous with the civil commonwealth for which the former is, in large part, the period of preparation. It is for this reason, if for no other, that your students need to look beyond the commonwealth of the classroom into the commonwealth of the civil society and know it as a social system. But their participation in it will be in a cadre different from that in which they were educated.

What I mean to suggest may be clarified by comparing the classroom with the barracks. In the latter, the cadre in which the recruit is prepared for action is, in large part, the same cadre in which he will operate in action. Not so with the cadre which the classroom symbolizes. Hence the classroom must make the most of the group spirit in the hope that the schooling of both mind and emotion will stand up under the rigors of life in the Great Society, which will in many if not in most cases be encountered in groups totally different from those in which one was a "comrade in books." Sometimes your students will have to go it alone, because the groups in which their life course is cast in civil life are mean and little.

Teacher and psychologist. And now briefly to the *who* aspects of the therapeutic climate. It has been thought that the teacher and the psychologist differ in that the attitude of the former, being concrete and ethical, is opposed to that of the latter which is abstract and analytical. These two orientations are obviously different but they do not necessarily need to stand in opposition. What is required in the teacher is such an interplay between them as will produce the ability to see the task abstractly and analytically, and thus enhance the art of teaching concretely and ethically.[21]

Some characteristics of the ideal teacher. Such a teacher is "charged with crisp meanings" and is like the one Professor Robert E. Park used to refer to as one who "pulled the kivers off and woke me up." But there is a quality in the teacher from Montaigne's view that has not yet been touched upon. He wrote:

It is a good thing if the tutor will make [the pupil] trot out in front, so that he may judge how far he must descend to the boy's level in order to accommodate his powers. For lack of this may spoil the whole thing. . . . It is the mark of a lofty and powerful mind to be able to condescend to childish needs and to guide them.

To do this the teacher must stay young, even in the "thick of thin things." The spiritual obsolescence of teachers is apt to go on at a much

---

[21] See William James, *Talks to Teachers on Psychology and Life's Ideals* (New York: Henry Holt & Co., Inc., 1900), p. 13.

faster pace than their biological obsolescence. Staying young in spirit is difficult because, to the conflict often involved in one's own advancing years, there is added the conflict between the generation of the teacher and the student. Great patience is required for youth is, as always, reluctant to take, much less put to use, the wisdom of its elders.

You must have the self-command you wish to inspire in your students. You must be slow to anger and plenteous in mercy. You must learn to listen with the "third ear," the ear of deep and sympathetic insight.[22] You must develop the skill of the Quaker in getting "the sense of the meeting," a sense which all the psychological training in the world cannot guarantee. You must do all these things, and many more, if you are dedicated to the creation of the therapeutic climate. In that climate your students will find something to know and believe, something to love, and something to belong to. In such a climate the rigors of disciplined thought may be near to a joy.

The prime virtue of the teacher. Finally, a word about the prime virtue of the teacher—the teacher who is possessed of a great faith. This is the faith that can bring every student to the top of his level of achievement: not merely to outdo someone else but to learn to make the best character which he is capable of making.

This is the faith that there is an undiscovered and an unachieved dignity in every student. This is the grain of mustard seed which is "indeed the least of all seeds: but when it is grown it is the greatest among herbs and becometh a tree, so that the birds of the air come and lodge in the branches thereof."

The Teacher of Nazareth used this parable in speaking of the kingdom of heaven. I do not know why it may not be used to speak of the kingdom of men, a kingdom of goodness and wisdom which had its beginning in a teacher's faith in human nature. This is the best teacher grown still a little taller.

Such a faith is a faith in love: a love of self as well as a love of others, for they are not alternatives and they are not separable. The depth and quality of the teacher's love of self is inseparably bound up with love of others. Each is based on care, respect, responsibility, and knowledge. These are the constituent elements of the democratic character.[23]

---

[22] See Theodor Reik, *Listening with the Third Ear* (New York: Garden City Books, 1951).

[23] See Erich Fromm, *Man for Himself* (New York: Rinehart & Co., Inc., 1947), pp. 128-129.

CHAPTER III

The Rhythm of Continuity
and Discontinuity
in Culture and Character

The teacher as priest and prophet. The teacher of the social studies is called upon to play two roles: one as priest, the other as prophet. As priest, the task is to pass on the culture in order that it may be continued and preserved. As prophet it is to interrupt its continuity. These roles are inherent in the nature of things: the spirit of conservation and the spirit of change. Nothing can be real without both. Conservation without change cannot conserve; change only is passing from "nothing to nothing."

This is but a way of bringing to mind the age-old problem of permanence and change. The French have a phrase for it: the more things change the more they remain the same. Our students are continually confronted by this fact. Always and everywhere in advanced societies, young people face the same question: What shall I do with my life? But always and everywhere in such societies, they face it under changing historical and cultural conditions. It is only the "practical man," as Disraeli defined him, who does not recognize this. He is the man who repeats the errors of his forefathers.

The rhythm of continuity and discontinuity. We do not face continuity *or* discontinuity, nor do we face permanence *or* change. We face a rhythm of continuity and discontinuity in the form of *changing permanence*. We cannot afford an attitude of disdain toward the past nor can we afford to idealize it as the only source of what is good and wise. The "insistent present" is always more than present: it is disappearing past and emerging future. Such enduring values, such Great Oughts as truth, beauty, courage, truth-telling, justice, and love, like themes of music, have endless variations. They are our bench marks but each requires fresh insight into its meaning for every age. They are kept, but embodied in new forms. They change yet have a quality of permanence or persistence. They change in form but remain constant in essence. We shall miss the truth if we mistake the letter for the spirit of them.[1]

The principle of changing permanence was in Thomas Jefferson's thought in the Declaration of Independence. It is stated almost explicitly in these lines:

. . . whenever any form of government becomes destructive of these ends, it is the right of the people to abolish it and institute a new government, laying its foundations on such principles and organizing its powers in such forms as to them shall seem most likely to effect their safety and happiness.

But such changes must not be for "light and transient reasons." By the same token, those changes which the teacher, in the role of prophet, makes in the interruption of the culture must not be made for "light and transient reasons." The teacher's roles, both as priest and prophet, will concern us in the next chapter. Our concern now is to explain what we mean by "changing permanence."

Change and civilization. The great ages have been, in significant respects, restless and unstable. "Every great advance in civilization begins with a new wandering," so wrote Karl Bücher, the German economic historian. Witness the Crusades, the periods of great migration, of exploration and colonization. The history of all peoples who have been involved in the processes of civilization has been a shuttling back and forth between periods of relatively stable equilibrium and great unsettlement. Through these the continuity of their culture was interrupted. They then took new directions. Then the course of empire changed.

The Americanization of the immigrant changed the culture to which he came. It likewise changed that which he brought with him and the one he left behind. With these changes his character was changed. The vigor, the dynamics, and the uniqueness of our culture is due to the cross-fertilization of many cultures, each of which was broken or interrupted in the process. The continuity of the cultures of city and country alike have been interrupted by the flood of rural migrants to the city. The characters of both ruralites and urbanites have not been unaffected by those changes. Discontinuities in cultures and characters take place when young people

[1] See Kenneth Burke, *Permanence and Change* (New York: The New Republic, Inc., 1935), pp. 227-236.

marry and leave their parental homes. They occur when casual laborers follow the harvest and when the Okies in Steinbeck's *Grapes of Wrath* sought a Promised Land. They occur, with more greatly disturbing effects, when wars and natural disasters come to a people.

The good of change. Cultural discontinuities are thought by some to be harmful both in their public and private effects. This is not to be denied. But they have their civilizing and progressive consequences. In those terms I now appraise them. But whether their consequences are good or ill, they appear to be inevitable. They put old institutions, old ideas, and old ideals to test. "The old order changeth, yielding place to new," not only respecting cultures and characters but also respecting knowledge.

The life course of restless and uneasy growth. The life course of persons in advanced cultures reveals, like that of the cultures themselves, a restless and uneasy growth. While such a course is different for each of us because we are individuals, we can abstract from it what is common to all. This may be done by the construction of an ideal type, as in the foregoing chapter. Such an ideal-type account of the life course from adolescence to adulthood runs somewhat as follows.

Ideal-type poles of family and public life. Suppose a wandering and up-and-down line between two poles. It is a life course. The ideal-type poles represent the ideal characteristics of two situations. We name these "family life" and "public life." We call the former a "who situation" and the latter a "what situation." The terms "who" and "what" represent not only the polar situations between which a life-course is run but also contrasting norms by which the value of a person is judged. The characteristics of these two situations are given in the following columns. They describe and differentiate between the two ideal-type situations.

An Ideal-Type Representation of the Life Course from Adolescence to Adulthood

"FAMILY LIFE"— THE "WHO SITUATION"	"PUBLIC LIFE"— THE "WHAT SITUATION"
(*a*) sacred attitudes are held toward persons.	(*a*) secular attitudes are held toward persons.
(*b*) personal relations are noncompetitive.	(*b*) personal relations are competitive.
(*c*) sentimental and nonrational means of social control are used: love.	(*c*) practical and rational means of social control are used: reason and law.
(*d*) one's status is ascribed, i.e., given.	(*d*) one's status is achieved, i.e., earned.
(*e*) security is inherited.	(*e*) adequacy is earned.
(*f*) "He's our boy!"	(*f*) "What can he produce?"

The characteristic "f" under both columns carries the moral of the entire scheme: "He's our boy!" is an affirmation and a judgment. It is not a question. It is something taken for granted. Moreover, it is a judgment before the facts, or even in spite of the facts. It is based on the presumed intrinsic merits of a person. No matter how deviate (especially in his younger years) be the child's behavior as seen by strangers, his parents and siblings love him. On the contrary, "What can he produce?" is not so much an affirmation of character as a performance standard. It is a question before the deed and requires proof. Similarly, the child has *security* in the family without earning it; *adequacy*, on the other hand, has to be demonstrated. These two characteristics are closely identified with ascribed and earned status respectively.[2]

The ideal-type "public-who situation" is that toward which he moves as he grows up. The tempo of the transition varies according to the sex and temperament of the child, the position of the family in the class structure, family tradition, the child's capacities, the occupation and employment of the father, and many other factors. For the lower-class child, as we have seen, the tempo is faster than for the middle-class child. The former is more on his own in just the sense that he makes the transition without as much guidance as the middle-class child and tends to begin it earlier. The journey is, however, not without storm and stress for both.

Growth and transition. As the child matures he acquires the knowledge and attitudes by means of which he gradually gains emancipation from the family situation and enters more and more into the public situation. (Our reference to "thresholds" in the preceding chapter is to this change.) That transition is, in reality, never complete because the stabilizing and humanizing factors which operate in the public situation are the sentiments which were laid down in the family. Throughout his life, the person's experience is a weaving backward and forward between these two situations.

Changing roles and statuses. The child's social education consists essentially in learning the roles and statuses appropriate to the family and public situations, respectively. The breaks or discontinuities in his character come in the form of changes in attitudes and behaviors which the transition entails.

[2] Although the ideal-type construct is a logical rather than an ethical one, it can posit certain ethical characteristics in typical social situations. This is evident in my implicit assumption that the family situation gets its unity through sentiment and the public situation gets its unity through law and reason. Here the fictitious nature of ideal-type constructs is revealed, because we know that real family situations employ both sentimental and rational means; similarly, public situations. If you will remember that neither situation exists in reality, you will be able to use them as ideal-type constructs to get at characteristic differences, here exaggerated.

The family and public situations.   In the family situation he has a relatively limited number of roles and statuses. (These vary as between middle-
and lower-class children.) In the public situation he has a greater number
of roles and statuses—that is, his social contacts are wider and more
numerous. In the family situation, complemented by the school, he is
given considerable counsel and guidance. In the public situation he is, as
we have noted earlier, more or less on his own. From this fact we derive
the conception that the student's education should be geared to learning
to manage himself, not to rote learning. The latter requires only remembering; the former, insight, knowledge, and skill in inquiry. This is what
Sir Richard Livingstone referred to when he said that "the test of a
successful education is not the amount of knowledge that a pupil takes
away from school, but his appetite to know and his capacity to learn." [3]
It is explicit in Whitehead's definition of education as "the acquisition
of the art of the utilization of knowledge." The most precious fruits of
good teaching are the unseen harvests. All the more need, then, that the
student's social education should be a cross-fertilization of theory and
practice for, without theory, practice is but routine born of habit.

The scientific view of success.   Among the many ways in which we
might trace the student's journey from early adolescence to later adolescence and adulthood, I choose what I believe to be a very significant one,
namely changing conceptions of the nature of *success.* As the objective
social scientist views it, success tends to be measured in the family situation in terms of *worthiness* which does not have to be proved. In the public
situation it tends to be measured in terms of *competence* which must be
proved and demonstrated. The student's struggle for success will, then,
go on under different rules of the game as he moves further from the
family-who and closer to the public-what situation. This experience is
characterized by both continuity and discontinuity. The teacher's task is
to assist the student in both. (We have seen that the rules of "the game
of success" vary considerably as between middle- and lower-class families.)
Characteristically, in our society, the competitive principle dominates the
public-who situation—when it is not denied by the practice of monopoly.
But the competitive principle conditions not only material success and
failure, but also moral success and failure.

The folklore view of success.   The prevailing folklore (operating with the
Horatio Alger and rags-to-riches myth) presents a quite different account.
According to it, success is achieved in the public-what situation first be-
cause one is worthy and second because he is competent. This is a com-

[3] *The Future in Education* (Cambridge: The University Press, 1942), p. 28.

plete reversal of the order which the objective social scientist finds. If this myth is examined the result may well be that its continuity will be broken. At the same time, phases of the student's culture and character orientation will also be broken. This may produce considerable shock. You must decide how to soften it, that is, if you choose to put the myth under critical examination. But all learning involves a slight frustration because thinking begins only when a student feels the sense or the shock of a problem of some kind.[4] Bertrand Russell has written wisely on this in his observation that "to tell lies to the young who have no means of checking what they are told is morally indefensible . . . if [however] the knowledge comes gradually, duly intermixed with a knowledge of what is good, and in the course of a scientific study inspired by the wish to get at the truth, it will have no such effect." [5] (Russell does not add that the whole matter will depend very much on the civil community setting.) My observations lead me to believe that all but the most sheltered and naïve students, of whom there are fewer and fewer, can stand much more realistic teaching than they sometimes get. In this matter, you must take your cues from the policy of the school, which reflects the attitude of the major policy-makers of the civil community whose school it is. All your teaching should be realistic (it is fact, not fancy, which is your bench mark) but about what situations and with what quality of critical study is yours to decide.

The prevailing folklore, furthermore, says that success is achieved chiefly by virtue of "good character." In large measure this is true but such other factors as education, training, health, capital resources, and even some luck are involved. The folklore's accounting for failure runs according to the same logic, except in this case it is due to "bad character." For the student to take the folklore account as authentic and reliable would be harmful and pathetic. Your task is, at least, to give him a choice: a folklore or scientific account of the nature of success and failure.

Likewise, the folklore says that those who are endowed "by nature" with the attribute of confidence in themselves and who are "worthy" succeed; those not so endowed fail. This denies the myth that the good are rewarded by success and that the wicked are punished by failure. The nub of the whole business is that the rules of ascribed status sometimes operate to a very considerable degree in the public-what situation, although according to a more rigorous view the rules of achieved status tend more often to operate in it.

[4] See Franz Alexander, "A World Without Frustration," *American Journal of Sociology*, XLIX, No. 5 (March, 1944). The burden of his thesis is that this would be a dull and monotonous life if it contained no frustrations.
[5] "The Function of the Teacher," *Harper's Magazine* CLXXXI (June, 1940) p. 15.

The process of growing up. If this discrepancy is discovered by the student, his character orientation may suffer considerable shock because his ideals have been challenged. But again, it will depend largely on the atmosphere of the classroom and your skill in revealing the difference between the folklore view and the view of objective social science. It is not your task to put either the student or the businessman on the spot. The proper focus of your concern is on the process of growing up. It is your obligation to establish truth about success and failure by as objective canons as possible.[6] You must, of course, take your directing cues from the maturity of the student in all your teaching, especially as respects its controversial nature. But this fact stands: unless your students are introduced to the nature of *change* there will be mighty little left around which you can fashion worthwhile teaching in the social studies. To a large degree, the only alternative is to admit that there is nothing much to study.

Family and public situations not totally different. Here it is necessary to point again to a limitation in the ideal-type constructs given earlier. I appear to have taken alarm at the fact that the rules of ascribed status continue to operate in the public-what situation. But if they did not, that situation would, in reality, be ordered only by the competitive principle. It is this principle to which our national economy is committed. It gives the public-what situation its basic set of rules. But these are modified by the family-who principle of sentiment, in order to insure that there may obtain between competence and worthiness that humane balance necessary for civilized social relations. This requires that success be judged in moral as well as economic terms, as indeed it is. This is the tempering fact of which you should not lose sight.

By the same token, success in the public-what situation does not, in reality, stand alone on proof of adequacy. There is also some security of the family-who type. Similarly, in the family-who situation, the child's status is determined by a mixture of security and adequacy—unless he is feeble-minded or has excessively indulgent parents. The mixture of these two in the public-what situation is apparent to all who understand that positive sentiment operates in all human groups, although it varies greatly as between the family-who and the public-what types.

In the foregoing, I have sought to offer two perspectives on the journey from adolescence to adulthood. One is that of the prevailing folklore, the other that of objective social science. In both perspectives, the reality was

[6] See Frank Abrams, "A Businessman Looks at Education," *The Saturday Review,* April 19, 1953. Mr. Abrams, one of the nation's leading business executives, makes an able plea for the right of the school to engage in critical education.

somewhat twisted because it was based on the ideal-type method of analysis. The facts are, of course, never as sharply "either-or" as these perspectives suggest. They are, nowever, useful for analysis. The polarity which they provide is an excellent way of taking a bifocal view of social reality. Folklore tends to err on the side of optimism; social science, unless properly understood, errs on the side of pessimism—by reason of the fact that it shows up the optimism and quasi-blindness of the folklore approach. Often they are in complete and total disagreement as to the part which worthiness and competence play and the question as to which weighs more heavily in the public-what situation.

Security and adequacy in balance. The extension of the principle of security into the area of life in which adequacy is the ideal-type criterion brings with it danger of the belief that *adequacy* has served its day. Young people should know that the former imbalance in which scant weight was often given to worthiness and excessive weight was given to competence (for that was the case in the era of the robber barons in our national economy) may conceivably be followed by another imbalance in which too *little* weight is given to competence and too much to worthiness. These are the complementary and balancing elements in the light of which the services of both private and public agencies (private charity and social security through legislative provision) might well be assessed. Awareness and study of their possible imbalance would certainly induce a more sober, objective, and discriminating perspective on recent politico-economic changes in our national life than a battle of angry words in which half the students charged that the welfare state has imperiled the American way of life, and the other half countered with the accusation that "the greedy capitalists" are ruining our country.

Personal and social needs. In this account I have sought to deal with two problems. I have sought to treat the process of growing up, viewed as a journey between two quite different kinds of role and status situations. I have also sought to show how, according to the maturity of the student, you may help him analyze the nature of the changes he undergoes in the journey from family-who to public-what. In this I have sought to show that his "real life situation" changes, and that his understanding of it involves his getting a *systematic* as well as a personal view of both situations. Implicit in all has been a concern with the satisfaction of his needs parallel with the satisfaction of the needs of first that phase of the society which we know as the family, and second that phase of it which we may designate as public life. Implicit throughout has been the rhythm of continuity-discontinuity-continuity, respecting both culture and character.

Success and the class structure. I wish now to develop somewhat more fully some ideas about the nature of success as different segments of our society view and appraise it. I shall place the discussion in the context of that view of our society which takes account of its class structure. I hope to temper the shock which mention of class sometimes gives by showing that our society is not rigidly class-structured and that we are dedicated to keeping it from becoming so.[7]

It is not clear how the present American class structure has been affected by change in the balance between worthiness and competence, security and adequacy, and ascribed and achieved status. Their effects would, however, certainly be reflected in a change in the value placed on upward mobility in the class structure.

Success and upward mobility. Success has, traditionally, been measured in our society by one's upward mobility. We seem to have written a new commandment which reads: "Thou shalt strive ever to move upward lest thou be judged guilty of wrongdoing." Such a view would seem to suggest that social-class organization is essentially hostile to personal freedom *but* that this hostility may, somehow, be reduced or escaped if one can move "ever upward" in the class order. A truly democratic order should, however, afford some options in the matter of rising or staying, and should recognize relative rather than absolute differences in class-based status.

The first of these options would be the freedom to rise from one class to another in the spirit of individual freedom as reflected in the standard of "careers open to talent." This freedom is for those of requisite capacity and ambition. If their capacity is truly superior they may, without necessarily stepping on the faces of others, move upward in the class structure. But if ambition alone were the motivation, there is only the will and not the humane way. But, if ambition be paired with genuine competence, the margin of success in upward mobility should increase.

Success without upward mobility. Upward mobility is an important freedom but not less so than another kind. This is the freedom for individuals who have neither the wish nor the power to leave the social class

[7] A poll taken by *Fortune* reported in the issue of February, 1940, showed the following social class identification of the persons polled *as stated by them:* upper class, 7.3 per cent; middle class 70.4 per cent, and lower class 22.2 per cent. The percentage of students who finish high school is very high among those from upper-class families, fairly high among those from middle-class families, and very low among those from lower-class families—something in the order of 95 per cent, 60 per cent, and 30 per cent, to strike a fairly representative national average. Correspondingly, the percentage of those who go on to college falls into something like the following rank: 90 per cent from the upper class; 15 per cent to 45 per cent from the middle class, and probably never higher than 10 per cent from the lower class. These figures are only general approximations and will vary from community to community and according to scholarship privileges which men and women from the various social classes enjoy.

in which circumstance has placed them. This freedom, no less than the first named, should insure justice, opportunity, and humane living. But in this case it is freedom, not to leave a given social class position, but to stay and be something in it. This would be the opportunity for those who make their living in the various trades, and with varying degrees of skill, to have comfort, security, and a good life without ceasing to be tradesmen.

How status and esteem differ.   We often take little or no account of the difference between status and esteem. The fact that those who are occupied as tradesmen can hardly expect to be considered equal in class status or prestige with those in more honor-bearing tasks (such as law, medicine, engineering, and banking) ought not, it seems to me, lead them to believe that prestige parity is all there is to success. Teachers might well call attention to the high esteem in which persons pursuing the trades are held when their performance warrants it.

The school and the class structure.   I do not believe it is the school's obligation to allocate students in the class structure. But the school cannot afford to be insensitive to or unconcerned about either the fact of the student's class origin or his class aspirations. But rather than allocate students to their "proper" class position (what a monstrous idea), I would view the school's task as that of providing both realistic and idealistic pictures of the student's life chances and of his roles and statuses which go with them. (In doing this the term "class" need not be used.) If the school should arrogate to itself the power to allocate students in the class structure, or worse, undertake to determine what the class structure of the society should be, it would cease to be an educational institution and become a political one. In what I believe to be its proper role as an educational institution, the school's task is to analyze the workings of the social processes by which human beings become identified with certain levels and standards of living and certain kinds of occupations and seek to bring students honestly to assess their competence and life-chances as that analysis might reveal it to them.

Status and success as problems in the social studies.   I should now like to pose some questions bearing on matters of status and success which teachers of the social studies might well ask themselves. The search for "answers" might provide highly useful experiences for their students.

1. What are the liabilities as well as the assets of the competitive principle as it relates to the tendency for young people to engage in excessive status striving?
2. To what degree have the market and technology set the norms for success and provided many of the symbols for it?
3. What politico-economic changes are necessary to create the climate in

which less materialistic symbols may arise and make a substantial appeal to young people? (I do not mean to suggest any necessary antithesis between material and moral.)

4. Is it possible for today's youth to maintain as wide a margin of difference in success and status between *their* present and future, as it was for their parents?

5. As our civilization matures and the older land frontiers are closed, what new cultural frontiers offer promise for success and status? (Despite our great national need for technological leadership I feel that we have quite as great a need for what I should call *sociological* leadership.

6. If we continue to believe that success, through status-striving, is in large part the measure of a man's worth to his society, how difficult do we dare make its attainment, short of imposing failure on many who, if success were conceived in less rigorous terms, might not fail?

The shock that might come to a student whose character orientation was challenged by pursuing such inquiries may be tempered by *what* you do and the *way* you do it—as well as the climate in which it is done. If you create discontinuity, you must do what you can to create continuity.

I should now like to comment on some phases of the analyses which might assist you in inviting character reorientation, for that is all you can do.

A new definition of success. Success may be defined as that which the community calls upon me to do because it is unable to call on anyone else. This does not assume that fame and fortune necessarily go with it. It is the quality of character which the mother in *I Remember Mama* exemplified so poignantly. It is akin to that which Emerson expressed in his belief that every man is made of "some triumphant superiority."

Success is a variable. Quite practical and attainable steps, by which such a conception of success may be realized, suggest themselves. I think that it is possible to demonstrate through case studies that several levels of success in power, prestige, and esteem may be achieved at any social-class level. It may also be demonstrated that students may achieve distinction in several ways. A student may be poor in history, he may lack the social graces necessary to be a good dancer, he may be too small to excel in athletics but when it comes to geometry, civics, or free-hand drawing "let 'em look out." Signal success in one realm may thus compensate for low-grade success in another. Hence the problem we face is not adequately defined as one simply of success or failure. Rather, it is one of evolving what James S. Plant called "a workable bundling of one's different personalities." [8]

However, if the view is taken that a worthy character can be achieved

[8] *The Envelope* (New York: The Commonwealth Fund, 1930), p. 128.

by success, unalloyed by failure at *any* time, high prestige bought at whatever cost in esteem, and striving which takes its pattern from what *others* do rather than from an honest assessment of one's own competences, the result will almost certainly be bungling rather than "bundling."

What shall I do with my life? Count Tolstoi posed the great question: "What shall I do with my life?" While I do not suggest that it be repeated daily in the manner of a secular or academic golden text, I do suggest that it be the persisting focus of all teaching. I do not recommend teacher-preachment; it does not produce legitimate social knowledge. I suggest, rather, that social education find its constant focus in the formation of character but with that balance of directness and indirectness in approach which will produce neither tedium nor anxiety.

Insight into success and failure. I believe it is possible to achieve far more than we now do in bringing students to know that they have standards for assessing their own success and failure, as well as those of mankind generally. There is considerable evidence that students are only dimly aware of the fact that these are moral standards. In order to develop these insights, we need to educate our students to be both actors and spectators. This will require that they develop the ability to see themselves in critically objective ways. They need to develop the ability literally to put their aspirations, ambitions, and future plans into rehearsal and see how the play ends, insofar as that can be known. They need to learn to play a whole series of imagined roles and judge their consequences, not in terms of the market canons of success alone, but in terms of their greater happiness and sanity as human personalities.

Social class not a problem to be solved. I have placed considerable stress and emphasis on social class. In closing, I should like to state what I hold to be the teacher's obligation respecting the whole "social-class problem" insofar as it may be so designated. It is not that of doing away with social classes. Rather, it is that of insuring, to the degree our position as *teachers* permits us, that our social-class system maintains its open character and affords dignity and security at all levels. Social classes and their role in our society do not constitute a social problem to be solved. They are not an evil, but rather the seams in the coat of a society which respects difference and does not censure men because they are not all alike. Social classes constitute phases or elements in the social process, called democracy, which requires to be directed by as humane rules as men can devise and control. If any people would undertake to do away with social classes, the surest thing we know is that they would spring up again. By the same token the presumed "withering away of the state" is not only sheer nonsense but impossible so long as human beings constitute societies. It is both inane and futile to anticipate either a perfect synthesis of social classes (as the prevailing communist dogma looks forward to but, in reality, moves away from) or their disappearance. The doctrine of the "class struggle" as the be-all and end-all of history is "weighted with the wish for eternal rest—for death." [9]

The need for equilibrium in the social-class system. But we want life, not death, and the way to get it is to manage the social-class system so that an equilibrium will be maintained. This is an equilibrium between competing conceptions of both desirable ends and desirable means. Struggle, divergence, difference, and the constant breaking and mending of the continuity of both culture and character are the conditions of social peace and welfare. Only that teaching of the social studies which is beholden to such a conception can, in my view, prepare young people to live wisely and well today and not only meet tomorrow but make it. That is, make it more like the democratic dream.[10]

[9] Frank Tennenbaum, "The Balance of Power in Society," *Political Science Quarterly,* LXI (December, 1940), p. 504.

[10] Much of the material of this chapter was taken from my article, "Social Class as Fact and Perspective in the Social Studies," *The School Review,* LX (April, 1952), pp. 203-212. Chapter XXIV deals with the pedagogical aspects of the journey from family-who to public-what situations.

CHAPTER IV

Indoctrination:
Avoidable and Unavoidable

Primitive and advanced cultures. It will make a difference that you will teach in the United States rather than in the Admiralty Islands or in New Guinea; that attendance at your school will be required, not optional; and that change is a constant feature of our culture.

I suggest these, among many other characteristics of an advanced culture in contrast to a primitive one, so that you may see yourself in the perspective of profound cultural differences. This may help you better understand the great obligation you have inherited and the importance of your task as teacher—despite the fact that it may not be seen in this light by everyone else.

In primitive cultures, the accent is on *learning;* in advanced societies it is on *teaching.* I say "accent" because I shall, as Mark Twain once put it, "exaggerate in order to make the truth stand out."

In primitive cultures, teaching is *sporadic;* it takes place chiefly when custom is not clear or when it misfires or miscarries. In advanced cultures teaching is *continuous:* things are so complex and in such a state of change that custom does not suffice to make clear how people ought to behave. Furthermore, there are many different and often conflicting customs.

In primitive cultures, teaching is done chiefly at the instance of the *learner;* in advanced cultures it is done chiefly at the instance of the *teacher.* In the former it is more or less *optional;* in the latter it is *required.*

In primitive cultures, when custom is not clear or when, for whatever reasons, it does not tell one what to do, the learner comes to the sage or the Old Man of the Tribe and says: "I met my mother-in-law in the

43

forest yesterday; the way she treated me makes me think that I did something wrong. Tell me what I should do." Or, "I think I have wronged my brother; tell me, if you will, what I should do." [1]

Thus, teaching in primitive societies is custom-bound. It tends to be *after* the fact or the event. Typically, the learner is taught what he asks to be taught and often in the instance of an emergency. The accent is chiefly on what is past.

In advanced cultures in which men are much less custom-bound, the accent is a divided one: on permanence and change. In them men face the task of resolving the conflict between tradition and dissent. In this complicated state of affairs the learner is taught, not what he asks for, but what the culture, through its agents the teacher and the school, decides what he ought to learn.

The teacher as priest and prophet. In our culture, advanced and modern, the teacher is cast in the dual role of priest and prophet, as we noted earlier. But, as we also observed, the teacher should not assume the role of prophet (or indeed that of priest) for "light and transient reasons." The moral and intellectual view which the teacher takes, as prophet, is that

. . . the primary task of a democratically inclined society is to develop ways and means of interrupting the continuity of cultural tradition in those areas where it is evident that the ideas and practices of the past are working to the disadvantage of human welfare and threatening to destroy the integrity of the human personality.[2]

The need to discriminate. But more than a premise is necessary. There must also be an informed mind which can discriminate between the genuine elements in the tradition of our culture which are alive and which make for emotional stability and intelligence and, on the other side, those attitudes and institutions which are in decline or decay because they have lost their function and meaning.[3] The teacher as prophet must, then, be informed, dedicated, and gifted with rare insight.

Change, conservation, and moral issues. It is a truism that our culture is dedicated to progress, human as well as technological. The great movements for the advance of human dignity have, as we noted earlier, always involved change as well as conservation. When social life is stable, when

---

[1] See Margaret Mead, "An Anthropologist Looks at the Teacher's Role," *Educational Method*, XXI (February, 1942), pp. 219-223.

[2] Lawrence K. Frank, "Social Order and Psychiatry," *op. cit.*, p. 155. This same premise has been stated by many others. Abraham Lincoln wrote that "we must disenthrall ourselves and then we shall save our country." See also James Harvey Robinson, *The Mind in the Making* (New York: Harper & Brothers, 1921), especially p. 22.

[3] See Karl Mannheim, "Education, Sociology and Social Awareness," *Diagnosis of Our Time* (New York: Oxford University Press, 1944), pp. 34-35.

custom rules and "everybody" knows his place and function, the problem of good and wise behavior is solved by adjustment to institutions as they are. But, in a time like ours, when many of the institutions and dogmas of the past are, in Lincoln's words, "inadequate to the stormy present," the problem for the teacher, as well as for the whole society, is the moral quality of the institutions and dogmas themselves.

It is under such conditions and for such reasons as these that you will be called upon to play the role of prophet as well as priest. This will involve you in creating discontinuities—the kinds discussed in the preceding chapter and many more. As we suggested, your teaching must be tempered not by anger toward the attitudes and institutions of the past but by an entirely different set of attitudes. It will be your task to show your students, not by mere declaration but through sober and interesting study, the genesis, in specific and particular situations, of some of the ideas and beliefs to which they hold and which give them their character orientation. It will be your task to study out with them, rather than point out to them, that some of their ideas and beliefs ought to be re-examined, not only because they can be refuted by more reliable knowledge and deeper insights but because they are no longer appropriate to their world and time.[4] These may range from the more complex conceptions of success we have just examined to other and maybe simpler conceptions, such as "saving is always a virtue," and that "a public debt is the same as a private debt." Such enterprises of inquiry will often involve you, not only with naïve and stubborn student-minds, but with equally naïve and stubborn attitudes in the civil community whose bearers may accuse you of "corrupting the mind of youth." But thinking is always thinking about change of some kind; if it is encouraged its risks cannot be avoided.

Teachers are critically important.   It is thus evident that what the whole community did informally in primitive cultures now falls more and more, in a culture like ours, on the teacher and the school. Hence *to the degree that teachers make whatever we decide our culture should be*, it behooves us to see to it that they are not regarded as mere by-products of our society's creative process. Unless teachers are critically important, they are unimportant; such is the nature of their calling. To transmit our heritage is to transmit the belief that we *ought not* transmit it uncritically.

Achievement and success differ.   I recall the observations of two great thinkers: one in the twelfth, the other in the eighteenth century. It was Abélard who said, "By doubting we come to question and by seeking we may come upon the truth." It was Voltaire who said, "One cannot be a

4 See Lawrence K. Frank, "Two Tasks of Education," *op. cit.*, p. 211.

critic of his own society and expect to enjoy the reputation of being a pa-
triot at the same time." To these I would add that if you choose to teach
you will be well advised to know that you may *achieve* but that you may
not *succeed*. The difference is this: achievement is doing something well,
independent of public acceptance and also independent of the fate of its
author. Success, as I now use the term, is achievement which has gained
public acceptance and acclaim.

In entertaining such an image of the teacher, to whose prophetic role
I have given special emphasis, your chief and continuous task is to aid in
the making and remaking of the character of individuals—not in making
and remaking the character of a society, *except* indirectly and in the
long run.

The teacher and the society. As teacher you have neither the mandate,
the tools, the power, the materials, nor the audience for directly changing
the society. You are, however, a party to such a task, but one step removed. You will contribute to a changed society by the priestly and
prophetic roles you play vis-à-vis your students who are representatives of
their culture (albeit unofficial) and who will return to it changed as to perspective, knowledge, and skill respecting those phases of their culture which
should remain unchanged and those which should be changed. It is for this
reason, especially, that permission or certification to teach should be the
sign of the full and unremitting approval of a society.

The position taken in these remarks does not deny that our society has
given the school a task far more complex than that implicit in the words
teaching and *learning*. It does deny, as I observed earlier, that the school
or the teacher should undertake to play the role of political partisan. Good
and wise governments have always resisted the temptation to make the
teacher the hired man of partisan politics but have instead sought to recruit
for its teaching roles those who were decent and responsible exponents of
their culture. The only political policy to which the teacher—*as teacher*—
is beholden is that of humanism, expressed through the institutions and
ways we call *democratic*.

While it is unquestionably right that all men of intelligent good will
would wish to

> Have power on this dark land to lighten it,
> And power over this dead world to make it live,

to use the school directly, or propagandistically, for that purpose is both
technically impossible and morally wrong. The school and the teacher
must undertake the task for which they are equipped and no other. But

to be one step removed from economics and politics is not to be aloof from them. Although the school is not the Great Lever, it can and does exert pressure on that lever, one step removed in time, in method, and in personnel.

Education and schooling differ. We need to understand how education and schooling differ. Education is all the process by which human beings, born with potentials for learning from their experience (if it is organized), are transformed into full-fledged members of society. Schooling is that more or less formal part of it which goes on in the school.

The "educative society." Hence it would be unrealistic to believe that the school is, or ever could be, the main educative agency. It is both aided and interfered with by the processes of education that go on in the "educative society." The educational means of the "educative society" are more formidable and probably more lasting than those which the school can employ. They are such as these: the side of the tracks one is born on; the wage scale; the bargaining process, both individual and collective; occupational opportunity, skill, and training; the conditions of employment; the newspapers one reads, and the quality of his ability to know what he reads —and through that the reality and reliability of his opinions; the organization of industry; the nature of politics and the degree of one's participation in it; and such imponderables as the great social trends which find their origin and rhythm in the stream of history. It is these which cast the mold within which the school does its work. It is through such channels and agencies that, in the final accounting, our society works out its goals and purposes and the tempo and directness with which it moves toward them.

Creating and mending breaks in social continuity. Although I shall leave it to a later chapter to examine the integrity of our culture, we know that if the teacher, in the role of teacher-priest, should attempt to pass on the culture uncritically the result would be that a lawsuit had been passed on. While it lies with neither the teacher nor the school to "settle" that lawsuit it does lie within their province to make known the facts at issue and hold a kind of continuous moot court on it. This is standard procedure in the education of lawyers. It is equally appropriate to the general social education of students who have inherited the lawsuit and who must devote themselves to the lifelong task of bringing it nearer to settlement. The teacher's role as prophet, however odd that designation may sound in connection with the study of a cultural lawsuit, is the role which is played in the process discussed in the preceding chapter: creating and mending breaks in the continuity of culture and character.

Propaganda and indoctrination.   This brings me to distinguish between propaganda and indoctrination. The propagandist looks in only one direction for truth, is sure he has found it for good and forever, and then proceeds to dictate it to his students, neighbors, or whoever it be whose mind and spirit he seeks to control. The teacher, on the contrary, looks in every direction which gives promise of aiding in the establishment of truth and then invites a class in social study to join in co-operative endeavor to check both the method and the findings. The propagandist subscribes to the "method of authority"; the teacher to "the authority of method." [5]

Avoidable indoctrination.   As for indoctrination, there are two kinds: the avoidable and the unavoidable. The avoidable is exactly the same as propaganda.

Unavoidable indoctrination.   An account of the unavoidable kind runs something like the following. There are bench marks for both belief and thought in our society. The ethics of democracy provide the bench marks for belief. These are the Great Oughts which we have already noted. Others among them are tolerance, humility, personal dignity, brotherliness, reasonable persuasion, well-being, and peace. These constitute our changing-permanents, whose forms, means, and conditions of achievement change but whose essence is permanent. The methods of science—both natural and social—constitute the bench marks for thought and inquiry. Its attributes are integrity, competence, and humility; its opposite is fraud.[6] Not to teach these bench marks to our youth would be a travesty on the liberal spirit. They are the ground and stuff of general education. They are the doctrines of democracy. A people without doctrines is a wolf pack. A teacher without them is a hired man or a phonograph. Doctrines are things held. If you have nothing to hold to, you have nothing to offer your students to hold to. In holding to them, they constitute your biases. As Goethe observed, you cannot be impartial but you can be sincere. It is about these doctrines that you must be sincere. Your problem is not one of doctrine or no doctrine. It is whether you will teach about and by humanistic and scientific doctrines or whether you will impose them.

How to think and what is worth thinking about.   The late Justice Jackson once said: "If there is any fixed star in our constitutional firmament it is that no official, high or low, can prescribe what shall be orthodox in politics, nationalism, religion, or any other matter of opinion." In being a teacher you will, unofficially, be one such official. It will be your task to

    [5] See Sidney Hook, *Education for Modern Man* (New York: Dial Press, 1946), pp. 112-138.
    [6] See Frank H. Knight, "Fact and Value in the Social Sciences," *Science and Man*, Edited by Ruth Anshen (New York: Harcourt, Brace & Co., 1942), p. 344.

define the rules of inquiry; not to dictate the conclusions. It will be your task to teach your students *how to think* and *what is worth thinking about* for their life and the life of their time. But sometimes, sadly enough, "you won't know what method to use about a problem which is not yet quite formulated." [7]

The teacher's task is both moral and intellectual. In making up your mind what your students ought to know to live wisely and well you confront a task which is inseparably a moral and intellectual one. You must decide what they *ought* to learn. With this emphasis your moral task is identified. With it you demonstrate your use of the standard of what you believe to be *significant*.

You must also decide what they ought to *learn*. With this emphasis your intellectual task is identified. With it you demonstrate your use of the standard of what you believe to be *relevant*.

It is not a matter of moral *or* intellectual, of significance *or* relevance. It is a matter of both. With these combined you will offer your students the materials for the making and remaking of character: a scale of values and a method of thinking about them.

In basing your instruction on these two criteria—and here I change the order of consideration—you will reveal to your students the nature of things as the method of social science inquiry reveals them. You will also reveal to them how it may be used to study the process involved in making moral choices as to the use to which these things ought to be put. The latter is much more difficult, for things which are not lovely often present themselves in the camouflage of being lovely. Your difficulty is further increased by disagreement as to what *is* lovely.

The method of inquiry. But this disguise is capable of being penetrated, in large part, through what the method of inquiry can tell us about the probable consequences of alternative choices. It cannot make the choice for us, for there is no science of justice, or of beauty, or of kindness. But it can fit us with the skills requisite for understanding not only the nature of means but also the nature of ends. It so happens that judgments of fact and judgments of value are both *judgments*, although the latter are more mixed with our passions than the former. They both involve the same logical processes.

The method of "Little Bo Peep." There is another method which I would be remiss not to mention. This is the method of "Little Bo Peep" which leaves inquiry and moral choice to uninstructed common sense, fate,

[7] See Margaret Mead, *The School in American Culture* (Cambridge: Harvard University Press, 1951), p. 41.

intuition, or worse, to a dictator in the belief that goodness and wisdom will, like sheep, "come home, wagging their tails behind them."

Problems of what, why, and how.   Your obligation to do something about the social education and re-education of your students reduces to a *what*, a *why*, and a *how*. The *what* is to pass on and at times to interrupt the continuity of their cultural heritage according to your judgment of what is significant and relevant. The *how* is the method of inquiry. The separation of the *what* and the *why*, which is never complete, will be briefly discussed here. The *how*—incapable of being separated from the *what* and *why*—will concern us in many of the following chapters.

Your options are the following.

Teach "the facts."   You may decide to "teach the facts" and let the values go. But facts were not, as some suppose, born "free and equal." Furthermore, you cannot avoid a choice of those you will take and those you will leave, and furthermore, they must be facts about something; what will that something be? It is not self-appointive. Even to choose to be a party to the dullest and most meaningless rote-learning is to choose to do that. Such a choice would be not only innocuous, although bad enough on that score. It would be immoral, for unless students learn how they assign values to facts they learn nothing.

Interpretation cannot be avoided.   If this option be interpreted as trying only to reflect the contemporary social scene rather than to reflect *upon* it in the spirit of loyal criticism this attempt at neutrality will also fail. Simply to reflect it rather than to reflect upon it will have the effect not only of endorsing "things as they are," but of sanctifying them. What your students will see in such a mirror will be without meaning. No teaching which seeks to avoid interpretation is teaching at all. But even under this option you cannot avoid interpretation. Try as you will, you cannot engage only in description. But to do even that will involve you in a choice of what you will describe. You cannot enter the room of neutrality through that door. You cannot escape the display of some preferences. This choice will find you involved in unconscious indoctrination—unconscious to both you and your students. It will cast you in the role of hired man or phonograph. In the attempt to be a "Know-nothing" you cannot avoid being a "Know-something"—but neither you nor your students will know what that something is.

But trying only to reflect the social scene is impossible on other grounds. The Great Society, or call it the "educative society," is not a mere theatrical backdrop against which a puppet show called teaching-learning goes on. No metaphor can fully suffice to indicate what it is. But it is stage, players,

plot, and audience. It is the whole of the social life which it is the obligation of the social studies to reveal and interpret. Teaching-learning does
not go on in *front* of it. It is *in* it, *of* it, and *about* it. It is human life in all
its manifestations with which the social studies deal.

The teacher as social planner. You may decide to throw your whole
energy into sketching the outlines of *the* good society. This will make you
a propagandist, pure and simple. It will cast you in the role of social
planner, but the blueprint you teach will represent the ideals of only one
sect, not of a nation. Insofar as your plan is indorsed by your school it
will cast it in the role of *the* political party. Like the ideology of the class
struggle, which is supposed to lead to that impossible thing called the
"classless society," it will lead to the death of the human spirit. It will
fool your students—if they are gullible enough—into believing that democratic humanism subscribes to fixed and final social ends. John Dewey has
spoken with penetrating clarity on this matter.

In order that education of the young be efficacious in inducing an improved
society, it is not necessary for adults to have a formulated definite ideal of some
better state. An educational enterprise conducted in this spirit would probably
end merely in substituting one rigidity for another. What is necessary is that
habits [i.e., attitudes] be formed which are more intelligent, more sensitively
percipient, more informed with foresight, more aware of what they are about,
more direct and sincere, more flexibly responsive than those now current. Then
they will meet their own problems and propose their own improvements.[8]

Defend the status quo. You may decide to make another positive judgment, that is to maintain the *status quo*. But it is a myth, for change is in
the very nature of social life. As we stated earlier, you must admit the fact
of change or admit that there is mighty little else around which you can
organize useful learning experience. It is silly to be either "for" or "against"
change. You might as well be for or against gravity or the seasons. The
question is: What account will you take of it? You cannot escape that
question in either your priestly or prophetic role. The least you can do
under this conception of your task and still give some meaning to your
teaching is to make your students aware of the fact that change is going on
in many directions. But if you leave it there, little has been accomplished.
You would give no insight into how they might assess the forces making
for these many directions of change or what their probable goals are. Thus
you would offer no reliable method for their making a choice as to the

---

[8] *Human Nature and Conduct*, p. 128. See also John Dewey, *Reconstruction in Philosophy* (New York: Henry Holt & Co.. Inc., 1937), p. 177, in which he writes of the
"process of growth."

movement and direction of change with which they might ally themselves. This method is another illusion.

The canons of significance and relevance. Finally, and this is the only professionally defensible alternative in a democracy, you may select, by the canons of significance and relevance, those aspects of the social scene which you believe will give your students a working acquaintance with facts and situations which will best equip them to meet and intelligently deal with their world and that which is a-making. You will seek to teach them how it works and, as objectively as possible, how well it works. The former will require that you teach them the method of inquiry; the latter, its use in judging between competing values. That judgment will be theirs, not yours. In doing this you will combine the priestly and prophetic roles.

Your task is defined. If you choose this option your task may be defined, in outline, as that of helping your students

1. develop an awareness of their own beliefs: their personal value system, which includes what they hold to be true and the method by which they fix that belief.

2. develop an awareness of the means which they employ to think and believe as they now do—this is, in reality, an extension of 1.

3. develop an awareness of the fact that the means and ends to which they are committed have not, like a spider's web, been spun out of their individual selves but are the product of interaction with their fellows in a myriad of social relations—at home, in their gang, in their school class, in their youth organization, their church, and so on—the elements of the "outer environment" with which their "inner environment" has made many transactions.

4. in the light of the foregoing, to make, voluntarily, those changes in their character which will bring their thoughts, feelings, beliefs, and acts more nearly in accord with the principles of democratic humanism.

An account of the *why* would involve us in the story of the nature of the democratic dream and how we came to espouse it. But that story cannot be told here. It is assumed that you know it and are committed to all it stands for.

Avoidable indoctrination. I return now to the nature of avoidable and unavoidable indoctrination. The avoidable, as I have observed, is propaganda. It gives not only answers, but final and false ones. It forgets that there was a Socrates, a Galileo, a Newton, an Adam Smith, a Tom Paine, a Jefferson, a Darwin, a Pasteur, a Freud, a Justice Holmes—all those who changed "the facts." Nor does it suppose that their kind will ever come again. It forgets the fact of change. It believes that democracy can be saved once and for all—by nondemocratic means. It does not understand Tennyson's

> All experience is an arch, wherethro'
> Yet gleams that untravell'd world, whose margin fades
> For ever and for ever when I move.

The absolutism of the propagandist, as Horace M. Kallen has remarked, traces to a deficiency in a sense of history and in a sense of humor. The propagandist is also blind to the dynamics of learning which require that the student *seek* rather than be dictated to. The propagandist is also ignorant of the fact that there is no freedom without choice and no choice without intelligence—that is, no freedom which is not illusory and bogus. He is content to turn the student out upon the world with "an acquired and artificial innocence" which is Dewey's equivalent for Veblen's "trained incapacity" for moral and intellectual existence. He produces inflexible people, unable and unwilling either to face change or help to bring it about by orderly and democratic methods.

Unavoidable indoctrination. And now, in conclusion, a few more remarks about unavoidable indoctrination. The teacher who knows the difference between avoidable and unavoidable indoctrination is not ashamed of being called a "pedagogue" which, in the Greek, generic, and best professional sense means "one who leads children." This is a "leading" through which, in Montaigne's words, the student is "not pledged to any cause but insofar as he approves it." Such a teacher believes that only a monster would manipulate a student's mind.

Such a teacher teaches principles, not formulas. These principles, whether they be those of economics, civics, social problems, or whatever, are principles in the sense that they discipline students to know and act in *principled* ways. These demand, in both teacher and student, trust in reason which manifests itself in habits of suspended judgment, legitimate skepticism (not the childish or nihilistic kind), an appeal to honest observation rather than sentiment, reliance on discussion rather than dictation, and on inquiry rather than the blind acceptance of traditional moralisms: in short, reliance on the method of inquiry which, of all methods, is the one which gives us "maximum correctness."

The teacher who knows that indoctrination is unavoidable will not fear to use "colored words," for those which are not colored are colorless—and meaningless. "All speech is a trigger for action." Such a teacher will not be so tolerant of error as to be indifferent to it, or so afraid of imposing a view that no student will be exposed to one. Views are to be given and taken only on a faith which is grounded on evidence. About the "penumbra of doubt" which will always surround such a faith, the teacher will not be disturbed for it is that "legitimate doubt" by whose door, as Justice Cardozo put it, "enters the judicial function."

Such a teacher knows that courage cannot be taught timidly nor tolerance intolerantly, and that the "propaganda of the deed" speaks louder than the "propaganda of the word." Such a teacher does not believe that "it is propaganda when you know what you are doing and education when you aren't quite sure."

All these things are contained in "the school" if you will but rephrase it to read, "to school," which is to subject your students to moral and intellectual discipline. They will thus be indoctrinated without having doctrines imposed upon them.

By these canons the teacher is committed not only to take account of social change, but to contribute to the kind which brings the progress which is measured by the advancement of human dignity through policies in which all share in the making. This progress is always a condition of dynamic, not static, equilibrium. What it seeks is found in faith and fixed by science. It is not an attainment, but a quest. To transmit our heritage, broken or unbroken as the case may require, is, in the final analysis, to transmit the faith that the quest is worth making and that we are worthy and prepared to make it.

CHAPTER V

Modern Society:
A Spatial Pattern
and a Social Order

THUS FAR OUR focus has been on the student and teacher. We now shift it to inquire about our society. In this and the following chapter we shall examine its structure and *how* it works. In Chapter VII we shall ask how *well* it works.

The chief characteristics of modern society. Thanks to the changes which have taken place in the past one hundred years, the chief characteristics of modern society, of which ours is representative, are *size, complexity, speed, mechanism,* and *freedom*.[1]

In *size*, modern society has reached the limits of the habitable world. All its future expansion will be in the direction of greater complexity rather than extension in space. It is a smaller world because it is one in which peoples who were formerly in isolation are now in close communication. Burma, Ceylon, India, Iran, Lebanon, China, and all the hitherto little known peoples of the Near and Far East are now the focus not only of world news but of worldwide concern. That we and the other Western nations lack an understanding of them and they of us and, to some degree,

[1] See Robert E. Park, "Modern Society," in *Levels of Integration in Biological and Social Systems*, Robert Redfield, Editor (Lancaster, Pa., Jacques Cattell Press, 1947). Your appreciation and understanding of modern society will be enhanced if you will read "The Folk Society" by Robert Redfield, *American Journal of Sociology*, LII (January, 1947), pp. 293-308. Take particular account of Redfield's treatment of the folk society in terms of its ideal-type characteristics. The characteristics which Park gives modern society are ideal-type in nature. That is, they are the dominant aspects of a so-called advanced society as contrasted with those of a primitive or folk society.

each other, is perhaps one of the most significant political facts of our time.[2]

It is a commonplace to speak of the "passing of the frontier," but its significance for our learning to live with our fellow men the world around we appear to understand darkly, if sometimes at all. In times past that phrase referred to a region or possibly a continent. Now it refers to a planet. The revolution in communication and transport has made it so.

The *complexity* of modern society is due to its diversity of races, nations, classes, castes, and creeds. These are not something new under the sun but, thanks to the virtual annihilation of time and space, are now next door to each other. We are all internationalists whether we know it or not, or knowing it, whether we are willing to admit it and act in the light of it. "We live upon a shrinking sphere, like it or not, our home is here." [3]

The *speed* of modern society confronts us in the rapidity with which men may move about and the consequent speed with which they may find themselves in communities with different and conflicting value systems. Karachi, Cairo, Tokyo, Rio de Janeiro, Moscow, Cape Town, Rome, Manila, Berlin, the Congo, New York, the Argentine, and Melbourne are not only places, but places with different and often conflicting ways of life.

The *mechanism* of modern society, in a sense its *raison d'être*, reflects its scientific, rational, and calculating character. This has often led to "the substitution of methods of manipulation for understanding in areas of life as distinct as politics, business, and education." Not only the terminology but the practices of the business world have found their way into education, for we read of the *management* of the reading program and even of the *management* of students.

Finally, the *freedom* of modern society, one of the by-products of the machine, is reflected in the growing emancipation, around the world, from tribal rule and tradition, except when these return in the form of communistic or fascistic conceptions of the nature of man and attempts to control him in such ways as to deny him an opportunity to direct his nature in humanitarian ways. Sometimes, however, the traditions of ancient and tribal ways have come to be the wellsprings of a strike for freedom by peoples who have been denied it under one form or another of colonialism. Witness the present stirrings in what was for so long referred to as "the dark continent," for manifestations of both the suppression and the resurgence of what are essentially tribal ways of life.

[2] Liston Pope seems to have had this fact in mind when he wrote that "a smaller world requires bigger men." See his article, "Man Is the Measure," *The Saturday Review of Literature,* February 10, 1951, pp. 7-8.

[3] Edna St. Vincent Millay, "There are no islands, any more."

The local community and the Great Society. These characteristics, which Graham Wallas brought together under what he called "the Great Society," [4] are reflected in one way or another in every local community in our society, each of which is not only a part of, but a *counterpart* of the Great Society.

Every local community is sizable, at least in the sense that it is tied to the Great Society by the newspaper, the radio, the television, the movies, the automobile (less than formerly, the railroad), and the mechanisms of the market. The so-called "little man" as well as the "big shot" now reads the daily quotations of the stock market and both are concerned with the ups and downs of the business cycle because, as never before, their lives and fortunes are told and foretold in such indices. The *Saturday Evening Post, Collier's, Life,* and the other best sellers among the popular magazines not only entertain us but tell us, in the advertising pages, what to eat, drink, and wear. Such journals of opinion as *The Nation, New Republic, Commonweal, Christian Century,* and *The Reporter* help to shape our views and opinions in matters of politics, economics, religion, and the arts. To these should be added the editorial columns of the great metropolitan dailies which, in becoming fewer in number, have made it more difficult for the average reader to become aware of and sensitive to the political and economic affairs of his local community—except it be in one of the great metropolitan centers. In that trend, the columns of the small city daily, and increasingly of the country weekly, have come to be filled (especially the latter) with "boiler plate" bought by subscription and the relatively little either can afford by way of the purchase of national and world news from the great press services. This loss has, to a considerable degree, been compensated for by the news and opinion we get by radio and television. But while these media may have the result of informing and advising us with respect to national and world affairs, they have tended to weaken the ties which bind us to the affairs of our state and local communities. The result has been, in large part, that we know *about* national and world affairs but find it difficult, if not impossible, to know what their bearing and meaning are for our private and local lives.

Every local community is less local than it was a generation ago because the range over which people travel has increased manyfold. The family car is now a common carrier. Youth knows not only the parish within whose bounds it can see the smoke from its own chimney, if indeed houses are heated by coal any longer, but it also knows, however uncritically, the sights, manners, and customs of cities and states near and remote. These

[4] New York: The Macmillan Co., 1916.

experiences give the lie, at least in an objective sense, to the notion that modern young people live primarily a local life.

Every local community is "speedy" in the sense that, in the brief span of life of only their adolescent years, young people enjoy a range of experiences (sometimes far beyond their years) which it took their forebears a lifetime to acquire. This has resulted, many times, in a false and thin sophistication which will continually confront you as a teacher. The Great Society is no longer only some place "out there." It is also, in varying degrees, "in here" —in every village, town, and city, although those who are dully perceptive, wrongly educated, or overprotected may not sense it.

Every local community is mechanized through its dependence upon the machine—"in politics, in education, and in business." This fact expresses itself, for instance, in the current emphasis on vocational training in which learning to operate machines sometimes takes precedence over learning to operate a self—the very self which is under the influence of an essentially machine civilization. A truly liberal education, on the other hand, is regarded by some as a too-costly luxury, especially for the "hand-minded" (see Chapter VIII).

Finally, every local community is free as reflected in our growing concern with social and economic rights rather than with only the more narrowly conceived political rights with which eighteenth-century thought was concerned. But emancipation from tribalism and traditionalism will bring in its wake a legitimate freedom only if we can come to know and understand that it involves obligations as well as rights.

From these characterizations of the local community we learn that we live in one in both a spatial and a social sense and, in varying degrees, depending on our knowledge and imagination, in a global community— the Great Society—more and more in both a spatial and a social sense.

The local community and the Great Society are interdependent. The local community or neighborhood—call it the parish in the secular as well as the sacred meaning of the word—is, by definition, apart from the world of affairs.[5] Especially for youth, the parish—whether of the pump or the chapel—is the locus of the experiences by virtue of which they become, in a true sense, persons. In that sense the local community is of preeminent importance both as a spatial and a social fact. But once character has attained its basic structure we tend, in the light of what we know about the Great Society, to live a social existence which far exceeds the bounds

[5] See Emile Durkheim, *De la division du travail social* (Paris: Librairie Felix Alcan, 1938), now available in translation by George Simpson, as *Emile Durkheim on the Division of Labor in Society* (Glencoe, Ill., The Free Press, 1947).

of our native heath. But whether we live *from* the parish, *in* it, or both—as is the certain fact—the pervasive forces of an essentially rational and secular society invade it and change it before our very eyes.

John Dewey has shown us how these two worlds are related.

In the deepest and richest sense a community must always remain a matter of face-to-face intercourse. This is why the family and neighborhood, with all their deficiencies, have always been the chief agencies of nurture, the means by which dispositions are stably formed and ideas acquired which laid hold on the roots of character. The Great Community [by which Dewey refers to what Wallas calls the Great Society] in the sense of free and full intercommunication, is conceivable. But it can never possess all the qualities which mark a local community. It will do its final work in ordering the relations and enriching the experience of local associations. The invasion and partial destruction of the life of the latter by outside uncontrolled agencies is the immediate source of the instability, disintegration and restlessness which characterize the present epoch. Evils which are uncritically and indiscriminately laid at the door of industrialism and democracy might, with greater intelligence, be referred to the dislocation and unsettlement of local communities.[6]

It is this relationship between the neighborhood and the Great Society which we sought to clarify in our discussion of the journey from the family-who to the public-what situation. There we pointed out that the "real life situation" of students, in which their needs arise, cannot adequately or intelligently be served without their taking account of the relation between their needs and the needs of the society. That relation is always reciprocal and as youth increases in age and maturity its life is cast, more and more, in an ever widening area of influences.[7]

The interplay between personal and impersonal worlds.   The nature of the interplay between youth's personal and impersonal worlds warrants further discussion.

Human beings are animals who live together. But they are much more than that. Other forms of life—even plants—live together; birds, at least in the mating season, and apes. There are others but these are enough to establish the fact that man is not the only gregarious form of life.[8] Human beings are also animals who live and work together, sometimes at cross-purposes, in order not only to survive as animals, but as creatures with

---

[6] *The Public and Its Problems* (Chicago: Gateway Books, copyright 1946), pp. 211-212.

[7] See Karl Polyani, *The Great Transformation* (New York: Farrar and Rinehart, 1944), pp. 159-160.

[8] In this connection Professor Frank H. Knight makes the pertinent observation that "It is misleading to call man a social animal, since it is not as animal that he is social," "Fact and Value in the Social Sciences," *Science and Man*, Ruth Anshan, Editor (New York: Harcourt, Brace & Co., Copyright 1942), p. 331.

ideas and ideals. This is the chief difference between man and other forms of life—plus the power of communicating by the use of symbols. Man's ways are manifold and whatever is instinctive in his behavior is so coated with custom, tradition, and law as all but to erase any trace of instincts. He is value-maker and value-pursuer. He is a culture builder—the only one.

Man viewed as a space-filler—the spatial pattern. The pattern which human beings constitute as animals living together we call a spatial pattern, that relationship in which we may perceive and study man, *as if* he were only a space filler. The process by which this pattern comes about we call the symbiotic process.[9] (The pattern is sometimes referred to as "ecological.") By a spatial pattern we refer to a unity of human beings based on useful or utilitarian rather than on sentimental bonds. The former are relations which are established through buying and selling. It is in this context that we speak of the "impersonality of the market." These relations, as such, do not come about through sentimental contacts. *As such* they are not social relations; hence they do not bind individuals into a common culture. (We are again dealing with ideal-type constructs which do not exist in reality.) That they are inevitably a part of truly social relations we do not deny and shall come to the implications of that fact shortly.

Man viewed as a communicator—the social order. By a social order we mean a relationship which is based on the sharing of common purposes and meanings through communication. Whereas in a spatial pattern the individual components treat one another as *things*, in a social order they treat one another as *persons:* hence the impersonal and personal aspects, respectively, of human relations. But, in treating one another personally, we do not mean that they always treat one another kindly because sentiment may be expressed in negative as well as positive ways.

The social order—an order of distribution of thing and not-thing values. We now define a social order as an *order of distribution of values.* This does not exclude persons from it for they are makers of, bearers of, and

---

[9] Symbiotic means, literally, "living together" but without communication and hence only in a spatial or a social relation. The classic illustration of symbiotic bonds was given us by the elder Huxley. It runs as follows. One of the important economic activities of Ireland is the growing of flax from the fibers of which linen cloth is woven. The pollination of the blue flower of the flax is brought about by bees. In fact, except for chance pollination by the action of the wind, the flax flower would, were it not for the bees, produce sterile seeds. It so happens that bees are hatched from eggs but if mice are about and eat the eggs, no bees will be born. However, if cats are about they will eat the mice and thus render, unconsciously, a service to the flax plant which, needless to say, is also unconscious of this relationship. But, so the story goes, it is not likely that cats will be about unless there are also spinsters who, according to legend, are proverbial keepers of cats. Here is a whole web or network of relationships which relates cat-keeping spinsters to the vitality of the linen industry through a series of symbiotic relationships.

pursuers after values. Values are of two kinds: thing and not-thing. It is these toward which we take positive and negative attitudes: thing and not-thing values which we like or dislike, toward which we are attracted or by which we are repelled and which, in extreme cases, we love or hate. Thing values are such as these: houses, money, stocks and bonds, furniture, clothing, jewelry, and machines and gadgets of all kinds. Not-thing values are such as these: respect, honor, deference, esteem, power, ideals, theories, and ideologies of many kinds. Neither kind is more real or unreal than the other, although we are prone to think of not-thing values as unreal because they do not possess weight, form, or mass.

Values are unevenly distributed.　In our society, and all others of which we have historical knowledge, these two kinds of values are unevenly distributed. The order of their distribution in any society we call the *pattern* of their distribution. This is what we refer to when we say that a social order is an order or pattern of distribution of values.

We have already noted how a social order differs from that which lower animals and plants constitute. To those we now add the order of rocks, and the order of heavenly bodies. These orders are spatial only and in no way social because no conscious or intended interaction goes on between their constituent elements.

Men constitute both a spatial pattern and a social order.　We now bring these terms, a spatial pattern and a social order, into relation. Human beings, unlike other forms of life, constitute both a spatial pattern and a social order. If we view them *as if* their relations were only symbiotic or utilitarian we view them as *individuals*. If, on the other hand, we view them in their sentimental relations and as bound together by a common body of purposes and meanings (but never without disagreement), we view them as *persons*.

How the spatial and the social are related.　Thus it is that the associations of human beings may be viewed in two contexts: spatial and social. We remarked about each in our characterization of our society as an exemplar of modern society. From the perspective of its size, our view was chiefly a spatial one but, notwithstanding, one which carried with it certain social implications. Our view of its complexity permitted us to see it, again, in both spatial and social ways: the cheek-by-jowl closeness of people of many creeds, colors, and political ideologies all of which make for great difficulties in building and maintaining a harmonious world. The account of its speed suggests how the movement of peoples and goods—even the rate at which the human voice may be sent across long distances—which are spatial ways of looking at man, implies changes in his social relations.

Next there is the mechanism of our society which has given us, among many other things, the instruments by which we have made the world one vast whispering gallery. Surely the latter is a social consequence of mechanism. Finally, we have the characteristic of freedom which, in a spatial sense, means the breakdown of the traditionally narrow boundaries of communities of all sizes and the consequent creation, in both a spatial and a social sense, of the Great Society in which freedom has become contagious. In fact all the other characteristics tend to focus on the creation of the freedom to move and thus create a new social order more vast in its potential form and extent than any man has hitherto known. That this is denied or retarded in significant ways by restrictions on immigration both behind the Iron Curtain and on our side of it does not gainsay the generic relation of freedom to move with wider and more social-like freedoms. It only confirms it, negatively.

What the concept "social" means. We now need to clarify what we mean by the term "social." By it we do not necessarily mean something good, or, for that matter, something bad. We mean only a set of reciprocal human relations which are always characterized by a quality of sentiment, positive or negative, such as love, admiration, hate, scorn, and feelings of right and wrong.

Symbiotic, the opposite of social. The opposite of *social* is neither antisocial, unsocial, nor bad. It is *asocial* or symbiotic, that is, relations from which all sentiment is absent. This distinction is an ideal rather than a real one, for all social relations are capable of being ranked or graded in terms of the quality and quantity of their sentimental content. It is impossible for a human being to act in a completely asocial way toward his fellows. Even to ignore another is to choose not to recognize his presence or show deference to him. Thus such an act has a negative social character. Both parties are affected by such a display. The distinction made here does not deny that we often use the term "asocial" in speaking of timid, withdrawn, or hostile persons but even in this common-sense use of the term we refer to a negative quality of social relations.

Varieties of the social. Whenever human beings communicate by word or gesture, social relations exist: in a gang of thieves and between rival gangs, in a civil war and at a peace table, in a race riot and in a citizens' group formed to prevent such forms of violence. A debate between an American and a Soviet representative in the UN would be a social relation, however wide apart the two were on the matter at discussion.

(If what I am saying contradicts what "people say" you will do well to remember that what is held to be true in common sense is sometimes in sharp disagreement with what is held to be so in social science. Your task is to decide whether you understand what I am saying, rather than whether it agrees with what "people say." Your mastery of a scientific view of the social order will rest first on your mastery of the terms used to set it forth.)

Thus far, we have said what a social order is, how it differs from a spatial or symbiotic one, and have defined both social and order. Although we have said that a social order comes about by reason of reciprocal interpersonal relations we need to reduce this total process to its constituent parts. If we can do that we shall be better prepared not only to understand it but likewise to control it.

The relation of order to process. We begin by assuming that its order may be discovered by reason of a "working." We call this a process. This is a major postulate of all science. Thus we assume that the patterns we have identified—one spatial, the other social—are not due to whim or caprice or, at least, they are not due *primarily* to them. We also assume that these patterns are determinate rather than fortuitous. This means that, within the limits of human knowledge, we can determine how they came about. (We readily admit that these orders are not as determinate as those of rocks, stars, and planets.) In making these assumptions we affirm not only a scientific fact but also a great ethical principle, namely, that there is order in the universe.

The scientist must imagine. Why do we do this, and how do we do it? The why is answered by the fact that the basic interest of science is in "how things work." This is not revealed through the eye of common sense. With such an eye everything seems to be helter-skelter. But we wish not only to know how things work—for even to the eye of common sense they appear to be active—but we also wish to control them. The scientist has no other recourse than to *imagine* how they work, for he cannot see processes; he can see only their results. Thus he imagines a process or a set of processes and tests each by applying it to observable facts. Thus the why and how are explained.

Meaning of the concept, "process." The concept *process* is thus the name not only of a "working" but of a regular and orderly working through which change takes place. We can control it, within limits, by *directing* it. A process is an emergence, a becoming—it moves *from* something *to* something.[10]

Free will and determinism. At this point objection may be raised by

---

[10] See Frederick J. Teggart, *Theory of History* (New Haven, Yale University Press, 1925), especially p. 46 and pp. 158-159. See also his *The Processes of History* (New Haven, Yale University Press, 1918).

those who fail to understand, have little faith in, or even reject the postulates and methods of science. They say that human beings are creatures of free will and hence that man alone determines what he does and what happens to him; that he is unaffected by factors which lie outside him. But happily it is not a matter of one or the other: pure self-determinism or *pure* determination by the environment. This is not to say that man's relations with his fellows are as determinate as those of plants, rocks, and stars. But it does not follow, because man is different from these classes of things, that there is nothing determinate about him. Despite the fact that much of his action reveals a unique kind of causation, namely *motivation*, which other forms of nature do not reveal, social science affirms that man's behavior is not to be explained solely on the basis of free will. Man molds and is molded by his culture. He is a result of the transaction between his inner and outer environment. He is both like and unlike others of his kind in significant ways. He is an individual. Our analysis throughout will be guided by these assumptions, which are confirmed in the postulates and methods of social science.[11]

What we have then is a pattern of values and/or a pattern of human beings who are creators of, pursuers after, and bearers of values. It is in this sense that men are not mere animals. But how did any given pattern of values come about? By the working of what process or processes may it be explained? Thousands of events are happening at any moment. It helps a little to say that they may be ordered by a social process, but it does not help much. It tells us only that the pattern of any social order is due to communication, which is unique to man.

Four kinds of communication.   What kinds of communication processes can we imagine? Shall they be four or four thousand? We choose the smaller number. The four are these: *competition, conflict, accommodation,* and *assimilation*. (I shall deal with another set of processes in Chapter XXI.)

But the four we have named are quite abstract. They are titles, rather than copies, of what goes on between human beings. They are convenient, economical, and useful ways of abstracting certain phases of reciprocal

11 In "Fact and Value in the Social Sciences," *op. cit.*, p. 341, Professor Knight writes in part as follows: ". . . man must be described in terms of at least a half-dozen fundamental kinds of entity or being. He is (*a*) a physical mechanism; (*b*) a biological organism, with characteristics extending from those of the lowest plant to the highest animal in the biological scale; (*c*) a social animal in the traditional-institutional sense; (*d*) a problem-solving individual in the economic sense, as economic man; (*e*) a problem solver at the higher level of critical deliberation about ends; (*f*) a social being in the sense of the free association of individuals with characteristics (*d*) and (*e*)." Professor Knight adds in another paper that man is also a problem to himself.

human activity. Hence they are simplifications of what "really" goes on. Furthermore, they are not tangible entities. You cannot touch them or see them, although you can both touch and see people engaging in activities which may be roughly correlated with each of them. Nor are they descriptions. They are *derivatives*, created by abstracting parts from a whole. They are a set of fictions or "as ifs" which permit us to say something like this: reciprocal human relations can be viewed *as if* they were regular and orderly and *as if* this regularity and order were due to the interplay of these processes. To the degree such fictions give us an ordered acquaintance with and insight into the behavior of people in groups, their construction and use is justified. At any given time our society, or any other, since these processes are universal to men, gets its orderly or patterned character from the complex interplay of four processes. What they are and how they operate and interrelate now concern us.

COMPETITION. The results of this process can be observed in pure form only among plants. In the plant community the *only* interplant process is competition. No plant has any regard for any other plant. None can communicate with another. Some are dependent on others and between some there is *interdependence*. The mistletoe, which is a parasite, is dependent on the oak. Between certain trees and moss there is an interdependence. The moss competes with the tree for sustenance from the soil which is common to the life of both. The tree serves as the home of the moss, which pays its rent by helping to hold and conserve the moisture at the base of the tree. In other cases of interplant relations the process is one of competition to the extinction of one of the species, as in the case of crab grass and bluegrass. But whether the case be one of living together (a form of commensalism) or of extermination, the relations are completely nonsentimental.

Among nonhuman animal forms, the competitive process is often modified by a kind of instinctive sentiment. This exists, for instance, between the mother bear and her cubs. It is not learned but inborn. Between some forms of plant and animal life a kind of mutuality exists. The yucca plant, for instance, provides food for the larvae of the yucca moth which, in turn, pollinates the yucca blossom. But obviously, neither plant nor moth is aware that it either gets or gives a service.

The interdependence of the plover bird and the crocodile is another instance of interanimal competition, but far short of the extermination of one by the other. Indeed, a form of co-operation ensues from such competition. The crocodile holds its mouth open to permit the plover to enter and pick off the leeches which suck blood from the gums of the crocodile.

The plover thus gets its food and the crocodile gets rid of a harmful parasite.

The competitive process goes on between human beings, but is always modified by some cultural influence: affection, conscious rivalry, hate, planning, compromise, and so on. But despite the intrusion of such forms of sentiment, competition among humans is the most impersonal of the four processes noted earlier.

Competition, always modified in some way, goes on between men in all societies—even in Soviet Russia. This is due, everywhere, to the fact of scarcity. Space and the conditions of sustenance are everywhere limited, to some degree. To the degree that all living organisms—plant, lower animal, and human—increase their numbers, the tempo of competition tends to increase. Competition underlies and pervades all aspects of human life, despite political policies which may be used to reduce or eliminate it. It has certainly not been eliminated in the civil and political life of the Soviet Union.

In our society competition, or rather modified competition, takes many forms. "Dear" labor competes with "cheap" labor although the persons affected may not be conscious of it. Children compete for the affection and attention of their parents. Political parties compete for the support of the voters. The dominant theme of business enterprise is competitive. But in each of these, as in thousands of other instances, pure competition is always modified by some form of sentiment: the policies of organized labor, love or the lack of it of parents, a sense of fair play at campaign time (sometimes conspicuous by its absence when name-calling is resorted to) and the many kinds of laws regulating business.

CONFLICT. When competition becomes conscious and personal it changes to conflict. War is its purest manifestation among human beings. But there are also trade wars between competitors in the market. Conflict also takes place between ethnic, racial, and occupational groups.

All conflict is conflict over both *thing* values and *not-thing* values. Likewise competition, to the degree that it can be distinguished from conflict, goes on over both of these kinds of values. What the values are depend on time, place, and the characteristics of given cultures or divisions within cultures. The process of conflict goes on between individuals, between groups, and also *within* individuals and groups. Indeed, thinking is itself conflict between alternative hypotheses as to how one might solve a problem or resolve a difficulty. In the group it takes the form of discussion.

Conflict is not to be regarded as something essentially evil. Without it there would be no progress, although this is not to say that conflict insures progress. One of your major tasks as a teacher will be to humanize the process of conflict, not only through formal and informal discipline, but through the effect which your teaching may have in helping to reshape our society so as to reduce its conflicts.

Among human beings, conflict may result in total victory as in the extinction of the enemy, but it is more often modified by some form of compromise or conciliation. When the differences between conflicting individuals or groups are thus modified we use the term "accommodation" to name the process which has taken the place of conflict—insofar as either process is ever found in pure form.

ACCOMMODATION. As we have already noted, competition among human beings merges into conflict and it, in turn, tends to run its course and merges into accommodation. As long as competition and conflict dominate human relations things are in a greater or lesser degree of unsettlement—depending on the vigor of each process.

Conflict tends to be intermittent, that is, to recur rather than to be ever present. The strain which it puts on us is too great to bear over a long period of time. It is modified and becomes accommodation. But accommodation is not eternal—our personal and group experiences tell us that. Even so, it seems to be required for however long or short a period it may characterize the relation of people in labor groups, in the family, in political parties, in business organizations, or between nation-states.

Accommodation is in the nature of "live and let live." It is the result of the making of terms, of compromise and conciliation. It may lapse into conflict or move in the direction of assimilation. At best it is *adaptation to* rather than complete *acceptance of* a situation. The life of the child from infancy through adolescence is normally marked by a slow but progressive change from relations of conflict to those of accommodation. This is the process of the child's socialization, to which your teaching should make an important contribution. But the period of adolescence is often marked by the storm and stress of the child's experience with others—a shuttling back and forth between relations of conflict and accommodation. The task of the adolescent as well as adult newcomers to any society is that of finding a place in its social scheme. In the experience of finding a place and of learning the roles appropriate to it, the processes of conflict and accommodation are largely the means through which these things are done.

Accommodation is aided by the formation of habits and the acceptance of custom and tradition by adolescent and adult newcomers into a culture, alike. Between organized groups accommodation may be illustrated by the recent merger of the A.F.L. and the CIO. It may also be illustrated by the agreements which were once entered into by competing corporations, who made what were called "gentlemen's agreements" to maintain a given price level.

In substance, accommodation represents the striking of a social equilibrium in which custom, law, and sentiment combine so that life is livable and without the constant threat of being upset by conflict. In a free society such an accommodation is, ideally, a relation between coequal individuals. But such a condition of coequality is ideal rather than real. Usually the relations tend to reveal something in the nature of what the sociologists call "social differentiation" which, in the extreme, would reveal a class order as sharp as that of master-slave. In any real society it would always reveal an uneven distribution of such values as property, power, deference, esteem, and respect. It is for this reason that every social order reveals an order of distribution of values which is judged by some to be fair, by others as unfair.

The main ordering factor in modern society is not love which, although it is the deepest and dearest sentiment, is an unstable one. In fact no society is organized on the basis of love or any other *single* sentiment. The unity and order of our society, and many if not all others, are due to a working balance between freedom and restraint through various forms of social organizations, i.e., social institutions.[12] This is to say that rules of the game, laws, adjudication, compromise, and other forms of accommodation, rather than full and complete agreement on what our values should be and how they should be distributed, are the devices by which our culture maintains itself. The larger the society in population and area, other things being equal, the greater the likelihood that the processes of conflict and accommodation rather than that of assimilation will characterize its human interaction.

ASSIMILATION.   This is the fourth social process. Under the conditions which it assumes, the people of a society are in reasonably solid consensus or agreement about what their values should be and how they should be distributed. To the degree that human relations have reached the condition of assimilation, to that degree complete socialization has taken place.

---

[12] See Frank H. Knight, "Ethics and Economic Reform," in *Freedom and Reform* (New York: Harper & Brothers 1947), pp. 102-112. Anarchy presumes that each human being is capable of disciplining himself in such a way as to produce social harmony. But no such society has ever existed. Anarchy is intolerable even to those who say they want it, once they have had a taste of it. It is also *impossible*, human nature being what it is the world around.

That this is an ideal rather than a real state of affairs goes without saying. It is more fully attained in simple than in advanced cultures and finds its fullest realization in the latter under conditions of fear, such as the threat or the fact of attack by a powerful enemy. Persons and groups may reach an understanding about values on the basis of accommodation more quickly than on the basis of assimilation—except when the latter is the consequence of the emotion of fear.

The processes form a contiuum.　We may think of these four processes as arranged on a contiuum as follows: The poles X and Y represent the

$$X \ . \ . \ . \ . \ . \ . \ . \ . \ . \ . \ . \ . \ Y$$

Competition　　Conflict　　Accommodation　　Assimilation

least and most intimate human relations, respectively. Between them lie conflict and accommodation, which represent intermediate states of intimacy and interdependency. If the pole X (competition) may be taken to represent the most secular kinds of human relations, the pole Y (assimilation) may be taken to represent the most sacred. No human situation corresponds fully to either, but any single one may be graded by being placed somewhere on the continuum.

Assimilation may lapse back into accommodation. In more aggravated situations, it may revert to conflict, even to competition. Thus it is that competition, conflict, accommodation, and assimilation—as abstractions created for the purpose of social analysis—are phases or cycles of human interaction. Dynamic cultures are dynamic in just the sense that they represent moving rather than static conditions of equilibrium. Ours is such a culture. It finds its balance in varying degrees and combinations of competition, conflict, accommodation, and assimilation.

Thus it is that through the interplay of these four processes any given social order is created and re-created. Thus it sustains itself in time and space. All forms of group behavior are subject to analysis in terms of the play and interplay of these processes.

We now inquire what the constituent elements are which enter into the interplay of these four processes. These are the "given things" in every society: nonmaterial cultural elements, material cultural elements, human resources, and the physical habitat.[13] The first may be identified as a body of custom and beliefs and the second a corresponding body of artifacts and technological devices. The human resources are the popula-

[13] See Robert E. Park, "Human Ecology," *American Journal of Sociology*, XLII (July 1936), pp. 1-15; also his article, "Symbiosis and Socialization: A Frame of Reference for the Study of Society," *ibid.*, XLV (July, 1939), pp. 1-25.

tion and the physical habitat, which is everything we include under the term, "natural resources." [14]

We have already given illustrations of the first two: they are the not-thing and thing values of a culture, respectively. The human resources are the sentient beings we call men, by which term we refer to both sexes, all ages, and all the racial and ethnic varieties. These are the biophysiological units of a society and the bearers or owners of all the nonmaterial and material culture traits. The physical habitat is the theater, with all its properties (minerals, flora, fauna, climates, and atmospheres) on which the drama of any social order goes on and which are taken up into its social processes in such ways as to be useful (and harmful) to man.

Three views of the social order. With these elements in mind we again turn to a somewhat more abstract and analytical view of a social order.

Assimila-
tion: When
social inter-
action has brought
humans to a condition
of assimilation, the optimum quality of a social solidarity has been realized. The
measure of it is the degree to which
there is consensus as to what the value-
set should be and by what means and
"rules" the values are to be distributed. Assimilation is subject to lapse into accommodation
and conflict.

Conflict and Accommodation: Conflict is conceived as
"conscious competition" but unless it is to be allowed to go
on to the annihilation of one of the parties to it, some ground
on which a working agreement may be reached is found. Thus
accommodation is a form of compromise. This is a degree of intimacy and interdependence less ideal and perfect than assimilation. It may
change to assimilation or revert to conflict.

Modified Competition or Competitive Co-operation: Pure competition is
never found between human beings. Between them the least intimate relation is
conflict. It may be called modified competition or competitive co-operation; this
transformation is due to the presence of some form of sentiment.

Competition: This is found in its pure form only among plants, and in degrees, modified
by animal instinct, between the lower animals. Wherever commensalism exists between plants
or between plants and animals, the law of the jungle is thus partly modified.

CHART 1. *The Processes of Competition, Conflict, Accommodation, and Assimilation*

[14] Two definitions ought to be given at this point. By a *culture* we mean the distinctive way of life of a people, i.e., the distinctive ways in which the four social processes "operate." Man is everywhere different and he is everywhere the same. By this we mean that these four processes are found in all cultures, all ways of life, but that in each they operate in distinctively different ways. By a *society* we mean a group of people who have learned to associate themselves in the way distinctive to a particular culture.

The structure of a social order, respecting the degrees of interdependence and intimacy which exist among its members, may be represented by a cone or, when projected on a flat surface, a triangle. Since we are forced to use a two-dimensional figure we shall use the triangle. This has been called the "human relations triangle"[15]—not to be confused with the "domestic triangle" of human tragedy and folly.

Nothing new has been presented in Chart 1. The vertical ordering of the four processes does, however, help to emphasize the fact that as human relations move "up" from modified competition, through conflict and

> The Cultur-
> al: A "resid-
> ual" order in the
> sense that relations
> not political or economic
> are cultural. It represents
> the optimum aspect of assimila-
> tion, the most solid condition of
> consensus.

> The Political: This order is achieved, ide-
> ally, through discussion on two related ques-
> tions: "What is 'the good' for this group, i.e.,
> what should its values be?" and "What are the most
> effective ways of realizing that 'good'?" i.e., by means
> appropriate to the values themselves. Here values are
> treated at a somewhat more rational level than in the cul-
> tural order.

> The Economic: This order is concerned with the distribution of scarce
> means among an unlimited number of ends. Ideally it is worked out by
> the process of modified competition, or competitive co-operation. Through
> this process three related questions are resolved: "What shall be produced?"
> "By what proportional use of land, labor, and capital is it most efficiently done?"
> and "How shall the value product be distributed?" The resolution of these questions
> involves man in activities which combine economics and politics so that, in reality, they
> are almost indistinguishable.

> The Symbiotic: This order, as such, is not found among humans because symbiotic relations exist
> only among plants and, modified by "animal sentiments," among the lower animal forms. Human
> relations may be viewed as if men were associated only in spatial and hence asocial ways.

CHART 2. *The Social Order Viewed in Terms of Its Component Suborders: the Cultural, Political, Economic, and Symbiotic*

accommodation to assimilation, they become more intimately human. They do this because positive sentiment enters more and more into them: thus the social bond between the members or participants is strengthened.

In Chart 2, the suborders of the social order taken as a whole may be viewed and correlated, roughly, with the processes in Chart 1. In both charts the several social processes and suborders are arranged on a vertical axis to show the degree to which human relations become more intimate and

[15] See Robert E. Park, "Physics and Society," *The Canadian Journal of Economics and Political Science*, VI (May, 1940), pp. 135-152.

sentimental and charged with greater interdependence, as human beings are involved in various phases or social organization. Chart 2 portrays the division somewhat more than the unity or men's associations. Each sub-order is presented *as if* it might be experienced apart from the others, although this interpretation is modified somewhat. To the extent to which it is, the data of Chart 2 present social reality as man experiences it. Charts 1 and 2 are also related in the sense that for each of the four processes taken separately there is a corresponding phase or suborder of the total social order. Thus the relation between *process* and *order* is again confirmed.

Our third and last chart in this series is based much less on fictions than the foregoing two.

The person
and his rela-
tionships

The family as the
most intimate or prima-
ry of one's relationships

Political relationships

Economic, or market relationships

Territorial or geographic relationships

CHART 3. *The Human Relations Triangle Showing a Series of Relationships*

The base of this triangle is the territorial or geographic phase of human existence. It is basic to human relations in the sense that they are conditioned in important ways by how far apart or how near men are in space and by the degree of their dependence on the physical resources of their environment. Likewise, it is important to look at human relations from the perspective of the extent to which the members of any society are mobile or fixed in space. Man's relation to his fellows in space and to the resources of his physical environment are immediately and importantly affected by changes in technology (witness the difference in human relations in the horse-and-buggy days and in the jet age), by new knowledge, by new forms of social organization (e.g., the UN), indeed by any and all factors which affect communication between human beings.

The rubric "economic relationships" reminds us that humans not only live together in space and on the land—close in the city and apart in the country—but that they compete with each other, not only for goods and jobs but for prestige, honor, and affection. Their competitive relations—whether of the market or nonmarket variety—are also immediately affected by changes in modes of transportation. As for economic relations alone, their importance can hardly be overstated since the ties which men have with their fellows are usually economic before they are political—to the degree that the two may be separated. (The earlier term for economics, namely political economy, carried this meaning.)

Thus it is that man's economic and political relations are highly interdependent. The bargaining which has gone on since human cultures were born has been modified in one way or another by political factors.[16] Man's political relations have thus been founded a great deal more on territorial and economic than on familial grounds, at least in modern times. His political relations are not, however, unaffected by changes in technology, new knowledge, and new forms of social organization.

These three orders of relationships—territorial, economic, and political —may be correlated with the symbiotic, economic, and political orders shown in Chart 2, as well as with the processes shown in Chart 1. There remain the two types of relationships at the top of the triangle in Chart 3. These are the group and personal phases of the cultural order (Chart 2) whose corresponding process is assimilation (Chart 1). Ideally, the family may be viewed as providing the protective and loving conditions necessary for laying down the basic human nature of the child. Its protective function is carried out by shielding the child from the rigor of the affairs which go on in the political and economic orders. Here the family-who and the public-what are again brought into view.

The "person" at the top of Chart 3 symbolizes the moral and intellectual human being. His moral and intellectual qualities will be conditioned, in large part, by the quality of the social relations which obtain in the orders and processes which lie between the apex and the base of the triangle. This person, symbolizing adult man come into the fullness of his capacities, was at birth little more than a biological or statistical entity related spatially to others in a territorial or geographic order. As his age and maturing process permitted, he has been drawn more and more into the economic and political associations of his society. He has found a place in a division of labor, and come to full citizen rights in a political system. He also symbolizes the question, "What kind of men does it make?"

[16] Philip L. Grierson, in *The Silent Trade* (Edinburgh: W. Green and Sons, 1902), writes of trade between warring tribes. A space is cleared in the forest to which each tribe brings what it wishes to dispose of and which it assumes, or knows by past experience, the other needs. The trading is not only silent but done without the members of either tribe seeing one another. Political factors are quite absent in these transactions.

CHAPTER VI

Modern Society:
Persons and Institutions

OUR DISCUSSION of the social order revealed that men are bound together by bonds of sympathy, which may express itself in negative as well as affirmative ways. We also observed that human relations may have a quite impersonal nature as well as an intimately personal one. Man is, obviously, capable of many moods respecting his relations with his fellow men. We did not, however, take account of the view that human beings and their society stand in not only an antithetical but downright antagonistic relation: not sometimes, but characteristically. This was the view of Thomas Hobbes in the "war of all against all." For him, society and its political expression through the state were needed to repress man's base and animal tendencies. This view was also in Herbert Spencer's thought, although in a modified form, when he wrote of "man versus the state." Moreover, it persists in some social theories in our own time. A goodly number of people are shocked if not angered by the concept of "the service state," believing it to be not only immoral but contrary to human nature.

No necessary opposition between man and society. It is not my purpose, however, to espouse any of the many partisan views on this matter. Rather, it is to examine the belief that a necessary, natural, and inevitable opposition exists between men taken individually and collectively.

My inquiry begins by asking how human beings come to be human. Nonhuman animals are born, so to speak, in their old age; human beings, in their infancy. By this I mean that the former are born with most of their education behind them; their instincts contain the bulk of it. Human be-

74

ings, on the contrary, are born with all their education ahead of them: this is the organized experience through which they develop and shape their human potentials. The facts are that human nature is something which man does not have at birth (except potentially), which he acquires only through interaction with his fellows, and which withers in isolation from them.

Thus, the process by which human beings become persons is the same process by which they become members of groups. Goethe stated it beautifully in these lines from *Tasso*:

> Der Mensch erkennt sich nur im Menschen, nur
> Das Leben lehret jedem was er sei.

When translated, and shorn of much of their beauty, they read,

> Only in man does man know himself; life
> alone teaches one what he is.

What society is and where it is located now becomes our concern. The first is given by Alexis de Tocqueville:

A society can exist only when a great number of men consider a great number of things in the same point of view; when they hold the same opinions upon many subjects and when the same occurrences suggest the same thoughts and impressions to their minds.[1]

Where is society located? As to its location, which is implicit in what de Tocqueville has said, there are two answers. One is given in the language of the Christian ethic, the other in the language of social psychology. In the language of the former it is, like the kingdom of heaven, within you. In the language of the latter the case is the same although the report is a little longer:

In order to have a society it is . . . necessary that persons should get together somewhere; and they get together only as personal ideas in the mind. Where else? What other possible locus can be assigned for the real contact of persons, or in what form can they come in contact except as impressions or ideas formed in this common locus? Society exists in my mind as the contact and reciprocal influence of certain ideas named "I," Thomas, Henry, Susan, Bridget and so on. It exists in your mind as a similar group, and so in every mind.[2]

If we understand these conceptions as to what a society is and where it is located we may understand the error which people practice when they tell us that "society is just a bunch of people." That conception is a

[1] *Democracy in America*, Vol. I (New York: Allyn and Bacon, Inc., 1899), p. 398. Reeve translation.

[2] Charles H. Cooley, *Human Nature and the Social Order* (New York: Charles Scribner's Sons, Copyright 1902), p. 84.

spatial, not a social one. As a "bunch of people" human beings constitute a statistical unit and nothing more. But, as "personal ideas in the mind" they constitute a social order. This does not deny that the members of a society are biological forms which have number, density, and spatial distribution. They can, of course, be seen and counted. But, in the sense in which they form a society, they may be felt and appreciated and attitudes taken toward them.[3]

The fallacy that there is a basic and necessary antagonism between a human being and his society also appears in the mistaken meanings given to two words, "individual" and "social." Not only the separation but the opposition of these two words has its roots deep in the past.

Man is never free from social restraint. The events and the way of life which were produced by the waning of the Dark Ages, followed later by the Enlightenment, may be seen as a break with a long period in which men lived under the strict controls of the church and the state. The new day marked their partial release from these controls. But what is forgotten is that they were not now free from restraint. The case is rather that they continued to live under a set of social conditions, but social conditions which permitted them wider and freer options than they had hitherto enjoyed. They had not escaped society. They had only found themselves in one organized on less authoritarian principles.

The error in supposing that they were now released from social restraints stems from the fact that only the old traditions and old institutions from which they were now released were identified with the social. Contrariwise, it was erroneously presumed that their new life constituted a cutting loose of something called "the individual" from "the social." Out of this view came something called "*the* Individual"—an absolute creature and absolutely free.

From the conceptions born of this transition from a more to a less restraining scheme of social organization, and hence the emergence of human beings with wider margins of choice, seems to have come the idea that the term "individual" refers only to freedom and the term "social" only to restraint. (Throughout this discussion I use the term *individual* as synonymous with *person*.)

Mistaken uses of "individual" and "social." Many of us are disposed to use "individual" chiefly as a *noun* as when we speak of "the individual,"

---

[3] It is my sober view that the result of much teaching of the social studies leaves many students quite unaware of the reality of the social or collective aspect of man's experience. It is regrettable that some people interpret "collective" as dangerous because the Communists talk much about it. The term "collective" refers to as solid a reality as does the word "individual."

nd "social" chiefly as an *adjective,* as in the phrase "social legislation." There is, of course, nothing intrinsically wrong in using "individual" in the noun sense or "social" in the adjective sense. But when we lose sight of the fact that they may *both* properly be used as adjectives to modify "human being" we divorce them from that which has both individual and social, or collective, aspects. We hear a good deal about "the individual" as though he were some lone and independent entity existing in a social void. And when we speak or hear others speak of "social relations" we often seem to be unaware of the fact that they are the consequences of 'individuals-in-communication." This new relation is not one which can be explained in terms of simple addition. Its explanation requires the calculus of a complex interaction.

If we think of any human being in the concrete, rather than in the abstract, there comes to mind a creature born so helpless as to be dependent on others for his very existence, and continuing throughout life to be dependent upon them—though not in such a helpless way. We could not, for example, account for the emergence and development of the mind if we omitted the part which language plays. One becomes and is a self only in the measure that he can identify himself with other selves in the collective relations we call a society. This does not mean that man is an inert mass, clay in the potter's hands. No such simple analogy does justice to the process by which he becomes individualized and socialized —at the same time. There is no such thing as the mere conformity of the individual to his society. The relation between them is always after the manner of a *transaction.* Out of it emerges the thing we call individuality which permits each of us to be different from others in significant ways.

All men act in a social context. If you think of any person in a concrete way you are forced to put him in some social context, in some functional and mutual relation with other human beings. He is parent, employer, employee, farmer, student, merchant, lawyer, teacher, and so on. In each of these roles he lives an associated life in a family, a business enterprise, labor organization, a gild of those who till the soil, a school class, or a profession. Each of these roles and associations contains elements of both freedom and restraint.

Society makes individuals. Furthermore, we are usually more aware of individual human beings than we are of a society. This is probably due in large part to the belief, so common in a democratic society which is as new as ours, that society is by nature and by necessity repressive—a paradoxical notion indeed, in a democracy. That individuals constitute society would be readily admitted, but that society *makes* individuals would strike many as a false idea. It is easier to consider the single or *distributive* aspect of human life as more primary and even causative, than it is to consider its *collective* aspect.[4]

To the view that individuals are primary and causal, this discussion has lent no aid. Above all, it has sought to indicate that the individual is not a datum, something *given*. On the contrary it has conceived him as formed in and by the social process, the process in which individual selves come into being through communication with others. Hence the notion of purely individual action (except in the case of biological functions, which is an animal rather than a social aspect of man's behavior) is "an analytical concept reached only by quite heroic abstraction."

The reality is human life. By the same token, society is an unreal abstraction when regarded as something apart from and outside of human beings. The reality is *human life* which presents itself in collective (social) and distributive (individual) aspects. Moreover, we shall have a more accurate sense of what both individuals and societies are if we look upon societies, not so much as means of obtaining something for individuals—happiness, security, and like values—but as means of *creating* individuals. Thus we may come to see that neither an individual nor a society is merely one thing. The word "individual" refers not to one thing but rather is a general and covering term for a great variety of specific reactions, habits, likes, dislikes, interests, attitudes, and powers of human nature. These are evoked, and evoked differently, in different individuals under the influence of associated living. And so it is with the term "social." While "society" may be but a single word, it is an infinite variety of things. It includes all the ways by which men, through associating together, share their experiences and build up common interests and aims. It runs the gamut of street gangs, trade unions, religious societies, "syndicates" of hoodlums, the "social sets" of the 400, co-operatives, corporations, school districts, cities, nations, and such international alliances as NATO and UN.

"Individual" and "society" not metaphysical entities. Thus if we conceive of either "individual" or "society" as single and unitary things we give them the character of metaphysical entities or "things in themselves" which defy empirical investigation. We fall into the same error if we take individualism and socialism in a like manner. We cannot subscribe to one without subscribing to the other. But neither need be spelled with capital "I" or "S." Neither need be the name of a political party. And certainly

---

[4] See John Dewey, "The Crisis in Human History," *Commentary*, I (March, 1936), the subtitle of which is, "The Danger of the Retreat to Individualism." The immediately preceding discussion owes a heavy obligation to this article.

they need not stand in opposition. If we would find the opposite of "social" we must find it not in "individual," but in such words as "animal," "sensual," or some other word implying mental or moral inferiority.

Social organization secures individual liberty. The problem of building and maintaining a democratic society does not call for striking a balance between the claims and counterclaims of the individual and the society. The problem is not one which can be stated or understood in terms of either bookkeeping or horse-trading. The task we face, insofar as a clash or conflict of individual and social interests is involved, is one of determining the degree and kind of social organization which will secure to the individual the greatest liberty as a result of a blending or balancing of personal and social liberties.[5]

The nature and function of institutions. This brings us to inquire into the nature and function of social institutions. They are the quasi-persistent units of human interaction. Indeed a society can be thought of as a pattern of social institutions. An institution consists of a concept, a structure, and a set of functionaries. These are an "idea, notion, doctrine, or an interest," and a framework or apparatus which holds the members of an institution together in their collective concern with some idea, notion, doctrine, or interest. The functionaries are the officers. The function of a social institution is to serve its own ends (the advancement of its "concept") and through it serve the interests of men in society.[6]

Our chief concern is with the fact that the structure "holds the concept" and provides the means by which it may be served in the interests of society. For Sumner's "concept" (idea, notion, doctrine, interest) we now substitute the term ideal, aim, or purpose. These are the things which the apparatus of the institution serves. Hence, those persistent social arrangements which we call institutions (the home, the church, the school, the corporation, the labor union) are composed, so to speak, of two parts: ideals, aims, or purposes which are their *ends*, and the apparatus, form, or *means* through which these are served.

Institutions are "social habits." It is widely known and accepted that habits serve individuals in such ways as to organize and integrate their activities. But it is not so widely known or accepted that institutions serve societies in a similar fashion. Were it not for social institutions, each newborn infant would enter upon a social void. But, thanks to the nature and function of institutions, his capacities, potentialities, tendencies, and im-

[5] See G. D. H. Cole, *Social Theory*, p. 185. See also the discussion on this point in Chapter II.
[6] See William Graham Sumner, *Folkways* (New York, Ginn & Company, 1906), p. 53.

pulses are shaped and fixed in purposeful ways—purposeful for his self-realization within the context of his association with others in some one or more of the myriad institutions of his society.

Thus the integration which a society enjoys at any time, as well as its existence through time, is possible because of its institutional organization. Institutions thus possess a kind of quasi-immortality. It seems that individuals take the short view, and institutions the long view. They can do this because their life span, at least as respects those which provide the basic structure of a society, is much longer than that of their founders.

Individuals go; institutions remain. But enough of institutions in the abstract. I recently visited the village of my boyhood. I wished to discover whether individuals or institutions possessed the greater immortality—at least "this side of Jordan." Three decades and more had passed since I had left it. My disappointment was great because the boyhood friends I had hoped to see were no longer there. I had forgotten, they too had left. Instead of old faces I found only old institutions.

There was the depot at the foot of Main Street. Old John Reynolds had gone, but the station-house was there: the potbellied stove, the click of the telegraph, and all the sights and sounds I had known as a boy. The man was dead but the institution, symbol and mechanism for insuring communication and transport, had lived on. It had been there before Old John. It was still there giving structure, balance, and pattern to activities which, without it, could not take place.

There was the building, little better than a shanty, where the *Enterprise* ran off the weekly ration of village and farmside gossip. Of course everybody already knew it but, nevertheless, it had to be institutionalized into print every Thursday. But Uncle Billy did not peer out at me over his steel-rimmed spectacles. He too had gone. And the old hand press, and some of the cobwebs. But the Press was there, and a new editor: never mind his name. The institution had lived.

The old frame school where I "went" to Kate Parmalee (my third grade teacher and my first love) was now the high school. A new building, hard by, housed the grades. But neither Miss Parmalee, nor Mr. Porter, the principal, nor any who had taught under him, was there. Only the institution remained: the school, pattern-maker for successive generations of culture-bearers.

The church house in which my father had preached had been destroyed by fire; a new building of greater beauty and utility stood on its site, and in the intervening years pastors and people had come and gone. But the church stayed on.

The events which had transpired since the days of my youth and this my first return had transpired *in* and *through* and *by* these institutions. How well they had served the ideals of village life I do not know. That is not now my interest. But whether those ideals had been well or poorly served, it was individuals working *in* and *through* and *by* institutions such as these which had served them.

The problem is not institutions "or" men. If anyone supposes that this emphasis on institutions does away with equal emphasis on individual human beings he is mistaken. The task of our time, in which social knowledge plays a unique role, is not that of producing good men *or* good institutions. It is one of producing good men *in* and *through* and *by* good institutions. If each generation took its institutions with it to the grave, its successor would have to start from scratch—the cave of Neanderthal man.

A conservative tendency in institutions. But institutions tend to grow conservative. Although their arteries harden and they fall sick, they tend to linger on. We bury our personal dead with the proper ritual and within a reasonable time after their demise. But even when, for all practical purposes, some of our institutions die we permit them to lie about—not only useless but harmful to our social welfare. In this senile state they become almost completely preoccupied with their form or apparatus and, in doing so, they either fail almost completely to serve the ends for whose service they first came into being or, with consequences which are equally out of place, they cherish those ends and attempt to serve them (however feebly) in the present in quite the same way they did in the past. Thus it is that social institutions tend to behave as if a given form (or structure) which was adequate and relevant to advance a given purpose (concept) in times past is, by that token, adequate and relevant to advance that same purpose in times present.

In permitting ourselves to be uncritical of the relevance and adequacy of our institutional forms to our ideals and purposes, for whose service they were originally designed, we engage in what Kenneth Burke calls "ethicizing the means of support." Its simple equivalent appears in the miser's practice of valuing the possession of his gold more nighly than its use for goods and services. The burden of our argument is that institutions have to be remade as well as established in their original form.

A great moral ideal and changing institutions. Let us now examine the institutional means which were once quite adequate to serve a great moral ideal and ask ourselves if they are still adequate to its service in our time.

"Thou shalt love thy neighbor as thyself." It can hardly be denied tnat the conditions required for the fulfillment of this commandment in our time differ from those in which it was first given. The Galilean social scene was a simple one. It was a rural and provincial society composed chiefly of closely knit and quite self-sufficient villages. Tribal and family ties were strong. There was little if any mobility. People knew each other intimately and throughout the entire span of their lives. In this setting they could practice the primary virtues of love, mutual aid, and brotherliness in truly personal and emotional ways, through the simple institutions of the tribe and the village.

If such a commandment is to be served in a society such as ours we shall have to distinguish between the letter and the spirit of the injunction to "love thy neighbor." Neighborliness as an ideal is still necessary for the good society but the means which were adequate for its realization in the long ago are no longer adequate.

It is, no doubt, possible for one to love his neighbor whom he knows personally but quite impossible to love people the world around whom he does not know, has never seen, nor shall likely ever see. If the ideal is to be served it must be understood as one not necessarily dependent on the institutions of a simple social system. We must distinguish between the ideal as still a precious end, and the conditions of a simple society as means which are no longer adequate. To learn that it can be served by different institutional means is our task and the task of our students.[7]

Thus, if we would take account of social change—to keep pace with it or seek to direct and control it—we must critically examine the serviceability of our inherited institutions. If our values are to be protected and advanced in a world in which change is a constant, we must continually reconstruct the institutional forms through which our personal service to them is rendered.

New times require new institutions. The dark and troubled days on which the discharge of personal responsibility have fallen is due then not only to the characteristics of modern society we have noted. It is also due to our ignorance, our unwillingness, our inability, or our ineptness in devising institutions which are fit and proper for serving the conditions which we face. Apparently, we must sometimes be almost frightened into devising them. But emotion has always been a stronger motivating force than reason. If we are not concerned about people on the other side of the globe

---

[7] To love one's neighbor is to love him because of the not-thing values which he honors. Chief among these are truth, beauty, goodness, and good workmanship. It is such ideals and attitudes as these which we may still love in men who live half a world away. See Frank H. Knight, "Religion and Ethics in Modern Civilization," *Freedom and Reform*, p. 172. We are here dealing with some of the Great Oughts of the democratic faith which we referred to earlier as "changing permanents."

in the old humanitarian terms we might well concern ourselves about them in terms of sheer biological survival. This is, however, only the least common denominator by which we can act.

To know distant people is to know them not so much in personal as in political terms. This is to know them in terms of the manifold ways in which we are related to them and they to us: what effects their fortune or misfortune have on us and ours on them, how we differ in what we severally stand for and what the grounds for a workable mutuality might possibly be, how our differences might be reconciled, indeed what compromises are required. To know others, near or far, is to know how we and they are related. It is not things in isolation but things in *relation* with which social study deals.

Improved human nature and improved institutions required. The gap between our ideals and our practices can be narrowed by bringing about two improvements. These are an improved human nature and improved social institutions. But the first can be had only through the second. And, paradoxically, we can accomplish the second only in the measure that the human nature of the good and the wise embodies and multiplies itself through better social institutions.

This is, however, not a counsel of good men *or* good institutions. It is a counsel of better men as means to better institutions and, in turn, better institutions as means to better men. It is better men, individually and collectively, that we need if we would bring our society nearer its ideals. Nor does this view deny the validity of Alexander Meikeljohn's question which must be asked of every society: "What kind of men does it make?" We argue, after the nature of human relations and the logic of the social sciences, that men are made through association, and association takes institutional form. We can no more secede from institutions than we can secede from the human race. It is the obligation of every generation in a democracy to bequeath to the one which follows it a better society than the one which was bequeathed to it. There is no way this can be done save through the improvement of institutions.

Confused ideas of change. But such a theory of social change runs counter to the prevailing folklore of our time. Many of us subscribe to two contradictory principles, (*a*) man is "infinitely perfectible," and (*b*) "you can't change human nature." Both cannot be true. Not until this confusion is cleared up can we get ahead with social improvement, or even believe that it is possible.

We must also understand the meaning of the paradox that "human nature is everywhere the same and everywhere different." It is everywhere the same in the sense that man is everywhere *man;* that everywhere he constitutes a common treasury of human potentialities. But human nature is also everywhere different because the cultures in which men live and which give pattern, direction, and meaning to their potentialities are everywhere different.

Everywhere men are pugnacious, but whether they display their pugnacity in humor, pantomime, or armed conflict is determined by the culture in which they live. Everywhere men are affectionate, but the institutional forms—the clan, the tribe, the family—which pattern and satisfy their affections are a cultural matter. Everywhere men love honor but what is considered honorable is a matter which their cultures define. But we are sometimes so blinded by our own cultural pride and ethnocentrism that we think any display of human nature which differs from that which our culture disposes us to manifest is necessarily inferior to ours. We even consider it unhuman.

Many of us believe that the motive for economic gain is a trait of original and universal human nature: that when the seller raises his price, if buyers increase their demand for a commodity, *original* human nature is being displayed. The facts are that it is *our* human nature which is a product of *our* culture to do so. It is not the human nature of the Trobriand Islanders, or the disciples of Tolstoi or Gandhi.[8]

When, for instance, we say that the TVA, the FEPC, or the UN is against human nature we argue on false grounds. The real grounds on which our objections rest is that we don't want to give up our accustomed and vested ways of running a civilization. We don't want to give up our traditional institutions. It is high time we quit making human nature the whipping boy for the shortcomings of a civilization.

The myth of the individual as absolute.   This is not a new perspective. It is only unpopular and hence readily forgotten or rejected. It is unpopular because it challenges the toughest myth of our time—the myth of the individual as absolute. To believe that the quality of either our ideals or practices is unrelated to the quality and vigor of our institutions, whose task is to hold them in trust, is to argue that the resolution of our difficulties will come about by every one's achieving moral and intellectual individuality without the help of anybody else.

The thesis in essence.   The essence of my thesis is this: life goes on in associated, corporate, and institutional form. These give it its organized character. When its ideals suffer it is necessary that we re-examine not

---

[8] See Adolf Löwe, *Economics and Sociology: A Plea for Cooperation in the Social Sciences* (London, George Allen & Unwin, Ltd., 1935), pp. 50-51.

only them, but the forms in which their protection and trusteeship is lodged.

Our difficulties are not chiefly in the realm of our ideals. Rather, they trace to the fact that we have not made those institutional changes necessary for effective and devoted service to them. As Dickens wrote, "Old Marley was as dead as a door nail . . ." the wisdom of our ancestors is in the simile—as well as some of the institutions which they founded. We are in a period, not only in our own country but in the whole round world, and in all the arts and crafts of mankind, which makes it imperative that we submit to critical examination the institutions we inherited from our fathers which are less than adequate to control a technology which we did *not* inherit from them.

The test is a simple one. If our old institutions, however old, still serve well such ideals as brotherhood, well-being, security, and peace, they should stand unchanged. If they do not, they should be revised. We ought to know which are expendable—old and still precious ideals *or* the old and ineffective apparatus of the institutions which hold them in trust. This is a genuine "either-or." But it is not a call to revolution. It is a call to sober, devoted, and critical re-examination and reconstruction of some of our social institutions. If we would have a better human nature and a better-integrated culture we must remake the patterns which will produce them. These are persons and institutions which will honor, better than today's, our democratic ideals.

> Give me the liberty to know, to utter, and to argue
> freely according to conscience, above all liberties.

Our own Roger Williams voiced the spirit of a new world when he declared:

> The sovereign, original, and foundation of civil power
> lies in the people . . . people may erect and establish what
> form of government seems to them most meet.

And it was Edmund Burke who said,

> I do not know the method of drawing up an indictment against
> a whole people.

In Burke's time, from our own Tom Paine and Thomas Jefferson come two great testaments of faith in truth and reason,

> But such is the irresistible nature of truth, that all it
> asks—and all its wants—is the liberty of appearing.

That from Paine, and this from Jefferson,

> Reason and experiment have been indulged, and error has fled
> before them.

The martyred Lincoln held that

> This country, with its institutions, belongs to the people
> who inhabit it,

which is one with his devout hope that

> . . . government of the people, by the people, and for the
> people, shall not perish from the earth.

The good grey Whitman, poet of democracy if there ever was, promised,

> I will make the most splendid race the sun ever yet shone upon;
> I will make divine magnetic lands
> With the love of comrades,
> With the life-long love of comrades.
> I will plant companionship thick as trees . . .

We are trustees of many values. Of testaments such as these, and countless others, our legacy consists. Of these, we are trustees: trustees of justice, love of truth, reasonable persuasion, human dignity, mutual respect, neighborliness, brotherhood, material well-being, peace . . . the list is long. These, and many more, are the points on the compass of our faith by which we set our course. These are the not-thing values to which we give lip service, but too frequently shameful infidelity in our acts.

We fail our trusteeship.   We mistake comfort for civilization and wealth for happiness. We are more concerned with freedom *from* than freedom *for*. We establish guilt by association and confuse condemnation with inquiry. We mistake bigness for goodness. We control our children more by force and fear than we lead them by love. For many of us the government is *they*, not us. We mistake a standard of living for a standard of morality. We alternately praise and condemn self-interest, forgetting that it is good or bad depending on whether it advances or retards the common good. We not only deny the ideals of our heritage but have lost the will to believe in them. We confuse fitness to survive as biological forms with the art of living the good life. We contemplate the law only as a means of forcing men to serve the letter of it, forgetting that it also permits them to honor its spirit. We hold that "everybody has a right to his opinion" even when he hasn't a single fact to support it. For many of us, thinking is little more than a search for more convincing ways to support our prejudices.[3]

More than crooked thinking.   Voltaire's dictum comes to mind: "As long as we think absurdities we shall continue to commit atrocities." But crooked thinking is not all there is to our difficulty. The plight we are in is both intellectual and moral. Our difficulty reveals a tragic confusion of means and ends. This confusion takes several forms. Among them are such as the following: [4]

We are ignorant of our ends; hence we are directionless.

We know our ends but deny them except through lip service; hence we are hypocrites.

We use means which are unsuited to the realization of those ends of which we are aware; hence we lack a sense of relevance.

We take our means for our ends; hence we fall into moral materialism.

We assume that our ends will be realized without the use of means; hence we practice self-delusion and sentimentalism.

"Whirl is king."   Thus far, our diagnosis has taken no account of the complexity of the world we live in. Much of what we face, do not under-

---

[3] For a critique of American culture see Robert Lynd, *Knowledge For What?* (Princeton: Princeton University Press, 1939).

[4] I shall not attempt here to deal with the many nuances of the means-ends problem or dilemma. The disjunctions noted here are all but self-evident. For further reading see Melvin Rader, *Ethics and Society* (New York: Henry Holt & Co., 1950); George R. Geiger, *Philosophy and the Social Order* (New York: Houghton Mifflin Co., 1947) and Wayne Leys, *Ethics and Social Policy* (New York: Prentice-Hall, Inc., 1941).

stand, and hence do not know how to face is a world which this generation did not make, but inherited. But, in Justice Holmes's phrase, "we are
in the belly of the universe; it is not in us." It is, however, more chaos than
cosmos. As Aristophanes wrote almost half a thousand years before the
Christian era, "Whirl is king, having driven out Zeus." The period of
modernity has been a long one.

It is not evasion to say that most of our difficulties have been inherited.
But it does not absolve us from the fear, the apathy, and the confusion
which grip us. The great tragedy is that men are no longer sure. This lack
of a sense of certitude is the function of the circumstances in which we
live and in our own character, as individuals and as a people.

What is a crisis in valuation? Let us now ask what a crisis in valuation
is, and name some of the uncertainties which we face.

A crisis in valuation is a time of great difficulties, of many alternatives,
and of decisions which we do not know how to resolve, or knowing, lack
the consensus and the courage to make those changes which are required
for their proper definition and action on them. We are not wholly without consensus, if it can be so called, but it is a consensus born of fear
rather than agreement reached through sober and rational discussion. We
are more disposed to excoriate the devils to whose evil machinations we
lay our difficulties than to search our minds and consciences.

A crisis in valuation is a time when we assume that the dogmas and
institutions we have inherited need no re-examination or, admitting the
need for it, lack the courage to make it. It is a time of moral imbalance and
bewilderment marked by frustration, bickering, conflict, and profound disagreement on both what we ought to do and the manner of doing it. It is
a time when a culture has lost its integrity because it has lost its integrity:
the first *integrity* meaning fidelity to declared purposes, the second meaning
our inability or unwillingness to act in concert and thus regain our moral
unity.

It is a time when the blacks and whites of an older world are gone, a
world with neat and trim borders around fields of both knowledge and
morals. It is a time when we have no clear-cut answer to any important
question: the nature of men, the "best" political system or social or economic arrangements, the destiny of the individual, the fate of nations or
even of the human species. No longer, for honest and dedicated men, are
certitudes certain or their philosophical and ethical metes and bounds clear
or fixed. The rules which, in an easier and more tranquil time, seemed to
carry their reasonableness and justification for all time written on their
foreheads, now reveal with equal plainness, their provisional and *ad hoc*

nature, their local and temporal limits. As Walter Lippmann has observed, "Our ancestors thought they knew their way from birth through all eternity; we are puzzled about day after tomorrow." [5]

How clear are our goals as individuals and as a nation? How universal and firm is our devotion to them? What respect do we have for the past? How well do we know it, or knowing it what relevance do its "lessons" have for our time? What alternatives do we face and what consequences might follow from each? What means do we use to discover these things? Are negotiation and appeasement the same? With whom and about what? Is it right to compromise; about what issues, when and with whom? Do we have enough facts? How inclusive-exclusive are our hypotheses? Are they about real problems? What are the real problems? What is the right thing to do, about what, how, and when? What are we willing to give up to get what we believe is right?

Teachers have special obligations. These are questions for all to ponder. They are citizens' questions. Teachers are citizens but they are citizens charged with a special task. Let us inquire what some of their problems are. Those I record here are from Dr. Margaret Mead's Inglis Lecture at Harvard in 1951. They are dated but they are not outdated, nor will they be in this generation or for many generations to come.[6]

Dr. Mead begins, not with questions but with an image of teaching, an image born of profound knowledge and insight not only into our culture but many others, strange and exotic as we are wont to view them.

. . . before we have devised a way of life in which to keep our teachers abreast of life, so that they can teach those things and in those ways which they now know how to teach, we need a new kind of teaching altogether. From the teacher of the traditional world we need a reunderstanding of history in the light of our new knowledge about men and their motives. We need this desperately, because otherwise, under the pressure of a changed world, the past—and all that it means in models and in communication with ourselves through the use of symbols our forebears used—may well be lost to us. From the teachers of little children we still need a cheerful willingness to preserve in the child that which is there, *to tolerate an impulse long enough so that it may be regulated rather than rejected.* We need not only a willingness to welcome the way in which the child unites its individual phantasy with the phantasy creatures of its culture, but we also need new inventions in which the child will be left free to integrate all through life—with the vividness and immediacy and concrete images so easily come by in childhood—each new experience. If we are to continue

---

[5] I have to thank Mr. John R. Seeley, former Professor of Sociology at the University of Toronto, for many of the insights of the immediately foregoing.

[6] *The School in American Culture* (Cambridge: Harvard University Press, Copyright 1951), pp. 38-41.

living in this changing world, we need an art which can face it and make sense of it, not arts which are the screams of the dispossessed and the forsaken in a world they never knew. But to have such an art we need to keep alive a type of awareness which it was once enough to cherish in childhood, so that the gifted artist and philosopher might use this access later, as he built new symbols for his generation. We must devise new ways, not of cherishing awareness of self a little longer, which is all that the current nursery school really tries to do and which is all that the child nurse and the peasant nurse did, but instead ways of making that early awareness a continuing part of the personality into adulthood and old age. We need, in fact, to do for many men what accidents of gift and history made possible in the occasional great geniuses of the past. (Italics added.)

The importance of communication. In all the literature on teaching, I know no statement which excels this in imagination and devotion. I know of few which equal it. In the following, with which she concludes her lecture, Dr. Mead speaks further of the problem of method—*method* of communicating, not technique—and closes with some of the questions which we all face but which fall to the teacher with unique singularity.

And finally, and perhaps most difficult of all, we need from the teacher who has relied on teaching how a tried method can be used on new materials, a totally new kind of teaching—a teaching of a readiness to use *unknown* ways to solve unknown problems. We are facing a world which this adult generation is unable to grasp, to manage, to plan for. The most we may reasonably hope for is that somehow the old unsuitable methods will get us through until another generation is able to tackle the job. But through history, each generation has stood on the shoulders of the past, each new learning has come from an old learning, if only by way of contradiction and explicit rejection. How are we who do not know what to do, who do not know how to live in one world, who have no faintest trace of habituated capacity to operate in a world which may actually destroy itself, who do not know how to carry in our hearts the weight of those who died yesterday in Burma or who may die tomorrow in Prague, or how to cope with the spectacle of machines, which can do problems which the men who design the machines could not do—how shall we, who are so unfit, prepare a generation which will begin to be fit to face the new problems which confront mankind? At first sight, it seems a hopeless dilemma, for men can teach only what they know. And yet it need not be, because what we need to teach is a technique which can be well communicated if we ourselves fully realize our own position. We need to teach our students how to think, when you don't know what method to use, about a problem which is not quite formulated. And is not that in a nutshell our actual position? So if we, who live now, can fully realize and incorporate into our every teaching word and gesture our parlous state, we will, as we transmit it to our pupils and students give them just the freedom, just the sense of an unguessed-at process which nevertheless *must be found*, which if they incorporate it, should equip them as no generation has ever been equipped to make the new inventions which are necessary for a new world.

The importance of method.   I offer no solution to any of the questions which have been posed. That is not my task or the task of any other single individual, assuming for the time that any one of us knows what their solution is. That task falls to the whole culture to be worked out through leadership by the good and wise and through the participation, under their stimulus and guidance, of all those who are of good will and possessed of different and varying degrees and kinds of knowledge and wisdom. And so it is to method to which I now turn, not to finalities.

In her allusion to "inventions," Dr. Mead is suggesting not only those in the field of mechanics or in the field of teaching; as I understand her, she is suggesting inventions in the several bodies of social knowledge—psychology, psychiatry, sociology, anthropology, economics, political science —which will contribute not only to greater reliability of knowledge in those areas but, through it, to the enhancement of the art of living together. Through this quest, undertaken by the disciplines singly and in co-operation, man may be brought better to know himself and use his powers for a fuller self and social realization.

We are responsible.   We must be wise and courageous enough to accept full responsibility for the fact that society introduced morality into the world. It was not here before men began to live in groups and it arose within their experiences, not outside them. This places the responsibility for the kind of world we make where it belongs, with us.

The enemies of democracy and the means to fight them.

Men suffer from *preventible* evils. . . . Having found anything wrong we should set to work to mend it; for *the woes of men are the work of their own hands* . . .[7]

For "the woes of men" we substitute the enemies of the democratic way of life. These are ignorance, muddle-headedness, and crassness. They may be called lack of information, which includes knowing a great deal which is not true as well as not knowing at all, lack of operative logic, and lack of imagination, or spiritual blindness. These are deeply entrenched in our social institutions and in our character. These foes suggest three opposite forces. These are reliable knowledge, operative logic or the method of inquiry, and imagination.[8] The fight against the foes of the democratic way

[7] "Introduction" by Archibald Robertson to *The Ethics of Belief and Other Essays,* by W. K. Clifford (London: Watts & Co.; The Thinker's Library, No. 111, 1947), p. x.
[8] See Hoyt H. Hudson, *Educating Liberally* (Stanford: Stanford University Press, 1945). This is one of the most perceptive and challenging books on liberal education with which I am acquainted.

of life and conception of the nature of man is one which Professor Hoyt Hudson says is a "real fight," hence "one that may be lost." Our attack on the problems of our time calls not only for the weapons which are here listed but the courage to use them.

The need for a rational faith.   The first requisite for that courage I sought to suggest in Chapter I. That is, a rational faith in our own powers. The full task which is involved in winning the fight against the enemies of our ignorance, fuzzy-mindedness, and moral apathy cannot be told here. Each of the foregoing chapters has been concerned with certain phases of it and the following chapters will continue to divide the labor of that task among them.

Morality is objective as well as subjective.   The method of intelligence, however, can help us little in our concern to achieve better selves and a better society as long as we think of morality only in subjective terms, that is as only personal, private, and in our conscience. If morality be only subjective, that is, good thoughts and right sentiments, it sets up a solitary self without social ties and the means of its maintenance. Such a conception ignores the most rudimentary social knowledge as to how one comes by a self which is a pattern of beliefs and attitudes—the internal stuff of morality. The facts are that morality is both subjective and objective in its nature and location. It is made up of ideals, ends, and obligations but it is not independent of concrete actualities. To be moral is to "practice a character" and, in doing so, to "hold fast to an ideal." But this can be done in neither a social nor a physical void. It involves our consort with our fellow men in a world of thing and not-thing values—natural resources, machines, stocks and bonds, laws, beliefs, theories, and dogmas. In the last analysis a man's character is revealed in his actions in and through such media as these.

John Dewey has stated the problem clearly and succinctly:

It is impossible to say how much of the unnecessary slavery of the world is due to the conception that moral issues can be settled within conscience or human sentiment apart from consistent study of facts and application of knowledge in industry, law, and politics. . . . A morals based on study of human nature, instead of upon disregard for it, would find the facts of man continuous with those of the rest of nature and would thereby ally ethics with physics and biology.[9]

Morals, which is the stuff of character, and conduct, which is its vehicle or expression, are then not concerns apart from humanistic and scientific

[9] *Human Nature and Conduct,* pp. 11 and 12.

knowledge, with the latter including the physical as well as the social. Nor are they adequately treated in narrowly conceived courses in ethics and religion which, like the McGuffey Readers, are usually more *about* morals than *of* them. Such courses are notorious for their conception of morals, conduct, and character as chiefly, if not entirely, subjective and personal in nature.[10]

The prerequisites for moral responsibility. Three things are necessary in order that men may be morally responsible for their actions. They are (*a*) the fact that they might have done something else, which is to say that their action was not wholly determined by external circumstances; they chose, within limits, to do what they did, hence they are responsible for the choice which they made; (*b*) the fact that they have a conscience which is "the voice of Man ingrained into our hearts, commending us to work for Man"; and (*c*) the fact that their action was one for the doing of which their conscience *might* be a sufficient motive. These three things are necessary but they are not sufficient. Their action must also be voluntary, which fourth precondition is implied in (*c*) above. A moral act is then one which, upon restrospect, reveals that it was *voluntary* rather than nonvoluntary, an act concerning which a certain portion of one's character has been consulted.[11] In any voluntary act we should know how much of "circumstances" and how much of "self" are involved, at least approximately.

The "best" hypothesis. Now we need to ask in what respect a moral act involves an hypothesis which, although it is but one of the tools of science, is a very important one. In the making of moral judgments or the carrying out of moral action we have to work out a social hypothesis, which cannot be done simply from one's own point of view. We have to look at it from the point of view of the *social* situation. The only answer which can be given to the question as to what is "the best hypothesis" is that it must take into account all the interests which are involved—those which are in accord with one's own and those which run counter to them. The temptation is, of course, to emphasize only those with which we are identified. This means that, in moral action, one cannot lay down in advance fixed rules as to exactly what ought to be done. As we remarked in Chapter IV, science cannot tell us what we ought to do nor can it tell us what

---

[10] This is not to say that direct teaching of morality has not been effective. It has been effective, not because of the power of words to organize attitudes, but because the instruction was part of the system of control of the institutions in which it went on. It was not due to teaching *as such*, but rather the enforcement of it by the whole regime of which it was an aspect.

[11] See Clifford, *The Ethics of Belief and Other Essays*, pp. 50 and 51. The quotation just given is from the "Introduction," pp. ix-x.

the facts are going to be. It can, however, give us a reliable method of approach to them, help us to recognize all the facts which belong to a given problem, so that our hypothesis will be a consistent and rational one. This will widen the range of our sympathetic understanding and reduce selfishness and fanaticism. "The moral act must take into account all the values involved, and it must be rational—that is all that can be said." [12]

Democracy and science are different. We observed that the essence of the democratic faith is belief in the capacity of men to achieve the good life by rational and humane means. The rational is the scientific; the humane carries its own identification. However much science can help us make a better society, its method is not identical with that of the democratic process. This distinction between them may be stated as follows: the democratic way of life will survive in the complex world of science only if a "considerable proportion" of democratic decisions are as right as science can make them. However, decisions in a democracy are right only if they are freely arrived at, whatever be the findings and verdict of science to the contrary. Furthermore, problems are resolved by science through the discovery of the order that is in nature and the use of that knowledge to control nature. Problems in a democracy are problems of policy; these are resolved, ideally, through the process of discussion among free men. What democracy "finds" is then the product of consensus; what science "finds" rests on the degree to which men, competent in the same field, get the same results from the use of the same methods in a given problem. It need hardly be added that the "findings" of both democracy and science are always eligible to be changed in the light of new knowledge and new interests.[13]

What are the alternatives? If we are not disposed to accept and use the methods of intelligence, through the use of science and discussion, what are the alternatives? The popular prescriptions run as follows: Some would have us recapture some earlier cultural period, some one of the golden ages of the past—medieval, classical, or oriental. Among them are the Spenglers and the Bellocs.[14] Others would enjoin us to accept the doctrine of race supremacy. Others call for a new Caesar. The racists rest their case with "the philosophy of blood," the new Caesar cult with "the philosophy of brawn"—specifically through "the proletarian revolution" which will take

[12] George H. Mead, *Mind, Self and Society* (Chicago: University of Chicago Press, Copyright 1934), p. 388. See Mead's full discussion of this problem in "Fragments on Ethics" (pp. 379-389), from which I have taken the structure of my discussion.

[13] See Richard McKeon, "Democracy, Scientific Method and Action," *Ethics, An International Journal of Social, Political, and Legal Philosophy*, LV, 4 (July, 1945), p. 269.

[14] See Oswald Spengler, *The Decline of the West*, (New York: Alfred A. Knopf, 1932) and Hillaire Belloc, *The Crisis in Civilization* (New York: Fordham University Press, 1937).

us, so they promise, to the perfect goal of "the classless society." [15] Others invite us to "ride the wave of the future." Still others, having misread Tennyson, "that good will be the final goal of ill," believe that the environment will be polite enough to change continually toward the better without any bother on our part.

The tragedy is that, as our problems grow more aggravated and our bewilderment and confusion deepen, the attractiveness of these alternatives may increase. Each would require the surrender of all the personal freedoms we have won from various forms of authoritarian control and our representative form of government.

Faith in our own powers. We must gird ourselves in the faith that we are equal to the problems which are now "heaped up in unrelieved immensity." If we want democracy to survive we must love it more, we must make it more intelligent, more capable of knowing who its enemies are, more conscious of its basic meaning, less open to attack with the weapons of apathy and cynicism. We must be possessed of a great emotion: a great devotion to the right of everyone to be his best self—to live in the light of the acutest self-awareness. This is the conscience of the "better angels of our nature."

In this faith we can know what our task is. In this faith we must use scientific truth—"not that which we can ideally contemplate without error, but that which we may act upon without fear." [16] In that faith we may find courage in the belief of Professor William E. Hocking that "the new conscience is finding its courage because man's soul is recovering the sight of both its eyes. It is taking the scientific conscience into the house, not as master but as partner."

Thus loving and thinking are joined.

[15] See Charles W. Morris, *Pragmatism and the Crisis of Democracy* (Public Policy Pamphlet No. 12, Harry D. Gideonse, Editor. Chicago: University of Chicago Press, 1934).

[16] Clifford, *op. cit.*, p. ix.

CHAPTER VIII

The Need for General Education

WE HAVE NOW looked at modern society from three perspectives: as a spatial pattern and a social order; as a pattern of persons and social institutions; and as a culture in a crisis of valuation. In these inquiries we have dealt with the environment of the school in terms of *how* it works and *how well* it works. Whether it works well or badly, it reveals a unity of sorts and in varying degrees of being whole or broken. In this chapter we shall inquire into the nature and need of a general education with particular emphasis on the social studies.

Youth needs a united view of social life. The unity of social life, whether whole or impaired, is what youth ought to understand. This unity should be pictured in both its ideal and its real character. It must also be seen in terms of both the division and the unity of man's activities. We need, in short, a bifocal view of human life: its parts and the ways and degrees in which they are integrated.[1]

The relationship which exists between the parts of human life cannot be revealed by the mere addition of courses about it. As we have observed earlier, neither society nor the self can be understood by the process of addi-

---

[1] The word "integration" has come into common use in attempts to find a concept which will express the central idea in general education. I understand that it refers to the interrelatedness of human life and the ways in which the methods and materials of the social sciences may be used to reveal the "altogetherness," at least ideally, of human life. In this regard, however, we should take heed of a scholar's warning that "we cannot hope to integrate by educational devices what is not yet integrated by the scientist and the scholar [for] our education in this respect will not be far ahead of the general state of our culture. It is one of our tasks to see that it is not lagging too far behind"; see Louis Wirth, "General Education, Its Nature, Scope and Essential Elements," in *General Education: Its Nature, Scope and Essential Elements*, Edited by William S. Gray, Vol. VI, Proceedings of the Institute for Administrative Officers of Higher Institutions, 1934 (Chicago: The University of Chicago Press, 1934), pp. 25-35.

tion. What is required is an understanding of the functional relations of their various phases. Mere addition tends to "tie them apart" rather than together.

The self and the social process. One of the fundamental axioms of social psychology is that the individual self finds its unity in the unity of the whole social process: any defect in its unity will, ideally or theoretically, be reflected in the quality of the self. In light of this fact, we cannot expect young people to grow up "whole" in a society which is presented to them through not only separate but *disparate* courses which, in splitting the organization of thought about life, split life itself. We never have a society which is perfectly ordered, nor do we ever find selves which are perfectly ordered, but we ought not to settle for less than the best unity we can get in both. An understanding of society, which we have shown to be persons-in-communication, demands a more realistic and useful account of it than students sometimes get in our secondary schools. Advances have been made and more are on the way, but on the average we are still far from the goal of achieving a truly effective and efficient general education in the social studies.

Life is the subject for education. No writer on educational theory has written with deeper insight and more substantial knowledge than Alfred N. Whitehead.[2]

There is only one subject matter for education, and that is Life in all its manifestations. Instead of this single unit, we offer children—Algebra, from which nothing follows; Science, from which nothing follows; History, from which nothing follows; a couple of Languages, never mastered, and lastly and most dreary of all, Literature, represented by plays of Shakespeare, with philological notes and short analyses of plot and character to be, in substance, committed to memory. Can such a list be said to represent life, as it is known in the living of it? The best that can be said of it is, that it is a rapid table of contents which a deity might run over in his mind while he was thinking of creating a world, and had not yet decided how to put it together.

It ought to be said that Whitehead wrote this some time ago and had in mind the English secondary schools of that time, but, despite the passing of time, his criticism is still appropriate to what may still be found too frequently in American high schools. Where such a curriculum is in use teachers are, without putting it into so many words, saying something like this to their students: "You stack it, you put it together; you make it give you a picture of life and you wrestling with life. You put it together, we

---

[2] ˌ̣New York: *The Aims in Education*, Mentor Books (The New American Library of World Literature, Inc., Copyright 1949), pp. 18-19.

don't know how, or we don't care." If you choose to teach, you must do much better by your students, for those who are forced to suffer instruction with such a curriculum are given, not a picture of life, but an unco-ordinated mass of "subjects"—a chaos instead of something at least resembling a cosmos. Although the picture of our culture given in the preceding chapter was somewhat more like a chaos than a cosmos, it has a working unity, however badly it now appears to work. Again, I suggest that we need to be careful to distinguish between an ideal and a real culture. If we make no attempt to show the degree to which it has a wholeness and the way in which its wholeness might be improved, we shall do badly by our task.

Subjects are "about" something. We know that subjects are not things-in-themselves. They are about something and that is life seen in the perspective of young people trying to understand it and find their place in it. On this matter let Whitehead speak again.

We must take it as an unavoidable fact that God has so made the world that there are more topics for knowledge than any one person can possibly acquire. It is hopeless to approach the problem by way of the enumeration of subjects which every one ought to have mastered. There are too many of them, all with excellent title-deeds. . . . What I am anxious to impress on you is that though knowledge is one chief aim of intellectual education, there is another ingredient, vaguer but greater, and more dominating in its importance. The ancients called it "wisdom." You cannot be wise without some basis in knowledge; but you may easily acquire knowledge and remain bare of wisdom . . . wisdom is the way knowledge is held.[3]

The bench marks for a general education in the social studies. Here we have the bench marks for a general education in the social studies: Emerson's "The great object of education should be commensurate with the object of life," and now Whitehead's "There is only one subject matter for education and that is Life in all its manifestations." It is clear that neither Emerson nor Whitehead is talking about an education in subjects, *added up.*

Lack of awareness. The effect of an education in unrelated specialisms has led to what Karl Mannheim has called a "lack of awareness." This manifests itself in little or no interest in real problems or a desire to study them. (*Real* problems in the social studies, we might remind ourselves, cannot be studied within the confines of a single discipline.) It has fostered dilettantism—a smattering of this and a smattering of that—or worse, the disposition to believe nobody—except the propagandist.[4]

[3] *Ibid.*, pp. 40-41.
[4] Mannheim, "Education, Sociology and Social Awareness," *op. cit.*, pp. 58-59.

A common humanity is the antecedent. The task of fashioning a general education in social knowledge is that of achieving a unity of view and social purpose among greatly diversified human beings through an integration of hitherto separated specialisms. (Note my earlier reference to the "homogeneity of knowledge" and the "heterogeneity of students.") It is this unity of view and social purpose which can provide the common humanity we so much need, whose expression will, withal, be individual. Such a common humanity is the antecedent of the moral and intellectual individuality toward which we have set our course in social education. It also, in turn, is enriched by individuality. It is my belief that unless an education, formal and informal, can provide at least a general view of the essentials and the totality of a humane existence, political and economic attempts at either national or world unity can accomplish little. A better society exists first in the minds of men.

But there is, despite the great diversity represented in the student bodies of our high schools and junior colleges, a commonality of interest and understanding among them. This must be made clearer, hence it must be both taught and retaught.[5]

The "feebleness of co-ordination" is our problem. The problem we face in constructing a general education and through it a related view of "Life in all its [social] manifestations" is the task of repairing what Whitehead has called "the feebleness of co-ordination." [6] Our problem is, then, not so much the fact that subject matter courses are separate but that, being *separated*—that is, without a common focus—little synthesis is achieved among them. Their mere addition does not bring this about. Their separation obscures the unity of human life, whether it be much or little in fact. It is to this condition that Whitehead's term refers.

"General education" is a misleading term. The term "general education" is somewhat misleading. A general education in social knowledge (or any other) is not obscure or abstract, thin, vague, or quickly come by. Nor is it for only the dull and retarded. It is for all and is to be found wherever there is an "explosive mixture of ideas" drawn from the various social science disciplines.

---

[5] Professor Robert Ulich holds that even if this commonality did not exist to the degree it does, it would have to be "insisted on" to the end that some unity of culture might be guaranteed among men. See his *Conditions of Civilized Living* (New York: E. P. Dutton & Co., Inc., 1946).

[6] The most profound critique of an education in unrelated special courses of which I know is to be found in Whitehead's *Science and the Modern World*, Chapter XIII, "Requisites for Social Progress." This volume is now available in a Mentor Books edition. A companion book is Graham Wallas, *The Great Society*, a treatise on the difficulties of effecting a humane social organization in the Great Society.

The nature of general education clarified. A general social education is general in the sense that it seeks to effect a synthesis by bringing separate subject matters together as co-ordinate means to study what is general, common, repetitive, and pervasive in human experience. No single body of subject matter based on any one of the single disciplines can "give the student his world." A general education is general in the sense that it relates thought to action and means to ends. In bringing hitherto separated knowledge together, it brings students' capacities and interests into focus. It is general in the sense that knowledge is prolific with new connections and with new and unexpected insights. It seeks not only an accommodation but an assimilation of social knowledge. It brings an awareness not only of values and their central role in social life, but also the rich and wide variety of values and how they are related. It thus increases the "depth of individuality." It is general in the sense that it seeks to reveal those aspects of social knowledge which are relevant to all human beings and to many situations and experiences. It is an education independent of the class, race, sex, creed, or the future occupation of the student. It is for Everyman. It seeks to insure that loyalty to principles with an adaptiveness to change which modern life requires. It thus rejects the thesis of "fixed men for fixed duties," which might have been applicable to times more tranquil and slower of pace than ours. It seeks to deal with *social* men, not only political or economic man. It takes account of the student as thinker, doer, appreciator, and believer. It is general in the sense that ideas are *working* ideas, useful for inquiry and for producing insight. It is general in the sense that it seeks to emancipate youth from the thralldom and muddle of mere events and isolated and sterile facts—from the accidental and the episodic. It is general in the sense that its task is to substitute a conceptual for a perceptual order and thus, by giving the student skill in generalizing, help him become the "lord of nature," including his own.

A new fable. A fable "which Aesop somehow neglected to record" has been invented by Professor Robert Redfield, which illustrates clearly the fallacy of "fixed men for fixed duties" as well as the need for loyalty to principles and adaptiveness to change. The fable runs as follows:[7]

A hen is making an effort to instruct her chicks about their future sources of food supply while she and they were balanced precariously on a chicken coop

[7] Robert Redfield, "Research in the Social Sciences: Its Significance for General Education," *Social Education,* Copyright 1941 (December). It is obvious that this fable also—and perhaps chiefly as Professor Redfield intended that it should—illuminates the unconcern of "research scholars" with the kinds of material and the outlook required for a general education, that is an education in adaptive principles. Nevertheless I use it to make the point indicated.

which was being carried down a river by a flood. It was a long time since she had studied the forest on the bank, and the account she was giving her chicks of forest resources was none too good. So she called to the wise owl on the bank for help. "You know the woods, oh owl, for you stay in this forest and study it," said the hen; "will you not tell me what to teach my chicks about life in the forest?" But the owl had overheard what the hen was telling the chicks about the forest as she came along, and he thought it was scientifically inaccurate and superficial. Besides, he was just then busy completing a monograph on the incidence of beetle larvae in acorns. So he pretended he had not heard the hen. The hen, turned back upon herself, proceeded as well as she could to prepare and put into effect an instruction unit on food resources of forests, meanwhile struggling to keep her chicks from falling off the chicken coop. The chicks took the instruction very well, and later the coop stopped at a point far downstream and the chicks went ashore—to begin their adult life in a treeless meadow.

Education is organized experience. An education is a systematic experience in *the organization of experience*. Or it may be seen in Whitehead's terms as "the art of the utilization of knowledge," which presupposes the organization of it. Each of these conceptions is based on the premise that education focuses on conduct. This requires that its final locus of integration be in the student through the integration of his character. But can the student, unaided, organize or "stack" his experience and the knowledge necessary to organize it in purposeful and artful ways? The evidence is that he cannot. Hence a general education has a double focus: an understanding of related subject matters and an understanding of the method by which their interrelations may be established. If our students are to be civilized they must know the method by which this may be done. Hence they must be *skilled* in order to be *civilized*. The emphasis must be not only on the interrelation of subject matters, but on the interrelation between substance and methods of dealing with substance.

New points of view are needed. A general education in social knowledge does not so much require new knowledge as a new view of the knowledge we have and a new method of dealing with it. This method has two phases: method as a means of inquiry and integration, and method as it is commonly and often exclusively conceived of in education, namely a method of teaching. A long step toward a general education can be had by changes only in the method of teaching. We trust that this may relieve the fears of those who think that a general education requires a special and esoteric talent.

A general education can be had without courses or a curriculum, so named. That it will require revision of old courses and old curricula goes without saying. But one thing is certain: it cannot be had by merely reshuffling old courses, by the method of a "survey" or the layer-cake stacking of "slices" or "slabs" of history, geography, economics, and the rest, overlaid on each other. A "grand survey" may do for Alice in Wonderland or for a Cook's tour but not for general education. Between these layers there is little discernible seepage or osmosis. The transfer of insight is not so easily achieved.

Co-ordination, not sampling.   Such a conception of courses in a general education has no center, unless it be the page or the time which indicates when they are half completed. But this is not a center; it is merely a middle. Co-ordination, not sampling, is the method for organizing a general education and for getting one. It can be had by drawing on and drawing together selected materials from a variety of social science disciplines so they converge on what is really the center of human experience, an integration of thing and not-thing values in such a way as to permit the organization and reorganization of character. This involves a concern chiefly with the How and the What (and indirectly the Why) of personal and social experience.

By the same logic, a general education in social knowledge cannot be had by a "method of distribution," arrived at by something akin to the doctrine of proportional representation in politics. True enough, each of the main bodies of social knowledge must be represented, but the student must master the art of legislation through which these representatives arrive at a consensus about man. He must, above all, come to know himself —the task which Plato enjoined us all to undertake. At this stage of our knowledge, the pattern of a general education will likely be the product of a compromise between a "federal" and a "states' rights" principle of the co-ordination of the materials and methods of the several disciplines.

Youth's experience is the content.   The content of a general education in social knowledge is, in the last analysis, the body of experiences which youth is now having. The task is not only to learn by experience but to learn *of* experience. Experience teaches, to be sure, but not all experience teaches. That experience is educative which establishes relationships; that experience is non- or mis-educative which fails to do so. Hence the axiom that "we learn by experience" must be revised to read that "we have to *learn* to learn by experience."

Special education is not abandoned.   This view of general education gives the lie to the view that it abandons special education. We can never deal with "life in general." Men are never either good or wise "in general." We always deal with life in concrete form, in particular and specific situations. To blink these facts is to conceive of general education as playing with empty abstractions.[8]

General knowledge is related knowledge. My point is that general knowledge is had by *relating* special studies. The trouble with special studies, that is separated ones, is that they are only special and thus unrelated to any "whole." The specialist is intellectually and morally crippled, not because he is a specialist but because he is only a specialist and hence does not see himself in the context of other specialties. A society held together largely by the aims of many individuals to get on only as specialists is held together on a precarious basis. It is really not held together at all.

It is largely in the process of acquiring a general and related acquaintance with his culture and himself that the student can hope to discover his special aptitudes and interests. Thus it is that subjects pursued for the sake of a general education are "special subjects specially studied," that is, in a related context. One of the most effective ways of encouraging and developing a thorough awareness is to foster a devotion to special interests. Only in a caste society can special and general education be separated.[9]

The separation of special from general education is perhaps no more dramatically and dangerously evident than in the divorce of vocational training from the social studies.

Vocational training is often narrow. Vocational training is all too frequently conceived and given in the narrow context of job preparation for various commercial, industrial, and agricultural arts and crafts. Thus it represents preparation in certain practical skills and techniques in contrast to the social understandings which the humane and social studies provide. But the arts of commerce, industry, and agriculture are phases of a common culture no less than those which are represented in civics, history, and literature. Youth must be educated to see them as interdependent arts.

The isolation of vocational from allied liberal arts traces, in part, to the split in education which we inherited from the Greeks. In classic Greece, masters were educated to reflect about substantive matters. Slaves were educated chiefly to control the reflexes required to hew the wood and draw and carry the water for their masters. While it is true that some slaves were emancipated and not only got the same education as their masters but also taught, this split was characteristic of the education and social life of that society.

[8] See Karl Mannheim, "The Social Education of Man," *Essays on the Sociology of Knowledge*, edited by Paul Kecskemeti (New York: Oxford University Press, 1952), pp. 230-237.

[9] See Louis Wirth, *General Education*.

We inherit a split view of society. This split is still evident in our society in the fact that sharp differences in deference and honor obtain between the so-called "higher" professions of law, the ministry, and medicine and such "lowly" occupations as carpentry, plumbing, and masonry. Certain fields of vocational endeavor, such as accounting and book-keeping, lie in a kind of twilight zone between the elite professions and the not-so-elite trades and crafts. The differences in deference and honor which we accord these two grand divisions of labor is overtly manifest in the different statuses and roles which their practitioners enjoy and play.

The importance of vocations. The logical ground for the integration of the vocational and liberal arts lies in the fact that they are both vocations, however much they differ in the deference paid those who practice them. The view of Robert Burns that "a man's a man for a' that" may, we hope, come to be held toward all men regardless of their occupation. The test is not which occupation, assuming that each contributes to personal and social welfare, but in how well and wisely tasks are discharged. But the changes in popular attitudes which would reflect such a view will come slowly—if and when they come. The school cannot produce them quickly or on the vast scale of the Great Society. It can, however, seek to redefine certain tasks, show their interrelations, and reshape attitudes so that, in the long run, the Great Society will be transformed in these respects.

The fact is that the liberal arts were and now are preparation for the vocations which we call the professions. They are vocations in the sense that men are *called* to them. But the less honored occupations are also vocations for the same reason. Both are tasks to which men, ideally at least, dedicate themselves. We now have, as we have always had, vocational education in American high schools. The difference is that some of it has changed its clothes from business suit to overalls. The high school now lays the foundation for both blue- and white-collar vocations. Both of them take the form of occupations in the generic sense that those who enter them are occupied by them.

Education changes its clothes. This change in clothing came about with the democratization of our public high schools in the middle 1900's. Since then they have become, increasingly, the secondary schools for the sons and daughters of all the people—except the children of the social elite who attend private high schools.[10]

---

[10] See Lloyd Warner, Robert Havighurst, and Martin Loeb, *Who Shall Be Educated?* (New York: Harper & Brothers, 1944) for a statistical and social analysis of the student make-up of American high schools.

With this democratization came certain significant curriculum changes. A single college preparatory curriculum gave way to a variety of other kinds. Important among these were the curricula in vocational training. But, all too often, they were added to rather than integrated with the older liberal studies. It is their mere addition which results in a separation that has given American secondary school education a rigidity which does not bode well for the development of moral and intellectual individuality.

The high school prepares for three roles. The task of the high school may be seen as preparation for three roles: to make a living, to make a life, and to mold a world. None of these roles can be prepared for by an education "for its own sake." Each phase of education must be for the sake of these related roles. I choose to view them as related in the sense that preparation for the third, which is an adult and public role, comes through the integration of the first two, which are both public and private and adult and preadult in nature. Education for both present and future are joined in secondary education as they must always be joined in education at all levels.

Making and living have been separated. The separation of vocational and social education, insofar as they are inclusive-exclusive aspects of general education, is the separation of making a living from making a life. It is no doubt true that *making* in the technical sense is easier than *living* in the cultural sense. It is also true that the work a man does represents his most important function in a society. But unless there is some kind of integral social background to his life he cannot know what the social ends of his craft are. Hence the only value he can assign to his work is that it makes him a living. We shall not produce integral human beings until we close this gap. The integrity of man is a function of the integral natural of what he works with and what he works toward.

A problem of the relation of means and ends. The separation of vocational (in the trade and craft sense) from social studies is the separation of function and substance, or of means and ends. But, because ends are given in the means, the ends of a narrowly conceived vocational education, or worse, a mere *training,* can only be narrow technical ends. They cannot be broad social ends. This does not require that education in the arts and crafts be abandoned. It requires rather that it be integrated with social education. The grand vocation is that of being a first-rate human being. This requires a harmony between culture (taken in its broad and legitimate meaning) and competence. This harmony can be achieved only if the competence is a part of the structure of the culture, not subsidiary to it. If the student is to be good he must be good for a specific something. If ne is to be wise he must be wise in the relation between many specific some-things. All these somethings have a technical phase which is the skillful discharge of the obligations which attach to them.

What "vocation" means. We shall not understand the meaning of vocation until we understand what its opposite is. The difference between them has been stated crisply and profoundly by John Dewey.

> A vocation means nothing but such direction of life activities as renders them perceptibly significant to a person, because of the consequences they accomplish, and also useful to his associates. The opposite of a career is neither leisure nor culture, but aimlessness, capriciousness, the absence of cumulative achievement in experience, on the personal side, and idle display, parasitic dependence upon others, on the social side. Occupation is a concrete term for continuity. It includes the development of artistic capacity of any kind, of special scientific ability, of effective citizenship, as well as professional and business occupations, to say nothing of mechanical labor or engagement in gainful pursuits.[11]

We remarked that the work a man does represents the most important phase of his life. It consists in the tools of his trade which become the tools of his status. Thus their tool-like nature has a double function. In one sense these tools are only technical. But, if their technical phase is socialized, related to their social function and consequences, they become also social techniques.

The "dignity of labor." The "dignity of labor," a term which we use in praise of all wage earners, inheres not only in his labor but in its integral relation to his life and the life of his culture. It loses its dignity when divorced from its social function. An automaton has no dignity, no matter how skilled he be. The absence of skill, for its importance is not denied, results in distrust and contempt of self, in feelings of personal inadequacy and in both psychic and material insecurity. These are the result not only of the absence of skills but of the separation of technical tools from their social ends. They are both the cause and effect of the lack of aware-ness of the not-thing values which it is the function of trade and craft techniques to assist in "tooling." The industrial worker, or any other for that matter, can ill afford to restrict his intelligence which is, in essence, the ability to see the relation between the means and ends of his conduct.

Social aspects of vocational skills. Aside from their purely technical character, the skills learned in the trade and craft vocations both imply

---

[11] *Democracy and Education* (New York: The Macmillan Co., Copyright 1916), pp. 358-359. It is obvious that the man who has no work is incapable of genuine leisure. In another place Dewey observes that men are dignified not only when they *do* but when they *make*.

nd require certain virtues which are generally applicable. Among these
re promptness, precision, the difference between accuracy and vagueness,
elf-reliance and honesty, careful and disciplined observation, an awareness that nature, to be commanded, must be obeyed, insight into the
omplexity of nature whether it be the properties of steel, the hardness of
. species of wood, or the growth process of a food-producing plant, and
he great virtue which lies in knowing the difference between words
bout a thing and the thing itself. But these virtues are generally applicable
only if they are generally applied. This requires that bridges be built, over
vhich they may transfer to social situations which lie outside the shop.

The value of concreteness. The great value of shop work lies in its
concreteness. Here the student has a chance to be "scared by a fact," and
overcome the shock of it by seeing its relation to a *body* of fact, i.e., the
elated phases of a given technical task. Here he may face certain facts,
irsthand, not secondhand, which, perforce and regrettably, are those with
vhich the more verbal social studies deal.

But shop courses and even laboratory work in the more respectable
ields of botany, chemistry, and physics may present the student only with
unrelated facts. The empirical may be overdone. If so, the student has only
'the facts" without knowing what "the case" is in which they are related.
If this be true, he will be only functionally trained; he will not be sub-
stantively educated.[12] Rote learning is possible in shop and laboratory
courses.

Education for many vocations, those of the crafts and trades especially,
s undoubtedly here to stay. The social changes which make impossible the
kind of apprentice relations which once obtained between father and son
and mother and daughter have taken most vocational education out of
the home. We can go back to home instruction in these areas only if we
are willing to go back to an agrarian society. This is not only improbable
but impossible. But we can go back in the sense that we can recapture
some of the meaning which vocational education had in those days.
This can be done by the integration of the technical arts with the liberal
arts, or more accurately, by teaching youth that they are all liberal arts
if they be employed to show the relation of their *making* to their *doing*.

The new vocational education. The new vocational education must
inculcate the habit as well as the skill of work. Our young people are not
only largely unskilled but, what is worse, they are out of the habit of

[12] Karl Mannheim's diagnosis of the culture crisis rests on the divorce of functional
from substantive knowledge. This is the divorce of techniques from their causes and
consequences. See *Man and Society in an Age of Transformation* (New York: Harcourt,
Brace and Company, 1940).

genuinely rewarding work. This is not so much a fault of the schools as it is a fault of a technological civilization. Young people have the same energies and drives that their pioneer forebears had, but a tailor-made and "you can buy it" civilization sets narrow limits for providing them much beyond make-work tasks and dead-end occupations. It is not to be wondered at that they have been called "the lost generation." In many communities the only channel in which they can direct their energies is that of "hanging around." If the school cannot find work for "idle hands to do"—which includes idle minds—we may be sure that Satan will. That he already has is evident in the many forms of juvenile delinquency from which none but the most isolated or exceptional communities are exempt. (The term "juvenile delinquency" is a misnomer; it is the civilization which is delinquent.) The thesis is tenable and provable that much of this delinquency is a reaction against uselessness which, as the elder Huxley remarked, "is the severest shock which the human system can sustain."

The high school is custodial.   If the high school has become a custodial institution, as the evidence clearly reveals, it behooves us to make the most of the time which youth must spend in it. It is custodial to a greater extent for those students whose prospect is gainful employment in the so-called vocational arts and crafts than for those whose life chances are of a more professional kind. The school's major obligation to the former is to effect an integration of narrowly conceived technical education with social and humane study.

The "hand-minded" and "head-minded."   We must honestly admit that among the more than six and a half million students in our public high schools an increasing proportion are more "hand-minded" than "head-minded." This classification is not a slur on their character; it is only an honest identification of significant differences. But we cannot subscribe to the education of a Greek slave for the former, and the education of a Greek master for the latter. The goal of moral and intellectual individuality demands that each shall be given the maximum opportunity to get it in the fashion and measure which is appropriate to his unique capacities, interests, abilities, and skills.

For those whose life chances lie in the professions we would argue that they would profit from a firsthand experience in some kind of technical course. This might well give them an immediate rather than a vicarious acquaintance with "the arts of making." It might also provide insight into the world of industrial labor even if it did little to improve the work of their hands.

But our concern here is more with those students whose life chances will find them in the trades. Their more or less narrow technical education must be broadened by integration with social and humane studies. What such an education might require by way of a specific curriculum I do not undertake to sketch. I shall, rather, suggest some of the lines of relationships on which it might be built.

The shop is the focus. Its focus would be the shop. This would require, first, the identification of the virtues which are basic and elementary in all trades and crafts. These would reveal to students aspects of technical training which, in all but rare instances, have never been brought to their conscious attention, despite considerable "talk" to the effect that they are taught. The not-thing values of technical training would then be identified as its social core.

The fact that students' interests focus on the shop would require that what it symbolizes be the point of departure and the constant point of reference. They are not only occupied in it but preoccupied by it. We must make the most of this. From the shop as a center, inquiry would carry them into the interrelations which obtain between it and the Great Society. It is these relationships which are now so characteristically missing in narrow vocational training. Such lines of inquiry as the following might be pursued: the social origin of skills and techniques, the relevance of the virtues noted above to out-of-shop situations, the standards of living and the kinds and qualities of social esteem or disesteem which are associated with various occupations, the political stake of various trades, the organization of industry, market operations and especially those of the labor market, the problem of leisure, labor-management relations, history viewed primarily from the perspective of the political, economic, and social consequences of the machine, wage systems, the nature and role of trade unions, and the changing conceptions of the place of government in a society which is knit together perhaps as much by machines as by sentiments. Studies along lines such as these would require contributions from both the social and humane studies.

Some problems of organization. Some problems, however, stand in the way of organizing and teaching such an integrated program. First and perhaps foremost is the fact that an honest and public identification of "hand-minded" in contrast to "head-minded" is an affront to a fallacious notion of democracy. There is, on the other hand, the view which glorifies the "common man" and makes him, not one of several types, but the "least common denominator" by which all achievement in our culture is to be judged. This is a leveling-down conception of democracy which confuses equal opportunity of access by individuals, commensurate with their potentials, with the *same* level and kind of opportunity for everyone.[13]

If the criticism of the kind I have assumed were vocally manifest, it would probably come in terms of the accusation that this is "class education." But we have always had "class education" in the American high school. It was for a single "class" when it offered only college preparatory work. The multiplication of its curricula has, in a way, been a response to the fact that a college-preparatory course does not suit the conditions and prospects of students from other segments or "classes" of our society.[14]

Waste of human energy.   The fallacy of such an accusation is revealed in the tragic waste of human energy which would follow if we held all students to the same intellectual tasks as those required by the courses which lead to college and professional education. Those most vigorously opposed would probably be among the socially elite, who are quite ready to accept the techniques of the new industrial order but are much less disposed to accept the changes in the social structure (the structure of education included) which those techniques have almost forced upon society. This is now revealed in the reluctance of some of them to support a thoroughgoing general education through the junior college for the children of tradesmen and the "lower orders" of white-collar employees. But, cast against them, is the great and growing awareness in our society of the need for such an education for all. The contribution which organized labor has made to this body of opinion is outstanding.

Unity of student life can be maintained.   Such a curriculum image as I have sought to set forth need not and in my most critical judgment would not result in a division of our high school student bodies into social or intellectual "haves" and "have-nots." Such a program would not exclude its students from competition in sports, drama, forensics, and all the many other curricular and extracurricular activities which round out the life

[13] See Joseph Wood Krutch, "Is Our Common Man Too Common?" *The Saturday Review,* January 10, 1953.

The distinction between "hand-minded" and "head-minded" is not the only basis for the allocation of many students into craft and liberal curricula, respectively. There is considerable evidence that such factors as lower socio-economic class status and "poor deportment," i.e., so-called "discipline cases" have much to do with the assignment of high school students to "vocational" or shop curricula. The lines of inquiry which I have suggested are based on certain interests which I assume to be native to shop situations. The learning which such inquiry would engender would, I trust, result in the skills and understandings essential to participation in a democratic society.

[14] Much of the storm and fury which rages over the standards of work done in the American high school stems, in my judgment, from failure or unwillingness to understand the effects which followed from the democratization of its student body. A plea for an understanding of that fact is not a defense of lowered standards. Where standards have fallen they should be raised. The central problem respecting standards (many of which were set before the turn of the century) is provision for a general education adapted to the varying abilities of many kinds of learners.

of the school. The boys and girls whom I have designated as "hand-minded" would find only the study-center of their school life in such a curriculum. Wide margins would still remain for the display of their talents, which number quite as many and are quite as honor-bearing as those which the "head-minded" possess.

The legend of the labyrinth of King Minos. In concluding this chapter I should like to draw a moral from the legend of the labyrinth of King Minos of ancient Crete. There the terrible minotaur was kept and hostages were yearly sent to be devoured by it. The hero of the legend was the youthful and valiant Theseus and the heroine his sweetheart, the beautiful Ariadne. You recall how Theseus, as hostage, made his way through the labyrinthian passages, found the beast and slew him and how, thanks to the thread which Ariadne had given him and which he let fall behind him, he found his way out.

The pattern of the labyrinth of Crete was thus *ordered* by a thread. But the pattern of the Great Society or any of its local counterparts is far more complex than the labyrinth of Crete. No single "thread of evidence" will suffice to order it; no one subject, no easy prescription or simple formula, no hasty or nervous attempt to solve old or new problems, no flight into the presumed security of the past. The synthesis we seek is not synonymous with simplicity.

The pre-eminent obligation of the social studies, in concert with the humane and natural studies, is to help the student discover the ordered character of the social pattern of his time so that he will neither be lost in it nor seek only to escape from it.

CHAPTER IX

The Place of the Social Studies
in General Education

SOME OF THE major problems posed by the separation of courses within the area of social knowledge and the separation of technical from social and humane knowledge have been presented, if not resolved. We now discuss the place of the social studies in a total pattern of general education.

The "given things" in any human community. We bring to mind again the "given things" in any human community which were presented in Chapter V. Their arrangement in the form of a triangle permits some comparisons to be made.

Man seeks to live better. Man's nonmaterial culture—his ends, purposes, and goals—arise out of his attempts not only to live but to live better according to the standards of his culture. They are components *in* his action, not outside it. The pursuit of these nonmaterial or not-thing values involves man in individual and group effort. The more permanent of these group forms we call social institutions. The sense in which no social action lies outside them was indicated in Chapter VI. All man's activities require, for their successful outcome, indeed for their very existence, the materials which the "world of nature" provides. These constitute the conditions of his achievement. Social action, whether engaged in individually or collectively, is, in effect, the action of mediating between man's ideas and ideals and the thing values of his physical habitat. In doing this, man is involved in the social processes discussed in Chapter V.

The moral, social, and physical. The not-thing values which make up man's nonmaterial culture we now call *moral;* his involvement in the four

114

social processes we now designate *social;* and the thing-values of his physical habitat we label *physical.* These are set forth graphically in the following chart.

Charts 4 and 5 suffer somewhat by reason of the fact that they suggest a real separation of the various areas and that they are static. Our earlier discussion has sought to negate such a view. The vertical arrangement of the areas in Chart 5 might also imply a fixed order from the top down of most to least important in man's experience. The sense in which this is a misrepresentation will be discussed later.

The
Nonma-
terial Cul-
ture, i.e., cus-
toms, beliefs, rules,
ideals, laws, theories,
conceptions of right and
wrong—and attitudes toward
them.

The Material Culture, i.e., all goods
and things, artifacts of all kinds which
man has made out of the "original environment" but whose transformation into usable
goods has been effected by interaction between
his ideals and the "original environment" through
the several social processes.

The Human Resources, i.e., human beings of all ages, sexes,
and races and in all stages of sickness and health. These are
the physico-biological units of a culture who are the loci and
bearers of the culture, both material and nonmaterial. They also
are something more than physico-biological units in that they are capable of reason, emotion, and goal seeking.

The Physical Habitat, i.e., the theater and its "props" on which the drama of
human life (socialization) is enacted and which are taken up into the social.
Through this drama, men associate through the social processes and use and transform
this phyiscal habitat in ways which will serve them.   It consists of all geological and
geographical phenomena, and all flora and fauna.

CHART 4. *The Given Things in Any Human Community* [1]

A popular fallacy is explored. The popular view is that the moral, the social, and the physical phases of man's experience are quite separate and distinct. The moral is popularly conceived as representing man's highest interest, the social not quite so high and the physical the lowest. We shall seek to show that the moral has its origin in man's social experience and that it is realized, insofar as it is, by man's interaction in the social processes with his fellows and the materials of the physical habitat. We shall seek to disprove the fallacy expressed in the term "man and nature." We

[1] Robert E. Park, "Human Ecology," *The American Journal of Sociology,* XLII (July, 1936), p. 15.

shall attempt to show that man is that factor in nature which is the most adaptable and changeable and that the human, that is, the cultural, is that toward which all other things tend. In sum, we shall seek to establish the "altogetherness" of man's experience. This will provide the ground for a general education and identify the social studies as its center or axis. Although man at birth is a part of nature he does not, at that time, have a human nature. He acquires it through interaction with others of his kind. He becomes acculturated by learning how to make and buy and sell, by loving and being loved, and by joining with his fellows in the dialectic process through which the question of "what ought we to do" both arises and is, in some way, resolved. In this recital we have come full circle and have brought within it the physical, the social, and the moral.

The Moral, concerned
with the "good life" in
terms of humanly originated
and conceived ends, goals, and
purposes. This phase of human activity arises out of:

The Social, concerned with all aspects of
human interaction in which we make practical differentiations of acts "more or less" moral
in their intrinsic character. It represents social organization by means of which mens' ideas and ideals
permit them to take up and incorporate within personal
and collective acts, the materials (including man at birth) of:

The Physical, concerned with those processes which belong to all
"natural" phenomena which include man, and all other nonhuman
but vital phenomena and all nonvital phenomena.

CHART 5. *The Moral, the Social, and the Natural*

But we have come full circle too swiftly. Hence, we set for ourselves a division of labor in which we shall first indicate the interdependence of the social and the physical and, second, not the interdependence of the social and the moral, but their identity.

Social and physical interact. That man cannot live outside nature is too simple to require proof. Death follows the separation of man from his physical environment. He lives not only *in* the physical world but *by* and *of* it. He cannot breathe without air. He cannot digest food except it be in his stomach. Whenever he moves it is through the medium of land, air, or water. Light, as well as the optic nerve, is involved in his seeing.

These observations give the lie to the view that social phenomena lie merely on top of physical phenomena. The fact is that they interact. In fact, all conduct is *interaction* between elements of human nature and the environment, physical and social. This suggests the sense in which the physical, in being incorporated in the social, is taken up into a wider and more complex and more delicate system of interactions so that it takes on new properties through the freeing of hitherto unreleased potentials. In this interaction between elements of human nature and the physical environment, trees become telephone poles between which the copper wires of communication are strung. Trees are processed into boards with which men build houses to provide shelter wherein the patterns we call the family and the home are woven and in which both infants and their human nature come to birth. The abundance or dearth of such natural resources as oil, coal, tungsten, uranium, and aluminum condition the place and prospects of whole nation-states in the power pattern of world politics. The miracle of irrigation transforms deserts into fertile fields from which men harvest the food and fiber which support life and provide clothing for ornamentation and warmth. Indeed, as civilization advances the physical environment becomes more and more humanized though too often in a negative fashion: witness the splitting of the atom and the fabrication of first the atomic and next the hydrogen bomb. What peaceful uses these great forces will be put to is just beginning to be suggested.[2]

The importance of the physical.   Geography tells us of the earth factors which condition (not determine) the interaction and conduct of human beings. The significance of the insular factor in the history and culture of the people of the British Isles cannot be ignored any more than the significance of the almost limitless expanse of the steppes of Russia, if we would understand the cultures of both people. Geographic factors are hence more than the "props" of a cultural stage. They materially affect the social drama. Hills and valleys, plains and prairies, tundras and icy wastes, mountains and river courses are media through which a people develop a way of life. They are stimuli, obstacles, and resources.

To be aware of the physical media in which social life goes on, to be aware of the function of the physical as that which both obstructs and facilitates human interaction and its moral consequences, is to be in command of not only physical but also social knowledge. The long struggle which man underwent to master physical nature by magic and his present attempt to master it by science have both involved the interaction of his ideas and ideals with the world of physical nature.

Some personal phases of physical and social interaction.   But the interaction of the physical and social is more personal than has yet been pointed

[2] For the theory set forth in this chapter I owe a special debt to two papers by John Dewey: "What Is Social Study," *Progressive Education*, XV, 1938, reprinted in *Problems of Men* (New York: Philosophical Library, 1946), pp. 180-183), and "Social as a Category," *The Monist*, XXXVIII (April, 1928).

out. The helplessness of the infant and the dependency of the aged have far-reaching social consequences. Both have had much to do with the form and function of the family. The "century of the child" in which we now live owes its name to the scientific and sociopolitical activity which has made pediatrics a fully developed medical specialty, greatly advanced the sciences of orthogenetics and orthopsychiatry, brought more anti-child-labor laws, and developed a body of literature on the child which ranges from the scientific to the popular magazines which the mother and house-wife buy at the chain store. Concern with problems of the aged has taken the form of the new science of geriatrics, for we have come to believe with Walter Pitkin that life *may* begin at forty—even at sixty-five and later. Plans for old age security run the gamut from the misguided and economically unsound policies of the now defunct Townsend Plan to increased provision for old age assistance and survival benefits under the aegis of both voluntary associations and the federal government. Sex is a physical phenomenon whose significance for social relations has become a matter of increasing study and importance as evidenced by the Kinsey report and the current dispute over the teaching of sex hygiene in the public schools. Witness, furthermore, the timeless part which sex has played in taboo practices, puberty and adolescent ceremonies in both primitive and advanced societies, marital sex adjustment, and the relation of bodily changes to changing interests and social roles. We deny that the social is merely *superimposed* upon the physical. It is not the social which is the superficial; it is those who conceive it thus who have a superficial view.

Number and density and social effects. The sheer number and density of human populations, from which perspective we treat men as mere biophysical things, have profound implications for the quality of life of both persons and nations. If the community is small in population and area, the number of things which its members can do in common and without either economic or political middlemen is increased. The problem of achieving democracy in the Greek city-state was relatively easy (made more so by the disenfranchisement of slaves and artisans), whereas one of the most pressing problems the modern world confronts is that of achieving the same humane ends for all, in populations which number hundreds of millions and which inhabit lands which cover half a continent. Hence, with every increase in population, aggravated by immense land areas, the possibility of the direct participation of all the people in the making of policy which affects the general welfare is correspondingly decreased. It has brought the faint-hearted, the unimaginative, and the crass, to argue that democracy is impossible under the new conditions of life. The principle of representative government and attacks on it, with all they suggest by way of the impossibility of direct democracy, cannot be understood apart from the sheer facts of great numbers and vast land areas.

The number and density of human beings in political divisions, as well as the magnitude and frequency of the movement of men in space (migrations either as whole peoples or as individuals) condition significantly the quality and quantity of social interaction. The slogan of *Lebensraum* (living space), whether genuine or spurious, has been a *cause célèbre* of war since time began. Indeed, human society may be studied from the symbiotic view—in terms of space, time, number, and movement, as we observed in Chapter V.

Man is a part of nature. To these observations many others might be added. But, in the light of those which have been given, who can say where the line falls between the physical and the social, or indeed between it and the moral? If we would be sensible in our attempts to understand man as a part of nature, we might well be less concerned with the lines of demarcation between man and the physical realm and more concerned with the interaction which goes on across those lines. The evidence increases that nature is one, however differentiated be its many facets.

Social and natural science. These interrelations have still another aspect. We refer to the impact which advances in the natural sciences have made on social life. The promotion of research in the natural sciences is itself a social matter. But we have been, until only recently, more concerned with the dearth of natural scientists than with the dearth of teachers of the social studies, as well as many others. Hence we have been more concerned to order physical than human nature.

This unbalanced emphasis traces, almost certainly, to the fact observed in Chapter I, that we are more concerned with what is around us than with what is within us—forgetting that the quality of each determines the quality of human life. But the emphasis may be explained on another score, namely that social life gives up its secrets more reluctantly than does the realm of physical nature. The pace of social science will always be slower than that of natural science. But the pace of social science can be increased. This will, however, not happen until we spend more money on it, expect less in cash returns from it, and are more dedicated to it.

We grant that beliefs, customs, laws, and the forms of social institutions are more resistant to change and control than are minerals, plants, and nonhuman animal forms. But we are not for these reasons excused from the obligation of trying to understand human nature and social institutions if we are really serious about our vaunted prowess to control nature.

The natural sciences tell us of almost inevitable cause-and-effect relations, but the best we achieve many times is a compromise with their truths—likewise with what the social sciences can tell us, with which we compromise even more. Both the natural and social sciences tell us much which would save us from a great deal of folly. But to both of them we are disposed to say, "Come now, you don't know everything. Let's look at the practical issues involved in this matter." ("Practical issues" usually mean "traditional ways.")

It is one thing to know what can be done to solve our social problems but it is quite another to reach agreement among sharply conflicting interests, as well as to overcome deep-seated prejudices, stupidity, and resistance to new social facts. This suggests the relation between the methods of science and the methods of democracy. Earlier, we indicated wherein they are alike and wherein they differ.

Science and democracy.   It is clear that from the marriage of the method of science and the method of democracy a happy domestic life cannot be guaranteed. The trouble is that men want contrary and conflicting things. Your task as teacher of the social studies is to reveal to your students that to the degree we increase the areas of reasonably sure knowledge—both social and natural—we may diminish the areas within which wishes contrary to personal and social welfare may be hidden from our view. Until the end of time interests will still be the major motivating force in our lives, however much we advance the frontiers of all the sciences. All social action is based not on what science tells us but what we tell ourselves respecting the values we seek. Feelings and judgments will continue to play a central and vital role in human affairs. The ideas, ideals, beliefs, habits, and the traditional concepts that "hang in the picture gallery of our minds" will always color much of our conduct even when they are no longer the major guides to it. An essential obligation of the teacher of the social studies is to make students aware of these pictures, to recognize them for what they are, good or bad, and seek to control the extent to which they enter into individual and group thought and action. Improvements in the actions of men will come, as they always have, by laws and education. The teaching you do must be more comprehensible than some of our laws to the end that *they* may be made less complex and finally that the need for them may be reduced. We may at least hope and work for the day when education will be the greater force. We dare not accept the alternative that only the crafty and the strong shall prevail. Full selfhood, we must believe, can be had by the good and the wise.

The impact of natural science on human conduct.   If we would live by the fruits of the natural sciences we must make known to our students that many of the conceptions about the nature of man and his relations with the physical universe, as laid down in the dogmas of a prescientific age, must be abandoned. They must become acquainted not only with the findings of modern science but with their bearing on human conduct. Those of modern biology, anatomy, and psychology, respecting the myth of a superior race, represent one such bearing.

Our failure to teach the meaning of the findings of natural science for living in our world is one of the great tragedies of modern secondary education. Many of our high school graduates are at least fact-filled in the area of the natural sciences but close to being socially illiterate as to what the implications of those facts are for their personal lives. The fault is not theirs, but ours. No wonder that many of them display the same bewilderment about the basic problem of our civilization as do their adult contemporaries whose education was, like theirs, split between fact and meaning. Young and old alike, most of us are "as helpless as wasps on a window pane" because of an unconnected education. We shall neither make nor discover "the moral equivalent for war" or our lesser ills until we translate the facts and generalizations of the sciences, natural and social alike, into patterns of belief and action in human conduct.

No thinker of our time has stated our problem more boldly than Lawrence K. Frank.

It must be emphasized that we need more than abstract scientific laws, generalizations, quantitative findings, and formulas; we are waiting for a statement of the *meaning* of scientific knowledge in terms of its emotional significance for living, so that modern cosmology, astronomy, geology and biology will provide the equivalent of "Now I lay me down to sleep," in which the traditional cosmology, biology and psychology was expressed. More concretely, we must courageously and imaginatively recreate the four basic organizing conceptions essential to culture—the nature of the universe, man's place therein, his relations to his fellows and his society, and human nature and conduct—utilizing our recent scientific knowledge and understanding for that purpose just as our predecessors utilized the best contemporary knowledge and understandings available to them for constructing the culture they bequeathed to us.[3]

Man and nature interact. The burden or the roregoing has been that the physical does not occupy one realm and the social another, detached, alien, and apart from it. This is not to suggest that there are not important differences between man and trees, minerals, plants, and other animal forms. We have not undertaken to establish their identity but rather to

[3] "Science and Culture," *op. cit.*, p. 284.

learn how they are mutually related. We have sought to point out some significant lines of their interaction. We have, in short, sought to indicate that physical things must be respected as the indispensable means and conditions for social achievement. It would, of course, be childish to confuse physical things taken as means with physical things taken as ends. But it would be equally childish to assume that social and moral achievement, as ends, can be had without resort to physical things. Consonant with the view expressed by Lawrence K. Frank, we have sought to indicate the necessity of educating our students to see the social bearings of natural studies.

The identity of the social and moral.   Just as I have sought to show that the social does not merely lie on top of the physical, I shall now seek to show that the moral or ethical does not merely lie on top of the social. Indeed, I shall argue that the social and the moral, or ethical, are identical.

We are, unfortunately, heir to the view that the social *ought* to be the moral on grounds of "ethical obligations." But the case is much simpler. Human conduct is social in that it has consequences for others in terms of better or worse, right or wrong, good or bad. In this sense the social *is* the moral, since moral distinctions are exactly those of better or worse, right or wrong, good or bad. Social acts are social, hence moral in their consequences. If we should disregard the values or goals to which our social acts take us we would miss the significance of many, if not all, of the facts involved. Each of the social sciences focuses in one way or another and immediately or remotely on the order which men constitute. This is a social order. In the terms of the foregoing, it is also a moral order.

The opposites of social and moral.   Social and moral are general terms whose opposites are symbiotic and amoral. The latter are spatial or asocial and hence amoral. We are not now speaking of any *specific* social or moral order such as that of people who hold to a particular religious creed. But such orders are moral or social precisely for the reason that, in them, conduct is judged to be moral if it conforms to the tenets of a given creed. It is perhaps unfortunate that the term "moral" is often thought of only in terms of either sex or religion. It includes these but it also includes all conduct which has consequences which may be judged in the terms given above.

The term "moral" viewed generally and specifically.   If, perchance, social conduct is of the kind which injures or fails to advance either self or society (bearing false witness, cheating, adulterating foods, etc.) it is referred to as immoral, although it still belongs to the *general* category of the moral. It is not *amoral*, that is without social or moral consequences. Thus it is that if we (or people with moral standards different from ours but quite as binding on them) judge conduct to be moral it is moral in a *specific* sense, as measured by our (or their) standards. However, in the generic sense the term "moral conduct" has that quality simply by virtue of the fact of having social consequences—whether we like it or not, or whether or not we believe in it.

In the specific sense there is "right moral" and "wrong moral" conduct; in the generic sense there is only moral and amoral conduct. The moral or social consequences of conduct are evident in two ways: (*a*) in objective conditions which are created—housing, employment, health, etc., and (*b*) in the judgments of better-or-worse or of right-or-wrong which are laid upon conduct.

"Ethos" and "Mores." The identity of the concepts "ethical" and "moral" is evident in their language origins. The term "ethical" derives from the Greek word *ethos*, which originally meant customs and usages, especially those of the "in group" ("our folks") as distinguished from the "out group" ("those folks"). The ethos of the in-group was different from that of the out-group because each had different customs and usages and hence different standards by which they judged the goodness or rightness of conduct. Each rejected the *ethos* or ethics of the other. An equivalent for *ethos* is found in the term *mores*, the Latin word for things "moral." The German word *Sitte*, meaning custom, is an equivalent for both *ethos* and *mores*.

The separation of the ethical, or the so-called "higher" manifestations of human conduct, from the social and physical, was given its classic formulation in the writings of Immanuel Kant. Kant conceived of two worlds: the world of appearances and the world of realities. The former consist of *noumena* or things-in-themselves (*dinge an sich*); the latter consist of *phenomena*, the things of everyday experience. The former are categorical in nature and can be known by "pure reason." The latter are hypothetical in nature and can be known by the ordinary senses, those used in empirical study.[4]

[4] The dualism implicit in Kant's theory traces to Plato and, in some respects, to Aristotle, although scholars differ in the interpretations given to both Plato and Aristotle respecting the dualisms charged to them. There is, however, considerable evidence that both Plato and Aristotle took a dualistic view of matters which later philosophers have refuted, especially in those systems which have been formulated in the light of scientific knowledge which was not available to Plato and Aristotle, or, for that matter, to Kant.

The dualism of "higher" or "lower." It must suffice, for our purposes, to say that the distinctions of "higher" and "lower" assigned to the "ethical" and "social" aspects, respectively, of man's behavior is a heritage which has stubbornly resisted its critics. Such dualisms or "either-ors" as "individual or society," "man or nature," and "social or physical" are of the same genre. This is not to deny that differences exist between them, as shown in our previous discussion. However, many scholars affirm that the terms set against each other in these "either-or" pairings are not as separate and not necessarily as conflicting as they are assumed in popular thought to be.

Ethical and social are equivalent. Perhaps the chief barrier to one's viewing the ethical as equivalent to the social or moral lies in the belief that some matters of conduct are not only "higher" than others in an ethical scale but are always "higher"—that is, they are *absolutely* higher. This traces to the view that they have their origin, not in man's experience, but outside it. This view is explicit in a passage in Plato's *Protagoras* in which it is related that Zeus "fear[ing] that the entire race would be exterminated . . . sent Hermes to them, bearing reverence and justice to be the ordering principles of cities and the bonds of friendship and concilia-tion." (Steph. 322.) A considerable number of modern scholars defend the view that such virtues as reverence and justice are the result of man's attempt, not only to live, but to live better.

This is not to deny that such virtues as these and many others work to order men's social affairs. It is the verdict of anthropological knowledge that all cultures are alike in that they have developed standards of moral conduct respecting the whole range of social relationships, however much they differ in their specifics. Thus, they and we are far from denying the fact of certain social, moral, or ethical universals. It is only in the most primitive cultures that these norms of conduct remain relatively unchanged. In our culture we have not so much permanence or change, as changing permanences in these respects. As we have noted earlier, our moral stand-ards stay; they also change.

The problem of "moral relativity." This suggests the problem of moral or ethical "relativity." It is taken by the uncritical to mean that everyone sets his own moral standards and changes them to suit his caprice. If this were the case, we should be in a state of anarchy and the fact or the possi-bility of a society would thus be denied. But a society is by definition the way people work and are bound together in social or moral bonds. The legitimate meaning of moral relativity was never of this sort, and most of those who use the term and subscribe to it have never given it such a ridicu-lous interpretation. Always and everywhere, as we have observed, men have

been conditioned, in the long run at least, not by purely individual standards of conduct but by group standards. While all do not hold to them
with the same devotion and rigor, they do not treat them in the fashion
suggested by the interpretation just given. These standards are the *mores*
or the *ethos* of their cultures. Without them they would have no culture.
It is a fact, not to be denied, that such norms do not bind men as tightly
as they would be bound if they did not interpret them differently, or find
themselves in life situations in which, according to their best and most
honest judgment, they cannot always be honored literally. But because
men do not live completely by such approved and expected standards is
not to say that they do not live by them at all. This is not a plea for
deviation from them; it is only a statement of fact about such deviations.
Furthermore, any divergence from them is not to be explained by some
innate moral perversity. It is the view of social science that any divergence
is due to causes which trace to the way men respond in varying situations.
In our society, such divergences may be traced to such causal factors as
these: the complexity of the laws, sheer ignorance, the clash and conflict
of men's interests, the fact of individuality on which we place such a high
premium, the great mobility which we enjoy and which permits us to move
freely from place to place and between groups with different moral views,
and the fact that we have not yet learned how to live in a world of such
complexity as ours.

Moral relativity has two loci. The moral relativity of which we speak
has then two loci: variations in what is considered moral or ethical *between individuals* within the same culture and variations of a similar kind
between cultures. Moral or ethical relativity does not mean that all conceptions of rightness go by the board—whether between individuals or
between cultures. Between peoples as well as among a given people we
have the problems of cultural pluralism and *pari passu* of moral or ethical
pluralism. We also have individual pluralism which, however much a
problem it poses, is one of our most cherished values. The basic requirement for the good life in a democracy is, of course, that the plural number
of moral codes will not be so variant, conflicting, and uncompromising as
to make certain common beliefs and collective action in their support
impossible.[5]

Some conduct more "central" rather than "higher." Within our culture,
certain traits of conduct have such an obvious and direct relation to social
and personal welfare, or goodness, that we assign them a special status. We

[5] For a convincing reply to those who make "relativity" mean whatever whimsy and
caprice might dictate, see Ralph Barton Perry, *General Theory of Value* (New York:
Longmans, Green & Co., Inc., 1925), pp. 127-137, and Abraham Edel, *Ethical Judgment, the Use of Science in Ethics* (Glencoe, Ill.: The Free Press, 1955).

not only refer to them as ethical or moral as distinct from social, but refer to them as earning a "higher" ethical or moral position than other traits. These are such as truthfulness, honesty, chastity, and brotherliness. But in being named "higher" they are not *more* ethical than such other qualities as thrift, promptness, and cleanliness. They may be more *central* or *pivotal* to moral conduct but not because they are isolated from, "higher than," or outside of human affairs but, on the contrary, because they are intimately tied up with and are central aspects of conduct which has immediate and profound social consequences. They are also central or pivotal in that to possess such virtues as honesty and brotherliness is not to possess only those separate virtues. To be honest and brotherly means to be involved in conduct which has many related aspects, such as promptness, thrift, and courtesy. It is not now denied that there are great differences in the *quality* of social conduct. However, we take the view that all our virtues, including those which are traditionally thought to be ethical in the sense of being "higher" than others, have their origin *inside* man's experience. This means that we know and identify the moral or ethical as we know and identify all other objects which we, as sentient beings, are able to perceive.

It is undoubtedly true that, in the normal run of life, certain values tend to be assigned a more central and pivotal place than certain others. The ones we have cited illustrate this fact. But those named may not always be pivotal and central—however much they may usually occupy those positions.

No "fixed" ethical principles.   We normally give truth-telling a pivotal and central place but there are enough exceptions to show that it cannot always be assigned such a place and hence cannot be said to be a fixed ethical principle. In other words, we are saying that lying is normally immoral, but it is not difficult to illustrate that it might be moral. There is, for instance, Professor Henry Van Dyke's *Story of the Other Wise Man*. When he was confronted by Herod's soldiers who were in search of the infant Jesus to put him to death, Artaban, the other wise man, lied and told them the child was not there—at the door of the very house in which Mary, Joseph, and the infant were then in hiding. Believing that Artaban spoke the truth, the soldiers went away. Van Dyke's story does not tell us what Artaban's feelings were. Asked if his act did not do violence to something inside him, he might have replied, "Yes, but that is the price I had to pay to protect the truth." The limitation of the dualism of "truth or falsehood" is thus instanced.[6]

[6] The axiom, "The truth, the whole truth, and nothing but the truth," does not, as I understand it, rule out what we know as "little white lies." It would, of course, apply in

The view of pragmatism. The view that a universal rule can be laid down as to what constitutes ethical behavior in *all* situations must, in the light of the pragmatic philosophy, be abandoned. If both human nature and social situations were impervious to change of any kind, such a universal principle could be stated and ethically applied. But, given the nature of human nature and the variable nature of social situations—both within a given culture and between cultures—any universal principle as to what constitutes ethical or "right" conduct is impossible. This does not rule out the hope that cultures may become more homogeneous as respects their conceptions of moral conduct. Nor does it permit us to subscribe to that interpretation of ethical relativism implicit in the axiom, "everybody for himself and let the devil take the hindmost."

Abstractions are confusing. Much mental confusion and suffering might be avoided if we would test our conduct by specific instances rather than engage in abstract talk about morality and ethics. This might have the effect of making us even more conscious of the value of our usually central moral standards.

Ideas and ideals. The distinction we have sought to make between different qualities of the social (as measured by their central or peripheral position) and hence of the moral and the ethical, is further illustrated in the distinction which may be made between ideas and ideals. Both are born in the reflective processes of man, for modern psychology does not permit us to believe that there are special faculties of the mind, one of which produces ideas and another ideals, or that there is a faculty for "good" or "bad" ideas or ideals. Ideals are ideas in that they are idea-ted. Some are more central than others to "right" conduct. Their presumed antithesis is further exposed as fallacious when we recall that the scientist constructs an *ideal* conception of the relation of certain factors in order to test his *ideas* about the order that is in nature.

The ideal-ethical constructs of seers, prophets, and priests are made by means no different from the ideal-logical ones of the scientist. Men *make* good, as well as they make bread, houses, and machines. The Reformation was man-made. But it was not made from ideas or ideals only. The silver mines and the silver miners of Westphalia helped to make it. By the same logic, what we call the good is, at any given time, the consequence of all the factors, social and physical, which have *made* it possible. As social and

---

a court suit but would be inapplicable to neighborly talk between housewives. If applied there, the gossip in which they sometimes engage would be worsened in its consequences. There are, in fact, many situations in which fixed standards for determining good ethical conduct would be quite inappropriate for the substantial reason that they would injure rather than advance the amity of human relations.

physical conditions and knowledge change so conceptions of the good change.

Ethical beliefs and scientific theories are both social products. Thus it is that ideals and ethical beliefs, like ideas and scientific propositions and theories, are social products. Like democratic government, they are things which arise *out* of men's experience and some of them, so to speak, are assigned by them to a place *over* their affairs, but never so far *over* that they cannot be modified and made better—and also worse.

Thing and not-thing values are interdependent. About the relation of the ethical or moral to the physical little needs to be said. They are not, of course, identical. But in the sense that the physical is taken up into the social—now defined as the moral or ethical—it provides all the material and many of the conditions for their achievement. None of our not-thing values can be even formulated as hopes without concern for things in the inorganic world and the human organism. No values are possible except man finds himself in a physical environment in which they are achievable. It is in this sense that we may properly speak of *decent* housing, *just* wages, and a *moral* world. Man's culture, a compound of thing and not-thing values, is achieved and experienced. It is achieved and experienced through man's interaction with his physical and social surroundings. In this we do not deny the profound significance of the difference between central and peripheral values. Nor would we minimize the sacredness of man's conduct. On the contrary, we have sought to suggest how man may clarify the meaning of his conduct by locating it where he can do something about it, by making its origins clear and by suggesting how he may control and improve it. Thus we have suggested an objective as well as a subjective ground for a thoroughgoing ethics.

Man lives in two orders, the social or moral and the spatial or biotic. His conduct, whether good or bad, is a function of the complex interaction of these two orders. The scheme of organization of these orders has already been treated in Chapter V. Together they constitute the "seamless web of life."

A classification of humane, social, and natural studies. We shall now undertake to relate the foregoing discussion (in both sections of this chapter) to the three major bodies of studies in which knowledge may be classified: the humane, the social, and the physical. This classification may tentatively be made as follows:

The *humane* studies: literature such as the novel, poetry, biography, travel, etc.; the arts including painting, sculpture, music, the dance, drama, ceramics, etc.; aesthetics viewed as the science concerned with the nature of beauty; the study of religions in their historical and moral rather than their dogmatic and theological aspects; ethics and philosophy.

The *social* studies: cultural anthropology and ethnology; economics, geography (in its human aspects), jurisprudence, history, political science, social psychology, sociology, and logic.

The *natural* studies: astronomy, anatomy, biology, chemistry, demography, ecology, geography (physical), mathematics, physiology, physics, statistics, and physiological psychology.

These studies differ in significant ways. These three groups of studies are intended to mark certain general distinctions in the total body of knowledge which man has elaborated. The "humane" and "social" studies are concerned with man as a sentient and moral being: as knower, appreciator, believer, and doer. From this perspective they deal with him in what we choose to call "intrinsic" terms, that is, as a social being who may know himself. The physical studies are concerned with man and not-man. Through them man may be known extrinsically, that is, as a biological organism. They are also concerned with aspects of the world outside his skin. That these perspectives on men have both a separate and a related character has been the burden of the foregoing discussion, although we have made only marginal reference to these subject matters.

These three families of studies may be differentiated in other ways. Such studies as aesthetics, ethics, and various forms of belles-lettres treat man in aesthetic and unqualifiedly "ought" terms, rather than only in informational or didactic terms. The arts (drama, music, painting, sculpture, etc.) create symbols whose exact meanings are not indicated. Thus, they create truly expressive forms which speak a various language. The social and natural studies permit much narrower margins of interpretation as to the meaning of the symbols which they create.

The social and physical studies, on the other hand, treat man and his world in qualified terms. They use such imperatives as "ought," "must," and "should," but always in the context of the qualifications provided by the "if-then" formula. For instance, the social scientist says: "*If* you wish to maximize your profits, *then* you ought to do thus-and-so." The natural scientist says: "*If* you wish to split the atom, *then* you must do thus-and-so." The social studies, furthermore, treat their data by naturalistic rather than humanistic methods as far as their basic logic is concerned. However, they employ techniques uniquely adapted to the nature of their data. Thus, on these scores, the social studies have more in common with the natural studies than they do with the humane.

Social studies closer to humane studies. The social studies are, however, closer to the humane studies than are the natural studies in the sense that the object of the humane and social studies is man as a social being. .This does not deny that the humane studies are also interested in non-human objects (the sea, the sunrise, flowers, etc.), but they express this interest in humane, subjective, or preferential ways. Contrariwise, the social studies treat man in objective, scientific, and fact-statement, i.e., naturalistic ways. It is not, however, denied that such components of the humane studies as grammar, rhetoric, and the rules of the various arts have a quasi-scientific character. The affinity or nearness of the social to the humane studies is suggested in the fact that the social studies are sometimes called the "scientific humanities."

Some difficulties of classification. The inclusion of separate studies under three classifications is only an approximate one and requires critical comment. We have placed history in the social studies but know there is a history of everything whose past can be known—even the history of rocks with which geology deals. Psychology has been split between the social and natural studies: that phase of it (social psychology) which deals with man as a group member has been placed in the social studies, and that phase (physiological psychology) which deals with him as a biophysiological organism in the natural studies.

Cultural anthropology, in its study of cultures-as-wholes, concerns itself with all man's conduct—from the religious and artistic to the demographic and economic. (Physical anthropology, a branch of anatomy, has not been listed.) There is, likewise, an economic, a political, a sociological, and a geographic aspect to all personal and group behavior. All forms of social and individual activity may be studied by the philosopher. Logic provides tools and methods to test the formal truth of all propositions in all the areas of man's activity as a reasoning animal. Its tool-like character is thus shared by mathematics, ecology, demography, and statistics.

In one instance, at least, we might have used the term "political economy," by which title what we now know as economics was originally designated. But we leave the classification as given, for we are concerned more with general characteristics and relationships than we are with trying to effect a strictly logical classification of the many studies which man has invented. If done, this would involve the use of several logics. But whatever we might attempt on that score would not find unanimous acceptance by a jury of scholars from the various sciences.

This classification may be viewed from the perspective of Chart 2 in Chapter V. Insofar as the cultural aspects of man's behavior are less rational than its economic and political phases, and insofar as the term "cultural" is taken to connote a direct appraisal of it in unqualified terms, we may say that the humane studies are more intimately related to the "cultural" (so interpreted) than are either the social or the natural studies. But this does not mean that cultural behavior, so abstracted and set apart, is not eligible for study by the social scientist as well as by the natural scientist. It depends on the phase of it which is singled out for special analysis. Our basic thesis is that nature is one, however differentiated it may be in certain respects; its cultural aspects are not exempt from examination by all the branches of knowledge or systems of inquiry—*within the limits of their methods.* There is, for instance, an ecology as well as a sociology and history of religious beliefs, and both physiological and social psychology have something to say about artistic talents and temperaments.

If we now take man's political and economic behavior as representing the core of his more rational and calculated social behavior, we have no difficulty in matching the social studies with those phases of his life. But these behaviors are also subject to examination, in selected aspects, by the natural studies.

The symbiotic order remains. It is exclusively the concern of the natural studies by reason of the fact that it is that order of human behavior which is subject only to spatial, numerical, and quantitative methods of study. All human behavior lends itself to study from these perspectives but it cannot, as *human* behavior, be fully known when studied only from these angles. Its essence has an intrinsic nature; its form an extrinsic nature. The natural studies can treat only the latter.

In these comments we seek to show relations rather than identities. We certainly make no claim that there are not marked differences between the cultural, the social, and the symbiotic. Nature is one; it is also many.

The preceding discussion gives us a picture of the diversity and unity of nature, and likewise a picture of the diverse or separate, as well as the related ways we may observe and study it. We now give a graphic representation of the division and unity we have identified.

How the humane, social, and natural studies are related.

The vertical XY axis is the one with which we have been concerned in the foregoing discussion. The fact that we viewed the social, moral, and ethical as equivalents has not, however, prohibited our making distinctions between relative degrees of "dearness" of certain values as expressed in their central, rather than peripheral or marginal position in certain situations. That any values are fixed *absolutely* in either a central or marginal position we have not agreed.

We have differentiated between the humane and the social studies. The latter deal with values in a way as objective and scientific as is possible; the former deal with them in more subjective and hence less scientific ways. It is, however, true that each has a *social* character.

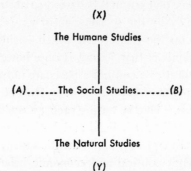

(X)

The Humane Studies

(A)........The Social Studies........**(B)**

The Natural Studies

(Y)

DIAGRAM 1. *A Two-Axial Schema for Relating the Humane, the Social, and the Natural Studies*

We have thus split the realm of the social. There remains the unsplit realm of the natural science studies, however much they represent a complex division of labor within their "total" field.

The social studies may be split into "goals" (or "ends") and "means." The split in the social studies gives us the following diagram:

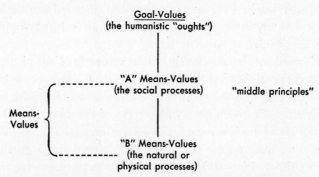

Goal-Values
(the humanistic "oughts")

"A" Means-Values
(the social processes)   "middle principles"

Means-
Values

"B" Means-Values
(the natural or
physical processes)

DIAGRAM 2. *Goal-Values and "A" and "B" Means-Values*

The split in the social studies is "temporary." The split in the social studies is represented by the *Goal-Values* (the humanistic "oughts") and the "A" Means-Values (the social processes). By this we simply mean that the values which are produced by man's interaction in the social processes are treated *temporarily* as "Goal-Values," and the processes through which they were achieved are treated *temporarily* as "A" Means-Values. But these do not work alone, for man does not make his values without interaction with "natural" things: soil, machines, minerals, and the like. These are here designated as "B" Means-Values.

With this split in the social studies, half assigned temporarily to the rank of goal-values and half assigned temporarily to the rank of means-values (which share their means function with the natural or physical processes), we conceive of the social processes as performing a mediating or "middle principles" function through which the physical means-values ("B" in the diagram) work *through* the social processes ("A" in the diagram) to produce the Goal-Values. They cannot work directly on the Goal-Values.

The social studies as "means" and "ends" illustrated. To any who charge that we are trying to have our cake and eat it, we plead "not guilty." We are only treating the social studies (or the social processes) now as *means* and now as *ends*. An illustration will help clarify this distinction.

Suppose the goal value to be "more and better health." As such, it is a humanistic "ought." It has emerged out of man's quest for a better life. But "more and better health" cannot be had only by wishing and speculating. It requires physical things and physical processes which, with the social processes, are the indispensable means for its realization. The medicines, clinics, staff, and all the paraphernalia of medical practice, laboratories, hospitals, and the like, which are the physical prerequisites for "more and better health," are brought into being by the interaction of men in political and economic activities. These go on in the social processes. They also require that men direct and control activities which belong to the category of physical processes.

Thus it is that the social processes play a "middle principles" role between men's dreams, hopes, aspirations, and plans for "more and better health" and the physical activities required for its realization. If we would know how any value (thing or not-thing) comes into operational reality we must (a) see it as something wanted or prized, (b) provide the physical things necessary for its being had, and (c) take account of the social processes in which men engage in the realization of it.

The foregoing analysis of Diagrams 1 and 2 has taken no explicit account of the interaction which goes on *within* the social processes. This is represented in Diagram 1 as the (A) . . . Social Studies . . . (B) axis. It will concern us in later chapters.

CHAPTER X

Attitudes:
How We Get and Change Them

THE FOREGOING chapters provide the background as well as context for an inquiry into the nature of attitudes. They are the ultimate focus of all the social studies. Inquiry into their nature and how we get and change them involves understanding of the nature of frames of reference, for without that knowledge we can know little about attitudes, how they are established or changed. Thus we must, at first, go somewhat far afield in order to understand something which is very private and immediate.

Our need for frames of reference. If we would be content to live in a world of unorganized sensations we would need no frames of reference. But such a world would be impossible to live in. Our perceptions would be as senseless as those of a newborn infant whose world, as William James expressed it, was a "booming buzzing confusion."

We do live in a sensory world and it does make sense to us, but only because we organize it through using frames of reference. They are the contexts in which attitudes arise. But they are more than that. They are the houses in which they live—sometimes past the time of their usefulness. A change in attitude requires change in a frame of reference.

Frames of reference help us organize our perceptions. A frame of reference is a heuristic tool, that is, a useful and man-made device which makes it possible for us to organize our perceptions into wholes or patterns. It is based on the psychology of the *Gestalt*, a German word whose nearest English equivalent is form, shape, pattern, or unitary structure. The psychology of the *Gestalt* is a psychology of perception. It affirms that we see things, not separately, but as parts of wholes. When, for instance, we see a tree we do not see leaves, twigs, branches, and trunk as separate things

134

which we then proceed to add up. We see it as a *tree*, a pattern of leaves, twigs, branches, and trunk. The same principle underlies the concept of a general education as one in which the separate bodies of knowledge are related in wholes. In these patterns or forms the separate bodies of knowledge take on new properties as we have shown.

Frames of reference we have used. We have used many frames of reference thus far and we shall use many more. Among those we have already used are the following: the productive in contrast to the non-productive character, the concepts of significance and relevance as aids in the selection of subject matter, likewise the concepts of goodness and wisdom, useful in giving pattern and structure to the democratic character, the four social processes as fictions to help us get an organized view of human life, the spatial and social orders and social institutions as ways of perceiving modern society, and new institutions as instances of changed frames of reference for perceiving an old ideal ("thou shalt love thy neighbor") under new conditions, the concept of a crisis in valuation as a way of selecting certain aspects of our society in order to view it in a critical light, the human relations triangles as fictions to aid us in social analysis, such ideal-type structures as the "family-who" and "public-what" situations, the concepts moral, ethical, social, and physical as names of related frames of reference rather than as separate and disconnected ones, vocational education viewed first in an isolated and next in a related frame of reference provided by social and humane studies, avoidable and unavoidable indoctrination as proper and improper ways of organizing the teacher's attitudes and roles, and common sense and science as contrasting frames of reference or perceiving systems.

We shall continue to construct other such systems in order to offer more organizing principles or schema without which you would be forced to fall back on quite imprecise and clumsy common-sense devices. We have insisted and shall continue to insist that such schema are useful not only to you but are the very essence of an education. Thus they are offered, not as your private possessions except that you use them to make their nature and use the private property of the students. Thus they will become, we hope, public property.

Some frames of reference are simple, some complex. Some frames of reference are simple; some complex. We use both kinds every day in ways such as the following:

1. The Marshall Plan was a pattern or schema by which we sought to reorganize the socioeconomic life of non-Communist peoples. An alternate plan is that currently expressed in the phrase "Trade, not aid."

2. Jurors have to distinguish between the frame of reference called "the facts" and the frame of reference called "the law"; a difficult task because they tend to overlap and interact.

3. When the demagogue quotes someone out of context, he quotes him outside the frame of reference in which his remark was made. The result is to falsify and twist his language, and thus engender hostile attitudes toward it.

4. The principles of "states' rights" and "federalism" are not only principles but Gestalts or frames of reference in which certain problems of law and government may be viewed.

5. The forms of literature we know as prose and poetry are frames of reference for expressing ourselves about various things; they differ chiefly by reason of the fact that the frame of reference which prose writers employ has more fixed boundaries than that which poets use.

6. The function of an hypothesis is to cut out a field within which a search is made for causal factors; thus the hypothesis constructs the frame of reference within which a net of causation may be examined.

7. Democracy, communism, and fascism are not only different and competing political ideologies; they are also competing frames of reference for perceiving human relations.

8. A Moslem does not eat pork; a Christian does. Each views pork meat in a different frame of reference or perceptive set. Thus their attitudes toward pork are formed.

9. President Coolidge is said to have remarked, respecting the money owed us by foreign governments: "They hired the money." This seemed to imply that they should pay their debts just as any debtor should settle his obligation to any creditor. But foreign and private debts are not the same in all respects. Such an attitude toward a debt owed by one foreign power to another thus confused a public with a private frame of reference.

10. On the occasion of destruction by fire of great stores of synthetic rubber during World War II, a government official is reported to have said, "What's all the hollering about; it was insured, wasn't it?" He thus placed the destruction of strategic war materials in the same frame of reference in which he was disposed, as a business executive, to place any loss by fire.

11. A ladder may be put in two sharply contrasting frames of reference: as an artistic pattern or art form made up of vertical and horizontal lines and as a device for climbing. Each of these perceptions engenders the attitude unique to it.

12. Custom requires that we wear bathing suits on the beach, not to a wedding, a formal dinner, or a funeral. In taking these different attitudes we place bathing suits in different frames of reference.

13. United States treasury officials are much more disposed to favor an increase in taxes during a time of inflation than in a time of deflation. In a time of inflation, increased taxation tends to check the upward spiral of prices; in a time of deflation a decrease in taxation tends to have the effect of stimulating the upward spiral of spending. They thus place tax policy in different frames of reference to suit different situations.

14. Similarly, the imposition of price controls under conditions of a scarce

supply of consumers' goods in wartime and the relaxation of such controls under conditions of more adequate supply of consumers' goods in peacetime takes account of the different frames of reference which wartime and peacetime, respectively, constitute.

15. In general education we seek to substitute such frames of reference as problems, situations, and processes for the more limited frames of reference which the traditional disciplines of economics, political science, etc., provide.

"Wrong" frames of reference produce "wrong" attitudes. It is evident that if we place things in inappropriate frames of reference we shall engender inappropriate or even wrong attitudes toward them. We have earlier argued that the mere addition of subjects does not constitute the basis for a general education. We might just as well have said that they do not constitute the frames of reference out of which a general education can emerge. If we now think of an education as a pattern of attitudes we see the relation between appropriate and inappropriate frames of reference and the attitudes engendered by an education in *related* and *unrelated* subjects, respectively.

Logic and morality are related. But we are not content to discuss the nature and use of frames of reference in terms only of a logical analysis, although that aspect is not to be overlooked because we want our students to know that the logic of their behavior is causally related to the moral quality of it. We would think a person odd, if not insane, who put his goldfish in a bird cage and his bird in a fish bowl. But worse logic and equally disastrous moral action would be practiced if our students do not know "what belongs where" in the many phases of their experience.

If, for instance, a student should place certain minority groups—ethnic or racial—in a fixed and categorical frame of reference as fit only for menial tasks, he would thus form attitudes toward them which would be prejudicial to the eligibility of such people to perform tasks for which their talents might fit them if they but had the opportunity.

How things get meaning. Our discussion will now focus on the relation between the frame of reference as a logical device and the process by which objects come to have meaning and, in that process, how our attitudes toward them are formed.

Whatever becomes an object of interest to a human being becomes, by virtue of that fact, a value. To take an interest is to act, however overt or covert the action be. As Professor George H. Mead has expressed it, a value is "the future character of the object in so far as it determines your action toward it."

Objects are such as these: trees, houses, human beings, machines, coins, foodstuffs, beliefs, attitudes and thoughts, poems, falsehoods, theories—in short, anything in which an interest may be taken. Objects do not have to possess weight, mass, form, or density.

Interests, attitudes, and values.   The transformation involved is a simple one. By our taking an interest, which is the same as *taking an attitude*, objects become values. Of all living creatures, man is the only one who is able to effect that transformation. Only human beings can take attitudes toward objects, hence only human beings can create values.

The capacity not only to get meaning out of experience but also to give meaning to it is nicely illustrated in a story which Professor Robert E. Park used to tell.

Animals do not understand.   A man was out walking with his dog when it began to rain. His dog had been trained to fetch his umbrella at the simple command, "Umbrella." That is, his reflexes had been conditioned to bring an umbrella when his master so ordered. And so away he went, only to return shortly with no umbrella. It had been moved from the place in which he had been conditioned to look for it. The man hurried home. Even his careful search failed to locate the umbrella but, close to the place where it should have been, lay his raincoat. Now if the dog had known the *meaning* of umbrella as a rain-protecting device and if he had been able to place it in the context of its use, he would have brought the raincoat when he failed to locate the umbrella. But, alas, he was only a dog. He had only been conditioned. He could only fetch objects, not understand them. The moral is obvious.

Many attitudes are inherited.   We inherit most of our attitudes, that is culturally—not biologically. The remaining few come by choice. How intelligent that choice is, is the real problem. The social studies teacher does not inherit the right to tell students what attitudes or valuations they ought to change, reject, or accept. The teacher's task is to make them aware of those they have inherited and those between which choices may be made and to test their significance and relevance for the world they believe to be a good one.

To have an attitude toward a thing is not only to prize and esteem it but also to apprize or estimate it, to judge its worth and to qualify it in many ways. Thus in valuing we engage in an act whereby we cherish or condemn, hold something dear or of little worth, and pass a judgment on it.

We hold attitudes toward both "thing" and "not-thing" values.   The "personal ideas in the mind" which constitute society—in the subjective sense—are personal attitudes or valuations. They are taken toward both thing and not-thing values. Our attitudes toward money and real property are attitudes toward thing values; those we take toward thrift, honesty, or theories are attitudes toward not-thing values. The means by which we get *en rapport* with our thing and not-thing environment is through our attitudes toward it.

Attitudes change by redefining values. Since our attitudes are subjective or "mental" in nature it follows that they may be changed only by our changing our mind—which includes our emotions. The only way this can be done is by redefining our values. But attitudes cannot be changed directly. They can be changed only through redefining the objects of which they are the subjective dimension. This is done by putting objects in different frames of reference. One of the most important principles in the whole realm of the teacher's education is that attitudes are changed indirectly. This requires that the teacher "works on" the student *by way of* "working on" the objects presented for study.

If, for instance, a student is to change his attitude (belief will do as well) toward the tariff, delinquency, or his own parents, he must redefine these objects. He must perceive or evaluate them differently. Note that it is *he* who does this, with the teacher helping him by unavoidable indoctrination.

The importance of interest. All learning, whether it be that through which the student develops an initial attitude or through which he changes an attitude formerly held, requires that an interest be taken. Interest is not something which the teacher demands; it is that which the very act of learning demands.

How attitudes are changed. Dewey has written with great clarity on the process by which attitudes are rightly and really changed.[1]

We cannot change habit [by which Dewey means attitude] directly: that notion is magic. But we can change it indirectly by modifying conditions, by an intelligent selecting and weighing of the objects which engage attention and which influence the fulfilment of desires.

We may desire abolition of war, industrial justice, greater equality of opportunity for all. But no amount of preaching good will or the golden rule or cultivation of sentiments of love and equity will accomplish the results. There must be change in objective arrangements and institutions. We must work on the environment, not merely on the hearts of man.

Change of attitude is "invited" by the teacher. Dewey's remarks bear chiefly on the method by which attitudes are changed in the Great Society. But the principle he states is applicable in the "society of the school." His remarks also suggest, as we have insisted, that a change in attitudes is an

[1] *Human Nature and Conduct*, pp. 20 and 21-22.

instance of re-education. Most of a student's attitudes were formed unconsciously. The task of the teacher is to invite him to look at those he has and ask himself if they are appropriate to the life situations in which he finds himself. He must be invited, not commanded, to change them. That is what we mean by education as "an invitation to learning."

The school works through symbols. Dewey speaks of "change in objective conditions and institutions." He also says that "we must work on the enviornment, not merely on the hearts of men." The school must be content to deal with both of these at the level of symbols. It is obvious that it cannot directly change the rugged objective conditions and the major social institutions of the Great Society. Nor should it undertake to deal directly with the "hearts of men," i.e., its students. It must deal with them through their attitudes.

A common-sense fallacy. One of the fallacies of common-sense sociology which we shall treat in Chapter XI but of which we now take a preview will help explain the school's role. This fallacy holds that it is "sufficient to create favorable or remove unfavorable conditions in order to give birth to given tendencies." For "given tendencies" we now substitute "given attitudes," because attitudes are tendencies or dispositions to act.

Humans react to meaning. The statement is a fallacy because a change in "tendencies" or attitudes is not automatically effected by creating favorable or removing unfavorable conditions. Humans react not to things, but to their *meaning*. The fallacy takes no account of this fact. The teacher's task is then a twofold one: to surround the student with new "objective conditions," that is, new objects of various kinds and/or with old "objective conditions" viewed in new and different frames of references. Through either or both of these acts the teacher works *indirectly* on the student's mind. What change of mind or attitude takes place is obviously conditioned by the teacher, but the decision to change or not to change lies with the student.

Propaganda is the wrong way. The easy but wrong way to attempt to change attitudes is to propagandize the student. This is the same as Dewey's "preaching good will or the golden rule." Good will or the golden rule is not ruled out—only the preaching of them is. You cannot escape the role of moralist, but you can escape the preaching of moralisms. It is a conspiracy against individuality. To such methods the student is an unwilling partner in a captive audience. The alternative method, that of unavoidable indoctrination, is not only more difficult but takes longer. Its merits lie in the fact that the results which follow are, if not also more lasting, those of which the student is consciously aware. He learns not only his thought, feeling, and belief but also their structure and origin. Feeling and believing are components in the social and humane studies much more than in natural science studies. The objects of the former two may be both known and loved; those of the latter may be chiefly known although there is nothing wrong—it is even a delightful thing and greatly to be cherished—if the student develops a genuine affection for principles in physics, chemistry, geology, or domestic science.

Some capacities and potentials of students. No student can be educated beyond his capacities and potentialities. (We often underestimate both of them.) They are of the following kinds: a different quality of imagination and more pertinent though perhaps not *more* imagination; the exercise of the conscience on more significant objects than now engage it; learning and using more critical and more reliable methods of examining attitudes; perceiving objects in more relevant and more significant perspectives; and seeing relationships and consequences which hitherto have been seen obscurely, if at all. These are some of the elements in the undiscovered and unachieved dignity of your students.

Inner and outer environment interact. Experiences such as these give promise, not only of changing tendencies or attitudes in the student, but of drawing out of him undreamed-of interests, concerns, and abilities. This involves him in a transaction between his inner and outer enviornment. Your teaching may not only arouse and draw out, but it may also create. But you will do this not by "working on the student" but rather by working on the objects which engage his interest and attention. Thus *your* control of the "objective conditions" is related to *his* control of "subjective conditions" or attitudes. These "objective conditions" must refer the student not only to himself and his personal knowledge and beliefs but to those of the Great Society. These are embodied in its institutions. Only by establishing this relation can his attitudes have both the personal and the public character required for their greatest usefulness. Only then may your teaching act as a bond to tie the student to life, rather than as scissors to cut him off from it.

If we would understand what is involved in the student's changing his attitudes, we must inquire further into the nature of the process by which any attitude is taken. This is, in short, the process by which things get meaning.

But it is more complicated than that, for we shall also need to inquire how it is that the "same" things have different meanings for different people, and the "same" person at different times.

False theories about meaning. We say that common sense tells us what things mean. For instance, we say that it is natural that a green traffic light means "go," and a red one "stop," or that the shout of "Fire!" means danger. In the common-sense view things don't "come to have meaning," they just *have* it "by nature." But in the view of the social studies they come to have it by virtue of *human* nature.

There is also the common-sense notion that things mean what they are named, called, or labeled. But we may know that a patent medicine contains sodium acetylsalicylate, or that some people die from arterio sclerosis and yet have no understanding of the meaning of either the drug or the cause of death. Our students may know that the name of a certain historical period was the Renaissance, and that the name for a certain theory of political authority was "the divine right of kings," without a glimmer of the meaning of either.

Thus the common-sense and practical explanations run. But neither of them is satisfactory. What we think we understand almost intuitively has a complex history, for we have Plato's word that "the knowledge of things is not to be derived from names." This does not deny the importance of names, but we must know that they serve only as symbols and are not the things themselves.

Meanings are assigned within our experience.   We now offer the proposition that: *things have the meaning(s) which are assigned to them by human beings, and these assignments are the result of the experience(s) they have with them.*

We have already distinguished between objects and values and have observed that the change from the former to the latter comes by way of our taking an interest. We now call that "having an experience with them." Furthermore, any given object may have many meanings, because we may have different experiences with it in different frames of reference, and thus take different interests in it.

The objects "men" and "women" may become the values we call parents if our experience with them is of a parental kind, but they may also become the values we call statesmen, inventors, thieves, or neighbors depending on the nature of our experience with them. The roles they play are, of course, important factors in the meanings they have for us and the attitudes we take toward them. These roles are part of the "objective conditions."

The object "hill" is capable of becoming the value of an "ore deposit" to the mining engineer, a "place to slide" to a boy with a sled, or a "place susceptible to erosion" to a farmer. The object "the house across he street" will mean different things to a mortgage banker than it will o the man who lost his owner's right to it because he could not pay off his mortgage. A lately adjourned session of the Congress may have the meaning of "honorable achievement" to one member, while to another of the opposite party it may mean "dishonorable achievement." The object called a "scientific theory" may possess the value or meaning of an "indispensable aid to practical action" to one man, but to another it may be the value or have the meaning of "impractical nonsense."

To any who may still be disposed to ask, "But what are things, really?" the only answer we can give is that they are really what they come to mean through the part they play in some experience we have with them. Objects, as such, are phenomena of nature. Values are phenomena of human nature.

The meaning of an object is the result of a frame of reference. These remarks suggest a second and complementary proposition, namely that: *the meaning of an object is the result of the context or frame of reference in which we put it.*

"Picnic" and "freedom." We may examine the truth of this proposition by asking the meaning of two words: picnic and freedom. What "picnic" means is not difficult to learn because it is easy to experience, although there are several varieties of picnic. But the meaning of "freedom" is more elusive. We must ask: freedom for whom, when, to do what, and from what? Everyone is in favor of freedom in the abstract; difficulties arise when specific kinds of freedom come under discussion. The difference lies in the general and specific frames of reference in which it is put.

The more we reflect on the process by which objects become values and engender attitudes, the more apparent it becomes that we are involved in deeply personal ways in that process. Things not only exist but coexist, and different patterns of coexistence give them different meanings.

Teaching does not start with "the facts." The orthodox view of teaching holds that one starts with "the facts." But which facts? In the light of our analysis two prior decisions must be made. We must decide which objects are significant to examine and which frames of reference are the more relevant for their analysis. Once these objects—be they principles, people, laws, processes, relationships—have been chosen, we are on the way to concern ourselves with the facts "in the case." Note that they are those "in the case," that is, in the frame of reference in which we have placed any given object. Meanings are attributes of objects placed in different frames of reference, and facts are the terms in which those attributes may

be known. Otherwise, they can be learned only by rote, or dictation.[2] Rote
learning is, however, a frame of reference. We call it "humdrum" or non
sense.

We need to teach the method of evaluating. These judgments are diffi
cult to make because we need to teach not facts but rather the *method* by
which our students may understand how they come to place certain
valuations on or take certain attitudes toward given objects. This does not
do away with facts. It only puts the objects of which they are the
facts into frames of reference whereby they may come to have meaning.
These are facts about such objects as the tariff, the law of supply and
demand, the nature of culture, the obligations of adolescents to their
parents, the western migration, the TVA, the control of atomic power,
and countless others.

The moral question is "which frame of reference?" But this does not
answer the question as to the context or frame of reference into which we
ought to place these objects. To that question we can only reply that we
ought to place them in alternate and conflicting frames of reference, because we want our students to learn that objects can be placed in many
frames of reference, and that in each they will have meanings as different
as the frames of reference are different. We want them to know that
controversy as to the meaning of any given object is not an evil thing but
that it is the consequence of the fact that human beings put the same
objects in different and conflicting frames of reference. Thus, our students
may come to know and understand that controversy lies in the very nature
of conflicting interests and that a society which puts a premium on individuality puts a premium on difference and must expect controversy. They
may also come to understand that when people see things in different and
conflicting perspectives they ask different questions and get different
answers.

"Wrong" questions give "wrong" answers. Once, in a lecture on the
teaching of social problems, I was speaking about the factors which are
responsible for the appearance and growth of slum communities. This
required that I deal with unemployment, low wages, absentee ownership,
and other factors which must be treated in such an inquiry. I pointed out
that the characteristics of the slum are not only substandard houses but
defeated, helpless, and poor people—poor in spirit as well as poor in
purse. It was my mention of the poor that "pulled the string" on one
student. He looked up at me with a kind of sad innocence and said, "But

[2] See Robert E. Park, "A Memorandum on Rote Learning," *American Journal of Sociology*, XLIII (July 1937), pp. 23-36.

thought the Bible said that 'the poor ye always have with you.'" I replied that I had read the statement in the New Testament but understood it to mean something quite different from the interpretation he put upon it. I said that the remark was made by Jesus of Nazareth by way of noting the continued presence of the poor in contrast to the statement which followed: "but me ye have not always." I suggested that one need not be an expert in biblical analysis to say that the use of an idiom about the poor in that day was not intended to recommend poverty or obstruct attempts to eradicate it. In that economy there were many poor and, given the quite natural assumption that the economy would undergo no marked change, the poor would remain. I questioned this student's intelligence, not his religious views. In failing to put the poor of today in a modern frame of reference, he failed to ask relevant questions. And, by the same token, he gave himself irrelevant—even unintelligent—answers.

Policy study is controversial. In the light of this view the most inane question that can be asked of the social studies is, "Should they deal with controversial matters?" Only in a society in which there was no change and hence no controversy would such a question make any sense, except that in such a society there would be no occasion for asking it. This is not to say that controversy makes up the entire body of social knowledge. There is a place for description, logical analysis, and those kinds of interpretation which do not require a concern with conflicting policy. But, to the degree that the social studies are *policy* studies (which they are to a great extent) controversy cannot be escaped. Whenever the facts of social study are dynamic, controversy enters. The task is then to analyze what is involved in the controversy, not to *settle* it, except at the logical level. Social controversy is settled, when and if it is, at the level of social action.

Students must learn to choose. The substance of my argument is this: our students cannot learn to make choices unless there is something to choose between. In the social studies that opportunity is given by their viewing the same objects or situations in different and often conflicting frames of reference: the tariff in the frames of "high" and "low"; the advancement of education within the frames of "states' rights" and "federalism"; the ballot in terms of the "short" and "long" one, and so on. Their emancipation from narrow if not outmoded ways of perceiving the possibilities in the world can come by no other means.

Reason and sentiment are both involved. I do not assume that the student's choices will be based entirely on reason, for sentiment is closer to the core of his life and purpose than definable thought. But it seems

to be true that we cannot search our souls without using our minds. W
discriminate on the basis of both reason and sentiment. Certainly Jea
Valjean searched both his mind and conscience when he chose to lift th
cart from the old man, although he knew that this display of strengt
would identify him as an escaped convict. But the freedom which senti
ment, rightly bound to reason, gives us is not the freedom to do only thos
things which do not matter much.

The method of the dialectic. The method of using comparative, con
trasting, and even conflicting frames of reference is the method of th
dialectic which Socrates used. It is told that Socrates asked his student
if the breath were hot or cold. One was quick to reply that it was hot
Of him Socrates asked how that could be since we blow it on our sou
to cool it. Another student, thinking he had the clue, volunteered tha
it was cold. Of him Socrates asked how this could be true since we blow i
on our hands to warm them. The fact is that the temperature of th
breath is determined by the frame of reference or the context in whic
it is placed. The dialectic which your students ought to practice is tha
which sets old and new attitudes against each other, as well as tha
which puts in contrast different kinds of new attitudes. Their choice
will then have a chance to be real ones.

To fail to employ the dialectic is to run the risk of giving your student
the impression that there is but one way of looking at the objects of thei
life, hence that only one attitude is possible toward them. To the fea
that this method would confuse them I can only reply that it were fa
better that they be confused in the protective, decent, and helpful atmos
phere of your classroom than to leave them to experience that confusior
in an atmosphere much less protective, decent, and helpful. The schoo
especially in the social studies, deals with life *now* as well as preparation fo
it "after school." In the measure that if fails to join these two "existences"
it almost certainly insures the innocence and incapacity of which I spok
earlier.

The mind is a harp. That these be your teachings is crucial. But how
you will teach them is of equal importance. I speak of the "how" of teach
ing as the realistic study of things that matter, tempered with insight int
how deep and all but almost immutable lie the attitudes which you
students have already formed about these things. Thus the rigor of you
teaching must be conditioned by the mental and emotional maturity o
your students. It is they who will undergo change, and only that amount o
it which seems good and wise to them. The remaking of character whicl
is their pattern of attitudes is not an easy and often is not a pleasant task

The mind is like a harp; all its strings throb together. These are the emotions, impulses, thoughts, beliefs, and attitudes of your students.

Evidence is not enough. What I seek to emphasize was done with great wisdom and in the quaint and charming language of seventeenth-century England by Richard Baxter.[3]

And I know not how hardly men's minds are changed from their former apprehensions, be the evidence ever so plain. And I have perceived that nothing so much hindreth the reception of truth as urging it on men with too harsh importunity, and falling heavily on their errors. For hereby you engage their honour in the business and they defend their errors as themselves, and stir up all their wit and ability to oppose you.

Attitudes are not appendages to social education. In the light of this discussion, what a foreshortened and erroneous view it is that attitudes are in the nature of appendages to social education to be added or left off as one chooses. The burden of my thought is that the teaching of them is inevitable, granted that it is teaching that induces more than rote-learning. But all teaching has meaning, if only the meaning of boredom, ennui, and tedium as it certainly must have if you subscribe to rote-learning. If it has such meanings as these you may be sure that it will engender the appropriate attitudes, not only toward yourself but toward social knowledge, the school, and life itself.

I have been greatly troubled by reading "units of instruction" which, in listing their objectives under the rubrics of skills, understandings, and attitudes, fail especially to show the relation between understandings and attitudes. If wisdom is the way in which knowledge is held, as Whitehead has told us, attitudes are the way in which understandings are held.

The continuum of teaching. The continuum with which we have dealt is this: objects, frames of reference, meanings, attitudes, valuations, and finally conduct. You cannot go much beyond attitudes, as we observed earlier. But that does not make your task less important, only more difficult—for your students will have little opportunity, under your guidance, to "try out" their new attitudes in the forms of conduct of which they are the mainsprings.

The logic of the method which has been presented is a kind of impersonal-personal conception of teaching. It suggests a pedagogy something like that expressed by Polonius in Hamlet: "by indirections find direction out." These are the indirect-direct methods by which your students may develop a mobility of mind through the mastery of conceptual frameworks

[3] Quoted by Sir Josiah Stamp in *We Live and Learn* (London: Macmillan & Co., Ltd., 1938), pp. 58-59.

which they have, so to speak, "on hand" in advance of the need for them
They will not then have to improvise them on the spot.

But frames of reference have a more personal value than this. If you
students will see their frames of reference as their basic postulates and
assumptions, they may become aware of what it is they think with. In
doing this they will develop independence of thought. That is one of the
great goals of teaching.

CHAPTER XI

Perception, Valuation and Conduct

THE TERMS and the process we shall now treat were introduced in Chapter I. Any change in the student's character involves him in the experiences implicit in the title of the present chapter. The valuation we place on any thing or not-thing value is the result of the attitude we take toward it. But, as we suggested in Chapter X, attitudes are conditioned by the frames of reference in which we perceive given objects and the attitudes thus formed are the mainsprings of conduct. The relation between perception, valuation, and conduct is thus made evident.

The student's character is a pattern of attitudes. The student's mind is not a clean slate upon which you may write the truth "with a firm, round hand." His present character orientation is made up of his present attitudes, which constitute the *Gestalt* within which he perceives himself and his world. It is not a piecemeal thing. Furthermore, it is both consistent and inconsistent in its structure, however much he may be unaware of its inconsistencies. If he is aware of them, he is troubled; if he is not, he is relatively content. Your task is to get him to examine his character *Gestalt* and change it, as the old Dutchman said, "by his own convincer."

Evidence of consistency and inconsistency. Let us now look at some evidence of both consistency and inconsistency in the organization of students' attitudes. These may be defined as the mental-emotional residue of what they think or believe is true. They are, in substance, their beliefs. How they fixed them, we do not know.

The following statements and student responses to them were taken from a random sample of 500 students (mostly freshmen and sophomores)

149

in ten colleges chosen at random from twenty-two. The Inventory of Social Understanding from which the statements are taken was administered during the studies made by the Twenty-two College Cooperative Study in General Education between 1940 and 1944.[1]

TABLE 1. *Student Responses to Controversial Statements* (*Paired*)

	PER CENT OF STUDENTS WHO		
	AGREED	DISAGREED	#5 RESPONSE
1. Human beings are so irrational you can't do anything to change them.	14.2	80.8	4.8
2. You can't change human nature.	48.6	46.6	4.6
(181 students or 36.2% disagreed with (1), but agreed with (2))			
3. Any real hard-working person can make about $2,000 a year in this country.	31.1	57.2	11.3
4. If people are poor it's chiefly their own fault.	18.2	76.6	5.0
(108 students or 21.6% agreed with (3), but disagreed with (4))			
5. Everybody has an equal chance in America.	42.0	56.2	1.6
6. No matter how poor people are, they can get all the medical care they need if they try.	46.1	50.6	3.1
(50 students or 10.0% agreed with (5), but disagreed with (6))			
7. Human beings are so irrational you can't do anything to change them.	14.2	80.8	4.8
8. It is useless to try to reform criminals.	4.8	93.5	1.5
(68 students or 13.6% agreed with (7), but disagreed with 8))			

[1] See Albert W. Levi, *General Education in the Social Studies* (Washington: American Council on Education, 1948), for a full account of the Inventory, which went through three editions. The responses in Table 1 are from my personal files as the former Research Associate in the Social Sciences in the Study; those in Table 2 are taken from Levi, *ibid.*, pp. 55-56.

The Inventory permitted five kinds of response: "agree," "disagree," "preference for," "preference against," and a No. 5 response which was, we assume, elected when a student could not make up his mind to use one of the other four. In the tables, the "agree" and "preference for" responses are combined, as are also the "disagree" and "preference against" responses. However questionable or impossible it be to add these two qualities of responses, we do it here in order to indicate two classes of response. In reality, of

The statements in each of the above pairs report similar, although not identical points of view. Whether they are true or false as to fact does not now concern us. What does concern us is the inconsistency in responses which is recorded for each pair. On logical grounds, a student's response to the statements in each pair ought to have been of the same kind. That is, if he agreed with the first, he should have—on logical grounds—also agreed with the second. Similarly, his disagreement with the first should have been matched with his disagreement with the second.

The statements in the following table are not paired. Nevertheless, the responses reveal some significant patterns of attitudes.

TABLE 2. *Student Responses to Controversial Statements*

| | PER CENT OF STUDENTS WHO | | |
	AGREED	DISAGREED	#5 RESPONSE
1. Unemployment benefits and things like that demoralize the people who receive them.	41.0	50.0	9.0
2. Plain human contrariness (sin, cussedness, etc.) is at the bottom of most of the world's troubles today.	68.0	24.0	8.0
3. It's undemocratic for taxes collected from the people in New York state to be spent for public education in Georgia.	29.0	60.0	11.0
4. It would be a good thing for the U.S. to deport the aliens who criticize the government.	55.0	41.0	4.0

Some factors which account for vagaries of mind. The responses in the two tables give evidence of many kinds of miseducation. But, rather than attempt to diagnose each response (which would require knowledge which is not available), I choose to make some general remarks which will at least suggest what some of the main factors are which account for the inaccuracies and vagaries of mind represented.

1. Man is a social being, hence his thoughts and attitudes reflect his group associations. It is only in a limited sense that the student, or any of us, creates

course, factual and preferential responses cannot be added. It should be further noted that the statements as given in the Inventory were not paired as they now appear in Table 1. We now pair them in order more clearly to indicate inconsistencies.

All statements in Table 1, except (8), were keyed as statements of fact. In Table 2, (1) and (2) were keyed as statements of fact and (3) and (4) as statements of preference, i.e., which are not amenable to proof. See Nathaniel Cantor, "The Teaching and Learning of Sociology," *American Journal of Sociology*, LV (July, 1949), for a critical discussion of some other responses from this Inventory.

his mode of speech or thought out of himself. He speaks the language and he thinks the thoughts of the group to which he belongs. His confusions in thought may arise from the fact that he belongs to several groups between which there is considerable difference in point of view.

2. The preferences to which students subscribe strongly or about which they feel strongly are often treated by them as proved facts. In so treating them, they reveal their attitudes, that is, what they take for granted. To know what one takes for granted is to know one of the most significant things about him.

3. Much of what students learn in formal education is really not learned at all. Rote-learning rather than insight-learning characterizes much of what students get at all levels of instruction. On this account, they often entertain traditional beliefs (folklore) side by side with scientifically established facts. The contradictions between them go unnoticed.

4. Man establishes his right to be called rational by showing that he can see himself and his world in an objective light.

5. Students are caught in the crossfire of the education they get informally in the "educative society" and formally in the "educative school." (This is closely related to (3) above.)

The nature of common-sense thinking.   Further light would be shed on the responses reported above if we could know more about the thought-ways of the culture from which they came. This can be done in general by inquiring into the nature of common-sense thinking. One of the changes which social study ought to produce is that of helping students become somewhat less persons only of common sense and somewhat more persons of science.

The words "somewhat less" and "somewhat more" need explanation. No reasonable person would expect or wish that all human action take its instruction from science. Indeed, it could not—given the nature of man. Hence, there remain, even for the mind most devoted to the accuracies and precisions of the method of science, large areas of practical use and enjoyment as well as what we believe life to be for, which ought not to be invaded by science, and which cannot be. A life devoid of the nonrational and the fortuitous, a life without "self-evident" evidence would be one without poetry, native insight, or any aesthetic or ethical quality. And so it is that the chief attributes of common sense, belief in the providential, and an affinity for the qualitative rather than only the quantitative are not lightly to be surrendered. Man can and has lived without science but never without a philosophy and a religion of some sort. Indeed, science would be meaningless without them. But the attributes of science are not to be denied their rightful place.

We need "good" common sense. I do not, then, suggest a choice and dependence on common sense *or* science but rather a sensible division of labor between them. The human mind is not naturally disposed to operate within sharply delineated and disciplined boundaries. We are disposed to take appearances for reality, to believe rather than to establish belief on the grounds of objective evidence, and to judge by "rule of thumb" rather than by scientifically valid principles. But these are not marks of human perversity. They are only the uninstructed ways of man.

Common sense defined. Webster tells us that common sense consists of the "unreflective opinions of ordinary men; the ideas and conceptions natural to man untrained in dialectic." The Oxford Dictionary tells us that common sense is "good sound practical sense; combined tact and readiness in dealing with the ordinary affairs of life." From these definitions it is clear that common sense refers to many notions and opinions which we have long been accustomed to regard as wholly reliable on their own account. We trust them because we have never found, indeed we have never tried to find, any reason to doubt them. It also refers to the somewhat chaotic and mixed-up view which almost all of us seem naturally to carry around under our hats; opinions and guesses, more or less vague and confused, which are echoes or shadows of old-fashioned but still fashionable dogmas. Common sense may also be thought of as the fleeting and subjective impressions we have of things but of which we are unable to give any clear-cut and scientific explanation. Moreover, it has about it a kind of sagacity or acuteness of sense impression which almost all of us have but which slips through our fingers when we try to define it—a fabric of hunches and prejudices that have not been and in most cases cannot be confirmed on rational grounds.

From these definitions and comments the impression follows that common sense is an inexact, practical, unreliable (though often reliable), and a more or less private and personal way of knowing. But science is also a way of knowing. They differ greatly in their reliability.

The "common-sense" and "scientific" mind contrasted. Despite these differences, science starts with common sense. It is rooted in it. Furthermore, unless science is able to justify the sensible qualities of men's minds, that is, *good* common sense, it can make only feeble claims to our acceptance of its findings. But it would be incorrect to say that science is "organized common sense"; it is rather a tool which we may use for organizing it. The following columns show how the common-sense and scientific mind differ.

"COMMON-SENSE" MIND	"SCIENTIFIC" MIND
1. Takes a restricted and partial view of facts and events.	1. Seeks to examine facts and events in as wide a context as possible.
2. Tends to confuse judging and explaining.	2. Recognizes the difference between judging and explaining and seeks to separate them.
3. Is committed to the idea of a single cause.	3. Knows that cause is multiple and complex.
4. Tends to explain things in terms of "will forces" and supernatural factors.	4. Explains cause in terms of the play of "natural" phenomena.
5. Is often controlled by wishful thinking.	5. Seeks to exclude wishes from that which is studied.
6. Looks for the evidence which will confirm or sustain a view already held. Tends to be intolerant toward contrary evidence.	6. Seeks to give due weight to negative evidence, and to be as objective as possible.
7. Is dogmatic and uncritical.	7. Rejects dogma and invites criticism.
8. Is credulous, that is, will believe "almost everything"; holds that "seeing is believing."	8. Is properly skeptical until proof is at hand; is suspicious of "appearances."
9. Is impressed by "authority" and is not disposed to question it; is reverent toward tradition.	9. Is unimpressed with "authority" until examined; is skeptical of tradition.
10. Believes in fatalism and destiny; asks, "Why did it happen?"	10. Accepts no fatalistic explanations; asks, "How did it happen?"
11. Careless in making observations.	11. Cautious in making observations.
12. Makes snap judgments; is reluctant to admit its ignorance.	12. Capable of suspending judgment; admits the limitations of knowledge.
13. Is negative toward "disagreeable facts."	13. Unafraid of facts, whatever they be.
14. Is conventional and often gullible.	14. Is unconventional; bases belief on inquiry.
15. Interested chiefly in the immediate; is impatient with theory.	15. Takes due account of the past; uses theory to guide practice.
16. Believes that facts have self-evident meaning.	16. Knows that facts may mean different things under different conditions.
17. Makes loose generalizations on the basis of unexamined hunches.	17. Disciplines generalizations by carefully testing the truth of hypotheses.
18. Interested chiefly in what is unique.	18. Interested in the relation between the unique and the general.

When, for instance, a man says that "night follows day," or when his wife says that "Duzie soap is better than Dozie soap," each is making a common-sense judgment. They ask for no proof other than that which their untrained senses and practical experience give them. The judgments of neither are related to any hypothesis or theory.

Most, if not all, of Poor Richard's axioms are common-sense. "Early to bed and early to rise, makes a man healthy, wealthy, and wise," may be true at times and false at other times. Such axioms do not allow for exceptions. So with all common-sense knowledge.

We muddle through. Despite the fact that common sense may see us through, it does so chiefly by requiring that we muddle through. It has a tendency to lead us to false as well as true conclusions. It is unable to cope with new situations and tends to degenerate into dogma and makes for mental inertia and sluggishness.

Some limitations of common sense. There is, for instance, the notion that if something happens after something else, it happens because of it (*post hoc, ergo, propter hoc*). But everything happens after something else, so that view tells us little about the causal relation between things. The scientist, however, makes no claim that he can explain everything. There are, have been, and will always be elusive factors in the causal process and the adventitious cannot be totally removed from human experience. In short, certainty is not to be had.

The limitations of common-sense thinking become sharply evident when we face a new situation which does not correspond with its fixed formulas or stereotypes. The farmer who, upon seeing a giraffe, said, "There ain't no such animal," practiced common sense. No such animal could be, because it was quite unlike any he had seen before. Common sense is "always wrong . . . in that it is never complete, and is never understanding in terms of theoretical and comprehensive generalizations." [2]

The "insider" and the "outsider." Suppose that a social scientist sets about to study a community. He will both depend and refuse to depend on the insights and reports of the layman. He will listen to what the layman says but will carefully check it to see if the facts confirm it. The social scientist does not believe that the layman is trying to deceive him; rather he recognizes that his observations are those of a layman and subject to impressions which he reports, in good faith, as statements of fact. They may or they may not be true. The layman is, so to speak, "on the inside"

[2] Robert Redfield's comment on Carl C. Taylor's paper, "Sociology and Common-sense," *American Sociological Review*, XII (February, 1947), pp. 10-11.

and sees things from the inside. He is not able to get "on the outside" and look at things with the detached and objective eye of the scientist. But the scientist, although a stranger and "outsider" can, by getting acquainted with the layman, become an "insider." He thus becomes both an "insider" and an "outsider." The two views give him a truer picture. The social scientist, by being both on the outside and the inside of the community, can see it in terms of other communities. This comparative view gives him a perspective far more critical than the layman has. It disciplines the scientist so that, in making general statements about community life, he does not go overboard and base them only on what he observed in a single community. This is just the mistake the layman is apt to make. But, to make matters worse, the layman is not trained in the methods of correcting his views—even if he should wish to. And so the social scientist "must be prepared to find the [layman] wrong as much as he is right." [3]

The role of unconscious bias. The operations of the common-sense mind can hardly be understood without taking account of the role which unconscious biases play in its observations and the conclusions which rest on them. Unconscious biases are what the layman is referring to (without knowing it) when he talks of "the human factor" in perception. Furthermore, he is apt to argue that nothing can be done about them. Here again, the layman is partly right and partly wrong.

Bacon's "idols." Francis Bacon in the *Novum Organum* called these unconscious biases the "idols and false notions which now possess the human understanding." Not only do they "so beset men's minds that truth can hardly find entrance, but even after its entrance, they will again, in the very insaturation of the sciences, meet and trouble us, unless men being forewarned fortify themselves as far as may be against them." These are the idols of the Tribe, the Cave, the Market Place, and the Theatre.

The Idols of the Tribe are "founded in human nature itself and in the very tribe or race of men." Human understanding "is like an irregular mirror, which distorts and discolors the nature of things by mingling its own nature with it." These mirrors created the idols of the tribe; we find what we want to find, not what is there.

The Idols of the Cave are the idols of "individual man." Everyone has "a cave or den of his own which refracts and discolors the light of nature." These idols owe their nature to such factors as these: one's own "proper and peculiar nature," "his education and conversation with others," "the reading of books," "the authority of those whom we esteem and honor," and the like.

The Idols of the Market Place are formed by "the intercourse and association of men with each other." They have their origin in clichés and wrong definitions

[3] Redfield, *op. cit.*, p. 11.

which "wonderfully obsess the Understanding" and "lead men away into innumerable and inane controversies and fancies."

The Idols of the Theatre enter men's minds "from the various dogmas of philosophies and also from perverse logic." These philosophies are "but so many stage plays, representing worlds of their own creation after an unreal and scenic fashion." They rest on "tradition, credulity, and negligence."

Biases need to be made explicit.   It is awareness of such idols or biases as these which marks the difference between the common-sense and the scientific mind. To deny our biases is to drive them underground where they continue to live a subterranean and subversive life. Hence, if your students would seek to become truly scientific in their methods of thought, they face the necessity of making their biases explicit. Only then may they be brought under conscious control.

But biases are not without foundation. They are based on assumptions, indeed they may be said to be the shadows which assumptions cast. If one's assumptions are known, his biases are known. Many students think that their assumptions are proved facts and hence do not recognize them for what they are.

Some fallacies of "common-sense sociology."   Another classification of biases is that provided in the "five fallacies of common-sense sociology." [4]

1. *We know social reality because we live in it.* A similar fallacy was practiced when men argued that the earth was the center of the universe and that the sun revolved around the earth. That was the way reality looked; "appearances" were enough. This fallacy is practiced in social affairs when people hold such opinions as, "All Negroes are lazy," "If the newspapers didn't print what the people want to read, they wouldn't buy them," "The people who complain about an unfair press are free to start a paper of their own," and "Where there's a will, there's a way."

2. The corollary to No. 1 is the fallacy that *we assume things and relations certain on the basis of only our empirical (uninstructed and untested) experience with them.* The practice of these two fallacies may be explained by the fact that one's experience is limited and constitutes only a small part of the whole complex of social reality. It usually extends over only one society, often over only one social class, and over only one community. This may be called one's *exterior* limitation, for, however wide in land expanse it be, the student may live in a relatively small world of perceptions.

In addition, there is the *interior* limitation. This is perhaps more important than the exterior. Interior limitations are such as these: (a) a large part of what is around us is left unheeded, hence we do not know it is there, (b) our interests and temperament dispose us to see chiefly what we wish to see; we are ruled more by subjective than objective factors; we tend to find it hard to be impersonal.

[4] William I. Thomas and Florian Znaniecki, *The Polish Peasant in Europe and America*, 2 Vols. (Chicago: University of Chicago Press, 1927), pp. 3-15.

3. *We launch investigations with immediate reference to and concern with only practical aims; in doing this we are guided by what we think is desirable or undesirable rather than by what a sober and objective search would reveal.*

This fallacy is double-barreled: (a) we do harm to our search for truth by our tendency to satisfy only immediate, personal, and practical aims; and (b) feelings of desirable or undesirable (right and wrong) distort, if they do not completely destroy our objectivity. This does not mean that social inquiry does not have practical uses; it means, rather, that if we are too much concerned with the practical side we will often be more concerned to *do good* than to *do it well.* "Haste makes waste." Recipes for immediate success are of dubious worth in the long run. We are afraid to be tentative; we want to be *sure.* Many quick answers are worth less than those which take longer to establish.

4. *We assume that problems can be solved "by themselves," that is, that delinquency can be solved only by working on delinquents as "bad men" with no concern for the community factors which have permitted or caused them to be "bad men."* This is the "devil theory" of human error and deviation. What it is that "makes Sammy run" is more than his legs; he is "afraid of something"—we need to find out what that something is. This fallacy is often practiced by reformers and "do-gooders" who, because of the narrow view they take and the "devil theory" which they hold, often fail to get at the root of the trouble. It is often practiced in politics under the slogan: "Vote the rascals out." Everyone who believes in good and efficient government would rather have good men than bad men in office. But the problems of corruption may be due, in large part, to worn-out and inefficient ways of doing things—in short, inadequate *institutional* methods. Likewise, depressions are not "cured" by government plans for work projects. The root causes of depression are far deeper. "Lazy" and inattentive students are often "lazy" and inattentive because they are not properly motivated: the teacher may be talking over their heads, or "under their heads"—something may be wrong with the school as well as with them. In fact, something *is* "wrong" with them which traces back to the "scheme of things."

If we would ask more often, "What made it happen?" rather than "Who made it happen?" we would be on our way to correcting this fallacy. There is, of course, a "who" in every situation; there is also a "what"—a process. Processes make people and people make processes; it is that simple, or complex—depending on our view. If we would change things, we must deal with both persons and processes: the "whos" and the "whats."

5. *We believe that people react in the same way to the same influences, regardless of their individual and social past; hence, we believe that it is possible to provoke (or evoke) identical behavior in various individuals by the same means.*

This is the fallacy that a given stimulus has the same meaning for everyone. But we know that "one touch of nature" does not always "make the whole world kin."

(a) We defend various forms of punishment as providing not only punishment for *this* offender but to "be a lesson to all of his kind." The history of law enforcement and prison commitment gives ample proof that frequently it provides no such lesson.

(b) People have different tastes; what will please one may displease another.

"One man's meat is another man's poison"—even this cliché helps to prove the point.

(c) You may scold some students and get improved behavior from them; you may scold others and get worse behavior. The same with praise. A map may interest one student but have no interest at all for another, or a movie, a film strip, etc.

(d) Propaganda which will get positive reactions from some people will get negative reactions from others. "Some people see the doughnut; others see only the hole"—another cliché which bears on this fallacy.

The point is that action *does not begin with the stimulus; it begins with the actor*—he may accept or reject the stimulus. What people bring with them to the stimulus is as important as what the stimulus may bring to them. (See Chapter XIV.)

6. *We believe that people develop certain tendencies, without any external influence, which enable them to profit in a full and uniform way from given conditions and that, therefore, it is enough to create favorable or remove unfavorable conditions in order to give birth to or suppress given tendencies.* (This fallacy was discussed by Thomas and Znaniecki under the fifth one. I treat it as the sixth in this account.)

Taken at its face value, such a belief assumes that proper and adequate housing *alone* will create good family life, or that the abolition of saloons *alone* will make men temperate, if not teetotalers. This is a form of determinism similar to that held by those who believe that if certain geographic facts are given then certain kinds of political policies or temperaments or what not *must* follow. All we can say is that geographic factors—or any others—allow or make possible certain things: they do not and cannot *determine* them. The geography of certain sections of New York is now the same as when they were inhabited by the Mohawk Indians—but the ways of life of those sections have changed much since the Mohawks left—with few, if any, changes in the geography.

How perception, valuation, and conduct are related. Changed behavior depends on two factors: changed conditions *external* to human beings and changed conditions *within* human beings. It is not as simple as "where there's a will, there's a way," or as "where there's a way, there's a will"— each is inadequate to explain change. "Will" and "way" are interdependent factors. Material conditions do help or hinder, to a large extent, the development of ways of conduct and thought, but only if the tendency is there or can be developed.

The foregoing must suffice to describe the folk or common-sense mind. With its characteristics in mind we now discuss what is involved in teaching your students so that they will develop insight into their attitudes, that is, really know what they believe. The following ten propositions are basic to your understanding the connection between perception, valuation, and conduct. Take particular note of the middle position of valuation, or attitude. Attitudes are the links between perception and conduct. They are often very fragile links, which is to say that there is no straight line or direct causal relation between attitudes and conduct.[5]

1. Normal or "right" attitudes and abnormal or "wrong" attitudes are formed by the same process. Men become saints or criminals by the same psychological process. The difference lies in the circumstances of life under which the person grows up (temperamental factors are not to be ignored). We do not know all the nuances of the process; if we did we would have perfect control over human nature.

2. A change in attitudes is equivalent to a re-education. This is brought about by a change in the person's culture whose subjective side is his attitudes. The "culture of the classroom" is an important aspect of it: our discussion of the therapeutic climate revealed that. But the "culture of the classroom" is not all the required new culture. Here the limitation which the school meets in changing attitudes is confirmed. The larger culture includes the social groups with which one is identified and the formal legal controls on his life. The school, as we have observed, can work on the larger culture only through the changes which it can make in its individual members. This limits it to individual rather than mass methods. For this reason it is important, even necessary, that the student who wishes to change his attitudes or, having changed them, finds a place in a group which will support and give strength to them.[6]

3. Exposure to new knowledge, whether first- or secondhand, is not enough to change attitudes. If this were true, the sixth fallacy noted would not be a fallacy. Change in attitudes depends on changes in the way the student perceives the things in his world. We shall discuss this at length later.

4. Social as well as physical action is directed by perception: the student's views of not-thing and thing values. If "seeing were believing" this would not be true; perceiving is more than sight. It involves all the senses. We are disposed to see things and evalute them in the context or *Gestalt* which we have shaped for ourselves. These *Gestalts*, or wholes, do not undergo piecemeal but total change if a genuine change in attitudes is effected. In this, reason and emotion are both involved. Teaching must attack the student's *Gestalt* or whole perceptive field through change in "objective conditions"; it cannot change him directly.

5. New and "correct" knowledge alone is not enough to correct faulty perceptions. (This is a phase of No. 3 above.) Genuine change in attitudes toward members of minority groups—ethnic or racial—requires that we see their individual members as individuals, not as stereotypes, e.g., Negroes, Jews, Wops, etc. Famous and "ordinary" members of such groups must be seen alike as *individuals*. This requires that we see them in intrinsic, not extrinsic terms. This is in terms of their worth as human beings, not as members of minorities.[7]

---

[5] These propositions are based on the discussion in Lewin, "Conduct, Knowledge, and Acceptance of New Values," pp. 56-68.

[6] See John Dollard, "Acquisition of New Social Habits," *The Science of Man*, edited by Ralph Linton (New York: Columbia University Press, 1945), pp. 442-464.

[7] See Robert E. Park, "Behind Our Masks," *Race and Culture*, edited by Everett C. Hughes (Glencoe, Ill.: The Free Press, 1950), pp. 244-255.

6. Incorrect or "wrong" stereotypes or "wrong" prejudices are, in the functional or operating sense, the same as "wrong" concepts. Stereotypes are not, necessarily, wrong or bad, although they have that reputation in common sense. Stereotypes are fixed images; without them we would have no social habits and hence would have to classify each object *every* time we met it. They are equivalent to theories about given objects: one's mother, oatmeal, going to church, and the like. We are largely unconscious of them; in that sense they are part of our social habit system. They carry with them the attitudes appropriate to them. The task of changing them, whether they are "good" or "bad," is a difficult one: they are parts of our fundamental views toward life. Simply being exposed to new knowledge does not change them.

7. Changes in sentiments, which express themselves in positive and negative ways, do not necessarily or automatically follow from changes in knowledge. They are, for the most part, the content of our stereotypes or prejudices. A student may change his words, but still be of the same mind. Verbal change is relatively easy to effect, but not change in sentiments. The test of a change in sentiment, or attitude, is a change in behavior. It is possible for people to become engaged in new forms of conduct and in that context take on, unconsciously, new attitudes. This has proved to be the case in desegregated schools and army units. The process which we have suggested may, then, be reversed: conduct, valuation or attitude, and perception.[8]

8. Changes in action and the values which guide it, new facts and valuations, and new perceptions are all part of the same process, as we observed earlier. Together they form a new *Gestalt* or "life scheme" for the student. (See No. 4 above.) Such a change, however, confronts the student with a choice between old and new loyalties. He must trade an old reality for what is at first little more than the promise of a new and more rewarding one. His new perspective must be strengthened by a new faith, which that new perspective has the major task of helping him establish. This new view must be voluntary; it must be not only got, but *accepted*—even sought after.

His old ways continue to struggle for dominance. They will not easily surrender. (Knowing is never passive.) He must decide to stick with the old ways or cast his life in the mold of new ways. He will, at first, be acting against his old personal interests; he must reorient his entire character. Here the tendency to rationalize, i.e., to find excuses for the old ways, enters. Between the old state of balance and the new one, the student is off balance. He may become a "marginal man," emancipated from an old life but not accepted or integrated into a new one.[9] He must change an old security which is quite comfortable for a new one which will not give him equal security at once. He will go through some such a series of experience as this: (a) he will likely resist the teacher's attempt to invite him to examine his old attitudes and points of view, (b) this resistance put him in "the middle." He is now in a state of imbalance or am-

[8] See *Studies in Reduction of Prejudice* (Chicago: American Council on Race Relations, 1948), prepared by Arnold Rose. See also Robin M. Williams, Jr., *The Reduction of Intergroup Tensions*, Bulletin 57 (New York: Social Science Research Council, 1947).
[9] See Robert E. Park, "Human Migration and the Marginal Man," *American Journal of Sociology*, XXXIII (May, 1928), pp. 881-893.

bivalence; (c) he now stands at the crossroads: he may choose to return to his former comfortable self or he may choose to identify himself with a new set of perceptions and take on new attitudes. This cannot be done without the *will* to do it.[10]

9. Acceptance of a new set of attitudes and values is not the result of logical proof. It depends quite as much on the climate of the classroom as it does on the materials which are studied. Re-education does involve a series of steps but these cannot be viewed in a mechanical way: rebuilding a character is far different from laying up a wall of bricks. The student cannot be pushed; your task is to surround him with new "objective conditions" in an atmosphere of friendliness. The nearest equivalent for what will happen to him is an experience of *conversion* to a new set of beliefs. New knowledge and new attitudes are not had by simple addition, or enumeration. They are got and felt as a new pattern. This is the artistic or aesthetic factor in perception. As Lewin remarks, his learning must relate to his "life space"—his way of life. Once this is changed, he is then prepared to translate the changes which have gone on in him into remaking old institutions, through his social conduct.

10. His acceptance of a new *Gestalt* of facts and values goes on, *pari passu*, with his coming to have a sense of "belonging" to the community of the classroom—as well as to all other communities to which his new attitudes belong. This phase of character change is duly taken account of in new penal theories and is evident in the organization of Alcoholics Anonymous. The traditional emphasis of all spiritual leaders—ministers, priests, and rabbis—is for the follower of a given faith to identify himself with its church or congregation. This is an invitation to *belong* and thus keep and strengthen one's belief.

The nature of perception. This brings us to inquire further into the nature of perception, change in which starts the process we have discussed. To perceive means to be *aware*. As Dewey remarks, "to par-take and perceive are allied phenomena." Perception is thus a way of entering into something, as well as taking it in. One is, however, motivated to perceive or partake of those parts of his world which will help him maintain his present self: hence perception is selective. In perceiving he does not put his emotions into a deep freeze and use only his reason. One perceives in order to know and, as a poet has lately put it, "to know is to care." Caring often expresses itself in what one *wishes* to perceive in order to know and survive.

It is natural to believe. "We are born believing," as Emerson put it. Hence most of us are quite unaware of our basic values, or those of our culture. We have inherited most of them, if not all. Justice Holmes said, "all I mean by truth is what I *can't help thinking*. . . . I have no means of deciding whether my 'can't helps' have any cosmic worth." They made up his "cosmic salad." Logic will neither prove nor disprove them for they are the fundamental assumptions which determine the kind of world we

[10] See Nathaniel Cantor, *The Dynamics of Learning* (Buffalo: Foster and Stewart, 1946), pp. 101-150.

want and that which we cut out. To the question about how far life is rational, an eminent economist tells us,

. . . not very far; the scientific view of life is a limited and partial view; life is at bottom an exploration in the field of values, any attempt to discover values, rather than on the basis of knowledge of them to produce and enjoy them to the greatest possible extent. We strive to "know ourselves," to find out our real wants, more than to get what we want.[11]

"Knowledge about" and "acquaintance with." Our concern with feelings as well as reason stems from the very nature of the data of social study. Physical objects can be known only in terms of "knowledge about" them; social objects can be known by that knowledge and also by "acquaintance with them." [12] Furthermore, it is exactly because a social fact is, at the same time, a *value* which makes it a datum for social study.[13] Hence, it is not a defect or a limitation of the social sciences that the knowledge they seek and can give is based more on interpretation than on description and explanation.

Ways of getting insight. There are three ways of getting insight: (*a*) by direct study of persons taken singly or in interaction with others; (*b*) indirectly through the study of symbols, words, and statistics about them, and (*c*) by sympathetic penetration. The arena for (*a*) is outside the classroom, through field study. Through such direct study students may talk with and see the social data which the textbook must treat secondhand. The rigidities of school schedules permit very little such study, to the detriment of the opportunity to know social life immediately instead of vicariously. Such study operates on the basis of sympathetic penetration. The means by which (*b*) may be accomplished have been stated: through words and statistics about social reality. The latter are, of course, more abstract than words since they deal only with the quantitative aspects of things: how many, where, when, and the like. But statistics are not to be discarded for they help students render their images of social

[11] Frank H. Knight, "The Limitations of Scientific Method in Economics," *The Ethics of Competition* (New York: Harper & Brothers, Copyright 1936) p. 105. I believe that this view holds as much for teen-agers as for adults, although teen-agers' real feelings are often covered with a bravado or are concealed behind a façade which does not permit us to know their true nature.

[12] See William James, *Psychology*, Vol. I (New York: Henry Holt & Co., Inc., 1890) p. 221. See also Charles H. Cooley, "The Roots of Social Knowledge," *Sociological and Social Research* (New York: Henry Holt & Co., Inc., 1930), pp. 289-312. He distinguishes between "spatial or material knowledge" and "personal or social knowledge." Cooley's and James's twofold classifications are almost identical in meaning.

[13] See Howard E. Jensen, "Social Methodology and the Teaching of Sociology," *American Journal of Sociology*, XLII (January, 1937), pp. 443-450. The term "sociology" may be changed to "social studies" with no violence to Professor Jensen's thesis.

things more exact than words do. Price levels, the phenomena of inflation and deflation, population, carloadings, bank debits and credits, sex ratios, and the like are important indices to social processes. The meanings which words have depend, as we shall show in Chapter XVII, on the sharpness and clarity of their reference. Finally, (c), sympathetic penetration. It is this method which is unique to the study of social things. By its use we may know persons and groups intimately. We may enter into and partake of their sentiments, aspirations, and ideals. The printed page does not exclude the use of this method of gaining insight although field study lends itself more fully to its use.[14]

The nature of insight. And now what *is* insight, how is it had, how does it work, what are its difficulties and dangers, and what kind of knowledge does it give the student? The following discussion will be based on the use of verbal symbols, that is, words in a textbook. (The methods appropriate to field study will be treated in a later chapter.) We now ask how the student perceives or gets insight into labor-management relations. They must exist in his mind as "pictures in his head." Only then can they become realities to him.

The nature of sympathetic imagination. The process by which these images come to have subjective reality is through imagination—or call it "sympathetic imagination." This is not sentimentality, engaging in charitable or kindly imagery, nor is it agreement. Nor does it mean pity. Sympathy, as used here and as it must properly be understood, may have a content of love, resentment, feelings of right or wrong, or any one of a wide range of positive or negative thoughts and feelings. One might imagine, for instance, how a suffering man feels and thus sympathize with him but be moved not to pity but to disgust or contempt.

The role of sympathy. Through the sympathy which the student may feel for labor-management relations he will have thought and feeling as distinct from mere sensation or crude emotion. He will get it through his image of those relations. Another student may get much the same or quite a different image of the "same" object.

The method of sympathetic imagination works chiefly with social objects. The single exception is that which comes through poetic license by which aesthetic attributes are assigned to inanimate things—flowers, landscapes, and the like. But this exception aside, the meaning of only social objects —persons, groups, institutions, and even nations—may be internalized.

[14] See Willard Waller, "Insight and Scientific Method," *American Journal of Sociology*, XL (November, 1934), pp. 285-297. See also Robert Redfield, "The Art of Social Science," *ibid.*, LIV (November, 1948), and a rejoinder to that article by Jessie Bernard, "The Art of Science: A Reply to Redfield," *ibid.*, LV (July, 1949).

The student's sympathetic attitude toward a social object may hinder his understanding of it unless he is able to bring his image of it under rigorous assessment.

Professor Charles H. Cooley observed there is "nothing more practical than social imagination." Without it we could not genuinely know friend or foe because without it we would be forced to resort only to "knowledge about" them. A moment's reflection will confirm the truth of this. We know some people much more intimately than others because of our acquaintance with them, rather than only our knowledge about them.

Sympathy and appreciation. The point needs reiterating that sympathy is not dependent on any particular emotion and hence may be hostile as well as friendly. Moreover, through its use the student does not need to agree with that for whicn he has sympathy, as we now use the term. As his talents permit—for insight is perhaps more native than acquired—he may relive the experiences of others. In doing this he *appreciates* them preliminary to *understanding* them. Sympathy and intellectual rigor are not necessarily strangers to each other, as common sense often holds them to be. The real enemies of a sympathetic or aesthetic approach are not intellectual things—they are dull and uninteresting things.[15]

The risks of sympathetic imagination. Thus it is that sympathetic imagination, as a means of getting insight, involves risks and offers certain difficulties. You will need to experiment a great deal as to the best methods by which your students may come to enter into the objects of their study. Those with which they are most intimately acquainted will be the easiest, but also fraught with the most risk. They may enter into them only in terms of their present perceptions and hence their present prejudices about them. They may capitulate to them because of favorable biases, or withdraw from them because of unfavorable biases. The risk of their capitulating, that is, coming into effective and affective *rapport* with them, is always present—depending on what they already have an affection for or against. They may be shocked or hurt; they may be disgusted, or they may take neutral attitudes. In short, the risks of too great emotion (for or against) toward the object called "labor-management relations" is always possible.

The risk of capitulation. Among these risks, that of capitulation to one

[15] See H. A. Hodges, *Wilhelm Dilthey, An Introduction* (New York: Oxford University Press, Inc., 1944). Dilthey conceives of *Verstehen* (understanding) as identical with *Nacherleben* (re-living). It is really appreciation and on it genuine understanding or insight rests. See also Theo. Abel, "The Operation Called *Verstehen*," *American Journal of Sociology*, LIV (November, 1948), pp. 211-218. Dilthey holds that we may understand "more than we may know."

"side" or the other is the most likely. The student's ability to delay his judgment is, of course, the test of whether he is student or partisan. It is likewise a test of both the depth of his insight and his knowledge. The five-year-old capitulates immediately to what he internalizes: this week or month to the role and values which he knows as a Space Cadet, next week or month to that of cowboy, engineer, fireman, or policeman, and thus through the range of adult careers for which he is undergoing a series of uncritical rehearsals. But the five-yer-old internalizes uncritically and un-reflectively. His quest is for expression and enjoyment. But the more mature student must be invited to a more serious quest: the quest of sober inquiry about that which he has internalized.

Provisional acceptance is the goal. Provisional acceptance by the student of the values of labor-management relations may never be achieved. It is, however, the goal which you may help him reach. The student's task is to internalize a form of the lawsuit to which we referred in an earlier chapter. The only place he can really assess the merits of labor-management relations is in his "head." This requires his temporary identification with all the issues involved. Only then is he in a position to assess them.

How we internalize values. This internalization will involve more than his mind and his reason, as we have meant to suggest. William James has stated the nature of the process or internalization in his classic essay, "A Certain Blindness in Human Beings." Some passages of it are pertinent to our discussion. First, the following:

> Our judgments concerning the worth of things big or little, depend on the *feelings* the things arouse in us. When we judge a thing to be precious in conse-quence of the *idea* we frame of it, this is only because the idea is itself associated already with a feeling. If we were radically feelingless, and if ideas were the only things our mind could entertain, we should lose all our likes and dislikes at a stroke, and be unable to point to any situation or experience in life more valu-able or significant than any other.[16]

The capstone of his comment, insofar as it bears on our problem, is put on in the following.

> The spectator's judgment is sure to miss the root of the matter, and to possess no truth. The subject judged knows a part of the world of reality which the judging spectator fails to see, knows more while the spectator knows less; and

[16] *Talks to Teachers on Psychology* (New York: Henry Holt & Co., Inc., Copyright 1910), p. 228. The blindness of which James speaks is "in regard to the feelings of creatures and peoples different from ourselves," *ibid.*, p. 229. He also speaks of the "stupidity and injustice of our opinions" concerning the "significance of alien lives." (*Ibid.*, p. 230). In the matter under discussion these are the thought, attitudes, values, and issues involved in labor-management relations.

wherever there is conflict of opinion and difference of vision, we are bound to believe that the truer side is the side that feels the more, and not the side that feels the less.[17]

We now take leave of labor-management relations and James' hill folk and apply the method of insight to the teaching-learning of history. Thus we shall test it on both present and past events.

Insight and the teaching-learning of history. The method of insight learning does not require that students are to study only good things. They are to get acquainted with values—theirs and others'—both good and bad in kind. Life is not made up only of the good: this is not a sugarplum world. Nor is it assumed that the student must distort the facts to fit his prejudices.

Suppose the French Revolution to be the social object under study. It, like a great many other events of the past, is one about which conflicting judgments have been made. But however great the disagreement among scholars as to whether its effects were good or bad, or how much of each, there is a rather solid consensus that it was a great historical event. How should it be studied? One way is to require your students to learn what historian X said about it (or both historians X and Y), store his (or their) remarks in memory until examination day, and then give them back to you. But there is another method which is more profitable. This is to seek to get them to enter imaginatively into the events of the Revolution, play all manner of imaginative roles, espouse this or that cause and thus both suffer and enjoy the Revolution. It goes without saying that this requires more than merely reciting what is in a book. They will, if they do well, re-enact the Revolution insofar as the means and methods of your teaching permit it. They may then come to see events as *values*, not as mere facts. These are not extraneous values; they are those which constituted the Revolution. The judgments which will follow cannot, of course, be final or infallible. But you may be sure that they will be more insightful and hence wiser and closer to what the Revolution actually was than by any other method.

Present and past must be made real. The relative ease or difficulty with which labor-management relations or the French Revolution may be either written about or taught so as to engender genuine understanding depends on the degree to which the writer or teacher is able to make both of them live so that they are penetrated by the heats, passions, and prejudices which men experienced in them. Unless this is done the account and the teaching will be unreal.

[17] *Ibid.*, p. 231.

What can be done about bias? The fly in the ointment of the method of sympathetic imagination and introspection is personal bias. What can be done about it? It intrudes, as we so well know, in our disposition to perceive what we wish to perceive rather than what is there. Thus we mix our private and subjective frames of reference with those of segments of the real world in which the objects of study ought to be placed.

The uses of logic. The canons of criticism which students must learn to use are those which logic provides. Its only function is to improve understanding: it is not a parlor game or a device to win them a high score in a quiz program. But do not ask too much of it. Logic never *made* anyone reason rightly; it only reveals *how* he reasoned if he will learn its method and have the will to use it. It does not provide the food which keeps our minds alive but is a kind of acid which helps us digest the contents of our mind. It orders our perceptions. Its task is to help common sense when it confronts a difficulty, a doubt, or a difference of opinion.

Logic is no "shell game." But logic has, traditionally, been a forbidding subject. The reason lies in the fact that it has often been taught in a detached way: a kind of intellectual shell game. It has not been related to real problems. We do not act *from* logic: it only puts before us the objects which are not directly or sensibly present. These are, in large part, our assumptions: what we take for granted. It permits us to locate the blind spots in our thinking, to reveal the intrusion of clichés and hidden assumptions, and has the power to make us humble before the facts.

How to detect bias. The method of detecting bias is as follows. Unstated premises or assumptions creep into and hide in our thinking processes; the inferences which we then draw contain logical flaws. What we need to do is to confront our conclusions with all the premises from which they stemmed; these are their origins. The task is then to find, if they be present, the *non sequiturs*. Our conclusions, which are our inferences, will be inconclusive and often untrue if all the premises on which they rest are not stated explicitly.

Biases and faulty observation. This method works as long as our biases are those which we deal with at the level of inferences. But these are not all of them. If they trace to faulty observations—in the field or in the text —the only thing to do is to repeat them and check for inaccuracies or omissions. This requires insight into the possibility that observations may be twisted by prejudices and stereotypes. For them there is no certain cure. In both of these searches your task as a teacher comes to the fore. It is your obligation to play "the devil's advocate." In that role you must continually ask your students if they looked for the exceptional case. Errors in recording may also be made but they are relatively easy to identify and repair.

The major difficulties which will be encountered are these: the intrusion of personal bias, faulty perception, inaccurate recording, and too limited demarcation of the field of observation.[18]

Logic helps to disclose unconscious bias. Now to some elementary illustrations of the use of logic. The first deals with a hidden premise or an unconscious bias. Suppose that a student says, "I like coffee better than milk because coffee is stimulating." Something has been omitted; an assumption is unaccounted for. The statement contains a value judgment ("I like milk") and a statement of fact ("coffee is stimulating"). But a value judgment or a value conclusion cannot be adduced from only a statement of fact, as in this case. If we repair the logic, we get the following:

> MAJOR PREMISE: Coffee is stimulating. (*This is a fact statement, to which may be added that milk is not stimulating.*)
>
> MINOR PREMISE: I like stimulating drinks. (*This is the hidden premise; it is a preference statement.*)
>
> CONCLUSION: I like coffee better than milk. (*A value judgment*)

Here the conclusion (which is a preferential statement) rests on two premises, one a preferential, the other a fact statement. It is logically correct.

The syllogism shows only "how" we think. The syllogism was one of Aristotle's greatest gifts. It is a foolproof device which reports how we solved a problem. But no problem is solved *by* the syllogism. We do not think syllogistically but searchingly, by trial and error. But we can report the nature of our thinking and check on its logical consistency by using the syllogism. As Francis Bacon observed: "It commends assent to the proposition but does not take hold of the thing." The syllogism gives us only formal truth; it does not give us empirical truth unless the premises are empirically true. One illustration will demonstrate this.

> MAJOR PREMISE: All blue animals are squirrels. (*A nonsense fact-statement.*)
>
> MINOR PREMISE: This animal is blue. (*A nonsense fact-statement.*)
>
> CONCLUSION: This animal is a squirrel. (*A nonsense fact-statement, although logically true.*)

Now suppose a student reasoned as follows:

> PREMISE: John Doe is an alien.
>
> CONCLUSION: John Doe ought to be deported.

[18] See Appendixes I and II in Gunnar Myrdal, *The American Dilemma*, 2 Vols. (New York: Harper & Brothers, 1944), Vol. II, pp. 1027-1064.

This is faulty logic because no conclusion can be drawn from a single premise. Something is omitted. Let us assume that the hidden assumption (a bias) has come to light. It is: "All aliens ought to be deported." If this premise is introduced, the syllogism reads:

> MAJOR PREMISE: All aliens ought to be deported.
> MINOR PREMISE: John Doe is an alien.
> CONCLUSION: John Doe ought to be deported.

However illiberal may be the view which the conclusion reports, it is logically true. The logical soundness of a conclusion does not depend on either the empirical truth or the "goodness" of the premises from which it is adduced. It is no better or worse, truth-wise and in ethical terms, than its premises.

Another *non sequitur* conclusion (literally, "it does not follow") is the following:

> MAJOR PREMISE: Communists believe in taxing the rich proportionately more heavily than the poor. (A *fact statement, whether true or false.*)
> MINOR PREMISE: John Brown believes in taxing the rich proportionately more heavily than the poor. (A *fact statement, whether true or false.*)
> CONCLUSION: John Brown is a Communist.

The syllogism fails to prove that John Brown is a Communist because the major premise is a case of "the undistributed middle." Communists hold such views on taxation but it also is true that people who are not Communists hold the same view; indeed it is the principle on which our income tax is based. We need only modify "Communists" by "only" to correct the major premise. If we do that the conclusion, as given, is logically true.

Wrong facts and ethnic prejudice. Let us assume that a student's conclusion is wrong because his facts are not accurate. We further suppose that his factual error traces to an ethnic prejudice. The syllogism might read as follows:

> MAJOR PREMISE: Naturalized citizens are not eligible for protection under civil rights laws.
> MINOR PREMISE: Jose is a naturalized citizen who was born in Mexico.
> CONCLUSION: Jose is not eligible for protection under civil rights laws.

The conclusion is logically true but empirically false because the major premise is false.

Logic cannot reform us.   But, as I have indicated, logic by itself cannot reform people. They must be willing to accept its conclusions. Short of that, all we can except from it is that it has revealed where the process of drawing a conclusion went wrong.[19]

Thinking is "enkindled by feeling."   What the foregoing implies for teaching may now be briefly stated. Thinking generates action only if it has been "enkindled by feeling," which means that it starts with an emotion. But emotions require examination. The fault of much teaching is that it commits the error of believing that students must choose between emotion and reason. Just as social science is partly art, so is teaching the social studies. Its task is to lay bare, to illuminate, to reveal, and to make things interesting and vivid. This cannot be done on scientific grounds alone. Students learn by "heart" as well as by "head," but the "heart" to which I now refer does not mean rote or humdrum. It refers to feeling. Knowledge is both effective and affective, touching both the mind and the emotions.

You will do no teaching if you only peddle facts. The task requires that you help your students create living images of the social realities. You must continually ask yourself: "Am I talking about the textbook or am I talking about the real world which it is supposed to treat?" Always your concern must be with what you are proposing to their belief and with it the most reliable method of examining and fixing it (see Chapter XII).

The social studies are not disinterested.   These observations confirm the fact that the social studies are not disinterested studies. When they are, it is because they are *uninteresting*. That great and constant difficulties will confront you is not denied. The social studies often occupy a place in the value system of many communities little better than that of a minority party or a minority racial or ethnic group. What you do must be done kindly, thoughtfully, and sensibly. It must be tempered by sound judgment and deep insight. Even then you may not succeed, but you may achieve. Above all, you will do well to keep in mind the progression: changed perceptions are necessary to changed attitudes and these, in turn, for changed conduct. Thus the principle of "indirect-direct" which was suggested in Chapter X is again affirmed.

[19] I have given only a very small sample of the uses of the syllogism. I suggest that you read further about it in any one of a number of excellent books on logic and the scientific method. Among them are: Frye and Levi, *Rational Belief*; Cohen and Nagle, *An Introduction to Logic and the Scientific Method*; Lionel Ruby, *Logic, An Introduction*; Harold A. Larrabee, *Reliable Knowledge*; Robert H. Thouless, *How to Think Straight*; Mander, *Logic for the Millions*; and L. Susan Stebbing, *Thinking to Some Purpose*.

CHAPTER XII

The Fixing of Belief:
The Method of Inquiry

WE HAVE BEEN speaking of the internalization of values, through sympathetic imagination. Once "inside the student," it is his task to introspect about them. This involves not idle musing or mere appreciation. It involves submitting values to the rigors of intellectual criticism. We now inquire about the methods he may use to fix the beliefs he has internalized.

Attitudes are beliefs. His attitudes toward what we have called thing values as well as not-thing values are beliefs. Toward the former his attitudes are relatively noncontroversial; toward the latter, relatively controversial.[1] This means that toward them the student, like the rest of us, is disposed to "jump to conclusions." He is disposed to accept or reject them without inquiry of any kind. If that course were followed, they would be fixed by the fiat of unexamined biases. We cannot afford to trust that method. We seek a more reliable method of fixing beliefs.

We need to fix our beliefs. Abundant confirmation exists in both ancient and modern thought that we need to fix our beliefs. In *Meno*, Socrates speaks of opinions (synonymous with unfixed beliefs) as follows,

. . . when they are bound, in the first place, they have the nature of knowledge; and, in the second place, they are abiding. And that is why knowledge is more honorable than pure opinion, because fashioned by a chain (98a).

---

[1] The controversial or noncontroversial quality of any object inheres not in the object, but in the attitude we take toward it. Under ordinary circumstances or in frames of reference in which we would normally place a ladder it would belong to the noncontroversial class. But if one were superstitious about ladders and believed that walking under one brought bad luck that attitude would change it from a noncontroversial to a controversial object.

172

While we might disagree with Socrates on the issue as to *how long* they are "bound" we are happy that he agreed with modern social science at least in the respect that there is a dependable way of fixing opinions. The thought of John Stuart Mill comes closer to the way modern social science would put it in his observation that "belief *independent* of, and *proof against argument,* will be in danger of being lost or enfeebled, and thus deprived of its rational effect on character and conduct" (italics added).

A belief is an attitude or a feeling about a thing or a not-thing value. However good or bad a given belief is, we share with Socrates and Mill the view that it ought not to go unchallenged by inquiry. Science holds that no value is too good to be excused from rigorous investigation. The perfect achievement in scientific endeavor is to produce that quality of certainty of our expectations on which conduct can be based. Right conduct is its "end."

The role of doubt. If the method of intelligence is to be used to fix our beliefs, we must first entertain doubt about them. Lacking that, they are accepted *without doubt.* The doubt of which I speak is not disbelief as it would be in a theological frame of reference. Nor is it nihilistic doubt, the view that nothing can be believed; nor is it cynicism. It is, rather, the doubt of which Tennyson wrote when he said that "there lives more faith in honest doubt, believe me, than in half the creeds," or the doubt to which Browning referred in "Rather I prize the doubt low kinds exist without, finished and finite clods, untroubled by a spark." It is the doubt of which Justice Cardozo spoke of as the beginning of a judgment. This is the judgment which is the settled outcome of inquiry.[2]

The terms of discussion. The terms of our discussion will be these: doubt, inquiry, belief. Doubt and belief are the terminal points of what we shall call "the purposive act." In it we move from the pole of "doubt" to that of "belief," through inquiry. This continuum is this:

DOUBT ⟶ INQUIRY ⟶ BELIEF

It is important to note that inquiry, thinking, or problem solving comes in the middle of this act, not at the beginning as common sense believes it does. This simply means we think or reflect only when we run into a

2 Both "doubt" and "belief" can be put in several frames of reference. Respecting "doubt" they are such as these. Shakespeare wrote that "Our doubts are traitors, and make us lose the good we oft might win, by fearing to attempt." Herrick wrote, "Attempt the end, and never stand to doubt; nothing's so hard but search will find it out." In these frames of reference the word "doubt" connotes something akin to cowardice or lack of courage. Dante's "Doubting pleases me no less than knowing," and Abélard's "By doubting we come to question and by seeking we may come upon the truth" belong to the frame of reference we are using.

problem or difficulty. Then we *doubt* what we ought to do. In order to resolve that doubt and bring about a state of belief, we think. The method of inquiry which we use is the method we use to *fix* such a belief, that is, unless we wish to take it on faith, hearsay, intuition, common sense, or other unreliable bases.

We now amend the continuum by adding some synonyms to each of its three terms:

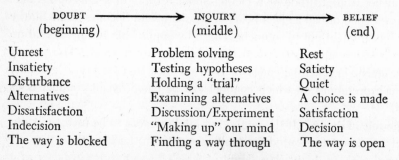

DOUBT ⟶ (beginning)	INQUIRY ⟶ (middle)	BELIEF (end)
Unrest	Problem solving	Rest
Insatiety	Testing hypotheses	Satiety
Disturbance	Holding a "trial"	Quiet
Alternatives	Examining alternatives	A choice is made
Dissatisfaction	Discussion/Experiment	Satisfaction
Indecision	"Making up" our mind	Decision
The way is blocked	Finding a way through	The way is open

The methods of tenacity, authority, a priori, and inquiry.   Our concern in this chapter is with the most reliable way of turning doubt into belief: the method of inquiry. But before we present it, we offer three less reliable ways; these in addition to the methods which we discussed in the foregoing chapter—common sense and dependence on personal bias.

THE METHOD OF TENACITY.[3]   This is simply the method by which men willfully adhere to their old beliefs without examining them. It is the method which mystics have long employed. We are disposed to use this method because doubt and an undecided state of mind often induce us to cling tenaciously to beliefs already held. It is, in effect, a method of fixing beliefs through taking an attitude of contempt, suspicion, and even hatred toward any method that might dislodge old and cherished beliefs. It is not to be denied that such a method of fixing belief gives great peace of mind. But it does not allow those who use it to weigh its advantages against its disadvantages. Such a test might reveal the danger which it hides. Peirce takes the view that the one who adopts this method will be unable to hold it in practice because he will learn that other men think differently from him and, in his sane moments, it will likely occur to him that their opin-

[3] The three unreliable methods of fixing belief which we now examine are based on the thought of Charles S. Peirce (pronounced *purse*). These are clearly set forth in the *Collected Papers of Charles Sanders Peirce* (Vol. V), *Pragmatism and Pragmaticism*, edited by Charles Hartshorne and Paul Weiss (Cambridge: Harvard University Press, 1934).

ions are as good as his. Peirce holds that this will reduce one's confidence in the method of tenacity. The final danger and damage of such a method lies in the fact that, unless one lives a hermit's life, the one who holds it will influence others' beliefs and thus spread its ill effects to the whole community.[4]

THE METHOD OF AUTHORITY. This method of fixing belief is based on the will of the state. There are two forms of it. One is "inevitable and reasonable." It is used whenever we are unable, for lack of knowledge and skill, to settle some problem which may range all the way from how to build a bridge to how to bring up our children. In such instances we leave the resolution of our problem to experts whose authority is acknowledged, dependable, and wise. Reliance on good and wise authority is involved in our reliance on the advice and counsel of those who head the social institutions with which our lives are intimately related: the banker, physician, editor, pastor, and political leader. Much of it comes through the newspapers, magazines, and journals we read and increasingly the news analysts and commentators we hear and see on radio and television. Much of their authority we must take on our faith in them which is established by the satisfaction we feel because we took their advice. We cannot individually be authorities on all matters. Our problem becomes one, then, of knowing how to choose good and wise leaders in all these phases of our life. This is the problem of the dependence of the layman on the expert. It confronts us perhaps most persistently in the area of politics. In short, without reliance on good and wise authority, an ordered society could not exist. Anarchy and chaos would reign.

The other form of authority is not inevitable, nor is it reasonable. It is the kind which invests certain sources of authority with perfect, unmistakable, and final authority. This is the authority symbolized by the Man on Horseback. It seems that the masses of mankind will be governed by this kind of authority for years to come if the present rage of dictatorship continues. The methods and principles of democracy are the surest, although the slowest, means of insuring against dictatorship, as well as insuring its ultimate defeat.[5]

THE METHOD OF A PRIORI. This is more intellectual and respectable from the point of view of reason than either of the two foregoing methods. But it is no more reliable. It bears close resemblance to the method of authority. In it the authority lies in a body of principles whose validity is established

---

[4] See Peirce, *ibid.*, par. 378.
[5] See Peirce, *op. cit.*, pars. 378-381.

on a purely logical rather than logico-experimental basis. It is the method of casuistry. Bacon both described and evaluated it in his observation that:

. . . it cannot be that axioms established by argumentation can suffice for the discovery of new works since the subtlety of nature is greater many times over than the subtlety of argument.

It was used by the Scholastics, who determined the number of teeth in a horse's mouth by argument, rather than by counting them. It was the method used by the early Greek astronomers to fix the path of the planets. Their taste for the circle as the highest form of beauty led them to "discover" that the orbit of the planets was a perfect circle. But the planets continued to describe elliptical orbits. Peirce speaks of this method of investigation as "something similar to the development of taste," that is, the taste of the dominant school of metaphysics. It differs from the method of authority chiefly in the fact that it substitutes the method of disputation according to certain fixed principles. In such disputation, the conclusions which are drawn are empirically true or false depending on the truth or falsity of the premises from which they are drawn. But the Scholastics engaged in no inquiry by which they might have tested the empirical worth of their premises; they took them on traditional grounds. They may have sharpened their wits but they added nothing to knowledge.

THE METHOD OF INQUIRY. We offer three illustrations of the "purposive act" which will reveal the method of inquiry.

An act in the practical affairs of everyday life. Suppose that you are in the *habit* of returning home from the movies by crossing a vacant lot. You have not been to the movies for a week or two, but as you set out for home, you *assume*, or take for granted, that nothing will interfere with your taking your usual or habitual way. The path is poorly lighted, as it has always been. But that does not bother you; you have traveled it many times and have no doubt about the way. And so, trusting to your past experience—the sure and certain auspices of an old and well-established habit—you start across the lot.

But halfway across, your *way is blocked*. Habit no longer serves you in the safe and secure way it once did. The area is strewn with building materials—lumber, sacks of cement, bricks, and kegs of nails. *Doubt* enters your mind. You make several attempts to get through and around these piles, but without success. These *trials* all end in failure. Doubt still possesses you. A low order of *imagination* has been at work, hardly to be distinguished from crude *trial and error* attempts to overcome obstacles. You now engage in a somewhat higher order of imagination. You begin to "talk to yourself"—that is, engage in *discussion* with yourself. You *imagine*, through the use of *memory*, how you can continue your way toward home. You *conceptualize*, that is you deal with ways and means which are not visible to your eyes. This involves your examining *alternative ways* "in your mind." You mentally *rehearse* several ways—"maybe if I go this way, I'll get through, or this way, or this way." Meanwhile you are standing still—the *action* you take is only implicit or imagined. You are testing some simple *hypotheses*. You then put these imagined alternatives to test or *trial*. But none gets you through the obstacles. The way is still blocked. At this point memory comes to your aid. You *recall* having read in the paper that the Smith Construction Company has started to build a new supermarket. That explains the piles of material that block your way. These now become the *facts* which sustain a *generalization* or theory. You then say to yourself something like this: "That probably means that the whole lot is strewn with materials of one kind or another; they've probably dug some trenches for the foundation and likely as not, I'll stumble into one and maybe break my neck (your *imagination* lets you *conceptualize* these facts). I'd better forget the whole thing." Whereupon you *decide* to turn around and take the "longest way 'round" which, in accordance with the old axiom, "is the shortest way home." Your doubt has been turned to *belief* and that belief has been fixed by intelligence.[6]

The components of this act may be reduced to the following: impulse, intelligence, and conduct. The impulse to get home was blocked, it could not "out" in its accustomed and habitual way; hence the need for a new definition or new stimulus to give it instructions. The older stimulus did not suffice. A more adequate one was not found at once, but only through trial and error. This was a low order of inquiry, i.e., hunting. While this purposive act had an end, namely your decision to go "the other way," it was not *the* end of your activity. It was only a temporary stopping place in the whole chain or series of purposive acts which, with *reflexive* acts, make up your life. Your whole life is capable of analysis only by cutting it up, so to speak, into its constituent and related parts. This suggests that a life of purpose is a continuum of experiences within which we resolve doubt and bring it to a state of belief through the use of intelligence. To live is not only to live, but to live better and more worthy of our ideals. Given a world of rapid change, we cannot do this on the basis of habit alone.

As goal-pursuing beings we act. Life is action, sometimes to "good" and sometimes to "bad" goals and by adequate and inadequate means. Much

[6] The italicized terms identify phases of the purposive act or the act of inquiry.

of it is habitual. Indeed, if we had to think through every situation we met, our life would be so problematic as to be intolerable. Habits do not, however, take care of new situations—that is, except the habit of thought. Normally, we rely heavily on our reflex habit patterns and thus leave our higher mental energies free for reverie, for imagination, recall of past experiences, projecting our behavior into the future, and for sober speculation and reflection.

An act of a scientist engaged in inquiry. (In this and the following illustration I shall italicize no terms. I leave that to you as an exercise in applying theory to specific instances).

Let us first note what an eminent mathematician said about the scientific method. Professor Gilbert N. Lewis writes as follows:

I take it that the scientific method, of which so much has been heard, is hardly more than the native method of solving problems, a little clarified from prejudice and a little cultivated by training. A detective with his murder mystery, a chemist seeking the structure of a new compound, use little of the formal and logical modes of reasoning. Through a series of intuitions, surmises, fancies, they stumble upon the right explanation, and have a knack of seizing it when it once comes within reach.[7]

I now take some pages out of the life of Louis Pasteur. The vintners of southern France faced a crisis. Their habitual way of producing wine ran into a problem. Something had happened which soured their wine. They were troubled and in doubt. They tried to find the cause of their difficulty but were unrewarded. Their problem came to the attention of Pasteur, a chemist. The vintners' problem became his. But his customary and habitual ways of dealing with problems of this kind did not avail.

This set him playing with some hypotheses. One after another they came to naught. But finally he hit upon an idea that became "the germ theory." He theorized that some microorganic form of life was the cause of the trouble. Through a series of planned experiences, in which he used experimental and controlled situations, he discovered how the germ worked and how it might be both controlled and prevented. From his work came what we now know as the *pasteurizing* of both wine and milk.

The components of this act are the same as those in the act just described. They are impulse, intelligence, and conduct. The impulse may be thought of as having two valences, the valence given it by the worried vintners and wine-makers and the valence given it by the sympathetic Pasteur. The impulse of the vintners and wine-makers ended only in

[7] *The Anatomy of Science* (New Haven: Yale University Press, Copyright 1926) p. 6.

random behavior—or merely common-sense attempts to find and remove the difficulty. They failed because they were short on theory. They could not imagine the "right" hypothesis. But not so with Pasteur. Through the use of intelligence in its most exact meaning, i.e., the projection and trying out of alternative hypotheses, and by tracing consequences back to causes, he came upon—even stumbled upon—the factors which caused the trouble. It was then a relatively simple matter to prescribe what should be done. We may properly call his experimental acts a series of trial-and-error behaviors because he had no certain image of the goal toward which any one would lead him, namely the identification of the germ which caused the wine to sour. But when the "right" hypothesis proved to be the "right" one, Pasteur was able to engage in what we call conduct, moving in the direction of a known goal in a fully conscious and purposive way. When he discovered what was "right" conduct for him, he also discovered what was "right" conduct for the vintners of France. The problem which an entire economy faced was thus resolved by the method of intelligence.

An act of inquiry by students in a social studies class. Let us suppose that a study of the causes and consequences of the black market in gasoline during World War II becomes the object of inquiry in a social studies class. The country is at war and there is widespread alarm over black-market operations in gasoline. This is accompanied by doubt as to the causes of the black market and how its operators may be apprehended and punished. They are violating a federal law through their operations in the major cities of the land.

To the common-sense mind such causal theories or hypotheses as these suggest themselves: the black market is due to Bad Men, a weakness in human nature, selfishness, lack of patriotism, and maybe the belief that the law-enforcing agencies are either lax or corrupt. But how make bad men into good ones, repair a weakness in human nature, change selfishness to altruism, turn "slackers" into patriots, and clean up the law-enforcing agencies? These hypotheses are all personal in nature; they take no account of process.[8]

We assume that through reading and discussion the class comes to believe that these are inadequate hypotheses. But more adequate ones must be constructed and belief in their findings confirmed through the discipline of inquiry. So, under the guidance and stimulus of the teacher, the class makes a factual study. Some hunches are followed through. Some are rewarding: some are not. But an image begins to shape itself in the minds

[8] The distinction between Who and What (bad or good men and social process) is convincingly given by Lincoln Steffens in his *Autobiography*, pp. 572-574.

of the class: the black market is due to an involved and complex process which has many facets. Now the hunt is on in earnest.

By means of the research made by the class through individual and committee projects and with the aid of such resources as the sheriff, head of the city police, some well-informed businessmen, a specialist in criminology, and studies of underworld operations, the image suggested above is put to the test of many facts. Among them are such as these: there is a greater demand for gasoline than the restricted supply can satisfy, the war "is over in Europe," hence not close enough to keep some people from doing unpatriotic things (there *are* people "in it" but they are in it through some process); the "predatory tendency" in the human nature of some is too strong to resist mere appeals to be loyal and obey the law; a ring of professional crooks exists—their *business* is evasion of the law; this ring has its staff of experts—counterfeiters, muscle-and-gun-men, "pushers" of counterfeit ration books; the ring provides its counterfeiters with copper plates, ink, and presses; a wide net of filling stations provides a system of distribution of the counterfeit ration books; the ring has its own legal staff and its "fixers"; a few filling-station operators willingly co-operate and many more are forced to. Such is the web or net of causal factors. In this web the belief is "fastened." Note that it is a *web* or net and not a *chain*. The outcome of the study gives understanding which comes through what Peirce has called "the action of thought." [9]

Again, in this instance, habit proved to be an inadequate guide through a new and complex problem. Furthermore, common-sense notions proved inadequate. The breakdown of habit and common sense created doubt, intelligence came to the the rescue, and a belief was fixed by the method of scientific inquiry.

The continuum of the purposive act. The foregoing analyses may be reviewed by relating them to the following continuum which constitutes the purposive act: (*a*) a human being is engaged in goal pursuit, that is, he is acting in his usual and habitual way; (*b*) this activity is blocked by something with which habit is not able to deal; (*c*) this blocking or interruption generates an emotion; (*d*) doubt, dissatisfaction, or unrest ensues; (*e*) reason or intelligence is called upon to find a solution, remove the block, and permit activity to continue; (*f*) this involves imagination and experimentation, overt or covert; (*g*) alternative ways of solving the problem are tried out; (*h*) one of these proves more satisfactory than the

[9] I am indebted to Joseph D. Lohman, my former colleague, for this analysis of the operation of the black market.

others; (*i*) this one is used to organize the behavior potentials of the person with the result that purposive conduct ensues. The terminus may also be called a judgment, namely, the settlement of an issue which can be stated verbally. The shorthand for all this is what we started with: doubt-inquiry-belief.

The logical structure of the method of inquiry. Our analysis still lacks something by way of logical rigor and precision. We now undertake briefly to show the logical structure of all the three foregoing illustrations of the method of inquiry.

Thought or reflection has five phases or aspects, but they do not necessarily follow one another in the order we shall indicate. In giving them, I shall not bother you with references to the foregoing illustrations but ask you to make the connections on your own.

1. A troubled or indeterminate situation: The emphasis is on both adjective and noun alike—something has "gone wrong," activity has been blocked, habit has proved inadequate, things are muddy, indeterminate. So much for the adjective phase. "Situation" suggests a lack of clarity, the absence of focus; it is problematic but *the problem* cannot be stated in explicit terms. This is the stage of general doubt and confusion; the form or pattern is not clear; there is no clear *Gestalt*. This phase is chiefly one of feeling, not thinking. The situation is questionable, but *specific* questions have not yet come to mind. A kind of vague and not wholly conscious kind of "casing the joint," as the vernacular has it, goes on. The doubtful character of the situation cannot be relieved unless we can imagine how to rearrange it; in doing that we will have to rearrange our "mind" at the same time.

2. The appearance of a problem: Things are beginning to be a little clearer; a *Gestalt* begins to *suggest* itself; relationships are less shadowy; it begins to "make sense," as we say. Ideas or suggestions begin to come "to mind"; we talk to ourselves. The indeterminate situation is now less indeterminate, hence *more* determinate. This means that we begin to sense or feel the terms and conditions which must be met if the problem is to be resolved. This is not idle speculation or thinking "in the dark"; we mentally manipulate the situation and some hint of order, sequence, cause, or consequence begins to come out. We seek to match this situation with some other we have met before and think or "wonder," as we say, how they may be related. All the while, we are being tempted to act but this temptation is pushed aside though not without some regret. Slowly the temptations *to act* on impulse fade out of the picture.

3. The suggestions, hunches, notions, or what-you-may-call-them which have *come* to us (they seem almost to invite themselves in) compete with one another. They now become more respectable; they become hypotheses. There is a kind of quiet rehearsal: *if* I do this *then* that will happen, and so on through the list. We now talk to ourselves but with greater clarity and precision. We now have somewhat clear *ideas* in the form of competing questions. We have

now *intellectualized* the problem; it is now in a form in which we can get evidence. The situation is less emotional in tone and more rational. By that token it is less only a *situation* and more a discrete *problem*.

4. Reasoning, or the mental testing of one or more hypotheses. This is thinking, which is always *thinking through*. This phase shades out of the previous one, almost imperceptibly. Sometimes it may leap out: the "right" hypothesis seems to stand out and we concentrate on it. This is the phase of mental testing, not that of overt action, although they are not as easily separated as are words *about* them. The "best" hypothesis gives order to disorder, the *Gestalt* or form of what we face is now pretty clear; lines of action, likewise.

5. The "lines of action" involve the overt test of the conclusion to which our reasoning has brought us: we abandon the attempt to cut 'cross lots, and strike out for home "the long way 'round"; we apply our theory of microorganic life and find that it works; we make sense out of the jumble of factors that earlier had muddled our minds about the origin and operation of a black market in gasoline. We now understand and we act on that understanding. Whether we verbalize our findings in the form of a proposition, a generalization, or a principle depends on the situation.[10]

The steps of inquiry grow out of each other.   We have reduced the process of inquiry to five phases or stages. We might have increased their number to eight or ten; that would depend on how we "set our microscope." Each stage blends, almost imperceptibly, into the next. They are not so much connected to as they are outgrowths of each other. We do not say that a bud is *connected* with the bush; we say that it *grows out* of the bush. So we have come out of the "bush of doubt" into the "bud of a judgment." It will become a full-blown flower as it proves itself adequate to handle a whole series of similar situations. But, most important of all, we have learned the skills of "flower-culture"!

There is no fixed order of steps.   An experience in problem solving may not take your students through these phases in the order named. The reason is simple: a problem is a *problem*, it is not an alphabet or a timetable. No book of rules or catechism can tell anyone what to do first; hence no one can tell him what to do second, third, fourth, or fifth—or however many phases the solution requires. Science, as we have suggested earlier, is half art and half science. Art and science are different but they are not opposed. The art aspect requires that we begin where a beginning seems appropriate and always with imagination. Having begun, science tells us to be cautious, precise, sure of our facts, and gives us general norms to satisfy. It can never tell us what hypothesis to use or what facts are needed. It tells us only that we must imagine within the limits of an hypothesis.

[10] See John Dewey, *Logic: The Theory of Inquiry* (New York: Henry Holt & Co., Inc., 1938), especially Part Two, pp. 101-280.

The facts which are needed are those which the "right" hypothesis demands.

A hypothesis may spring up at the start, or it may "wait in hiding" until we have muddled around for some time. Feeling exists throughout the entire experience. The mind shuttles from crude hunches to less crude ones. One hypothesis may take us part way and then peter out. Then we have to start over. The field narrows and we come upon the "answer"— even stumble on it, as Gilbert suggests. But we must have wit enough to know when we have stumbled onto it.

Inquiry involves "painful suspension." The entire act of inquiry is one of "painful suspension" which eases up gradually. Thinking means keeping the mind in suspense. It cannot ride off in four directions at once, although at first our impulse is to do just that. But finally we must narrow the field, which tends to shape and clarify itself as we proceed. We may jump at a conclusion and land in the middle of a secure hunch which may at once become a respectable hypothesis—from there on it may be quite simple. Or, we may land in a worse muddle. Jumping to a conclusion is usually an attempt to escape the tedium, the tension, and the pain of careful work. It cuts inquiry short. But even if the conclusion to which we have jumped turns out to be a sound one we have to back up and trace through the process by which it came to be. We thus fix our belief in it.

The method is subject to being checked. To withhold a judgment is disturbing. For that reason thinking or reasoning runs contrary to our nature as emotional beings. But it is the price we must pay if we would get a reliable warrant for what we assert. Thus our beliefs are fixed by a method whose reliability and accuracy others may check. Always it means a challenge to and the breaking of habit, which is never easy. The course we run in most thinking is from dogmatism to negative skepticism and then to genuine criticism, that is, if we really go through it.

What and where thinking is. In conclusion let it be noted again that thinking, which each of the foregoing cases illustrates, lies within the purposive act, not outside it. It goes on only when there is something to think about, and think through. The interruption of habit provides that occasion. But the stuff of thinking is not thoughts; they are its products. Its stuff is possible and alternative modes of action, facts which will clarify these alternative ways, and an image of the events which would ensue if one or another of these actions were carried through. Thinking is the process by which these things are related and patterned.

Science is an exacting master but the tasks it sets are worthy ones because they indoctrinate us with the method of intelligence.

CHAPTER XIII

Science and the Value Problem

THE PREVIOUS three chapters have confronted us with a problem which now requires explicit discussion before we proceed with some of the more practical aspects of teaching-learning. This is the problem of how the method of inquiry can help us with what is known as "the value problem." It is the problem of the relation of the method of intelligence to the making of moral decisions.

Science does not give certainty. The truth is that social science can give us only certitude—not certainty. As Dewey has put it, it can give us "warranted assertibility"—the warrant for making a value assertion. The attributes of its method were noted in Chapter IV: integrity, humility, and competence—whose opposite is fraud. Its method is not only the method of intelligence; it is also the method of morality.

What science demands. It requires disciplined, patient, and honest observation and the demand that we report with unscrupulous honesty what we find—not what we wish to find. Thus those who use it honor the conditions which produce not only reliable knowledge but also the traits of the democratic character: care, responsibility, and affection. These are the criteria of the obedience which the scientific method demands. It assumes a passion for truth. It requires the humility which demands that the thinker forget about himself. To *see what is there* is one of the truly great moral achievements of the human race. The scientific maxim, "In order to master, we must first obey," bears close kinship to a maxim of the Christian ethic: "In order to find our lives we must lose them." Both condemn self-assertion as the method of mastery of anything having to do with truth. Back of science, as we have observed, lies not only a great emotion but a profound ethical principle.

184

"Value" as noun and verb. Earlier we distinguished between the meaning of the term "value" as noun and verb. In its verb form it means to prize, to esteem, and also to apprize or estimate. We are now concerned with how the method of science can help us apprize or judge the values which we prize: examine and fix our belief in them. For "apprize" we now use the word "evaluate." It so happens that we apprize our values only when we face a problem, when they are in jeopardy. Otherwise, we simply take them for granted.

Judgments of fact and value. In the field of the social studies there is far from complete agreement on the role and importance of values and the process of evaluating. There are those who take the position that the only judgment of value which the study of social things is required to make is the judgment of which facts are relevant to a given problem. This is the question of the kind of hypotheses which are needed; how wide a net of investigation needs to be cast.

But this is the kind of value judgment which the natural scientist must also make. As we have observed several times, the study of social things is not as easy as the study of physical things. The former have a way of presenting themselves in the camouflage which our biases throw over them. What is lovely or true is a judgment not easily come by.

Man belongs to many universes. Man with his ways, unlike physical things with their ways, is a member of many universes. We have noted his characteristics earlier but call them to mind again. He is a physical mechanism and a biological organism. He is a social animal with a history some aspects of which only the individual himself knows, or thinks he knows. He is a problem solver, he is capable of manipulating both things and the symbols which stand for them, he deliberates about ends and fashions means for achieving them. He communicates with others of his kind and both are changed in the process. Finally, he is interested in changing himself. He is, as the psalmist told us, "a little lower than the angels," and is crowned "with glory and honor."

Man is aware of his history. The fact that man has a history makes him a unique object of scientific study. It is true, in one sense, that everything has a history. But in another sense only man has a history. The earth, in common with all other inanimate and nonhuman animate forms, has a history but one of which it (and they) are in no sense aware. It is not a "possession" of theirs. But man is not so limited, for he is the only organism that is aware of its own history as well as the history of other forms, animate or inanimate. He is thus able to get some systematic and enduring knowledge of the history both of himself and all other things and profit from it. Thus he is able to change, not what has been, which is quite beyond his power, but to determine in part, at least, what the future may be.[1]

Some difficulties of social inquiry. Physical objects, furthermore, unlike the objects which the social sciences investigate, are not trying to understand and use the investigator while he is studying them. The natural scientist may be content to discover and formulate a law or theory about the behavior of his objects of study. But when the investigator of human motives, attitudes, sentiments, and beliefs seeks to secure the co-operation of his subjects he can never be sure that they are not "play acting." Although guinea pigs and rats may have wills of their own, they have never been known to plot against one who is seeking to fathom the secrets of their behavior. Moreover, the social scientist may and does arrive at generally true propositions about his objects of study but he still does not know what attitude they will take toward the generalizations which he may formulate. On the contrary, the reports which the natural scientist publishes cannot be read by his objects of study. But not so with those of the social sciences. The social scientist hopes, however, that when his problem is solved, if it is solved, the world will be different on that account. Natural scientists entertain the same hope, insofar as it is appropriate to the discoveries which they make. Indeed, the real radicals are the natural scientists for it is the result of their work which, in large part, renders social institutions and customs out of date and inadequate.

Hence, it is obvious that the natural scientist who works with nonhuman and nonanimate objects is far less hindered in his search for truth than is the social scientist, at least as far as intrusion of his personal biases is concerned. The objects of his study are, as we have suggested, less ambiguous than those which the social scientist studies, that is, they tend to stay put and are not changed by the "winds of opinion" and the vagaries of temperament.

The relation of "ought" to "can." But now, given the fact of the student's bias because he is a human being, that is, one who values objects and takes attitudes toward them, we must ask how clean and absolute a separation can be made between "what *ought* to be done" and "what *can* be done and the manner of doing it?" The former is the citizen's question; the latter is the social scientist's. Our students will think, question, and act in both of these roles (as indeed the social scientist also does, since he is man first and scientist second). Our concern is that our students do not

[1] See Carl L. Becker, "The Function of the Social Sciences," *Science and Man*, edited by Ruth Anshen (New York: Harcourt, Brace & Co., 1942), pp. 243-269.

confuse them. We would wish them to get the stimulus for their study from the "ought" and their directions from the "can."

How social science can help us choose between values.   We now list the ways in which the method of social science inquiry can help us when we face the task of choosing between two or more values. These may be as different in their moral quality as whether to go to New York by train, car, or plane, or whether to espouse an authoritarian or a democratic political doctrine.

1. Social science seeks to examine the relation between means and ends. This is explicit in the form of the conditional proposition: "*If* I would do thus-and-so, *then* I must (or ought to) employ these means." In other words, it permits us to say that *if* we want "this" we must also want or use "that"—with "this" standing for an end and "that" standing for a set of means. Thus social science can tell us of the fitness or appropriateness of given means to given ends. It thus affects, however indirectly, the ends themselves. Thus social science establishes guide lines or bench marks for what is achievable. It tells us what we must give up if we would achieve certain ends. Life is a series of just such choices.

2. Social science can tell us of the probable consequences of our acts. This is but a phase of No. 1 above. That is, it can tell us what the ends which we have in view will cost us in financial and social or moral terms. Thereby, it helps us assess the cost of a given end. We then know more critically what it is we seek.

3. Social science can also tell us of the origin or causes of the values or the ends which we seek. This assumes, of course, that they did not just "happen." Thus we can, so to speak, "think backward" as well as "forward" in our concern to know our values.

4. Social science enables us to examine and criticize our ends as well as our means.

Ends, as well as means, may be examined and criticized.   The last of these is the least understood. If we assume that the scientific method is applicable only to studying the relation between means and ends, that is telling us that "*if* you do this, *then* you will find yourself at this goal," we sell it short. It may also be used when the problem is one involving not only the choice of alternate means but likewise when it involves a conflict among ends. This may be illustrated in many fields; I take the field of public health.

An illustration in the field of public health.   A number of values have competed with its advance and have impeded it. They did not, of course, compete without human competitors and their values being involved. These competing values have been such as the following: (*a*) cheap child labor defended by certain business interests, (*b*) the complete control of children by the family even to the point of refusing to let them be vaccinated, (*c*) foolish and unscientific notions about health, defended by

188 THEORY AND PRACTICE OF THE SOCIAL STUDIES

frauds and quacks, and (d) the doctrine of individual freedom which would brook no interference by the state respecting sickness and disease. These and other values held as absolutes, i.e., subject to no challenge or change, have from time to time been used to block the progress of scientific public health programs.

But, through the accomplishments of such measures as vaccination, quarantine, epidemic control and prevention, and the like, those who have defended their "absolutes" have either reconsidered them and changed them or been forced to do so by the state. Thus conflicting ends have, in part, come under the domain of science, both natural and social. The acts which were involved in reconsidering such ends were not only acts through which certain groups changed their minds. They were acts through which they made choices between competing ends.

Insofar, then, as there is an issue between the methods of science and moral conduct, i.e., ends or goals, it may be stated in these terms: "If the community is seeking an end by the intelligent method of science and in doing so runs counter to its habits in attaining and maintaining other ends, [the absolutes we have noted] these ends are just as subject to restatement as are the means themselves . . . in other words, its attitude toward conflicting ends is the same as its attitude toward conflicting facts and theories in the field of research." [2]

Science cannot tell us which values to choose. Despite these uses of social science respecting choice between values, whether of means or ends, it cannot *tell* us which to choose. It was Thomas Jefferson who said that "He who made us would have been a pitiful bungler, if he had made the rules of our moral conduct a matter of science." But, even so, the so-called fact-value division is neither simple nor absolute. If facts are sometimes colored by valuations, valuations are also influenced by facts. Even as the social studies must work one step removed from the determination of political, economic, and social policy, so does social science work one step removed from the declaration of what constitutes the good. It does, however, insist on the morality of its method for determining what its effects are, and how they may be had.

A critical view of three rules. Despite what has just been stated, there are those who argue that the value problem is of relatively minor importance and may be adequately handled by doing the following three things: (a) by "keeping to the facts," (b) by a thorough understanding of and expert use of the rules of scientific procedure, and (c) by refusing

[2] See George H. Mead, "Scientific Method and the Moral Sciences," *International Journal of Ethics,* XXXIII (April, 1933).

to state conclusions in ways which will make them useful in practical situations.

With respect to (*a*) the problem is, of course, *which* facts. The world is full of them and what they mean or what they are good for is not written on their foreheads. They are, as we have observed, *facts about some values*, hence the question of "which facts" cannot be settled until we have decided which values are relevant and significant to study. When we finally take our facts we *take* them. They are usually called *data*. But they may quite as properly be called *taka*. Hence we agree that one ought to "keep to the facts" but in doing so we find it impossible to escape being involved in the making of value judgments.

One can, of course, always argue that the facts are not yet all in, and that we must be careful about what we conclude on the basis of less than all the facts. But the facts are never all in; we neither need nor want "all the facts," we want and need those facts which any given hypothesis requires in order to be rigorously tested. Furthermore, all scientific conclusions are subject to revision and correction. (Here Dewey's term "warranted assertibility" applies.) The history of science is the history of man's being mistaken many times—and learning better for it. But whether the facts are many or few, the social scientist must treat them with the greatest care and respect.

As respects (*b*) above we would certainly agree that the social scientist should understand and expertly use the procedures of the scientific method. But our understanding of its nature forces us to state that these procedures include awareness of the value premises about which we have been speaking.

There remains the third point. Let us examine it as a way of emancipating ourselves from bias and valuation.

One may seek to escape the risk of concluding something that may be useful in practical situations by arriving at findings which are quite unfavorable to certain established institutions and then try to balance them by a more favorable conclusion. Such a balance is considered by some to be strictly scientific. The substance of such a procedure is that it displays a will to please rather than a will to discover. It is not the task of science to please, or for that matter, to displease. Its business is to seek truth within the limits set by the fact that the social scientist is a human being disposed to err. Biases are not honestly dealt with by being "spread" now in favor of this side and now in favor of that.

There is a vast difference between genuine scientific work and the manufacture of pleas for political and economic reform. But if problems press in upon our society with such force and persistence that they threaten the values upon which it rests (the value of the scientific method among them) the conclusions of the social scientist about what might be done, and how it might be done do not fail on that account to be truly scientific. We fail to be truly scientific when our conclusions follow from hidden or buried premises or when they are the result of the inexact use of the method of inquiry.

Social inquiry is interested in practical matters. We may, until the end of our days, slavishly follow the techniques of physical science, as some social scientists contend we should, but those techniques will not permit us to deal adequately, accurately, or honestly with social science data. Any problem of social inquiry that does not grow out of actual or practical social conditions is, by definition, not a problem of social inquiry. In the social sciences, genuine inquiry starts from a genuine curiosity in and concern with actual social situations which are, by their nature, confused and problematic. Indeed all science has grown out of a concern with problems out of which have come methods more reliable than those of simple intuition and common sense. In social science inquiry, no matter how carefully it may be done, nothing but busy work is accomplished unless social action, which is action toward a value goal, is informed. All science is interested in consequences; social science is interested in social, hence, moral consequences. If its conclusions or judgments do not combine to help man achieve some value, they give us nothing but a display of technique. Whenever we study the operation of any set of social means we study the means by which acts are engaged in which have social or moral consequences. Social science is not and cannot be, if it be truly scientific, remote from life. It is not remote from life when the problems it investigates are socially significant, that is, bearing in one way or another on the good life.

A false view of science. Science has, however, earned the reputation of assuming that there is no longer any place for purpose in human life. Some scientists have designed experiments for the *purpose* of proving their belief that animal operations are motivated by no purposes. Some have, perhaps, spent their spare time in writing articles to prove that human beings are as other animals, so that "purpose" is a category irrelevant for explaining their bodily activities—including those of the scientists themselves. But such a view seems to have had its day.[3]

---

[3] See Alfred N. Whitehead, *The Function of Reason*, p. 12. One needs to read only the writings of Professor Edmund W. Sinnott of Yale University to learn that such a view is not representative. See his "How to Live in Two Worlds," *Saturday Review of Literature*, December 23, 1950, the theme of which is further developed in his book, *Two Roads to Truth* (New York: The Viking Press, 1953). See also J. W. N. Sullivan, *Limitations of Science* (Pelican Books).

Man has purpose and we dare not disregard it. For if we do, we disregard the values and goals of his acts and thus fail to see the significance of the facts about them. How tragic and impossible it is to believe that facts are about nothing but themselves: they are, as we have sought to demonstrate, facts about both the means and ends which man uses to seek a better society and a better self.

CHAPTER XIV

The Psychology of
the Teaching-Learning Act

The method of inquiry is the method of teaching-learning. We have now set forth and examined four methods of fixing belief. The fourth, the method of inquiry, has the greatest reliability. Moreover, it is self-repairing. We have given three illustrations of its use. We have referred to it as the method of inquiry and as a purposive act. In being these it is also the teaching-learning act, as our third illustration confirms. It provides us with the method of teaching-learning, the joint quest for truth by teacher and students. It shows how we may move from a difficulty to a judgment—from doubt to belief.

In its very nature it is experimental. It is not an exercise in logic although logic may be used to check where we erred, as we showed in Chapter XI. Problem solving is a matter of hunch, wit, imagination, and method. It is, as we have said, half art and half science. It is a *practice* and teachers and students may become its practitioners.[1] It demands searching, delving, trying out, failing, and trying again and coming to a conclusion.

Method and technique are different. It is *the method* of inquiry; not a *technique*. There is the one reliable method of inquiry and it provides the one reliable method of teaching-learning. There are, however, many techniques—as many as there are ways to get students to use their talents in the experience of discovery. The method is the constant; the techniques are the variables.

[1] For explicit discussion of the method of inquiry see Dewey, *Logic: The Theory of Inquiry* and *How We Think*.

Techniques complement method. This distinction is one of the most important in the whole realm of pedagogy. The method of inquiry is *necessary;* it is both *necessary* and *sufficient* when complemented with appropriate techniques. Their function is to make it work for students with different abilities, interests, and concerns.

The psychological act. Because the act of teaching-learning is the act of inquiry I shall offer no more illustrations or analyses of that act. My concern is now with its psychology. I shall refer to it now as the "psychological act" as Thurstone did: "the history, or course of events, by which a craving or want becomes neutralized in satisfaction." [2] This is familiar language.

The stimulus-response fallacy. I begin with what the psychological act is *not.* According to the old and now discredited stimulus-response theory, action begins with a stimulus which comes along and irritates us into doing something. It assumes that we are passive until the environment makes us active. According to it, we wait around, Micawber-like, waiting for something to turn up. According to it, action begins with the outer rather than with the inner environment. It is related to the "push from behind" theory of causation. It may be represented by the stimulus-response arc as follows:

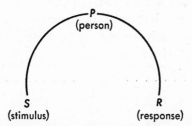

DIAGRAM 3. *The Stimulus-Response Arc*

According to this conception the stimulus is primary. It is thought to be the whole cause of action. Moreover, it assumes that everybody is pretty much alike and that a stimulus to one is, with minor differences, a stimulus to all. It belongs to the *tabula rasa* theory of mind as a blank slate on which the environment, in the form of various stimuli, writes instructions for human beings.

[2] L. L. Thurstone, *The Nature of Intelligence* (New York: Harcourt, Brace & Co., 1927). See especially Chapter I, "The Stimulus-Response Fallacy." This book is a clear, comprehensible, and exacting discussion of "the nature of intelligence." It owes its conception largely to G. H. Mead from whose writings we have drawn heavily. The following discussion owes much to Thurstone's formulation of the problem.

The theory of the dynamic self. The theory of the *dynamic self*, as the psychological basis for the teaching-learning act may be represented by a circle.

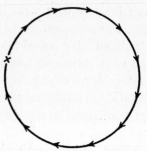

DIAGRAM 4. *The Dynamic-Self Circle*

X marks the spot! This spot is the potential learner. The arrows mark "the history, or the course of events, by which a craving or want becomes neutralized in satisfaction." They also symbolize a hunt for the "right" stimulus, that which will change unrest to rest, dissatisfaction to satisfaction, tension to its release—any one of the changes indicated in the discussion of the act of inquiry in Chapter XII. The circle is significant in that it symbolizes the fact that action begins with the actor, not in the environment. Moreover, it ends with the actor—that is, pro tempore because he continues to act but now on a more informed basis.

To facilitate our diagnosis of the psychology of the teaching-learning act we straighten out the circle into a line.

Student . . . . Stimuli . . . . Conduct

This sequence shows that action begins with the actor and not with the environment. This suggests the dynamic self and the self-expression conception of the psychological act.

Now we modify the student-stimuli-conduct continuum as follows:

THE DYNAMIC SELF	STIMULI	UNDERSTANDING
the student whose dynamic attributes are: needs, wants, drives, urges, difficulties, emotions, impulses, confusion, doubt, uncertainty, tensions, misgivings—some kind of block to his activity as a living and seeking organism.	the "objective condition," the real and symbolic environment—of varying qualities respecting their "ability" to direct the "tendencies" of the dynamic self (see discussion in Chapter X).	attitudes, meanings, valuations which are the dynamics of conduct—these take the form of conclusion, judgments, or generalizations which provide the directives for overt behavior (see discussion in Chapter X).

Tendencies and objective conditions. The attributes of the dynamic self are "tendencies," the stimuli are "objective conditions." See Chapter X. The three phases of the continuum constitute the act of inquiry or the purposive act, now called the act of teaching-learning or the psychological act. The understandings, conclusions, judgments, or generalizations are the outcome of inquiry. Through it they are fixed.

For this view of the psychological act we now submit a complementary view.[3]

Drive . . . . . Cue . . . . . Response . . . . . Reward

This continuum symbolizes that the student must *want* something, *notice* something, *do* something—then he will *get* something.

The purposive act. This is the purposive act which every human being *enacts*, in school and out. Through it our impulses maintain our life process by selecting certain stimuli—those which we believe we need to maintain ourselves. Thus we *create* our environment. The stimulus or cue is the occasion for the expression of the impulse or drive. It does not cause it. Stimuli are means, conduct is the end. Intelligence is the selection of the stimuli which will set free and maintain our energies and aid us in the task of continually rebuilding our character. When this process goes on in the school it is called learning; we call it the teaching-learning act. It is, in sum, the experiences through which a response and cue-stimulus get connected.

Teaching is manipulating stimuli, not students. Teaching consists in helping the student match his drives or impulses with the right stimuli, those which will make him intelligent. The teacher is then not only the manipulator or broker-of-stimuli but, as teacher, *is* stimulus. The teacher manipulates the stimuli, or the "objective conditions"—not the student. Attitudes are changed *indirectly*. This act of brokerage or manipulation is the way the teacher dramatizes an "invitation to learning." The stimuli are the objects of study and everything which is done to give them meaning: texts, the blackboard, discussions, talks, lectures, field trips, movies, and all the many so-called "aids to learning." Students may become co-partners in the manipulation of the stimuli through their participation in discussions, planning field trips, carrying them through, and the like. The final responsibility, however, rests with the teacher whose ultimate responsibility is to educate students to become masters of the manipulation and choice of stimuli.

[3] See John Dollard and Neal A. Miller, *Social Learning and Imitation* (New Haven: Yale University Press, 1941).

Constituent elements in the transaction between inner and outer environments. We have now identified the constituent elements of the transaction between the inner and outer environments: students, teacher, impulse or drive, stimulus or cue, response and intelligence. Our discussion will find us shuttling back and forth between them for they are not related in a straight-line or first-this-and-next-that manner. What we have is a field or *Gestalt*. Ordering it or giving it a systematic pattern is the experience of learning.

Stimulus and response come together. By discussing stimuli first we do not mean they come first. In fact neither stimulus nor response comes first: they come *together*. "Together" has a double meaning: (*a*) at the same time, and (*b*) interaction. They are correlative. The old stimulus-response theory held that stimuli come first, then response. But that was a "nickel in the slot" conception of the nature of learning: you show the student *this* and he does *that*. It allowed for no individual differences, indeed it ignored them. Stimulus and response are part of the same *Gestalt*. When an impulse—drive, desire, need—meets up with the "right" stimulus then there is a transaction; then the impulse is defined, channeled, and given direction.

The teacher helps the student complete "unfinished business." We speak of stimuli only when a situation is inadequate, when an impulse has been blocked, doesn't know where to "go" or what to "do." (Chapter XII gave three illustrations.) By the same token we may speak of students as being inadequate, even incomplete. They achieve adequacy or completion by finding the "right" stimulus for the expression of their drives. We suggested this earlier when we said that human beings are born "early in life" and have their entire education ahead of them. Through it, they achieve greater and greater "completion." They even make themselves over in the process. The business of the teacher is to help them complete their "unfinished business," or their "unfinished selves."

No natural stimuli. Stimuli are stimuli only if they are defined as such. There are no "natural" stimuli. Whether or not an object of study becomes a stimulus depends not on its being "there," but upon its being *chosen* by the student as something which will help him give direction and meaning to his drives or impulses. No stimulus is "sure fire," although some pan out better than others among modern teen-agers. But it always depends on the situation or the *Gestalt* in which the student is at a given time.

A beautiful scene is not a beautiful scene to one who has no impulse or taste for beauty. Hence it is not a stimulus to him. America was not a stimulus to European explorers until they were stirred by curiosity or adventure, or commissioned by a trading company or monarch who had an interest in exploration. Of course it was there as a land mass as it is now. But that did not make it a stimulus. It was only an object eligible for becoming a stimulus. By the same token food is not a stimulus to one who has just finished his dinner.

Dethrone the stimulus. Thurstone advises that we "dethrone the stimulus." It is not the king of conduct. But he does not advise that we cut its head off. He simply advises that it be made a commoner, coequal with response. Without a need of responding there would be no need of stimuli, and without stimuli—(granted that we admit the facts of "unfinished business" and "unfinished human beings")—neither the business nor the human beings could be "finished."

Environment is what is perceived. And now something about the "objective conditions," the "outer environment," the objects potential for becoming stimuli. We have already said that we create our environment. We do it by defining it as useful to us in the experience of self-maintenance. The environment is not all that is "out there." At any given time, it is only that part of it which conditions us to interact with it to meet a need, satisfy a curiosity, relieve a tension. It is what we *perceive* as environment. From former discussion we know that we perceive what we want to or can afford to perceive in our task of self-maintenance. The environment, or a part of it, is perceived by us only in terms of the problems which we are trying to work through at a given time. It enables us to act. Furthermore, there is no such thing as mere conformity to it. It affects us and we affect it. Even a clam modifies its environment to some extent. The higher the form of life the more it is engaged in an active reconstruction of its environment.[4]

We are, however, disposed to take a much simpler attitude toward our environment. We are disposed to approach it from the standpoint of a pre-existing thing—just *there*. We now know differently.[5]

The nature of interest. This brings us to the nature of interest. It is what the student focuses *with* and what you must focus *upon*. There is no mental development without it. This requires that you have an abundant supply of knowledge and illustrations at your fingertips. Your major attention, which you are teaching, must be on the interests and attitudes of your students. You must know what they perceive, for their perceptions

[4] See George H. Mead, *Mind, Self and Society*, pp. 246-247, and *The Philosophy of the Act* (Chicago: University of Chicago Press, 1938), p. 364.

[5] Williams James's chapters on "Interest" and "Attention" in *Talks to Teachers* are still unsurpassed as introductions to these concepts and processes. See also Dewey, *Interest and Effort in Education*.

are the function of their interests. These will be dictated by the values of their culture and that part of it which they have cut out for their private worlds.

You must appeal to interest.   To take account of your students' interests is not equivalent to capitulating to them. You need not accept them but you had better respect them, for they mark the place you must start. They are your students' present foci of attention. Their interests are not so much *in* objects as they are kinds of relations *with* objects. If you wish them to become interested in other objects you must make them interesting. This is done by showing that these objects are worth attending to because of the consequences which will follow from establishing relations with them. These are both *knowing* and *doing* relations. Interest in an object is the first thing. The reason for it is second. Indeed, interest in it is "reason" enough in the beginning. This is equivalent to saying that feeling and appreciation, which are related more closely to sentiment and aesthetic dispositions than to reason and analysis, are the best starting places.

What it means to take an interest.   You will know what interests your students have by seeing what they attend to and are curious about. Take due account of the fact that interests are often more *taken* by them than *given* by you. You may undertake to be an interest-broker but they may not choose to buy your stocks. To take *an* interest is to refuse to take another one. It requires discipline. It is a voluntary act. Thus it requires inhibition as well as exhibition. It will be difficult or easy depending on the drive which is involved and the promise of the environment as to the kinds of stimuli which it offers.

For an object of study to become a value and thereby an interesting stimulus the student must "turn off" other and competing stimuli. He may not have the self-discipline required to do that. What teachers often call inattention is nothing of the kind. Rather it is attention to things other than those which are under study. Daydreaming, "idle" reverie, and autistic thinking are ways of attending but they are usually designated as ways of *not* attending.

Stimuli are variable.   The most egregious error you can make is to suppose that what is a stimulus to the interest of one student is a stimulus to the interests of all the others. You will also be mistaken if you assume that, because something you seek to teach is "in the student's interest," he will be interested in it. Truth is not so self-evident to youth. No objects are naturally interesting.

Interest is not impulse.   Interest is thus not to be taken for impulse.

Impulses may become interests as students wave them about somewhat as a vine waves its tendrils. Each seeks something to catch on to. Impulse is the initial stage of any complete experience: it is the feeling which enkindles thought. Feeling and impulse proceed from a need, urge, or drive of one kind or another and can be satisfied only if they are transformed into an interest. This, in turn, renders the hunt for satisfaction more specific and direct.

We may learn something about interest by noting its origin from the Latin *inter + esse*, "to be between." Interest is the link between an impulse and some object eligible to become a stimulus which will give it direction and an intelligent outlet. By the same token, but negatively, if there is no interest there is nothing to tie an impulse to a stimulus. If there is interest then there is attention. But there is always interest of some kind—vagrant, fleeting, or of whatever quality.

You redirect or arouse interest. Students have interests and we ought to be glad of it. Emerson wrote, "Happy is the child with a bias, with a thought which entrances him, leads him, now into deserts, now into cities, the fool of an idea." On the whole it is probably easier to redirect interests than to create or arouse them. The student with an interest is at least alert to the world around him; the student who seems to lack an interest (always a mirage or an illusion when the truth is known) protects his relatively disinterested state with an armor of lethargy which is often difficult to penetrate.

Knowledge begins with sensation. Neither let us mistake sensation for anything but the fact that the student is alive. Sensation is not knowledge, but it is the beginning of it. Unless the student feels or senses some unrest, curiosity, or tension he will have no incentive to seek a condition of rest, satisfaction, or release. Sensations and impulses are the same. They are raw material but they have to be tamed, domesticated, and given purpose. We remarked at length about them earlier and now add only that impulses or sensations have to be educated to give a good account of themselves. As Dewey expressed it, they have to be compressed—that is, put under discipline, to be expressed in intelligent ways.

The virtue of patience. Impulses are to be directed, not thwarted. Here enters the principle of "let's do" rather than "don't do." But impulses make *us* impatient; they are "disobedient." They resist being redirected. On this point we may well ponder Dr. Margaret Meade's words, "We . . . still need a cheerful willingness to preserve in the child that which is there, to *tolerate* an impulse long enough so that it may be regulated rather than rejected" (italics added). If impulse is crushed, motivation is put to death.

Neither impulse, emotion, nor desire knows the answer to its unrest. But this does not preclude its trying to find it. The path each takes is that of unguided and unreflective manifestations. They will "out"—and any out is as good as another. They seek release—any release is as good as another. This is to say that they are not practical. They are not to be trusted. They are unintelligent. They do not "stop and think"; they simply seek escape.

Thinking is problem solving. It is only when emotion, impulse, or desire is impeded or checked that thinking sets in. We saw it in each of the three cases: the impulse to get home by the shortest route, the impulse to discover what sours wine, the impulse to try to understand the operation of a black market. If the path had been clear the habitual act of going home 'cross lots would not have been interfered with; if catastrophe had not threatened the wine industry the vintners and wine-makers would have pursued the usual tenor of their ways; if a wartime emergency in the gasoline market had not restricted supply there would have been no "field" or occasion for the illegal operations of the black-marketeers, at least in gasoline.

Thus it turns out that, within the act, impulse is primary and intelligence is secondary, and in some ways derivative. That is, it derives, in a way, from emotion and impulse. Desire, impulse, and emotion without intelligence are directionless, and intelligence without them has no task set for it. Under these conditions activity would go on in the old habitual channel.

The role of intelligence. Intelligence is not the slave of the passions, to do their bidding. Its task is to inhibit impulsive action, to ask it where it is going. But it does more than that: it supposes a number of places to which it might go and offers a picture of the probable consequences which would follow from each. The task of intelligence is thus to inhibit so that time may be had for reflection, choice, and reasonable expression of emotion. Thus the "act of painful suspension" is required if we would teach our students to master their impulses.

The problem is not that men should act: they *do* act. The problem is whether they are to act from sheer impulse unaided by reason or whether they will take counsel with their impulses by the use of reason. Warm emotion and cool intelligence can work together and we must teach our students how they may co-operate.

Here and in Chapter XII we have dealt with the logic and psychology of inquiry. We have identified three acts: the purposive, the psychological, and the teaching-learning act. They are but different names for the same quality of experience. The point we would emphasize is that the method of inquiry, by whatever name it be called, is *the method of social study*.

CHAPTER XV

The Structure of
the Teaching-Learning Act

The unit of instruction. Teaching-learning always goes on within a *Gestalt*. Otherwise it has no organized character. The psychological *Gestalt* has just been discussed. It is the all-inclusive form. A less inclusive but necessary form is the unit of instruction.

Obviously it is impossible to study everything at once, hence the necessity for some logically useful division of "everything." A unit of instruction is such a division. It cuts out a field or phase of study.

The unit in historical study. An analogy from the field of historical research will help explain what a unit is. The historical scholar, like the teacher, cannot study everything at once. Hence, he has to cut out some segment of historic time. He calls this an epoch. It is an arbitrary unit of the continuous stream of human experience which was not, while it was being lived, felt to be separate and distinct.

Such epochs are the Athens of Pericles, or the England of William the Conqueror. Where the lines shall be drawn which begin and end such epochs is, of course, the problem. Here the historian must be arbitrary. Any given date on the rather wide margins of an epoch belong to an earlier or later epoch, depending on the historian's viewpoint. So with the unit in teaching.

But this limitation may be largely overcome by the continuity and overlap of units, not only in history but all the social studies. Only thus is the continuity of the processes in which we are interested made known and preserved. The principle of continuity between units will be discussed in a later chapter. We are now concerned with the several logics which must be employed in cutting out a unit of instruction in any field.

The logics necessary for unit construction. We shall start from our point of scratch as we see the task. The logics are these:

The psychological. This issues from the fact of the student's interest, and what he can think about and get hold of. According to it, the unit of study must be determined, as far as possible, by the span of his attention and his willingness and ability to see it through. This can be known by you and him only on an experimental basis.

The historical. This relates to the concern which any unit has with the historical background of the object of study. Hence, it is applicable to all social study, not merely to history.

The sociological. This is closely related to the historical in that it helps to cut out those forms of human association—the family, the market, the state, the corporation—through which the several social processes work.

The scientific. This is based on the need that inquiry be engaged in (see Chapter XIV.) [1]

The contents of a unit. The basic assumption we hold is that every unit contains something which is unknown to the student or something which is less than clearly known. Hence each must provide for inquiry. The function of a unit is to economize the task of inquiry. It also contains a set of aims. How detailed, explicit, and many they are is a matter of taste rather than anything which can or should be set down in fixed fashion. I would counsel a minimum of aims, those which the teacher believes are paramount and to which the materials of study are uniquely appropriate. Each unit should also contain a set of operations, or call them activities. They are the roads to the aims. How straight or deviate these roads are no one can say, for students often learn far more than they are taught. At least, they often learn things other than those we think we are teaching them. For this reason there is no sure-fire relation between any set of activities and any set of aims. A classification of aims and illustrations of units—some quite specifically structured and some less so—will appear in later chapters. [2]

The concept of the unit clarified. I do not understand that a "unit" is a *method*. Rather it is a segment of experience which is cut out for study; within it method is employed. It is my understanding that every unit is a

[1] For a critical discussion and a good bibliography on unit construction see B. Othaniel Smith, William O. Stanley, and J. Harlan Shores, *Fundamentals of Curriculum Construction* (Yonkers: World Book Co., 1950).

[2] The pedagogical pamphlet and journal literature is rich in sample units. See those in a series on problems in American life (Nos. 1-21) prepared under the auspices of the National Association of Secondary School Principals and the National Council for the Social Studies (Washington: The National Education Association, 1945).

project. It is a project in the sense that one projects inquiry into it. Further-more, every unit has a *topic, theme,* or central tendency or whatever name you choose to call it. Otherwise it could have no unity. Every unit is a *contract* in the sense that the student enters upon a contract or obligation to study how the things which it contains are related, how they work, how cause and effect are identified and related, and how a conclusion is reached. Every unit is also a *problem:* a problem of significance and meaning in some unknown or less-than-thoroughly-known phase of human experience.

In light of the foregoing, it is impossible to teach without some unit treatment of subject matter. Hence it is not against the unit which this discussion inveighs. It is against the unit as a kind of self-operating mech-anism or fetish and the view that there is one best kind. What teachers need is a broad related education in social knowledge, mastery of the method of inquiry, a knowledge of the life and times of their students, and imagination enough to put these together into a dynamic demonstration which will catch the interests and engage the loyalties of students. Teachers need far less of cookbook prescriptions and recipes for success, call them what you may—the Dalton plan, the contract method, and the like.[3]

A critique of Herbartian psychology. Many of the difficulties in this matter stem from the psychology of Herbart. Herbart set five stages or steps through which the student must go if he is to learn. They are preparation, presentation, comparison and abstraction, generalization, and application. Under *preparation* the teacher reminds the students of certain facts or experiences with which they are already acquainted. This step teaches nothing new; it only stirs up what Herbart called the student's "apperceptive mass." Following this comes *presentation* in which new facts are added to the old ones, or to the "apperceptive mass" which has been aroused or stirred up. Then comes *comparison and abstraction* in which the new and old are welded together through the relation which they may be shown to bear to some principle or fact. The formulation, in more precise form, of this abstraction comes in the next step, *generaliza-*

---

[3] The statement which should have given the *coup ae grâce* to the almost endless verbiage and largely aimless discussion about method and "the unit" is the following: "When the philosophy, program, and purpose of instruction in the social studies are thus clearly recognized and provisions made for the thorough preparation of teachers in knowledge and thought, the various forms of pedagogical prestidigitation [sic] such as the unit method, the correlation method, the radiation method, the fusion method, the concomitant method, the dioptric method, and the penetralia method, appear in their true light as empty formalisms," *Conclusions and Recommendations, Report of the Commission on the Social Studies* (American Historical Association) (New York: Charles Scribner's Sons, 1934), p. 113.

tion. Finally comes the step of *application* in which the principle or fact is applied or used to explain further facts, that is, applied to new situations to see how it works.

According to Herbart, these steps must be followed *seriatim.* They are the *fixed* steppingstones to understanding. Failure to take them in this order would, we suppose, land the student in the ditch.

Herbart held that the student perceives the objects of study and then responds to them. This theory is now thoroughly discredited, as we have shown in Chapters XII and XIV. The student perceives the objects of study in terms of the responses which they arouse in him. Objects of study are what they are to the student, not because of their natural qualities but because of the qualities which his perceptions give them. An analogy will make the point. The outfielder does not see the ball in the air and then respond to it. He sees it in terms of the responses which he is already making to it. Likewise the student does not see the tariff, the western movement, the TVA, or the cold war as something already "there." He sees them in terms of the responses which they invite or fail to invite. An object of study is an object of study only in the sense that the student is disposed to respond to it as one.

Herbart did take account of the state of mind which the student possesses. But he supposed the student to be somewhat more an apperceptive mass than a *human being with an apperceptive mass.* His theory put the teacher in the driver's seat. The class was supposed to go where the teacher drove and no other place. Thus Herbart's theory permitted little if any spontaneous inquiry on the student's part. Inquiry was not absent but was chiefly, if not entirely, determined by the teacher. Moreover, the conclusions to be reached seemed to be foregone. The teacher knew them; he would lead the students to them.

If there was a *problem* in Herbart's theory it is almost completely hidden from the student's view. Hence there was little genuine inquiry, that is, inquiry initiated and followed through by students in terms of their individual interests. There was also little if any recognition of students' attitudes. There was great concern with their knowledge and "the facts," but little about how they might *feel* about them.

The Herbartian steps. Let us now trace through the steps in the Herbartian method in a "lesson" in history. It is the battle of King's Mountain in the Revolutionary War.

The step of *preparation* involves a survey or recapitulation of previous classroom work. This requires the use of maps and books in order to get the geographical and military setting of the battle. In the step of *presenta-*

ion the story of the battle is set forth, by teacher and text. Under *comparison and abstraction,* this battle is compared to others, for instance Bennington in Burgoyne's campaign. Under *generalization* it is brought out, chiefly by the teacher, that "all" battles may have a great influence on the fortunes or misfortunes of a campaign and hence that the interest of the colonists in the two battles was about the same. In the step of *application* other battles are studied and compared—Bunker Hill, Saratoga, and Stony Point.[4]

The "lesson" on the battle of King's Mountain is typical of the operation of the Herbartian steps. Little, if any, room is given to imagination, interest is assumed rather than created, and the sense of a problem or of a task of inquiry is almost completely absent.

A critique of the Morrison method. The Herbartian method persists, with changes, however, in what is popularly known and rather generally used as the "Morrison method." The structure of the Morrison method is "the learning cycle" and the "teaching cycle." These go through three phases: *stimulus, assimilation,* and *reaction.* Included in the phase of stimulus is *exploration,* which is a pretest of the students' apperceptive background. This is followed by *presentation,* which is a broad expository enterprise in teaching to reveal the major essentials or ideas to be striven for. Under *assimilation* comes supervised study, independent student work, lectures, discussions, and other activities which will give the student the materials which he is to assimilate. Under the third phase or step, *reaction,* or what Morrison calls "organization," comes the construction of an outline in which the argument is developed in logical and convincing order, and finally, recitation, through oral discourse in which the students share with their peers what they have learned.[5]

Each of the foregoing steps is accompanied by what Morrison called the mastery technique, reported in the rhythm of test-teach-and-test again. After each pretest, students' failures are identified and, in the light of what they are, each step is retaught and tested again. This process is repeated until mastery is achieved.

As the authors of a text in the teaching of the social studies have observed, the technique of the Morrison method in its pure form is too

[4] This account is suggested by Boyd Bode's critique of the Herbartian method which was based on an illustration given in F. and C. McMurry, *The Method of the Recitation,* pp. 270-281. See Bode, *How We Learn* (Boston: D. C. Heath & Company, 1940), pp. 151-152. Bode remarks that Herbart did not break completely with the theory of the "substantive mind" or the "mental states" psychology but rather "retired [it] on a pension" (*ibid.,* p. 152).

[5] See Henry C. Morrison, *The Practice of Teaching in the Secondary Schools* (Chicago: University of Chicago Press, 1926), pp. 220-316.

complicated to be very practical in the classroom and too deadly to stimu late interest or learning in the student. I cannot disabuse myself of the view that it is committed to the old stimulus-response psychology. On that ground alone it has long ago served its day.

The method of inquiry. The discussion in Chapter XII on the fixing of belief and the method of inquiry may now be brought to bear on this matter. In it five stages or phases were identified in the act of problem solving which, we took pains to emphasize, did not need to come in any fixed order. They presumed the following phases: a state of doubt caused by a problem, tension, or blocked activity; the emergence of a problem from this inchoate state; the formulation of hypotheses; the testing of them; the choice of the most appropriate one and, through its use, the formulation of a judgment which resolved the doubt.

This analysis led to our identifying the teaching-learning act, which is the act of inquiry. The main beams in its structure are impulse, a problem, inquiry, and the resolution of doubt.

The teaching-learning act reviewed. A brief review of the teaching-learning act, aided by the following graphic form, will bring us to a further examination of that act.

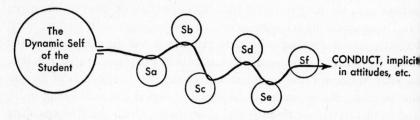

DIAGRAM 5. *The Teaching-Learning Act*

There are three elements, or constituents, in the diagram: the student, the teacher, and the "thing learned." These are represented by "the dynamic self," the field of the stimuli which the teacher manipulates (instead of manipulating the student) and "conduct," which may be translated into "attitudes" and/or a proposition, conclusion, judgment, or generalization of some kind. These exist subjectively in the student's understanding, which is hardly to be differentiated from his beliefs.

The hunt for the "right" stimulus. Note the sinuous course of the impulse which is seeking a stimulus which will interest it (a far cry from

Herbart's or Morrison's conception of the beginning of the teaching-learning act). It takes a bite of *Sa, Sc, Se, Sb,* and *Sd* but rejects them; it chooses *Sf.* Let us assume that these several stimuli are such things as: a reading assignment which may have been read but which offered no invitation to learning, a map or graph, the requirement that a chapter be outlined (almost certain to be ignored or, if sampled, spurned), a discussion not too tightly structured, a vital teacher who made a brief talk (not a lecture), and a movie. Which one "pulled the string" on a given student we do not know. We do know that a potential stimulus became a real one because it was selected by the student. It turned his impulse into interest. It (or two or three) found the student "at home." It gave direction to the subsequent act of inquiry. Thus was confirmed the first principle in teaching: the student is what he is at the moment you are teaching him. He is not what he will be after you have taught him.

The method of inquiry is tentative. The method of inquiry has none of the lock step, certainty, or the cocksureness of the Herbartian or Morrison methods. It has a tentativeness which does not permit the teacher to know the exact order of steps to be taken respecting a given problem of inquiry. This is just the state of mind in which the scientist, bent on scientific research, finds himself. The absence of certainty as to the order of steps is, however, more than compensated for by the thrill which accompanies inquiry which takes its cue from whatever lies at hand.

An ideal order of the steps in inquiry. The method of inquiry is a *method*; hence it does not operate at haphazard. Each phase or step seems almost to suggest if not dictate the next step. This is true, wherever you start. I shall now show the ideal order of its steps or phases. I shall leave the area of study unnamed and I shall not give a name to the problem on which it is used. I wish to make it clear, however, that the method of inquiry is applicable to all *problems* in the area of human affairs—and which are not necessarily *social* problems. They are all, however, problems of cause-and-effect. What now follows is only a slightly changed version of the analysis given near the close of Chapter XII. Do not attempt to match them with minute exactness.

1. The identification or creation of a problem situation of some kind: "Who killed Cock Robin?"—or its social studies equivalent. Note that it is a problem situation, not a discrete problem. The *Gestalt* or form is not clear; there is a field of things which appear to belong together but the lines of relationship are obscure. The *Gestalt* has no clear center.

There is an "idea" in it, but do not worry if it cannot be stated at once. That is just why it is a problem situation rather than a problem. If the idea is readily apparent then you have nothing about which to invite a search. It is "too easy" and the task is over before it is begun. Even if the idea which is central to the problem situation were stated that would not, of itself, guarantee that its meaning is known. Only to "say it" is not to find it.

You try to excite the class: the response is variable. You are manipulating stimuli. All sorts of exploratory activities might be employed: a movie, a short talk, suggestions from the class, etc. These are to serve the purpose of putting the class in *a tension* to bring it to *attention*. This is an ever-so-slight frustration not more than that. Or call it the creation of a block or a doubt. You want to get the class in a "slight jam"—from which you wish to help to rescue it. If there is nothing to overcome, if there is no tension to release, then there is no beginning. If no beginning, no middle; and if no middle, no end.

In short, in this phase—which may reappear in the course of the enterprise because the path of inquiry, like true love, seldom runs smoothly—you try to create such a state of concern and interest that every other object except the one at hand is banished from the minds of all. That takes some doing.

You and the class have but one objective at this time: to get a clue which will give insight into how the problem may be stated in explicit terms. The more the class shares in the planning of it, the greater interest you start with. If your students press you to teach about it, you may be sure that they have some views and opinions on it—whatever the "it" turns out to be. These will range from cocksure to cloudy ones.

But what is your aim or objective? Only this: to get a sharper picture of what makes something "tick," how something works, etc. You state your objective only in a very general way: one or more hunches, clues or call them hypotheses if you wish, so that the act of inquiry may begin and go forward. You are simply "going hunting"—what explicit game will be bagged no one knows. Scouting for game is the first objective; the more specific objectives will follow when the game shows up—rabbits, quail, or maybe larger "animals."

2. Throughout this phase you are doing your best to suggest clues without giving the plot away. *You* know the answer but you are not going to take your students by the hand and lead them to it. You want a *hunt*—not a sure-fire *find.* Your attempt to stimulate interest takes the form of raising and planting questions. I say "raising questions" rather than "asking questions." The difference is this: to ask a question suggests a direct answer response; to raise a question connotes that some time must elapse before it is "lowered"; it is for consideration not for immediate answer.

Many kinds of assignments, many enterprises or projects may enter here; if questions are asked facts will be needed, and facts suggest further questions. The problem situation is beginning to clear up—a problem is emerging. The questions tease it out of hiding. They might be such as these: to whom is this a problem? To whom not and why in both cases? What facts seem to suggest this? How did the problem arise? How widely is it felt? What specific interest or stake do various groups have in it? What facts are known about it? What would happen if it were solved? Would new problems be created in the very solving of this one? What resources—machinery, finance, leadership—are needed to solve it? Are the causal factors simple or complex? How readily can they be seen by

rdinary people? How deeply is the community affected by the problem? Who
ill be hurt if it is solved?

3. These questions help to narrow the field of your students' perceptions, and
elp to sharpen the *Gestalt* by putting things into place. They have their origin
n wild, vague, or random hunches but they are the raw materials for specific
ypotheses. They give you the search leads. Research is quite as appropriate
ecause there is always a trace of common-sense wisdom at work which needs to
e reworked or researched. Assume that two or more promising hypotheses (*née*
unches) come to light. That's right, come to light. They spring to the mind
y the provocation which questions create. (Teaching is always more provoking
han "telling.") These hypotheses suggest a division of labor which will be
lled out in terms of the different interests and ideas that have been aroused and
nanifested. Some students will work alone—don't force people to co-operate;
e want some lone wolves, the good kind! Committees may be formed: research
ommittees who will dig and delve. Such activities as these may be tried out to
ee what they produce: interviews, "resource people" brought into class, bibliog-
aphies assembled, a map may be appropriate—it is better hand-made than
bought"—all learning has a kinesthetic aspect—biology is part of thinking;
 movie, a filmstrip may throw some light on the problem, a field trip, etc. At
ppropriate times, difficult if not impossible to plan with calendar precision,
he findings will be pooled—discussion may ensue, even ought to.

4. In this net of experience, the "right" hypothesis is caught.

5. This "right" hypothesis has earned its place through competition. It is now
ut to work. It leads to the appropriate data. These data are the ground for a
udgment or conclusion. Once the data confirm it, it is put to test in similar
ituations. This may require some changes in it and subsequent changes in a
udgment or conclusion. But this depends on the size of the universe which is
eing examined as well as its complexity. Once these revisions have been made
he inquiry is satisfied.

The teacher's role in inquiry. This continuum of learning experiences
pplies to both you and your students. For them it should have a fresh and
xciting character. For you it may be pretty routine, even "old stuff," be-
ause of your greater knowledge. You may, nevertheless, find a great reward in a new experience in *communication* rather than in the discovery
f new truth. This suggests what your role is, as distinct from your students'.
You have an idea (or more than one) in the back of your head. It is as
lear and precise as you can state it to yourself. This is the bull's-eye of the
nterprise, which may be a whole unit or a part of one. (For your students
t is much less clear, even unknown.) If the matter at hand has to do with
he provisions of the Constitution you have, in your head, the *idea* that
earning them by heart will be well-nigh worthless *unless* they are seen as
neans to insure justice or whatever else you wish to emphasize. This *idea*
f justice is your central and crystal-clear idea. You will, eventually, seek to

make it as central and crystal-clear to your students. Suppose that the enter prise has to do with the importance of *distance in space* as a factor related to the ability of the people, in a country with such great land expanse as ours, to act in concert on some public issue. Many other factors are, of course, involved but at this time you want to drive home the significance of "distance in space." That is *your* central idea. And so it goes. But, not until you are sure of *your* central idea, or sense one that the students seem to be trying to work out, can you know which stimuli to manipulate. Your selection and manipulation of them is guided by an idea.

Although, ideally, everything I have said involves the fullest participation of your students, the responsibility which you have inherited as *leader* cannot be minimized. This involves you in suggesting, correcting, demonstrating, asking questions, giving encouragement, praising, and the many things which no teacher can completely delegate to students. Nothing can escape *you*. You are all eyes and ears. You are the teacher and it is your business to *teach*. (I shall return to this phase of your task in Chapters XIX and XX for it can hardly be given too much emphasis.)

While I would not for a minute suggest that you arrogate to yourself the role of authoritarian, you have every right to think of yourself as an *authority* in both method and substance. This requires the balance of a sense of humility and genuine pride—in what proportions I cannot tell you.

The conception of your role which I have in mind was given by H. G. Wells.

I want simply this world better taught . . . I will not suppose that there is any greater knowledge of things than men actually possess today, but instead of its being confusedly stored in many minds and books and many languages, it has all been sorted and set out plainly so that it can easily be used. . . .

When I ask you to suppose a world instructed and educated in the place of this old traditional world of unguided passion . . . a world taught by men instead of a world neglected by hirelings, I do not ask you to imagine any miraculous change in human nature. I ask you only to suppose that each mind has the utmost enlightenment of which it is capable instead of its being darkened and overcast. Everyone is to have the best chance of being his best self. Everyone is to be living in the light of the acutest self-examination and the clearest mutual self-criticism.[6]

A classification of aims. Although a later chapter will deal with aims, it is appropriate now to identify those which are basic to every unit of study: reliable knowledge, skill in inquiry, and attitudes. These will, we hope, defeat ignorance, muddle-headedness, and apathy. New methods of per

[6] *The Undying Fire* (New York: The Macmillan Co., Copyright 1919), pp. 182 and 184.

-eiving will be learned, new facts acquired and these, in turn, will engender ~ew attitudes and patterns of conduct. Thus knowledge, policy, and action will be related. Doubts, dissatisfactions, and states of unrest will take the form of ideas and these will be tested. The *activities* in which you and your students co-operatively engage will mediate the whole enterprise. In it all, the fallacy that the mind is first sharpened and then used will be exposed for what it is. The mind will be sharpened by its *use*. Learning will be interpreted as problem solving. Interest will be the shaft which gives unity and continuity to the whole experience. Thus the course of productive thinking will run.[7]

The rhythm of romance, precision, and romance. There is a cyclical rhythm to its course. This is the rhythm of romance-precision-romance. In giving structure to the teaching-learning act, this cycle performs a useful function which is, of course, the purpose of structure. These phases of the teaching-learning act are not sharply and distinctly separable because they are *phases* rather than fixed steps. Whitehead calls them "distinctions of emphasis," each one of which is present throughout the act. There is only "alternation of dominance" among them.[8]

Manifestations of romance. The hallmark of romance, wherever it enters into inquiry, is imagination. Inquiry begins with it, for the thing sought must be sought first by imagining *how* it may be sought. Without curiosity there can be no quest: the thrill of the quest is the romance of it. Rote learning is dead, unimaginative, provokes no curiosity—hence is unromantic. Romance is the art phase of the work of the scientist. Work does not dull romance, only make-work dulls it. Assignments that have only the purpose of setting tasks that are unrelated to anything but a teacher's notion that through them the student will be made to learn are also death to romance. If you would encourage your students to learn you must appeal first to their imagination and from that, romantically invite them into reasoning and thinking.

Romance is the affective phase of learning without which it will be idle to expect much on its effective side. It inheres in the very nature of the experimental outlook and attitude. It inheres also in the thrill which attends discovery. It is part of the ferment with which all genuine inquiry

[7] An account of the dynamics and logic of productive thinking is to be found in Max Wertheimer, *Productive Thinking* (New York: Harper & Brothers, 1945). See especially "Introduction," pp. 1-13, in which Tables I, Ia, and II set forth the course of thinking under the rules of deductive and inductive logic, and the association theory, respectively. Read "Conclusion," pp. 189-215, in which these theories are examined and compared with the logic of the method of inquiry which I have used.

[8] See Whitehead, *The Aims of Education*, Chapter 3, "The Rhythmic Claims of Freedom and Discipline."

begins, and which exists throughout its course. If affection for the objec of study can be fixed there will be something to deal with through sym pathetic imagination.

Interest is another name for romance. This is the dynamic which sustain the student when the discomfort of thought, the "painful suspension" o inquiry seems more than he can bear. It renders difficulties less difficult It keeps him from losing heart.

It may, sometimes, impede or forestall inquiry by jumping over i Human interest in consequences is sometimes so romantic as to seek t escape the discipline of reason. Pascal once said that most of the evils o life arise from man's being unable to "sit still in a room." That is hard he wants to be up and doing.

The demands of the romantic mood in learning dictate that you begi not with abstractions but with concretions. The abstractions they ma illustrate will then come easier. This means that you begin where th student is: with his own involvements which, if not romantic, are at leas emotional. There is also some danger in overdoing reference to the purel contemporary. It is often too commonplace and the task of rendering i uncommon is not easy. Knowledge sometimes requires that it be *suffered* romance can relieve some of the suffering, but not all of it, for disciplin cannot be denied its claim.

But there is some discipline and precision in the romantic phase. N part of an education can do without discipline, rigor, and precision. Bu do not forget that the adult world is not like the world of youth. Th former is more complicated and will repel inquiry about it if it is thrus on the student in its demanding and complex form.

Romance will persist throughout if learning can be made a game. Th essence of a game is continuous novelty. The sheer joy of playing i overcomes the ardor of playing it. Without this spirit knowledge is inert Without romance, knowledge may even be held in contempt.

The cadence changes.   But the cadence changes and the act of inquiry becomes more demanding. If romance has dominated the beginning i has put the student in the mood for doing more precise things. Th phase of precision calls for patience, waiting, and ultimate rather thar immediate rewards. It demands an investment which does not pay of at once. It changes the emphasis to concentration, to the use of skills to studying, figuring out, making connections, and arriving at conclusions

Precision is misunderstood.   Not infrequently this is the only stage, no by necessity but by virtue of a teacher's believing that you have to "mak 'em work." This is the view which Mr. Dooley reported in his aphorism that "it doesn't matter what you teach the child so long as he doesn't like it." But teaching does not find its genuine directives in seeking to please the student. It finds them in making learning as rewarding and hence as pleasurable as possible. The limit of precision is reached when imagination is stifled; when rules are followed in rote fashion, when the student is commanded to do this or that. Precision does not inhere in teacher authority. It inheres in the attractiveness of the enterprise.

Skill demands repetition but this need not be rote. It can be made to combine romance and precision by the will to solve a problem. Order is not enough. The requirements of precision are more complex than that. Precision permits order with a touch of novelty in it. Without it, precision degenerates into punishment. It is brute facts with which your students must work. Only by a mixture of novelty and romance can their nature be tamed.

Romance and precision co-operate. Hypothesis-making is both romantic and precise. Here the rhythm is one of up and down and of shuttling between. Facts come hard. The printed page is often uninviting; it is too impersonal. But hard work may be no less hard but less onerous, and the printed page may be worth interpretation if the pitch of interest can be kept high. Thus romance serves precision. The truth and the hardness of a fact or a proposition may be the more rewarding if they can be presented with an appeal not only to reason but also to sentiment.

If the object with which you are dealing is abstract show its nature in concrete examples. If it be unfamiliar show, by analogy, that it is like something the student already knows. Students cannot imagine anything with which they have had no acquaintance. The approach to the unknown is through the known. This makes it no less precise—only knowable. If the matter be difficult and almost beyond their reach, couple it with their interest. Theirs will be the gain. It is not the precise truth of an idea that leads to its acceptance as much as its truth-appeal; it must be as congenial truth as you can make it.

The transition from romance to precision. The big problem comes in the transition from romance to precision. At this time the breadth of treatment narrows and you seek what is exact, more than what is picturesque. This is the state of "the grammar of science." This is the phase when activity is more than play. It is the activity of analysis under rules of the game. The rules are dominant; the game spirit is recessive. Still there can be what Whitehead calls "the adventure of thought." But hard work need not be irksome, however much it demands precision. It need not turn into drudgery. Right and wrong ways must be distinguished.

Romance again dominates. Then follows the phase when romance is again dominant. Whitehead calls this the phase of generalization. Its romance inheres in the fact that doubt is now turned to belief. The roadblock is down; action can go on. The judgment which has been made can now be tested—even played with to see how well it works in like situations. This is the fun of proof. The garden which was weeded in the middle stage of precision now yields its crop. This is the stage of consummation.

Romance becomes orderly. Romance is not unorderly now, as it was in the beginning. It is orderly and in that fact lies a sense of accomplishment. Order has been *created:* this is the productive, the creative, the working act. Synthesis brings its own reward. The student may now show what he has learned. He is now effective and finds even an affective thrill in being that. He is now in command of principles; his conduct may thus be principled in both intellectual and moral ways. He can now direct his thinking. He can now generalize; he is relieved from the pressure of mere events; facts are now clothed with meaning. He may sense the meaning of Emerson's belief that "generalization is always a new flux of divinity into the mind: hence the thrill that attends it."

CHAPTER XVI

The Nature and Origin
of Aims in Social Study

THE AIMS OF and conditions for social study have been matters of concern in each of the foregoing chapters.[1] But it is not my purpose, even now, to provide an inventory or finding-list of aims. In so far as anything of that nature is undertaken, it will be found in later chapters. My purpose now is to say what aims are, how they arise, and how they ought to be stated. Chapter XVII will treat the more technical phases of the statement of aims in the context of the construction of tests.

Aims are acts of faith. Any statement of aims is an act of faith. It is a transaction in futures. But it is also a present transaction. The future issues from the present, which has its roots in the past. This is the insistent present, made up of disappearing past and emerging future. Each of these time-frames conditions our vision of what the purposes of social study ought to be. There is a past which we dare not deny and there is a future which we cannot afford simply to let happen. What we may do about it rests with the direction we take in the present.

Aims are dynamic. Aims or ends are not static things. They are the dynamics of individual and social life. Neither are they fixed and absolute. They are ends-in-view, the view which our present knowledge and dedication permit us to state and work for. In being ends-in-view, they are those we can envisage from where we now stand. They are not the ultimate termini of our effort but rather those things which we now set ourselves to

---

[1] I use the term "social study" here, as earlier, rather than "social studies" to suggest what the social studies have in common. Social *study* suggests a unity rather than a division of labor although it does not deny the fact or usefulness of such a division.

achieve, in the achievement of which we hope to come upon a grander view and, from that point of vantage, fashion the new ends-in-view which it will permit.

Aims are derived.   To state an aim is to state what one *aims* or *means* to do. They are beliefs which one aims to realize. They are derived, not by induction, but by deduction. We take them, not from facts but having taken them must know what facts we shall need to bring them to pass. As the aims of social study they are secondary or derivative aims. They derive from our social philosophy, in wonder—for it is in wonder that philosophy begins, as Socrates taught. They are the fruit of our ideals. Hence *they* are ideal. In being ideal they are ethical. They are willed, not found except that we find them in our hearts and minds.

In a democracy we find the aims for social study in two images: the image of a better and wiser social order and the image of better and wiser persons. These are now, as they have been, our bench marks. The first tells the kind of society we want, the second the kind of people required to run it. Each is to be efficient and civilized: thoughtful and loving. These images are impelled by the faith that they are attainable: that we may not only come closer to our ideals but that we may improve upon them.

Aims are tentative.   Let us not mistake the origin of these aims. They trace to no Rosetta stone, they come from no opinion surveys, or from Mount Sinai or Mount Olympus. They come from "a living picture of the choice of thoughtful men about what they would have life be and to what ends they would have men shape their intelligent activities." [2] They come out of human experience. Hence they are experimental and, being experimental, are tentative. But this is not the tentative of a faint heart or of hands that are afraid to grasp. It is the tentative which settles for no finalities—the tentative of the very process of life itself: the tentative of an adventure in humanism.

A frame of reference for developing aims.   Aims, like the objects of social study themselves, are developed within a frame of reference. The one we have used is the following:

1. What is "the good society" and what are the attributes of the persons who are to make it a reality? This is the philosophic perspective.
2. What are the present social realities as they are revealed in the behavior of persons and institutions as the several social sciences permit us to know them? This is the scientific perspective.

[2] John Dewey, *Reconstruction in Philosophy* (New York: Henry Holt & Co., Inc., Copyright 1937), p. 26.

3. What are the present needs of both persons and institutions as we may know them by their declaration and weigh them by the canons of goodness and wisdom? This is the perspective of needs.

4. What does the teaching-learning process require respecting the way in which aims should be stated so they will affect conduct? This is the perspective of operationalism.

The foregoing chapters have dealt in one way or another and both explicitly and implicitly with the first three of these perspectives. In the immediately foregoing remarks we have dealt with the first one. The second and third are difficult sharply to differentiate. Hence we shall treat them together through a discussion of the concept of *need*. The fourth will follow.

The importance of needs. All purposive social study must be motivated and directed by a conception of a need. Otherwise, it cannot be purposive. With what needs, or rather whose needs, should the social studies be concerned—the needs of the social order or the needs of individual persons? With both, of course, and through the division of labor implied in an earlier discussion, that is through institutions and persons (see Chapter VI). But the school can meet the needs of institutions only through meeting the needs of their individual constituents. It is needful individuals, not needful institutions, that the teacher confronts. These are the young people who are somewhat more molded *by* than molders *of* the institutions in and through which they live, but who in their adult years will be able to establish a different ratio between molded *by* and molders *of*.

The needs of institutions and individuals differ. The needs of institutions and the needs of individuals may be differentiated. Institutions have needs in the sense that the patterns and organizations within which human beings carry on their public and private lives require improvement so as to provide a better environment for the improvement and a better expression of human nature. Individuals have needs in the sense that they require improvement in knowledge, skills, and loyalties respecting the remaking of their characters and their institutions.

The needs of institutions and individuals are not identical. They are related, but they are different. If this distinction is not admitted we shall run the risk of concentrating too narrowly on the needs of individuals. This distinction and this relation were discussed in Chapter VI in the observation that "It is better men, individually and collectively, that we need if we would bring our society nearer to its ideals"—"better men as means to better institutions and, in turn, better institutions as means to better men." Better institutions are such as these: more effective means of handling problems which individuals cannot handle by themselves—the great controls which came through legislation and the programs of voluntary organizations and which result in the great freedoms. By better men I think of more efficient institution-builders, better leaders, and better followers; men who are brave, talented to imagine, and informed as to the ways in which what they imagine may come to be.

The importance of institutions.   There is disquieting evidence that we do less than we can to make our students conscious of the nature and role of institutions. We are too much disposed to take only an individual view, the view of the "real life situations" of our students seen in less than their real dimensions which are social and institutional. Hence the needs of institutions often lie quite outside the ken and concern of many students. But if public as well as private needs—the needs of institutions as well as those of persons—may be brought into the common focus which they really occupy, we may make an important and long-delayed advance in thinking and teaching about needs in terms of *we* as well as *I*. This is the sense in which the needs of individuals require to be related *outward*.

Aims have a dual purpose.   From this dual perspective, the general aims of social study may be stated: the further *socialization* and *individualization* of the student. One becomes socialized, that is, a sharing member in group activity, only as he develops a fuller selfhood and this develops only through his fuller interaction with his fellow men.

A need defined.   But what is a need? The following statements give us a variety of views, if not definitions.

1. a lack or want which must be met if persons are to be happier, more effective, or more "complete" in one way or another.
2. an unsolved problem.
3. the dynamic, driving, or projective element in a human being.
4. that which is caused by the fact of an imbalance (biological or psychological) in a human being—such imbalances as those we know as hunger, fear, ignorance, and loneliness.
5. a condition of unrest or dissatisfaction which manifests itself through tensions of various kinds.
6. a condition or state of incompleteness in the sense which suggests that a gap exists between where one (a person or a group) is and where one (a person or a group) ought to be, as measured by some scale of values.

It would be futile to attempt to reduce human needs to any fixed number. Moreover it would be impossible, inasmuch as they are as many and as variable in kind and quality as the imbalances with which human beings may be beset. Nor are they to be thought of as a new version of human instincts. Although the above statements differ, their common denominator may be identified: *needs are dynamic conditions of human beings which imply states of unrest or imbalance to which the human organism seeks, in a variety of ways, to give expression.*

Felt and unfelt needs.   So conceived, a need may be *felt* or *unfelt*. As a felt need it may be sensed and accompanied by only random and trial-and-error attempts to satisfy it. That is, it may be little more than only felt. Or, it may be felt and accompanied by quite appropriate and purposive attempts to satisfy it. Important among these is the ability to state what the need is and thus inform others about it so that they may help one's attempt to satisfy it. To feel a need and be able to identify it "by name" is to make statements such as: "I am lonely and need companionship," or "I am uncertain about the part that biases play in my thinking and I need to know how much they disturb it." Such statements contain an element of fact, e.g., "I am lonely" and "I am uncertain." They also contain an element of preference, e.g., "I need companionship" and "I need to know how much they disturb it."

The preconditions for reporting felt needs.   Hence three things are required for needs to be felt and reported: appropriate sensitivity to one's states and conditions; some knowledge, however vague or clear and accurate or inaccurate it may be, and the ability to make a valuation or a judgment. Of these three, sensitivity is probably part of one's innate equipment; the other two must be acquired. One can, of course, be mistaken about his judgment concerning both biological and cultural needs. For this reason it is necessary that he be educated to sense more accurately what the nature of his imbalances is and to make more discriminating judgments about what should be done about them.

But one may have needs which he does not feel. Such a need is hence not his in any self-conscious way. A need which is unfelt is, obviously, one which cannot be named, talked about, or made known to another in a conscious way. It may, however, be *inferred* by another.

At the biological level one may have that kind of organic imbalance which incipient or active cancer or tuberculosis may cause but may have no feeling of it or know anything about it. How then can he be said to have a need? Such a judgment is the consequence of the knowledge of persons competent in diagnosis who are capable and willing to express the need for treatment. Likewise, at the cultural level a person may feel no dissatisfaction or unrest because of his lack of skill in perceiving both himself and his world. Such a person may be judged to need better insight into his biases and the way in which they distort his perceptions.

Neither of these judgments can be made by such a needful person. Hence the role of the teacher as one of Dewey's "thoughtful men."

How felt and unfelt needs differ.   The distinction between felt and unfelt needs is an important one. Those which are felt may be or may not be reported and, if so, the report may be accurate or inaccurate, likewise the judgment made about what ought to be done about them may be wise or unwise. Unfelt needs place the burden of judgment initially on someone else. That person may be able to state what another's need is with accuracy or inaccuracy as to its nature, and make wise or unwise judgments as to what ought to be done about it.

Needs may be mistaken for other things.   This poses the question: what is the value, importance, and validity of students' conceptions of their needs for the teacher who seeks to state the aims of social study? The first thing to note is that students may mistake their wants, interests, desires, wishes, and whims for their needs. For so they may be, as *they* see them. But are they genuine needs, those which are *really* needed?

The teacher must discriminate.   Let us compare two felt and articulated needs. Let us suppose that a student thinks he needs the latest model "hot rod," a basement rumpus room with bar, indeed with all the gadgets and trappings of the "Joneses" in order to be happy and successful. Is the teacher to accept such a statement of felt needs as eligible for an aim in social study? Hardly. If, on the other hand, the student gives expression —whether in so many words or by some behavior from which a valid inference may be drawn—that he believes he needs to be clearer about the criteria he ought to use to make a reasonably dependable choice of career, no sensible teacher would deny that such a felt need was highly eligible for consideration as one of the aims of social study. (The former would, of course, be eligible for study and might be said to qualify as a negative aim for social study.)

However much the teacher may wish to take account of and use to a warrantable extent the felt and expressed needs of the students as suggesting aims for social study, it appears they cannot be taken at face value. The teacher must distinguish between genuine and spurious student-stated needs. But does the teacher have the moral right to pass judgments on students' expressions of their needs? Certainly. The teacher has not only the right but the duty to do so—and the necessity.

Certainly no sober person would argue that the aims of social study are to be determined, in whole or in part, by unexamined and uncriticized acceptance of students' expressions of needs.

Needs and self-direction.   The examination of expressed needs and the judgments made about them involve both student and teacher. The task of education is to develop in students the acutest self-consciousness concerning the worth of their knowledge, the reliability of their skills, and the moral quality of their beliefs. In this view, the student is conceived as one who learns to direct himself in the formulation and realization of his goals, both for himself and for a society of similarly self-directed persons. This conception contains no element of anarchy, as the concept "self-directed" may suggest to some. Hence it does not subscribe to the view that a society is either created or held together by the "need" of many individuals to get on by themselves. Such a conception would not permit a society to come into existence, much less persist.

The teacher's task is to aid rather than dictate. If the student's conception of what he needs is faulty, it is the teacher's task to help him examine and reformulate his needs-beliefs and see them in enlarged and more enlightened terms. It is not the teacher's task to tell the student he is wrong about his expressed needs. It is not the teacher's business to declaim upon the rightness or wrongness of any of the student's views or acts. Competent persons are not made by moral injunction. Final judgment to change and to change in a given way rests with the student. It is hoped that this judgment will be made less difficult because the climate is a friendly and permissive one, made so by the teacher who is an exemplar of the culture at its best and artful in creating the atmosphere in which right judgments are shaped.

The teacher not a "hired man." The opposite conception of the role of the teacher, respecting students' expressed needs, is that of a hired man who does the bidding of students, motivated and directed by their felt needs—whatever their quality or appropriateness might be. The best that this could produce would be a completely individualized and purely *ad hoc* education except when the expressed needs of students, whether worthy of being satisfied or not, were identical enough to instruct two of them in the same things.

A false conception of needs. Such a theory of education sometimes comes perilously close to being practiced. It grew out of an attempt to establish the aims of social study on what was presumed to be a scientific basis. Instead it was only on a *statistical* one. The practice was to make studies of the frequency of both student practices and felt needs. The root fallacy was that what students practiced and felt they needed should be taken as warrant for the rightness and appropriateness of such practices and feelings. This method, furthermore, presumed to take the identification of the aims of social study "out of the thin air of speculation" and put it on the solid grounds of empirical study. But the mere fact of greatest frequency of either practices or needs—even their universality among youth—does not establish their validity as aims of conduct. Such thinking subscribed, in effect, to the view that the kind of education which young people get quite unconsciously through their relatively undisciplined social relations is what the schools ought to give consciously—without regard to its defects, distortions, or perversions.[3]

A technique mistaken for a philosophy. The fallacy implicit in this method is patent. It mistook a technique for a philosophy. (Someone has said that it confused pediatrics with pedagogy.) It appears to trace, in part at least, to Rousseau's belief that, since the child was created in the image of God, the expression of his desires (mistaken as genuine needs) must be appraised as coming from divinely instructed sources. The doctrine of the divine right of kings was thus revised to the divine prescience and omniscience of students. Education was to consist in the nurture of desire.

The chief errors in this notion of education may be summarized as follows:

1. It mistook desires for needs and assumed that they could be accepted as valid at face value.

2. It declared, in effect, that student judgments were infallible and held that criticism of them was unwarranted invasion of individual freedom.

3. It had the effect of discharging teachers from the duty of discovering how a great deal of genuinely needed, useful, and necessary knowledge might be made attractive.

4. It brought back the equivalent of the elective system—everyone was to choose what he wanted to do.

5. It bordered on the theory which holds that instinctive tendencies should not be "instructed."

6. It defined the teacher as little more than hired man or shepherd.

7. It mistook a statistical technique for a philosophy of education.

8. It failed to recognize that needs are culturally derived but individually expressed.[4]

Students' interests, wants, wishes, and desires have significance. The distinction between genuine needs and such manifestations as interests,

[3] See Dewey, *Education and Experience* and Boyd H. Bode, *Progressive Education at the Crossroads*, the chapter "The Concept of Needs"; also I. L. Kandel, *The Cult of Uncertainty*, for critical observations of the needs-approach as sometimes practiced.

[4] On this last point, see Dorothy Lee, "Are Basic Needs Ultimate?" *Personality in Nature, Society, and Culture*, edited by Clyde Kluckhohn, Henry A. Murray, and David M. Schneider (Cambridge: Harvard University Press, 1953), pp. 335-341. I believe that an advance would be made if we threw away the concept of "need" and substituted the concept of "requirement." The question might then be asked: What do human beings require, individually and collectively, to sustain and advance the democratic way of life?

wants, wishes, and desires is not meant to imply that they are of no significance in determining the aims of social study. Short of being evidence of genuine needs they are important in the sense that they make known to the teacher what it is that interests, occupies, or pre-occupies students. Within reasonable limits, which the teacher must locate as lying someplace between pure fantasy and the most informed sobriety, the things which students might want, wish for, and be interested in might well be *increased*. This is premised on the view that it is within the widened and deepened scope of such a field of expression that students may come to discover genuine needs, with or without teacher guidance and co-operation. The concept of "one's best self" is a concept which requires broad ranges of imagination in the many possible areas through which the self might become its best. Right aspirations, beliefs, interests, wants, and needs are more discovered than they are made. Teacher judgments which are prematurely *negative* respecting felt needs may have as destructive effects as those judgments which are prematurely *affirmative*.

The importance of individual differences. Informed and devoted teaching requires all the evidence that can be had on the human nature of students. Their honestly making known their interests, desires, wishes, and needs, whether they turn out to be genuine or spurious, contributes to that end. And these are perhaps better "betrayed" than given in response to formal request. Human beings are their realest selves when they behave, so to speak, *ad libitum*. Free and honest expression of these things likewise tells us who is like whom and who is different from whom and in what respect. To overlook or to blink individual differences is to underevaluate one of the basic human realities. The liberal society is liberal in the sense that it allows for an infinite variety of types. But they must be individual types in the sense that they are individual expressions of something common and dear to all. There is a vast difference between anarchy and the individualism which expresses, in unique but not antagonistic ways, the nuances of meaning of some general and basic values. My meaning is implicit in "E pluribus unum" or the observation of St. Paul that "For as the body is one, and hath many members, and all the members of that one body, being many, are one body." Democracy requires that men know what their common obligations are. It permits them to discharge them in various ways but expects that they will be harmonious.

The insightful teacher. Teachers need all the light they can get on what makes Sammy run. But his true individuality is often coated over by false etiquette, hidden behind anxieties, or twisted out of shape in his attempts to conform to the polite and mediocre expectations whicn are held up to him. This being the case only the most insightful teacher can succeed in finding out what he really is.

The individual is not a finished datum. To do these things is not, as the radical "progressives" supposed, to deal with the individual as a finished datum. The completeness of "the individual" or even his existence in the absolute terms in which he was conceived by this group is a stubborn myth. He is, like democracy itself, an instance of unfinished business. But even so, the teacher no less than Thomas Jefferson might well have a "decent respect for the opinions of mankind" as they come in the statements of needs—whatever be their final value in the determination of the aims of social study. They may at least tell us in what specific ways the student is unfinished. Furthermore, an awareness of needs as the student may express them may help us avoid the error of arriving at aims which have little if any bearing on what human nature really is, whether it be good or bad, wise or foolish.

Needs are the basis for general and special education. If, in the teacher's best judgment, students' statements of their needs are acceptable as aims in social study, they will have two uses. Those which are judged to have value for *all* youth will aid in determining the aims of *general* social education—that which all students need and hence which should be required. Those which cannot meet that criterion will aid in determining the aims of *special* education, to be made available as electives.

But such an allocation of needs, as determinants of aims, is difficult to make with anything like precision and finality. This follows from the fact that, given the ambiguity of many needs and their strong impulsive charge, a great many of them may be met in a variety of ways. Thus the probability is increased that any given need may qualify as an aim for general social education.

The role of needs summarized. The role of needs in the determination of the aims of social study may now be summarized. If a case can be made for them, needs which students can state may qualify as aims for general or special study. Those which do not qualify are by no means lost. They provide significant clues to the kind, intensity, quality, and direction of students' interests, aspirations, desires, and wishes. Although there is no defensible alternative to the needs approach—whether they be the needs of institutions or of persons—the teacher's judgment on the validity of the felt needs of students is weighted with heavy obligation. The final judgment as to which needs shall be taken for aims lies with the teacher.[5]

[5] Call this "judicial review," or the assent or "veto by the executive." So conceived it assumes that students have shared in the discussion if not the choice of aims. There

Likewise the teacher must make judgments about the needs which students have but of which they are unaware. They will almost certainly be greater in number than their stated needs. These are both private and public in kind. The latter are those for which students seldom, if ever, have a feeling. They must come to know what these public needs are as certainly as they must come to know that the richness of their individual selves is a function of the richness of the institutions which are the source of their sustenance and growth as personalities.

These two kinds of needs, appropriate needs reported by the student and/or inferred by the teacher, whether personal or public, provide a basis for the aims of social study. Both are, however, necessary rather than sufficient factors.

Needs not the only basis for aims. There is a sense, of course, in which all the aims of social study must be justified in terms of their meeting the needs of students—but not only as they feel and can state them. This suggests that the teacher must have access to sources far more inclusive and profound than what students are able to say about what they need. These sources are the social sciences and what they can tell us about the nature of the social realities—society and individuals as they are. Furthermore, they can tell us what the characteristics of the society are which condition the realization of such grand aims as the promotion of the general welfare and the securing of liberty and justice. These were given in previous chapters on modern society. In Chapter VII we went outside the realm of the social sciences and undertook to assess our culture in terms of ethical norms.[6] These are the kinds of knowledge of which the teacher's general education consists.

Needs noted in earlier chapters. The foregoing chapters may now be assessed, in part, in the light of what may be drawn from them illustrative of some of the needs with which they dealt. These are not only needs but themes and content around which highly useful learning experiences might be fashioned. A random choice includes the following: the components of the democratic character—care, responsibility, respect, and knowledge, in which terms students might come better to know themselves; the continuous and discontinuous nature of culture and character viewed,

---

is, however, considerable sham and even deceit in some pupil-teaching planning practices. In these, the teacher permits the discussion to proceed on a quite equalitarian basis and then "pulls the rabbit out of the hat"—the rabbit of a judgment already formed. In any event, the commonwealth of student-peers should be under the regency of the teacher, on both legal and intellectual grounds.

6 See Dewey, *Human Nature and Conduct,* "The Nature of Aims," pp. 223-237, and *Democracy and Education,* Chapters VIII and IX, pp. 117-143, for a clear and profound discussion of aims in education.

for instance, in terms of the changing tempo, if not of the breaks and mends in the economy through prosperity and depression and full employment and gross unemployment, as well as in the cultural terms of the changes in roles and statuses involved in the journey from the world of the family to the world of the market; the need to know the difference between propaganda and education and what they denote by way of independence of thought and belief; the structure of their own community viewed as both a spatial pattern and a social order; the resistance of institutions to change and the resulting harm to many of our cherished values; the relation between the vocational and the liberal arts; the function of frames of reference which they use but of which they have no critical awareness; the *belief* nature of social knowledge, and the reliability of the method of inquiry.

Through the study of such needs as these (probably unfelt but eminently teachable so that they be both felt and known) students might come into a more realistic and useful acquaintance with reality and greater harmony with its changing forms, the ability to live more sensibly and more sensitively in a world of increasingly more abstract symbols, e.g., from "mother" to "co-operation" or from "ward and neighborhood" to "wide world" and, in these growths and transitions, increase their capacity for self-direction, learn to balance success and failure, and above all come into a fuller and more self-conscious selfhood.[7]

Aims ought to be stated operationally. Having discussed the origin and nature of aims we now come to the problem of how they should be stated. Their function is to give *an aim to activity*, hence they ought to be stated in *operational* terms. However noble they may be as you conceive them as teacher, they must be something more than the frieze which adorns the temple of learning. They must have utility.

We want our students to get ideas, for it is ideas rather than uninstructed impulses which are the goals of teaching. We want them to *do* something with ideas, to *act* upon them rather than only *retain* them. Indeed, the normal destiny of an idea is to express itself in some form of action or power over the environment. True ideas are workable, actionable; false ideas are unworkable and unactionable.

Ideas and effects. We sometimes seem to think that an idea, to be a "real" idea, must have a kind of inscrutable character, be even a bit

---

[7] See Daniel A. Prescott, *Emotion and the Educative Process* (Washington: American Council on Education, 1938), "Ego and Integrative Needs," pp. 118-125. See also James S. Plant, *The Envelope,* and *Personality and the Cultural Pattern.* Note the somewhat general but real nature of the needs given above. It is apparent that none can be solved per se. Each requires knowledge of the interrelation between person and culture, self and society, and many of the processes by which each is ordered.

ambiguous. Nothing could be further from the truth. Peirce has told us that "mysterious ideas are those which give no hint of their portent for action," and that "our idea of anything is our idea of its sensible effects." Earlier we observed Whitehead's injunction that the thing to do with an idea is to "prove it—to prove its worth."

The importance of the present participle—the "ing" ending. This does not deny that ideas have a latent quality but in being latent they are full of power, potential for action. What things mean is what they *purport*, that is, the action which lies with them. This can be the action of appreciating, covertly doing, believing, or feeling. Note the "ing" ending of these terms. We need to *ing* our aims and purposes, that is, we need to convert our aims from their more or less inert form as *nouns* into their more dynamic form as *present participles*. If we do this we shall ask our students not only to think but to *be thinking*, not only to plan but to *be planning*, not only to feel but to *be feeling*, not only to love but to *be loving*, not only to know but to *be knowing*. And for each ing-word there is an implicit *what*. What shall they be thinking *about*, planning *about*, feeling *about*, and so on? What things mean to them is what they are prepared to do about them and act toward them. Therein lies the power of attitudes which are the wellsprings of *action*, even though we cannot know what *particular* behavior will spring from any one. If we take heed of this we shall give our students an education for what is real.[8]

Just as we are sometimes disposed to think of ideas as inert because they are latent, we are also often disposed to think of mind as something static. Our remark in Chapter I that the task of teaching was to help young people inquire what is good and wise *to mind* and *to purpose*, suggested action. We may now change and enhance its meaning by saying that mind is *minding* and purpose is *purposing*—whether it be covert or overt. There is, then, no necessary antithesis between teaching which seeks to nurture the life of the mind and that which seeks to fit students for action.

Definitions of mind. The view that the mind is a static thing was laid to rest by William James long ago when he corrected the "mental states" conception of it by showing that mind is a *stream* of consciousness—a moving and dynamic thing. This view was endorsed and extended by Dewey in his observation that

. . . mind is not a name for something complete in itself; it is a name for a course of action that is intelligently directed in so far, that is to say, as aims, ends, enter into it, with selection of means to further the attainment of ends.[9]

[8] See Earl C. Kelley, *Education for What Is Real* (New York: Harper & Brothers, 1947).

[9] *Democracy and Education*, p. 155; see also p. 153.

To this we add two other definitions of mind which Dewey has given us:

Mind as a concrete thing is precisely the power to understand things in terms of the use made of them; a socialized mind is the power to understand them in terms of the use to which they are turned in joint or shared situations. *And mind in this sense is the method of social control.*[10]

and

Mind is capacity to refer present conditions to future results, and future consequences to present conditions. And these traits are just what is meant by having an aim or a purpose.[11]

The dynamic conception of mind.   But the belief in "mental" states still persists, despite the fact that abundant testimony is at hand to the contrary. James and Dewey are only two of the later thinkers who have sought to scotch such a view. The history of the dynamic conception of mind may be traced by recalling the wisdom of many great thinkers. In the *Ethics*, Aristotle knew and stressed the action side of knowing by saying that "Men become builders by building and lyre-players by playing the lyre; so too we become just by doing just things, temperate by doing temperate acts, brave by doing brave acts." Spinoza's definition of the good was "that which we certainly know is useful to us." Nietzsche said that he hated everything that merely "instructs me without increasing or directly quickening my activity." The elder Huxley wrote that "the great end of education is not knowledge but action." Emerson wrote that "without action, thought can never ripen into truth." Clerk Maxwell's concern with all knowledge was "the particular *go* of it." Whitehead sensed the same thing in his remark that "general training should aim at eliciting concrete apprehensions, and should satisfy the itch of youth to be doing something." George H. Mead said that "Thinking is not a field or realm which can be taken outside of possible social uses." The philosopher William E. Hocking observed that "to believe in an idea is to begin to form habits about it."

What and how are joined.   Thus in being operational and useful, aims must readily permit the student to express them in action; not only the "action of thought" but also overt action or doing, that which reflection helps him plan and fashion. They can be operational only if the knowledge which they provoke may express itself in the playing of roles—imaginary and real. Social knowledge is not only to be entertained, it must be put to work. If aims may be stated in operational terms, the *what* and the *how* are joined. This was my emphasis in Chapter XI in which I discussed the

[10] *Ibid.*, pp. 39-40.
[11] *Ibid.*, p. 120.

relation between perceiving or knowing, evaluating or taking attitudes, and conduct. But I also noted that the school is not an "action institution" or, if so, in only an attenuated sense. This limitation can, however, be compensated for by teaching which is so realistic that our students may, through sympathetic imagination, enter into the experiences of others— in the past as well as in the present. Thus they may internalize thoughts and values and reflect upon them—turn them over and about, examine their meaning, motivation, purpose, and consequences. (That this does not mean they must agree with the ideas or actions of others I took pains to emphasize.)

The need for operational aims. The idea of operational aims and functional learning is old in such fields as geography, geology, physics, chemistry, in fact in all the bodies of knowledge which readily permit an operational acquaintance with the objects of their inquiry. These fields have their laboratories, but about all the social studies can provide are *observatories*. Despite the fact that we often talk of the community as an experimental area, it is that chiefly in the sense that we can do little more than observe the experiences or the experiments of human beings. We can do little to set up laboratory experiences or experiments. We must depend pretty much upon history to provide us with experiments "on the fly"—and catch them if we can. But the things we may observe and, in a sense, experiment with are by that token no less important. They are only more restricted in the sense that we cannot plan neat experimental and control situations, observe or manipulate them, and discover their alternative effects. That is why social study is often so quiet, sometimes so quiet as to be almost unreal. Hence, all the more reason that aims be stated operationally, within the limits of what can be done in quiet study about them. What field trips and other aids to instruction may offer on this score we shall discuss later.

Some of our difficulty lies in the fact that social education, unlike medicine, has no *specifics*. That is, we do not know what particular activity will contribute directly to the realization of a given aim. The distinction between "knowledge about" and "acquaintance with" throws considerable light on our problem. The latter kind comes through participation—imaginative or real. Of the two, it is the least spectator-like. Of the former kind of knowledge we have far too much—from athletics and voting to social learning.

Aims become real through and in action. It is *through* and *in* activity that aims come to be real. They become operational in the sense that, through activities of various kinds, aims *arise*, come into view, and may be worked toward. Thus meaning involves *doing*, as mind involves *mind-ing*. (The meaning of "mind the baby" is to be engaged in some activity toward the baby; similarly toward an assignment in social study.) How pathetic, then, that we find teachers who conceive of activities—other than listening and reading—as more or less gratuitous additions to the apparatus of teaching-learning. This is not to suggest that listening and reading are not activities and worthy ones, but they alone often fail to satisfy the "itch of youth to be doing something."

Operational aims illustrated.   How then may aims be stated so that facts may be *represented*, as well as *presented*? How can they be made *evidence* of something besides themselves? How can they induce role-playing—overt or covert? The answer to these questions lies in what we may do to connect them with an experience, or call it an *experiment*.

Suppose the aim has to do with critical thinking. It is not enough to state it as "learning to think." So stated, it offers no bill of particulars. But if the skills implicit in and necessary for "learning to think" be set forth the student will get explicit instructions as to what he is to learn to *do*, namely: discriminate between fanciful and realistic thinking, identify *non sequitur* conclusions in samples of his own and others' reasoning, learn to use the syllogism in order to identify the premises in his reasoning and test his conclusions in the light of them, and set forth clearly the criteria by which one decides what constitutes valid evidence of proof. Such words as discriminate, identify, use, test, and set forth imply quite specific be-haviors. In this sense aims which are stated operationally are stated in behavioral terms. If it is behavior we wish to change and discipline through social study our aims must be stated so that they at least suggest, if they do not explicitly indicate, the behavior which must be engaged in to realize them. To engage in such behaviors as these is to play specific roles. That they are not as dynamic as we might wish they were is a fact we must face. Your obligation is to make them as dynamic as possible.

Objects of study vary in just the degree to which they may be known through more or less dynamic kinds of activities. Computing the increase in railroad mileage, figuring the rate of population increase or the changed ratio of owned to rented farms or residences, comparing tariff rates of cer-tain commodities under higher or lower duties, dividing the tax dollar into the various expenditures to which it is put in local, state, and national budgets, making maps, drawing graphs of family expenditure for food, clothing, medical care, and the like for different income brackets, and making definitions involve the kinds of behavior to which I refer. To these may be added the more imaginative behaviors and roles involved in appreciating the difficulty Washington had in holding his army together, of the various feeling reactions in the Senate and in the country generally to the Webster-Hayne debate or, outside the walls of the Congress, to the Lincoln-Douglas debates, sensing the beliefs of opposing groups in the current discussion between those who support the principle of voluntary interstate conservation programs and those who support the federal form, or feeling what discrimination in education or employment means to the one who is affected by such a policy.

Aims are influenced by the nature of assignments. The possibility of students engaging in such overt or covert behaviors or roles depends, of course, on the nature of the assignments you make. If they are only in terms of pages rather than in terms of themes, situations, and problems they will deaden, discourage, and make well-nigh impossible what I think of as *personal* learning. The concept of *coverage* in teaching must then give way completely to the concept of *meaning* in all the terms implied above. As I observed earlier, too much teaching is about too much which lasts too short a time.

The principle of *operationalism* does not, of course, give us our aims.[12] But it does give us insight into the importance of stating them in terms that permit students to *do* something about them and thus real-ize them.

Some concluding propositions about aims. The following propositions about aims may be made:

1. Aims must grow out of existing conditions, that is, out of activities already going on; otherwise they cannot be ends *in* action. They must take full account of what newspaper men call "the local angle" or the merchant's concept of "the point of sale." This view is implicit in George H. Mead's observation that "you cannot build up a society out of elements which lie outside the individual life process."

2. Aims must take account of the "readiness" of the student. This is the matter of their *meaning* to the student rather than merely how old or mature he is. It is obvious that the meaning of aims is advanced if they are stated in terms which permit action.

3. Aims, as ends-in-view, cannot be completely known by the student before he is involved in an attempt to realize them. This does not outlaw lesson plans

[12] A heated debate is now going on among social scientists over the meaning of operational knowledge. I have illustrated rather than defined what I understand it to mean. I do not understand that it requires that all social understanding be expressed in statistical form—by operating with numbers and other mathematical or abstract symbolic forms. My view is that such operations may be mental, manual, or verbal. See P. W. Bridgman, *The Logic of Modern Physics*, and his article, "Operational Analysis," in *Philosophy of Science*, April, 1936 (Vol. V). See also Geo. A. Lundberg, "Operational Definitions in the Social Sciences," *American Journal of Sociology*, XLVII, No. 5 (March, 1942), and Harry Alpert, "Operational Definitions," *ibid.*, XVLII (May, 1942).

and units of instruction prepared beforehand. It does, however, suggest that they contain the proper expansion joints in order to meet unforeseen conditions. Aims must *come* to the student rather than, as we so often assume, be *given* to him. They are, in effect, generated in and through activity. It is the function of aims to release the action which is potential in the student.

4. Aims must be both particular and general in quality. This is not the kind of *general* which is abstract in the sense of being obscure and abstruse. It is general in the sense of being alive with connections; general in the way that brings particulars into families and enhances their meanings; general in the sense that concepts become working ideas. Aims are not only worked *toward* by the student but may, if stated in operational terms, be worked *with* as guides to understanding and action. They must help the student organize his experience; they are general in that sense.

5. Aims should suggest and permit, when appropriate to their nature, co-operative and joint effort. This is not a never-to-be-broken principle but one applied when sensible. The student should, of course, develop independence of thought but it may be recalled that co-operative and joint activity provides the challenge and stimulus in which such thought is generated.

Three major aims.   The aims of social study may be divided into three major groups: factual knowledge, understanding or insight, and skills. Factual knowledge is the content, understanding or insight represents its meaning, and skills are the means by which its meaning is established.

Skill knowledge includes such abilities as these: generalizing within the limits of valid evidence; making valid inferences which includes the elementary skills of logic; defining concepts; distinguishing between statements of fact and statements of preference (what is, and what ought to be); imagining hypotheses and using them in the search for data which will explain some situation, relationship, or process; distinguishing between denotative and connotative terms; using appropriate analogies; employing judgment as well as suspending it; framing definitions; and distinguishing between reliable and unreliable evidence. Every unit of instruction will, if properly conceived and constructed, provide practice in each of these.

Effective and affective aspects of knowledge.   Both skill and understanding knowledge have their *effective* and *affective* dimension. That is, they have a *knowing* and a *feeling* quality. What students *know* lends itself to being shared and hence tested formally more easily than what they *feel*. What they feel consists in their interests, appreciations, attitudes, and beliefs. These are much more private than what they know. They constitute what I think of as the *wisdom* aspect of knowledge. They are the ways in which knowledge is held and the way in which it provides a unique kind of intellectual and moral dynamics. They are the *ultimates* of learning.

Affective knowledge ought not to be judged. Students may be judged in terms of both skill and understanding at the knowing but not at the *feeling* level. We should seek to discover what their interests, appreciations, attitudes, and beliefs are respecting both skill and understanding. But we have no right to "pass" or "fail" or qualify in any way their affective learning. That is theirs: private and sacred. It is, however, a clue to the effectiveness of our teaching. The only thing we have a right to do with it is to use it as the basis for further teaching, in so far as it reveals a quality of thought and feeling which is at variance with the consensus of "the choice of thoughtful men about what they would have life be and to what ends they would have men shape their intelligent activities."

Effective and affective need to be understood. It is a common practice for teachers to list interests, appreciations, attitudes, and beliefs for each unit of study. Sometimes, as I remarked in Chapter X, these appear to have little bearing on the objects to be understood and in the service of which the skills of inquiry are used. Moreover, I have yet to find in them the distinction made between effective and affective learning. I read much about the "effective citizen" discussed under the rubrics of attitudes, appreciations, and interests. These certainly contribute to his effectiveness but, it seems to me, in *affective* ways. Until the distinction between effective and affective learning is understood we shall not know what basis we are using for qualifying the performance of students.

I find such things as the following listed under the "effective" aspects of learning: a feeling of responsibility to do certain things, belief in the goodness of certain actions, open-mindedness toward certain changes, cheerfulness in supporting certain causes, accepting disappointment, failure, criticism, and the like. All these are worthy but I cannot believe that they qualify as legitimate ground for *grading* a student's work. I do not mean to quarrel about words. I seek only to indicate that such results of teaching as these are affective as well as effective. The meanings which are attached to these terms are the crux of the matter.

We need to suggest attitudes, interests, and beliefs. That some of the things which I have called the affective dimensions of both skill and understanding knowledge may be identified and listed in units of study I agree. But in seeking to do that, we should take full account of an observation made earlier, namely that students learn much more, and many things different from those we think we teach or even intend to. What we need to do is to suggest what some attitudes, interests, and beliefs might be. How we can go beyond that I do not understand. We should certainly wish to raise the horizon of every phase of their affective learnings but to seek to make inclusive-exclusive listings of them is, as I view the problem, quite beyond both our ken and our right.

The central task. If we stress skill and understanding and seek to assess the quality of our students' responses in these matters we shall have task enough. The depth and profundity of each will take them far down the road to "right" affective consequences. But this can never be guaranteed, any more than their effective learning can be.

Can virtue be taught? These observations raise the question which has intrigued men since the days of Socrates: Can virtue be taught? That it can be taught *about* I am certain but that virtue will certainly follow on that account I cannot accept. The teacher's obligation is to make that precious value we call *knowledge* available about things which matter to the dignity of man. The spirit, the effectiveness, and the dedication with which this is done will go far in bringing about the great metamorphosis of education, the turning of knowledge into wisdom. This is the nearest we can come to teaching virtue. Consonant with my view about the nature of attitudes (or call them beliefs) I am forced to take the position that "moral education" must be implicit rather than explicit.

CHAPTER XVII

How Well Did You Teach?
Testing and Evaluating

THE BIAS WHICH is implicit in the title of this chapter ought to be made explicit. It is meant to suggest that the quality of your teaching is quite as much subject to being tested and evaluated as the quality of learning by your students. This does not mean that the entire onus of "bad learning" nor full credit for "good learning" falls on you. It means only that teaching and learning are mutually related. Hence teaching is tested and evaluated when learning is, and vice versa.

By this token, testing and evaluating are not to be viewed as punitive devices in the nature of "the goblins 'll git you, ef you don't watch out." Nor does it permit the doomsday approach which will be commented on shortly.

Testing and evaluating are different. Between testing and evaluating there is a great difference. The first connotes *asking;* the second, *judging.* The only genuine function of asking is to provide a basis for judging. No matter how "objective" a test may be, your evaluation of the student's performance on it can be sublet to no machine or other mechanical device.

However difficult judging may be, testing is also difficult. Its difficulty lies first in the fact that the ultimate concern of the teacher ought to be in the growth in goodness and wisdom of those who have been taught. For this, pencil-and-paper devices can take you only part way. Professor Fred Clarke writes that "to test Civics [by which I understand him to mean any of the social studies] by a written examination is to put the crown on absurdity." [1] He may well have had in mind Montaigne's observation that

---

[1] Fred Clarke, *Foundations of History Teaching* (New York: Oxford University Press, copyright 1929), p. 21.

"the true mirror of our speech is the course of our lives," for it is the operational value of all knowledge which is the pre-eminent value we seek. But, despite the wisdom of Clarke and Montaigne, you must rely heavily on pencil-and-paper means of testing and evaluating.

Your difficulty is further increased by reason of the fact that your students often understand more than they know. But do not be too much daunted by these or other difficulties. Take full account of what somewhat formal testing permits you to know about your students. Use formal tests but use them wisely.

Right and wrong conceptions. The purpose of testing and evaluating is not that of separating the "sheep" from the "goats," dividing a class into those who "passed" and those who "failed," or of devising lesson units merely as difficulties to be overcome. The obligation of teaching, of which testing and evaluating are integral parts, has become one of discovering the "right education" for the "right pupil" under the "right teacher." While levels of achievement must be set, the ultimate success of an education in the social studies ought not to be measured merely by the "passing" or "failing" of examinations. It should seek to provide the kind of education from which each student is capable of receiving the maximum profit. For this conception of social education, the traditional type of examination which stressed chiefly memory, if not memory only, is totally inappropriate. Testing must be diagnostic of a great range of abilities.

The purposes of testing and evaluating. The purposes of testing and evaluating are five: (a) to find out how your teaching has gone, (b) to find out what each student has mastered by way of substantive knowledge, understandings, or insights, and intellectual and other skills, (c) to inform you as to the ways you may help individual students, (d) to help you improve units, courses, and whole curricula, and (e) to provide a record.[2]

Misconceptions about testing and evaluating. Many misconceptions are still widely held concerning testing and evaluating. Among them are such as the following: [3]

1. *Evaluation and measurement are limited to pencil-and-paper tests of information, interpreted generally as "true" or "false" statements of fact.* The acquisition of facts is not, nor has it ever been, the cardinal concern of an education in any field of knowledge. This is not to demote facts but rather to insist

---

[2] See Max Marshall, *Two Sides to a Teacher's Desk*, p. 157. Professor Marshall's chapter on "Evaluation" is both gay and useful.

[3] I have drawn on the insights of my colleague, Professor Harold B. Dunkel, for these remarks and added some of my own. See his article, "Common Misconceptions About Testing and Evaluation," *School and Society*, 57, (May, 29), 1943.

that what they mean and what attitudes and action they inform is their ultimate function. Skills, interests, personality traits, and a host of other characteristics are legitimate objects of concern and for the discovery of their kind and quality testing devices have been developed.

2. *Tests can tell the experienced and competent teacher nothing* (or little) *more than can be found out through "living with a class" and through interviews, and hence that formal evaluation is a waste of time.* While experience and competence are valuable, they do not constitute omniscience and there may be some things which they do not tell us about our students. Tests of all sorts can, however, help us get information quickly and efficiently. Certain kinds of information provide initial and all but indispensable data about our students which the wisest intuition cannot provide. Furthermore, it can be funded, that is, recorded and preserved. It can give us an initial bench mark for judging how and what to teach as well as the "kind of person" the student is. Being funded, such information may be used by teachers other than those who collected it originally. Whatever evidence we can get about a student by as "objective" means as possible will serve as a check and corrective on more subtle and informal appraisals we may make about him. We can "spread ourselves" only so far and if we depend on only our native talent for judging students we may miss some of them as well as some part of each of them. Try as we will, we cannot get as close to some students on a personal and informal basis as we might wish. In order to know them, as the best testing devices will permit us, we must know how to make and use such devices.

3. *Testing takes too much time away from teaching, which is our main business and that for which students come to school.* But teaching and testing are not mutually exclusive activities. Tests can be teaching as well as testing devices. This will be the case, however, only if tests are viewed as diagnostic and are useful to the student as well as to the teacher in revealing strengths and weaknesses. They will not serve this purpose if the teacher uses them only as the basis for assigning a "grade" and/or the student looks on them only in terms of "what did I get?" If they are used as diagnostic devices they may serve all the four functions noted earlier. One of the major functions of testing and evaluating is to make known to the student where he is, where he ought to go and what changes are involved in his getting there.

4. *Tests are an attempt to mechanize teacher-student relations and hence rule out the rapport, camaraderie, and informal insights which the skilled teacher can gain from purely personal contacts with students.* This alarm arises from a misapprehension and a misconception about testing and evaluating. Tests are not infallible and provide no substitute for sound common sense. They need always to be checked against the kind of evidence we can get about a student by knowing him as personally as possible. No test gives more than probability; none gives certainty. Furthermore, no tests serve us with "answers"; rather they provide the bases for a number of cues and hypotheses which require further investigation and follow-up. Tests are as much points of departure for teaching as they are terminal appraisals of what has been taught and learned. Their results bear immediately on ways we may help individual students. But no test can replace the teacher. They are only aids to better teaching.

5. *A certain magic effectiveness inheres in the administration of tests even if the teacher does nothing about the results.* This misconception is not as much the "straw man" it may appear to be. Tests are not infrequently administered because "it is the thing to do"—they are "in style" or the prevailing fad. Such a view is less and less in evidence but still persists in places. But, taken at its worst, such a use of tests may reveal a sign of growth. If comprehensive testing is begun there is a fair chance that some of its results may be ploughed back, not only into courses and syllabi but in the whole range of human relations in the school.

6. *You cannot measure any of the really important things which teachers wish to find out about students.* This position was more tenable in the days of the true-false examination but is no longer valid. Some of the "really important things" can now be learned, but not *all* and no sensible proponent of testing and evaluating would take any such position. We need to recall that tests give us probabilities, not certainties; but they give us a wider range of probabilities than we can get without them. True enough, you cannot always buy the test you need or want. But the "mail order" or "you can buy 'em wholesale" notions about tests is, happily, becoming a thing of the past. "Home-grown" and "hand-made" tests are coming increasingly into use. Indeed, you will find them more appropriate to many phases of your work than those which can be bought. The development of them requires good common sense, their experimental use, much perseverance in order to get "the bugs" out of them, and not a little ingenuity. But a teacher without ingenuity cannot even design a useful unit of instruction, not to speak of designing ways of testing and evaluating its effectiveness.

The steps in testing and evaluating.   Testing and evaluating involve the following steps:

1. Formulate your objectives under the three major categories of factual knowledge, understanding or insights, and intellectual skills. To these may be added interests and attitudes. However, consonant with the view expressed in Chapter XVI, these latter two objectives are not to be used to affect the student's academic standing.

Your objectives should, then, represent much more than a sampling of content to be tested for memorization. Furthermore, they should be stated in operational terms for it is the student's ability to demonstrate certain behaviors in which you ought to be interested.

2. Imagine and formulate situations which will permit such behaviors to be demonstrated. If this is done your objectives will be relieved of vagueness and ambiguity and you will respect the operational principle.

It is all but self-evident that the precision you achieve in testing rests with the precision with which you imagine and formulate test situations. If you are not sure of your aims you cannot, of course, be precise in the fashioning of test situations. If you should approach the obligation to formulate a test with the query, "My, oh me, what shall I ask them?" it is pretty clear that you are unclear as to what you have undertaken to teach. In such a case, you may be importuned to give them an ambiguous essay question or dash off a miscellany of true-false items with little certainty in your mind as to the bearing of either on the range of factual knowledge, the nature of understandings or insights, or the intellectual skills you may hold as your objectives.

This is the doomsday approach. You must "turn in a grade" and so you concoct a test. Genuine testing and evaluating are not achieved by such a method. Certainly, the fact that you face a deadline for handing in grades is the least legitimate among the reasons you might assign to such a gesture. Although grading periods come at regular periods, say every four to six weeks or at the end of the semester, testing and evaluating are appropriate any time you wish to determine how your teaching has gone, what your students have learned, or how you may gain evidence which will help you help individual students and improve your own work as teacher. A record only for the sake of a record is mere academic bookkeeping.

3. Submit these test situations across the entire range of objectives (although not necessarily at any one time or in any single test) to your students. Thus you will offer *tests of situations*. These situations should be a representative sample of the objectives which they seek to test. The emphasis here is on their being representative. You cannot test every possible situation any more than you can teach all "the facts." Hence you must seek to provide a representative sample of situations.

Tests of understanding or insight and intellectual skills should be fairly independent of what Professor Ralph W. Tyler calls "parochial content." This means that the situations should be drawn from sources different from but, of course, of the same kinds or families as those from which the original instructional materials were drawn. The reason for this is obvious: teaching is teaching the transfer of learning, hence, your tests should seek to reveal whether your students can apply or transfer certain learnings from the situations in which they were originally instructed to *new* but similar ones. Otherwise you may be testing only their ability to recall.

The reliability of your tests will depend on two factors: the *number* of items in a given test and the *variety* of situations. It is impossible to lay down a fixed rule as to the "right" number of items in a test. If, for example, you are testing for an understanding of concepts or terms you should assure yourself about the number which will constitute a representative sample—more than three and perhaps less than thirty. Subsequent tests of the same understanding can, of course, extend the sampling and increase the total number of items. Likewise, if you seek to test your students' ability to establish the "goodness of proof" of certain propositions or conclusions you would, in a given test and over a series of such tests, give careful thought to the number and the variety of situations in which such an ability might be demonstrated.

4. Interpret the responses of your students in terms of as specific criteria as possible. (See the following summary for some of these.)

5. Report the results of your evaluation to your students.

Except for the record which is provided, all testing and evaluating has a *diagnostic* function. Every test should be followed by a thorough discussion of the strengths and weaknesses which it reveals for individual students or the class as a whole, if such be the case. Such a diagnosis is best done in such a way as not to embarrass any student. It is legitimate diagnosis, not an inquisition in which you and your students are co-operatively engaged.

Such a diagnosis, done in class (or in consultation privately with those students whose poor responses seem to warrant it), has two main concerns: to measure the student's progress and indicate his level and quality of mastery of the objectives under examination. Progress is a matter of "better" work. The matter of the level or quality of mastery is more difficult. It raises, rather than settles the question as to whether you should set absolute standards for mastery, or set different levels for students of different abilities. Of these two functions, the first, namely progress, presumes some "floor" below which a student should not fall or a "ceiling" toward which you expect him to rise. My only comment on this point is that you distinguish between these two functions or bench marks. The standards by which you will evaluate a student's "final" position are, for the most part, set by administrative officers although such standards may permit you considerable margin of latitude in interpreting them.

My position is not that "anything goes." There must be, in every legitimate teaching-learning enterprise, a "floor" below which you cannot permit a student to fall and still "pass." But the "floor" for a given student may be a variable one, although his "average" may still be lower than the standards for "passing" permit. You are under a sacred professional obligation to share with your students, as well as with the administrative officers of your school, the criteria by which their work was qualified. If a student must repeat a grade or a subject, his teacher (who may be you) ought to know, as clearly as they can be recorded and made available, the definitive characteristics of his varying abilities.

What indices should you use to report a student's achievement to him? Quantitative indices, e.g., 96, 88, 72, or 45 always require interpretation in terms of the qualities of behavior which they represent. If your school uses only such numerical indices (often translated into A, B, C, D, or Fail) you will have to abide by that logic. But that need not deter you from reporting to your students the particular quality of response which was "worth" a given numerical score. Such qualities as the following come to mind: ability to draw valid inferences from a paragraph of material on an historical trend, a social process, or a social problem; elementary skill in logical reasoning demonstrated by the ability to identify flaws in simple syllogisms or to construct logically correct ones; "place knowledge" in the area of geo-ecological study; historical mindedness, that is, the ability to identify men and events and know what was "before" and what was "after" something; the establishing of casual relationships—in short, many kinds of evidence that learning has been solid and that it has transferred.

We need to take our cue from the methods of the physician. He diagnoses in order to prescribe. So should the teacher. The physician does not tell the patient or patient's parents or spouse that he is "A, B, C, D, or F" respecting his bodily functions. He tells him (or them) in precise diagnostic terms what is wrong with the patient's physiology and/or biology and what should be done to bring him to an improved state of health. This is a theory of testing and evaluating which teachers might well emulate. The problem in a nutshell is this: if a grade is a symbol, of what specific behavior is it a symbol?

The time for such diagnoses should, ideally, be set by the initiation of a unit (when a pretest is appropriate), some point in time within a unit to get your bearings and give your students their bearings, and/or to terminate a unit.

Whether you give a "final" examination at the end of a semester or at the end of the year will depend on the kinds of general and over-all evidence you believe appropriate. But in no instance should your motivation be that of testing only to provide the basis of a grade. A grade will be assigned and it will reflect your evaluation but the mark will, per se, tell neither you nor your students anything about specific achievement or mastery.

6. Use your evaluations of student performance for whatever evidence they suggest for needed revisions in unit construction and content, as well as for revision of courses and entire curricula. Thus your findings will be ploughed back in such a way as to improve both teaching and learning.

The structure of testing and evaluating—a summary. The structure or anatomy of testing and evaluating may now be set forth, with emphasis on the phases shown in the tabular presentation.

The Abilities to Be Tested (1)	The Kinds of Situations with Which to Confront Students (2)	Content of a Test (3)	Criteria for Evaluating Student Responses (4)
Identify assumptions.	A political speech or editorial in which assumptions are implicit rather than explicit.	The kinds of situations suggest the nature of the content. It may range from statistical tables through charts and graphs to case studies and political and economic theories. It may be geographic, historical, economic, political, sociological, or psychological. Certain behaviors manifest in field trips and in research projects, as well as those demonstrated by term papers, may be observed and evaluated.	These vary according to the content and potentials of a given test. For No. 4 (in Column 1) they would be truth or falsity, accuracy, inclusiveness, and completeness. For No. 7 they would be the kinds of social views revealed in the preferences given as well as the consistency of preferences. For No. 2 they would be of a similar kind. For No. 8 they would be accuracy or correctness of definitions. For No. 11 they would be such as these: Relevance: are the principles identified relevant to the situations? Comprehensiveness: have the major principles been identified? Understanding: are the implications of the principles understood? Objectivity: what is the evidence respecting freedom from bias and the discounting of slogans and clichés? Caution: is ability to suspend judgment revealed? and Attitude toward evidence: what
Reveal awareness of bias.	Same as above, or a series of statements like those given in Chapter XI.		
Judge the "goodness" of proof.	Statements about the need for a given tax, reasons for delinquency, etc., with supporting proof or reasons.		
Recall factual information	Matters of who, what, when, and where.		
Determine the logical consistency of an argument	The same as No. 3, but with the emphasis on types of logic employed.		
Interpret the meaning of data: verbal, graphic, or statistical	Charts, graphs, maps, case studies, editorials, etc.		
Reveal preferential position	A speech, editorial, statements like those given in Chapter XI, etc.		

The Abilities to Be Tested	The Kinds of Situations with Which to Confront Students	Content of a Test	Criteria for Evaluating Student Responses
(1)	(2)	(3)	(4)
8. Define terms or concepts	Give a list of terms to be defined or give definitions and ask for the terms.		discrimination is shown specting kinds of evidenc
9. Reveal understanding of a theory	Statements about penal methods, causes of delinquency, the operation of a tax, etc.		It is not suggested that such criteria can be appli to every test of the kin suggested in Column From this fact, it follo that tests draw from representative sample situations each of whi permits some more or le unique ability to be vealed.
10. Judge the validity of generalizations	General statements about human nature, authority, cause and effect relations, etc.		
11. Apply principles	Descriptive statements to which certain principles may or may not apply.		The abilities identified Column 1 are among tho but are not meant to all which the social studi afford. It is also appare that the line between so of them cannot be sharp drawn. Thinking cann be cut up into complete inclusive-exclusive phas or segments.
12. Show acquaintance with "best" sources of data	Description of a research problem in which certain data will be needed.		

The forms of tests. Something may now be said about the various forms of tests. Unfortunately, the view is sometimes held that the form of a test is more important than its content. The fact is that they are mutually related. The first question to ask, however, is, "What do I wish to learn about my students?" rather than "Which test form should I use?" Diagnostic knowledge about your students is your end; the form of the test you use is your means.

The chief characteristics of various test forms, the so-called new-type, and the essay may be stated as follows. Some cautions and advice are also given.

TRUE-FALSE

(a) This is, rightly or wrongly, the most widely used form. The fact that it is easiest to construct does not guarantee that it is the best form. It is, however, easy to construct only if you consider it in a quite uncritical light, namely the recall of inert statements whose truth or falsity the student is to judge. The more dynamic the items, the harder it is to construct. It is perhaps the least appropriate for testing and evaluating in the social studies since only the "plainest" and most "self-evident" fact-statements can be readily scored by a simple True-or-False response.

(b) It lends itself to "chance answering" which can only in part be corrected for. Incorrect responses may prove the student's ignorance but correct ones may represent guesses. A greater number of items gives some insurance, through comprehensiveness, that the "guessing" student may be caught in his own device. But this makes the test too cumbersome for general use. A score of "minus 1" for incorrect responses, zero for failure to answer, and "plus 1" for correct responses is advised. The "minus 1" is designed to discourage guessing.

(c) It tends to place emphasis on "photographic recall."

(d) It can be used to test opinions as well as facts. In that case the response "undecided" should also be provided. It is quite as significant to know what students are *not* certain about as that about which they are. Such an adaptation is ideal for a short pretest in a unit or field in which student opinion is especially important to know.

(e) It has some advantage over the "multiple-choice" form since in the latter the "wrong" answer may be somewhat difficult to disguise as such. Hence the True-False test is recommended in such instances.

(f) If students are to write T or F, they should be advised to do so clearly since a "lazy" T may look like an F, and vice versa. Mimeographed or dittoed test forms may be prepared which require only that the student draw a circle around the appropriate letter, T or F, given in the margin.

(g) Be as certain as you can that the statements are unambiguous. If you say: "The Sherman Anti-Trust Act, passed in 1870, declared combinations in restraint of trade illegal" the student cannot be sure whether you are testing a year or the provisions of the act. The statement is better phrased as follows: "The Sherman Anti-Trust Act which declared combinations in restraint of trade illegal was enacted in 1870."

(h) Write no "catch questions."

(i) Avoid "bookish" language. It is easily recognized and if the question is answered correctly, it may reveal only that the student has remembered the answer by having read and remembered the words of the text.

(j) Do not use such terms as "never," "none," "always," and "everyone." If you do, it is pretty certain that they will identify an item which is palpably false. Social studies facts are seldom of such an "over-all" or "all out" nature. There may, of course, be exceptions.

(k) Avoid double-barreled statements such as is given in (g) above.

(l) Avoid such ambiguous terms as "good," "bad," and "important." In any event, true or false statements are neither "good" nor "bad"; they are only "true" or "false." We assume that every statement worth the testing is "important."

RECALL (memory)

(a) A test of recall only gives no evidence of the student's measure of the importance or significance of an item.

(b) Recall items are appropriate in identifying men or events, and in such connection as "who," "what," "when," and "where."

(c) As in True-False, avoid "bookish" language.

(d) Take full account of the fact that recall tests test only memory. How much stress do you wish to put on it and with reference to what?

COMPLETION

(a) The variety of answers to this type are so many that you may get responses which you did not anticipate. What do you do then? If you ask: "Abraham Lincoln was born in ...." the student may reply, "Kentucky," "1809," or "a log cabin." How can he know what is required?

(b) The completion test is too much chiefly a test of what "the teacher holds in his hand behind his back." It is more a puzzle than a test.

(c) Recommended never to be used.

MULTIPLE CHOICE

(a) One of the best test forms because it lends itself to many uses, e.g., inference, understanding, judgment, and fine discrimination.

(b) It is easy to score.

(c) Requires unusual skill and precision in construction because every response should have the appearance of being the "right" one. If the items do not have this quality, the student's choices are, to that degree, limited and his chance of answering correctly is enhanced.

(d) Be sure that each option fits grammatically and might, for that reason, be the "right" one.

(e) Avoid "bookish" language. Likewise avoid making the "right" choice either the shortest or the longest. It is best that all options be of approximately the same sentence length.

(f) Options greater than seven in number are of no advantage. Moreover, it is very difficult to write seven discriminating statements each of which may plausibly be "right." Five options are "about right" but three will provide a difficult task. Less than three is not enough.

MATCHING

(a) Provide a few more items as options to be matched than those given in the left hand of the two columns. Avoid using more than ten items in either column.

(b) Offer options that might be correct in more than one instance but, if you do, be sure to make this known in the instructions.

(c) The items in both the left and right columns must be mutually homogeneous. Do not require students to match men and events, dates and treaties, events and locations in the same test.

(d) Construct your options so that any given response might be satisfied by more than one "right" one. This cannot, of course, hold unless the items in both lists are of the same family or class of objects, i.e., mutually homogeneous.

ESSAY

The wide use of new-type tests has brought some teachers to conclude that essay examinations are obsolete. A review of this position is in order.

The proper use of the essay examination seems to be implicit in the meaning of the word "essay." Certainly it does not suggest that it should be used for recall of factual data. If memory of these is to be tested, one or more of the new-type examinations should be used.

The essay type lends itself admirably to the discussion of principles and points of view, the interpretation and analysis of ideas, comparison of principles or propositions, and the organization and interpretation of factual knowledge. It is also appropriate for testing the student's ability to express himself cogently and convincingly. In sum, essay examinations might well be classified under types such as outline, description, comparison, contrast, explanation, interpretation, discussion, evaluation, and summary.[4]

Unlike the new-type tests, essay examinations are relatively easy to construct. They are, however, more difficult to evaluate. Several factors account for this difficulty. Among them are such as these: (*a*) subtle subjective factors tend to distort the objectivity of the teacher's judgment; (*b*) the criteria of evaluation, however sharply defined, are difficult to hold constant given the wide variety of student responses; and (*c*) fatigue may set in to dull the precision of application of criteria.[5]

Essay examinations may be improved by respecting the following principles:

1. Do not use them to test chiefly or only the recall of factual knowledge. They are better used to require that the student perform some intellectual operations on "the facts." These may be given in the test or supplied by him. If you wish to provide "the facts" this may be done by the "open book examination." It is then the student's obligation to "do something" to them. A student may be quite able to perform such operations—see below under (2)—but may not be able, at the time, to recall the necessary factual data. In that event he is embarrassed in revealing his ability to interpret, analyze, or explain. The point at issue here is that you ought to know what you wish to test and are testing, e.g., memory and such abilities as have been mentioned or only memory. If you wish to test the student's ability to recall as a precondition for his doing other things, take full account of the fact that those are the demands of the test.

2. Make as explicit as possible the kind of skill you wish the student to demonstrate. Devise an essay question for each skill or make it clear that several abilities are to be demonstrated in the same essay. Among these would be such as interpretation, analysis, evaluation, and/or comparison.

[4] See J. W. Wrightstone, "Are Essay Examinations Obsolete?" *Social Education*, September, 1937.

[5] It should be noted that subjective factors are not completely absent in the determination of "right" and "wrong" or "best" answers to new-type tests. Such determinations can, however, be made *before* such tests are administered. New-type tests permit the student to make completely unambiguous responses to questions by using the appropriate symbol or marking the "right" response. In essay responses the student's answers are weighted with his own peculiar language and are less subject to objective marking or evaluation.

3. If the test has more than one part, score each separately.

4. Write out an ideal response to each part of the essay examination or better, prepare several scaled sample responses ranging in quality from "poorest" to "best." Something approximating such a scale of sample responses may be discovered in the students' papers. If these are used they constitute norms of performance which may only approximate the "poorest" or "best" (and qualities in between) responses which you yourself may compose.

5. Use the "guided" or "restricted" type of essay question. Such a structure is illustrated in the following:

> Explain the reasons for the strike in the XYZ industry so as to show the relation between (i) the grievances of the employees, (ii) the policies and practices of management, (iii) the prevailing attitude or sentiment of "the public" as it bore on the strike, (iv) the presence or absence of a rival union, and (v) the quality of leadership of both labor and management.

(Instructions to analyze, interpret, compare, contrast, or evaluate may be given the same kind of specification as are given here to explaining.)

Working bibliography. The task of providing a representative sample of test forms is too unmanageable to be undertaken here. They are of many kinds and are suited to many purposes. Your acquaintance with and skill in devising various tests and learning how to use and evaluate them is a task in itself. In its service there are many excellent resources. Among them are the following:

1. O. K. Buros (Editor), *The Fourth Mental Measurements Yearbook*, Highland Park (New Jersey): The Gryphon Press, 1953. Contains critical reviews of all the important published tests.

2. Benjamin S. Bloom (Editor), *Taxonomy of Educational Objectives*, New York: Longmans, Green & Co., Inc., 1955. Elaborates and discusses a system for classifying educational objectives and gives sample tests for each type of objective.

3. Nelson B. Henry (Editor), *The Measurement of Understanding* (Forty-fifth Yearbook of the National Society for the Study of Education), Chicago: University of Chicago Press, 1946.

4. Ralph W. Tyler and E. R. Smith, *Appraising and Recording Student Progress*, New York: Harper & Brothers, 1942.

5. Benjamin S. Bloom and Lois J. Bruder, *Problem-Solving Processes of College Students*. Chicago: University of Chicago Press, 1950.

6. *Examinations and Their Substitutes in the United States*, Bulletin No. 28. New York: The Carnegie Foundation for the Advancement of Teaching, 1936.

7. Howard R. Anderson (Editor), *Teaching Critical Thinking in the Social Studies*, 13th Yearbook of the National Council for the Social Studies; see also the Yearbooks noted in Chapters XXI to XXVI.

8. *The Social Studies in General Education* (A Report of the Committee on the Function of the Social Studies in General Education for the Commission on Secondary School Curriculum), New York: Appleton-Century-Crofts, Inc., 1940.

9. Horace T. Morse and George H. McCune, *Selected Items for the Testing of Study Skills*, Bulletin No. 15 of the National Council for the Social Studies, September, 1940.

10. William L. Wrinkle, *Improving Marking and Reporting Practices in Elementary and Secondary Schools*, New York: Rinehart & Co., Inc., 1947.

In addition to these resources, such journals as *The School Review, The Social Studies, Social Education,* and *Educational Leadership* frequently contain materials on testing and evaluating. The Educational Testing Service at Princeton University is another excellent resource. Experience suggests that you begin with the simpler forms and give particular attention to the writing of clear and unambiguous items and instructions. Like any skill, the making of tests requires much practice.

Grading on "a curve." A number of aspects of testing and evaluating invite brief discussion. The question arises, "Should you grade 'on a curve'?" The alternative, of course, is to grade in terms of the norms set within a given class. A curve is a "curve of probability" and is appropriate as a basis for the distribution of grades only if the number of students is large enough to give you, in a given class, a "normal distribution" of student abilities. The smaller the class the less is the likelihood that its membership will represent such a normal distribution.

In any event, a curve has no intelligence of its own nor is there any magic in it. It is your task to set standards and use them as the norms by which to judge your students' progress in and mastery of the aims you set. Much will, of course, depend on the policy of the school as set by its administrative officers and teachers as well as the general caliber of its students. Different curricula tend, almost automatically, to set different standards. But in any case there must be standards and you ought to stand by them. It is rank dishonesty to yourself, to your students, and to the aims of social study to employ a scale of standards which is so variable that it ceases to exist as a set of bench marks.

The problem of cheating. What about cheating and what can be done to reduce it? Many of the problems associated with cheating might be solved if a natural and legitimate rather than a frightening and punitive function were given to testing and evaluating. Coupled with these negative qualities is the fact that testing is often, if not always, only of a very formal kind. It is formal in the sense that it is set apart from teaching and learning, and in that it is done in an atmosphere of too great tension and competitiveness. In such a climate, students sense that their fate or fortune rides upon the outcome of every test. This conduces to cheating among students who are, in other matters, quite sincere and honest people. The tense and highly competitive atmosphere seems to invite them to cheat.

Students are more or less success-bound, and moral rules are apt to go by the board in their endeavor to "make the grade," which is done by "getting a good grade."

Certain procedures can be adopted which will minimize cheating. All examinations should be proctored; seating should be spaced wherever and whenever possible; and tests should and can be devised which will make cheating next to impossible. Cheating which originates in copying from smuggled notes can easily be made impossible by giving "problem questions" for which students can make no adequate memoranda which will help them during the test. If, however, all we ask of them are true-false responses, they may both smuggle in answers and "peek" at their neighbors' paper, if their neighbors sit near enough for them to copy from them. The "open book" examination has great merit in and of itself and is a pretty secure guarantee against cheating. The facts are given, hence they need not be "cribbed." It is difficult for a student, under such conditions, to copy an analysis or explanation from a neighbor's paper.

But more than physical devices are available to reduce cheating and to create the climate in which it may not be resorted to. The main factor which will minimize cheating is the creation of a climate and with it that set of expectations which says, implicitly, "Let's see what we can do by way of proving that we have accomplished our objectives." Indeed, a test need not be announced as a test. This can be done by making testing an integral part of all teaching. The almost certain effect will be that objectives will be clarified and their relation to study tasks made clear.

A test as the object of inquiry.   This may be done by making a *test* the object of inquiry. It may be, in effect, a kind of informal dress rehearsal for a somewhat more formal experience in testing but it is sufficient unto itself in this setting. Such a procedure will permit you to concentrate on certain objectives under the guise of a quite normal teaching-learning experience. Not a little of the fear that attaches to a test experience and the cheating which issues from it may be traced to the fact that not until "test time" are students aware of what the objectives of their labors have been—and then it is too late.

The how and why of testing.   Such an inquiry would provide an ideal setting in which to instruct your students in the "how and why" of testing in general and, particularly, in some of the more or less obscure and novel aspects of the new-type tests. There is evidence that students have to learn how to take some of these tests, granted that, if they understood the logic of their organization without formal instruction, they might do well on them.

Testing and reading ability. No test should require that the student should "pass a test" in the interpretation of the structure and instructions relating to a test. An appropriate level of reading ability is, of course, always required for both the instructions and the test itself. You are advised to take full account of your students' abilities in this respect. The alternative to printed tests is not to dictate questions but rather to write all instructions and the test items themselves at the language level which your students can handle. Complexity in either form or language is not the mark of a fair test, rather simplicity and clarity. In order to observe and meet these requirements you may have to revise or remodel some of the standard tests which, in their original form, may be too difficult for your students. Here it may be suggested that, other things being equal, there is no need for you to devise your own tests if the standard and "ready-made" tests suit your situation. But whether you use them without modification or not, they are highly useful in helping you master the rudiments of the art and skill of test construction.

The test analysis just referred to may help much to reduce cheating, even its genuine discouragement. Students may accept a "low grade" without fear or disgrace if, in the analysis, they learn the nature of their errors. You will thus help, rather than punish them for their errors. This procedure will help to redefine a test as the occasion on which a student may learn to ask "How well did I do?" rather than merely "What grade did I get?"

Make it a good and fair game. The substance of these observations may be reported in the remark that testing may become a good and a fair *game*, in the playing of which the student will *learn* rather than merely be "graded." Rightly understood and used, tests are learning devices. If a student gets from them only a "grade" he is given occasion chiefly to vaunt himself on his superiority or become discouraged and unduly apprehensive because he did not "make the grade." The ultimate gain from such analyses is that which comes from both you and your students knowing precisely wherein corrective learning needs to be instituted as well as that certitude which comes from knowing precisely what one has achieved.

Every day is "test day." If testing can be defined and experienced as a good and fair game, every day is, in the nature of the case, test and evaluation day. If that view can be indoctrinated through its practice rather than by its declaration in a frightening, anxiety-producing, and punitive manner, testing and evaluation may become, as they ought to, integral with teaching and learning. We still practice far too much the "retention and return" principle of testing and evaluating. This comes from valuing knowledge as something to be "given back to teacher," rather than to be lived by.

Knowledge, understanding, and skills must, of course, be acquired but not only to be displayed on "test day."

Implicit in all this is the principle that the time to test is, ideally, determined by the need for diagnosis which may come at any time. Testing and evaluating are not, however, primarily temporal matters. They are primarily intellectual matters.

The "terminal" examination. This observation suggests the query, "What is the meaning, nature, and purpose of a terminal examination?" To that it may be replied that all tests are terminal in that they mark the initiation of a unit, its close, or some place "in between." No test is "terminal" in the sense that something may not be gained from it which is useful for both you and your students. Only if tests are considered in this light may they contribute to growth in goodness and wisdom.

Do not despair if you cannot test and measure every phase of your teaching. With your more or less formal testing can go the kinds of informal evaluation which will, while not of the pencil-and-paper kind, help to give you the knowledge and insight into those which depend on those devices. It is integral human beings whom you are not only teaching and testing, but with whom you are also living. Together they constitute the great adventure. In this adventure, many things both formal and informal in kind make it possible for the "word to be made flesh" and dwell with you and your students.

Critical thinking and factual knowledge. In the event that you are troubled by the fact that critical thinking has been stressed in this chapter more than the recall and retention of factual knowledge it may be said that stress need not be placed on intellectual skills at the expense of factual knowledge. As was noted in Chapter XVI, knowledge is tested and given meaning only through the use of the tools of inquiry. To know is, in the final analysis, to know *how* and to know the ground for action, included in which is "the action of thought." [6]

The grading of term papers. A phase of teaching and testing which has not been mentioned is that involved in the "grading" of term papers.

[6] A careful study of the effectiveness of instruction in critical thinking *pari passu*, with ample attention to factual knowledge which provided the "stuff" of thinking, showed the following results: (i) interest in the social studies was increased, (ii) problem-solving skill was not achieved at the expense of acquaintance with factual knowledge, (iii) the number of dropouts decreased, (iv) teachers' conceptions of their task were markedly changed, and (v) no one teacher personality type was shown to be significant. (Hyman M. Chasow, *The Organization of Learning Experiences to Achieve More Effectively the Objective of Critical Thinking in the General Social Science Course at the Junior College Level*, an unpublished doctoral dissertation, Department of Education, the University of Chicago, 1955).

Although they belong to the general category of essays they are not the same. Many times such papers are dull, stereotyped, and quite unimaginative. Nothing less than great patience and fortitude is required to "wade through" many of them.

The importance of the assignment. As in every other phase of teaching-learning, the assignment of term papers or reports is a matter which demands clear and specific identification of what is to be done. If this is made understandable, the criteria by which they will be evaluated are thereby laid down. The object of inquiry must be sharply identified as well as the intellectual operations to be performed on it. This does not require giving back to "teacher" words and phrases which have been put into notebooks. Nor does it require wholesale copying from encyclopedia or other sources. These are proofs only of rote learning, not of independent thought and its organization.

But here, as in all teacher-student relations, the nature of the assignment is greatly conditioned by the quality of rapport which exists. What a student might be willing and able to say over a cup of coffee or a "coke" gives us the standard for what he might be invited to write in a more formal way. If such a "coffee or 'coke' " atmosphere and rapport can be established your students will likely give you what they think rather than what they believe you want them to say and think.

Ideas, not words, are the focus. It is ideas with which you wish them to deal, not with mere words, many of which they do not understand but which when copied perform the function of filling a given amount of "paper space." It were better that your students be caught in the trap of incorrect but fairly clear ideas than in that of mere words. But ideas will not be discussed, clearly or unclearly, if they are not made clear in the assignment. If you can give yourself and your students fair assurance on that score, both you and they are on the way to something worth doing.

This chapter began by remarking on the difficulty of testing and evaluating. The overt social behaviors which it is the ultimate function of the social studies to fashion can be brought into neither the laboratory nor the classroom. Despite this limitation, you can help to create the incentives and forms for them. This is the one step of removal from the affairs of the Great Society to which earlier reference has been made. But it is an important step, however removed it be. It is the step in which interest can be aroused as well as that through which the principles and skills of dedicated living may be rightly indoctrinated. It is faith in such an outcome that will, above all other things, sustain you.

CHAPTER XVIII

The Logic and Sociology of Communication

IT IS APPROPRIATE now to treat certain phases of teaching-learning in the social studies which are common to the entire range of inquiries into human affairs. The first of these phases is the logic and sociology of communication.

Two phases of communication. John Dewey wrote that "of all affairs, communication is the most wonderful." Its wonder lies in the fact that it is the mechanism through which human nature and society come into being. It has two phases, one of which is logical, the other sociological. Dewey calls them the instrumental and the consummatory.[1]

The story of the Tower of Babel illustrates how the logical and the social are related. "The whole earth was of one language, and of one speech." This huge family set about to build a city and a tower whose top "may reach unto heaven." But the Lord, seeing what the people were doing, was displeased and bethought to "confound their language, that they not understand one another's speech." And "the Lord did there confound the language." With their shared means of communication destroyed, the tower was not consummated.

The harm of ambiguous language. The social or consummatory phase of communication may also be injured by the use of ambiguous terms in the same language. An editorial, under the caption "America-Lasters," appeared in a Chicago morning newspaper shortly after the nominating convention of the Democratic party in the summer of 1947. It read in part as follows,

---

[1] *Experience and Nature* (Chicago: Open Court Publishing Co., 1926), p. 166. See the chapter "Nature, Communication and Meaning," pp. 166-207.

Events and speeches at Philadelphia make it manifest that the word "internationalist" is no longer serviceable as a description of a particular kind of politician. . . . Accordingly, we are dropping "internationalist" from the vocabulary of this page because the word means a variety of things to a variety of men. Hereafter, instead of saying that a man believes in internationalism we shall say that he believes in America last. Such a man is an American-Laster. These aren't elegantly formed words but they have the great merit of being free [*sic*] from ambiguity.

If I should say, "But deliver us from evil," you would recognize the phrase as a part of the Lord's Prayer. But if I should say, "And initiate protective measures to safeguard us against any antisocial activities or tendencies to recidivism," no image of the Lord's Prayer or anything else but a jumble of words would come to your mind.[2]

The social depends on the logical. These illustrations illustrate how the consummatory or social phase of communication depends on the quality of its instrumental or logical phase. If we do not know what a person talks *with* we cannot know what he talks *about*. It is, of course, possible, in the latter two illustrations, that the speakers may have had a clear understanding of what they were saying but their language was either so ambiguous or so esoteric that their readers or auditors would hardly know what they meant by what they said.

Meanings are never absolutely definite. However, the meaning of words is probably never absolutely definite. Many of them have about them a "penumbra of doubt." Their meaning depends on their arrowlike character, but arrows which are not too much encumbered by feathers.

Meaning is an *area*, like a target. If it is very clear it may "hit the bull's-eye," but the outlying parts of the area may still be more or less within the intended meaning. They are, however, gradually less and less within it as they lie farther and farther from the bull's-eye. The more precise language becomes, the less of its meaning lies outside the bull's-eye, and the bull's-eye itself grows smaller and smaller. But it never shrinks to a point. There is always a doubtful area, however small, surrounding it.

Scientific and expressive words. What we have a right to expect of words depends on the kind of language which is being used. A rather simple twofold classification identifies two kinds: scientific (logico-experimental) and expressive (emotive). This does not mean that scientific language does not express, but rather that its language comes closer to the bull's-eye than

[2] Ivor Brown, "The Pudderers," *Saturday Review of Literature*, December, 1940, p. 16. See also Samuel T. Williamson, "How to Write Like a Social Scientist," *Saturday Review of Literature*, October 4, 1947, and S. I. Hayakawa, *Language in Action* (New York: Harcourt, Brace and Co., 1941).

expressive language. Whereas scientific language denotes, expressive language connotes. Words which denote leave narrower margins of interpretation than do expressive ones. Words which denote, signify; words which connote, suggest. Thus, if I say "It is twelve o'clock," I signify the time of day; but if I say "The day is half spent," I only suggest the time of day. My words thus differ in the clarity of their reference to time. Scientific language describes, identifies, and permits clear classification. Expressive language is expletive in that it deals in metaphors; it may even be poetic.[3]

Charles H. Cooley has written with insight and beauty about words.

A word is a vehicle, a boat floating down from the past, laden with the thought of men we never saw; and in coming to understand it we enter not only into the minds of our own contemporaries, but into the mind of humanity continuous through time.[4]

Conditions change but words often fail to change. Although I would not wish to mar the beauty of the truth of Cooley's statement, I would observe that "inherited" words and their meanings are not always relevant to contemporary affairs. Thurman Arnold has remarked on our continued use of "the language of private property to describe an industrial army." He cites, for instance, the fact that a man may own an automobile and refer to it as "his car" but he does not know what is under its hood and can neither buy nor run it without depending on a great deal of outside help: the mammoth industrial organization that designed and built it, the finance company which helped him buy it, the refineries and the pipe lines that provide him with gasoline, the filling station and the repair shop, to name only some of the great organizations that assist him. Certainly in this frame of reference the term "private property" has a meaning different from what it had for his pioneer forebears who practiced a high degree of self-sufficiency and hence whose property was "private" in a much more exacting sense of the term.[5]

Meaning and context. As I. A. Richards has phrased it, "a word means the missing part of its context." The seven-letter word "capital" may have any one of four meanings, depending on the context:

[3] See Robert E. Park, "Reflections on Communication and Culture," *American Journal of Sociology*, XLIV (September, 1938). A four-fold classification of language is the following: reportorial (which reports or gives information); expressive (which uses songs, slogans, or terms of a ritual); directive (which gives orders, commands, threats, appeals, or promises); and stylized (which takes the form of such expressions as "So what?" "Do tell," and "O.K."). It is quite difficult to draw a hard and fast line between the expressive and the stylized.

[4] C. H. Cooley, *Social Organization* (Charles Scribner's Sons, copyright 1923), p. 69. See Part II, "Communication," pp. 61-103.

[5] See *The Folklore of Capitalism*, especially pp. 118-135.

> This is the capital city of the state.
> They say that the food at the hotel is capital.
> Capital and labor get along better than they used to.
> Some people do not believe in capital punishment.

As the context varies the meaning of the word is as different as a noun and an adjective and as the quality of food differs from a form of punishment. In every instance the sound is the same. No wonder that Whitehead remarked, "What an appalling task, the correlation of meanings with sounds!" The meaning of a word lies in our knowing how to respond to it, which involves a response to it through its frame of reference. It is thus clear that a *literal* education which is an education only in words is not the same as a *liberal* one.

Language is symbolic. A great deal of the difficulty which we all encounter in the use of words is due to the fact that language is not only a system of words but a system of symbols. Of these there are two kinds: verbal and nonverbal. They are both gestures in the sense that they are not the things to which they refer but rather are ways of denoting or connoting those things.

Verbal gestures are such words as "pretty," "mother," "shoestring," and "winter." Nonverbal gestures are such as a clinched fist, a flag, a monument (in the German it is *Denkmal*, literally "think once"), a wink, a shrug of the shoulders, a white or yellow line down the middle of a highway, and a stop-and-go light. Both verbal and nonverbal gestures have meaning in the sense that they call up images and even patterns of behavior. Both may miss, by a considerable distance, the bull's-eye.

Only man makes and uses symbols. Man is the only creature capable of making and using symbols. Animals react to signs; men respond to symbols. The reactions of animals are only those which they have been conditioned to have; men's responses are also conditioned but do not depend only on their reflexes. Symbols bring objects and their meanings to mind; signs announce the presence of objects. Man lives in a world of both signs and symbols. Storm clouds announce wind and rain; barometers and thermometers supply readings which mean certain atmospheric pressures and temperatures. A sign causes us to think and act *in the face of* the thing signified; symbols cause us to *think about* the thing symbolized, which may be present or absent. The dog in Dr. Park's story in an earlier chapter illustrates this difference. The dog was trained to react only to the command "umbrella" as a sign; he was unable to symbolize it as a "rain-protecting device" and, failing to find it, was unable to substitute a raincoat for it. This would have required his ability to deal with symbols or with a concept. Only the dog's reflexes were conditioned, not his reflections. He could be ex-cited but not in-sighted. Man constructs his symbols. For instance, when he is confronted by an object which has no meaning to him or symbolizes nothing, he says "I can make nothing out of it." That is, he cannot *construe* or construct its meaning.[6]

Some common errors.   Our failure to understand the symbolic nature of words leads us into a variety of errors. Some of the most common of these are the following.

1. Words used as if they had magical power: Teachers sometimes assume that the command "Be quiet" will, like some magical incantation, produce quiet. They fail to take account of the fact that words are sounds (even noises) and do not, as such, have any magical power. Their use in such a case ignores the fact that such factors as fear of or respect for the commanding person and a willingness to respond in accord with such a command are involved.

2. Words without referents: It may be that a word always has some referent but some appear to reach the zero point. Such are the words which are rote-learned. We might avoid this error if we would take Justice Holmes's advice to "think things, not words," which cannot, of course, be taken literally. Charles Peirce once remarked to the effect that good language, by which he meant clearly referential terms, is not only important to good thought but the very essence of it. When we think, we converse with ourselves; hence, if the words or "things" (to follow Holmes) with which we think do not have clear referents we shall be unclear as to what we think about.

Slogans tend to be words without referents except those which the readers or auditors of them supply. But that is the intent of the slogan-maker: he wishes the slogan to be all things to all men. "Keep America Ahead" is such a slogan. Each reader or auditor is free to supply his own image of what it is of which America is to be kept ahead.

3. Words considered to be identical with their referents, or as guarantors of certain facts. This is the error of reification. Shakespeare's "a rose by any other name would smell as sweet" affirms the fallacy of such a fixed and real connection between a word and that to which it refers. The little girl who said that "we have to call it a pig because it is so dirty" did not understand the fallacy she was committing.

4. Emotive words used in place of those with sharp reference: slogans belong to this category as do certain "tag" words such as "egghead," "Communist," to denote a left-winger whom we don't like, instead of a *real* Communist.

Rote learning is only word learning.   The fallacies identified in 2 and 3 deserve more extended discussion. The classic narrative on rote learning was told by William James. He recounts the experience of a friend who

---

[6] See Ernst Cassirer, *An Essay on Man*, pp. 41-62. See also Susanne K. Langer, *Philosophy in a New Key, A Study in the Symbolism of Reason, Rite and Art* (New York: Penguin Books, Inc., 1948). "The Logic of Signs and Symbols" is treated on pp. 42-63.

visited a class in geology in a secondary school. He was disturbed by the teacher's sterile, unimaginative, and rote methods. He asked if he might take over. The text had stated that the center of the earth was in a state of "igneous fusion"—a molten mass. James's friend wished to know what that term symbolized to the students. (The teacher's methods had been only to require them to repeat it in response to his question, "How does one find it in the center of the earth?") He hoped to stimulate some genuine responses, even a little discussion as to the meaning of the term, and so he said, "Suppose you could dig a hole hundreds and hundreds of miles into the interior of the earth; how would you find it there, hotter or colder than on the surface?" He got no response except blank and expressionless faces. He tried again and got the same silence. At this point the teacher, sensing that James's friend must be embarrassed by his lack of success, asked if he might take the class. Then, word for word as the book had it he asked, "How does one find it in the center of the earth?" In chorus, the class responded, "At the center of the earth one finds a state of igneous fusion." There was no symbolism in their response; there was only repetition of words, rote saying. Neither was there genuine communication.

The error of reification.   The view that words are identical with their referents is called reification (*res* meaning "thing" and *facere* meaning "to make"), that is to make the symbol identical with the object to which it refers. This is a form of magic practiced by both advanced and primitive people. Among some primitive cultures it is commonly believed that to stick spears or arrows in the image of an enemy is to inflict pain on the enemy himself. This is reification through nonverbal symbols. Blasphemy is held by some to be a sin not only because of their objection to the curse but because they believe the Deity is actually harmed by it.

Reification illustrated.   Instances of the practice of reification might be cited in abundance. The folk saying, "Speak of the Devil and he's bound to appear," is a form of it. A good deal of advertising is based on reification. The advertisement of a certain beverage announces, "You've earned it; now you can have it." Somehow, to the naïve mind, this declaration is little short of one's actually having it. The pretty girl who graces the advertisements of commodities ranging from the service of banks to cosmetics is not only a "becoming lass"; she all but *becomes* the service or product itself.

But advertising has no monopoly of the use of reification. The political demagogue who promises prosperity, lower taxes, or whatever (with no power or intent to deliver on them) leads the gullible to support him since they have "his word for it." (The late Harry Stack Sullivan, the eminent

psychiatrist, once remarked that "plausibility" is the outstanding characteristic of human beings. It is close kin to gullibility.) During the great depression of the thirties, one of Chicago's leading newspapers seldom, if
ever, used the word "unemployed." Its editorial term was "the idle." One
suspects that it was used in the magic view that the country's millions of
unemployed might thereby be *made* to be the shiftless persons that the
word "idle" suggests.

Reification comes even closer to the classroom when we permit our students to mistake the textbook for the reality with which it is designed to
acquaint them. Rote learning is a kind of reification: the words are the
realities, never mind what they symbolize.

There is also the fatal error which is enacted when students take their
repetition of the oath to the flag as allegiance itself. The phrase, "with
liberty and justice to all," is a great and noble one. But merely repeating
it does not bring those precious things to pass. It is not the same as the
words for it.

The triangle of reference.   We have insisted that the word and the thing
it symbolizes are not the same. They are, of course, closely related, otherwise the word would not be a symbol. The inverted V, or the triangle
without a base given below, will help us understand their relation.

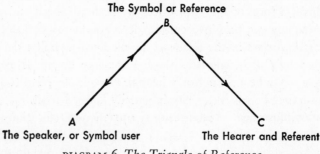

DIAGRAM 6. *The Triangle of Reference*

Assume that Brown is the symbol user and Smith the symbol hearer.
They stand at points A and C. Brown says, "I'm going on a picnic; won't
you come along?" Smith hears him and understands his invitation because
there immediately comes to his mind the meaning of the symbol "picnic"
which Brown has used. In other words, he and Brown place the word
"picnic" in the same frame of reference. (We have shortened this to "the
reference" at the apex B.) We can say that Brown and Smith live in the
same frame of reference because the symbol "picnic" has the same meaning for them. It is a common term and the image of what it implies readily

comes to Smith's mind. But note that the route which the symbol "picnic" travels is that marked by the arrows: from A to C *through* B. Likewise the route which Smith's response follows is that marked by the arrows: C to A *through* B. In neither case does their communication go from A to C or from C to A, *directly*. It has to go *through* its meaning, that is *through* B. If Brown and Smith were not in the same frame of reference, that is, if each did not entertain a very similar (though not identical) image of the symbol "picnic," their communication would be interfered with. Here the logical and the social phases of communication are again illustrated.

Now let us suppose that Brown says "I believe in freedom." Again we assume that he and Smith live in the same general frame of reference and that Smith has some inkling of what Brown means. But "freedom" is a much more ambiguous word or symbol than "picnic." This causes Smith to wonder what Brown's *specific* reference is. Smith then engages in the following dialogue with himself: "I don't know what Brown means. He believes in freedom; so does everybody. But still I don't know what kind of freedom he refers to. Freedom to do what? Freedom from what? Freedom, freedom!—by itself, it doesn't mean anything to me. I could understand his invitation to the picnic but 'freedom'—I give up." Thus, because Brown's use of the symbol "freedom" is too general he gets only a quizzical look from Smith; he gets neither agreement nor disagreement. If they arrive at a common understanding it is only because Brown gives him some specific instance of his belief in freedom.

Again, the path of communication is along the route ABC, not the route AC. Whatever meaning was communicated had to come by the longer route. Again, "the longest way 'round is the shortest way home." Here the imprecision of Brown's logical instrument, the ambiguous word "freedom," made clear communication and hence clear understanding impossible.

The teacher must know the students' language. The meaning of these illustrations for the teacher is obvious. Unless we speak in the verbal frame of reference of our students we shall not be understood. Rather, we shall be misunderstood. We must begin with their common-sense language or, in using a more precise language, we must give ample illustrations which lie in their "universe of discourse," which is the universe of their experience and the words they use as they live in it. Our ultimate aim is to make their discourse less commonsensical and more scientific, because we wish them to use words which have as precise meaning as possible.

A problem in economics. Let us assume that a discussion in a class in economics brings up the problems of inadequate housing and unemployment. The crux of the discussion is the old problem of the relation between the individual and his society. Assume that a student says: "Let 'em build their own homes; my grandfather built his; he wasn't looking for any government handout and there wasn't any goofy old FHA in his day." Or suppose, respecting unemployment in time of depression, a student gives the old argument that "anybody can get a job if he's got guts enough." (I do not think ill of high school students; I seek only to give illustrations which will permit me to elaborate a point. However, truth to tell, I have heard expressions as ill-informed as these.)

The teacher's role. Obviously your obligation in the face of such arguments is not to tell the students that they don't know what they're talking about—although the truth is that they don't. Your task, in the role of one who practices unavoidable indoctrination, is to get them to reflect on their words—or more accurately their attitudes. Your problem is not one of merely repairing their speech; it is one of doing what you can, without propagandizing them, to invite them to take a new perspective. This will require that the facts which underlie their arguments get into competition with more realistic and truer facts. The facts on which they have based their judgments are false, at least for the economy of our times. (They may have been true for the economy of their grandparents.) These are the facts about the "objective conditions" we treated in Chapter X.

How attitudes are changed. Attitudes are not changed through exhortation as we shall show. Nor are they changed solely by language reform. If you would seek to effect only the latter change you would come close to subscribing to reification. What is needed is not only new words but new meanings. Old words may be given new meanings. We remember that words are only the *tools* of thought. We also remember Justice Holmes's injunction to "think things." Hence we suggest that if the terms or words which students use are changed they must be changed, not by your dictation but by getting them involved in some precise observations: directly through field study or indirectly through reading the literature on housing, incomes, and the labor market.

The social reference of words. Take the misuse or misunderstanding of such words as "strike" and "scab." If your students know only these words and the meanings which uncritical common sense assigns to them your task becomes one of providing the experiences through which those who use them in an imprecise and even dogmatic way may come to perceive that they refer to specific situations which involve human beings. They may then come to understand that such words have a social reference.

But the task is difficult because the words with which the social studies deal are often heavily weighted with emotional overtones. They are such "trigger words" as control, freedom, government, opinion, worker, capitalist, strike, and so on. Some are less "triggerlike" than others. It is interesting to note that the words in the Declaration of Independence (one of the most magnificent and effective propaganda documents ever written) belong to the category of expressive language. They were designed to incite men to revolution. On the contrary, those in the Constitution are more sober; they belong much more to the category of scientific language. They were designed to bring men to act on a reflective, even a legal basis.

The danger of generalizing. The situations into which the social studies inquire also lend themselves readily to the making of very broad generalizations. It is easy for students to talk about "the Negro," or "the foreigner," or "the market" rather than about specific people who are Negroes or foreigners, or a specific market. But generalizations are worth no more than the specifics on which they rest, hence the need to get "the facts in the case."

The importance of language tools. It is *with* words that our students will need to think, hence they must be able to think *about* the reference which they bear to a society of human beings. Their conclusions, that is, what they "consummate" or conclude with, will depend directly on the truth and clarity of the tools they use.

Perceptions and facts must change. In changing their language habits they will be obligated to change their facts. Only then will their language relate to something more than the words themselves. Only if their *expressions* are as correct as reliable facts can make them will their *impressions* be true and relevant. In so far as language alone is involved we must help them see that the world they perceive will be a different one if they will but remove some words from "their eyes." They may then come to understand that they look *with* words as well as *at* them. In the process of doing these things we shall err badly if we make the mistake of supposing that because what they may say makes no sense to *us*, it makes no sense to *them*. Their language may be more or less counterfeit but it is the only coin they have and it buys them something. They are saying *something*. Your obligation is to find out what they mean and then try to provide them with more legitimate word-coins. While the dictionary may help some, it has its limitations. It contains definitions which are, in many instances, chiefly words about words, rather than their meaning in *context*. Lacking such a context, their definitions have little use value. (Illustrations are often better than definitions.) Another important obligation is that you do not paralyze, by too severe criticism, what little expressive power they have—however inexact and truthless it may be. What "too severe" is, you must judge.

My point is that language is a vehicle; it can carry a cargo which has quite precise meaning if it is a good vehicle. Your task is to help repair the vehicle and improve the content of the cargo. If any object that this is "teaching English" the reply is that the vehicle is English. Literature has its own concern with language, different in some ways from that which the social studies have. Each has its unique task to perform with the instruments of language to the end that appreciation and understanding be enhanced.

The nature and use of symbols.   After this somewhat technical excursion into the land of words we return to the central topic, the nature and use of symbols. Man's ability to make and interpret symbols is the basis of his intellectual freedom. Poetry is perhaps its maximum expression. But in the social studies, likewise, his ability to symbolize permits him to escape the bonds of time and space. He may, with symbols, exchange the world of the present, of accident, and of percepts for a word of the past and future, of essence, and of concepts. We cannot see the "lilacs [that] last in the dooryard bloom'd" of a Whitman but we can, by the means of the symbols he has given us, enjoy their beauty and understand his grief at the death of his "captain," the martyred Lincoln. In like manner we can feel, as Vachel Lindsay did, the strength and loneliness of the tall shawl-clad figure that walked at midnight in a prairie town. We can stand watch with Columbus, and feel the tired march of a Lewis and Clark because we have symbols at our command. It is through symbols that man has come, in truth, to enjoy *freedom* of speech.

Charles H. Cooley has also written about words and the mind.[7]

A mind without words would make only such feeble and uncertain progress as a traveler set down in the midst of a wilderness where there were no paths or conveyances and without even a compass. A mind with them is like the same traveler in the midst of civilization, with beaten roads and rapid vehicles ready to take him in any direction where men have been before.

Words and past events.   Through the power of words as symbols we can relive past events. True, we cannot talk events but we can talk about them, examine them, classify them, and frame general propositions about them. We can ask questions of them and, if they are sensible and perceptive questions, get sensible and perceptive answers. By the use of words we

[7] *Social Organization,* pp. 69-70.

can contemporize the "Western movement," the Lincoln-Douglas debates, the Crusades— whatever the past contains. The history you teach will be as dull or lively, real or unreal, peopled or full of dead men's bones as your ability to create the symbols which will reveal that what happened in the past *really* happened.

Words and role-taking. But what is the bearing of all this on the social relation of teacher and students? As we observed, communication is the mechanism through which human relations exist and develop. By the same token, it is the mechanism by which teacher and student share ideas, attitudes, and understandings. In short, it is the means by which they get on a common ground of fact and sentiment. This is done by each entering into the mind of the other, through role-taking.

The "significant symbol." This is done through what Mead calls "the significant symbol." A significant symbol, a word or gesture, is significant in that it arouses in the one who uses it the same response which it arouses in the one who hears or sees it. Thus it is a stimulus to the hearer or viewer, and it is stimulus *and* response to the speaker or actor. As stimulus to the speaker or actor it arouses in him the same general response as it does in the hearer or viewer. If this were not true the speaker or actor could not know how his symbol would be received. In responding to his own stimulus, he thus takes the role of the other—the hearer or viewer of his symbol.

The hen and her chicks. Take the hen and her chicks. When she clucks and they come running to share the worm she has found or to seek shelter under her wings she does not know that they come because she clucks. She is incapable of being aroused by the same stimulus which arouses them. What she does she does by instinct, not by insight. She is not capable of entering into the role which her chicks play. She and her chicks are members only of the same spatial order.

A mother and her children. But the relation of a human mother to her children is greatly different. When she calls them to supper or warns them of the approach of some danger, she can enter into their experience. She can be, and is, stimulated by her own speech, or vocal gestures. She acts on the basis of insight, rather than instinct. She both *is* and *has* a self, because she is able to enter into the experience of others. She and her children are members of the same *social* order.

The basis of human nature and society. This ability to take the view, the meaning, or the role of others is the basis of both human nature and society. It is the ability to direct one's own life in terms which have that degree of congruence or agreement with others which makes consicous human co-operation possible. As Professor Mead expresses it, "The . . . social group which gives to the individual his unity of self may be called 'the generalized other.' " The "generalized other" is the attitude of the whole social group of which the individual is a member. When he "internalizes," so to speak, this "generalized other" he thereby becomes a self and a member of a society at the same time. If we take human beings as members only of a spatial order they have no sense of others, and hence no sense of the "generalized other"—of the society, however large or small it be.[8]

Mead describes the process in the following way:

The final outcome of human social conduct is that the individual in exciting, through the vocal gesture, the response of another, initiates the same response in himself and, in that attitude of the other, comes to address himself in his own conduct. It is this attitude which is commonly called "consciousness." . . . The individual can then indicate to others what he is at the same time indicating to himself, that is, the gesture of indication becomes a significant symbol.[9]

Chess as a form of communication.   Imagine a game of chess. Each man has the response of the opponent in his mind. This means that A's moves call out in him the response which he imagines it will call out in B. Thus in playing his role well he must also play well the role of his opponent. In fact, his success at the game depends on his ability to anticipate what his moves will evoke in B. Thus he conjures up moves which he, taking the role of B, believes cannot be checked. The winner, other things being equal, is the one whose guesses about the reaction of "the other one" are closest to what the "other one" actually does or fails to do. But A and B are engaged in more than a game. They are engaged in communication —"a conversation of gestures," as Mead implies.

[8] George H. Mead, *Mind, Self and Society* (Chicago: The University of Chicago Press, copyright 1948), p. 154. Thus it is that "only so far as [a human being] takes the attitude of the organized group to which he belongs toward the organized, co-operative social activity or set of activities in which that group is engaged, does he develop a complete self or possess the sort of complex self he has developed [and only on this basis can he] direct his own behavior accordingly." *Ibid*, p. 155. It is obvious that this can be more readily and completely done in a therapeutic climate. Mead is quite explicit in stating that such a relationship cannot be fully explained by mere imitation. He writes ". . . there is no particular faculty of imitation in the sense that the sound or sight of another's response is itself a stimulus to carry out the same reaction, but rather that if there is already present in the individual an action like the action of another, then there is a situation which makes imitation possible" (p. 68, *ibid.*). See pp. 51-61 for Mead's refutation that language (the use of verbal and nonverbal gestures) has its origin in imitation.

[9] *The Philosophy of the Act* (Chicago: The University of Chicago Press, copyright 1938), pp. 189-190.

The Good Samaritan as role-taker. In the parable of the Good Samaritan, Jesus of Nazareth showed that the distress of the injured traveler on the Jericho road became a stimulus to the Good Samaritan; at the same time it was his *response* to it. Thus it called out in him the response of which his nature was capable, but of which the nature of neither the priest nor the Levite was capable. Only the Good Samaritan was able to take the role of another, the injured traveler.

The attributes of the Good Samaritan. The attributes of the Good Samaritan were three: a *capacity, knowledge,* and *absence of prejudice.* The first is a capacity for great imagination through which the teacher may enter into the thoughts and sentiments of the students. It requires great sympathy and wide and reliable knowledge about each student. Although it is not confined to friendly attitudes, we now think of it chiefly in that sense.[10]

The second attribute, *knowledge,* is knowledge of both subject matter and human beings. It is used in the teacher's attempt to surround students with new "objective conditions, i.e., knowledge of facts which they do not have and do not know. Thus are attitudes changed, if they are changed. No amount of techniques or gimmicks can make up for inadequacy in either of these kinds of knowledge.

The third attribute, *absence of prejudice,* is simply that attitude which refuses to charge students with guilt for deeds which neither they nor their parents have committed.

Teaching and imagination. Of these three attributes, the first and third are humane, the second scientific. In practice, indeed in the *practice of teaching,* they are combined in such ways as mutually to re-enforce each other. When a native capacity of imagination may be lacking in some respect, it may be provided, in part, by knowledge. The greater the scope of the teacher's knowledge, the greater is the likelihood that the illustrations used will "pull the right string" on students of all types. Indeed, imagination never works in a vacuum. Rather it provides a certain kind of canny insight which seems to advise just what illustration or project will appeal to a particular student. Thus it is that insight and knowledge supplement each other. On the basis of knowledge gained through a study of students'

---

10 "One's range of sympathy is a measure of his personality, indicating how much or how little of a man he is—there is nothing more practical than social imagination: to lack it is to lack everything." So Cooley wrote in *Human Nature and the Social Order,* pp. 140-141. (We would be disposed to use the word "character" in place of "personality.") As we have observed earlier, sympathy may be positive or negative, friendly or hostile. In either case, it requires that one have the capacity to put himself in another's place.

life histories, through the use of anecdotal records and such materials as the files of the principal and the counselors might provide, the teacher may work out a kind of rough "table of prediction" as to what objects, illustrations, and projects will make the greatest appeal to certain types of students. This requires highly specialized techniques and presumes more time than most teachers have. But if the school's records on students' achievement, temperaments, capacities, and all the other attributes about which more and more statistical and case-study data are sought, are not available to the teacher, much of their value is lost.

The student's inner life. The greater the number of students *per* teacher, the greater the need for the use of such materials. The inner life of the student is accessible only if we know enough about him to know his roles and attitudes and, in that knowledge, be able to *take* his roles and attitudes. The real social facts are our imagination of others. The more accurate it is, the more useful will be the social knowledge we can make available to them.

Prejudice is a barrier to communication. The third attribute, absence of prejudice, is not a special demand made on the teacher as the other two, in a sense, are. It is a demand made upon all persons of good will. Its relevance as an attribute of the teacher is not far to seek. Prejudice toward human beings is a barrier to communication. In being that it is a barrier to the creation of a sense of community—the therapeutic climate. For communication is not something that runs itself. It requires some sort of co-operation in which teacher and students are actively engaged. Ideas and meanings have no existence prior to communication. They are the fruit of it and, being achieved, enrich it. A thing is fully known only when it is shared, that is, socially accessible. It must be more than merely "found out."

Conversation with yourself. The teacher must be not only sensible but sensitive, that is, stimulated to respond to the same significant symbols which are used to arouse the response of students. This may be illustrated in the area of personal relations in such a way as to imply how the mechanism operates in general. Assume that you start to say something to a student, we presume an unpleasant something. When you start to say it you realize, from your *sensibility* and *sensitivity*, that it would be cruel; you even feel its potential cruelty. Its effect on you brings you to check yourself. You have engaged in a conversation with yourself and come out with the judgment that you ought not to say what was on the tip of your tongue.

The same principle holds with reference to a metaphor, an analogy, a reference, or an illustration. Each of these must be not only "kindly" but within the frame of meaning or reference of your students. Otherwise, you will get no response except perhaps reluctant agreement, which is not agreement at all. You must, as Max Marshall expresses it, be on "both sides of the teacher's desk."

Meaningless soliloquy. If what you try to communicate is not communicated, that is, taken in by your students in something approaching its meaning to you, about all you have done is to engage in a meaningless soliloquy by which you disturbed the silence of the classroom. This same principle applies, of course, on the student-to-student axis of which we spoke in Chapter II. Your obligation is to help meanings along on *that* axis, as well as that which runs between you and them.

Teen-agers' world of meaning. I do not mean to suggest that communication is always difficult. There is, I suspect, a common background of meanings among modern teen-agers which, if we can sense it, will greatly facilitate communication between them and their teachers. If, however, we depend too much on rationality, this background or *ground* may not be there. We may easily err in believing that an idea which is clear to us *must* be quite as clear to them. By the same token, meanings which are emotional rather than rational in their intrinsic nature may be quite difficult to communicate. As P. W. Bridgman has observed, we cannot communicate the beauty of an evening star to a blind man. Neither can we communicate either the beauty or the ugliness of many phases of human affairs to those who have never perceived them. All the more need then that we understand the life-space or frame of reference in which our students live.

You must listen. Perhaps your greatest difficulty will be to *listen*. Your first question, in case of doubt about a student's response, ought to be this: "What does the thing mean to *him*?" It will be only natural for you to ask yourself, "How do I *like* it?" The proper question is: "How does he like it, what does it mean to him, how does he feel about it?" If you fail to do this you will play the role of the executive (the "Big Shot" type) who always refers his remarks and orders to *his* understanding of their meaning and fairness, never to the reactions which the members of his staff might take toward them.

A new Tower of Babel. The confusion of tongues at the Tower of Babel was due to language differences, tongues which fellow workmen could not understand. That will not be your problem. The English language is the lingua franca, with but rare exceptions, in all American secondary school classrooms. But you may find yourself in another Tower of Babel.

This will be a confusion, not of tongues, but of symbols: a confusion as to the *meaning* of justice, freedom, brotherliness, equality, and the other Great Oughts of the democratic faith.

This will be the manner in which the crisis in valuation will confront you as a teacher, as it confronts our whole culture. The clash of interests, the differences in beliefs and expectations which your students will hold toward the good life as it is envisaged in the democratic dream will find expression in your classroom. Such a Babel can be resolved, insofar as is possible, by your playing the role of the Good Samaritan as I have sought to describe it.

The teacher as leader. This requires that your role as teacher be expressed through the role of leader. This is one who is able to relate social knowledge to the life conditions, interests, beliefs, and expectations of many kinds of students—those which we suggested in Chapter II. This is the precondition for leadership in every group committed to the principles of democratic organization. Such a teacher-leader will never use students to get results without deference to their emotional and intellectual dispositions and consent. To do otherwise would be to deny and violate the nature of true communication and the true community.

Communication and democracy. If communication can be carried through and made perfect—and only when it can—is a perfect democracy possible. For a perfect democracy is that society in which each individual carries within himself the same response that he calls out in others in his community. The method by which it may be achieved in the classroom is no different from that by which it may be achieved in the Great Society. Only then can the student or citizen be "at one" with his fellow men.

CHAPTER XIX

The Nature and Purpose
of Discussion

THE SECOND PHASE of teaching-learning in the social studies which is common to them all is discussion. If, as Dewey remarked, communication is of all affairs the most wonderful, discussion is perhaps the most difficult of all its forms.

The "age of discussion." Walter Bagehot called ours the "age of discussion." Although his remark was directed to government by discussion it is equally applicable to education by discussion. In both government and education, discussion has come to challenge the authoritarian methods by which both were once carried on. But discussion is not only difficult; it is dangerous. "Once effectually submit a subject to that ordeal, and you can never withdraw it again; you can never again clothe it with mystery, or fence it in by consecration; it remains forever open to free choice, and exposed to profane deliberation."[1]

Discussion is private and public. Discussion is common to both private and public thinking. Privately it is an inner conversation: Talking with the mouth shut. Publicly it is that manner of thinking which goes on *between* individuals. It is social action in its purest form: the solution of a social or group problem through the establishment of agreement or consensus.

A conflict of values. Discussion always has to do with a problem, an issue—some phase of a conflict of values. It may be about the logic and moral quality of Justice Taney's decision in the Dred Scott case, the factors responsible for our government's unwillingness to share in the construction

[1] *Physics and Politics* (New York: Alfred A. Knopf, Inc., copyright 1948), p. 167.

of the St. Lawrence waterway and its subsequent change of mind, the constitutionality of granting off-shore oil rights to the states, adolescents' rights and privileges respecting parental authority, the increasing power of the executive in modern governments, the "good" of advertising, the merits of public and private forms of charity—even the time, place, and cost of the Senior prom. In short, any situation in which, as we say, there is a difference of opinion.

The coin of human affairs.   The topics just given appear to divide into what one might call private and public, or individual and social problems. But in being private they have a public aspect, and in being individual they have a social phase. The presumed antithesis of personal and social is always cropping up in the social studies. We remarked in Chapter VI that much of this confusion might be avoided or remedied if we would think of individual and social as adjectives, as well as nouns. Our inability or reluctance to view them as adjectives has much to do with the view that discussion among teen-agers ought always to be about individual or private matters because social and public matters are too remote or too difficult for them. The position we have taken and shall continue to take is that private and public are but opposite sides of the coin of human affairs.

The constituents of a discussion.   The constituents of a discussion are a leader, a group, a problem, and a content. We assume that the teacher is the leader. We shall show how important and difficult that role is and the danger which may come from its being assumed, without proper instruction and too soon, by a student. Such a role is not prepared for only through observation or by mere practice. As we observed in Chapter XVIII, the major prerequisite for it is the ability to enter into the life experience of every student. This depends not only on technical training, but on an understanding of and deep insight into one's self and other selves. It consists in far more than governing a discussion by Robert's *Rules of Order*. The function of a discussion is to educate young people in the process of group thinking, a process in which they are continually engaged in a more or less amateur fashion. It is not, as many appear to believe, the mere demonstration of skill in parliamentary procedure. That is a means, not an end. The excessive or wrong use of it may block rather than facilitate the meeting of minds. The belief that leading a discussion consists chiefly in manipulating such rules explains much of the insistence that the teacher should be a mere "watcher" in a discussion.

The group is, obviously, the students in a class in economics, social problems, history, or whatever the subject matter be. In all but a few groups there are the quick- and slow-witted, the talkative and the silent, the stubborn and easy-minded—indeed all the varieties of minds and temperaments of which an average student body is composed.

The topic or problem of discussion must be one which the students at least feel, although they may not be able to state their feelings with any precision. If they do not initially feel it, they can be brought to do so. The language which they use to state their feeling or understanding may be more expressive than scientific. Their experience in the discussion should correct that. This will improve the quality of their symbolism by making it more precise and exact. Although the teacher may play a considerable role in nominating the topic, it must be more than *nominal*; it must be a real one. Problems are problems, in part, exactly because students are not able to state them in the terms which analysis requires. The terms of that analysis always involve consideration of their public as well as their private phase. If this fact is not honored the problems of the students will continue, for the most part, to appear to them as purely private, that is, without public causes or consequences. Their needs have this two-sided nature, as we observed earlier.

Every topic, problem, or issue has a private and a public phase. This two-phase quality is more apparent in problems of social policy than in those of only logical matters—although all social problems have their logical phase. But, to the degree that logical problems may be separated from social problems, they also have a private and public character. Their private phase is the confusion in the manner in which students think about social problems. This is but the private manifestation of the confusion which stems from the imprecise and illogical (even nonlogical) way in which "the folk" think about them. The quality of such thought was stated in our earlier discussion of the difference between common-sense and scientific ways of thinking.

The content of the discussion is the body of knowledge—facts and generalizations—which must be drawn upon if any problem is to be discussed and resolved. Nothing can come from a discussion but deeper confusion and bewilderment unless there is constant resort to facts and generalizations. Facts, of course, cannot be discussed; they can only be proved true or false. But propositions, which are statements about values, may be discussed as to their meaning, their truth, and their significance. It is about these that difference of opinion arises.

Discussion is not "thobbing." The nature of discussion may be sharpened by contrasting it with what it is not. It is not "thobbing"—a strange mixture of thinking and sobbing. The greater the number of students in the class, the more likely that thobbing rather than thinking may go on. The difference between them is the difference between a *crowd* which is disposed to act without thinking and a *public* which thinks how and when to act. A crowd emotes and views with alarm; a public thinks and seeks to be dispassionate.

Discussion is not a "bull session."   A discussion is not a cracker-barrel argument or a "bull session." These are chiefly opinion-swapping, the pooling of ignorance, harangue, disputation, fact-mongering, and idle oratory. Often they consist only in imitation or citation of what someone "seen in the paper." Discussion, on the contrary, proceeds under the control of the rules of scientific inquiry with order and continuity maintained through a moderator who uses some standard rules of procedure. Ideas are initiated, not imitated or copied. There is exchange of opinion but it is accompanied by a search for its factual basis. Speech is not only free but responsible. Values are not quarreled about; they are created.

Discussion is critical examination.   The assertion and dogged defense of unexamined preferences is not discussion. Discussion is the critical examination of them. In it they are sifted, examined, criticized, and subjected to restatement.

Discussion is not a debate.   Discussion is not a debate in which one takes but one view or, if pro and con views, only those to strengthen the "side" which he defends rather than examines. The debater argues that his facts lead to his "resolved" or conclusions. But it is just the other way around: He has been assigned to find those facts which will support a "resolved" already formulated. The debater seeks to annihilate his opponent by logic or trickery. It is combat by words rather than by fists or swords. It rests on an "all or none" principle. The debater seeks only to win an argument. Compromise is foreign to his task. Discussion, on the contrary, is a sharing and weighing of all sides which are as many as there are conflicting interests or values. The participants are interrelated in a process of competitive co-operation. Agreement, rather than annihilation, is the declared purpose of a discussion. Trickery is outside the rules. Compromise is a legitimate and useful device.

Discussion is the dialectic.   By resorting to discussion we assume that subject matter is not an inert mass of facts to be stored against the day of its use. Facts, as Whitehead has observed, "keep no better than fish." Discussion is a way of teaching which puts the question mark to work. It guarantees no answers. It may result only in the restatement of the question which is a gain since, as we have remarked, the kind of answers we get depends on the kind of questions we ask. Discussion assumes a culture committed to progress, and the fact of change in human affairs. In society in which there is little or no change it is custom, not discussion, by which whatever issues arise are resolved. The method of discussion is the dialectic: a "conversation of gestures" out of which new perspectives and values may emerge. It is an ordered process of collective decision-making. It seeks agreement but, if it is not reached, it has the value of clarifying and sharpening the nature of disagreement.

Not the only method of instruction.   As a method of instruction, group discussion combines the spirit of honest inquiry with the spirit of responsible membership in the community of the classroom. It is not the only method of instruction. It does not teach students to read with understanding, nor write with clarity. It provides no experience with concrete things such as the field trip does. It deals with reality through the medium of symbols—words about it. Thus it depends heavily on the method of logic. It takes time—a great deal of it. Its aim is mastery, not coverage. In this attribute it has great merit for too many students often learn too little about too much which lasts too short a time. It acknowledges the truth, perhaps more than any other form of instruction, that students can learn no more than they can think about at the time.

Gives knowledge a round trip.   It likewise has the merit of giving knowledge a round trip. It is not the one-way affair of the lecture. It engenders more reflection than the "ping-pong" of the question-and-answer recitation. Of all the means of instruction it is furthest from rote-learning. It employs reasonable persuasion in place of cajolery, threat, coercion, or propaganda.

Discussion is discovery.   In discussion a student may find out what he did not know, what he has overlooked, and wherein he is mistaken both as to facts and the method of interpreting them. Equally important, he may find out what he knows and with what surety he knows it; likewise, what he believes. Discussion can be no more lively or rewarding than the intelligence of its participants and their willingness to enter into it. It readily degenerates into mere talk and the idle and pointless exchange of unexamined, groundless, and worthless opinion. Through it issues may be clarified and sharpened and new ground discovered for both agreement and disagreement. Assumptions may be laid bare and their relation to social reality tested. Students may thus come to know what they have taken for granted and from what their thinking has taken its departure. Old values may be replaced by new ones.

Through discussion students may come to know and understand that difference in perspective need not result in disaster and that people may believe in the same thing for different and acceptable reasons. Through it, objective proof may be given to the fact that those who live differently perceive, think, and evaluate differently. Thus, it may engender toleration for views which are at variance from those one holds. It is potential for enjoying the thrill which comes with a change of mind, the intellectual equivalent of religious conversion. It may also produce the pain which often comes with a new idea. It makes for objectivity through the student's speaking his mind and listening to how others respond to it.

Discussion and overt action are different.   Although its judgments and conclusions provide the basis for action, discussion is itself action only in the sense that thinking is "the action of thought." Discussion, as such, cannot clear the slums, reduce unemployment, or stop the spiral of inflation. While it is true that discussion is " 'pure' social action" because it is the joint intellectual quest for the solution of *value* problems, it does not include acting out its decisions and agreements. This fact may create impatience among those students who are "hot for certainty," that is, the certainty of making material changes. But, in being something short of that kind of action, discussion shares the quality of all social *study*, which is one step removed from the major theaters of action in the Great Society where "the Big Show" goes on. There is some danger, how great I do not know, that some students may confuse the judgments which are arrived at through discussion with overt action itself. In this matter, as in all social study, we must rest in the faith (with all the evidence we can get) that students' minds and affections are changed through discussion. These changes may have such a lasting quality as to affect, in time, the institutions of the culture.

Discussion must be disciplined.   But none of these things are the certain or automatic outcomes of discussion. They are only some of its potentials. But none will come, except by chance, unless discussion is disciplined. This comes through the effectiveness of its organization.

The "physics" of discussion.   The most manageable phase of its organization is its physical aspect. The traditional seating arrangement—students lined up at desks like soldiers on parade—needs to give way to an arrangement which permits face-to-face relations. This reform is long overdue in American classrooms in which students now "talk behind each other's backs." There is great merit in a seating pattern which a large table permits. We have evidence that a table produces a feeling of one's being less vulnerable. If there are not places for all at the table let some occupy a row behind those who sit at it. This position constitutes a kind of "psychological bay' from which they may test out the situation and feel less exposure and compulsion. Let the place in which a student sits be his choice, rather than one assigned to him. The reasons for this are implicit in the foregoing comments. But whether in a circle, a hollow square, or around a table, the discussion will be improved because the student's sense of isolation is reduced and, by the same token, the *esprit de corps* of the class raised. Such seating arrangements have the further advantage of providing a focus on which all may fix their eyes. The task of the teacher, as leader or moderator, is thus greatly aided.

But, despite the value of an appropriate physical structure, the mere circular ordering of students in space does not insure a good discussion. It is a necessary though not a sufficient cause of it. (The relation between a spatial and a social order is here illustrated.)

Discussion is the interaction of ideas. We assume that one does not engage in discussion merely to give his own ideas. If that were all, he might just as well phone them in or submit a memo. Its purpose, on the contrary, is to create a group idea, judgment, or conclusion. This is not the sum of the ideas of all but a *function of the interaction* of the ideas of all. We reject the principle of addition in discussion as we rejected it as the principle by which a general education may be had. In fact, the principle of addition is directly contrary to the aims of discussion; furthermore, it is psychologically impossible.

What is genuine discussion? This gives us the test by which we may judge whether genuine discussion is under way. Do our students come together to register the results of their individual thoughts or opinions, to compare the results of individual thought in order to select the best or do they come together to create a new idea? Therein lies the problem of the discussion: to bring about a genuine meeting of minds.

The psychology of discussion. As a psychological process, discussion may be described as follows. A speaks and B responds to A. This gives us, not "A plus B" but "A times B." C now speaks. In doing so he responds not to "A and B" but "A times B." We now have the equation [C times (A times B)]. Now D speaks. This gives us D times [C times (A times B)]. By "times" we mean to suggest a dynamic of interaction which "plus" does not signify. Each equation is composed of what was said and the interpretation of what was said in which the biases of each are included. The process is not one of bricklaying nor the mere mixture of physical things. It is after the nature of a chemical reaction, in which the participants are not mere catalysts.

It goes without saying that the process is more complicated than our figure of speech indicates. Irrelevant contributions are made. Mere opinion, rather than sober thought, enters. The participants may attack each other, forgetting that the issue is *propositional*, not personal. Discussion may be abandoned.

The continuum of discussion. We now offer, not recipes for "keeping them quiet" or devices for maintaining discipline; rather, we offer two ideal-type procedures within which discussion may go on. First, however, we present a continuum which an observer might discover in students' behaviors in a discussion. The items are arranged according to the principle of whether or not a student is being required to organize his learning.

1. The student listens to the instructor expound a point.
2. The student asks questions in order to clarify in his own mind what the instructor has said.
3. The student challenges the instructor's statements.
4. The student propounds his own solution to the problem and has it approved or corrected by the instructor; if incorrect, he listens to the instructor's reasons for modifying or rejecting.
5. The student propounds his own solution to the problem and is led by the instructor to elaborate it and defend it against attack, to relate it to other ideas, to modify it, if necessary, in the light of the attacks, etc.
6. The student *participates* in a *group effort* in which Step 5 is done by other students as well as by himself.

(The same continuum would occur if the suggested exchange between teacher and students were changed to report exchange only between students. My own view, as I shall make clear later, is that the teacher must play a dominant role in discussion. The phrase "first among equals" does not exactly describe the function of the teacher as discussion leader.)

Two ideal-type discussion procedures. With this continuum in mind we now suggest two procedures in which discussion may go on. The first we call "Procedure-D." The teacher who consistently uses it we call "D-teacher." Its use seeks to call forth an increasingly larger amount of the kinds of behavior represented in the continuum as one moves from Step 1 to Step 6. Conversely, a set of procedures which seeks to call forth in the students the steps toward the *upper* part of the continuum, with an increasing tapering off from Step 4 downward, we call "Procedure—U." The teacher who consistently uses it we call "U-teacher." Similarly we shall speak of the "U-session" and the "D-session," respectively.

The meaning of "down" and "up." These labels may appear to complicate the mechanics of discussion. Actually, however, without these or similar procedures, discussion would be impossible. "D" and "U" have been chosen in order to indicate the direction (down, up) on the student behavior-continuum just given. It should be clear that "Procedures-D" and "Procedures-U" do not constitute fixed sets of classroom techniques, but rather, they represent tendencies in given directions. "D" gives the discussion an orientation "down" to the students; "U" gives it an orientation "up" to the instructor.

Discussion shuttles. We have noted earlier what the constituents of a discussion are: a teacher, students, a problem or issue, and a content. From the interaction of teacher and students, as the discussion moves ahead, teacher-concepts about the problem and its solution emerge; similarly student-concepts. Either may become the focus: the point of beginning or ending, or the point to which the discussion refers at a given time. The discussion may shuttle between the more precise teacher-concepts and the less precise student-concepts. It cannot focus on both at once. Such a mixture of terms of discourse would produce a babel of sounds, not communication.

AN "UP" SESSION. A discussion in a U-session would contain units something like the following:

The teacher has just evaluated a response about element Y—let us suppose that it is one of several factors in the prevention of delinquency; similarly for element X.

Teacher: And what is the significance of element Y? (A student answers.)

Teacher: That is not quite right. You see, you have failed to take account of the fact that . . . (Steps 4 and 1 in the continuum are being taken here.)

Or, a student asks a question and the teacher answers it. (Steps 2 and 1 of the continuum are being taken here.)

A "DOWN" SESSION. In a D-session the units would be something like these:

A problem has been clarified and a solution is asked for. A student gives his solution. The teacher asks a second student to evaluate the solution. The second student evaluates unfavorably. The teacher asks the second student for *his* solution. (Step 6 in the continuum is being taken here.)

Or, a student asks a question. The teacher calls on a second student and asks if the question is clear. The second student says "Yes." The teacher asks the second student to restate the question and attempt an answer. (Step 6 in the continuum is being taken here.)

The role of the U-teacher. In the role of U-teacher, we would seek to satisfy the conditions of Step 5 and Step 6 by doing the things indicated ourself, that is, *we* would play the role of student. In the role of D-teacher, we would seek to elicit those responses from the students as the continuum indicates.

Techniques of the U- and D-teacher.   We now offer some general comments on the techniques used by the U-teacher and the D-teacher, respectively. The U-teacher indicates agreement with a student's response by restating what the student said. The D-teacher does likewise but in a different manner. Whereas the U-teacher's response implies *agreement,* the D-teacher's implies *neither* agreement nor disagreement. The difference lies in the teacher's tone of voice or facial expression.

The teacher in the D-session.   In the D-session the teacher's evaluation of students' responses will take the form of "Do you agree?" "Are you satisfied?" and "Do you think that A's statement is a good one?" In asking these questions the teacher will not invite a yes-or-no response either by tone of voice or facial expression. Probing and cross-questioning will take such forms as, "Could you support that statement with evidence from your readings or observations?" or "How would you answer someone who felt that the point you were making is inconsistent with fact X?" In these latter comments a point has been made for *other* students through the teacher's noting a possible inconsistency. This should aid other students in their own evaluation of the reciting student's statements.

The D-session, in its concern to "push" the discussion toward the students rather than toward the teacher, should not be confused with the bull session in which the attitude often is, "Well, this is all just a matter of opinion; any answer is as good as any other." It is just this attitude which the D-teacher seeks to prevent and at the same time refrain from giving the answer, until the possibilities of Steps 5 and 6 have been exhausted. If this should prove impossible for the teacher to achieve, it is probably unwise to continue with the D-session for that class.

Differences between U- and D-teachers.   We now consider some differences between the U- and D-teachers' attitudes and procedures for insuring a free flow of communication between members of the class. The U-teacher is primarily concerned with the adequacy of communication between *teacher* and students; likewise, of course, in communication between students and himself. The latter is a simpler matter for it is easier for the teacher to discover that he has not understood a student than to discover whether a student has understood him. It appears to be less important in the U-session for students to understand what their classmates are saying than it is for them to understand what the teacher is saying. (The U-session is more teacher-oriented than is the D-session.) When a student in a U-session gives a response which the teacher takes as *correct,* the teacher generally restates the point—often with amplifications or illustrations in order to make it clearer to the class. When a student in a U-session makes a response that is *inaccurate, incomplete,* or *irrelevant,* the teacher often calls upon another student, either after giving an unfavorable evaluation or without any comment. (Failure by the teacher to comment is usually taken by the class in a U-session as a sign of unfavorable evaluation.) The second reciting student's only concern is not to say *exactly* what the preceding student said because it was evidently not acceptable. Eventually the U-teacher will *restate* (or state, if no reciting student has done so) the correct answer to the question. Nothing much is lost, then, for students in a U-session, if they have not listened carefully to their classmates' remarks or if they have not understood what they said. It is, obviously, *better* in the U-session for students to understand one another's comments, but in most cases the attainment of aims is not seriously interfered with if the students have not understood each other but have understood the teacher. The procedure of the U-session, other things being equal, may be best for a student group which does not speak articulately; it is assumed that the teacher's speech is always articulate.

The D-teacher insures and checks. In the D-session, however, the progress of the discussion and the attainment of aims are both seriously hampered if other members of the group do not understand what the reciting student is saying. This makes it mandatory that the teacher do all possible to insure the adequacy of communication between members of the group. In the D-session the teacher seeks, by a variety of comments, to insure and check the adequacy of interstudent communication. Such comments as the following may be made: "B, do you understand A's question?" or "I see. So you would say that X is true?" or the D-teacher may submit the reciting student to a series of cross-questions with the object of clarifying the student's point to everyone, teacher included. A D-teacher may go so far as to encourage students explicitly to cross-question the reciting student.

The U-teacher will rarely use these techniques when he understands the student's comment, even though almost certainly other members of the class have not understood.

Some techniques of the D-teacher. The D-teacher will use such techniques as the following in order to aid the group to understand a student's point or general position. Even when the student's point has been well formulated but proves to be rather complex, the D-teacher will restate the point in a different way and follow it with such questions as, "Is that what you're saying?" If the U-teacher does this, the student is tempted to say "Yes" unless the teacher's facial expression or tone reveals disagreement, even though a more truthful answer would have been "No." This is because a U-teacher usually implies agreement by restating the response. In the D-session, however, if the student answers "Yes," even though a more truthful answer would have been "No," he is likely to find himself in the position of having to defend the truth of a point he did not make.

Students may restate.   If communication is to be adequately established, restatement of a student's point is particularly necessary after the point has been drawn out of a student piecemeal by cross-questioning. But whenever restatements seem necessary, it need not be the teacher who does the restating. In the D-session especially, he may turn to another student and ask him to restate the point which has been earlier drawn out by questioning or which the reciting student made with difficulty or in too wordy a manner.

"Yes" and "No" replies.   The teacher may combine his desire to insure communication *between* students with his desire to *check* whether communication has been established by asking, "Is it clear?" He may be satisfied with a "Yes" reply, or he may ask, following the "Yes" reply, for a restatement or summary. If a "No" reply is given the instructor may restate the point himself or ask still another student whether it is clear to him, and if so, ask him to restate the point.

In addition to these techniques the teacher who is concerned with communication between students will seek to help the group understand the *difference* between two or more students' comments on the same point. The teacher may himself state the difference, or merely indicate that there is a real one.

Communication between students.   Generally speaking, the difference in attitude behind the concern shown by U- and D-teachers with communication between students seems to be this: the U-teacher is eager that students understand what a reciting student has said in order that *his own* comment upon and evaluation of that comment may have the greatest possible meaning. The D-teacher is eager that students understand what a reciting student has said in order (*a*) that they may become aware of the factors which they had not themselves, perhaps, taken into consideration in thinking about the problem and (*b*) because clear understanding of a point must precede an attempt to evaluate it. These reasons do not operate strongly with the U-teacher because (*a*) if there *are* other factors of which students ought to become aware and if these are brought forth by the reciting student, the U-teacher will restate them with his approval, and (*b*) because students will not be called upon, generally, in the U-session to evaluate comments made by other students but will wait for the instructor to do so.

U- and D-teacher face some pitfalls.   We now turn to some of the pitfalls which U- and D-teachers face. First, those common to the U-teacher

1. He may incur the resentment of those students who insist upon leaving the road he has set up and who then find themselves blocked by him, that is, they refuse to take his "answer" and he will not take theirs. Very often there is nominal but not *real* acceptance of their part. While resentment may in some cases hasten the learning process, it will generally impede it.

2. He may reduce large segments of the session to a lecture.

3. By inducing students to expect a statement of "the answers" from him, he may encourage them not to work out problems in advance, and thereby prevent them from discovering the errors they might have made had they attempted to do so.

4. He may encourage students' impatience with time spent on student responses and comments, since time spent on the *teacher's* comments appears to be so much more valuable in terms of forthcoming examinations. Therefore, he may encourage students to *want him* to talk as much as possible.

5. There may be excessive formality in the class which will have the effect of stifling spontaneity and a feeling of good fellowship.

Now, the pitfalls common to the D-teacher:

1. He may lose control of the group.

2. There may be excessive informality.

3. He may allow students to waste time in making irrelevant remarks; an excessively permissive attitude on this score breaks into the structure of a discussion and obscures it.

4. He may lose status with students for not being sufficiently authoritarian when occasion demands; aside from loss of status, there may be wasted time or an obscured structure, *if, under the appropriate circumstance, authority is not used.*

5. He may frustrate the students by not indicating what the answer is.

Pitfalls may be avoided. How may these pitfalls be avoided? Those associated with the U-teacher may be avoided by his adopting the techniques of a D-session. As for those dangerous to the D-teacher, there is an element which may be added to the Procedures-D which will help in avoiding all but the last pitfall named; he may give "the answer." Pitfalls 1, 2, 3, and 4 will not prove dangerous if, to the elements of the D-session already discussed, there is added one other, namely, structure. Both the U-session and the D-session may be either structured or nonstructured.

The structure of a discussion. Other things being equal, a discussion session will more nearly attain its educational aims if it is a structured session. A structure would be somewhat as follows: [2]

[2] By "structure" we mean a sequence, exhibiting an order of parts which may be comprehended and justified; each individual part of sufficient complexity as to be capable of having a progression—a beginning, a middle, and an end; the sequence of parts is not incidental but intentional and both teacher and students are conscious of it.

1. Summary of preceding discussion given by a student with the aid of the teacher.

2. Consideration of the question: "How shall we proceed to discuss today's topic?" This question is raised by the teacher. In this phase a clear statement of the topic is made; basic terms are identified and defined in so far as they can be known at this time. Others may be considered in the next step.

3. The discussion of the topic. This involves the identification of relevant facts, the determination of alternative perspectives or "value positions," analysis of the logical problems involved, the statement of alternative solutions if such there be and a consideration of their actual or hypothetical consequences. This may be done under Procedures-U or Procedures-D.

4. Summary—by teacher and/or students.

5. If time permits, brief consideration of the topic for the next discussion and its relation to the one just considered.[3]

The "Eros" or affective phase. Skill and insight knowledge as the aims of discussion are implicit in the foregoing. These I have called the effective phases of aims. Their affective aspect is still to be noted. In the language of psychotherapy, this may be called the "Eros aspect" of learning. It is made up of the deep personal satisfactions which come from association with an understanding and loving teacher, genuine affection for the topic discussed, the sense of pride in having helped to effect the outcome of the discussion and having also affected others, as well as a desire to act out the conclusions reached. That the teacher may also share in this "Eros aspect" hardly need be added. Respecting this phase of a discussion, indeed this phase of all genuine communication in all types of instruction, both teacher and student may say, "I have affected, therefore I am." [4]

Discussion and a sense of self. As I implied in Chapter XVI, it is the affective phase of learning with which the student's self is most immediately

---

[3] The foregoing coverage of the U and D types of discussion procedures is adapted from *Teaching by Discussion in the College Program*: Report of a Study Made by Five Members of the Faculty of the College of the University of Chicago, 1947-1948. The report was based on tape recordings of many discussionns, and reports of an independent observer as well as student-participant observers. All judgments are based on what this particular study revealed. It is my belief that the same judgments would be arrived at in almost any student body of secondary school ages. I have used materials from pages 24 to 57; some I have taken verbatim. I have omitted parts which I should have liked to include but could not for lack of space. I have restated some parts and added some comments and interpretations of my own. My colleagues are in no way responsible for my selections, editorial changes, or comments.

[4] This is a parallel of Descartes' *"Cogito, ergo sum"*—"I think, therefore, I am." I owe this insight to my colleague Professor Joseph J. Schwab, Professor of Education and Professor of Natural Sciences. My entire elaboration of the "Eros aspect" of learning and the three-phase "structure" of the discussion which is to follow is based on an unpublished paper by Professor Schwab, "Eros and Education: A Discussion of Discussion." It is the most brilliant and penetrating contribution to this topic which I know. Its relevance to all instruction, i.e., teacher and students in communication, gives it a value beyond its immediate relevance to discussion as a method of teaching.

and fully identified. In Chapter XVIII I remarked on the relation between role-playing and the development of the self. Discussion is uniquely appropriate for developing this sense of self, granted that the discussion is conducted in a manner which respects the right of all students to participate. Through it, a genuine feeling of community may be achieved. What I have in mind is better expressed by George H. Mead in his observation:

> You cannot build up a society out of elements that lie outside of the individual's life-processes. You have to suppose some sort of communication within which the individuals are themselves actively involved as the only possible basis for participation in communication.[5]

Three phases of discussion. The three phases of a discussion within which both effective and affective aims may be realized are these:

I. The substantive or knowledge phase in which the students arrive at a specific understanding of the object under discussion.
II. The method phase. Through this students move in the direction of understanding. Possession of skill in the use of the scientific method of inquiry is, for the student, an "exemplar of power." Through its use the substantive knowledge is made substantive.
III. The "Eros phase," or the affective side of the experience. Through it, the student is provoked and stimulated; in it he develops a genuine affection for the whole experience.

The "Eros" phase persists. Let us again focus on the "Eros phase" and take account of its function throughout the discussion. Professor Joseph J. Schwab writes as follows:

> If discussion is to achieve this purpose (the full effect of the "Eros phase") it must do more than import specific learnings. It must take cognizance of its "erotic" purpose *and* its intellectual aims, and it must take action in respect to them together. The movement of Eros and the movement of the mind cannot take place separately, converging only at the end. In . . . the student, they interact and interpenetrate. They must be treated so in transactions with a person. They must be moved together. Consequently, the quality of effective discussion will reflect this conjoint purpose.
>
> The quality of discussion appropriate to this conjoint purpose can be stated as three functions which, ideally, every discussion, and every segment of discussion, will serve. (It is not practically possible, of course, that every query and every hour of discussion will serve equally well all three functions. It is enough if the three show a proper balance in the long run.) First, each query or discussion must serve as an efficient means of arriving at a specific, intended understanding of some specific object knowledge. This is the function of discussion which is most commonly understood. Second, each query or discussion must

[5] *Mind, Self and Society*, p. 257.

function as an instance of movement toward understanding. It must represent that kind of attack upon the problem at hand which would be found appropriate and proper, defensible as a part of the discipline in question, by a master of that field. We are trying to impart, not only knowledge, but a species of activity ("method," if you will) as well. We are concerned that the knowledge we impart be sound. If activity is also our aim, we must be equally concerned that this be sound, and the activity which matters in the teaching of it is not the "method" we talk about, but the method we actually employ in the sight of our students and persuade our students to employ. Third, each query or discussion must function as a stimulus to the student to try the activity in question, the activity which can eventuate in the immediate understanding sought. It is this function which most obviously involves the Eros.

The balance between phases is dynamic.   We need to take special note of the fact that no equation can be given which will determine the way in which the three phases will be balanced. The "balance cannot be described, for it is a dynamic mean." Schwab continues,

It varies from group to group, from instructor to instructor, and from time to time in the course of discussion. The group of low energy or of scattered interests needs more of the stimulative, for example, than of the exemplary and the substantive. A tense and anxious group, hounded by competition, by social or economic pressures, requires little of the stimulative. But it may need much of the substantive which can provide assuagement of anxiety through concrete signals of achievement; and certainly it needs much of the exemplary in order to mediate the headlong and uncritical rush toward the substantive which its anxiety motivates.

The teacher with a flair for insights and inspiration, whether about the subject-matter or about the course of discussion, is one who must attend much more to the criterion of exemplariness than to the substantive and the stimulative. Conversely, the teacher in whom circumstance has created a remoteness from the young needs to be most attentive to the problem of the stimulative.

With respect to the time-factor, also, the balance-point is variable. For an average student-group with a well-balanced teacher, for example, the stimulative will exceed the other functions, and the substantive will exceed the exemplary, early in the discussion. But soon thereafter the exemplary must be introduced more and more until it exceeds, first, the substantive, and later, the stimulative aspect of the situation. The means or balance cannot then be given both a general and a precise formulation. The extreme however, can; and in terms of these, the teacher may locate the mean for himself.[6]

Some dangers of imbalance.   If the substantive phase predominated the session might well become excessively authoritative. In the extreme it

---

[6] Schwab's three-phase theory appears to be closely related to Whitehead's conception that teaching-learning involves romance, precision, and romance. My interpretation is that Whitehead's phase of precision is found in Schwab's substantive and exemplary and Whitehead's phase of romance is, in general at least, related to Schwab's stimulative.

would become much like a question-and-answer process. If too much emphasis were given to the exemplary phase the session might be dull and unrewarding by reason of the divorce of method from substance and the tendency to cut short the stimulative. If too much emphasis were given to the stimulative the result might well be one of overstimulation with too little concern with substance and method. Thus, intellectual growth would be discouraged—even stunted. The students would simply have "a good time" in swapping uncritical opinions. If it were only stimulative the cracker-barrel conception of a discussion would be enacted since the discussion would consist chiefly in affirming unexamined authority—that of the students or some quoted expert. Genuine substance would be lacking. What substance the discussion had would be purely in the nature of opinion. No challenge could be given it other than the challenge of one opinion to another on common-sense ground. The judgment of the "rightness" or "wrongness" of such opinion would then rest only on the degree to which it departed from the "consensus of opinion" already present in the minds of the students. It would be submitted to none of the critical canons of examination provided by the exemplar phase. The result would be the re-enforcement and confirmation of only common-sense knowledge which it is the declared purpose of discussion to examine and test. Not only would no reliable method of inquiry be employed but, more's the pity, the different frames of reference which the exemplary might provide would not be used. Regretably, we observe that much classroom discussion is of the extreme substantive *or* stimulative phase type: the teacher runs a question-and-answer session or the students run amuck.[7]

The "mental health" phase is integral.   It need hardly be noted that the great merit of Professor Schwab's theory is that it treats the so-called "mental hygiene" aspect of the discussion as an integral part of, rather than as an amendment to, the process of learning. This is a contribution long overdue. Teaching cannot afford to treat the human nature aspect of learning in a kind of "left-handed" or "also" fashion.

The teacher's obligation.   From the foregoing it is clear that the task of leading a discussion falls heavily on the teacher. This does not deny that it is a training ground on which the student may learn, by slow and difficult stages, to undertake the leader role. But that role, as we remarked in Chapter XVIII, comes only to one who is able, imaginatively, to play the roles of every student in the class and, in that knowledge and skill, respond

---

[7] Schwab does not relate his theory to Procedures U and D. It is my view that each would take account of the three phases of the discussion process in ways unique to it. What that balance would be cannot be stated; it can only be sensed and properly implemented by the perceptive teacher.

to each in terms of his own role conception. This ability comes only with an intellectual and emotional maturity.

Specifics of the teacher's obligation. Some specifics of the leader role need to be noted. These transcend any directly teachable techniques. The talkative need to be controlled with a minimum of damage to their egos. The silent need to be stimulated to speak. (It should be remembered, however, that sharing and participation need not always be vocal.) The spirit of discussion as well as the direction of its course is a leader responsibility. This is insured through subtle as well as overt guidance. Co-operation can only be invited; it cannot be demanded. The discussion must be kept on the track by the display of a minimum of authority. The "right" questions must be asked of the "right" students at the "right" times. The discussion needs to be moderated in the sense that the leader is moderate in giving it direction and, in doing that, giving it continuity. This permits arbitrary but fair intrusion. The leader must know that compromise is not a first principle but, by that token, not an inappropriate method of reaching a consensus. The true leader knows that no discussion can proceed on the basis of a fight between "I wants" but rather between propositions which translate "I wants" into statements which report varying value positions. Only then can the quest for truth arise above a competitive quarrel and become a truly co-operative experience. The leader must continually discourage attack upon persons and seek to bring the participants to focus their comment on the *proposition*—not the person. Interest must be sustained. This requires change in the balance between the three phases which only a master of the art of moderating can effect. Irrelevant contributions may be handled by asking that discussion of them be postponed, or, if the situation warrants, their irrelevance may become part and parcel of the discussion.

The teacher is weaver. These roles and competences make the teacher much more than catalyzer, mere watcher, or order-keeper. They require, in sum, a masterly, even clever, weaving of contributions to the end that the discussion move toward its conclusion. The teacher must certainly show the way, both as to means and the direction in which they take the session. In this the blackboard may be used to good advantage. It serves not only to record certain stages of the discussion, provide explicit definition of terms, and the structure of the discussion but, in doing these things, provides a strategic point of focus.

A discussion as a clinic. A discussion may be used by the teacher as a kind of clinic. In a session which "lets 'em talk" or one in which more positive direction is enforced, the teacher may observe many things which will aid not only the course of other discussions but which will provide significant insights into the capacity and temperament of each student. A record may be kept of the frequency with which students contribute, as well as of those who do not speak at all. The cogency of their logic, their command of facts and disposition to use them as well as their ability to use clear and truly communicative speech may be observed. Certain types of contributors may be noted: those who speak chiefly on a compulsive basis and those who speak more thoughtfully. The kinds of questions asked, and by whom, may be noted. Something may be learned about those who seem to assent although they do not participate verbally, those who seem to approve but probably do not understand, and those who tend to argue rather than discuss. In short, through the clinical use of a discussion the teacher may learn how students *do* think in order that they may be taught how they *should* think. Such findings as these may become the content per se of later discussions or they may be used as occasion permits in run-of-the-mill ways. The teacher's own behavior is not exempt from such clinical observation. This will include such things as frequency of intrusion and the tendency to state personal opinions with objective check on their effect. Last, but not least, the teacher may move more certainly in identifying those students who have a potential for becoming genuine leaders.

What does discussion accomplish? Finally, we ask what can or what does a discussion accomplish? By this we have in mind something different than whether Procedure-U or Procedure-D was rightly manipulated or whether the phases of substantive, exemplary, and stimulative were properly balanced—important as they are. Nor do we ask only about the degree of participation, or whether a good discussion was had. We are not concerned with what a vote may have reported, if one were taken, for voting is the least of the important outcomes of a discussion. The "fetish of the majority" could well be less honored with the result that better discussions might be held.

We are concerned with such results as the following. What is the evidence that any student has changed his mind? This will hang upon his *discovery* of his mind for he cannot change something which he does not possess. Has he learned the true meaning of freedom of speech, which is that he has a right to express his thoughts only if he has some? Does he take delight chiefly in the clash of opinion but is not disposed to contemplate the truth which may come from a genuine meeting of minds? Does he understand the meaning of "peaceful assembly" and the rights and duties which inhere in it? Does he voluntarily submit to new findings of fact, does he display a will to conquer rather than persuade with sweet reasonableness? What is his attitude toward compromise: when and how it is rightly used? Has he discovered that the thing which human beings principally want is to find out what they *really* want because they believe they *ought* to want it? Does he know a genuine issue when he confronts one? Has he developed more logical habits and does he see how they may serve to improve his moral behavior? Does he mistake a filled mind for an informed one? Has the discussion given so much emphasis to procedural rules that he believes that mastery of Robert's *Rules of Order* is the chief end of discussion? Has he learned, a little at least, to trust more to intelligence? Has he learned that facts do not speak for themselves, unless he be their ventriloquist? Does he know the difference between opinion and conviction? Has he learned what it will cost him to keep his prejudices? Is he willing to *act out* the conclusions which have been reached?

But, perhaps most important of all, does the student know that once he has committed himself to the use of intelligence he nor anyone else can predict where he will come out—except that he and his world will be different? If the French proverb be true that "from the clash of opinions the truth spurts out," is he willing to accept it? [8]

[8] You will find *The Journal of Social Issues* useful in your approach to many phases of teaching. See, for instance, the Spring, 1948, issue, "The Dynamics of the Discussion Group." See also B. S. Bloom, "Thought-Processes in Lectures and Discussion," *The Journal of General Education*, VII (April, 1953), and Sidney J. French, *Accent on Teaching* (New York: Harper & Brothers, 1954).

CHAPTER XX

Teaching Skills and
Understandings That Persist

THE TITLE OF this chapter reports my approach to the *what* and *how* of the persisting elements of an education in human affairs. It is my way of stating the problem of the "transfer of training." Certainly it is common to all the social studies.

"Transfer of training" is an unfortunate term. That term, "transfer of training," is a somewhat unfortunate one. "Transfer" connotes carrying something of mass and bulk over in time and space. "Training" connotes the fixing of reflex habits. Neither is appropriate for matters as creative as intellectual skills and understanding. The latter, as Professor P. W. Bridgeman observed, is "as private as pain."

Some general principles about transfer of learning. The present state of knowledge respecting the transfer of learning (which term I shall use to cover both skill and understanding) may be reported as follows: (*a*) the greater the native intelligence of the learner, the greater the transfer; (*b*) rote learning produces a minimum of transfer; (*c*) the greater the similarity between situations, the greater the transfer; (*d*) the fewer the similarities between situations, the more the "higher" intellectual powers are required; (*e*) some transfer takes place without formal instruction, depending on the native intelligence of the learner but such transfer is less than was once thought, and (*f*) learning transfers best if what is taught in one situation is taught in terms of its applicability to other situations.[1]

[1] See John Dewey, *Democracy and Education*, pp. 63-80, and *Logic: The Theory of Inquiry*; George Katona, *Organizing and Memorizing: Studies in the Psychology of Learning*; Guy M. Whipple, "The Transfer of Training," 27th Yearbook of the National

Teaching is teaching transfer.   I take my cue from (f) above. Teaching is *teaching the transfer of learning*. Learning may be said to persist only if students are able to apply what they learn to new situations. That is the nub of the problem of transfer. The reliability with which they do this depends on their ability to abstract from present situations something which is common to other situations of the same type or class. This is the ability to get the theory of what they learn, for theory is "nothing but the consciousness of the way in which one adjusts his habits of working to meet new situations." [2]

This adjustment may be illustrated at a simple level by the ability of a Boy Scout to build a fire in the woods according to the principle or theory which disciplined his building one in a training session. In the woods he does not do it in the same place or with the same sticks. But he does it the same way. He abstracts from both situations certain basic and general phases of behavior.

The effective aspect of transfer.   This illustration carries the full weight of the *general* nature of transfer and hence the persistence of skill and understanding. On its effective side, it is skill in and understanding of a process or situation. A Boy Scout employs the implicit hypothesis that "If certain things are given and treated in a certain way, then a certain outcome may reasonably be expected." His fire-building behavior is not random but structured and systematic. Moreover, it is both covert and overt behavior: it demands the manipulation of materials, muscles, and mind. That it is done almost automatically or by habit does not gainsay that it contains elements of understanding as well as skill.

The affective aspect of transfer.   His behavior also has certain affective concomitants. These are interest, appreciation, and attitude. He has an interest in fire-building, he appreciates it, and has an attitude of pride or achievement in mastering the art of it. (Memory, of course, operates throughout.) I know of no way to assess the weights of these affects of his experience. I only know that his behavior involves both effective and affective phases as does all learned behavior.

A Boy Scout might come by these effective and affective results of learning without formal instruction, just as some of your students might come by the effective and affective results of social study without it. But, if you wish to "make assurance doubly sure" you are advised to teach them so

---

Society for the Study of Education; E. Boring, H. Langfeld, and H. Wald, *Introduction to Psychology*; Arthur F. Bentley, *Behavior, Knowledge, Fact*; and Lloyd G. Humphreys, "The Transfer of Training," *Journal of General Education*, V (April, 1951).

[2] George H. Mead, "Industrial Education and the Working Man and the School," *Elementary School Teacher*, IX (1908-9), pp. 377-378.

that they may transfer their learning. It is for *use*. Why not take your cue from that fact?

Concepts and practices related to transfer. Let us now review some of the concepts and practices which bear on the transfer of learning. They are such as these: frame of reference, operational aims, developmental constructs, principles, problems, theory, method of inquiry, processes, introspection, order, essence, symbolism, ideal type, cause, and generalizations, propositions, and judgments. To these others will be added in this chapter and in those which follow. Opposed to these as inadequate for teaching transfer are such as rote or fact learning, slogans, clichés, exhortation and commandments, signs, and conditioned reflexes.

The acid test of transfer. In being concepts and practices these are the "right" and "wrong" tools, respectively, for teaching so that learning persists. Each of the "right" tools contributes to the student's ability to generalize. This is the acid test of transfer.

Acquaintance with three pairs of concepts is basic to an understanding of the transfer of learning. These are fact-generalization, percept-concept, and formula-principle.

Facts and generalizations. Justice Holmes observed that "a generalization is empty so far as it is general. Its value depends on the number of particulars which it calls up to the speaker and the hearer." The particulars are the facts. But they are not just "the facts"; they are "the facts in the case," that is, those which provide the materials for the making of a generalization. It is families or classes of facts about which generalizations are assertions. Thus, "explorations and migrations are important events in history," or "young people today are less respectful of authority than they were fifty years ago" are generalizations whose truth depends on what the *facts* are about explorations and migrations and the behavior of young people now and fifty years ago. Generalizations abstract from a welter of facts those which "go together." Thus they reduce to order what would otherwise be a meaningless hodgepodge of disconnected facts. Without the power to generalize, our experience would be chaotic and unorganized. Thus it is that facts and generalizations are the reverse and obverse of the coin of thought. If either side were missing the coin would lose its purchasing power. Facts and generalizations are co-operating factors in the organization of experience. Emerson's remark that "the power of generalizing differences men" gives you the gauge by which you may distinguish between agile and slow minds and thus decide the extent to which, and the level at which, you will try to teach generalizations. All students generalize but the level at which and the precision with which they do it differ greatly. Their generalizations are usually known to them as opinions. They often generalize or opinionate on the basis of quite inadequate facts. Sometimes they do it without any facts. It is then that they tell us, paradoxically, that the "facts speak for themselves."

This brings us to "the facts in the case." Heaven help the student who has never faced a fact, that is, who has never discovered that his words must always refer to the facts of which they are the symbols. He must, moreover, be challenged to reveal what the facts are which lie behind and give credence to his opinions. His facts must always face trial. They must always be tested by such criteria as these: Are they true or false? What are they the facts of? What are they good for? What will they permit him to know more clearly and more certainly? What action is implicit in them? Words are thus the insigne or shoulder patch of either clarity or confusion in thought.

The phrase "the facts in the case" means the facts in a given inquiry. Facts in isolation are worthless and hence to conceive of an education as a process of amassing facts is a worthless conception. (The cartoonist James Thurber once depicted the man who "didn't know anything but facts" as the lonesome man at a party.)

When we say that the facts in the case are those in a given inquiry we mean what Charles Darwin meant when he said that "all observation must be for or against some view, if it is to be of any service." We get our facts by observation. We then classify them and seek to learn what is common to each class. We generalize them. Thus it is that facts do not come first. They come because we have an interest, because we are curious, and because we look for those which will satisfy our interest and curiosity. In the light of this sequence it is meaningless to talk about "the facts"; they are never *the*, but *these*. Nor are they taken at random. They are selected to serve some view and establish some proposition. Facts are data or evidence about something other than themselves. They must always be interpreted, accounted for, and explained. They are not to be collected as curios. We look not only at them but *with* them. The latter fact is still too little known.

But these statements and cautions make facts no less important. Your obligation is to teach respect for them, to enjoin that those pertinent to an inquiry be not overlooked and that none are withheld. For your students to fail in any of these matters would mean that they had not given facts a fair trial.

As conditions change, so do facts and generalizations. They change much faster in an advanced culture such as ours than in a primitive one. For this

reason you will have to play the role of prophet as well as priest. As priest
you will treat of facts and generalizations which have not changed. As
prophet you will teach new facts and help frame new generalizations.

Percepts and concepts. A discussion of percepts and concepts will,
necessarily, cover some of the ground over which we have just traveled. It
was the philosopher Kant who said that "Perception without conception
is blind, and conception without perception is empty." He and Justice
Holmes were talking about much the same thing. They were speaking of
the interdependence of facts and generalizations, and of percepts and concepts, respectively. Concepts single out or abstract types and classes of
percepts and give them general or class names. Thus your students may
perceive such things as overcrowded land and overcrowded rooms, unsani-
tary and ramshackle dwellings, a mixture of residential and industrial land
use, and alleys littered with trash and garbage. These separate percepts,
when classified and related, become the concept "the slum." Thus percepts
are the raw materials out of which concepts are formed, in the same way in
which facts are the raw materials out of which generalizations are formed.
If we take our life in its most elementary state it is but a stream of percepts
or experiences. If we classify, order, and sort them we turn them into concepts. We thus conceptualize and simplify them. Without concepts and
generalizations we can deal only with what is unique. With concepts and
generalizations we may deal with what is general. A general education is
general in just the sense that it seeks to effect the substitution of a conceptual order for a perceptual one. We may generalize about or conceptualize things and experiences which are not present. With them we may
deal with past, present, and future. They thus give us a greater mobility of
mind in the three time dimensions in which we live. We can only *sense*
facts and percepts; we can *think* generalizations and concepts.

One of the consequences of a fast-changing society is the flux and the
welter, if not also the richness, of the experiences by which our students
live. The task of learning how to order those experiences into useful conceptions of life falls heavily on the school. This introduces the vexing problem of the use of concepts in such ways as to convey clear and unmistakable meanings. This problem is aggravated by the fact that the more complex our world becomes, the more complex become the concepts needed
to deal with it intelligently. The matter is made still more difficult by virtue
of the fact that there are two sets of concepts: the one which makes up
the conceptual system of teen-agers and the one which teachers use. The
former set is pretty certain to be more picturesque than precise; the latter
set is pretty apt to be more precise than picturesque.

Formulas and principles.   Formulas and principles are so different in kind as to make them antithetical rather than complementary. The former deal with certainties; the latter with probabilities.

By formulas I refer to recipes for understanding and conduct; by principles I refer to general guides to them. Formulas are in the nature of "thou shalt" and "thou shalt not." They order and forbid; they do not explain. They prescribe and hence anticipate explicit behavior. Principles are in the nature of general propositions or statements of relationships. Principles are of two kinds: unconditional and conditional. "The apathy of voters varies with their interest in and understanding of the issues in an election" is an unconditional principle. It states a relation between a constant (voters' apathy) and two variables (interest in and understanding of issues). It tells no one what he ought or ought not to do. It does, however, tell him what he may expect. "If delinquency is to be reduced, then we ought to know more about the kinds of control which will prevent or cure it" is a conditional principle. Its "if clause" identifies an end to be achieved; its "then clause" states what is necessary to achieve that end. It states nothing categorically. Thus principles tell us what might be done or what relationships exist. Formulas tell us what to do.

From these differences, it is clear that formulas provide the basis for an education in cultures characterized by permanence; principles for an education in cultures characterized by change. Formulas induce fixed and simple habits. Principles induce reflection as the basis for examining the adequacy and relevance of old habits and provide the basis for changing them to meet different situations. Your students cannot do without habits. The problem is whether they are to form them by formulas or principles.

"Slow-minded" and "fast-minded."   Those who can master only formulas are the "slow-minded"; those who can master principles are the "fast-minded." You will be tempted to make a quick and quite final judgment as to the category in which a given student falls. You will also be disposed to teach formulas to the former and principles to the latter. The only injunction given here is that you try to educate all on the basis of principles. This will require your taking full account of such individual differences as IQ, interest, preoccupations, reading skill and speed, and every factor you can identify which appears to interfere with the ability to deal with principles. The problem may turn out, in part, to be that of a teacher who is too "fast-minded" rather than students who are too "slow-minded." Students who are incapable of simple reflection and abstraction are perhaps not as numerous as we believe. Yours will likely distribute over a fairly wide range respecting such capacities. Hence your task is to match the level of your teaching with the level of the capacities of your students to deal with principles. Unless you follow this principle you will shortly discover, if you do, that you are making sense to only a few. Among these will be some who are quite capable of teaching themselves, once they have mastered the fundamental tools.

The problem of individual differences. The discussion of these pairs of terms and their implications for general education has immediate bearing on the problem of individual differences. Some of the nontechnical aspects of that problem were mentioned in Chapter II. While I shall not now undertake to deal with all the technical or strictly pedagogical phases of individual differences, some comments of a precise nature are appropriate.

Absence of emotional incentives. The first is, however, nontechnical. Perhaps never before have young people been expected to work from motives so detached from emotional incentive.[3] This is school work, as well as "work work." You will seldom need to transfer impulse to your students; rather you will need to direct or redirect that which they have. I am now talking about *interest*, which you will need constantly to think about, that is, think about ways of arousing and directing it. The doing of this involves many things, some of which have been touched upon in earlier chapters. But if I repeat, I offer no apology. Are you asking them to re-cite, before you *ex-cite* them? Furthermore, are you asking them *only* to re-cite, which is to give back what you gave them—maybe dull and worthless facts. If you gave them empty containers, they can give you back nothing better. They may be shiny, but empty.

Real questions or negative commands. Are your questions the kind that create curiosity or do they make it impossible? Questions that do not stimulate are not really questions at all. They are only negative commands. But you will ask stimulating and "curious" questions only if you can stimulate yourself at the same time you try to stimulate your students. *You* must be in the act you wish them to enter. Questions are a form of near-magic. When properly used they do two things: they open the path for students and incite students to open it themselves. Montaigne taught us that.

Inert and dynamic ideas. I am speaking about the difference between inert and dynamic ideas. For some, ideas must be quite simple, for others much less so. But you will never know which can handle either kind and which are incapable of doing so unless you experiment with them—"them"

[3] See Jane Addams, *The Spirit of Youth and the City Streets* (New York: The Macmillan Co., 1910).

refers both to students and ideas. Inert ideas offer no invitation to learning; they only require that students listen, and that without reward except that they have "paid attention."

What is the object?   How certain are you that you have made clear what the *object* is to which you wish them to attend? An object of study is any datum having an empirical content accessible to the members of a class. This means that it must lend itself to experience with it. Thus it becames accessible. It must *be* something which lets your students *do* something. Thus the mode of approach to any object of study to be known is dependent on the nature of the knower.[4] No objects are naturally interesting, as I observed earlier.

The object must be significant.   You do not start with abstractions. You start with concretions. Appreciation is first, understanding is second. Field trips, movies, recordings, and abundant illustrations are good beginners. It is activities such as these which will make the object of study a *significant object*. It will be significant to different students through different approaches to it. Your beginnings will need to take account of what will arouse interest in it for students with different capacities. Their capacity to attend to it depends on many other conditions: their preoccupations, their doubts, their aspirations, their power of imagery, their ability to reflect, and many more. None of these may be taken for granted. You must know as much about your students in these terms as is humanly possible.

To whom is it significant?   I so well remember once lecturing to a class of policemen. The object with which I was dealing was significant to me and I naïvely assumed that it was significant to them. I had spoken, using maps and slides, for about twenty minutes when one interrupted me with the query, "Say, professor, what is all this about, anyway?" Only then did I come to sense that I had not been teaching at all. I had only been disturbing the silence. I started all over. This time, it was from *their* point of scratch, not mine. The moral is that there can be no transfer unless there is first *communication*. The test of communication is whether what you say is somewhere within the "bull's-eye" of your students (see Chapter XVIII).

What can students "make" of an object?   What can your students *do* with the object of study? Can you make them feel it? What is something *like it* to which you can refer, something now in their experience? Can it be handled? or drawn? Can a chart or graph be made which will rep-

---

[4] See Karl Mannheim, *Ideology and Utopia* (New York: Harcourt, Brace & Co., 1936), pp. 76-77. See his excellent bibliography on many phases of the nature of social knowledge.

resent some of its meaning? I mean what can they *make* of it. What will quicken their activity toward it? (Nietzsche once remarked that he hated anything that merely instructed him without increasing or directly quickening his *activity*.) Are you aware of the truth that your students' ideas of what the facts are may determine their conduct more than your ideas of what they are? Are you only trying to pull something out of their memory and, if so, what does it have to do with something other than remembering? Is the textbook the authority which you are now asking them to re-cite? Are you punishing them with "Why didn't you read what I assigned?"

The assignment is important. How clearly and eagerly did they anticipate this session? That depends a great deal on your conception of an "assignment." To assign may mean to dictate or prescribe. It may also mean to point out clearly, to designate, and to preview. Did you make it by "pages in a book" or did you make it by indicating where the class is in a co-operative enterprise and what the next steps in it might be? If the enterprise has already enlisted their interest and participation, why not ask *them* what the next steps are? This will be a test, not only of them, but of you.

Students' attitudes are your cues. You must be free to give your undivided attention and energy to the attitudes of your students. They are your cues.[5] Above everything else, you will need constantly to keep in mind that the complexity of present-day problems is much greater than the capacity of present-day minds, of both young and old. Simplify. Whatever intellectual food you give your students will do little good or mean little to them unless you give them the appetite, without which they cannot digest it. •

The nature of "make-work." If you are artful and deceitful enough you can *make* your students work. But this will be "make-work," and largely unrewarding toil. What an awful name we have given to a certain "aid to instruction"—a *work-book*. The name alone is enough to make it distasteful. I do not mean by this that you are to conceive learning as a "pushover." But your students will never push it over unless they can find some curiosity, some wonder, and some challenge in it. Many so-called "workbooks" are bound volumes of blank spaces which students must fill in only because "teacher" told them to. I do not suggest work-books be outlawed. I only suggest that they have the quality of *worth* which will make the work they entail rewarding. You will have to depend on many such devices

[5] See John Dewey, *Democracy and Education*, "The Nature of Subject Matter," pp. 212-227. This book is still the classic in its field.

but take care lest they demand only that something be *done*, rather than understood.

Some student expectations.   Suppose that you find yourself in a school in which students are habituated to being *commanded* rather than taught. You will be confronted with something close kin to a dare: "Go ahead and teach us if you think you can." What will you do? You will launch a long-term campaign whose rewards both to you and them will be far from immediate. You will need to redefine their conception of the whole experience of education. This can be done, if it can, not by preaching but by *teaching*. But on this point I have no nice package of advice to give you. The first thing is to recognize the problem for what it is. Your biggest asset is the quality of *person* you can show yourself to be. Some of the things I said in Chapter II may help you. Beyond those I shall not go. The test will come, and you will know it when it comes, in the form of respect for you and, through that, respect for learning. This will mean that you have already begun to win them. But no "fad" will save you, only ingenuity and sometimes something close to genius. They will become less blasé. They will begin to demonstrate something like interest and with it a quality of genuine humility. They will not become a room full of Uriah Heeps. You would not wish that. If you get something less of the attitude of "O, yeah?" you will know that the climate has changed. The great change, for them, will be in a teacher who does not conceive of teaching as a series of "tell me."

You must economize.   In all these matters you will need to stretch yourself over a very wide range of activities and responsibilities. Hence you will have to *economize* your nervous and intellectual energy. This can be done through legitimate standardization, not the kind which kills the spirit but the kind which gives life to it. Standardization does not, necessarily, mean mechanization. You will not dispense with originality and initiative but you will conserve them for application at the points of greatest efficiency. Teachers are required to do an almost unconscionable amount of "bookkeeping." Delegate what you can and streamline what you must do yourself.[6] Many of these matters relate to the wisdom, foresight, and cooperative vision of your "superiors" and genuine reform may have to wait upon changes at the level of administration in which, ideally, you and your teacher colleagues ought to have a share.

Knowledge must get a "round trip."   Finally, respecting the art of teaching, be sure that every bit of knowledge gets a "round trip." It is not

[6] H. G. Wells, *The Salvaging of Civilization* (New York: The Macmillan Co., 1921) p. 158.

enough just to "say your say," or for your students to "say their lesson." Each needs to wait for its "echo." When you talk, get them to "play it back to you." When they talk, get them to play it back among themselves, with you taking the part you believe appropriate. Your tools are the gimlets of "how," "why," "can you illustrate it," and the like. Only a reply of "yes" tells you little, if anything, for *sure*. The great danger is not that your students will do ill, but that they will do nothing. But unless the climate is a friendly one, many will not hazard anything but silent or vocal agreement. Half of your task may be to listen, the other half is to be worth listening to. The final test, if there be anything so simple, is this: what are you proposing to your students' *belief?*

The art of teaching and individual differences.   I am still talking about individual differences because I am talking about some of the arts of teaching. Transfer goes on, not on a mass but on an individual basis. The art of teaching always reduces to the art of teaching *individuals*. You cannot separate teaching from teaching individuals. But you can separate *them*, and that may be one of the things you will be faced with. This means some plan of segregation according to ability to learn, and to transfer learning. Whether it is legitimate depends on the consequences for the students concerned. That must be your bench mark. If the range of abilities is very great, some kind of segregation seems justified. That may mean different tasks for different students in the *same* room or a different program for different students in a *different* room. The latter is obviously the more manageable. But that choice is almost certainly beyond your power. It is a matter of facilities, teacher-talent, and administrative provision. (You will constantly need to make a distinction between problems which are properly yours to solve and those which, by their very nature, are administrative problems.)

The good and bad of segregation.   Segregation may have good and bad consequences. It gives both the "bright" and "dull" a better chance in that teaching can be done with greater efficiency. But we must ask what such efficiency may cost in social terms. It may cost the "dull" students segregation with *only* their kind. They may, in such cases, never see or hear students superior to themselves. (They may still mix with them in out-of-class activities.) It may rob them of a kind of stimulation for which there is no substitute. The "bright" students will, almost certainly, be helped because they can now progress at their own pace, as can also the "dull." But, on the other side, they will lose whatever value accrued to them by reason of being "looked up to"—if such was the case—by their less able peers. To none of these problems do I give any pat answers. I can only say that there is a point past which, in a class of very wide range of abilities, spatial segregation seems indicated. Unless it is done, everyone will suffer. The practice of democracy requires some leveling down, but it does not require that the "common man" become the "highest common denominator" (see Chapter VIII). We must do all we can for the "leader types" as well as all we can for the "follower types." [7] *Each* requires individual attention.

Learning is intensive and extensive. I now address the problem of the transfer of learning from another perspective. Teaching must have an *intensive* and an *extensive* quality if learning is to transfer. It must be intensive in the sense that it is *principled* in what it treats intensively, and extensive in that these principles be applied to other contemporary and future situations. It must be concerned with what is *general*.

This observation suggests a caution: to know "in general" has two quite distinct meanings. One may know in more or less general terms, that is, he may develop the habit of thinking. This requires that he grasp the elements common to similar situations. But, given the fact that one may develop such a habit, he cannot do it unless he has learned to generalize from specific cases.[8]

How intensive and extensive learning differ. Learning *this* example is intensive learning. Learning *by* example is extensive learning. In doing this, your students must learn *this* example as something which has a general or generic quality which is referable to examples or situations of like *genre*. Great importance does and should attach to *this* example, as our mothers are wont to tell us. They mean by that that if *this* "lesson" or example is really learned it will have general "lesson value" through its automatic transfer to other "lessons" of a similar kind. An "example" or "lesson" is, by

[7] The immediately foregoing discussion makes no claim to a complete treatment of the problem of individual differences. It takes a myriad of forms and you will constantly confront it in one way or another. It is universal. I assume that you will subscribe to and read one or more of the journals for teachers of your craft, in which problems such as this one are being continually discussed. No textbook can keep you abreast of advances in your art. I shall have more to say, explicitly, about the problem of individual differences later in this chapter. See Edward Krug and G. Lester Anderson, Editors, *Adapting Instruction in the Social Studies to Individual Differences*, 15th Yearbook of the National Council of the Social Studies, 1944.

[8] See Chapter VIII for discussion of this view. I have the feeling that some of the literature dealing with prejudice, tolerance, and allied attitudes holds that such dispositions may be acquired or got rid of *in general*. Such notions are quite erroneous. Attitudes are the subjective aspect of the shield of reality, the other side of which is the objects toward which attitudes are held. Attitudes cannot be acquired in a general way any more than objects can. Each is, by definition, a quite discreet thing, although the expression of attitudes will depend, to a large extent, on the nature of the situation.

definition, an example or lesson of a principle which has general validity and applicability. It stands for a principle, process or situation. That it *does*, needs to be explicitly taught. Thus both intensive and extensive learning are necessary for its transfer.

How intensive and extensive learning are related. The relation of intensive to extensive learning may be illustrated in many ways. It is not enough to teach that the Pilgrim Fathers left Holland to seek their fortunes in a new world, or that they entered into a compact before they landed. The generic nature of their behavior needs also to be taught. Otherwise their migration and their formation of a solemn pact are only interesting episodes. Some general transfer value may leak from such episodes but we cannot afford to depend on its leaking only. The trek of the Pilgrims was an example of great faith and courage. The Mayflower Compact was an historic example of the formation of a political association which sought to effect a working balance between freedom and authority. Each was an event in time; each was also an illustration of timeless processes and values. If, for instance, the Erie Canal is known only by its date and the kinds of cargoes carried on it, it is not learned as an example of a mode of transportation which had much to do with a phase of the westward expansion of our economy. It is both event and symbol of a process.

Do not leave transfer to chance. This again raises the question of the level of abstraction at which you should aim in your teaching. Some transfer is, perhaps, inevitable for the brighter students. But even for them you cannot afford to leave it to the chance factor of native ability. They may be able in many ways, the least of which may be the ability to transfer their knowledge.

The four-year-old who calls all four-legged animals "doggie" has abstracted the common element of four-leggedness from his pet and applied it to all the other four-legged animals which he sees. (Or it may be that it is a creature covered with fur which conditions him to call all other fur-covered creatures "doggie.") By the same token, some students may be able to make some simple transfers. But the differences between social objects, as well as their similarities, must be taken account of. The problem is more complex than one of "doggie."

Teach both specifics and generals. The law of diminishing returns is a principle in physics, but it also has applicability to economic—even dietary —matters. Of leaders there are many kinds, but all symbolize *leadership* so far as their general qualities are concerned. Compacts, ententes, charters, and constitutions have a general quality in common, but rote learning of

them will not insure that their common attributes will be learned. (Rot
learning is only saying, it is not *knowing*.) Each permits examples to b·
learned, intensively and extensively.

How principles may be taught.   Principles cannot be taught by dicta
tion, nor by senseless drill. How they apply may permit something lik·
repetition to help fix them in memory. But this must be memory of thei·
applicability, not only of them as terms and sentences. The view is curren·
in some quarters that students can be taught the meaning of the Constitu·
tion by the mere repetition of its provisions and/or by patriotism being
preached to them. Patriotism is no cult; it is a code of ethics. The Consti
tution can be learned for *good* (by which I mean for its lasting and ethica·
qualities) only if its provisions are related to universal situations in which
the social controls which it set up may be understood. If its meaning were
self-evident we should not need a judicial system to interpret it. How
pathetic then that any should suppose that students do not need to in·
terpret it, which is to know its meaning and generic quality. Only if it be
seen in these terms will it contribute to the student's general education. In
all these matters the apparent "homogeneity of knowledge," of which I
spoke earlier, can be revised to address the levels of understanding of a
very heterogeneous student body.

Continuity and interaction.   The problem of the transfer of learning requires that social study serve the requirements of both continuity and
interaction. These are the "longitudinal and lateral aspects of experience." [8]

A ninth grade illustration.   Assume that a teaching-learning situation
at the ninth grade level has to do with an understanding of family budgets.
Should you try to get your students to think of themselves as parents and,
in that social role, deal with budgetary problems chiefly from the parental
perspective? I doubt if the bridge of understanding can span a river of
that width. I suggest a narrower stream and a shorter span of transfer.

Ninth graders are from eight to ten years away from marriage, let alone
parenthood. In light of this fact you might have fair success with a project
which deals with spending money, the purchase of clothing, carfare, lunch
money, amusements, and the like. Beyond this time-frame you can go only
at the risk of losing your audience. Once their interest had been secured
in these things, as they see and feel them, you would then seek to achieve
continuity and interaction by showing the relation of these personal aspects
of finance to those with which they may be functionally related. That

[9] See John Dewey, *Experience and Education*, p. 42 (New York: The Macmillan Co.,
1938).

might take you into matters of family income, and the principle of the budget in more general terms. You might be able to develop this topic as an aspect of the relation between rights and duties.

Extend the radius of understanding by teaching principles. Whatever the specific content, your task is one of extending the radium of understanding and hence increasing the area of life over which a *principle* might be applied. To succeed at it you will need to depend quite as much on your art and good common sense as on the aid of the psychologists and sociologists. Science follows common sense rather than precedes it. The social sciences, particularly, cannot come into their own except men find themselves in social problem situations and, on the basis of a good deal of trial and error, simple empiricism, and theory, build up, bit by bit, the kind of knowledge which can rightly qualify as scientific. Your students must, to a great degree, travel this tedious route—and so must you.[10]

The principle of subsidy. Now let us examine the problem of teaching the principle of subsidy which was implicit in the foregoing. You might begin with the teen-agers' allowance (a characteristic of middle-class families and maybe enjoyed by only a few of your students). You might begin with federal subsidy to ex-GIs, or, if the school is in a rural area, with farm produce price support. These are cases. The principles lie deeper. They lie in the fact that our society is one which practices mutual aid in many ways, among them such as have been suggested. Local and county governments get various kinds of state subsidy—for roads and schools, for instance. The federal government has given and still gives aid through various kinds of subsidy: the tariff, grants to colleges (the so-called land-grant schools of mechanics and agriculture), land grants to railroads; money for education and roads; for conservation projects, old-age assistance, social security, aid to dependent children, and unemployment benefits. "Subsidy" may not be the most appropriate term. If not, you face the task of distinguishing between various kinds of aid and giving each its proper definition. Assume that you identify a number of kinds of aid which may be brought under a common term. This term is a concept. You seek to develop understanding of it: how it applies in a variety of situations through inquiry into a variety of examples. (See Chapter XXI for the social processes with which the principle of subsidy may be identified.)

Tariff as an example of subsidy. Suppose that you concentrate on the tariff as an example of subsidy. This may be quite a new idea. If so, it will require the mastery of new terms. It may throw new light on the concept

[10] See John Dewey, "Social Science and Social Control," *John Dewey's Philosophy*, edited by Joseph Ratner (New York: Modern Library, Inc., 1939), pp. 949-954.

of the "service state," which ours has been, tariff-wise, for a long time
But the tariff is only one illustration. If it is appropriate as a typical in
stance of subsidy, you will then relate it to others which may be more
or less typical. The degree to which they are or are not typical needs to be
taught. The ideal arrangement would be to provide for the study of a series
of situations which illustrate the same concept and principle. Thus you
have some insurance that the experience will not be dully repetitive.

Some sample generalizations. A number of general propositions or
principles might be derived from such inquiries. Their derivation should
be a co-operative affair. They certainly must not be dictated by you: teacher
dictation and teacher-student derivation of propositions are as different as
night and day. Such generalizations as these might be formulated: "the
principle of subsidy is common to several kinds of 'protective' situations,
among them being the tariff, differential freight rates, and GI tuition
grants," "to grant a subsidy means to grant a form of assistance to someone which will give him certain advantages over others to whom it is not
granted," "subsidies are granted according to clearly stated rules which
determine the conditions under which they are given," and "subsidies are
usually defended in terms of the way they contribute to the general welfare or the good of all, rather than in terms of the advantage which they
give to special interest groups."

Generalizations and particulars. Such generalizations as these will, of
course, be worth no more than the particulars which are in them. They
thus suggest the particulars of your approach to them. The entire enterprise will provide for a great variety of intellectual skills. Such as the following suggest themselves: distinguishing between adequate and inadequate evidence (the nature of valid proof); using proper analogies; checking the validity of inference by using the syllogism; communicating clearly
in oral and written form; making clear and succinct explanations; defining
terms; identifying causal factors; and distinguishing between statements
of fact and statements of preference, what *is* as distinct from what *ought
to be*. This last skill suggests that "ought principles" are not ruled out but
it is hoped that your students will learn both "ought" and "is" principles.
A great deal of teaching in the social studies tends to forget the is-ness of
its subject matter and engages, excessively, in its ought-ness.

Method and content are related. It is my belief that the use and mastery
of such skills as these must not be considered as merely the by-products of
teaching-learning. You do not "teach the facts" with your right hand and
the method of inquiry with your left hand. Facts become pertinent and
useful only as they are processed by the method of inquiry. The ultimate

goal is the fixing of belief in propositions which rest on facts. Hence, method and content are inextricably woven together. Methods are methods of managing material, as we observed earlier.

The bridge of understanding. I have spoken of the playing of social roles and of the bridge of understanding. The theory of transfer to which they belong may now be stated: the bridge of understanding, which is the bridge over which transfer of learning must cross, can span a river of social roles which is as wide as the student's ability to imagine himself playing roles more advanced than those which he now plays and this, in turn, depends on the degree to which such roles (different and also more advanced) can be shown to be associated with and the natural extension of his present social roles.

On this whole matter Montaigne has words of wisdom for us.

Let the tutor demand of [the student] an account not only of the words of his lesson, but of their meaning and substance, and let him estimate the profit he has gained, not by the testimony of his memory, but of his life. Let him show what he has just learned from a hundred points of view, and adapt it to as many different subjects, to see if he has rightly taken it in and made it his own.

The role of imagination. A means indispensable to effecting the transfer of learning is imagination. But this never operates in a vacuum. Given the power to imagine—in varying degrees—and access to abundant facts, imagination may go to work. Although facts do not produce imagination, your students will have nothing to imagine about unless they have some facts. Imagining is assuming things similar to (or different from) those at hand. The making of hypotheses is imagination pure and simple. But hypotheses do not spring from a mind barren of facts. Given fair talents of imagination and access to interesting and provoking facts, you will be surprised at the crop of hypotheses which will be produced. The more you can define hypothesis-making as a game, the more rewarding it will be.[11]

If, as teachers, we fear imagination we fear thought itself, for thought requires that we construct something which has not been constructed, at least by us. To think is to imagine alternative ways of solving a problem. If we fear imagination we fear our own ability to discipline it. We often

[11] The making of an hypothesis is, to a large degree, an exercise in analogy. Harvey's theory of the circulation of the blood was suggested by the analogy of the water pump.

See "Creative Talent" by L. L. Thurstone (The Psychometric Laboratory of the University of Chicago, No. 61, December 1950). See also "Dissent: The Stuff of Democracy" in *Minerva's Progress* by Alfred E. Cohen (New York: Harcourt, Brace and Co., 1946). Dr. Cohen suggests that to dissent is to imagine something new and better in the realm of freedom. The partial paralysis of the will to dissent is one of the most serious manifestations of the crisis in valuation; see Chapter VII.

suppress it in our students, almost without knowing that we do it. Whe
we rule it "off limits," the mind has literally no place to go beyond th
commonplace. In doing so we hinder the intellectual growth of our stu
dents and the development of their creative talents upon which democ
racy, of all forms of government and ways of life, places the highes
premium.[12]

The value of analogy.   Your chief stock-in-trade is analogies. These ar
models *of* and models *for* imagination. They may take the form of simile
metaphor, allegory, parable, or myth. They are always couched in illustra
tions. They require your saying: "Did you ever look at it this way?" "Wha
do you think would happen if . . . ?" or "I wonder if what we have beer
talking about is like this?" Thus will you weave the old and new togethe
in a fabric which will support a generalization about a class or a type
You will take account of both similarities and dissimilarities and exercise
due caution lest you give the notion that you are referring to identities. I
you follow James's advice you will do this in a "lively and entertaining
way." Thus you will teach intensively and extensively.

The transfer of "moral training."   I have been speaking of the problem
of transfer chiefly as it relates to similarities between situations in the
present, although some illustrations have been concerned with the transfer
of learning from present to future situations. I should like to illustrate these
in a somewhat negative way, that is, by reference to certain common-sense
notions of the transfer of "moral training."

Some fallacies about "moral training."   It was once and still is supposed
that certain skills, understandings, and attitudes which may be quite
throughly established in the time of adolescent years and outlooks and in
private or at least only quasi-public situations carry over into impersonal
and completely public situations. The theory of formal discipline made
that assumption. (The McGuffey Readers well illustrate it.) It was, for
instance, supposed that something called "good citizenship" would, if
practiced in primary group situations, persist and manifest itself reliably
and loyally in secondary group situations. The old-fashioned schoolmaster
believed and many of his successors persist in the belief that a student fixed

[12] The most revealing study of the imagination of which I know is John Livingston
Lowes's *The Road to Xanadu* in which the imaginative workings of the mind of Samuel
Taylor Coleridge are set forth. If you know "The Rime of the Ancient Mariner" you
know something of Coleridge's ability to imagine—he had no immediate experience with
the sea (had never even crossed the English Channel) yet through reading and imagining
he gave us a picture of the sea which is perhaps unsurpassed. Lowes speaks of "the deep
well of unconscious cerebration" from which Coleridge drew the materials for the picture.
See also Hoyt Hudson, *Educating Liberally*, Chapter V, "The Arm of Imagination,"
pp. 57-74.

the qualities of "good citizenship" almost for all time if he did not cheat (was honest) in doing his assigned tasks both at school and at home, willingly cleaned the blackboards and erasers and monitored younger children (was co-operative and assumed and carried out his obligations on a more or less voluntary basis) and stood up well under the rigors of athletic competition without flinching (courage). But is teen-age honesty in academic matters and personal matters a certain guarantee that financial and civic honesty will naturally follow when the student has attained adulthood? Is co-operation with his political and civil co-equals inbred because he co-operated with the teacher and with his age peers when he was a schoolboy? Does the courage shown on the athletic field by a youth transfer so as to insure that, as an adult, he will stand up for unpopular causes?

One would like to believe that the answer to each of these questions is, "Yes, of course." But the matter of transfer either of knowledge or moral behavior is not as simple as these illustrations presume. If you will now review the discussions in Chapters II and III you will find theory and fact which will have pertinent transfer value for your reflection on this matter.

The danger of jumping to conclusions. Let us return now to the principle of subsidy. If some of your students get an understanding of it, almost automatically it becomes their obligation to confirm the method by which they got it. Otherwise neither you nor they have any reliable way of knowing how they came by it. Some may have jumped to their conclusion. If so, it is their obligation to step off the distance over which they jumped. This may reveal that their conclusion was unwarranted. Or, if it was correct, they may now confirm the method by which its correctness may be fixed. This is the fixing of belief. For those less well endowed the task is more difficult. We come again, in this remark, to the problem of individual differences.

Feeling and thinking, or affective and effective learning. The concepts of feeling and thinking come again to mind. Their correlatives are found in the affective and effective aspects of learning. They are inseparable, although one or the other may predominate. We thus identify two types of student: those who learn more by affective than effective identification with the objects of study, and vice versa. What we wish in both is what Mannheim has called "social awareness." [13] We also wish that the awareness of all may be fixed by appropriate methods of inquiry. On that score, however, some concessions must be made for those students who are intellectually less well endowed. The degree to which such a concession is

[13] Karl Mannheim, *Diagnosis of Our Time*, pp. 68-69.

made will depend on your knowledge about and acquaintance with your students and the skills and abilities they demonstrate (see Chapters XI and XVIII).

Affective learning and forms of art.   The techniques of teaching which stress the affective aspects of learning are, obviously, those which maximize the use of various forms of art. I do not suggest that they be used only in teaching those students whose intellectual capacities are of a relatively lower order. I suggest that they be used wherever appropriate and for all students. Learning begins best with romance and the various forms of art provide romantic techniques. Maximize your use of them and let their value rest with the quality of responses you get from both types of student. The limits of individual instruction are much narrower than we might wish and for that reason the range of your techniques must, to a large extent, be depended upon to address that problem. In any event the problem of individual differences in the rate and quality of learning is the problem of closing the gap between what you teach and what your students learn.

The pre-eminent value of art is that its many forms are perhaps the most effective resource for developing awareness, and a unique quality of understanding. In his chapter on "Art and Living," Lawrence K. Frank writes as follows:

> More than we realize, significant education occurs through aesthetic experi-
> ence of stories, drama, and poetry wherein a person realizes the valuations and
> the patterns that emotionally satisfy him. He identifies himself with the char-
> acters of the artist's creation whom he strives to emulate, or develops an aver-
> sion to others who affront his sensibilities and outrage his values.[14]

Some artistic aspects of learning.   We have pointed out many times that emotion initiates thought. We have emphasized the importance of sentiment and appreciation. We have stressed the necessity of attention.[15] These are but various ways of identifying the artistic aspects of learning. It begins with them. For some it may also end with them, but we should make every effort to fix belief by means which are more rational and logical.

[14] *Society as the Patient*, pp. 267-268. Although Mr. Frank emphasizes the role of art in education, he does not offer it as a substitute for science. He would, I am sure, subscribe to my view that thinking and loving are joint agents. We must find the right amalgam of the rigor of the Socratic method, the poetic and loving view of Kahlil Gibran, and the aesthetic theories of Plato. (For Plato see especially, *The Republic*, III, Steph. 401-2). See John Dewey, *Art as Experience;* Herbert Read, *Education Through Art*, and *Education for Peace;* and Lawrence K. Frank, "The Arts in Reconstruction," *ibid.*, and Jean Piaget, *The Language and Thought of the Child.*

[15] See "The Decline of Attention" by Clifton Fadiman, *The Saturday Review of Literature*, August 6, 1949. He writes of the need for students to become attentive "to knowledge, wisdom, and the works of the creative imagination." See also Walt Whitman: "Behold a Child Went Forth" for one of the most profound insights in all poetic literature on the subtle factors which help to shape the character of a child.

If that cannot be done with some students let us not believe that they have been taught nothing. We must not spurn imagination. It can be had quite unalloyed and it can be had as a part of science itself which, through its use of imagination, places a high premium on the thinker's ability to suppose what does not exist. We need not choose between unbridled emotions and "pure reason." We must find ways in which they may work together. I now suggest some of these ways.

Some artistic tools. SOCIODRAMA. The theory of sociodrama as a teaching technique was implicit in the discussion in Chapter XI on sympathetic imagination and in Chapter XVIII on the process of identification. It is an effective means of achieving affective learning. It permits the internalization of values by both covert and overt means. I now speak chiefly of its overt practice through role playing in dramatic skits of various kinds. Its power in creating imagery is well illustrated by Hamlet's words in Act II, Scene II, of *Hamlet:*

> . . . I have heard
> That guilty creatures sitting at a play
> Have by the very cunning of the scene
> Been struck so to the soul that presently
> They have proclaimed their malefactions, . . .
> I'll have these players
> Play something like the murder of my father
> Before mine uncle; I'll observe his looks;
> I'll tent him to the quick: if he but blench,
> I know my course. . . .
> The play's the thing
> Wherein I'll catch the conscience of the king.

All sociodrama has a psychodramatic quality. I now think of the socio-drama as appropriate for simulating such group situations as the Constitutional Convention, a citizens' group discussing some policy concerning neighborhood welfare, the session of a town or city council, and the like. I do not suggest elaborate staging. It may be done effectively with no more "props" than were used in Thornton Wilder's *Our Town*. Often, the fewer the props the more effective and the more affective the result. Students may also enact such roles as relief client, delinquent before a court, explorer, social worker, day laborer, political candidate, and many others. These may be done solo or in groups, as the roles suggest. Perhaps group settings are best for we seldom engage in pure soliloquy as human beings.[16]

The sociodrama, like all art forms, is metaphor and has all its suggestive

16 See Arthur Katona, "Sociodrama," in *Social Education*, XIX (January, 1955), and Jacob L. Moreno, *Who Shall Survive?* (New York: Beacon House, 1946).

and vital quality. Moreover, in common with all artistic techniques, the sociodrama has the quality of play whose relation to character was expressed by the poet Schiller in his observation that man is man in the full meaning of the term only when he plays. But do not mistake play for either fun, amusement, or entertainment in the narrow sense.

DRAMA. I refer here to plays and the theater. Drama is depictive. It permits the reliving we spoke of in Chapter XI. Many of the themes in social study may be dramatized and, even though fictionalized, made more real. What can match Synge's *The Playboy of the Western World* for picturing the ways of a simple culture? I have referred to Wilder's *Our Town*. I doubt if it can be surpassed in modern drama as a vehicle for portraying the foibles and virtues of human nature as well as the intimacies of small-town life. I think also of Milne's *Mr. Pim Passes By*; Connelly's *Green Pastures*; Kaufmann's *The Butter and Egg Man*; and Van Druten's *I Remember Mama*. To these add the plays of Shakespeare, Ibsen, Shaw, Barrie, and many others. These can be read or acted. They will portray literature; they will also portray life. The expertness of the teacher of English might be availed of and thus a breech be made in the wall which has too long separated the humanities from the social studies.

THE NOVEL. Perhaps many of the realities of social life are best treated through fiction. It is fiction by declaration, in form, and in fact—but it is not fiction in truth. But, fact or truth aside, it gives us a "lens on life." Let Wallace Stegner state the case.

It is fiction as truth that I am concerned with . . . fiction that reflects experience instead of escaping it, that stimulates instead of deadening . . . if it deals with make-believe—as it . . . must—it creates a make-believe world in order to comment on the real one . . . Because he writes fiction in order to reflect or illuminate life, [the writer's] materials must come out of life. . . . The flimsy little protestations that mark the front gate of every novel, the solemn statements that any resemblance to real persons is entirely coincidental, are fraudulent every time. A writer has no other material to make his people from than the people of his experience. . . . Any good piece of serious fiction is collected out of reality . . . it is [the] capacity for generalizing meaning that gives serious fiction its illuminating and liberating effect. But no fiction should be asked to state its meaning flatly, in conceptual terms, any more than a ghost should be called upon to come out and stand a physical examination.[17]

I have nothing to add to Stegner by way of indicating the place of fiction in the social studies, except to suggest a range of authors:[18] Dreiser,

[17] Wallace Stegner, "Fiction: A Lens of Life," *Saturday Review of Literature*, copyright April 22, 1950, pp. 9-10.

[18] See James McDonald Miller, *An Outline of American Literature* (New York: Farrar & Rinehart, Inc., 1934); Vida Scudder, *Social Ideals in English Literature* (Boston: Houghton Mifflin Co., 1898); *The American Mind* (2 vols.) edited by Harry R. Warfel,

Ferber, Richard Wright, Adamic, Cather, Farrell, Pearl Buck, Rolvaag, Sinclair, Edith Wharton, Steinbeck, Garland, Thomas Wolfe, and Mark Twain.

POETRY. This is perhaps the greatest resource for getting insight into human affairs. In common with almost all other art forms, it is often conceived as an isolated accomplishment and its enjoyment merely an exotic taste. What a pathetic view of the grandest of all literary forms. How can New England in the eighteen fifties be taught without Whittier, the South without Stephen Foster, or the Middle West without Carl Sandburg? Frankly, I do not know. Shakespeare is the poet of feudalism, *Piers Plowman* is indispensable for understanding fourteenth-century England, Shelley is the poet of social democracy and Byron of its political phases. Are the social studies to teach only utility and not beauty? I think not, nor do I believe that they stand in opposition. Indeed the field of art is all poetry; that of which I now speak is only the *form* so named. But do not kill the beauty of it by calling it "collateral reading." [19]

To these art forms should, of course, be added biography, short stories, literature on travel and exploration, music (why should not the songs of nations and regions be proper for social study?), sculpture, paintings, and every other verbal or nonverbal form of symbolism which constitutes so precious and eloquent a part of every culture. (The role of such symbolic forms as the newspaper, radio, and motion pictures will be treated in a later chapter.)

Ralph H. Gabriel, and Stanley T. Williams (New York: American Book Company, 1937); Vernon Louis Parrington, *Main Currents in American Thought* (New York: Harcourt, Brace & Co., 1927); Merle Curti, *The Growth of American Thought* (New York: Harper & Brothers, 1943), and Otis W. Coan and Richard C. Lillard, *America in Fiction* (Stanford: Stanford University Press, 1941). The latter lists over 1,100 titles by more than 650 authors. The titles are classified under such rubrics as "Pioneering," "Farm and Village Life," "Industrial America," "Politics and Public Institutions," "Religion," "The Southern Tradition," and "Minority Ethnic Groups." See also Ernest Horn, *Methods of Instruction in the Social Studies* (New York: Charles Scribner's Sons, 1937).

I am fully aware of a difficulty associated with the use of such art forms as have been suggested. Students may become so much interested in the plot, the story, or the characters that their import for social understanding may suffer. This difficulty can be overcome only by the teacher's artfulness in capitalizing on such interests and showing the way in which they are symbolic of general and pervasive aspects of human affairs. The great virtue of art forms is the richness of their symbolism. They speak a various language. We should not become so much enamored of *our* interpretation of what they "say" that the meanings which students read into them are lost to view.

[19] See *Social Understanding Through Literature*, prepared by G. Robert Carlsen and Richard S. Alm for the National Council for the Social Studies. You will also find excellent references of this type, and many others, in *Social Education* and *Educational Leadership*, which are the journals of the National Council for the Social Studies and the Association for Supervision and Curriculum Development, respectively. For critical thinking see *Teaching Critical Thinking in the Social Studies*, Howard R. Anderson, Editor, 13th Yearbook of the National Council for the Social Studies, 1942, and *Skills in Social Study*, Helen McCracken Carpenter, Editor, 24th Yearbook, *ibid.*, 1953.

Effective depends on affective.   Respecting the role of the arts, it seems that we often ask our students to take a *detached* view of social life before we even try to *attach* them to it. This is only another way of emphasizing the primary role of appreciation in all social learning. I do not know how human beings can be truly effective without also being affective. In seeking to get them to be both we must open to our students the avenues of every sense. Social life has color, depth, shape, scope, feel, touch, sound. Each suggests an approach to its intimacies. Moreover, these approaches may discover to students talents of which they never dreamed. We want them to be readers of books but we also want them to be poets, dramatists, novelists, painters—artists of every kind. Thus they may find bonds which will tie them closer to their community and tie those closer to it who are touched by their expressions. Lest you despair, all these things can be thought about as well as enjoyed.

Textbooks as tools.   Finally, and I trust not in anticlimax, I should like to make a few remarks about the textbook. "Blessed be the Phoenicians, or whoever it was that invented books." It is, however, regrettable that we owe little, if any, thanks to those who *wrote* some textbooks. But, on the whole, they are much better than they used to be.

How appropriate and useful are they as means?—for they are not ends. But they are not a means whereby to threaten students as some teachers of whom I have heard are wont to do with them. The hickory stick has all but vanished as a means of punishment, but not the textbook. It is one of many means to understanding and skill. Increasingly more of them are also means for creating delight in reading. Would that all of them were. The final test by which they are to be judged is in their power to make the social realities real.

But therein lies a danger. Some students may *mistake the books for reality.* This will be more likely for those who lack experience in life. It is they who may canonize the textbook. Hence, the greater the need that it treat reality in *its* terms.

Many textbooks introduce, but fail to prepare. Between these there is a wide difference. My bias is for trade books. They are often much more interesting but contain few, if any, illustrations, are not organized in units, and provide none of the excellent "aids to learning" which characterize the best textbooks. Whatever your choice, if you have one, don't make any book a fetish. Its merit lies in its readability, its clarity, and its utility in creating images which bear as close a resemblance as possible to the world which lies outside the windows of your classroom.

CHAPTER XXI

The Social Process Approach to the Study of Human Affairs

BEFORE WE discuss teaching-learning in the various areas of inquiry within the social studies, which we shall do in Chapters XXII to XXVII, we need to develop a *Gestalt* or frame of reference which includes all of them. The social process approach provides it. This approach will permit us to view the needs of individuals and the needs of society in their inter-relations. These will be found to be needful phases of human affairs which have a systematic character.

The four social processes described in Chapter V are too abstract for this purpose. In their place we choose those which Leon C. Marshall set forth in *Curriculum Making in the Social Studies: The Social Process Approach*.[1]

Tentative approach. This approach is for us, as it is for Professor Marshall, "frankly opportunistic," that is, tentative and workable rather than final. It would be a sad day for scholarship when *the* approach to human affairs has been made and when there is perfect agreement on it. And so, like human life itself and its "workings," it is a tentative way of looking at it process-wise.

We need such a view, not only as a matrix within which to place and relate individual and social needs but also in order to look at human life as something more than the shifting relations of bits of human matter in space and time. We need a universal picture, one which will be good for studying man in all times, places, and circumstances.

[1] Part XIII: Report of the Commission on the Social Studies, American Historical Association (New York: Charles Scribner's Sons, 1936). Professor Marshall's daughter, Rachael M. Goetz, shared the authorship of this work. See pp. 7-22 for the authors' rationale for this approach.

A "table of contents" of all cultures. We want a "table of contents" of all cultures. We also want a matrix which will help us relate the social studies to each other. We want to discover the basic themes in what is social so that we can develop a sensible division of labor in order to study it. The social studies are separate in the sense that certain of them treat certain social processes and certain others treat other social processes. But we wish to show their interrelations, hence the need for a universal set of such processes.

You will discover a close kinship between Marshall's account of the social processes and the account given in Chapter IX. Their logics are similar but not identical. The following vertical arrangement of my revision of Marshall's terms permits comparison with the triangles in that chapter.

9 Man Molds His Character
8 Man Faces the Problems of Change and Continuance
7 Man Organizes His Efforts to Secure Adherence to Values
6 Man Works to Secure Adherence to Values
5 Man Establishes Value Standards
4 Man Lives and Conserves His Life
3 Man Makes a Spatial Pattern
2 Man Adjusts Resources to his Needs
1 Man and Nature Interact

From man and nature, to man's character. The account of the several social processes begins with the bottom of the series above and moves to the top. This is Marshall's order of treatment; it conforms to my previous analyses.[2]

1. THE PROCESS OF ADJUSTMENT WITH THE PHYSICAL ENVIRONMENT, OR THE PHYSICAL WORLD

(a) man's mastery of his geographic base through the use of the natural sciences and the technology they have permitted him to develop.
(b) the distribution of man in space: the ecology of the human species.

Through the operation of this process man secures a base for the development of a culture: in fact, his adjustment with the physical environment is itself a cultural task. He interacts with his physical environment and seeks to change it to suit his plans and purposes.

He contends with the geographic and geological environment and also

---

[2] I assume full responsibility for modifying and interpreting Professor Marshall's scheme. Processes 5, 6, and 7 are, in effect, related phases of a single process. They are divided here for purposes of more discreet analysis. Process 8 is implicit in all the others.

with the world of plants and animals and rearranges them—in so far as he is able—so that they serve him. He domesticates animals, he develops plants to provide him with food and fiber, and he changes the surface of the earth and takes minerals from beneath its crust so as to advance his human desires. In this process he distributes himself over the face of the earth in patterns of varying sparsity and density.

The activities in which men thus engage and some of the things that might be studied are suggested in the following:

Draining swamps; dredging rivers of silt deposits; clearing the land of forest cover for farming uses; digging canals; laying steel rails; sinking mine shafts; extracting ores, smelting and refining them; domesticating plants and animals; harnessing the wind through the use of the windmill, water by the millrace and the power dam, and electricity by the dynamo; tunneling under mountains; building turnpikes and highways; converting lumber into building materials—likewise clay and building stone; stringing wires for communication; predicting the weather; developing the weaving and dyeing of cloth; making fabrics from chemicals; using natural products as medicines as well as making medicines synthetically; replenishing oyster beds and developing game and wildlife preserves; breeding stocks of animals for food and power purposes; making machinery out of raw physical resources—laborsaving devices, machines to make machines, etc.; fighting microbes through pest and disease control, through pasteurization, and the advance of medical science; developing X-ray machines to aid in the diagnosis of disease and the structure of metals; in short, the development of all the arts and sciences by which man has made useful things through the interaction of his mental powers with the raw materials of physical nature.

These activities are organized through the institutions of the market; they make the world habitable and are related to the distribution of the population as well as to its increase and decrease; they provide the material base for all activities; advances and retardations in these activities help to sustain and advance cultural change—are indeed some of the ways in which cultures change; provide the materials essential to spiritual and social advance; constitute, in themselves, a set of standards or goals—namely the mastery of man's physical environment; the activities in which men engage in order to perform these changes in nature involve their association with their fellows in mines, factories, and laboratories, and the social organizations which control and manage those and other enterprises; they permit men to play various roles—engineers, executives, managers, skilled workers, etc., through which they develop not only skills but a place in a complex division of labor, a place in the esteem and status system of their organization and the society in which they live and work, and a position in the spatial order.

2. THE PROCESS OF USING THE RESOURCES OF THE NATURAL WORLD SO AS TO SERVE HIS NEEDS: ECONOMIC ORGANIZATION

Man has to solve the following problems or answer the following questions in order to do this:

(a) what goods and services shall be produced and in what quantities?

(b) how shall the resources which are available to him be apportioned: that is, who will get how much or what of the goods which are produced?

(c) how shall resources and population be brought into balance?

(d) what kind of social organization—market organization—shall he devise to effect these things?

(e) what standards shall be set up by which these things are to be done?

In solving these problems man develops *a form of economy*: capitalism and socialism are the two main forms—but every economy is, to some degree, a mixture of these.

This process involves men in socioeconomic organizations—companies, corporations, trade associations, labor unions, etc., through which they find a place in the division of labor. Every activity has its economic problems and its economic base: these are its economic "ways and means."

The activities involved in these organizations include such as the following: growing, mining, manufacturing, transporting, storing, selling, developing banking and credit systems, etc. These activities are directed to the ends of "economizing," i.e., allocating relatively limited stores of goods among an almost endless number of needs or desires. The whole economic process is one of means and ends: deciding what to produce and devising ways to produce it. This is a process of making policy—a phase of setting standards or norms—and carrying out policy. In this complex process there is a division of function between men in their private and collective but voluntary capacities, and men in their capacities as citizens of political systems—represented by the intervention of the government in various phases of the economic life of a community.

There is a government *in* economic organizations (businesses, corporations, co-operatives, trade associations, labor unions, etc.) and there is government *over* them in some aspects of their activities. We sometimes have government ownership of certain economic enterprises, e.g., the post office and municipal utilities; such economic "experiments" as the TVA represent active governmental participation, control, and/or ownership of certain basic economic activities; there are trade laws, tariffs, subsidies, and many other kinds of governmental intervention in the economic process. The coinage of money and the granting of patents are government monopolies; the government engages in many kinds of research which affect economic life.

Economic activity is closely related to the well-being and security of the population: periods of "prosperity" and "depression" have their immediate consequences on the family, the birth and death rate, the distribution of the population in space, the growth and decline of cities, and the standards of living of the people. Taxation, licensing, permits of various kinds, and basic standards of purity and quality are factors which affect economic activity and the physical and mental security of the population.

Economic organizations are themselves examples of agencies of social organization as the foregoing suggests. Through the vigor and the well or poor working of economic activities, the rate of cultural change is advanced or retarded. They are social contexts in which men take on various responsibilities, achieve varieties of respect, prestige, and esteem—or the lack of them—and thus provide some of the main theaters for self-realization.

3. THE PROCESS OF ADJUSTING POPULATION WITH THE EXTERNAL PHYSICAL WORLD

This process has been mentioned in No. 1 above and is implied in No. 2. It is, however, important enough to be treated separately. In reality, it is closely related to not only the two processes already named but to most of those which are to follow.

This process is often referred to as the "population problem." It includes such matters as these:

(*a*) individual or mass movement of people: to seek employment, escape drought, flood damage, etc.

(*b*) mass movements of people: the great migrations such as the Crusades, colonization, and "folk wanderings," from which mixtures come new ideas and new cultural forms.

(*c*) adjustment sometimes goes on, not through movement, but through increasing the resources necessary for man's survival: irrigation, fertilization, development of new methods of manufacture and new forms of crops, e.g., winter-resistant wheat.

(*d*) adjustment also is effected through the control of population by lengthening the span of life and by various kinds of birth control.

In all these ways man seeks to find what is called the "optimum population balance"—not too many people, not too few but "just the right number in the right places."

This process is not only "statistical" or "spatial"; it is also *social*. All the major activities of man affect, in one way or another, how many people there are in a society, where they live (rural or urban communities), how long they stay in a given community, whether or not they move and whether as individuals or as members of groups, the "social distance" which exists between them—whether they are neighborly, apathetic, friendly, or unfriendly to each other, and hence the degree to which they enter into community life.

The age, sex, state of health, occupation, and marital state of the population affect all the other processes. Population movement, density or sparsity and its make-up, may be taken as a useful index to many phases of social life: immigration, overpopulation (too many people for the present state and quantity of material resources) or underpopulation (the reverse), crowding in housing and land coverage, and standards of living.

4. THE PROCESS OF BIOLOGICAL CONTINUANCE AND CONSERVATION

This process is part of No. 3 but, again, important enough to be given special and separate treatment. Central to this process is the form and function of the family, reproduction rates, care of the young and aged, and all the things that man does which guarantee his continuance and conservation as a living organism. Concern for his mental as well as for his physical health is involved in this process.

This process has been explicit or implicit in the discussion just above but some additional remarks may be made on it. The family is the social institution most closely related to the birth and death, the long or short life span of the population. It is also connected with the vigor of the economy, the standard of living, the adequacy of wages, and the provisions for public and private health and welfare. All these phases have their political, i.e., policy, aspects. They are matters not only of private and family decisions but of the policies and activities of governmental bodies. The health of the people affect their economic, political, and cultural activities and these, in turn, affect their health, life expectancy, and general worth to their community. Of special and increasing importance is the mental health and vigor of the population. One who is burdened with worry, who is distracted, if not mentally sick and an inmate of some type of mental-disease hospital, is worth little to himself, his family, his job, his church, or his political party.

Man as a biological organism is the raw material for all the social phases of community life; if the biological stock is poor the whole social order suffers; if it is vigorous, the social order has, at least, a strong and vigorous "human animal" out of which an effective participant in and contributor to all its activities may be shaped.

5. THE PROCESS OF GUIDING HUMAN MOTIVATION: ESTABLISHING VALUE STANDARDS OR NORMS

This process is difficult to state or even identify with the precision to which those processes already listed lend themselves. It is continuously in operation and takes a myriad of forms.

It goes on in all social institutions: the family, the church, labor organizations, merchants' associations, women's clubs, etc. It also goes on in the major political institutions: the county commissioners, the city and village councils, state and federal legislatures. The "business of living" is the "business of living *for something*"—these various goals are the value standards or norms of all social organizations. They take the form of ordinances, laws, customs, manners, constitutions, charters, and every manifestation of what it is that associations of individuals strive toward.

Perhaps a simpler and better known term for this process is that of making choices. This is the task and process of deciding between the many alternative things human beings might take for their goals and purposes. This process goes on in every enterprise: what is the well-done job, what is a happy family, what is a good and safe investment, what is the right amount of tolerance in the working parts of a machine or engine, what should we do with our leisure, what should be the specifications for a building, a dam, or a highway, what is beauty in the arts, what are the standards of health and welfare for persons and groups, and many, many other phases of the whole round of life; what liberty shall the people have, what restraints ought to be placed upon them since liberty is always the result of both freedom and restraint—this "balance" is established, a moving balance or equilibrium—in all phases of life: in the family, in all forms of voluntary associations—Scouts, merchants and workers' organizations, clubs of all kinds, etc., and perhaps most noticeably in the area we call "politics," that is in what "the government" at its various levels does or leaves the citizen free to do on the basis of his own choosing.

This process has two phases: the individual or personal phase and the collective or social phase. All judgments of choice are made by individuals, but seldom, if ever, without some kind of group influence. The choice to buy or sell, the choice to enter this or that profession—all choices between alternative goals or standards always reflects individual judgment modified in some way by social influences. Thus it is that the kind of person one becomes and the kind of groups persons form depend on the value standards or norms by which each "erects," makes or constructs itself.

The core of every society is its value standards or norms; likewise the core of every character. Such choices are often made almost unconsciously. The task of teaching about these things is to make students more conscious of them.

All the other processes are related to this one either in terms of the standards and values or norms which men seek individually or in groups or in terms of the means they employ. The process of manipulating the forces and materials of physical nature provides the material base for setting standards. Economic organization is the way men decide what to produce —itself a judgment of standards or norms—and all the other questions of norms or standards listed above. The process of adjusting population to resources always goes on in terms of standards or norms—it does not just *go on* without concern for the purpose and the "goodness" of the adjustment. The process of biological continuance and conservation is one of keeping life going and conserving it; these are themselves standards— they involve such standards as health and welfare, the care of children and the aged, and all the provisions necessary to improve the quality of the human stock—not only for survival purposes but in order to live more happily and securely. When minimum adherence is sought to standards and norms the things which will permit men at least to meet them if not exceed and revise them are being done. Men have many motives; it is the task of the process of securing minimum adherence to standards to educate their motives in "right" directions: those are the directions set by the standards and norms themselves. This task requires organization; it cannot be left to the efforts of men in their purely individual capacity. Thus social organizations which will bring about social solidarity and integrity *around* standards and norms are necessary. Finally, these value standards and norms are what individuals take as their own personal guides in life— they "internalize," as well as produce through their interaction with their fellow men, the value standards. Thus they develop centers for the development of their own characters.

6. THE PROCESS OF GUIDING HUMAN MOTIVATION: SECURING MINIMUM ADHERENCE TO VALUE STANDARDS OR NORMS

This is the "means" aspect of No. 5, above. The problem is this: What kind of instruments, means, institutions, and associations are necessary for guiding men's motives in such a way that at least a minimum adherence to the standards or norms is secured? Society exists in the degree to which people are committed, at least generally, to the same ends or goals. This process is concerned with the *integrity* of groups and communities: the degree to which they have common purposes and toward which common purposes their activities are directed. Involved in this process are all forms of ritual and ceremony; religious and patriotic special days and practices; laws, customs, regulations of all kinds; the effect of the press, the pulpit, the schools, public opinion on various issues; propaganda; taboos; gossip, desire for prestige, etc. These means may be classified as formal and informal, individual and social or collective, and conscious and unconscious. They involve the power of the "majority" and the power of the "minority" —the latter so that all forms of social organization may protect themselves against the "tyranny of the majority." They all work to get a "decent degree of conformity" in any association or institution, as well as in the society-as-a-whole.

The relation of this process to the others, given above and to follow, is of the following kinds. Securing adherence to value standards and norms depends on many things: on the adequacy of material provision—houses, roads, food and clothing. People who do not have the basic necessities of life are not apt to be interested in the moral standards which the community seeks to maintain. Thus it is that man's control over the physical universe and his skill and success in producing and distributing the economic goods by which men live as biological forms are basic prerequisites to securing even minimum adherence to value standards. The quality and quantity of the population is a further precondition: how many people are there, do they move or tend to stay put? It is difficult to get agreement on basic value standards when people move about; if they stay put the "cake of custom" is more readily formed. Standards undergo strain when the population turns over too fast. Do they have jobs and adequate wages or salaries? How steadily are they employed? Such economic questions as these are closely related to the securing of people's loyalties to value standards. Adherence to value standards cannot, of course, be achieved unless there are adequate social institutions. These institutions must, moreover, keep "up with the times"—they must undergo continuous revision. Value standards are sometimes borrowed from groups outside the community; they are also sometimes "exported"—these are aspects of cultural continuance and change which are closely related to the securing and changing of adherence to value standards. Finally the molding of personality is the test of both the quality of the standards and the adherence of persons to them.

7. THE PROCESS OF DEVELOPING AND OPERATING THE AGENCIES OF SOCIAL ORGANIZATION

Social life is an individual matter; it is also a social or collective matter. Men exist but they also *coexist* and they are modified through the fact of their coexistence. This coexistence takes on an organized form—groups of various kinds: the family, the church, the agencies of government in both voluntary and nonvoluntary organizations—in fact, all the myriad forms of organization in which people work together and among which many forms there are various degrees of co-operation and competition. These many forms of social organization undergo revision and change— the pattern within any organization and the pattern of "all" the organizations of a society is always fluid and changing to some degree. It is a "moving equilibrium" in each case; members come and go, leaders arise and are succeeded by others, policies are determined and modified—in short, change is the rule of social life. But despite all this change there is a quality of permanence to social life: always there are agencies of social organization. They change and they persist. The mode and process by which they arise, remain stable, and change is the concern of this process.

As already indicated, the task of effecting adjustment with the forces and materials of physical nature requires organized action—hence institutions or social organizations. These have already been identified. To the degree that man's activities have an organized aspect, agencies of social organization are needed. These may be classified for general purposes under three types: economic, political, and cultural. We have mentioned examples of each. Social organizations are immediately affected by whether people stay or move and how long they stay and how often they move. They are also dependent on the quality of the human population. Likewise the age, sex, and marital status of the people affect the kinds of social organizations that are formed. Social organizations are, in brief, collective and organized ways which men set up both to set value standards and to seek to bring men to adhere to them. Each social organization tends to focus on a somewhat special standard: the family, the standard of establishing basic rules of conduct and conceptions of right and wrong; the school, the standards of knowledge and preparation for a wide variety of tasks, each of which serves some value standard; the church, the standards of value as held by various sects and denominations; the market, to set and meet the standards for the exchange of goods; the political apparatus of the community, which works through parties and governing bodies of various kinds—and so on through the whole catalogue of many social organizations. In fact, a community may be said to be not only many people working in varying ways to advance (and sometimes retard) its value standards, but it may also be seen as a constellation of interrelated patterns of social organizations.

We have already commented on the forms of social organization necessary to solve our economic problems. Similarly, in political and cultural activities—striving after political and cultural goals—men are always involved in some kind of group effort. These range through the institutions of the market, the family, the school, the club, the political party, etc. All these agencies effect certain group controls over people; they set the limits of how free they are to make individual judgments and engage in individual acts and how restrained they ought to be, as each group works out what is for it the "proper" balance between freedom and restraint.

The "life and labor" of every social organization can be viewed from such vantage points as these: what give rise to it, i.e., why did men form it; how was the question decided as to what power the group should have over the lives and fortunes of its members; what provisions are made for the members to voice their views and to engage in discussion about the ends which the group is designed to serve and the proper means to use; how are leaders chosen, or how do they arise; what freedoms do they enjoy and what restraints are put upon them; how widespread in the group is the making of major decisions—by laymen or experts or both; what basic rules and bylaws are necessary; how will the group finance itself; how will it act in situations of great stress or crisis; how well does it survive such situations; what kinds of problems recur and what provision is made to deal with them; what kinds of problems (such as those in crises) arise which can hardly be foreseen and how are they handled; how does the organization recruit new members; what education and/or propaganda does it engage in; with what other social organizations does it co-operate or compete; what is its relation to the government of the community in which it is located; what unique problems, if any, face those social organizations which are governmental in the traditional political sense—the school board, the county commissioner, the city council, the state legislature, planning boards, and the federal congress; what division of labor is set up within such organizations which might be thought of as legislative, executive, judicial, and administrative; what variety of duties and obligations or personal roles does each organization provide; what education or training is necessary for the members of the group, for its leaders and experts; what causes groups to cease to be; etc.?

8. THE PROCESS OF CULTURAL CONTINUANCE AND CULTURAL CHANGE

This is included in No. 7 above, but is stated here to distinguish between the development and operation of agencies of social organization and their changing and persisting tendencies. The two are closely interrelated. But this process of continuance and change may be looked at in a special way by inquiring what certain cultures borrow from each other, what causes some parts of the culture to change more rapidly than other parts (we invent machines but are slow to adapt ourselves to them: their social effects are more difficult to control than their invention in the first place); how do cultures change when looked at from the point of view of increase or decrease in populations (by births, deaths, in-migration and out-migration), etc.?

It is obvious that men change the way by which they achieve adjustment with the physical universe—the advance of science and technology bears witness to this fact. In fact, every phase of human life—all the processes we have noted—undergo continual change. But despite this they manifest a permanence and continuance. If this thought is applied to all the processes, the relation of No. 8 to all the others will be made clear.

9. THE PROCESS OF CHARACTER MOLDING

This is the process by which character is formed. Again, it is not a separate process but all the other processes, seen from the point of view of what kind of men they make.

In examining this process we would ask about opportunity, the different biological and intellectual qualities of people and how they affect one's character, how secure people are physically and spiritually, what freedoms and restraints are placed on them, what groups are advantaged and which disadvantaged, race and cultural contacts and how various groups get along together and produce symmetrical or distorted characters, and every social influence which provides the mold within which character is formed and brought to some degree of fulfillment or realization.

This process is "the sum" of all the processes in which each human being plays a role. These processes are the means by which the socialization of each person goes on: he becomes a human being by playing roles opposite other human beings in the processes which make up social life.

"What kind of men does it make?" This is the great question to ask of society which we have here treated as the result of an interdependent pattern of processes. Thus it is that the ultimate concern of the social studies with the social processes is the kind of human being they produce. All human action is individual action. But this is always conditioned by the presence of other individuals, that is, by group life in myriad forms of association.

The focus of the social processes. The focus of the social processes is on men engaged in their self-maintenance and the maintenance of a social order. The roles they play may be classified as economic, political, and cultural. If to these roles be added the fact that they have both an historical and a geographic setting, the parenthood of the traditional "subjects" is thus identified. These, in turn, suggest the formal disciplines from which each has drawn its substance.

Which of these—the social processes, the traditional "subjects," or the formal disciplines—shall be taken as the constituents of a curriculum in the social studies? I find my answer to this in something other than a clear "either-or" because I believe that each has a somewhat unique contribution to make.

A division and a unity of labor. It is idle to suppose that the social studies can ever be taught without some differentiation in subject matter. This follows from the simple fact that we cannot talk about everything at the same time, and also from the fact that there is a *division* as well as a *unity* of labor in social life. We must, I believe, continue to respect the major roles which men play as well as the historical and geographic settings in which they play them. This presupposes that we shall continue to respect the fact that social knowledge has a *corpus* or form. The problem is to insure that it be not *too* formal.

A liaison is needed. The tendency of the disciplines and the traditional "subjects" is toward too great formality, so great as to make them unreal. What we need is an expansion or opening of both to the end that not only their interrelations but their interdependence be made known. The social processes give us the major clues to the "points" and "surfaces" at which the most helpful liaison might be effected.[3]

A core curriculum on the social studies. We might, for instance, conceive of a core curriculum in the social studies which would undertake to show how each of the disciplines might help illuminate the nature of two concepts: *consensus* and *character*. The contribution which each might make is shown in Diagram 7.

Here the units to be related are the disciplines of social science, to which ethics has been added. The social processes may be correlated fairly closely with them. Indeed, we shall be obliged to attempt such a correlation until

[3] See John Dewey, "Unity of Science as a Social Problem," in *International Encyclopedia of Unified Science*, Vol. I, No. 1. *Encyclopedia and Unified Science* by Otto Neurath, *et al.* (Chicago: The University of Chicago Press, 1940), pp. 29-38. See also *Eleven Twenty-Six*, Edited by Louis Wirth (Chicago: The University of Chicago Press, 1940), especially "The Social Sciences, One or Many," pp. 112-152; Adolf Löwe, *Economics and Sociology: A Plea for Co-operation in the Social Sciences* (London: George Allen & Unwin, Ltd., 1935); *The Social Sciences: Their Relations in Theory and in Teaching* (London: LePlay House Press, 1936); and *Further Papers on the Social Sciences: Their Relations in Theory and in Teaching*, Edited by J. E. Dugdale (London: LePlay House Press, 1937).

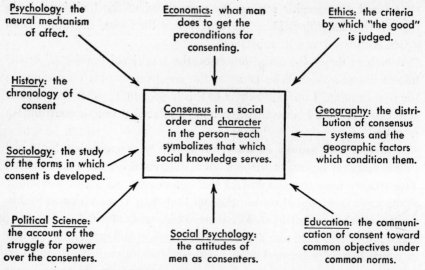

Psychology: the neural mechanism of affect.

Economics: what man does to get the preconditions for consenting.

Ethics: the criteria by which "the good" is judged.

History: the chronology of consent

Consensus in a social order and character in the person—each symbolizes that which social knowledge serves.

Geography: the distribution of consensus systems and the geographic factors which condition them.

Sociology: the study of the forms in which consent is developed.

Political Science: the account of the struggle for power over the consenters.

Social Psychology: the attitudes of men as consenters.

Education: the communication of consent toward common objectives under common norms.

DIAGRAM 7. *The Disciplines as Sources of Knowledge in a Core Curriculum*

the social processes are used, more than is presently the case, as the frames of reference within which research in human affairs is done.[4]

"Subjects" as "Perspectives on Human Affairs." I should now like to comment briefly on the approaches taken in the next five chapters. They do not constitute a blueprint for a curriculum in the social studies. They seek, rather, to take the present organization of the curriculum in terms of the major areas of subject matter as a kind of base line from which some departures are made. The major departure is that of showing what the dominant *perspective* on human affairs is which the traditional "subjects" have taken for a long time but have neglected to make known. The "subjects" and their hitherto undisclosed perspectives are as follows:

SUBJECTS	PERSPECTIVES ON HUMAN AFFAIRS
(a) history and cultural anthropology	(a) cultural change, culture, and human nature
(b) social problems	(b) conflict of values
(c) civics	(c) associations and the problem of consensus
(d) economics	(d) unlimited wants and scarce means
(e) human geography	(e) the spatial distribution of social phenomena

[4] See Louis Wirth, "Consensus and Mass Communication," *American Sociological Review*, V (February, 1948).

Theory and practice are mutually related. It is readily apparent that the perspectives given here are fewer in number than the social processes. Furthermore, in Chapter XXIV I shall develop a different set of perspectives based on the social science disciplines, as shown in Diagram 7 (Education excluded). Indeed, you will discover that I have used several logics in working out my idea of perspectives. The structure of none of the next five chapters corresponds to a single logical principle, nor is any one meant to be a complete outline for the perspective (or perspectives) which it employs. Each seeks, implicitly and/or explicitly, to suggest both theory and practice respecting each perspective. Indeed, the mutual relation between theory and practice is the controlling perspective of this entire book. I cannot disabuse myself of the belief that the education of teachers in the social studies has been inordinately concerned with practice to the great neglect of theory. How the former can be intelligently engaged in without knowledge of its theoretical basis I do not understand.

In all the logics used, I have sought to de-emphasize the term "subject," which is an unfortunate one because of its static connotations. My implicit and explicit emphasis is on *perspective*, even though I have used that term in two quite distinct yet not contradictory ways.

It has been said that there is no "royal road to learning." If "royal" be interpreted as "without effort," I should agree. But, from another point of view, I believe that there are many roads to learning and each can be royal in the sense that it can lead to deep insight and high purpose respecting human affairs. I look upon the various *perspectives* as offering some of these latter royal roads. Or, to change the figure of speech, they might be called loci of study, the ultimate focus of each of which is the moral and intellectual individuality of the student.[5]

[5] See *The Social Studies in General Education*, A Report of the Committee on the Function of the Social Studies in General Education for the Commission on Secondary School Curriculum (New York: Appleton-Century-Crofts, Inc., 1940); William F. Ogburn and Alex. Goldenwesier (Editors), *The Social Sciences and Interrelations* (New York: Houghton Mifflin Co., 1927); Robert S. Lynd, *op. cit.*; and *Education for Citizen Responsibilities*, Edited by Franklin L. Burdette (Princeton: Princeton University Press, 1942).

CHAPTER XXII

The Perspectives of Cultural Change, Culture, and Human Nature: History and Cultural Anthropology

The canons of selection. The historical scholar is concerned with the *writing* of history, you with the *teaching* of it. Otherwise you face the same problems. These are selection by the canons of relevance and significance, periodization, explanation, and interpretation.

Neither of you can deal with the totality of the past. Both of you must select from it. Both the writing and the teaching of history are from a point of view, that which one age finds worthy of note in another. Thus all history is prejudiced by the problems which are before the community. That is why history is rewritten and that is why Daniel Webster was mistaken when he said the "the past, at least, is secure." [1]

You and the research scholar are faced with a "glut of concurrences," millions of facts which were not born free and equal and which are in a "state of dispersion," and with events in flux—all of which would tell you nothing if they could all be treated in chronological order, which is impossible. What must you do? You must decide what is important for our time and for the youth of our time. In doing this you will use your standards of relevance and significance.

[1] See "Should American History Be Rewritten?"—A Debate Between Allan Nevins and Matthew Josephson, *Saturday Review*, February 6, 1954, pp. 7-10, 44-49. See also Carl Becker, "Some Aspects of the Influence of Social Problems and Their Influence on the Study and Writing of History," *American Journal of Sociology*, XVIII (March, 1913), pp. 641-675. See also Erling Hunt, "Scholar's History *vs.* School History," *Social Studies*, XXVI (December, 1935), pp. 513-518.

What is relevant and significant? But what is relevant and significant? The answer is not found by the inductive method. It is found by the deductive method which uses the perspectives noted earlier: philosophic, scientific, needs, and operational. These provide your basic frames of reference for selecting and organizing historical as well as all other data for social study.

You must ask yourself such questions as these: What ought history to *do* to my students? What has it to offer youth now? What ideas and visions are in it which may help to make them better and wiser now, and tomorrow? If there are topics or events which can give no satisfactory answers to such questions they ought not to be taught.[2]

Other questions. Still other questions must be pondered. They are such as these: What does youth and our society need? What are the bench marks for the "good society"? What was significant in the past which is still significant? What light can history shed on present social realities?

You cannot begin with "the facts." But none of these and many other questions can be satisfied by an *ad hoc* approach. Obviously, you cannot begin with something called "the facts." There are too many of them and, by themselves, they are too abstract. Standing alone they tell nothing and improve nothing. They must be facts *of* something. That something is cultural *change* in time, but change, not time, is the true historic concept.

Let Professor Fred Clarke tell it.

The importance of constant emphasis upon the idea of change and of abundant illustration of it can hardly be exaggerated. It is not too much to say that a reasonable and adequate grasp of it is a main essential for the healthy life of a democratic community. For its presence in full strength reduces both fear of the future and impatience with the inheritance of the past, the two factors which, from one side or the other, are always tending to rend apart the texture of a democracy.[3]

A conception of wholeness is required. Your selection must be made on the basis of some conception of *wholeness*. This is a whole view of both past and present, but always a selective whole. For this you will need a set of universals and the particulars which will give them operational meaning. You cannot choose these without a bias. This is implicit in your stand-

---

[2] The book which has been of greatest worth to me in developing the theory of history teaching which I shall set forth is *The Foundation of History-Teaching* by Fred Clarke. It is a book of only 171 pages but the "biggest" little book on the teaching of history of which I know.

[3] *Ibid.*, p. 63. Clarke does not mean that the time factor should be ignored. It is important, for instance, that students know that from Jamestown (1607) to the end of the American Revolution (1783) was a longer time span than from 1783 to 1914.

ards of relevance and significance. The facts and events you will choose will not nominate themselves because the past course of events is never separated from someone's idea about them. The research scholar takes those facts which fit his theme of change. So must you. This theme is a process of one kind or another—indeed, many processes. The element of process is the life of history. This is the process, or processes, through which something changed into something else.[4] There is no history except in terms of movement toward some outcome which was an issue in its time. History deals with change, becoming, emergence, hence with the processes by which change, becoming, and emergence went on.

A "table of contents" about man.   You will need a "table of contents" about man in past and present. Or call it "the common denominator of all cultures."[5] Such a "table of contents" was given in Chapter XXI. The social processes are the paths of historical development, "species of action," the means by which past and present are related. Through their use, the history you teach may achieve *continuity*. But do not mistake development for progress. We must, however, believe that progress is possible for man has achieved a considerable measure of it. We must believe, with Archibald MacLeish, that "History was voyages toward the people." Even in these days of the mushroom cloud we must continue to believe that it is still "toward the people."

Processes and facts.   The social processes provide you with a set of rubrics by which you may select and organize your facts. The processes are your universals; the facts are your variables. If you subscribe to the criterion of wholeness, you will neglect none of the processes and you will select only those facts about them which you believe are relevant and significant.

The analogy of a rope.   I choose the analogy of a rope to illustrate the relation of facts to processes and processes to the wholeness of a culture. I begin with the hempen fibers. These symbolize the facts. They are related to form strands. These symbolize events related in one or more of the social processes. These strands are woven to form a rope. This symbolizes the social process *in toto*.[6] This is the longitudinal view of history. All the strands run its full length.

Now we look at the rope horizontally. We cut it at various time points.

[4] See R. G. Collingwood, *The Idea of History* (Oxford: Clarendon Press, 1946), pp. 163-164.
[5] There are many such "tables." See Clark Wissler, *Man and Culture*, pp. 74-78, for his "universal culture pattern"; George P. Murdock, "The Common Denominator of Culture," in *The Science of Man in the World Crisis*, Edited by Ralph Linton; and *Introduction to the Study of History* by C. V. Langlois and C. Seignobos, pp. 234-235.
[6] I have taken some liberties with Fred Clarke's analogy. See *op. cit.*, pp. 67-68.

These are the median years of such epochs as Pericles' Athens, the Rome of Justinian, the Europe of Metternich, the England of Disraeli, and the America of Lincoln. Look at the strands. For each period they are the same and for each they are different. Viewed as the same basic social processes, they tell you of permanence or persistence throughout history. Viewed as different facts and events, these processes tell you of change. Again we find, not permanence *or* change, but changing permanence.

An "underlying tendency." How do you locate these stopping places? You start with a time line. You make rough common-sense divisions in it: a revolutionary period—political or industrial; a time of revolt against plutocracy—a period when the common man speaks out; an era of civil strife—our own Civil War and the whole cultural history that goes with it; the era of "the old South" and so on. You find approximate dates which begin and close such divisions. You have now identified what Paul Klapper calls "an underlying tendency" which dominated a period of time.[7] But time is only the boundary; it is not the *thing*. The thing is the movement, the processes, the interweaving which makes an epoch. (See Chapter XV for the application of this same general logic to the identification of teaching "units.")

Two measures of wholeness. We now have two measures of wholeness: *forces* and *forms*. The forces are the social processes which give us *continuity*. The forms are the epochs which give us *unities*. These are the "stream" and the "pools" of history. Both are fictions and rest on analogy which, despite its limitations, is useful.

Present and past are both structured. Now we need to inquire how past and present are related. We must see each in its wholeness—the wholeness which you choose. But this choice must be disciplined not by the principle of *ad hoc*, but by the principle of the structure of cultures in past and present.

The past is big and varied. It is not one, but many. Which past shall you choose? A past to match the present. This is an abiding past to match an abiding present. It is also a changing past to match a changing present. "Changing" calls for variables—facts and events. "Abiding" calls for constants—the social processes. Together they provide the cultural approach to history.[8]

"What's past is prologue." The past about which you teach must have meaning for the present. It can have meaning only if it is a past of the

---

[7] See Professor Paul Klapper's book, *The Teaching of History* (New York: Appleton-Century-Crofts, Inc., 1926).

[8] See Caroline Ware (Editor), *The Cultural Approach to History* (New York: Columbia University Press, 1940).

same human genre as the present. This is the "insistent present," the present of "holy ground" as Whitehead put it. It must be a past as plausible as the present; a past which not only happened but which is portrayed with such reality that your students will believe that it *could* and *did* happen. It cannot be made contemporary but it can be *contemporized*— by being infused with the heats and passions of the present. It must be a past to suit the tastes of Mr. Dooley who said:

I know histhry isn't true Hinnessy, because it ain't like what I see ivery day in Halsted street. If any wan comes along with a histhry of Greece or Rome that'll show me th' people fightin', gettin' dhrunk, makin' love, gettin' married, owin' the grocery man an' bein' without hard coal, I'll believe they was a Greece or Rome, but not before . . . histhry is a post-mortem examination. It tells ye what a counthry died iv. But I'd like to know what it lived iv." [9]

Only that conception of the teaching of history can be relived, for of such are the uses of the past.[10]

The limitations of some textbooks. Sadly enough, some textbooks will not picture the past in terms of its uses. Most of them are what they can hardly avoid being.

. . . small-scale histories which give the results but not the long, tedious, and doubtful struggles that produced the results. We see the last scene of the play but miss all the scenes that led up to the happy marriage or tragic disaster at the end. Everything seems easy to them; the difficulties are smoothed out; one wonders what all the bother was about, why so many mistakes were made, why the statesmen were such fools. . . . There are no final moments in human affairs, no Armageddon, no decisive battle which settles everything. There is only a long campaign for a better world, lasting centuries and indeed millenia; and for such long campaigns we ought to have short-term objectives, but very, very long-term views.[11]

You will do well to use several texts. Also use trade books, of which there are many. Above all use your imagination and incite the imagination of your students. The brightest book in the world will hardly deliver them from a dull teacher.

The necessary criteria for teaching history. The cultural approach satisfies, as none other can, the criterion of wholeness through continuity and unity. It also satisfies the criterion of representativeness—the opposite of

[9] Finley Peter Dunne, *Mr. Dooley at His Best* (New York: Charles Scribner's Sons, copyright 1938), p. 201.

[10] See Herbert J. Muller, *The Uses of the Past: Profiles of Former Societies* (New York: Oxford University Press, Inc., 1952).

[11] Sir Richard Livingstone, "The Road Ahead," copyright *The Atlantic Monthly*, November, 1948. See also Livingstone, *Some Tasks for Education* (London: Oxford University Press, 1946), pp. 25-33.

ad hoc. The other criteria which you must use are these: *nearness, suitability, intelligibility, actuality,* and *significance for self.*[12] Their interdependence is obvious. If what is past can be made near it will be suitable, intelligible, actual, and significant. The nearness of history is not its recency. It is the qualities just mentioned. If these criteria are met you will disclose something that mattered in the past and can be made to matter now to your students.

These criteria are not contradicted if we say that the past must be studied for its own sake. If not, it cannot be actual, and failing to be actual it cannot be suitable, intelligible, or significant for self. It must be a past told in such ways as to arouse not only your students' interests but also their affections. It must be a living past.

The necessity of continuity. The relation of present to past is one of continuity which, as Justice Holmes said, "is not a virtue [but] a necessity." Only beasts live unhistorically; [13] they have no past. But your students are heirs to a great heritage, a great permanence, and history holds all of it. Just as the past is big and varied, so is the present. But each is, paradoxically, both big and little. It depends on how we look at them. In the perspective of history, men and events often shrink to mere specks on the horizon— the view we get when we look down a long stretch of railroad track which appears to meet at the horizon's line. This optical illusion in history can be overcome only by new perceptions on the past.

How present and past are not related. Let us first ask how present and past are *not* related. Not as a row of dominoes standing on end: the first falls and topples the second, it falls and topples the third, and so on. Such a view is too neat, too predictable, and too mechanical. It allows for no sudden changes, no surprises, no setbacks. Nor can past and present be related through merely connecting facts and events, unless they be taken as significant moments or signposts in a continuing and sometimes broken process which has its temporal as well as its timeless aspects. Chronology alone cannot connect them. It tells us only that something happened before or after something else. But there are too many such "somethings." That way is too simple and too complex. Antiquarians follow it but they are interested only in the curious, not in the significant. The past has a wholeness which must be compared and contrasted with the wholeness of the present. We want a garment of interwoven processes, not a necklace of facts.

How present and past may be related. How then may past and present

[12] See Clarke, *op. cit.*, pp. 79, 86, and 127.
[13] This is Nietzsche's observation.

be related? By revealing the changing permanence of the social processes. Despite the breaks, the leaps, and the setbacks in history the present had a past. It must be captured. The process by which it may be captured is the *tentative* process of change and growth and of decline and decay. Rome fell but it also stood. It still stands—I mean the symbolic Rome of law and administration and the roots of our language. We seek a logic of change. No straight line can connect past and present. It must be sinuous and up hill and down. The things that grow and change, decay and die are ideas, institutions, and whole cultures.

The need of balance.   Now back to epochs, which are the phases of societies and cultures, which are the largest objects of historical study. The epochs are sections of the rope of change. We must keep our eye on both the sections and the society. We must also keep a fair balance between the temporal and the unique, and the typical and the timeless.

EPOCHS AND ERAS.   The history of our society may be divided into many epochs and eras. Following are two representative sets:

"Europe Finds America," 1000-1775; "A Nation Is Born," 1775-1800; "The Young Republic," 1800-1825; "Growing Pains," 1825-1870; "A Businessman's Nation," 1870-1900; "Imperial America," 1895-1915; "A New Century," 1900-1920; "The Great Boom," 1920-1930; "The New Deal, World War II, and Peace," 1930-   .[14]

Here is *sequence* and *consequence,* but not consequence in *all* matters. History is not that simple. Here also is overlap which cannot be denied. The focus is chiefly on the political and economic.

Another set with a focus on American thought is the following:

The American Adaptation of the European Heritage to the Conditions of Colonialism and to a New Physical and Social Environment, 1620-1775; The Growth of Americanism, Cultural Nationalism and the Expanding Enlightenment, and the Conservative Reaction, 1775-1800; Patrician Leadership, 1800-1830; Democratic Upheaval, a Reaction against the Patrician Leadership and the Dominance of the Spirit of the Frontier, 1830-1850; The Triumph of Nationalism and Business Ideology, 1850-1870; The Assertion of Individualism in a Corporate Age of Applied Science, 1870-1900; and Optimism Encounters Diversion, Criticism, and Contraction, 1900-   .[15]

The "right" pattern.   Each pattern or epoch has its own logic and focus. Which one is right? The one which satisfies the criteria already

[14] *United States of America* by Robert E. Reigel and Helen Hough (New York: Charles Scribner's Sons, 1949).

[15] Adapted from Merle Curti, *The Growth of American Thought* (New York: Harper & Brothers, 1943).

given. Courses in history may, like tribal lays, be written in any of "sixty-and-nine ways," and each of them is right—or so Kipling held.

The problem of periodization. Your attempt at periodization will be, at best, experimental. It may require that you follow the textbook or rearrange it. The basic criterion is what you take to be the "spirit of the age," its *Zeitgeist.* This is revealed in the dominant social trends: concern with the form of government, laying down the pattern of political divisions, the great mass movements, the dominance of certain factors in economic life, the uniqueness of leadership, trends in ownership and the socioeconomic organization of both industry and labor, the prevalence of protest, and the like. Neither cultures nor their epochs are primarily rational matters. Nor are they mere patchwork. They are a "working" in which now one process and now another is dominant. Hence different epochs will be characterized by different valences or weights among the several processes: there are no "carbon copies." But epochs will appear as unities only if the processes are interwoven and interrelated. The social studies deal with things in their relations: the form of the economy and the form of the family, the size of civil communities and the complexity of its social problems, the calm or disturbed nature of a time and the quality of its literature, the scope and power of government and the expense and numerical size of the domain, the homogeneity or heterogeneity of the population and the problems of social control, immigration and the rise and dominance of urban and state political machines, even the multiplicity of the laws and the number of law-breakers.

History is "from" something, "to" something. Implicit in the interrelation and interweaving of processes is the fact of movement *from* something *to* something. This view is mandatory since developmental change cannot be from "nothing to nothing." This problem is met by the use of what Lasswell calls "developmental constructs," sets of "to-from" termini. Representative of them are the following:

. . . police state to service state; sparse to dense population; desert to fertile field; isolation to world involvement; country to city; self-sufficiency to complex interdependence; handcraft to machine; single proprietorship to holding company; debtor to creditor status; states' rights to federalism; individualism to collectivism; dear money to cheap money; layman to expert; social control by custom to social control by law; separation of powers to concentration and integration of powers; spoils to merit system; and owner to renter status.

"From" and "to" are termini of processes. These are not sets of "either-ors." They are sets of "both-and." They are the termini between which the social processes run: sometimes forward, sometimes backward, and over longer and shorter periods of time. They may be used to chart the course of social processes within societies and between them. Medieval and modern times may be set in interesting contrast by similar developmental constructs. They are such as the following: activities ordered by night and day and the seasons, to those ordered by the time clock; steady work and full employment under serfdom, to cyclical employment under industrialism; children serving as valuable economic assets, to the prohibition of child labor; occupational succession of father-to-son, to the principle of individualism in choice of occupation; numerous rest days and holidays, to the "work week"; security as the chief concept of society, to freedom as its chief concept; a premium on conformity to local standards, to dissent and protest; and fixity in the class order, to upward mobility in it. With these, the dialectic of history may be taught to great advantage. Students will learn what *is*, in contrast to what *was*.

Stress development.   It were better, I think, to err on the side of the nicety with which you cut out epochs than to miss the history of such developments. They are the grooves of change in which the social processes run. Historical study requires both intensity and broad sweep. Settle for no "either-or" of any kind. Facts are facts about events, events are phases of social processes, and social processes are the warp and woof of changing cultural patterns.

The unit in history.   We now look to "units" of study in history. Like epochs, they are cutouts. They involve projects, topics, themes, and problems. These have been defined earlier. To them we need only add the concept of *chronology*, the time setting. Each project is one of inquiry into the working of some aspect of change, some emergence or becoming. Your students will likely state them as "whys" but only philosophy can deal with the *why* of things. History must stick to the "what" of them. "Why" must be changed to a search for relationship, cause and consequence.

History is not self-evident.   History is the story of what man has done to man, aided and interfered with by the forces of nature. It is the story of both the disappearing and the reappearing aspects of the making of cultures and characters. But these things are not self-revealing. The "self-evident" propositions which Thomas Jefferson recorded in the Declaration of Independence were so called in order better to make the case against George III. Their recitation was a magnificent propaganda gesture. But they are now part of a great heritage which it is your obligation to make known so they may be lived by.

The emphasis is on unity in epochs.   If an epoch is to be seen in its unity, the processes which worked to give it that unity must be shown in their interrelations. There is, of course, a division of labor among the processes but there is also a unity of labor among them. We now stress the unity, for interrelations must be *taught*. It is too much to ask that they be left to inference and native insight. Societies and cultures and their epochs are not skeins of yarn; they are garments.

The "Critical Period" as a unit.   Take the "Critical Period" from 1783 to 1789 in our history. The Revolution had been won and we stood on our own feet. Our destiny was now in our hands. But the unity which a common enemy had given seemed about to dissolve. Radical and conservative forces contended for mastery. Which would win or how might compromise bring a working unity? What kind of compromise? Shays's Rebellion was a symptom of unrest. It was, to some degree, the critical period in miniature. It gives you a point of departure. If it may be understood the spirit of the entire period may be understood. But whatever you do with it, keep true your allegiance to history.

Threads of connection between the revolt of the farmers and the destiny of an entire nation can be unraveled. The Articles must be revised. Radicalism and Conservatism have two theaters: we have found a theme and a focus, even a double focus. Shays's Rebellion is a symptom of popular unrest and the problem of the revision of the Articles is a symptom of the limitations of a former but now inadequate conception of political unity.

The need for inquiry.   We now have a hunch about issues and ideas in conflict, the main issues of the great debate—federation or confederation. We must find the leading proponents of each view. We must find the stake which the small states had, and the stake of the large states. But the period had another issue: that between slave and free states. Issues aplenty now, and leaders and followers. Who were the leaders? Who was their following? How did the Convention divide? The names of Hamilton, Madison, Adams, Morris, and others come to mind. There was the wise Franklin and the honest and optimistic Washington: "The Constitution that is submitted is not free from imperfections. But there are as few radical defects in it as could be well expected . . ." And then the contest in the states and the slow process of ratification. The climax came on June 21, 1788, when New Hampshire signed, followed in a few weeks by Virginia and New York. The new nation could begin business, "Little Rhody" and North Carolina to the contrary, notwithstanding.

The problem of significance.   What is the significance of the events, what are the facts about them? How close to the brink of failure did we come? What was the effect of the Federalist Papers? Why did Shays's Rebellion fail? Did it fail in all matters? What was the division of interests?

Who had a stake in what? What does Carlyle's theory of the Great Man tell us? Is this the place to examine what a social movement is? What are the steps or stages in the revolution brought by the Massachusetts farmers? [16]

Appreciation is first. Here are the makings of both past and present: facts, events, issues, and processes. Out of these must come insight into the issues, the stage, the drama, and the character of the time. The first fruit of it must be appreciation. The teaching of it must take account of the necessity that your students internalize the whole period. It will then be "inside" them where it must be if it is to be real. Only then can the past be contemporized. They must feel the issues, the greatness, the pettiness, the near-defeat and the final victory: a Constitution.

Propositions report understanding. Understanding may be reported in terms of propositions of one kind or another. The whole enterprise must have the right balance of romance and precision. Do not be afraid to use analogies. They are your chief device for showing similarities between past and present. Through it all take heed of Whitehead's advice: "Do not be deceived by the pedantry of dates." Here then is a pattern. You may have a better one in mind. In any event the consequences ought to be insight into and great dedication to the labors of the Founding Fathers.

A period in medieval history. Now let's take a period in medieval history. The time-span is long—maybe too long. It is from late Roman times to the Peasant's Revolt in the late fifteenth and early sixteenth centuries. The topics which identify the problems of inquiry and understanding might be such as these:

(*a*) Late Roman times: hereditary serfs living on latifundia.
(*b*) 6th to 11th century: a decaying society, anarchy, and then feudalism.
(*c*) 12th century: the rise of the middle-class towns.
(*d*) The role of the guilds.
(*e*) 14th to 15th century: the Peasants' Revolt.

How contemporize the past? Contemporization is more difficult. Or is it? Use analogies: "latifundia" are big estates (*latus*, broad; *fundus*, estate), as big as a Texas ranch; serfs were something like share-croppers; a "decaying society" is an organic concept the analogy for which is not "rotten apples" but something like a New England town that lost its textile mill. Feudalism can be defined as a social system based on lords and serfs, almost purely agricultural—what was the division of labor? What was a baron? Protection by the lord was traded for labor by the serfs. Study the pattern

---

[16] See Louis Gottschalk, "Causes of Revolution," *American Journal of Sociology*, L (July, 1944), pp. 1-8. Professor Gottschalk identifies the structure of revolutions. He demonstrates the narrow margin which separates history for general sociology.

of medieval fields and show how the total yield could not be great—what were the "baulks of earth" which divided the plots? What were the factors which caused towns to appear? Where did they appear? At crossroads of transportations—how come there? Did modern cities arise in the same manner? What were the guilds like? Like trade unions? Yes and no. How did it come about that the guilds had a big hand in government? What does the term "the city air makes free" mean? How was the rise of towns related to the Crusades? What was the significance of the rise of a "middle class"? How big were these towns? Where were they on a map of that period? Are they on a modern map? Have they grown much? The Peasants' Revolt: what was a peasant? Are there peasants in the United States? In Mexico? What was the revolt about? Who won? Did anybody win? Did feudalism pass away? By what steps? Had the world become too complex to be well run by a feudal system? What did trade have to do with the decline of feudalism?

Questions, inquiry, and activities. For each question there is an enterprise in inquiry. Each demands the appropriate activities. Romance and precision follow each other, again and again. What major propositions can be adduced? Maybe some like these: "There are several forms of society, each appropriate to the conditions of its time"; "A static society is one in which there is little mobility of people from class to class"; "Early medieval society had no middle class—only lords and serfs"; "Later medieval society had a middle class"; "Later medieval society was more like ours, classwise, than was early medieval society."

Begin where interest is. Where and when do you begin? To that there is no standard and pat answer. Begin where you can arouse interest. Do you teach history backwards or forwards? Does it have to be one or the other? Can it not be both? You weave past and present together on the loom of understanding of social processes common to past and present. Education offers no specifics. The past and present can meet no place but in the present. That they meet there is more important than where you start. The chances are perhaps greater that you will start with the present if Baron von Humboldt was right when he said that "man ever connects on from what lies at hand." Your problem is one of strategy, not of fixed rules. The long-agoness of the past may make little difference. The days of Attila may be nearer than last week. Proceed on the basis of what Karl Lowith calls "didactic expediency."

The techniques of teaching history are all and any that will serve to make the past real through inquiry and insight. Secondary school history is pretty much ready-made. Hence you can practice little of the method of inquiry which the research scholar uses. You face the problem of helping your students get understanding rather than establishing the historicity of the content of their textbook.

Knowledge about and acquaintance with.   The two roads to understanding were noted in Chapter XI. They are "knowledge about" and "acquaintance with." Of the former we have had enough and more. But it has proved ineffective in the teaching of history. It tends to run to rote learning. Historical account there must be and it must be known. But it must be more than known; it must be felt. It must permit roles to be played. This requires sympathetic imagination. Romance is the key to it.

The role of symbols.   The writing and teaching of history require the interpretation of symbols. For the research scholar these are every type of evidence he can bring to hand: manuscripts, coins, monuments, archives, and every other object which speaks of the past. For you and your students, the evidences of the past will be chiefly of a secondhand kind: words chiefly, and any other symbols available. These include pictures, dramas, poems, historical fiction, sound recordings, motion pictures, cartoons—anything that will aid the reconstruction of the past. These are the tools of romance. Through these your students may, pro tempore, live in the past. Use every device you can lay your hands on or conjure up to make the past real: fiction, pictures, maps, "movies," pageants, plays, biographies, recordings, music, etc.[17] Only then can they "live it up."

History is personal.   Again, I remind you to use analogies. They are metaphors. Although they are artificial devices, they make communication vivid and poetic and are indispensable to apprehension and appreciation. Without them past and present can hardly be woven together. They help to move from the known to the unknown. Use them generously but remember that they refer to things which are alike, not identical. They may be kept in check by "historical mindedness." But without them the teaching of history can be little better than a second burial of disinterred bones.

[17] There is a wealth of literature on techniques and devices: Ernest Horn, *Methods of Instruction in the Social Studies*; Richard E. Thursfield (Editor), *The Study and Teaching of American History*, 17th Yearbook of the National Council for the Social Studies, 1916; Edith West (Editor), *Improving the Teaching of World History*, 20th Yearbook of the National Council for the Social Studies, 1941; Howard R. Anderson (Editor), *Approaches to and Understanding of World Affairs*, 25th Yearbook of the National Council for the Social Studies, 1954; Henry Johnson, *Teaching of History* (New York: The Macmillan Co., 1940); Gunnar Horn, *American History in Fiction*, Personal Growth Leaflet, No. 206 (Washington: The National Education Association); Samuel Selden, *The Production of Local History Plays and Pageants*, Vol. I, No. 6 (April, 1943) (Washington: The American Association for State and Local History, 1943); and George M. Trevelyn, "History and Fiction," *The Living Age*, June 3, 1922.

History is violently personal, as is all life. Take your cue from the Prologue of Leoncavallo's "Pagliacci,"

Your author intends . . . to draw you a bit of life true to nature . . . you'll see love shown as human beings do love each other; you'll see too, of hatred the direful ending, witness woe's sharp agony. Howlings of rage will reach you and scornful laughter. . . . Watch you the plot unfolding before you.

History is the pageant of mankind.   Do not be afraid to make history sound like fiction. Hold heroes high but do not forget the nonheroes. Use biography but do not mistake it for history. History is more than Great Men; it is the pageant of mankind. Do not forget the little people: the foot soldiers, the coal miners, the mariners, the hostlers, the farmers, the trappers, the immigrants, Jews, Gentiles, Negroes,—all of "God's chillun." "Walk with kings nor lose the common touch." (Read again Carl Sandburg's "The People, Yes," and Whitman's *Leaves of Grass*.) Give your teaching the touch of "once upon a time." Try your best to create a nostalgia for the past. The integration of history and literature poses no problems other than those of mechanics and administration. Much literature *is* history. Don't spend too much time on the movements of arms and legs; find out what the attitudes were which lay behind them—likewise the decisions men made. These are the *realities* of history.

Introspection must be disciplined.   Once romance has engendered sympathetic imagination, you will need to help discipline your students' introspection. What do things mean? What is their significance? What kind of inferences may be drawn? What kinds of generalizations? These are all aspects of *inquiry* which is the Greek word for "history." But generalizations come second, for without appreciation there can be little to understand.

History permits generalization.   To any who may object to history's concern with generalization I would reply as follows: (*a*) the historian generalizes and (*b*) your students generalize. Hence it is both proper and necessary to teach them about the kind of generalizations which history requires and permits. If, as Emerson put it, the "power to generalize differences men," let your students become able generalizers. Professor M. Postan of Cambridge gives us full justification.

Every social generalization successfully constructed is a step away from the infinite expectations of an infant, or of a culture at its pre-scientific state, and a step towards the more limited range of expectations of a man "wise" about

life, or of a generation in the possession of an ordered and classified experience.[18]

A caution about generalizations. The generalizations which history
permits are not universal laws, such as Brooks Adams and Edward P. Chey-
ney sought to establish. They are generalizations only about the past but
they have relevance for the present to the degree that it is like the past.
Some are simple; some, complex. When the historian writes of a "Seven
Years' War" or "The Great Depression" he is generalizing. In fact, none of
us can talk without using concepts which are simple generalizations.

More complex generalizations. All generalizations are abstractions
which are the fruit of inference. Those just given are illustrations. Others
of a more complicated kind are such as these: "The Indian menace made
for a close pattern of settlement in the colonies and on the frontier"; "The
great political leaders have been followers as well as leaders"; "Dictators
tend to arise in periods of great unrest"; and "The prevailing pattern of
railroads in the pre-Civil War days was from east to west."

Equally factual but somewhat more controversial, if not contentious, are
such generalizations as these: "The building of the Chinese wall diverted
the migrations of the tribes of central Europe towards the South and was
a causal factor in the decline of the power of Rome"; "America's failure to
change its tariff policy when it shifted from a debtor to a creditor economy
after World War I was an important factor leading to the Great Depression
of the 30's"; "Economic factors weighed more heavily than humanitarian
ones in bringing about the Civil War"; and "The defeat of the Populist
movement was a severe blow to economic democracy."

Appreciations and judgments. The cultural approach not only permits
but requires generalizations, or call them judgments. They are the summa-
tions which give precision to the study of history. But they are not its
total outcome, for appreciation is not to be denied its share—a large share.

---

[18] *The Social Sciences: Their Relation in Theory and in Teaching* (London: LePlay
House Press, 1936), no author or editor, p. 67. Postan also observes: "If history is to
regain its place in the general intellectual movement of our time, it must restore to the
full its erstwhile connection with social generalization. Some such connection is always
present. Social facts, like all other facts, are not concrete and complete phenomena with
a real and objective existence, but merely 'relevances,' aspects of reality relating to the
interests of the observer," *ibid.*, pp. 62-63. See also M. Postan. *The Historical Method
in Social Science* (Cambridge: University Press, 1939). Here Postan says that "whereas
antiquarians collect facts, historians study problems," and that "the nearer the question
is to a social problem, the more completely it dominates a fact, so much the nearer to
history and to the true business of social science," pp. 14, 15-16.

When the historian Leopold von Ranke emphasized "what actually happened" as the
concern of the historian, he was not speaking against the making of generalizations. He
was merely insisting that historians first get their facts straight.

But it would indeed be pathetic if the teaching of history left appreciation to stand alone. If students appreciate the role of certain presidents, is
it too much to require that they master the concept of "the presidency"?
Does the romance of the building of the railroads excuse them from knowing the meaning of "transportation"? These, in being concepts, are generalizations—however "lower case" they may be. Facts never speak for
themselves and more than the memorization of them must be required.

There is no escape from these aspects of historical method. They belong
almost as certainly to sound common sense. The only question you must
answer is this: Shall I treat these phases of historical method as a thing
apart or as integral with substantive study? If they are to serve the purpose
for which they were designed they must be integral with it. They are some
of the fruits of it.

The fallacy of "single cause."   This brings us to the nature of "cause."
Historical cause is the same as all social cause—complex and difficult to
establish. The dramatic and personal interpretations of history have led
some to believe in a theory of single cause. That is not only bad history
but bad politics: Truman's War and Hoover's Depression. There is also
considerable misunderstanding concerning remote and precipitating causes.
The firing on Fort Sumter was the precipitating cause of the Civil War—
the last straw. Its remote causes run far back into the economics, politics,
and culture of the North and the South. Precipitating cause may sometimes be more visible but it is not total cause. It is always, of course, closer
to the effect. Cause is, furthermore, a matter of *what*, and *how*, not of *why*.
Its netlike or field rather than chain character has been noted earlier.

Cause is a net, not a chain.   The net of cause may be illustrated as follows: If the event X appears when the variables a, d, m, r, t, v, and w appear, then we may say that those variables are causally related to X. If X
does *not* appear when they appear, then we have no ground for saying that
they are causally related. The hunt for causal factors is the hunt for what
Dewey calls "relevant antecedent conditions": the emphasis is on *relevant*.
History allows for no experimentation. We may have to wait a hundred
years or more to study the cause of revolutions in order to arrive at a
dependable causal statement. Social cause is difficult to establish because of
the intervention of attitudes. A factor that may cause a certain response
in one person or generation may not produce the same response in another
person or generation. That is why social study is controversial and interesting.

A frame of reference for teaching world history.   We come now to
world history, a view of ourselves in the temporal perspective of great

change and as inheritors of the experience of the ages. The logic of it has been presented in the foregoing. I shall undertake to suggest only a general frame of reference for it.

If the theme be an historical study of our cultural inheritance, the selective principle is thereby given. The world is old and wise, and man is older than civilization. Yet the need was never more insistent that our young people know what the westward movement of the star of empire means.

I suggest that we need first to estimate what we inherited from the Greeks, the Romans, the Arabs, indeed all of Islam, the many phases of European culture, and our great debt to the experience of the people of the British Isles. To this should be added our inheritance from the Orient. To that we need to add some knowledge of the prehistoric: the age of the cave man. Here lies the origin of civilization.

The principles of continuity and unity, the timeless, the dated facts, events, and processes will have to be kept in proper balance. The principle of continuity would, as in our own history, have to take account of breaks, surprises, and divergences. In any event your students ought to know the sources of their language, technology, and science, the arts, ideas, and philosophies, indeed as many of the elements of our way of life as possible.

The tempo of history. History moves at various tempos, now fast, now slow. It is always massive. As modern times approach, the tempo seems to increase and the body of lore becomes so great as to be almost unmanageable. Throughout, your students must be guided by the selective principles contained in the "table of contents" and the "least common denominator" to which we have referred.

From prehistoric to modern man. First is prehistoric man; then the origins of civilization of historic time—Mesopotamia, Egypt, and Central America. After that the Greeks, Islam, China, and whatever in the Orient we are debtors to; Rome, medieval Europe, modern Europe—the Renaissance and the Reformation and the great revolutions as the transition stages or bridges which spanned the "great middle years" of European history.

The Greeks' gifts were early science, philosophy, logic, law, and much of our language; the contributions of Islam—algebra, astronomy, and whatever else we owe them. What we owe the Romans—more law, administration, the beginnings of military science, most of our language—by way of stopping places in between, French and the mother tongue—and the spread of Christianity. Then the Dark Ages—the work of the monks who kept learning alive, and then the dawn of medieval times with all their riches—the treasures of Italy in art and literature, the power of the Papacy, then the Renaissance. The culture of middle Europe, France, and the Low Countries—the beginnings of modern medicine, the roots of our political philosophy, the concept of the nation-state, even before them the Crusades. Next explorations and colonization—a European world. Even earlier, the growth of towns and trade and the beginnings of modern banking; then mercantilism and the beginnings of the modern market and imperialism. Finally, the great revolutions, the French and our own, by which we made the dramatic break with England. Then the beginnings of industrialism. Before we know it, the New World is upon us.

Each of these inquiries must be set in the context of *societies* for the meaning of our inheritance cannot be known unless its social paternity is known.

The importance of transitions. The transitions are quite as important as the unities, for history is the process of transition. Sometimes the course of history springs surprises on us, the Renaissance, the Reformation, and the Enlightenment to name only a few. How they came to be we are not sure. The Crusades helped to tie East and West, as did also the great migrations, and with them the cross-fertilization of both races and cultures. Centers of power and influence shifted. Do not suppose a six-lane highway from start to finish, rather be willing to take history as it may be told—footpaths, fords, connections as clear as the system of "roads" (real and metaphoric) of the Roman Empire and whatever will give insight into continuity. Our inheritance is varied and often enigmatic as to the route it took.

The "great" and the "small." Do not neglect the "giants in the earth": Alexander, Aristotle, Galen, Mohammed, Genghis Khan, Dante, Petrarch, Leonardo da Vinci, Michelangelo, Machiavelli, Joan of Arc, Luther, Spinoza, Shakespeare, Mozart, Napoleon, Montesquieu, Victoria of England, Pasteur, Ibsen, Madame Curie, and others of their stature. But, again, do not neglect or forget the peasants, the foot soldiers, the slaves and serfs, the diggers of coal and gold, the squatters—commoners of many kinds.

How may such a study terminate in order to bring it to focus on the modernity of our day? I suggest the criteria given in Chapter V: size, complexity, speed, mechanism, and the presence or absence of personal freedom.

Textbooks and romance. What about textbooks? There are many world histories, some excellent, some dry as dust. Why not try a trade book: Hendrik van Loon's *The Story of Mankind*.[19] It is picturesque in language and in sketches, and *readable*. Don't try to teach world history

[19] New York: Garden City Publishing Company, Inc., 1938.

down to half-past four of yesterday. Stop when you believe your students have an understanding and appreciation of the backlog of their time. But whatever the text and wherever your stopping point, supplement your teaching by every device that will transport your students in time and space—and in rapture. It can be a great adventure but only if viewed and learned as one. Its great aim should be to bring an awareness of the long struggle, up hill and down, through which man has come to call himself *modern*. Let romance run amuck.[20]

The world today and comparative study. There is another version of world history about which I should like to speak briefly. This is the study of the world as a whole today. This is a comparative study of contemporary socioeconomic and cultural systems: the democracies, the dictatorships, and whatever types lie between. All cannot be taken. Your selection must depend on your canons of relevance and significance for identfying what is both manageable and appropriate that modern youth may know the world neighborhood in which it now lives. Such a study might well take on the character of an enterprise in international relations with the emphasis on the great contest between the United States and Soviet Russia and its satellites—most, if not all, unwilling satellites. Such a course is best placed in the senior year. Materials would have to be drawn chiefly from newspapers and journals: *The New York Times, Current History, U.S.News and World Report, Time, Modern World History,* and such excellent monthly digests as those provided in *Atlantic Monthly*.

The contributions of cultural anthropology. This brings me to the perspectives of culture and human nature. These are by no means the monopoly of the approach of cultural anthropology. It is only that its methods are uniquely appropriate to them. A study of human affairs from these perspectives would be a study of our way of life in contrast with that of some alien and little known culture: the Chinese peasants of the thirteenth century, the people of Lapland, the Andaman Islanders, the peoples of New Guinea or Samoa, a central African tribe, a Guatemalan village, or one of our own native Indian peoples such as the Navaho. But such a study is something more than and different from the mere

[20] A pretty good education in the whole of civilization can be had by spending less than ten dollars. Here are most of the books you will need if you feel that your own education is less than adequate on this score: A. D. Ritchie, *Civilization, Science and Religion;* Clive Bell, *Civilization;* and W. J. Perry, *The Growth of Civilization* (these three are all available in Pelican Books). V. Gordon Childe, *Man Makes Himself;* Crane Brinton, *The Shaping of the Modern Mind;* and Arnold J. Toynbee, *Greek Civilization and Character* can be had in the Mentor Books editions. Add Gordon Childe, *What Happened in History* to the Pelican Books. For good measure add C. D. Hardie, *Background of Modern Thought* (Thinker's Library).

contrast between a so-called advanced and a primitive people. It is an enterprise in the study of *culture* and *human nature*. It would be organized by the same "table of contents" and "common denominator of culture" that have been suggested. This keeps it from being random and *ad hoc*. This makes it systematic, but no less exciting. Continuity has little place in it. It is the study of two unities: one primitive, the other modern. It will contain history but it will be chiefly a comparative study of two cultures.

Such a course would give general education in social knowledge a new, long neglected, and vital dimension. It would not center on the strange, the queer, and the exotic. It would center, as I have suggested, on what culture and human nature are, wherever found. It would show differences, but, underneath, it would reveal *man*.

Seeing ourselves in the mirror of another culture. It would bring familiarity with, insight into, and sympathetic understanding of a culture other than ours. Ours would be studied more or less by inference. The focus would be on "the other." It would permit your students to know another culture almost as another personality. They would find it unique, complex, and self-consistent. It would reveal that the primitive is not as simple as they believe. It would require depth study; it would be intensive. It would, we hope, permit your students to see themselves better because they have looked into the mirror of another way of life.

It would be local, even isolated. Which culture, is of no great matter. It is the *type* we are after. It would illuminate and make self-conscious, as perhaps no other study could, those things which your students take for granted. It would, we hope, engender perspective, curiosity, and the ability to live in another culture as though it were one's own. Both culture and human nature would be seen afresh. Students could get deeper into their own knowledge of both by getting outside that which they know, but know uncritically.

From the strange and exotic to the familiar. Such an alien culture would first appear as if it wore a mask, even as repugnant and fearsome. But, if its spirit is caught, its people will become human beings, even as you and I. The common things in culture and human nature will emerge. Thus it would deepen your students' acquaintance with themselves. They would learn the equivalent of a universal language.

The study of a primitive and simple culture would show our own in its true light: complex, lacking in integration, and multiple rather than single in its character. Acquaintance with a culture more quiet, solid in its integration, and single rather than multiple in its make-up would provide an experience which can be had in no other way. This, in turn, would increase awareness and understanding of our own culture—and make your students no less devoted to it. But they would know it more objectively.

Strange people would become much less strange; they would be revealed as types like those in our own community. The universal and basic traits in human nature, irrespective of simplicity or complexity of their culture, would come into view. What is common to man would be seen. If this would not provide an antidote for pettiness, smugness, and ethnocentricism it is not to be had. Need I say that this is one of the great obligations of the cultural approach to all social study?

A suggested grade placement. As for the grade placement of such a study, I suggest the ninth year. Social and humane study would be combined in a delightful way. No emphasis would fall on the skills of inquiry. The freshman's introduction to the high school and to the social studies can be achieved in no more rewarding way. If given later, the basic structure would not change. There would be only a slight shift in emphasis to include the tools of critical analysis and perhaps the application of the anthropologist's methods of study to the local community.[21]

The aims associated with the perspectives presented above fall into the three general classes noted in Chapter XVI: factual knowledge, skills, and understandings, each of which has its effective and affective aspects. I trust that those which I shall note have now come into your view.

The claims made for history. As for the perspective of cultural change or historical study, more claims have been made for the good it may do than for perhaps any other area of social study. None of them has been proved by objective evidence. The difficulty lies chiefly in the nature of historical study and in the foolish insistence on rote learning: "that frost of fact by which our wisdom gives correctly stated death to all that lives." This kind of learning has never proved worth a candle in the development of either skill or insight.

Knowledge about culture as a specialized study of the ways in which human beings work together to make a society is new as a perspective in the secondary school. It is, however, implicit in all the social studies, or can be made so. This has been my emphasis throughout. It would be difficult to say exactly wherein and to what degrees the historical and

[21] I owe the basic pattern of this discussion to my colleague, Professor Robert Redfield, a professional anthropologist and a great teacher. See his article, "The Study of Culture," *Social Education,* XI (October, 1947).

anthropological perspectives differ either as to skills or understandings. The same aims might be realized quite as readily and effectively by either. The differences would be chiefly in emphasis.

Some skills are suggested. Each provides the context for critical reading and interpretation, the making of valid judgments, the differentiation between valid and invalid evidence, and the ability to relate facts to situations and processes. Both may provide experience in the gathering of data if field opportunities and pieces of amateur research were devised. This is possible through the writing of local history (which I shall discuss briefly later) and the application of the methods of the anthropologist as he works in the field, for they are appropriate to advanced and local communities as well as to primitive and distant ones. These might well include the skills involved in interviews, examining cultural artifacts, delving into old records, and the like.

A sample of understanding. The understanding which might be developed in each of these fields is as broad as the whole range of human understanding. I list the following as representative, but leave it to you to allocate them to the perspective most appropriate to their realization:

1. Growth in disciplined imagination, the *sine qua non* of the ability to live in the past or in another contemporary culture.

2. Awareness of the fallacy that "history teaches," for it "teaches" chiefly what our biases dispose us to find in it by way of support of views already held.

3. Understanding the difference between interpretation and judgment. Past and contemporary cultures are interpreted in *their* terms; they may be judged in *our* terms, but usually falsely.

4. Understanding of the fact that no cultural study can be unbiased. No historian ever approached the study of the past with "an empty stare or an empty head"—likewise no anthropologist in his concern with primitive cultures.

5. Awareness of the fact that progress is made by overcoming difficulties, but that it is not inevitable. Moreover it is not the chief characteristic of many cultures.

6. Insight into the nature and cohesive function of values which is an aim common to all social study.

7. Awareness of the fact that change is uneven, partly accidental and partly purposive, but that it is usually full of surprises.

8. A sense of identity with the human epic wherever and whenever enacted and, with it, insight into the nature of human nature wherever expressed.

9. Understanding such concepts as continuity and unity; a respect for facts; and knowledge of significant dates as milestones in the life of a people.

10. Respect for the great who were truly great and scorn for those who were falsely so.

11. An attitude of patience at the slowness of social change.

12. Respect for the present and insight into its relation to the past and its implications for the future. With this, insight into the illusion of permanence.

13. Willingness to look at one's own culture objectively.

14. Delight in reading history and all literature which throws light on man's common characteristics.

15. Understanding of the fact that history cannot predict the future but that it may help us meet it and even shape it.

16. A sense of piety toward the accomplishments and virtues of our own culture.

You take it from there.[22]

---

[22] See Langlois and Seignobos, *op. cit.*, pp. 316-321, for aims in historical study.

CHAPTER XXIII

The Perspective of Conflict
of Values: Social Problems

THE STUDY OF social problems has no monopoly on the perspective of conflict of values. To the extent that each of the social studies is concerned with some phase of *policy*, conflict of values must be treated. The study of social problems is distinctive in that it takes *value conflict* as its major concern.

Conflicts over policy cause social problems. Practically everybody is in favor of adequate housing, public education, good mental and physical health, and everything else that makes for personal and social welfare. Disagreement arises chiefly as to the "right" policy by which these values shall be secured. It is chiefly in this sense that social problems are caused by conflicts over policy. Or call them value conflicts, the fact that men disagree about the ends or means, or both, by which social welfare may be achieved.

Conflicts of value are, as they must be, conflicts in attitudes. These are attitudes about such matters as housing, education, medical care, conservation, immigration, and whatever else is or may become an issue about which people take sides.

Two dimensions to social problems. Thus it is that social problems have two dimensions: one is subjective, the other objective. The former are dispositions and attitudes, the latter are objective conditions. But objective conditions, whatever their "condition," do not constitute a social problem unless men's attitudes define them as such.

Value conflict illustrated. Suppose that the citizens in three different communities are asked about the state of housing in a given section. How

351

will they respond? That will depend on what their standards of value are. If they deplore leaking roofs, inadequate lighting, sagging foundations, and the other indexes to inadequate housing they will perceive them as indexes to such housing. If they deplore them strongly enough to say that "something ought to be done," they will have identified the condition of housing as a social problem. If they perceive such conditions as normal or non-problematic they will not constitute, for them, a social problem. Housing as a social problem is thus defined as one according to the divergence of certain conditions from the norms which people hold as standard. It depends how they look at things, that is, through the lens of what norms of fitness, goodness, or adequacy they perceive the objective conditions in their community.

"Ought" and "how" differ. A majority opinion that "something ought to be done" does not settle the matter. This is agreement only on ends. Sharp disagreement may exist as to the "right" means. That it *ought* to be done is one thing; *how* it ought to be done is a very different thing. The difficulty lies in the fact that many interests are involved in every social problem and each one tends to have a somewhat different notion about the *ought* and *how*.

Variety and conflict of interests. Look at the wide variety of interests involved in either the cure or the prevention of "bad" housing. (It is significant that we assign the term "bad" to housing rather than to the attitudes which permit "bad" conditions to exist.) Interests of the following groups and persons come to mind: the building trades may be for or against "dry walls" or certain regulations relating to the glazing of the windows; the standards set by the building code introduce a variety of interests and standards about which there may be wide difference of opinion; the problem of financing involves the banker and the building and loan association whose interests may conflict; planning experts may take the view that the houses should be razed and the site used for recreation space or a parking lot; the interests of those who believe in private financing may conflict with those who believe in public financing as well as the ratio which ought to obtain between these two sources of money; public health experts will have their angle, and so on.

A conflict of interests is a conflict between different "I wants"—not on the basis of only whimsy and stubbornness but often because of quite reasonable and legitimate differences.[1] The solution of every social problem requires a working agreement on three matters: that it *is* a problem, that

[1] Students sometimes take the naïve view that a social problem has only two sides, a "right" and a "wrong" one.

it *ought* to be attacked, and that it ought to be attacked by a *given set* of means. Every social problem is settled, when it is, on three levels: the level of agreement on ends, on means, and in collective action.

The core of social problem study. The essential task of social problem study is to inquire how conflicting interests may be brought together. This involves students in projecting various hypotheses as to how this might be done. Hence, the net of hypotheses must be cast wide in order to include all the conflicting interests. This is the task in all ethical (or policy-conflict) situations. (See discussion of this in Chapter VII.)

Some phases of inquiry. This will involve the class in the study of public opinion, methods of compromise, propaganda analysis, and all the factors which enter into the making of consensus and the organization of collective effort. It may be that compromise cannot be reached. It is then a matter of which "side" wins and which loses. This inquiry can go on chiefly at the level of analysis, rather than at the level of social action by the class. You will recall my observation that the school is not an "action institution." The forces in contest are rugged ones and the school has neither the mandate nor the political power to manipulate them, *except* at the level of how they operate.[2]

In the light of these facts, it is sobering if not almost frightening to hear that the students in a social problems class have "solved" a social problem. They may have, but do they know that it was done at the level of social analysis and not at the level of social action?

The scope of social problem study. Social problem analysis is political study, par excellence. This requires that all the social processes be taken into account, because all of them are involved in both the creation and the resolution of every social problem. If this fact is acknowledged, a social problem study may rightly become an enterprise in every phase of social analysis. The degree to which the study of social problems now meets this criterion is, I suspect, not very great. But that is the scope of the task. Social problems arise by virtue of a breakdown in some one or more of the several social processes and all are ultimately involved in both their analysis and their resolution through social action.

Difficulties in social problem study. Dangers, difficulties, and disadvantages inhere in the study of social problems. As they say in the movies, "let's face it." Among them are such as these: symptoms rather than real causes may become the focus of study; analysis may be made chiefly in terms of "good" and "bad" men rather than in terms of men pursuing inter-

---

2 See Spencer Brown, *They See for Themselves* (New York: Harper & Brothers, 1945) for an excellent report of field work in social problem study.

ests which serve or dis-serve the general welfare, whichever the case may be; preferences may get the upper hand of facts, that is, what "ought to be done" may paralyze thought about what can be done and the method of doing it; solutions may be conceived as final, or the naïve view may be held that the "right" solution lies hidden just "around the corner" only to be spied out and put to work; the view may be held that the solution of a given problem will not create new problems at the same time; students may get only a pathological view of their community and will thus be depressed and discouraged; they may be so concerned with cure that prevention may escape their notice; their "itch to be doing something" may suffer because they cannot work on the real problem; and they may fail to see that one of the great values in social problem study is to learn to live with problems and "make the best of it."

These things are not said to discourage the study of social problems. They are meant only to indicate how difficult and complex such study is and to suggest that it come in the later years of secondary education—preferably the senior year. High school students are, for the most part, "hot for certainty" but the analysis of social problems will reward them only with "dusty answers."

All social study involves the problem approach. The study of social problems should not be confused with the *problem approach* to all social learning which uses the method of inquiry. All social study must focus on "how things work" in order that they may be understood and that, insofar as appropriate, students may learn to "work the world" toward the goal of a better one. Social problem study involves, as no other problem study does, both *how* and *how well*. Thus it involves, as perhaps no other kind of social study, the cheek-by-jowl closeness of facts and preferences.

Three kinds of problems. Students need to know the difference between problems of knowledge, problems of technology, and problems of policy. Problems of knowledge are scientific problems. They are due to the absence of reliable knowledge. They exist when the relationship between two or more factors or events is unknown. The cause of malaria was once a scientific problem but it is no longer one because the relation between the bite of a certain kind of mosquito and the onset of a certain kind of fever is now known. What causes the "common cold" is not yet known; hence it is a problem of knowledge. We are far from certain as to the causes of depressions, prosperity, inflation, and many phases of social life. These are all problems for the scientist.

Problems of technology are problems of means, pure and simple. We might call them engineering problems. They assume that agreement has been reached on the desirability of doing something: building a bridge, planning a city, reorganizing the courts, and the like. They are problems for technical experts. Hence they are matters of efficiency and know-how.

Policy problems are moral problems. Problems of social policy are, as we have said, policy problems. Hence they are moral problems; they arise out of a sense of ought, their resolution requires agreement on both ends and means. They are problems of the layman who, in working on a given problem, needs reliable knowledge and effective ways and means. Thus, in a sense, the study and solution of social problems involves problems of science and technology. But they are, at base, moral problems. Which of these three types of problems is the most difficult will depend on the standard you use. But we know that social problems are neither correctly analyzed nor their solutions even sought unless attitudes provide the dynamics for those tasks. Furthermore, social problems involve, in a unique way, scientific and humanistic energies and skills. Their analysis is largely scientific; their solution, through social action, is largely humanistic, for there is no science of politics or, if so, it is so weighted with human factors as to render it, at best, a mixture of science and art.

Social problem study in the high school assumes the following things as given: that the scientific knowledge is available, that technical know-how is at hand, and that agreement on both ends and means is the focus of inquiry.

The role of institutions. Now enters the role of social institutions. We discussed their nature and function in Chapter VI. Suffice it to say now that social institutions give every social system its form and organization; they are the "immortals" in the scheme of social things. But, as we observed, they tend to outlive their usefulness, at least in the form in which they were first conceived and set up. They are resistant to social change. Again we confront the eternal paradox of permanence and change. The timeless question which all societies face is how to set the pace for and control social change so as to preserve certain permanences, or "changing permanences." It is in this context that all social problems arise.

Organizational and humanitarian mores. The institutional set which any society has at a given time constitutes its "organizational mores." Those who seek to challenge and change this set must organize their efforts in the form of new institutions. These are the "humanitarian mores." [3] Social problem study must, if it be realistic, involve an understanding of

[3] See Willard Waller, "Social Problems and the Mores," *American Sociological Review*, 1 (1936), pp. 922-933.

the role of social institutions in social change. We hear a good deal about "vested interests." They are groups whose interests are not only vested but *invested*. Institutions are the form their "investments" take. This means that they are organized, and that if they be challenged they must be challenged in a form which is able to meet them in something like their own terms of strength: institutional terms. All this is implicit in the fact that social problems are group problems, that groups are not evanescent but fairly permanent things—at least those which give every social system its basic structure.

Cultural lag and moral divergence. The tendency for institutions to persist in their original form, or at least to change slowly and reluctantly, has been called "cultural lag."[4] This suggests a lag in time which cannot be denied. That conception of the difficulty may be helped by adding another concept, that of "moral divergence." This connotes chiefly a fault in will and purpose. Both concepts are useful for understanding the conditions under which social problems arise. The modern family has not yet adapted itself to the impact of the automobile which has made possible new kinds of personal freedom through escape from traditional authority, perhaps chiefly that of the family. Teen-age clubs, youth movements of various kinds, the enforcement of sterner curfew laws, stricter laws respecting the licensing of drivers, and realistic studies of youth's problems in the school suggest the kinds of institutional changes which are going on but which have not yet resolved many of the problems which arose from this greater freedom. The traditional institutions of community life were badly damaged by the impact of the Industrial Revolution and new institutional forms were slow to emerge and effect repair. Illustrations might be multiplied but the fact of uneven rates of social change as well as the time factor have been identified.

But time is not the only factor. Disturbances to the equilibrium of a society bring what I have called moral divergence. Suppose a vertical column which represents the Great Oughts to which we are committed. Now suppose lines drawn from the base of such a column so as to form angles of varying degrees. The width of each angle would measure, so to speak, the "amount" of moral divergence of our practices from the Great Oughts. The exact measurement of such angles is difficult, for who can say by how many "degrees" delinquency departs from a normal and healthy community and family life, or by how many "degrees" the cheapening of the dollar through inflation departs from sound fiscal policy?

[4] See William F. Ogburn, *Social Change* (New York: B. W. Huebsch, 1923).

We have now two somewhat objective measures of the presence and severity of social problems: the time lag between what is and what ought to be according to the standards of a community, and a moral divergence between the values we affirm and the malpractice in which we engage. The latter are our "sins" of both commission and omission. The facts of both lag and moral divergence tell us, again, that change and progress are not identical.

The importance of the time factor.   The time factor still concerns us, because it takes time to fashion institutions strong enough to challenge the power of those grown old and decadent. The panic of 1893 taught us a great deal, but it was not until 1916 that we created the institution called the Federal Reserve System to give us a greater measure of control over credit. It seems to have taken the great depression of the thirties to spur us to the creation of federal insurance of bank deposits. These time lags were due not only to the technical problems involved. They were also due to disagreement on both the need for such action and the most effective ways to take it. The public conscience is awakened slowly on many issues; we do not wish to be disturbed in our traditional modes of living. The new is not only strange but it is also likely to appear to be dangerous.

The logical stages of a reform social movement.   The phases in the evolution of a new institution may be identified in ideal-type form. We call them the logical or ideal stages of a reform social movement. They represent a continuum similar to that of the act of inquiry. The chief difference is that the course of a reform social movement involves collective rather than individual action and ends in a new institution, instead of a judgment or conclusion. Thus the movement becomes crystallized, loses its amorphous form, and becomes institutionalized. That the process may be repeated many times goes without saying.

1. Presume first an on-going social process, i.e., individuals in some form of collective enterprise (family, church, nation, business firm, sect, etc.) whose purpose is the satisfaction of individual and group needs. Seen as a whole it is simply the manifestation of some segment of life going on—a collective pursuit after some values which are considered necessary.

2. This on-going process finds itself, for whatever reason, thwarted, blocked, or confronted by something which threatens its continuance, and hence threatens the pursuit and consummation of the desired values.

3. The immediate result of this threat or blocking is the creation of a sense of unrest. It can hardly be given a more specific identification because it is ambiguous, vague, and ill-defined. Its personal counterpart is the shock effect of "bad news." All that people know is that "something has happened."

4. Through the process of "circular reaction" this unrest tends to spread and

become intensified. This takes place among the persons whose individual and collective interests have been threatened. This unrest is heightened in the very process of being communicated. This communication may take place through words, gestures, and all sorts of implicit and even unconscious gestures. It involves suggestion and imitation, the former of which tends to contribute directly to the heightening and intensification of *feeling* about the situation.

5. Gradually, what was at first only a vague fear or misapprehension and which found expression in ill-defined unrest and a random-like display of behavior (rather than *action*) comes to be defined more sharply. This takes the form of *a positive definition of the situation*. The subjective dimension of this clearer definition as to "what has happened" or "what impends" is the emergence of an attitude or a pattern of attitudes. The problem situation now takes more definite form and one or more specific problems come to be named as such. Parallel in time the sentiment that "something ought to be done about it" is made vocal.

6. Concurrent with this clearer definition of what the trouble is, or at least following closely on its heels, is the emergence of certain persons who come to be identified as leaders. The emergence of leaders is accompanied at one and the same time by the emergence of a definite following—a bond is thus cemented between the affected persons.

7. The affected persons now begin to achieve something like the form of a group with a conscious purpose. The sentiment that "our interests are in jeopardy" is important in the cementing of this bond. Leaders play an important part in this stronger feeling of mutual interest. A group begins to take form and organization.

8. This greater social solidarity comes gradually to take the form of a deliberately planned social institution or organization to "right the wrong." It begins to develop a program of action. The earlier stage of merely milling about has passed on to a stage when a program of overt and directed action has come into being.

9. In this process there develops a group morale; an ideology begins to take shape. This ideology consists of a doctrine, beliefs and myths, and operational tactics. The group thus achieves *direction* toward its goal.

10. The action which the group takes depends on many factors. It may rely on its own efforts; it may enlist the aid of others; it may engage in a propaganda campaign; it may attempt to get others to join its "movement"; it certainly will seek to appeal to public sentiment and develop public opinion in its favor. By whatever means, it will seek to address its problem and if possible to resolve it.

Thus what began as ill-defined unrest comes to be a social institution. If the problem is solved the group may be said to be "at rest."

Individual problems have a social phase. We now need to inquire into the relation which individual problems bear to social problems. Each represents a block, a disturbance, or some form of dissatisfaction with existing conditions. Each engenders attitudes of deep concern. It is

obvious that the final locus of a social problem is in the mind and conscience of individuals. Thus every social problem has a personal locus and
dimension. But it is not as clear to many that what are thought to be
personal problems always have an interpersonal dimension. The view that
personal problems are *only* personal is not only the mistaken notion of
students; it is the mistaken notion of many adults.

Individual-social problems illustrated. The sense in which personal
problems have a social phase, or are in fact only an unshared phase of a
social problem, was implicit in the discussion in Chapter VI. That analysis
need not be repeated, but some illustrations will help. Students are disturbed because they do not see clearly the career road which they should
follow, because they cannot get a job, part- or full-time; because there are
not adequate recreation facilities or because their parents "do not understand them." Each of these disturbances arises in a social context. This
is a problem context rather than a social problem, pure and simple. But if
enough young people come to agree that "something ought to be done
about it," the "it" being their common disturbances and dilemmas, a
social problem comes into being. Thus social problems arise through communication among those who are affected by some disturbances in the
equilibrium of their lives and in the life of the community.

This change in point of view on what were thought to be only intimate
personal problems may have a shocking and discouraging effect. They are
bigger than they were thought to be. But, in being bigger, they are more
manageable, at least analytically. They can now be stated in terms of the
interpersonal or interinstitutional maladjustments which have given rise
to them. Thus it is that students' personal problems must always be
redefined as *both* personal and social. Unless this is done all that can be
accomplished is to wallow around in a slough of self-delusion, the result
of which will be to deepen the personal problem.

A new perspective is needed. But this shift from personal to social is
important in another respect. We observed that students may assess a
problem in terms only of "bad" men. But the perversities of human beings
are not sufficient clues to social problems. We need to look at them in the
context of cultural patterns and the divergence of group action from social
norms. Only then will we address either personal or social problems in
their real terms.

The limitation of the personal view of social problems. But this view
is hard to take. Most of us are obsessed with individual matters and tend
to see our difficulties only from a personal angle. This explains, in large
part, why we are disposed to depend chiefly on amiable sentiment and

personal honesty and pay little heed to the roles of law, politics, and the rugged processes of the market. The concept of a *transaction* between the inner and outer environments is appropriate here.

Some years ago the following editorial appeared in a Chicago morning newspaper. The heading was "Honesty Alone Can't Stop Pressure Against Spurring Inflation." It read in part as follows.

. . . opponents of price control, anxious to prove themselves right . . . take great comfort from the fact that many retail establishments are still standing firmly by the old ceilings.

But this type of data proves almost nothing at all; it is an argument about the honesty of men, which is *not* the issue [italics mine]. Naturally there are many honest sellers who will try to keep prices down. But inflation does not take place because some rogues, laughing hideously, raise their prices to cheat the public. Inflation is a cyclical process which forces even honest men to raise their prices against their wills, and the question before us is not whether American merchants are honest but whether this cyclical process has begun.

When pressure for price increases becomes too great, the question of honesty becomes irrelevant. . . . The question is whether we have embarked on a process in which one set of price increases forces a second set of price increases which forces a third set of price increases and so on. If we have started on that process, we are in inflation regardless of whether Americans are honest or dishonest. . . .

Morality is institutional as well as personal. Such a view does not relieve individuals from honesty. It requires only that they institutionalize their honesty so that the environment may be so rigged that men will find it increasingly impossible to be dishonest. Morality is an attribute of institutions as much as it is an attribute of persons. Charles J. Fox, Member of Parliament in the 18th century, once said, "I do not impute the spirit of cruelty to individuals; it is the inevitable consequence of slavery." His moral was that if men were to be made less cruel, the institution of slavery must be abolished.

Let me again warn against the old but persistent "either-or" of individual *or* institutions. Right social change requires courageous, wise, and dedicated individuals but it also requires change in the objective conditions of the outer environment, not only changes in the hearts of men. Social problem study should keep these two factors always in view and always in balance.

The causes of social problems now concern us; likewise, what may prevent or cure them. Cause may be seen from two points of view: (*a*) as a field in which certain constants appear and, with them, certain consequences; and (*b*) as a cycle of causal factors. The net or field view was set forth in Chapter XXII.

The cycle theory of cause.   The cycle theory of cause is known as the vicious or beneficent circle: it may move down to worse effects or up to better ones. Take the case of such minority groups as Negroes, Puerto Ricans, or Mexicans. Suppose that the consequence of the play of a set of cyclical factors is prejudice and discrimination in housing, employment, and even the enjoyment of certain civil rights. Assume also that each of the following elements in their plane of living is considerably below the average for the whole civil community: level and regularity of employment; degree of skill; adequacy and frequency of wages; fitness of their housing for decent family life; quality of diet and adequacy of nutrition; state of physical and mental health; degree of literacy and level of school grade attained; stability of family relations; quality of manners, cleanliness, and law observance.

These constituent elements in their planes of living are the chords which make up the "net of life" in which such minorities are often caught. They are perceived in such contexts as unworthy, not to be trusted, and in many other negative and inhumane ways.

The principle of cumulative change.   Such attitudes may be changed by changes in their "net of life." A favorable change in any one or more of these conditions, if it can he held long enough, will ideally tend to have a favorable effect on the others. If these gains are maintained, the social position of the group will tend gradually to rise and engender more humane attitudes. The cycle may also move downward and bring with it increased prejudice and discrimination.[5]

Many points of departure for social problem study.   The merit of this view of the operation of causal factors is that it reveals their dynamics somewhat more clearly than the field view set forth in Chapter XXII. The cyclical view suggests more readily that inquiry about a social problem may begin at any one of many points or several at the same time. Improvement in one tends to make for improvement in all the others. Each of these causal theories (different chiefly in the manner of presenting them) denies the straight-line or "falling dominoes" theory of causation, which is much too simple. But whichever causal theory you teach, do not forget that it is attitudes which must change if social change is to be effected.

A range of social problems.   The following outline suggests a range of social problems. If one of each is studied, what might otherwise be a purely *ad hoc* choice could be avoided. But it would not necessarily preclude the maximum participation of your students in the choices which

[5] See Gunnar Myrdal, *An American Dilemma*, Vol. II (New York: Harper & Brothers, 1944), Appendix 3, "Note on the Principle of Cumulation," Vol. II, pp. 1065-1070.

are made. I mean to suggest only that those chosen be representative of some systematic view.

1. Material well-being of the population including
   a. physical health: medical, dental, and nursing care, the sale of patent medicines or nostrums, and the care of the aged.
   b. adequate supply of material goods and services: standards of living, wages, diet, housing, and police protection.
2. Psychic security, or good mental health: the problem of the incidence of insanity, care of the insane, programs for rehabilitations, and the problem of worry.
3. Job opportunity: opportunity to compete for jobs and, through employment, for the thing values which are the material base for not-thing values; discrimination; up-grading; career requirements; and the organization of the labor market.
4. Citizen opportunity: opportunity to play an active part in the making of political decisions; study of voter apathy, the complications in registering for voting, the complexity of issues, ease of access to reliable news and opinion; and propaganda.
5. Responsibility of elected and appointed officials: bureaucracy, ethics of politics, the problem of the layman vs. the expert, the political machine—how it works and how it is controlled, the function of the ward committeeman, and the behavior of candidates in campaigns for election.
6. Maintenance of civil rights, including
   a. freedom of speech
   b. freedom of press and publication
   c. freedom of assembly, association, and petition
   d. freedom of worship.
7. Opportunity for self-development
   a. freedom of choice of occupation
   b. parent-child relations
   c. marriage and family life
   d. the freedom of the consumer, the nature of advertising, etc.

The elements in this outline may be matched, approximately, with the several social processes described in Chapter XXI. But whichever scheme is used, the purpose is to insure, insofar as possible, that the choice of social problems is representative of the format of the entire set of social processes and that the analysis reveals the degree to which more than one process is related to each of the problems studied. At all costs, an *ad hoc* conception of social problems is to be avoided.

Some criteria for judging social problems. In addition to a range of related topics which will reveal the breadth of choice of social problems, some criteria are now offered as a basis for understanding the kinds of judgments which are involved.

1. The extent or degree of divergence of a problem from the declared normal, i.e., how "bad" is the problem measured in those terms?

2. The number of basic values from which a given problem diverges. All social problems involve divergence from many norms; from which does a given problem diverge? e.g., juvenile delinquency, parent-child conflicts, divorce, inadequate medical care, political corruption.

3. The number of persons affected by the problem, i.e., local, state, regional, national, or international—what age groups, what sexes, nationalities, racial and ethnic groups.

4. The duration of the problem—of how long standing? Are there vested interests which profit from its continuing as a problem? What attempts have been made to solve it? Why did they fail? What attitudes are now taken toward it—apathy, defeat, militant concern?

5. The spatial extent of the problem (related to No. 3)—what land areas, what communities? How can those affected join in attacking it?

6. The position of the value diverged from in the value-hierarchy of the community: is it a minor or a major problem, to whom, and why?

7. The range of undesirable effects which flow from a problem (part of Nos. 3 and 5). Who is most immediately affected, who least? What light does this throw on what is done and how successful the attempts are?

8. The relative ease or difficulty involved in the solution: what finances, leadership, knowledge, technical know-how, etc., are needed? What can individuals do by themselves? How great is the need for collective and continuous action?

A general scheme of analysis. However much the forms of analysis and the means and order of presentation may vary, the following general scheme is suggested as a rough outline.

I. Nature of the problem.
   a. How does it appear to the "man on the street"? Is he aware of it? What ideas does he have about it? What is his attitude toward it? How do different students in the class think and feel about it? What range of interests is involved in it?
   b. Who are the people affected, i.e., who has a stake in it? These may be as diverse as bankers, merchants, politicians, experts, women's clubs, youth groups, Kiwanis, Rotary, churches, labor unions, age groups, sexes, social scientists, ministers, and lawyers.
   c. How does the problem appear to each of these groups? This will reveal how many "sides" it has; it may also include the spatial area over which it is a problem to various kinds of people.
   d. Why is the problem significant? Number of people affected, intensity, what other problems are related to it, what are the chances that it will get worse instead of better, how critical is it, what news stories or editorials have appeared about it?
II. Origin or etiology of the problem.
   a. What is the social context out of which the problem arose? What dis-

turbed the equilibrium of the community? Are the causes quite apparent and easy to get at or obscure and difficult to isolate? What social trend does it relate to—population movement, change in prices, new ideology, some factory in the area of business or industry?

b. What are the ramifications of the problem? What is its connection with other problems? Is it difficult to give it a clear and precise name? What other problems stem from the same course? To what deep-lying disturbances in personal and community life is it related?

III. Goals which are sought through its solution.

a. What images do various persons or organizations have as to what the conditions would be if the problem were solved? Do these appear to be practical or quite utopian?

b. Are alternative solutions possible and who suggests them? How great is the difference between them in terms of cost, time, personnel, depth of analysis, probable results?

c. What benefits will accrue and to whom if the problem is solved? Who would benefit the most? Who would be hurt the most?

d. What do the experts recommend? How do laymen react to their suggestions? Is there the feeling that this is a job for laymen, i.e., that there is no need for any expert advice?

IV. Means required for solving the problem.

a. Can the problem be approached directly, or indirectly? Why? What tactical issues are involved? How easy would it be to do the wrong thing?

b. Is the problem a short- or long-range one? Are some aspects short- and some long-range? What do people think ought to be done first? How does the cumulative principle apply to it?

c. What do experts recommend should be done? How much faith do people have in them?

d. What are some of the chief obstacles?—the state of public opinion, support or attack from powerful groups in the community, the vested interests who want the problem solved or wish to keep it from being solved? What technological obstacles are there? Is there sufficient scientific knowledge to solve it? Are the dominant social trends running with or against an attack on the problem?

V. Sources of information, teaching materials, and techniques:

a. films and film strips, recordings, maps, etc.

b. printed materials, reports, etc., from organizations interested in the problem: public and private agencies, and propaganda groups.

c. newspapers, scientific journals, and popular magazines.

d. resource persons, and experts, statistical data of many kinds.

e. field trips, propaganda analysis.

f. discussions, group projects, panels, individual research, reports.

Practical suggestions for inquiry. The way in which the method of inquiry relates to the study of social problems may now be suggested in outline form.

1. Begin with the personal experiences of the students. Their responses will likely be in terms of personal problems.

2. Stimulate discussion as to the intensity of these problems and push the discussion in the direction of putting them in a social context. The students will be reporting their personal needs, or what they take to be needs. Your task is to work in the direction of getting them to see that these needs can be resolved only in an *outward* direction.

3. Once the personal and public phases of their problems have been related, the ramifications, through the various social processes, might well be explored. The techniques you will employ must be dynamic, vivid, and interesting—and informative by way of clarifying the personal-public nature of the problems under study.

4. If a given problem (because only one can be taken at a time) can be located in a particular social process, make the most of that. Every problem will have a somewhat unique nature and hence be somewhat more referable to one social process rather than to another. But do not undertake to make too tight a "fit." The best you can do is to identify the process which suggests the best point of departure.

5. The reason for joining personal with public problems is to emphasize both the social origin of problems and the social context in which they must be resolved. "Operation Bootstrap" will not get the job done.

6. Emphasize the interests of others in a given problem: whether to "good" or "bad" ends, and the degree to which these interests are in conflict. How stubborn and uncompromising do these interests seem to be? What common ground suggests itself for bringing them together? You have now reached one hypothesis stage although hypotheses are part and parcel of every step. Your students do not *know*; the thing to do is to imagine what they might do and follow these imaginings through as hunches and turn the best of them into hypotheses.

7. This brings you to the very essence of the data-gathering phase of inquiry. You and your students will now *seek* through, *inquire* through, and *follow* through certain lines of inquiry.

8. Once analysis of causes is well under way, methods of solution begin to suggest themselves. This is the problem of what can be done about the problem. Here the division of labor between individual and group effort should receive emphatic attention. Zeal may flag and discouragement may ensue if the problem is seen only in its remote and strictly social or collective terms. Find, if possible, the individual or personal angle that has appeal and promise and play it up. But don't overdo it. Some problems may be quite uniquely teen-age and peer problems whose dimensions may be somewhat less society-wide than certain others. Find that framework for solving the problem which will engage the interests and energies of your students. If it is a purely local problem, even local to the school as a social institution, that task will not be difficult. Even so, never ignore the civil setting of the problem and the fact that the school is a public institution. If the solution is far beyond teen-age capacity and power to engage in social action, the emphasis may well fall on your students' becoming more informed about it and, through this, sustain their interest in it. The

least they can do is to understand it, identify false and bogus schemes for its solution and learn to live with it.

9. The final step, always provisionally fluid, is to bring the entire enterprise back to focus on the field of experience in which your students now live. Thus the shuttle of experience flies back and forth between personal and social or social and personal, whichever way you wish it.[6]

Several kinds of thinking involved. Social problem study involves several kinds of thinking. Some of these are more or less unique to it and some are of the kind involved in all inquiry. They may be thought of as various skills of thought.

1. *Awareness of basic values*: this may be called "goal thinking." It requires consideration of the basic values of democracy, which are the bench marks by which we judge when a problem has arisen and the norm which the community must reach if the problem is to be solved. This skill requires that students know how these basic values were derived, and how they are related functionally or operationally to the concrete events and problems with which they are concerned.

2. *Trend thinking*: this requires the identification of the changes or trends which offer realization of or damage to the basic values. Representative current trends are such as these: increase in internal migration and decrease in immigration, decrease in the size of the family, reduction of the work week and the increase in leisure time, increase in the power of communication media—radio, TV, books, etc.; changes in the patterns of skills and occupations—the increased dependence on machines and the trend toward automation; increase in the birth rate with corresponding long-run increase in school enrollments, longer life expectancy and the problem of the aged and the retired, increased social mobility, the trend toward consolidation in religious groups, labor groups, industrial ownership, etc.

3. *Scientific thinking*: the relation between the variables of a changing social world and the permanents, i.e., the Great Oughts, and the skills required in inquiry.

4. *Projective or developmental thinking*: this implies and requires projecting into the future and inventing schemes of social organization which will advance and protect our basic democratic values better than those we now have. Invention is not only a mechanical task; it is also an important social task. This kind of thinking is thinking about the future, to new problems and difficulties and how best to meet them. It is the proper balance to historical thinking.[7]

[6] See *Contemporary Social Problems: A Tentative Formulation for Teachers of Social Studies*, Edited by Louis Wirth (Chicago: University of Chicago Press, 1940). I have based some of the foregoing formats on materials in this pamphlet. It contains an excellent model resource unit on the housing problem.

[7] See Harold D. Lasswell and Myres McDougal, "Legal Education and Public Policy: Professional Training in the Public Interest, *Yale Law Journal*, Vol. 52, No. 2 (March, 1943), p. 294, and Lasswell, *Power and Personality* (New York: W. W. Norton & Company, Inc., 1948), pp. 203-204.

Thinking involves doing. These various skills of thought will involve your students in (a) the gathering, manipulating, and interpreting statistics (the chief method of natural science), (b) sympathetic imagination and introspection (the method par excellence of the social sciences), and (c) judging, assessing, and evaluating (the method of "ethical" thinking).

How rationalizations operate. To these may be now added a format which shows how rationalizations operate. Social problems are indexes to various degrees of divergence of our behavior and practices, both personal and public, from our declared goals. In defense of these divergences we often engage in rationalizations which are little more than alibis for continuing to act in divergent ways. The process is as follows:

We subscribe to the principle of equal opportunity to compete for all occupations and professions but we depart from this subscription in the practice of various kinds of discrimination. The result is that men work at tasks below their level of capacity, their expectations remain far from satisfied, and they get less moral and material reward than they might if they had the opportunity to compete on the basis of their ability and training. This divergence worries us, so we invent alibis, excuses, or rationalizations for continuing to restrict open competition for occupations and professions. We do this to save our face. These rationalizations are of the following kinds: "competition is all right in theory but it won't work in practice"; "many workers have a low standard of living; hence they can get along on less pay and less frequent work than other workers"; "it isn't a good thing to mix the races—colored people are happy by themselves"; and "there would be a lot of trouble if we let 'just anybody' work at this job."

An excellent project for inquiry would be to examine these rationalizations for the truth and error they contain. The test of a rationalization is not only that of its logical inner consistency, but whether it is based on humane premises. The rationalization that men should work at menial and low-paying jobs because they have a low standard of living may be justified on logical grounds—their expenses are low, hence their income need not be high—but it is obviously not to be justified on the grounds of our cherished belief in the competitive principle. The rationalizations which students offer in class will usually provide more than enough raw material for projects of this kind. The tendency to rationalize is a weakness in mankind, but a very *strong* weakness.

Skills in social study. The skills and skill knowledge which may be used and developed in social problem study run the full gamut of those involved in the method of inquiry. I have dealt with them in Chapters XVI, XVII, and XXII, and shall not repeat them here. Many have been suggested in this chapter.

Understandings through social problem study. As for understanding and insight and their affective concomitants, there are a great many. Among them are such as the following: the altogetherness of every social system, the nature of institutions—how they grow stale and renew themselves, the relation between so-called personal problems and social problems, the difference between problem analysis and social action, the multiple nature of all social causation, the difference between facts and preferences, the operation of the cyclical theory of causation, the nature of rationalizations, the difference between change and progress, the use of democratic values as bench marks by which the divergence of social behavior may be identified and assessed, the nature of individual interests and their relation to the *general* welfare, the importance of the virtues of courage and patience in solving social problems, the role and power of propaganda, and the difference between prevention and cure.

Study a few problems thoroughly. One final observation: the great variety of social problems, the wide range of student concerns, and the limitations of time force the judgment that it is far more important to study a few representative problems thoroughly than many of them in a hop-skip-and-jump fashion. You can never deal with all "the facts" but you can deal with enough of them to illustrate the nature of social problems and do a thorough job in providing experience in analysis.[8]

[8] The following excellent sources on methods are noted: *Social Problems* (a journal published by The Society for the Study of Social Problems), and *Action for Unity* by Goodwin Watson (New York: Harper & Brothers, 1947). See also the resource units in the Problems in American Life series, *op cit.*, and Norman Daymond Humphrey, "Social Problems," *New Outline of the Principles of Sociology*, Alfred M. Lee, Editor (New York: Barnes & Noble, Inc., 1951), pp. 3-63.

CHAPTER XXIV

The Perspective of Associations and the Problem of Consensus: Civics

Civics closest to ethics. This perspective focuses on the political, the civic or policy approach. Of all the social studies, it is the most controversial because it is the nearest to the study of ethics. It seeks to learn how every form of human association, from the family to the state, resolves two questions: (*a*) "What is the 'good' for this group, or what shall its values be?" (*b*) "What are the most effective ways of realizing that 'good'?" Civics is, then, everybody's business—young and old, rich and poor.[1]

We live under many governments. This view of civics makes it no less a study of *government*. It only defines government as a means of social control in *all* associations rather than only in the state and its subdivisions. Each of us lives under a whole series of governments, each of which makes certain claims upon our loyalty. Among them are the church, fraternal societies, local improvement groups, political parties, labor unions, YMCA and YWCA, teen-age organizations, Boy and Girl Scouts, chambers of commerce, taxpayers' leagues, literary and scientific societies, and business organizations. Each has a constitution which, whether simple or elaborate, written or unwritten, is a "way of life," which disciplines part of our life.

Our membership in these voluntary associations does not deny that the supreme civil association is the state. But this fact does not require that civics choose between studying the state and its subdivisions and some of the voluntary associations to which we belong. It requires that we study the nature of *associations*, including voluntary and nonvoluntary types. This

[1] See Chart 2, Chapter V, for the position of the political order in the triangle of human relations.

is the study of government, policy, control, and allied matters in a variety
of organizations. It is also the study of how these two types are related
and what they have in common.[2]

The "right" balance between freedom and authority. The chief thing
which voluntary and nonvoluntary associations have in common is the
task of effecting the "right" balance between *freedom* and *authority*. This
is the ultimate problem which all associations face and the terms in which
consensus is achieved within them. Man has faced this problem throughout
all the ages of community life. It involves a limitation on individual freedom in order to create the conditions under which community life is
possible. The equilibrium which has been struck between freedom and
authority has always been tentative and shifting. Many mistaken notions
have been entertained about their relation. Before the Christian era
Aristotle wrote,

> Anyone who either cannot lead the common life or is so self-sufficient as not
> to need to and therefore does not partake of society, is either a beast or he is
> a god.

When Abraham Lincoln asked, "Must a government of necessity be too
strong for the liberties of its own people, or too *weak* to maintain its own
authority?" he was concerned with the balance of freedom and authority.
Justice Holmes's dissent in the case of Lochner *vs.* New York spoke to the
same great issue. It reads in part as follows:

> The liberty of the citizen to do as he likes as long as he does not interfere
> with the liberty of others to do the same, which has been a shibboleth for some
> well-known writers, is interfered with by school laws, by the Post Office, by
> every state or municipal institution which takes his money for purposes thought
> desirable, whether he likes it or not.

Justice Learned Hand spoke of the same mistaken notion when he said,

> A society in which each is willing to surrender only that for which he can see
> a personal equivalent is no society at all; it is a group already in process of dis-
> solution . . . it would be a hard choice between it and a totalitarian society.[3]

Rights and duties, and freedom and equality. Other pairs of terms may
be substituted for "freedom" and "authority." *Rights* and *duties* is one.
To claim a right is, at the same time, to attribute it to others. Their duty
to respect my right is balanced by my duty to respect theirs. *Freedom* and

---

[2] See Alexis de Tocqueville, *Democracy in America,* for commentary on the tendency
of our people to form voluntary associations; we are a nation of "joiners."

[3] See William E. Hocking, *The Lasting Elements of Individualism,* for a critique of
John Stuart Mill's theory of liberty, pp. 72-84.

equality is another, for freedom begins to operate significantly only when a plane of equality has been established. Such a plane is created by limiting the freedom of a few in order to guarantee freedom to the many. Equality thus puts a floor under man and sets the bench mark for what we call civilization.[4]

Note that each pair of terms was joined by *and*. Their "and-relation" is, of course, the basis of the controversial nature of politics. The controversy arises and persists in the tendency for men to take an "either-or" attitude toward them. It is evident that such a view would reduce the choice to anarchy or tyranny, as Justice Hand makes clear.

The "right" balance differs. The "right" balance between freedom and authority, rights and duties, or freedom and equality is not, of course, the same in all associations. But no matter how much they may differ in that respect the problem is there. The rules, regulations, laws, or ordinances of associations exist in large part for the purpose of defining the rights and duties of the members. These may differ as widely and significantly as the Mayflower Compact does from the charter of a local improvement association or a literary society but the differences are in *degree*, not in *kind*. The terms in which the "right" balance is struck between individual rights and duties are thus one of the distinguishing features of associations. It goes without saying that the "individual" may be single human beings, as in the case of the Mayflower Compact, or both single human beings and *states*, as in the case of the Constitution of the United States.

Imbalance and the crisis in valuation. The crisis in valuation which was discussed in Chapter VII is, in large part, due to the imbalance of freedom and authority not only in our national society but in the whole world. Our image of the "generalized other," or the community, is obscure and ambiguous. We are on the threshold of a cultural, economic, and political tomorrow whose dimensions we can only dimly sketch and about which there is grave disagreement. At such a time we need a reaffirmation of the creed on which our civil way of life is based. This is, in essence, a religious experience in the sense that religion means "to bind fast." This is the "religion of democracy."[5]

Such a reaffirmation was made in the time of Moses when the tribes of Israel had fled the land of their long captivity and were in the wilder-

[4] Rousseau's conception of the ideal democracy, as set forth in his *Social Contract*, was based on the assumption of a society in which the individual maintains himself as a citizen only to the degree that he recognizes the rights of everyone else to belong to the same community. See George H. Mead, *Mind, Self and Society*, pp. 286-287.

[5] See Horace M. Kallen, "Democracy's True Religion," *Saturday Review of Literature*, July 28, 1951.

ness of Sinai. It came in the form of the Ten Commandments and "divers laws and ordinances" which defined a constitution or a "way of life" for a people about to enter a strange and alien land. It is no sacrilege to believe that we now need to reaffirm our faith in our Constitution as a way of life. We must take its provisions

> . . . not as mathematical formulas having their essence in their form [because] their significance is vital not formal, it is to be gathered not simply by taking the words and a dictionary but by considering their origin and the line of their growth.[6]

The role of priest and prophet.   Our Constitution may then be taken as the study of the supreme civil association which encompasses all other civil units and ties them all together. The teaching of civics will cast you in the role of both priest and prophet as perhaps no other social study does. You will need to keep those roles in the most dedicated and informed balance.

Constitutional study is secondary.   There is a sense in which constitutional study is secondary. I find this thought in Aristotle's observation that

> He who proposes to make the fitting inquiry as to which form of government is best, ought first to determine what manner of living is most eligible; for while this remains uncertain, it will also be equally uncertain what government is best.

This defines your task as that of instructing your students so that they may understand the nature of democratic human relations and, in the light of that knowledge, study the Constitution as the basic civil instrument designed to make them a reality.

The demands of critical loyalty.   Such are the demands of critical loyalty. The wisdom and probity with which you address your task must take full account of the maturity of your students. This will require, at all levels of instruction, that you make clear that education in civics requires the wisdom and conduct not only to obey the government but to *be* the government, to make it, to inspire and control it. The government of any democratically conceived association is not *they*, but *us*. Furthermore, education for citizenship is not only the "civitization of teaching: it is a matter of the organization of the whole school . . . to suit the civic ideal." [7]

Only such a conception as this will reveal the relation between good men and good citizens as *all* who share in the civic life of "ruling and

---

[6] Justice Holmes in Gompers *vs.* United States, 1914.
[7] See Sir Ernest Barker, *The Citizen's Choice* (Cambridge: The University Press, 1937), pp. 166-167. This emphasis was my thesis in Chapter II.

being ruled." [8] What we seek in the teaching of civics is Aristotle's "nobleness and justice" which he taught in his *Ethics* and through the service of which men may live together "in peace and with reasonable happiness."

Associations in a democracy.   So much, briefly, on what associations in a democracy have in common. Now we ask how they are related. They are related competitively and co-operatively as the organized agencies making for or against, as the case may be, the cohesion and integrity of the entire nation which contains them all and whose supreme authority is the state, or, as we say, "the government."

It would be a mistake for your students to suppose that the political power of the state and its many subdivisions was the only force binding us together as a people. Although the many forms of the state lay down not only the general dimensions of law and order but also make rather specific provisions and requirements, they leave wide areas for the formation of voluntary associations. These broad lines and specific provisions are both permissive and mandatory. It is in the permissive zones that voluntary associations arise and multiply.

A changed balance between freedom and authority.   Because of the reciprocal relation between freedom and authority, or any of the substitute pairs of terms used, it is difficult to say what their changed balance has produced in the past one hundred years by way of greater or lesser personal freedom. This is the basis of the argument in much political discussion. We do know that the state has expanded its operations. This expansion has changed it from the police state of the middle nineteenth century to the service state of the middle twentieth century. This change is often referred to as the decline of individualism and the rise of socialism. But such labels are ambiguous and hence misleading. It would seem to be more sensible to ask what changes have gone on, what the circumstances were which brought them about, how democratic the process was, and what their effect has been respecting the welfare and security of the people. What the role of the civil government ought to be is not the prerogative of the teacher to declare. It is, however, a legitimate matter for inquiry, with the judgments arrived at those which the students make on their own. Any judgments in the nature of an *ought* must, of course, follow many prior judgments in the nature of *is*. Otherwise facts have no function.

[8] See Aristotle, *Politics*, Chapters V and XI. I do not, of course, accept his belief that those who practice the menial arts are to be excluded from the rights and obligations of citizenship. The status of children or those not of voting age does not exclude them from reverence and veneration toward the values of the associations of which they are members and in which they share different degrees of participation.

The "police" and the "service" state. The terms "police" and "service" state give us the termini between which we may describe and assess the changes in the balance between "freedom" and "authority" in our national, state, and local life. This will involve study of the changed relations between the state as the supreme nonvoluntary association and voluntary associations, chiefly in the area of economic life. The time span we suggest is between 1791 and the present time. The contrast we suggest finds its focus in changed conceptions of the nature of civil liberties.

The conception of civil liberties held in 1791 is reported in the first ten amendments to the Constitution which, by that year, had been ratified by enough states to become the law of the land. The conception held at the present time combines those with a great deal of legislation which, although it has not been as precisely reported in a Bill of Rights, may be stated in quite precise terms. Such a statement was contained in a new "bill of rights" proposed in 1943 and restated in similar terms in 1947.[9]

A copy of the first ten amendments may be found in almost every high school history or civics text. That suggested by the National Resources Board reads as follows:

A NEW BILL OF RIGHTS

1. The right to work usefully and creatively through the productive years;
2. The right to fair pay adequate to command the necessities and amenities of life in exchange for work, ideas, thrift, and other socially valuable services;
3. The right to adequate food, clothing, shelter, and medical care;
4. The right to security, with freedom from fear of old age, want, dependency, sickness, unemployment, and accident;
5. The right to live in a system of free enterprise, free from compulsory labor, irresponsible private power, arbitrary public authority, and unregulated monopolies;
6. The right to come and go, to speak or to be silent, free from the spyings of secret political police;
7. The right to equality before the law, with equal access to justice in fact;
8. The right to education, for work, for citizenship, and for personal growth and happiness; and
9. The right to rest, recreation, and adventure and the opportunity to enjoy life and take part in an advancing civilization.

Change in political philosophy. A little more than one hundred and fifty years lie between these two conceptions of the nature of basic

---

[9] The first, which is given here, was set forth in the National Resources Development Report for 1943 and appears in House Document No. 128, Part 1, 78th Congress, 1st Session, p. 3. The second appeared in *To Secure These Rights*, Part IV (Report of the President's Commission on Civil Rights). The chairman of that commission was Mr. C. E. Wilson of the General Electric Company. Its other members were drawn from the ranks of labor, religion (Catholic, Jewish, and Protestant), the bench, and representative laymen.

civil liberties. How can their differences be explained? The most general reply must be in terms of profound changes in the outlook of the American people brought about by equally profound changes in both our domestic and international relations. I should now like to trace the change in political philosophy which the two statements illustrate. The political philosophy which held in the western world when our Constitution was written and adopted (and within two years the Bill of Rights was added) owed its nature to a school of thought with which John Locke was closely identified. This was the school of political thought to which Thomas Jefferson subscribed. The core of its philosophy was to be found in the theory of "natural rights." This was the theory with which its proponents and advocates confronted and contested the institution of absolute monarch. Its essence is faithfully reported in Jefferson's words in the Declaration of Independence:

We hold these truths to be self-evident, that all men are created equal, that they are endowed by their Creator with certain unalienable rights . . .

Those "unalienable rights" were natural rights which man was entitled to enjoy because he was a human being.

A theory of natural rights. According to the natural rights view, each man is endowed by nature not only with certain unalienable civil rights but also with certain capacities: the capacity to think, the capacity to speak, and the capacity to use natural resources. These rights were conceived to be *natural* in the sense that they did *not* derive from communal living. But these rights and capacities, in Locke's and Jefferson's view, had to be made secure. On this need the case for government was established. But it was to be a minimum or negative government. This idea was made explicit in Jefferson's axiom: "That government is best which governs least."

"Natural rights" and the negative state. The state envisaged by the philosophy of "natural rights" has come to be known as the negative or police state. Its task was conceived, in the main, to guarantee that degree of law and order within which men would be free to develop their nature-born rights and capacities: that framework of civil order in which individuals would be left pretty much on their own to work out their destinies. But there was another important assumption in this philosophy, namely that man's rationality would insure, generally at least, that the use of his rights and capacities would be restrained by reason and, governed by it, he would not injure or reduce the rights and expression of the capacities of others. Natural rights and the supremacy of reason thus being taken for granted, it is easy to understand why government was looked at askance, or even feared in the period when our Constitution was written.

The emergence of the natural rights theory and its defense did not, however, happen in a social vacuum. While a theory of social classes can by no means completely account for it, such a theory and a unique set of class conditions were important factors in its development. Its chief proponents were members of the rising middle class composed of merchants, shippers, and manufacturers. In the latter part of the seventeenth and the early eighteenth centuries the members of this class were chafing under and struggling against what they considered to be unwarranted control of economic activities by the Crown. They were contending against mercantilism and in that struggle the theory of natural rights had both emerged and been seized upon as a rationalization for their demands for greater economic freedom. Thus it was that political and economic freedom were twin-born. The freedom which the rising middle class sought found its philosophical justification in the theory of natural rights.

The climate of the Bill of Rights. Thus it was that the theory of natural rights and the police or negative state furnished the political climate for our Declaration of Independence and, within fourteen years, the Constitution. It is in this climate of opinion that the Bill of Rights—the first ten amendments to the Constitution—must be viewed.

Civil rights are basic not-thing values. Those mentioned in the first amendment are of the first order of importance, in 1791 and today. They are: freedom of religion, speech, press, assembly, and the right to petition for redress of grievance. These are the classic freedoms of democracy. These constitute, in Jefferson's expression, what "the people are entitled to against every government on earth."

Note the words, "against every government." They reflect a negativism characteristic of the time, which found expression not only in the explicit prohibitions laid against "the government" in the Bill of Rights, but in the attitude which men held toward government in general. But in those days "government of the people, by the people, and for the people" was new and quite "unpractised." Government as the symbol and embodiment of tyranny and oppression was still fresh in men's minds and they were alert to make explicit what powers the Congress shall *not* have respecting basic liberties.[10] Most if not all of the states had made constitutional

---

[10] These basic civil liberties owe their paternity to such documents and traditions as are reported in Magna Charta, the Petition of Rights and the Bill of Rights in English constitutional history. These trace, in various ways, the gradual emancipation of the people of England from the arbitrary power of lords and monarchs. Each should, however, be studied with a view to learning explicitly *by whom* and *to whom* what freedoms were

provision for a bill of rights but the Constitution, which set forth what
the federal government could and could not do, had originally contained
no such provisions. A demand that the federal constitution make them
explicit respecting limitations on its powers was widespread. As George
Mason of Virginia phrased it, a federal bill of rights would "give great
quiet to the people." This was given in the first ten amendments to the
Constitution.

The Bill of Rights in historical perspective. My reference to popular
attitudes toward the new federal government needs further elaboration.
However much the climate of opinion of 1791 may have been due to the
prevalence of the natural rights theory, not to mention the recent experience of a colonial people with an arbitrary and tyrannical Parliament, more
should be said about the economic and cultural life of the day.[11] This will
put the Bill of Rights in its true historical and social perspective.

The details of such a picture, when filled out, would need to take account
of such as the following: the spirit of independence, even of revolution,
which prevailed in the minds of many; the tradition of religious freedom
and toleration dear to Protestants and Catholics alike; Puritanism, which
was a dominant factor in colonial thought and ideals; the sentiments which
citizens attached to their colonies, now become states; the great land expanse and the small and sparsely distributed population; the essentially
agrarian basis of the economy; the inviting frontier with all its promise of
freedom and fortune; the freehold system of land rights, marred only by
the short-lived patroon system in New Netherlands—in short, such a comprehensive view of the way of life in the new Republic as would provide
the "sociology of its political ideals."

This, in brief, is the account which characterizes the kind of society out
of which came those explicit restraints on the new federal government set
forth in the Bill of Rights. *In toto,* it constitutes a description of the 1791
pole of a continuum of social change whose opposite pole is the present
with all that it symbolizes concerning the status of civil liberties in our
time. Between them lie more than one hundred and fifty years of mo-
mentous and almost revolutionary events.[12]

---

given to *do what* things. It would be regrettable if students thought that the freedoms
won by the barons at Runnymede in the form of Magna Charta were the same freedoms
and for people in the same station in life that were insured in our Bill of Rights.

[11] Although the Declaration of Independence offered a bill of particulars against
George III, it was the Parliament which had imposed the restrictions, tyrannies, and in-
dignities which Jefferson so eloquently recounted to the court of mankind.

[12] This polar view of civil liberties was suggested by David Riesman in "Civil Liberties
in a Period of Transition" (*Public Policy*, Vol. III, 1942). This is a closely reasoned and
well-documented treatment of the conception of the state as guarantor of civil liberty. He-

Redefinition and enlargement of civil liberties. The present-day pole or conception of the nature of civil liberties may be reached by following the route of the "nationalization" of those stated in the original Bill of Rights. This continuum of social change will also take account of the redefinition and enlargement of the idea of civil liberties.

The processes through which the civil rights of 1791 were thus "nationalized" were, in fact, the major economic, political, and cultural processes in which the American people have been involved. This is simply to affirm that changes in the basic values of a people cannot be accounted for short of acquaintance with the changes in their major social activities.

These changes may be viewed in general and particular terms. From the *general* view they would include such as the following: the closing of the frontier; the maturation of an economy through its evolution from a small enterpriser and small landowner structure to a large and increasingly corporate scheme of organization (in finance, manufacturing, trade, transport, and lately in agriculture); the concomitant growth, organization, and political activity of the wage-worker population; the emergence of the "new middle class" of employed rather than of self-employed or employer status; the concentration of great populations in metropolitan cities and their immediate hinterlands; changes in the time-cost aspects of both transportation and communication, which have tightened the web of human interdependence; and with them the uneven rates of social development which have produced, in both states and regions, significant disparities in wealth and poverty, literacy and illiteracy, sickness and health, and the consequent tendency to enlarge the participation of the federal government as equalizer or at least as mediator.

From the *particular* view, and because the trend we examine is that of the redefinition and enlargement of the idea of *civil* liberties, the continuum of social change from 1791 to the present requires that explicit account be taken of laws and their judicial interpretation. It is the *particular* view which we shall now develop, leaving to you the task of relating the changes in law and its interpretation to the basic social changes reported in the *general* view.

Way stations in the route of change. We can deal here only with the main way stations along the route of legal and judicial development. That route until about the middle 1920's traced a serpentine course of advance and retreat. After the middle 1920's the route traces a path of fairly steady advance.

---

ably defends the thesis that civil liberty has come to rest on a great deal more than the vigilance of individuals acting only in their capacity as *individuals*.

You must make an independent judgment and selection as to what the main way stations are. The following can hardly be omitted: the Emancipation Proclamation (an act of the President as commander-in-chief of the army and without basis in the law of civil affairs); the 14th and 15th amendments; the Civil Rights Act of 1875; a series of Supreme Court decisions including the invalidation in 1883 of the Civil Rights Acts, a succession of 5-to-4 decisions in which the redefinition and extension of civil rights was defeated by a single vote; the "turn in the road" which came in such decisions as Gitlow *vs.* New York in 1925, and Near *vs.* Minnesota in 1931; the contest *pro* and *con* over a child labor amendment; minimum wage and safety legislation; provisions for social security and its expansion and extension; the sporadic and largely abortive attempts at "trust-busting"; the Wagner Labor Relations Act and its treatment at the hands of the courts; the story of bills designed to address such national problems as education, health, housing, and fair employment practice; down to such significant and recent Supreme Court decisions as those dealing with religious freedom (e.g., Jehovah's Witnesses) and the recent Supreme Court decision against racial segregation in the schools. This continuum of social change, with its advances and setbacks, its temporary and permanent gains and losses, is in short, the history of a people's attempt to achieve a new conception of social and economic democracy. Without some such historical preview, the changed conception of civil liberties can have little meaning.

Civil liberties and group affiliations. It would be a gross oversimplification to believe that demand for civil liberties was ever a purely individual affair. It has always been, and it continues to be, a matter of the liberties of men who are related more or less consciously and purposefully in associations of various kinds: farmers, artisans, bankers, tradesmen, shippers, financiers, and merchants. In the securing and guaranteeing of their civil liberties, men have always had to choose between affiliation with this group or that group. Thus is it that the state has always responded more to group than to individual pressures.

It is quite true that in the early years of our economy the associations of men, particularly among the poorer and "lower" classes, were evanescent, tenuous, and inarticulate. Contrariwise, those of the "captains of industry" were more permanent, well knit, and articulate. In our time this imbalance has been materially reduced. This provides the cue to the nature of the contest over civil liberties; their extension or nonextension, for whom, and in what areas of life. The contest is between voluntary groups and for this reason the judgment which individuals must make (sharecroppers, steel workers, housewives, merchants, shippers, etc.) concerning their stake in civil liberties is this: With which voluntary association shall I affiliate?

In the foregoing I have sought to show how a change in the balance of freedom and authority has brought a new set of relationships between the state as the supreme association and the many voluntary associations which are the informal representatives of a people. If this pattern be taken as the basis for several units of study it would be quite appropriate for the senior year.

The "journey of citizenship."   I should now like to offer a frame of reference for the teaching of civics which takes its departure from the concepts of continuity and discontinuity set forth in Chapter III. What was called the "life course from adolescence to adulthood" now becomes the "journey in citizenship" from the family to the state. Its continuity is found in students' membership and participation in the voluntary associations with which they are successively affiliated in their "growing-up process." Each would be studied in terms of its goals and the means used to achieve them. Each would also be studied with respect to its relations to the family and the local community. In this perspective students might come to understand more clearly what emancipation from family controls means and the nature of the right and duties which ensue. This perspective would also introduce and illuminate the concept of discontinuity, which would focus attention on the transition stages from simpler to more complex associations and from the sheltering climate of the family to the more rugged and competitive climate of the world of political affairs.

From familiar to public things.   Such a series of units would take full account of the fact that the student is "not a little man now." It would take him for what he is at every stage, a member of some of the community's many associations, his family, and of one or more less familial (or familiar) types of association. The journey of citizenship would travel between the poles of *res familiae* (familiar things) to *res publicae* (public things). At every stage the relation of his nonfamiliar associations to both the family and the larger civil community would be a matter of inquiry.

The criteria of study.   Criteria such as the following might be used for the study of each association, beginning with the family: (*a*) its nature, origin, purpose, and number of members, (*b*) the age range of its members and its significance for the creation of consensus, (*c*) the degree of formality or informality in its organization, (*d*) the kinds of power employed, by whom and to whom the power-users are responsible, (*e*) the kinds and complexity of issues faced and the machinery for dealing with them, (*f*) the concept of civil liberty which exists and in what manner it is served and enforced, (*g*) crises, if any, which the association has faced and how they were resolved, (*h*) significant changes in the association through time, (*i*) case studies of typical issues, that is, how consensus was threatened, the way issues were resolved, and the practical activities involved.

Continuity.   The concept of continuity might lead to the discovery of some such progression as the following: (*a*) from younger to older average ages, as well as the increasing absence or more remote relations of adults, teachers, counselors or sponsors, (*b*) from very informal and unstructured groups to more formal and more highly organized groups with accompanying specialization in the roles played and the development of a more complex division of labor, (*c*) from small to larger or more select membership, or from membership based on kinship and neighborhood residence to that based on interests, (*d*) from quite simple issues to more complex ones, with a growing difficulty in getting "the facts" and the more frequent use of the method of compromise, (*e*) from issues which affect only or chiefly the members of the group to issues which affect persons outside the group, i.e., the widening scope of the social influence of the group, and (*f*) from group activities in which the relation between impulse and action is direct to those in which impulse is mediated by and involves considerable thought and perhaps the aid of experts. Throughout, the problem of how consensus is achieved is the major focus.

Discontinuity.   The concept of discontinuity is, in effect, only another view of the progression just indicated. Whereas concern with continuity would center on the pervasive and persistent factors in group experience, concern with discontinuity would emphasize the elements of change. Thus the two concepts central to all social study would be served.

Life themes, not textbooks.   Such a scheme of study would have unique merit. It would find the subject matter in the past and present experiences of the students. These would be, not their textbooks, but their life-theme. It would honor the "citizen impulses" with which they are presently preoccupied. It would give the study of civics the romance which far too much of it lacks. It would combine rather than separate the study of form and function. In doing this, it would balance the spirit and the letter of the law. It would, for a given age group (ideally first or second year in high school), permit them to *practice* democracy in the terms in which their life experiences permit it. Thus it would, ideally, combine knowing and doing. It would, *contrary* to Aristotle's view, make the young man a "fit student of moral philosophy" because he *has* experience "in the actions of life." It might even prove the truth of Professor Fred Clarke's view:

There is at least as much civic value in knowing how to care for the feeding and health of a baby, or in being able to express oneself clearly and precisely in the mother tongue as there is in knowing the exact procedure by which a Bill becomes an Act . . .[13]

Politics is natural and unavoidable. Above all, it would provide the context for the study of *politics* as a natural and unavoidable phase of all group life. The skills involved would run the full gamut of all forms of thinking and the making of judgments.

Another view of civics. The basis for a core curriculum in the social studies, given near the end of Chapter XXI, now serves as the pattern for still another view of the study of civics. The degree of consensus in any association is the measure of its cohesion or agreement on both ends and means. Its corollary is character. They are but the collective and individual sides of the coin of human affairs.

As in Diagram 7 in Chapter XXI, I shall use the various social science disciplines (to which ethics is added) as the near-equivalents for the several social processes. Each contributes to an understanding of civics and the knowledge of each is a constituent element of it. By that token, civics becomes a general social study.[14] The pattern will deal with government per se, with the major emphasis on the federal system. But whatever its focus, it is applicable to all kinds and levels of social control through the many agencies of government—voluntary as well as nonvoluntary. The perspectives will overlap, as will also the various associations. No realistic description can avoid these things.[15]

THE GEOGRAPHIC AND SPATIAL PERSPECTIVE. This perspective derives from geography and ecology. They are concerned with location and spatial position as they affect human affairs.[16] They deal with matters relating to the base of the human relations triangles given in Chapters V and IX. They may, if you wish, be expanded to take account of the bearing of all phases of the natural science studies on man.

The state, with its many subdivisions, is unique in the sense that, of all associations of social control, it exercises supreme authority over all persons occupying a given *territory*. The fact that a population should exercise and enjoy common political rights and duties simply because they happen to live within certain territorial limits was strange and unthinkable in primi-

[13] Fred Clarke, *Foundations of History-Teaching*, p. 21.
[14] I shall treat Education only implicitly as the science and art of organizing and communicating what the other disciplines provide.
[15] The charts in Chapters V and IX and the discussion in Chapter XXI should prove useful in interpreting what now follows.
[16] Chapter XXVI will deal with this perspective much more extensively.

tive antiquity. Man has lived a community life since Cro-Magnon man—for perhaps 60,000 to 75,000 years—but not until the modern nation-state arose was political sovereignty equated with a given territory. Before then it was based on kinship. (The kingdoms and empires of the ancient world, as well as feudalism, offer some exceptions to this principle.)

The immediate implications for the study of civics of the territorial basis of sovereignty is the place and importance of law as the ultimate bond giving cohesion to a civil unit.[17] Here is the first instance of overlap of perspectives. But, except for courses in commercial law, the contribution of the study of law to civic education has been largely overlooked.[18]

The geographic or spatial pattern of associations may be viewed on a global, continental, national, state, and local basis. For each, the problem of where boundary lines fall is significant. Do they delimit areas on the basis of simple and arbitrary geometric forms or do they follow the contours of topography? What differences, respecting the problem of political cohesion, follow in each type? In the case of the nation-state, what bearing does its geography have on its defensive position in time of war? (Perhaps less and less a decisive factor in a thermonuclear age.)

Geography can tell of the kinds and quality of natural resources, the kinds of soil, and of climate and rainfall. These matters bear on the degree of self-sufficiency of national economies and on their import-export balance. What is their location in the land mass of a continent and its significance for trade and internal security? (Beware the neat and simple geopolitical thesis which places too great importance on position in the continental pattern.) To what extent is the conservation of natural resources a hot political issue and what is its effect on consensus, nationally and regionally?

What have geographic factors to do with "regionalism"—the corn belt, the wheat states, the cotton states? What is the difference between geographic *determinism* and *possibilism*? To what extent have machines reduced the time and distance factor in political units? What bearing does geography have on political isolation?

In so far as the ecological approach differs from the geographic such questions as the following are pertinent: What is the pattern of distribu-

---

[17] The term "the state" will be used throughout this chapter to refer to the supreme civil authority, no matter how large or small the territorial area be or whether it be the central government or one of its many subdivisions to which reference is made.

[18] See Max Radin, *The Law and You* (Mentor Books) for a witty and highly readable book suitable for high school use. See also Rod and Lisa Peattie, *The Law: What It Is and How It Works* (New York: Henry Schuman, Inc., 1952), likewise suitable in the high school.

tion of the population by states, counties, and municipalities? What are the shifts in population, the kinds of mobility—individual or en masse? What are their implications for the formation of consensus in cities and towns? What political problems arise in "down-state—up-state" rivalry, city and suburbs? What natural areas are significant for understanding municipal politics, such as Nob Hill, the Gold Coast, and the slums? Can voters, by political party affiliation, be shown to live in concentrated patterns? What bearing does this have on the ease with which the party machine may appeal to them?

What differences in political outlook can be traced to differences between farm and city? Can areas of absentee owners, owner-dwellers, and renters in cities be identified and what are their political differences?

THE ECONOMIC PERSPECTIVE. If the state be conceived of as a service-agency how are its services paid for? What are the kinds of taxes and what is the equity of each type? How are budgets computed: where does the tax dollar come from, how is it spent? How do periods of depression and prosperity and inflation and deflation affect the major political parties? In what ways does the state participate in sharing the nation's wealth? What aid does it give to business, to education, to the aged, etc.? What are the various bases of taxation, e.g., ability to pay, benefit received, ease of collection, etc.? How do debts held, respectively, internally and externally differ?

What groups are for or against various kinds of tariff policy? What is the relation between tariff rates and employment, capital investments and standards of living? How does running a government differ from running a business? Is it the business of a government to make a profit?

What groups make what claims and by what arguments, for government aid? How are taxes "hidden"? How does the government aid or hinder business enterprise? What is the equity of spending tax money collected in New York and Illinois for flood relief, education, or disease control in Mississippi or Arkansas? What does the Preamble to the Constitution say about "the general welfare"? Is the basic economy of the United States an unmixed one, i.e., "pure capitalism"? If not, how are departures from it justified in the public mind? Does the Constitution provide for any particular economic system? Does the road to democracy run through the factory gate as well as through the polling booth? What differences of political view are held by various groups toward co-operatives?

THE SOCIOLOGICAL PERSPECTIVE. This perspective has to do with the *forms* of association, some of which have already been noted. It overlaps with certain aspects of the spatial perspective already treated and the political approach to be treated next. On the spatial it would raise such questions as these: What is the numerical size of the association? What is its rate of increase or decrease in numbers? What problems of consensus and social control arise when an association grows very rapidly (a trade union, a city, or a nation)? What are the differences in literacy, nationality, and race which affect the difficulty or ease with which consensus may be achieved? How is it that custom will maintain consensus in small groups better than in large groups in which law must complement custom? (These matters affect the simplicity or complexity of the "political apparatus," e.g., techniques and areas of administration and representation.)

This perspective invites inquiry into those phases of associated living which are the most and least competitive, those in which sharp conflict arises, and in which accommodation is reached, for these are not only the basic social processes (Chapter V) but aspects of consensus. Differences in the ethnic, racial, and "class" make-up of the membership of an association would be reflected in the dominance of one of these subprocesses. In what areas of associated life and under what conditions is the phase of assimilation achieved? What is the relation of the number of people and the nature of issues to any one of these subprocesses? How do sharp differences in wealth and poverty affect the solidarity of consensus in various types of association? How fixed or mobile is the social-class order? What has position in the social-class order to do with the quality of leadership? How does leadership affect a peaceful and orderly succession—both in the formal voting sense and in the informal sense of natural leadership? What are the major groups in conflict, over what issues and how are they resolved?

THE PSYCHOLOGICAL AND SOCIOPSYCHOLOGICAL PERSPECTIVE. These perspectives combine to permit inquiry into the role which attitudes play in all associations. The importance of attitudes can hardly be overestimated. They are the "middle principles" which stand between persons and stimuli. (See Chapters X and XI.) This dual perspective on associations of all kinds raises such questions as these: What is the nature and importance of persuasion in the making of consensus? (Are we not disposed to make the study of consensus too rational?) What kinds of symbols are manipulated, by whom, and under what conditions to secure whose consent? What is the value of such stereotypes as, "Turn the rascals out," "America first," "Keep Podunk ahead," and "Give till it hurts"? What "deals" are made to gain whose consent? What is the diagnostic value of Harold D. Lasswell's phrase: "Who Gets What, When and How?" What are the major issues over which the contest for power goes on?—for executive office, in budgetary matters, fiscal policy, control of utilities, the "best" form of charter, revision of a basic constitutional document? What measures are used by whom to judge a member's (or citizen's) loyalty? What types of leaders are there in the association through time? What personality traits are associated with "the politician"? What are the campaign issues? How genuine or bogus are they in terms of the "real" issues? How do various pressure groups operate? What is public opinion and how is it formed? How do political leaders secure loyalty to the "machine"? Is the "machine" necessarily bad? Could a group gain or maintain power without one? Are "machines" more typical of national political parties than of conflicting groups in corporations, labor unions, or co-operatives?

THE POLITICAL PERSPECTIVE. The political and sociological perspectives differ chiefly in their concern with different types of association and with the apparatus of social control appropriate to each type. This is a quite arbitrary division of concern in which the study of the state and its subdivisions has fallen to political science. Hence its concern tends to be with the *forms* of nonvoluntary association, the "mechanics of government" as more or less formal sets of social controls, government's division and unity of powers—legislative, executive, judicial, and administrative—and the various services which it performs in its protection and advancement of civil liberties which are the specifics of its conception of the "good."

In both the sociological and the political perspective the study of form must always be viewed as the form in which *functions* are carried out. To separate them is to separate means and ends or worse, to treat forms, which are means, *as ends.* It is this error, more than any other, which has given death to the vitality of civic education. This has been practiced largely through rote learning of formal laws and provisions, sections of the Constitution, and any aspect of political study which permits *formal* study.

This is not to discourage acquaintance with constitutions, laws, ordinances, and other forms of government in both voluntary and nonvoluntary associations. It is only to insist that forms are means which can have no operational significance if separated from the function they serve. No association sets about to create *any forms whatsoever* unless it has a problem which requires them as *means* for treating it. Problems, issues, and processes come first; the forms which serve them come second. If you do not respect this distinction, your teaching of civics is certain to be not only dull but unrewarding and useless.

The teaching of civics, in common with all the social studies, requires that the criteria noted for the teaching of history be served: nearness, suitability, intelligibility, actuality, and significance for self. The fact that it is largely contemporary study does not guarantee that the criterion of nearness will be automatically served. Hence it is as important and often as difficult to achieve in civics as in history. Above all, do not suppose that student interest in civics will be motivated by a sense of duty. For all but a few students, politics is conceived as pretty dirty business or at least something too remote from their lives to make it either interesting or important. It can, however, be made the most provocative study of all, but not unless it deals with the operations of the civic and political in which they presently have a stake. These are your points of departure into the world of *Realpolitik* which is, for most students, out of sight, out of mind, and out of reach.

Your over-all task from this perspective is to reveal how, in form and function, *popular* government arose, how it operates, changes, and persists. This will involve historical and contemporary study. It will involve related study of the local precinct, the town or municipality, the state and the national processes of government. It will involve inquiry into problems of the following kinds: is "good government" the manifestation of only the *will* of the people, or informed and dedicated will? How effective is the most streamlined organization without informed and devoted public servants or how effective can the most informed and devoted public servants be without effective means of translating their knowledge and devotion into useful and needed services? What is the role of the expert in government? How does government employ science and technology? Do democracies and dictatorships differ only as to the power of their central government or do they also differ as to the source of their power, its uses, and the degree of responsibility of the power-wielders to the people? Is "big government" an evil? What is the relation between the size and scope of governmental power and the size and scope of the power of the great corporate forms of voluntary associations? What are the factors which make it so difficult to make major changes in the size and number of such legislative and administrative units as counties and townships? What is the logic for the division of the nation into various governmental units such as precincts, townships, and counties? Have any of these outlived their usefulness? Does their persistence have anything to do with the costs of government? Does it follow that county units established in the horse-and-buggy days are equally effective and necessary in the days of the auto and airplane? What do sentiment and tradition have to do with their persistence? Is popular government chiefly a rational matter?

What studies can be projected which will deal with the invention of new political forms and administrative techniques? Is it appropriate to think of civics as the study of the future as well as of the present? What is the need, local and national, for the invention of new forms of association? What reforms in voter registration, ease in voting, change in residency laws, etc., might provide stimulating and useful study? Might not inquiry be launched into the problem of the relation between the complexity of modern government and the fact of popular apathy toward it? What are the kinds of issues which arouse the people and which get out the vote? How might *world* political conditions and *personal* insecurity be related? What has been and what is the role of planning in popular government? Is planning a concept and practice alien to the American tradition? Is the Constitution a plan? The Northwest Ordinance? A municipal charter?

The base line for all inquiry into the forms and functions of government is their relation to consensus. It is that which determines the moral strength of a people in their attack on both their outer and inner enemies. This is the persisting integrating concept. Through it, all civic study can be systematized and related. Without it, such study can hardly avoid being *ad hoc* and unrelated for it is the political *order* which provides the context for all facts and events about the political life.

THE HISTORICAL PERSPECTIVE. This is an inherent element in all perspectives. It is used whenever the course of inquiry requires depth in time. It has to do with origins and changes. It saves contemporary study from hanging in mid-air, that is of being only contemporary.

THE ETHICAL PERSPECTIVE. Logically, this might well have been noted first since it directs inquiry to the conception of the good which every association serves. The Preamble to our Constitution, the Bill of Rights which constitutes its first ten amendments, the "new bill of rights" noted earlier, and the varying and often conflicting conceptions of the democratic way of life illustrate the ethics or the "good" of our federal system. It is served directly and indirectly through legislation, judicial decision, administrative orders, the findings of various commissions, the personal example of leaders both elective and nonelective, through laymen and experts—indeed through all individual and collective acts which affect the general welfare in the various subdivisions of the nation and in the nation at large.

Neither local nor national politics is ever a clear and definite matter of "left" or "right" concerning conceptions of the "good." It is rather one of a balance between "left" and "right." It is this because *compromise* rather than *conquer* is the basic principle in every democratic society. Only in totalitarian societies is compromise denied but in them, as Machiavelli taught, "the Prince" must know the limits to which he may go as tyrant. Adolf Hitler was always concerned with the popularity of the Nazi political ideology, which explains his persistent propaganda attempts to get it accepted. Even the governing *élite* in the Soviet Union must take due account of the impact of all political policy on the attitudes of the Russian people, even though it require continuous propaganda to make the Kremlin's policies acceptable.

The basic assumptions of democracy. I should like to close this discussion of perspectives with the statement of the basic assumptions implicit in democracy. They were written by the late Professor Charles E. Merriam.[19]

1. The dignity of man and the importance of treating personalities upon a fraternal rather than upon a differential principle.
2. The perfectibility of man, or confidence in the development, more fully as time goes on, of the possibilities latent in human personality, as over against the doctrine of fixed caste, class, and slave systems.
3. The gains of civilization and of nations viewed as essentially mass gains— the product of national effort either in war or in time of peace rather than the efforts of the few.
4. Confidence in the value of the consent of the governed expressed in institutional forms, understandings, and practices as the basis of order, liberty, justice.
5. The value of decisions arrived at by rational processes, by common counsel, with the implications, normally, of tolerance and freedom of discussion rather than violence and brutality.

It is around such a body of assumptions that consensus is organized and it is in their service that the balance between freedom and authority strikes its changing equilibrium.

Difficulties in teaching civics. Certain difficulties attend the teaching of civics. The temptation to propagandize is perhaps the greatest and most persistent of them. But genuine loyalty to democracy is best shown through the practice of the very civil liberties to which it is dedicated. Among these is freedom to think and speak, which does not permit the teacher to think and speak for or coerce any student. (Thought, to *be* thought, can never be anything but free.) As wise men have told us, when men cease from saying what they think, they soon cease to think. If you offer your opinion be sure to give the reasoning behind it and encourage your students to do the same. Unfounded and ungrounded opinion is mere wordmongering.

Do not make a fetish out of citizenship. It is, from one point of view,

---

[19] *What Is Democracy?* by Charles E. Merriam (Chicago: University of Chicago Press, copyright 1941), p. 8.

the goal of all social education but it is too omnibus a term to use without noting what the specifics are to which it refers. Citizenship has many facets. It is, in essence, the experience and the process of belonging, thinking, sharing, believing, judging, and acting in the interests of the good of many forms of association. There are as many areas for the practice and enjoyment of it as there are associations to which one may belong.

My emphasis in the foregoing has been to show the interdependence of the practice of citizenship in many forms of association, nonvoluntary as well as voluntary. It requires the study and understanding of man as a *policy-maker* and policy enacter. It can be practiced by students as citizens in the most inclusive sense, and by them as citizens in the several little corners of associated life in which they now express much of their concern with social life. The great and immediate problem for public policy today is that each person find a place in the community in which his work can count for more than his own goals.

Civics, in common with most social study, offers few hard facts. Those which it provides will not be working facts if they are only "learned by heart." The tendency to resort to rote learning increases as community pressures against the realistic study of the political process increase. Ideally, the study of those very pressures would constitute the materials par excellence for study.

The aims of civic study. Many of the aims of civic study are both implicit and explicit in the foregoing. In common with other perspectives on human affairs it provides the full range of opportunity to practice all the skills of inquiry and the making of simple propositions or judgments. I shall not detail these here.

On the side of insights and understandings and the appreciations and attitudes appropriate to them the list is well-nigh endless. To those already noted I add the following: democracy is competitive politics; democracy is not without its *élites* but these are ideally *élites* of performance rather than of wealth; representative government is not always "good" government; an education in civics should be an education which will prepare for adversity as well as success; [20] "the only thing necessary for the triumph of evil is that good men do nothing" (Edmund Burke); the community is as real a social fact as the person; [21] political institutions are quite as subject to obsolescence as are industrial machines; although a few may initiate a policy, all are politically free to judge it; the motto, "Let George

[20] See Julius S. Bixler, *Education for Adversity* (Cambridge: Harvard University Press, 1952).

[21] It is significant that the only crime defined in the Constitution is treason, a crime against the community, the *whole* people.

do it," may result in the *wrong* George doing it; politics is not bad but its practice will be, if used for evil ends; laws are permissive as well as regulatory; and we are both a republic and a democracy, the first in form, the latter in spirit.

Almost no end of concepts could be named as important for understanding in the study of civics. Among them are such as these: consensus, power, consent, influence, public opinion, bureaucracy, expert, layman, right and obligation, policy, compromise, and justice.

Finally, I should hope that your teaching of civics might correct the view expressed by Bertrand Russell:

Education has two purposes: on the one hand to form the mind, on the other to train the citizen. The Athenians concentrated on the former, the Spartans on the latter. The Spartans won, but the Athenians were remembered.[22]

I cannot believe that we must choose between these two; it is my faith that we can have both. But we cannot have either if civics is made a "subject."

[22] *The Scientific Outlook* (Glencoe, Ill.: The Free Press, copyright 1931), p. 243. An indispensable reading for the teacher of civics is Lincoln Steffens' *Autobiography*. Other readings of great values are these: Charles E. Merriam, *Civic Education in the United States*; John Dewey, *The Public and Its Problems*; Graham Wallas, *Human Nature and Politics*; and Harold D. Lasswell, *Democracy Through Public Opinion*. See also the author's article on "Civics" in the 1952 edition of *Encyclopaedia Britannica*.

CHAPTER XXV

The Perspective of Unlimited Wants
and Scarce Means: Economics

We can't have everything. The perspective on human affairs of un-limited wants and scarce means brings to mind the rhyme that "The world is so full of a number of things, I'm sure we should all be as happy as kings." But kings, of whom we have fewer and fewer, and even dictators —not to speak of hundreds of millions of common folk—must choose, whether it be among a number of things or only a few. None of us, high or low in the estates of men, can have everything.

The problem of disposing of scarce means among unlimited wants is the problem of *economizing*.[1] Economics has no monopoly on the study of it. It does, however, treat it in the set of terms and processes which we know as the market. There the problem of economizing is treated in terms of the disposal of scarce and saleable goods and services among unlimited wants. It bears eventually on the great question, "What shall I do with my life?"

Economics and the Good Life. Hence, however important may be the role which economics plays in revealing the "goods" aspect of choice, we ought to examine it first in terms of its relation to the Good Life. Frank H. Knight, himself a theoretical economist, tells us:

Our thinking about life values runs too much in terms of material prerequi-sites and costs. It is an exaggeration which may be useful to say that economic goods as a class are predominantly "necessary" rather than truly valuable. The importance of economic provision is chiefly that of a prerequisite to the enjoy-ment of the free goods of the world, the beauty of the natural scene, the inter-course with friends in "aimless" camaraderie, the appreciation and creation of

[1] Scarcity is, of course, always a relative matter.

392

art, discovery of truth and communion with the Nature of Things. Civilization should look forward to a day when the material product of industrial activity shall become rather its by-product, and its primary significance shall be that of a sphere for creative self-expression and the development of a higher type of individual and of human fellowship. It ought to be the first aim of economic policy to reduce the importance of economic policy in life as a whole. So it ought to be the highest objective in the study of economics to hasten the day when the study and the practice of economy will recede into the background of men's thoughts, when food and shelter, and all provision of physical needs, can be taken for granted without serious thought, when "production" and "consumption" and "distribution" shall cease from troubling and pass below the threshold of consciousness, and the effort and planning of the mass of mankind may be mainly devoted to problems of beauty, truth, right human relations and cultural growth.[2]

A problem of means and ends. The economic process is a succession of operations through which means are adapted to ends. The whole series may be simplified and set forth as in the following continuum.[3]

(a)	(b)	(c)	(d)
"Ultimate" resources	Intermediate and indirect goods	Direct consumption of goods and services	Want satisfaction

Included under (a) are the "human resources" (labor) and the materials of the "physical habitat" (land) shown in Chart 4 in Chapter IX. Under (b) are the items of the "material culture" (Chart 4) consisting of machinery, tools, buildings, and all useful artifacts conceived now as capital goods. Under (c) come those items of the "material culture" which are the thing values we consume including food, clothing, houses, books, automobiles, and all the occupational and professional services. Finally, under (d) are such as physical subsistence, gratifications of many kinds, esteem, honor, power, benevolence, and the not-thing values of the "nonmaterial" culture in Chart 4.

Theoretical economics usually studies the interaction among these factors in terms of the play of only the process of competition. The limitations of this view of the way man interacts with his fellows will concern us shortly.[4]

---

[2] "Social Economic Organization," *Second-Year Course in the Study of Contemporary Society. Syllabus and Selected Readings* (Chicago: University of Chicago Press, copyright 1934), p. 127.

[3] Based on Knight, *op. cit.*, p. 165.

[4] All references to theoretical economics are to the classical and neoclassical school. Note also that both of these schools do admit of monopoly. I trust that you will not be misled by my concern with theoretical economics. I do not suggest that it be taught to secondary school students, although it has a place at the junior college level. I mean, rather, to review for you the outlines of classical and neoclassical economics so that you may be self-consciously aware of its nature and its limitations.

The four constituents of economic behavior. Taking no account for the moment of the process of competition, we now list the four elements necessary to constitute economic behavior in the restricted sense in which theoretical economics seeks to explain the disposal of scarce means among unlimited wants.[5]

1. A human subject with a plurality of ends.
2. Scarce means which can be applied in different ways (otherwise there would be no choice of disposal at all).
3. The power of the subject in question to dispose of those means.
4. A maxim by which the human subject arranges his means, so as to secure the satisfaction of his ends according to their relative urgency.

Theoretical economics takes no account of the cultural influences or the "social ingredients," to use Dr. Löwe's term, which affect these premises. On the contrary, it invents a fictional person called "economic man" who is conceived as entirely rational, infinitely wise, motivated only by his self-interest the satisfaction of which is presumed to serve the general welfare, who is legally free to behave according to his self-interest and also free to move about without let or hindrance in order to economize his scarce resources. This behavior involves him, so theoretical economics holds, only in the process of competition.

These things are said, not to disparage the study of theoretical economics or to attack it, but rather to indicate the restricted perspective from which it treats the process of choice. That perspective, however, sets a task for us. It is to open the closed system of theoretical economics so that its relation with the other perspectives, disciplines, and social processes may be known and treated. You will recall that we are dealing here, as in the immediately foregoing chapters, with a single perspective on human affairs which, although single, is a focus to which all the manifold aspects of human affairs may be related.[6]

Some requirements of practical economics. We now propose to look at the four premises given above and ask what the cultural influences are

[5] Adolf Löwe, *Economics and Sociology: A Plea for Co-operation in the Social Sciences* (London: George Allen & Unwin, Ltd., 1935), p. 42. This is an indispensable reading for all teachers of the social studies, at whatever level of instruction.

[6] Karl Polanyi, *The Great Transformation*; R. H. Tawney, *The Acquisitive Society*; Caroline Ware and Gardner Means, *The Modern Economy in Action*; Adolph Berle and Gardner Means, *The Modern Corporation and Private Property*; Barbara Wooton, *Freedom Under Planning*; John M. Clark, *The Social Control of Business*; F. A. von Hayek, *The Road to Serfdom*; Frank H. Knight, *The Ethics of Competition* and *Freedom and Reform*; and J. R. Hicks and Albert G. Hart, *The Social Framework of the American Economy* are suggested as sources which give a number of interpretations of theoretical economics.

which operate in the case of each, but of which, as we have just noted, theoretical economics takes no account. This examination will suggest some of the things necessary if the closed system of theoretical economics is to be opened to include factors necessary for the understanding of the more practical aspects of economics.

The subject in question may be an individual, a family, a corporation, or a nation. Each faces the necessity of disposing of scarce means among unlimited wants. Viewed from the perspective of individuals we know that each of us has a limited life span, that is, our years are "scarce"; each of us is limited in physical energy; limitations are placed on each of us which reduce our freedom to compete with others; we have limited knowledge; and none of us is infinitely mobile (we are more or less "space bound") and hence we cannot go wherever we might wish in order to economize our scarce means. Limitations of a similar kind characterize corporations and nations.[7]

The scarce means, referred to in the premises given above, may include other people's skills and services, the financial resources of others, as well as goods which may be acquired through theft or force, by inheritance and gifts, and through the process of exchange in the market. The power to dispose of scarce means may be limited by law, custom, tradition, sentiment, by reason of the limitations on mobility, as well as limitations in knowledge, and many other factors. Finally, the maxim or standard by which we determine which wants shall have preference is conditioned by such cultural factors as ability to pay, all kinds of fortuitous (accidental) circumstances, the availability of credit and our eligibility for it, taste, style, custom, the influence of advertising, and the like.

The recital of these things shows how unreal "economic man" is. He is not only unhistorical and uncultural, he is ahistorical and acultural. He is quite unlike you and me and Mr. and Mrs. John Doe. His fictional character is further revealed by the fact that competition among human beings is never pure but always conditioned by positive or negative sentiment (see Chapter V).

A simple exchange illustrated. Let us test some of these amendments to the premises of theoretical economics by taking a very simple example of exchange. Suppose that the mother of a seven-year-old boy has given him a dime to spend as he pleases. How he pleases to spend it starts our

[7] Even in time of war we have been far more able to provide both guns and butter than has, for instance, the Soviet Union. One of its constant and very difficult problems is to allocate its scarce means so as to build up its capital goods and, at the same time, allocate enough of its limited resources to maintain the physical vigor of its population through the provision of consumer goods.

inquiry with the maxim or standard of preference in terms of which humans arrange their means. What is this boy's maxim or standard respecting his dime? He likely has many wants but has only a single dime. It might be spent for a number of things: a ball of twine, a candy bar, a comic book, a kite pattern, and the like. This reports his "plurality of ends." In the competition which goes on in his head (and also in his stomach) these possible wants "pass in review." He decides to buy a candy bar. In making that decision he has employed both reason and sentiment, as all humans do in making any choice. How it came about that a candy bar won out we do not know.

The power of the boy to dispose of his dime is limited by the fact that his mother has given him no carfare, hence his mobility is limited to the neighborhood. In being limited to that area, it is limited to the one candy store which the neighborhood affords, with its limited supply of candy bars as to size, taste, cost, and "customer appeal."

The boy is not in a position to "dicker." The candy store keeper is a small business enterpriser, has a limited stock, and the prices at which he sells his goods have been determined by elaborate competitive factors with which he as a single and "small merchant" has had little if any part.

The boy enters the neighborhood candy store. But his preference problem has not been completely solved. He has chosen to buy a candy bar. But which one? His options as he perceives them are these: the candy bar that "the other kids" are currently buying, one with a premium included in its wrapper, one with nuts in it, the biggest one, and so on. Again the boy engages in a conversation with himself in terms of his tastes, his social status, his appetite, what he considers to be a "good buy," and the like. He makes up his mind and chooses "X" candy bar. He pays his money and picks up his purchase. The exchange is over.

We have described, very briefly, the sale-purchase end of a transaction in the market. If this is all your students are to see and know about economics the term *caveat emptor* (let the buyer beware) will have little meaning for them. Hence, their need to know much more about the economic system in which they live and in which they will one day participate much more actively and significantly than they now do.

The perspective of theoretical economics. The frame of reference in which the theoretical economist works may now be restated, with the accent on the negative. He takes no account of political, historical, or sociological factors as they affect the economic process. The only psychological factor which he admits is that "economic man" is motivated by self-interest. His interest is in a study of relations, but the things between which the relating process goes on lie outside the scope of that interest. He only *refers* to extraeconomic data; he does not investigate them.[8] It is just these extraeconomic data with which your students must be acquainted if they are to get a general education.

The skeleton framework within which the theoretical economist makes his analyses may now be stated in its simplest form as follows: the terms of exchange (goods and services) are settled by individuals and organizations competing in the market, in which the price at which the exchange will take place is determined by the point at which supply and demand curves intersect. This assumes, obviously, "perfect competition"; hence it takes no account of any monopolistic factors.

The requirements of practical economics. Let us now ask what needs to be added to this framework if your students are to think about and use economics in the world of practical affairs.[9]

They will need to know a good deal about the size and distribution of the population. This would include knowledge of talents and skills, the education, age, state of health, and location of the potential labor supply. It would also comprehend the kinds of organizations through which they express their economic and political opinions and through which they also bargain with employers. These would include the great labor organizations. It might well also include the major professional organizations, significantly the American Medical Association. It would include knowledge of birth- and death-rates, life-expectancy and morbidity rates: in short, the size, sex, age, and the health and "illth" of the nation's labor supply. It would also need to take account especially of the problem of the "over-aged," i.e., the factors associated with the employment or nonemployment of men and women past 65, if not also past 45. It might also take account of movements of population both intranational and international.[10]

---

[8] See J. R. Hicks, "Economic Theory and the Social Sciences," *The Social Sciences: Their Relation in Theory and Teaching* (London: LePlay House, 1936), p. 131.

[9] Books almost without number, which treat economics in the practical and realistic setting of western society, might be cited. Among them are these: Gertrude Williams *Economics of Everyday Life* (Pelican Books); *Economic Education*, Edited by Harold E. Clark (11th Yearbook of the National Council for the Social Studies); Louis M. Hacker, *The Triumph of American Capitalism*; J. Frederic Dewhurst and Associates, *America's Needs and Resources*; *Financing American Prosperity*, Edited by Paul T. Homan and Fritz Machlup; William Van Til, *Economic Roads for American Democracy*; and Stuart Chase, *A Budget of Our Needs and Resources*, and *Democracy Under Pressure: Special Interests vs. The Public Welfare*. See also Prince Petr Kropotkin, *Mutual Aid* (Pelican Books) which is a counterargument to the competitive thesis in human affairs. The Public Affairs Pamphlets provide stimulating and readable materials on practically every phase of economic study.

[10] An excellent but very brief discussion of the economics of population is in Hicks and Hart, *op. cit.*, pp. 65-75.

The location and accessibility of raw materials would need to be known. This would involve knowledge of economic geography. Closely associated with this would be the location of industry and means of transportation. Technology, inventions, and the technical and theoretical sciences which contribute to each would be included. The problem of automation looms large and menacingly at this time and is certain to play an increasingly significant role in production and employment.

Respecting the individuals and organizations who are the demanders and suppliers of economic goods and services, a great deal of knowledge could be had from sociology and social psychology. This would help to explain fashions, standards and planes of living, tastes, customs, the effect of advertising (both as descriptive and persuasive), the importance of what Veblen called "conspicuous" rather than necessary consumption, waste and foolish expenditures, the psychological factors associated with yearly models in automobiles, attitudes toward saving and spending (delayed and immediate consumption), and many other matters which bear on the standards of preference which condition the behavior of both suppliers and demanders.

Law and political science would also have to be called on for the kinds of knowledge they are able to supply. Law would deal with such factors as property rights, contracts, patents, and copyrights. Political science could tell of the role of the government in policing market activities in many ways, in subsidies and taxes of many kinds, in setting standards of purity, the bureaucratic structure of organizations of suppliers and demanders, labor-management relations, and the like. Many kinds of social science knowledge would need to be used to study the process of collective bargaining, the social system of factories and offices, leadership in business enterprise and allied concerns.[11]

The five basic economic questions. Your students' preparation for "making up their minds" about economic questions will involve their understanding how our economy resolves the following questions: [12]

1. What goods and services shall be produced and in what quantities?
2. How will the value-product be distributed, that is, who will get what and how much goods and services?
3. How shall resources and population be brought into the balance necessary to have the "right" people with the "right" skills and knowledge in the "right" place at the "right" time?

[11] See P. Sargent Florence, "Economic Theory and the Social Sciences," *The Social Sciences: Their Relation in Theory and Teaching*, pp. 141-163. See also Adolf Löwe, *op. cit.*

[12] The questions given here may be posed in a variety of ways. These were taken, with slight changes, from Chapter XXI. See also Chart 2, Chapter V.

4. What kind of socioeconomic organization must be devised to effect these things, i.e., (1), (2), and (3) above?

5. What shall the standards of preference be and how shall they be determined?

These questions, now conceived as tasks to be performed or values to be served, can be separated only at the conceptual level. In reality they are inextricably interrelated and work together as the economic system operates. (This view is borne out by the account of the social processes given in Chapter XXI.) But, if they are to be studied, some scheme must be devised by which they may be treated somewhat separately. Here again we meet the problem of the division and the unity of scholarly labor in pursuing social study. The discussion which follows represents one pattern of approach to these questions. It is conceived as applicable to the grade levels ninth to twelfth (and even the two years of the junior college). In this I refer to its logical rather than to its pedagogical nature. It is logical in the sense that it sets forth a systematic and related framework for the study of human affairs from the perspective of unlimited wants and scarce resources. Its pedagogy has been stated, implicitly and explicitly, in the foregoing chapters. The basic pedagogical principle on which I have placed great stress is that individual needs can be met only through the individual's participation in the affairs of the social system in which he lives (see Chapters II and VI).

The choice-making process.   The perspective we are now treating is that which emphasizes the making of economic choices. What could be more appropriate, then, that a course of study on the choice-making process, as well as each unit in it, begin with a problem? (Inquiry demands something to be inquired into in all social study, as I have indicated many times.)

The "average" high school student is something like the man from Mars, in that he is not very well informed about the indirect process by which wants are satisfied in modern life. Hence, we suppose that the student, like the man from Mars, is apt to say that if, for instance, we need houses why don't we go ahead and build them? We have plenty of skilled labor, materials are plentiful, architects and builders are eager to construct them, and the need for them is great. Why, then, all the "wherefore and why" about property, wages, rights, taxes, titles, contracts, and the many things which lie between the need for housing and the satisfaction of that need? [13]

---

[13] See Lawrence K. Frank, "Social Problems," *op. cit.*, pp. 10-20; Willar Wallard, "Social Problems and the Mores," *op. cit.*; and Isaiah Bowman, "Science and Social Effects: Three Failures," *Scientific Monthly*, April, 1940. Each of these provides excellent substance and method for treating the problem aspect of economics.

A systematic view of how our economy operates.   The "wherefore and why" require systematic study of how our economy operates. That study is bounded by the questions (1) to (5) given above. The order in which they may be studied is more or less arbitrary but, whatever the order you choose, all must be included. Otherwise, your only recourse is to teach, in an *ad hoc* and random way, a series of more or less disconnected problems. Such a series of problems may be "practical" but it will be related only by accident or because a few "bright" students are able to discover the continuity which their *seriatim* treatment may permit.

Any problem with which you begin will allow, even invite, attention to the fact that it cannot be resolved without money being paid. Ours is not a barter but a money economy. This suggests that you deal first with the problem of income. Statistics will permit you to examine a table of income of individuals and families for the nation as a whole. This will be divided, or can be so divided by you and your students, into given income brackets. These ought to be translated into the levels or standards of living representative of each bracket. The task is then to estimate what proportions of income are spent for various goods and services by the individuals and/or families in selected brackets. Materials are available on representative family budgets which will bring your study closer to reality. Study might well focus on what constitutes necessities and luxuries, respectively, in the budgets of "rich" and "poor." Account should be taken of such items as medical care, insurance, and recreation as well as such staple items as food, shelter, and clothing. Savings ought also to be included. It will be found that some families have "negative incomes," that is, their expenses are greater than their income. How do they continue to carry on as an economically solvent concern?

The study of income (wages, salary, and investment returns) might well lead to inquiry into the economic services which are provided by various levels of the government. (The concept of the "service state" would be given explicit meaning.) These are paid for through tax money which suggests the need to study the kinds of taxes levied on various kinds of goods and services, that is, whether they are progressive or regressive in character. The equity and inequity of various kinds of taxes might also be studied. I do not suggest that the budgets of governmental bodies and subdivisions be studied at this time. The concern is now with family rather than public income and expenditure problems. The difference between economic and free goods and services might be made at this point. It will be found that free goods are not quite as free as they are supposed, since their enjoyment is conditioned by one's having some minimal amounts of freedom which come directly from the possession of economic goods— food, clothing, shelter, and the like. Voltaire's famous axiom that "the rich and poor are both free to sleep under bridges" comes to mind in this connection.

The major characteristics of our economy as one based on "exchange" might appropriately come next. This section might be prefaced by a brief historical survey of its evolution. This could also, appropriately, take account of different kinds of contemporary economies: the autocratic or militaristic economy of Soviet Russia, democratic socialism, and capitalism. Each of the historical and contemporary types of economy might well be assessed from the point of view of the freedom of choice which individuals living under them enjoy. This inquiry will reveal the many-sided nature of economic freedom. Complementary emphasis should be given to the kinds of restraints which each imposes. The balance between freedom and restraint would give a useful account of each.[14]

Inquiry would then center on what is meant by money as a "medium of exchange." This would require study of such specifics as these: wages, salary, profit, interest and dividends as "money in hand," banks and their function, the changing value of money, and the activities of the government in relation to inflation and deflation.

Next would come a study of the organization of industry, including the processes of production and distribution of goods and services. The central roles or figures here would be employer, worker, and consumer. Important aspects of this section would be such as these: the location of industry, specialization or the division of labor, the management and integration of labor, the nature of various forms of ownership (single proprietor, partnership, the corporation, and the co-operative), the discipline of the factory, the assembly-line process and its social as well as economic implications, wholesale and retail distribution, the changing pattern of retail services, and advertising, in both its descriptive and want-producing function. (What is called "consumer economics" might be stressed, but not without

---

[14] Julius H. Boeke, *The Structure of Netherlands Indian Economy* (New York: International Secretariat, Institute of Pacific Relations, 1942) will give you an excellent description of the way in which the people of a "primitive" economy respond to changes in demand. To the degree that their level of wants is relatively fixed they will tap fewer, rather than more rubber trees, if the demand for rubber rises. See also Russell A. Dixon and E. K. Eberhart, *Economics and Cultural Change* (New York: McGraw-Hill Book Co., 1938), Mary L. Fledderus and Mary van Kleeck, *An Inquiry into the Changing Technological Basis for Production as Affecting Employment and Living Standards* (New York: Russell Sage Foundation, 1944); National Resources Committee, *The Structure of the American Economy, Part I, Basic Characteristics* (1939), and Part II, *Toward the Full Use of Resources* (June 1940), and N. S. B. Gras, *An Introduction to Economic History*.

stressing at the same time the relation of the consumer to the complex matrix signified by the "organization of industry." Otherwise, the consumer appears to hang in mid-air.)

Individual freedom and our economy.   The foregoing is but one pattern or frame of reference for the study of choice-making as a socioeconomic process. Throughout, stress should be placed on the relation between individual freedom and the structure of our economy. Any section might be expanded to suit local circumstances. Such special emphases as these might well be added where they seem best to fit the outline: (a) unemployment and activities designed to prevent or cure it; (b) the problem of full employment under peacetime conditions (we normally have little unemployment under conditions of war or the threat of war); (c) study of federal and/or local governmental budgets—here the principles are more important than the amounts; (d) the problem of automation as the latest and most pressing instance of the relation between technology and wages, work and welfare; (e) the import-export balance and the problem of foreign markets and tariff policy; (f) the function of the stock market; and (g) the participation of the federal government in the economic process by way of conservation, waterways, and subsidies to health, education, and welfare.

Respecting any phase of economics which is basic to every form of social life, teachers face the temptation of undertaking to solve the problems which it presents. Students likewise chafe under the fact that economic problems press in upon them from many angles. Chiefly for these reasons, the teaching-learning of economics may have the effect of increasing impatience and deepening anxiety about economic matters. But in this area of study, as in all others, the school's task is what its role dictates it ought to be—a place where study rather than social action goes on. It is a hard fact to face at times but, unless it is accepted, only disappointment can come as a consequence.

The great social problem.   Teachers and students are beset with many problems, which they usually see as somewhat separate and distinct. The *great* social problem tends to escape us all. This is how it is possible that a society as complex as ours functions as well as it does. This is the problem toward the understanding of which all separate problems of social study ought to focus.

Emphasis on principles.   Some of the immediate concerns of students can, however, be at least clarified, but they may not be resolved in the terms they anticipate. Such questions as "How can I get a job?" or "Why can't I get a job?" "What is the best way to invest my money?" (would that more students were interested in that), "What career should I follow?" and "Why do we have depressions and unemployment?" can at least be set in the context required for their objective and critical study. Beyond that we cannot go. Any promise or proffering of answers is a form of fraud. Here the principle of the *teaching of principles* is the only professionally honest recourse. Again I remind you that education offers no specifics and no ultimate solutions. But it will appear to unless all personal problems—no matter in what area of human affairs they arise—are treated as the personal phase of a complex and sometimes almost inscrutable social system. The best we can do is to simplify the account of that system without distorting its real character too much in the simplification.

Students are wage-workers.   Certain circumstances in the life of modern youth ought to make the study of its socioeconomic aspects much more challenging and useful than was the case a generation ago. Many students are now wage-workers. I do not refer only to their activities as paper-carriers, as week-end helpers in stores, or as baby-sitters, however real these activities are. I refer also to the fact that a considerable number of students have part- or full-time jobs in industry, carry union cards, and are deeply involved in our economy.

Limitations of common-sense economics.   These involvements do not, of course, insure that their common-sense notions of economic affairs will now be seen in a critical light. The area of economics is notoriously one about which "everybody" has an opinion and these opinions have a very low mortality rate. These facts suggest that every unit of study begins with a sampling of economic opinion. (This procedure is quite as appropriate in all the areas of social study but has special relevance to economics and politics.) Such a beginning would give a stimulation and romance to inquiry and set up some quite specific bench marks for guiding inquiry. Such an inventory is not a test but rather a diagnostic probing. I do not suggest that students be graded on their responses. Nor do I suggest that you use their responses as the only content of a unit. Their chief function will be to give you a gauge of the climate of opinion that prevails respecting some problem or issue.[15]

Skills in socioeconomic study.   The range of objectives in socioeconomic study is very wide, as to both skills and understandings. The quantitative emphases which are possible from this perspective suggest elementary skills

[15] The propositions to which their response is invited are, in my view, best stated in language as unlike "teachertalk" as you can use. Thus they will tend to be in the vernacular of the students and, by that token, seem more real. See Albert W. Levi, *General Education in the Social Studies* (Chapter XI) for sample propositions in many areas of social study. See also Kenneth Boulding, *The Economics of Peace* (New York: Prentice-Hall, Inc., 1940), pp. 205-251 for "right" and "left" fallacies in the area of economics.

in statistics and the making of charts and graphs. These should, however, not be the only emphases in the development of skills, for the disposition to make snap judgments gets perhaps a somewhat greater chance to express itself than in, say, the area of history. This suggests unique emphasis on the making of inferences, the nature of proof, and elementary skills in the use of the syllogism as a check on faulty reasoning. All the other intellectual skills which have been noted in other chapters are, of course, relevant and necessary.

The concepts of economics lend themselves to reasonably exact definition. Ability to define them may, then, be tested with somewhat greater exactness than in the other social studies. I think of such terms as corporation (which many students confuse with co-operative and co-operation), capital goods as distinct from consumer goods, cost and price as distinct from value, interest, debt, rent, leisure (not only as time spent outside of work but as relatively free and chosen *behavior* as distinct from work behavior, which is a great deal more disciplined), economic services as distinct from economic goods, collective bargaining, union shop, the strike, and free enterprise. Closely allied to skill in the definition of such terms as these is the need to stress the difference between statements of fact and statements of preference. This seems to me to be particularly appropriate in this perspective because of the ease with which opinions are bandied about which are, characteristically, statements of preference but not infrequently taken and used as statements of fact.

Understandings in socioeconomic study.   Respecting major understandings and insight, the following suggest themselves as uniquely appropriate: (a) major changes in an economic system come not only through changes in personal valuations but through new institutions, and hence slowly; (b) "the consumer" is a highly fictitious entity since everybody is a consumer but the different interests of each make their concerted action, only *as consumers,* very difficult; (c) there is an economic phase to all group activity: religious, educational, recreational, scientific, to name only a few; (d) economic issues are, at one and the same time, social and political issues; (e) "economic planning" is not a concept or practice alien to our experience: the problem which it poses is the integration of many plans through the processes of the impersonal market and/or the more direct approach through the action of a people through various channels and agencies of their government; (f) the Constitution makes no mention of or provision for any particular economic mechanism; and (g) economic activity is not an end in itself.

Field study.   Economic study lends itself readily to field experience: the opportunity to "go and see." Through field observation, verification may be given to many phases of the operation of an economy which the text-book can only tell about. The deeply personal interest which students have in economic affairs tends to give you, ready-made, a lively quality of concern with them. But this will not be served or informed unless you show how the working of an economic system bears immediately on their problems, dilemmas, and concerns. I am reminded here of the doggerel which reads,

> I'd like to learn a lot of things;
> With curiosity I'm cursed.
> But teacher tells me that I must
> Complete my education first.

I do not know that the teaching of economics, any more than any other field of the social studies, insists on the student's education being completed before his curiosity is satisfied but that danger is far from remote or impossible. The economic order, like all phases of the Great Society, is directly available and mere words about it will not suffice to make it the rugged reality which it is.

This perspective also permits a great deal of "doing-learning" to which the use of field experience is immediately appropriate. Many phases of the economic process lend themselves readily not only to observation but also to role-playing. Such roles as those of shop steward, banker, advertising copywriter, consumer (in almost unnumbered situations), borrower, accountant, and many others suggest themselves.

The perspective we have discussed above, with each of those discussed earlier, lends itself to making clear the basic characteristics of a specific view of human affairs (here, that of economizing), concern with the value problem (however remote and impersonal), and the method of inquiry.[16] These box the compass of human affairs in all social study.

[16] Each permits and demands the various kinds of thinking noted in Chapter XXIII. You will find the format for the study of social problems (Chapter XXIII) relevant in many ways to the study of the socioeconomic perspective.

CHAPTER XXVI

The Perspective of the Spatial Distribution of Social Phenomena: Geography and Human Ecology

IN CHAPTER V, the distinction was made between the spatial pattern and the social order as complementary ways of looking at human affairs. This chapter will focus on the spatial pattern of the human community.[1]

Four factors interact. We shall examine the interaction of the following factors as they condition the spatial pattern of social phenomena: (*a*) geographic, including climatic, topographic, and natural resources; (*b*) economic, which includes a wide range of phenomena such as the location of industry, rents, land values, land use, and standards of living; (*c*) cultural and technological, in which are included attitudes, voting behavior, customs, dialects, and all the artifacts which the technical sciences and arts have made possible; and (*d*) political, including executive, legislative, judicial, and administrative, whether exercised by the state and its subdivisions or by voluntary associations. Together these factors give us the geographic-ecological approach to the spatial distribution of social phenomena which include both thing and not-thing values as well as the human population.

Place and position. The spatial distribution of all social phenomena—people, industries, customs, dialects, voting behavior—which may be plotted on a map, may be viewed on two axes. The relation of social phenomena

[1] See also the discussion in Chapters IX and XXIII and Charts 1 to 5 in Chapters V and IX.

406

to the physical habitat and whatever changes man has made in it such as canals, harbors, filled-in land, and crops of many kinds, gives us the *place* of such phenomena. This is the *vertical* axis. The second, which is the *horizontal* axis, gives us the *position* of social phenomena in a spatial pattern, that is, the phenomena vis-à-vis each other. The concept of *place* refers, then, to the relation of man and his cultural achievements to the "soil," plus whatever changes he has made in it. Correlatively, the concept of *position* refers to the spatial relations which obtain among the social phenomena conditioned by all the factors noted above.[2]

Place and position are interrelated. But the play of factors on the vertical and horizontal axes is, in reality, reciprocal. Suppose, for instance, that high winds and lack of rain over a period of weeks have created a dust bowl in a wheat-growing area. The result is a severe blow to the economy of the region. Man's relation to the soil has been changed, likewise his spatial and social relation to his fellows. The precipitating cause was the drought and the wind. But "behind" it is the causal factor represented by the fact that man converted grazing lands to crop use and thus helped to create the conditions for the devastation which winds and lack of rain brought about.

The emphasis is on the social. The human results of the creation of a dust bowl by man and nature may be viewed and assessed on both the vertical and horizontal axes. Man's relation to the soil is changed by reason of his migration to new places. Likewise his *position*, that is, his relation with his fellows, is also changed by reason of his change in *place*. It is the disturbance of the *social* equilibrium in which we are chiefly interested, due to whatever factors. This disturbance has many facets: new occupations, effects on family life, change in economic and social status—whole families may be made dependent on relief agencies, eligibility to vote may be affected by virtue of change in place of residence, interruption in school attendance by children, and many other effects. These

[2] R. D. McKenzie, "The Scope of Human Ecology," *American Journal of Sociology*, XXIII, No. 1, Part 2, 1926 (Papers and Proceedings of the 20th Annual Meeting of the American Sociological Society), p. 142; Robert E. Park, "The Concept of Position in Sociology," *ibid.*, p. 2; and H. H. Barrows, "Geography as Human Ecology," *Annals of the American Association of Geographers*, XIII, 1923. See also Robert E. Park, "Human Ecology" and "Symbiosis and Socialization," *op. cit.*

In making the comparison between vertical and horizontal axes (as symbols of the perspectives of human geography and human ecology, respectively), I am seeking only to clarify complementary rather than conflicting points of view. I am not challenging the right of any body of scholars to study what they wish to. Rather, I am drawing upon and drawing together various perspectives (to the degree that they take complementary views) so that we may deal with all the factors which condition the spatial distribution of social phenomena. This was the thesis which was argued in Chapter VIII. It is social life in which I am interested, not in the prerogatives of any group of scientific specialists.

changes in the spatial relations of the migrants to their fellow men affect the nature of their *social* relations.[3]

Significance of natural areas.   Any inhabited area of the earth's surface is, of course, eligible for study from the geographic-ecological perspective. I choose, however, to develop my discussion around the "natural area." I define it as geo-social unit which gets its integrity or unity through the interdependence of the geographic, economic, cultural and technological, and political factors noted above. It may lie within a political division or subdivision, e.g., a nation-state, a state or commonwealth, or a county, or its boundaries may overlap those of such political divisions or subdivisions. School districts are often "natural areas" whose boundaries are established, albeit by the fiat of a school board and whatever other civil jurisdictions may be involved, by virtue of certain time-cost and convenience factors respecting attendance at school. Other "natural areas" which become administrative areas are such as conservation districts, mosquito-abatement districts, recreational, and water-supply areas. In each case, the boundaries are due to something more than the arbitrary fiat of a civil governmental body. These boundaries often overlap such formally defined and delineated areas as states, counties, townships, villages, towns, and cities. The Tennessee Valley Authority is a civil-administrative area coextensive with part of the watershed of the Tennessee River, which is a natural geographic region. But topographical factors do not alone account for the "natural area" over which the Authority exercises jurisdiction. They provide, so to speak, the physiographic frame for a complex cultural unity.

Other examples of "natural areas" are such as these: urban slums, areas of wealthy and aristocratic residence, e.g., the Gold Coast in Chicago or Nob Hill in San Francisco; the trading area of a country town identified by the zone within which commercial relations go on between farmers and merchants, including such items as grain, cattle, machinery, and domestic supplies; the metropolitan areas surrounding such great cities as Chicago, Detroit, and Cleveland; and such "natural areas" as the wheat or corn belt which are not only land areas in which a certain crop predominates, but which also represent a somewhat unique cultural complex.[4]

[3] John Steinbeck's novel, *The Grapes of Wrath*, would be a highly appropriate reading in this connection, likewise Selma Lagerlöf's *Jerusalem*, although with a different emphasis and focus. Historic examples of the social effects of migration due to many factors are such as the Crusades, the seasonal migrations of people whose economy is based on the keeping of herds, the migrations of the Goths, and the whole story of exploration, colonization, and immigration (see again Chapter IX).

[4] This discussion does not deny that there are several kinds of "natural areas" as viewed by the geographer. These "possess entity because of contiguity of surface extent" and are

I have chosen to place special emphasis on the "natural area" because "man, proud man; dressed in a little brief authority" has tended to be preoccupied with the formal political units which he has established on the land: nation-states, commonwealths, counties, townships, and municipalities. The importance of politically determined divisions of the land is not to be denied as was suggested in Chapter XXIV when we commented on the relation between political control and the inhabitants of a given territory. But many, if not most, such political divisions owe some (if not, in certain cases, all) of their boundaries to natural physiographic factors: our New England states, for instance. But even when the boundaries of such civil divisions are set by physiographic factors we would do well to remember that they were chosen by the fiat of man. They did not nominate themselves as boundaries. The "middle principles" function of human attitudes and purposes is thus confirmed. Thus it is that "natural areas" are *natural* in the sense that physiographic and human nature factors combine to cut out an area within which the affairs of man may be viewed.

No determinism. By token of this fact such geophysical factors as rainfall and the location of a flat plain do not constitute data for the approach we are taking *unless* they are related to some cultural manifestations, the growing of certain crops, or the location of a railroad or a highway and the way in which both crops and means of transportation affect human relations. There is no determinism respecting any factor which influences human behavior. There is only *possibilism*. Areal *place* does not *alone* give us an adequate account of the totality of the factors which influence human relations any more than the alphabet and spelling give an adequate explanation of literature.[5]

Two pedagogical principles. Thereby hangs a basic pedagogical principle

---

natural in a physiographic sense. Other areal units recognized by the geographer are "geographic regions" which are "characterized by unity of human adjustment to the natural environment," and the "political unit" which is delimited "through possessing polity and territorial integrity" (C. Langdon White and George T. Renner, *Geography, An Introduction to Human Ecology,* New York: Appleton-Century-Crofts, Inc., 1936, pp. 603-604). These types of area units may be illustrated, respectively, by Samoa, Vancouver Island, the cotton and wheat belt, and such nation-states as France, Italy, and the United States.

[5] Roderick Peattie, *Geography and Human Destiny* (New York: George W. Stewart, 1940) p. 21. Dr. Peattie's book is ideally suited to high school use. See also Hendrik van Loon's *Geography* (New York: Garden City Publishing Co., Inc., 1940). These are two excellent trade books with far more romance and interest than a great many texts in human geography. Respecting the concepts "determinism" and "possibilism" see Lucien Febvre, *Geographic Introduction to History,* and Ellen C. Semple, *Geographic Conditions in American History,* Jean Bruhnes, *Human Geography,* and Derwent Whittlesey, *The Earth and the State.* These, and many other geographers, give the lie to Ratzel's remark that "the earth serves as a rigid support to the humors and changing aspirations of man and governs their destinies with blind brutality."

respecting the physical habitat and any changes which man has made in it. The *place* of plains, mountains, climates, cities, and the number and density of a population may be known without significance for social study *unless* such place identifications are shown to be causally related to the *position* of social phenomena in the spatial pattern of human affairs. A second pedagogical principle is that natural geographic features are not mere scenery or staging in front of which, or on which, the human drama is enacted. These features are taken up in the social processes and, by that circumstance, are humanized as we sought to indicate in Chapter IX. Our interest in nature is a means to our greater knowledge of *human* nature. But both the geographical and ecological approaches give us only social morphology. They do not, as such, treat the social consequences of that morphology.[6]

A rural natural area. I now choose to explore the geoecological approach to the distribution of social phenomena in two settings, rural and urban.

The rural setting is a "natural area" enclosed within a village-farm community of 1,500 people, only 350 of whom reside in the village. The area is in the form of an ellipse of some 25,000 acres whose east-west axis is slightly longer than its north-south axis.

The modal-sized farm is 160 acres and the average square-mile section is occupied by four families and approximately 22 people. Some sections have as few as two families and others have as many as seven or eight. Land on the modal-sized farm is divided, typically, as follows: 45.4 acres to corn; 54.5 acres to several varieties of hay or forage crops; 28.4 acres to small grain, chiefly oats; 16.2 acres to pasture; and 15.5 to buildings and feed lots. The chief motive power is gasoline-powered machinery used for plowing, cultivating, harvesting, and transporting grain (chiefly corn) and hogs and cattle to the village as the shipping point from whence these products find their way into the national and world markets.

This village-farm community includes parts of four townships and lies within one county. The village is incorporated and serves chiefly as a trading center for convenience goods, implements and parts, and mail service. It is platted to form a gridiron pattern of ten streets which order the arrangement of its business and residential structures. There are two churches and a consolidated grammer-high school in the village. There is one district school in the rural area outside the village.

The dominant social unit in this "natural area" is the family which

[6] A clear exposition of this point of view may be found in Nicholas Spykman, *The Social Theory of Georg Simmel* (Chicago: University of Chicago Press, 1925).

gets its living from the land. (The only concentration of families is in the village in which trading activity complements farming as the basis for livelihood.) Geographic factors (fertility, rainfall, etc.) are dominant in ordering the spatial arrangement of the population. The soil is exceedingly fertile and the community contains no eroded land. Thus any place in it is as eligible for cultivation as any other, the village site excluded.

The size of the farm as the production unit is, however, conditioned by such economic factors as the cash, resources, and credit of a given family; such cultural factors as its size (children are an economic asset), the degree to which inheritance has conditioned the amount of land owned (excluding the few rented farms from our account), and the use of horses and power machinery as the prime movers. Ethnic factors have little influence on either the size or location of farms. Civil political factors operate to define quarter-section, half-section, and section lines, as well as townships, and the location of the district school. Political as well as technico-economic factors condition the position of the consolidated grammar-high school in the village. It is these rather than geographic factors which operate in this instance because of the family car and the school bus. Time-cost rather than linear distance factors are thus chiefly responsible for the location of the consolidated school in the village. To these observations should be added the fact that the village is the "center of population" of the community.

The telephone serves as another technological factor to tie the inhabitants of the community together, both socially and economically. Its effect on the location of farms is, however, negligible. Such political factors as state laws respecting contracts operate uniformly throughout the community and hence give no preferential advantage to any farm site. Likewise, no advantage accrues to any spatial position in the community by virtue of special provisions for mail service. Every farm in the community is served daily by rural free delivery.

If, however, we look at this village-farm community from the perspective of attitudes, we would discover some significant spatial patterns. Attitudes toward federal policy on price support, control of acreage, the grain co-operative, school taxes, the curriculum in vocational agriculture, and the "youth problem" would likely be correlated with political party identification, renter and owner status, active or "retired" status, and perhaps size of families. In any event, the spatial distribution of such categories of attitudes would, almost certainly, reveal some significant divisions in the community. The factors "behind" such attitudes would be economic, cultural (religious, social status, etc.), and political in nature. They would all relate "near or far" to opinions taken on values, all of which are closely identified with a crop-and-animal-growing economy.

All such spatial patterns would give us a social morphology, i.e., certain spatial forms. These would provide significant leads to the factors which make for or against the ability of the community members to act in concert through the various associations, chiefly voluntary, within which consensus is achieved. Thus, knowledge of spatial relations would enhance our understanding of social relations. We have here something akin to the "geometry" of social affairs. It does not, however, *cause* human relations. It gives us, rather, a spatial perspective on them and thus tends to give them a realistic quality which is a considerable aid in our understanding of them. The unique "power" of any given factor making for such spatial patterns or forms would be difficult, if not impossible, to assess. The factors would, however, *in toto* permit us to get a more exact, though only approximate, view of the reciprocal effect of the processes of competition, conflict, accommodation, and assimilation. Thus the "web of human affairs" is not altogether seamless, even if we have to invent and suppose the "seams," i.e., the four social processes just noted.

In sum, we can say that this village-farm community is a reasonably homogeneous one: in its economy, its ethnic stock and language, and generally so in its sociopolitical attitudes. Its family units represent, we suppose, the "highest" manifestation of a condition of assimilation; social relations outside the family distribute across the spectrum of competition, conflict, and accommodation as attitudes toward the various issues of community life, condition social solidarity. The community is fairly free of the kinds of social problems which beset the people of a great city, although those which do exist are, for these village-farm folk, no less real and serious.[7]

An urban natural area.   I turn now to examine the spatial pattern of social phenomena in an urban setting. I choose the Chicago Metropolitan Area which is a "natural area" in the sense that Chicago and its suburban satellites are bound together as a socioeconomic unit which transcends many civil political jurisdictions. It is uniquely appropriate for study because it has no all-inclusive politico-administrative apparatus. Like Topsy in *Uncle Tom's Cabin*, it "just growed," but in doing that it did not "grow" a set of co-ordinated political controls.

[7] A series of monographs on rural communities may be purchased from the U. S. Department of Agriculture, Bureau of Agricultural Economics. These are titled *Rural Life Studies*, 1 to 6, 1942. Many, if not all, of the land grant colleges make extensive rural community studies. These may be had by writing the Extension Division of your state agricultural college.

Since the turn of the century the metropolitan areas which have grown up around our great cities have come to pose many difficult problems in civil administration. The former simple designation of our population as "rural" and "urban" has given way, in part, to a new term, namely "rurban." One quarter of the nation's population is now concentrated in twelve urbanized areas of 1,000,000 or more people. Their combined numbers in 1950 were 37,595,460. If to these twelve metropolitan areas be added all those which contain a population of 50,000 or more, the number of such areas increases to 157 and their population to 68,787,978 or close to 47 per cent of the nation's total.

The metropolitan area of Chicago (sometimes referred to as a "region") extends over part or all of fifteen counties and 165 townships, and includes parts of three states. The number and range of various administrative units within it is very great. Within an area of 4,800 square miles live nearly 5,000,000 people, of whom 3,620,000 are residents of Chicago. In this area (as of 1930) there were 204 cities, 978 school districts, 167 public water systems, 74 park and forest systems, 350 police forces, 343 health agencies, 190 drainage districts, 556 independent courts, and 11 sanitary districts.[8]

We now inquire into the factors which condition the spatial distribution of land, by various types of use, in this area. These uses may be divided, for our concern, into the following categories: farming, industrial, retail, wholesale, banking and administration, recreational, and residential. I shall treat each of these types briefly, seeking to indicate how each of the factors noted earlier operate.

Farming: Such geographic factors as soil fertility, climate, and rainfall are obviously important. These condition the *place* where farming goes on. General farming, that is, land devoted to corn, wheat, and oats as well as to the feeding of cattle and hogs, is conditioned by the factors which operate to explain the agricultural economy of this section of the Middle West. Respecting dairy farming such factors as *position* in the Chicago regional milkshed (another type of "natural area") must be noted. These are economic, e.g., proximity and/or accessibility to a large central city and suburban market; technological as illus-

[8] These data for 1930 are from Charles E. Merriam, Spencer D. Parratt, and Albert Lepawsky, *The Government of the Metropolitan Region of Chicago* (Chicago: University of Chicago Press, 1933), pp. xv-xvii. By 1935 the number of school districts had increased to 1,246. (John A. Vieg, *The Government of Education in Metropolitan Chicago*, Chicago: University of Chicago Press, 1939, p. 87.) A few consolidations have been effected in late years but the figures given here are representative of the great number of unco-ordinated administrative and judicial agencies. You are again enjoined not to be fooled "by the pedantry of dates." It is process and pattern in which we are interested. Minor increases or decreases in the number of agencies do not materially reduce the gravity of the problem of "too many governments."

trated by tankcars and trucks which transport the raw milk (sometimes separated into milk and cream) to retail and wholesale distributors; cultural as illustrated by such a factor as a family tradition to engage in milk production; and political through civil, political, and voluntary setting of standards and inspection. (The great enterprises engaged in the sale of milk have their own inspection staffs which supplement those of the civil authorities.) [9] Truck-garden use of farm land is conditioned by fertility, climate, and rainfall (with rainfall sometimes supplemented by irrigation which introduces a technological and cultural factor), nearness to a market for "green groceries" which require immediate delivery after being taken from the field, which is a factor of *position* in a time-cost spatial network as well as *place* in a geographical setting; the cultural tradition which in this area is uniquely related to people of Dutch ethnic stock (especially in the growing of celery and onions); and such politico-economic factors as are involved in the costs of production under various legal controls.

Industrial: Heavy industry tends, on the whole, to be located on sites of large acreages which, because of their distance from areas of close settlement, are relatively cheaper than smaller land plots. Geographic or place factors operate significantly in such industries as quarrying and rock crushing, steel production on lake and river harbors, and some industries which require rock subsoil to support their heavy machinery. Proximity and/or accessibility to labor supply and to transportation (through trunk and belt lines) and to allied industrial activities operate significantly to condition the position of industry in a complex spatial-social pattern. Such factors as light and air for baking industries and food processing do not, as they once did, depend on place factors. Such technological developments as air conditioning and provision of artificial light now permit such enterprises to locate almost any place in the area. Industries engaged in slaughtering and packing locate with reference to switching facilities, relatively cheap land, and regional and national transportation facilities.

Retail: Retail activities are more closely related to the factors which make for population (consumer) distribution than do farming and industry. Great department stores are located at the foci of local and regional lines of transportation and tend to stay put, despite the outward trend of population from the central city. This trend has, of course, conditioned the location of shopping centers in suburban communities. Smart shops are highly dependent for their position in the spatial pattern by proximity to the residential areas of highest buying power. Retail stores which deal in convenience goods (domestic supplies, groceries, and meats) are the most mobile in this category of activities. They must find a position close enough to consumers to make their sites accessible by walking or by the use of public and/or private transportation. Geographic factors, per se, have little influence on their position.

Wholesale: These activities demand relatively low-cost land sites and tend to locate on the margins of the central business district. This makes them accessible to retail outlets and to local and regional transportation facilities. Warehousing of nonagricultural products is similarly affected. Some wholesale and warehousing require waterside positions, depending on the bulk of the commodities in

[9] Proximity is measured by linear distance; accessibility is measured by time-cost factors, i.e., how long it takes to get to a certain place, and at what cost in money.

which they deal. They share with all urban (and many suburban) land uses, the effect which zoning ordinances impose.

Banking and administration: The great central banks (and exchanges) find a position in the central business district in a spatial matrix which is closely interdependent with the managing, executive, and administrative functions which characterize the economy of great central metropolitan cities. Much of their business is carried on by wire or correspondence, in contrast to retail which requires, for the most part, the physical presence of the parties to a transaction. Banking and administrative functions can afford to pay for a position in the central business district, despite the very high land values. That position also makes them accessible to central city and suburban residents who are employed in various capacities. "Neighborhood" banks (and building and loan companies), by the nature of their functions, tend to take a position near to and within the residential districts. Like retail functions, they tend to follow the outward shift of the population.[10]

Recreational: Recreational land use in the Chicago metropolitan area divides roughly into forest preserve areas, golf courses, and city, town, and village parks. The location of the forest preserves is conditioned, to a considerable degree, by geographical factors such as areas of forest cover and the banks of streams. Political factors, of course, operate in the process of land acquisition and choice of exact sites and the fixing of boundaries. Golf courses, except those which are municipally owned and located in public parks, tend to find a position in the suburban fringe where land may be bought or leased at "acreage" rather than "lot" prices. The lake-front parks of Chicago are either all or in part man-made. Hence technological combine with geographical factors to condition their position. Economic and political factors operate through such means as relative costs, taxation, and policy in land planning. Smaller park areas tend to be located with reference to both proximity and accessibility factors; the smaller the park the more the factor of proximity conditions the site.

Residential: This is by no means as simple a category of land use as one might imagine. Income, land value, accessibility or proximity to place of employment, public and private recreational facilities, location of churches, schools, and shopping areas, ethnic and racial and owner or renter status of occupancy are among the most important factors making for the residential pattern. Geographic factors tend to become less and less dominant, thanks to man's ability to improve or mar the landscape as far as its use for residential purposes is concerned.

If residential land use be approached from the perspective of a suburban

---

[10] Geographic or place factors should not be overlooked respecting the complex of activities which makes up the land users of Chicago's central business district. It tends to stay put by virtue of vertical rather than horizontal expansion through the service which the skyscraper affords. The Chicago River has, by and large, had a considerable effect on its upward rather than outward spread, but exceptions may be noted. Oddly enough, Chicago was the "birthplace" of the skyscraper although the geological structure underlying its central business district was not naturally suited to the construction of tall buildings. The first skyscrapers were on foundations consisting of steel rails "floated" in concrete and lying many feet above the stratum provided by hard clay. Thus technological factors had an important part in the development of land use in this business district.

rather than a central city site, different factors operate in different types of community. Some are inhabited almost wholly by industrial or wage workers, some by a large percentage of families whose head is a high-salaried executive, and others have a highly heterogeneous make-up respecting their employment, size of families, standards of living, and ethnic and racial composition.

Residential land use in the central city tends to conform to a pattern of concentric circles whose center is the central business district. Exclusive of this district, whose residents fall into hotel flophouse dwellers, the city's residential pattern may be classified by such categories as "slum," "Gold Coast," "workingmen's cottages," "apartment house," and "single and detached residence." These are, avowedly, ideal-type categories and are not as sharply identified in space as in the words used to denote them. In Chicago, however, they tend to be all but visible to the layman's eye because only very minor topographical factors intrude to twist or distort the concentric pattern.[11]

The ecology of economic, educational, and marital status. I wish now to illustrate and discuss briefly the spatial distribution of social phenomena which tell us a great deal more about the social organization of a community than the kinds of land use which have been presented. The following maps show not only the spatial distribution of families by economic status, the educational status of individuals (18 years and over), and the marital status of the population but suggest how these various social indexes are interrelated.

The thing which first strikes the eye is a sense of pattern, that is, the ordered and systematic arrangement of the phenomena. It is obvious that the distribution of Chicago's population in terms of these three statuses is not haphazard and accidental. All three distributions suggest the working of processes, the one which is the most dominant being competition, modified as we know it is by cultural factors.

The distribution of the population by economic status (Map 1) shows an orderly shading, generally from the center outward. The same pattern holds, with some exceptions for educational (Map 2) and marital status

[11] There is a rich and abundant literature on human ecology, much of which has been little used or referred to by the human geographers. The following sources give an excellent working acquaintance with both the methods and results of the ecological approach to human affairs: R. E. Park and E. W. Burgess (Editors), *The City* (Chicago: University of Chicago Press, 1925); R. D. McKenzie, *The Metropolitan Community* (New York: McGraw-Hill Book Co., 1933); Paul K. Hatt and Albert J. Reiss, Jr. (Editors), *Reader in Urban Sociology* (Glencoe, Ill.: The Free Press, 1951). (This volume would almost, by itself, provide a thorough education in the ecological approach.) A. B. Hollingshead, "Human Ecology," *New Outline of the Principles of Sociology*, Edited by Alfred M. Lee (New York: Barnes & Noble, Inc., 1951); L. L. Bernard, Editor, *The Field and Methods of Sociology* (New York: Ray Long and Richard Smith, Inc., 1934); Robert E. Park, "Sociology," *Research in the Social Sciences*, Edited by Wilson Gee (New York: The Macmillan Co., 1929); and *Our Cities: Their Role in the National Economy* (Washington: Government Printing Office, 1937). See also Clyde F. Kohn (Editor), *Geographic Approaches to Social Education*, 19th Yearbook of the National Council for the Social Studies, 1948.

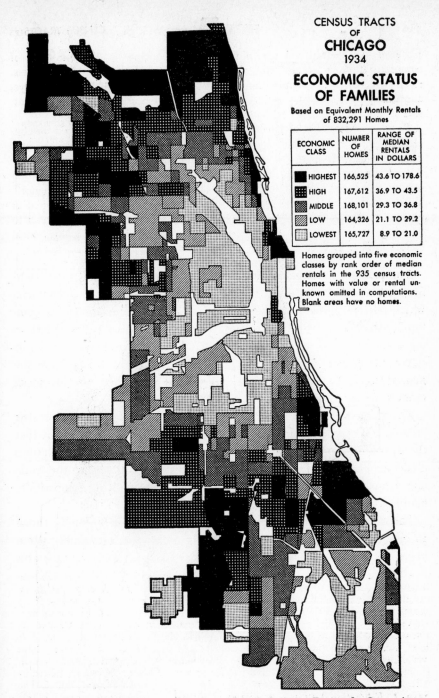

CENSUS TRACTS
OF
CHICAGO
1934

**ECONOMIC STATUS
OF FAMILIES**

Based on Equivalent Monthly Rentals
of 832,291 Homes

ECONOMIC CLASS	NUMBER OF HOMES	RANGE OF MEDIAN RENTALS IN DOLLARS
HIGHEST	166,525	43.6 TO 178.6
HIGH	167,612	36.9 TO 43.5
MIDDLE	168,101	29.3 TO 36.8
LOW	164,326	21.1 TO 29.2
LOWEST	165,727	8.9 TO 21.0

Homes grouped into five economic classes by rank order of median rentals in the 935 census tracts. Homes with value or rental unknown omitted in computations. Blank areas have no homes.

MAP 1. *Economic Status of Families* (Social Science Research Committee, University of Chicago) [12]

[12] "The Distribution of Some Selected Social Phenomena,' *Third-Year Course in the Study of Contemporary Society* (Social Science 3, formerly Social Science II), Vol. I, 10th Edition (Chicago: University of Chicago Press, Copyright September, 1942), p. 15. Distributed by the University of Chicago Bookstore.

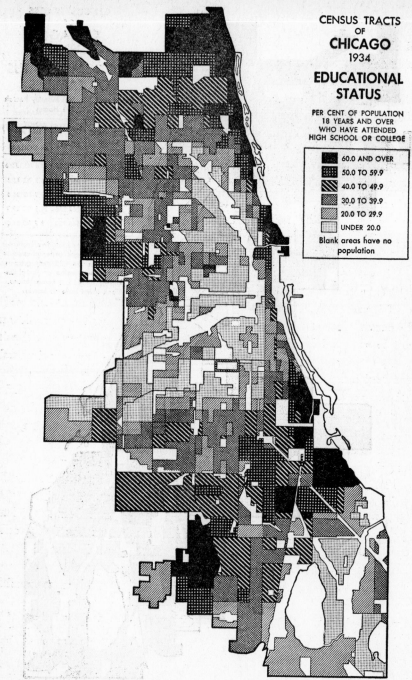

CENSUS TRACTS
OF
CHICAGO
1934

**EDUCATIONAL
STATUS**

PER CENT OF POPULATION
18 YEARS AND OVER
WHO HAVE ATTENDED
HIGH SCHOOL OR COLLEGE

	60.0 AND OVER
	50.0 TO 59.9
	40.0 TO 49.9
	30.0 TO 39.9
	20.0 TO 29.9
	UNDER 20.0

Blank areas have no
population

MAP 2. *Educational Status* (Social Science Research Committee, University of Chicago) [13]

[13] *Ibid.,* p. 16.

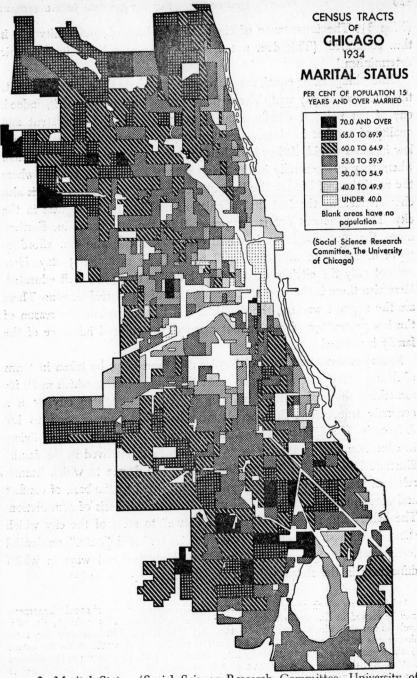

CENSUS TRACTS
OF
CHICAGO
1934

MARITAL STATUS

PER CENT OF POPULATION 15
YEARS AND OVER MARRIED

70.0 AND OVER
65.0 TO 69.9
60.0 TO 64.9
55.0 TO 59.9
50.0 TO 54.9
40.0 TO 49.9
UNDER 40.0

Blank areas have no
population

(Social Science Research
Committee, The University
of Chicago)

MAP 3. *Marital Status* (Social Science Research Committee, University of Chicago) [14]

[14] *Ibid.*, p. 17.

(Map 3). The importance of the economic base of community life is thus confirmed. (This does not, however, support a belief in economic determinism.)

Other things being equal, people tend to live where their income permits them to own or pay rent. The right to live where one wishes is, indeed, one of our political freedoms but it is conditioned by the extent and quality of another freedom, namely economic. A great many people with low incomes would, if they had their preference, live in places other than where they do—generally in the oldest part of the city, its center—where the conditions of life are the least attractive. In Chicago this area is also characterized by the fact that population mobility is the highest in the city. The movement out is far greater than the movement in. Furthermore, that out-movement is selective in that those who can afford to move do so; those who cannot afford to (with exceptions) stay. Here are not only the city's poorest people but also those less well educated. Here also there is the greatest concentration of unmarried persons. These are the migrant workers, the derelicts, and the bohemians. By reason of the low percentage of persons not married, the cultural influence of the family is reduced.

Spatial patterns and the social order.   If these maps be taken in terms of their general patterns one may sense the kind of factors which make for something short of cultural unity in a great metropolitan city. It is a generally true axiom that people who live differently respond to life differently. The differences which these maps reveal in standards of living, in education, and in the degree to which one's life is lived in the family illustrate both graphically and dramatically the degree to which human relations in a great urban community are organized on the basis of conflict and accommodation a great deal more than on the basis of assimilation. The beliefs and attitudes which are "native" to areas of the city which stand in such sharp contrast as do the "inner" and "outer" residential sections of Chicago are, of course, the deeply personal ways in which differences in the statuses shown are ultimately represented.[15]

[15] The factors which operate to produce the distributive patterns of social phenomena may be viewed in almost their ideal manifestation in Chicago. This is due to the relatively minor role which geographic factors play. The spatial distribution of the same phenomena in such cities as New York, Seattle, and Pittsburgh would reveal the extent to which geographic factors intrude to distort the almost perfect symmetry of the Chicago pattern. But the same general factors operate by reason of the fact that the cultures of these cities are, in all major respects, of the same genre as the culture of Chicago. Of all large cities in our country, the ecology of Chicago and Cleveland are most alike due, of course, to the fact that both their geography and culture are of the same general kind. The pattern for Milwaukee is similar to that of Chicago and Cleveland.

The substance of the foregoing discussion, especially as it relates to any metropolitan city, may be reported in the observation that the expression "the wrong side of the tracks" (which suggests also "the right side") refers to a pattern of human affairs which owes its nature to the interplay of all the factors we have noted. If the kinds of maps which this approach affords do not add several cubits to the stature of "visual aids" then I confess I do not know where one could find more graphic and almost self-revealing ones.

Some unfinished business relating to the metropolitan area remains to be dealt with before I turn to a brief discussion of demography and some other phases of the spatial perspective.

The ecology of associations and consensus. The land-use data did not deal with the multiplication of the administrative areas referred to in my introductory remarks about the Chicago metropolitan area. If these had been plotted (police, sanitary, and many other kinds of administrative areas) a graphic and almost eloquent case might have been made for the ecological approach to the problem of associations and consensus. The inefficiency and excessive costs of the great multiplication of administrative areas suggest the need for the elimination and/or the consolidation of many of them. This constitutes a study in the pressing need for the creation of political institutions more appropriate in their powers and the areal range of their controls than those which now exist.

A new focus for social study. Such a study has relevance for rural as well as urban schools by reason of the fact that "country" and "city" are both affected by the inefficiency and excessive cost of local government. Indeed, the old division of "rural" and "urban" is, as I have suggested, almost passé if our students are to understand the significance of metropolitan areas as units of social control: economic and cultural as well as political. One of the most inviting frontiers for social study is the present status and prospects of a nation's population patterned, as it is and will be increasingly, around its great cities. Problems of state and local government do not thereby become ineligible for study. The case is rather that the pattern of millions of our people in metropolitan areas gives us a new and urgent perspective from which to study local and state governments and their socio-economic problems. The light that such study would throw on an understanding of our national life would be no less important. There is some evidence that we have taken far less account than we ought of the effect which urbanization has had on our entire way of life.

The demographic approach. The demographic approach to various aspects of social study is common to both the geographic and the ecological perspectives. Its focus is on the number, density, movement, age, health, and "illth," and the sex ratio of the population of communities.

The following chart shows the distribution of the nation's population for 1920 by age and sex. The vertical axis is divided into five-year age brackets, except the bottom one which includes those "under five" years of age. On the horizontal axis are given the percentages which all the males and females, respectively, constitute, by appropriate age brackets, of the nation's total population. Thus, if the nation's population in 1920 was 105,000,000 and its entire male population under five years of age totaled 3,625,000, you would compute the percentage which that number was of the total population (5.25 per cent) and extend the bar of the bottom age category to the *left* of the vertical axis to the 5.25 mark. Correspondingly, if the entire female population under five years of age totaled 5,775,000 you would compute the percentage which that number was of the total population (5.50 per cent) and extend the bar of the bottom age category to the *right* of the vertical axis to the 5.50 mark. You

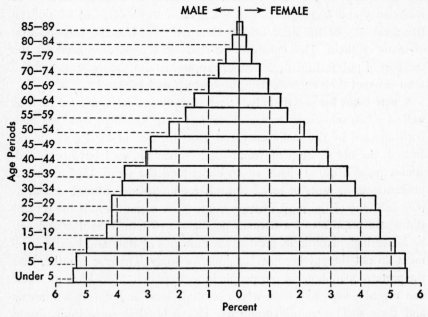

CHART 6. *Distribution of Age Periods and According to Sex of the Population of the United States, 1920* [16]

[16] Charles Newcomb, "Graphic Study of Urban Population," *Second-Year Course in the Study of Contemporary Society* (Social Science II), *Syllabus and Selected Readings,* 7th Edition (Chicago: University of Chicago Press, Copyright August, 1938), p. 239. Distributed by the University of Chicago Bookstore.

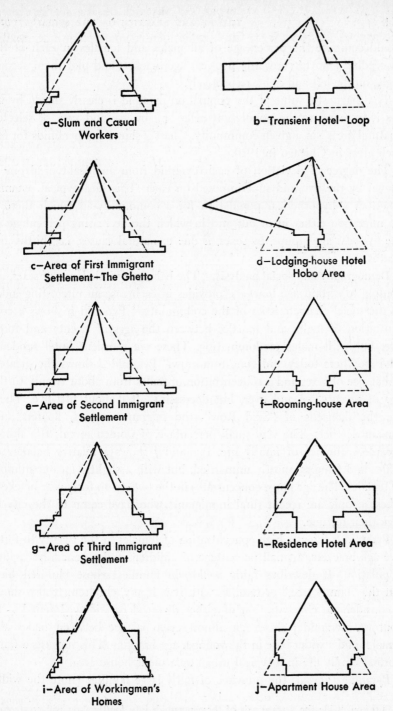

a—Slum and Casual
Workers

b—Transient Hotel—Loop

c—Area of First Immigrant
Settlement—The Ghetto

d—Lodging-house Hotel
Hobo Area

e—Area of Second Immigrant
Settlement

f—Rooming-house Area

g—Area of Third Immigrant
Settlement

h—Residence Hotel Area

i—Area of Workingmen's
Homes

j—Apartment House Area

CHART 7. *Populations of Selected Census Tracts in Chicago (1920) Representing Types of Age and Sex Distributions in the "City."* [17]

[17] Newcomb, *ibid.* p. 245.

would compute the percentage of all males and females in each of the succeeding (moving upward) five-year age brackets and plot them accordingly, on the left and right, respectively.

The diagnostic value of the population pyramid is clearly shown by using it to compare the population make-up (by age and sex) of selected "natural areas" in a given community. Chart 7 shows the pyramids for ten such areas in Chicago in 1920.

The degree of deviation of each pyramid from an ideal-typical one is shown by the pyramid superimposed on each. This ideal-typical pyramid describes a hypothetical population for a community in which there is no migration either in or out and in which the decreasing percentage of the five-year age groups, by sexes, is due to natural causes, i.e., births and deaths.

Demography and social analysis.   The balance or imbalance of sexes, according to certain age brackets, provides in each case an interesting index to the social characteristics of the community.[18] Pyramid *b* shows a concentration of males and females between the ages of twenty and forty-five, but with males predominating. These are transient hotel residents who are "here today and gone tomorrow." Pyramid *d* shows the greatest imbalance of sexes and a concentration of males from about twenty to the age of seventy-five and over, but decreasing after about fifty-five. These are the denizens of "Skid Row"—the migrant workers, floaters, and human derelicts. The very small percentage of women reveals the almost complete absence of family life. Pyramid *f* shows a relative balance of males and females, mostly unmarried, but with a slightly greater number of females. The age range concentrates in the twenty- to forty-year brackets. These people are recent rural in-migrants who have come to the city to seek their fortune.

Pyramid *h* shows a high concentration of females in the twenty to forty-five age brackets, a small percentage of children, and a generally "aging" population. It describes fairly well-to-do families whose children have left the "family tree," or families with few, if any, children. It also shows a considerable concentration of either divorced or widowed females. In contrast, pyramid *j* shows an almost even balance between males and females and a wider base in the younger age brackets. This suggests a fairly normal family life in a typical urban apartment house area.

Pyramid *a* reveals the presence of fairly large families (note the width

---

[18] If you divide the vertical axis of these pyramids into fourths, you will create four age brackets of roughly twenty-two years each. This will help you make some quick approximations of the age-distribution of a given pyramid.

of the base) and a slightly greater percentage of men than women in the twenty- to forty-five- or fifty-year age bracket. One may well surmise that the living standards in this community are low, given the status of "slum" and "casual workers" who usually do not have regular employment, and the large percentage of children. The imbalance of males in pyramid *c* is greater than in *a* and suggests unattached males who have come to America to seek their fortune, like the rural migrants represented in pyramid *f*, except in the community of pyramid *c* they are foreign born. Pyramid *c* shows the next greatest percentage of all the pyramids in the age brackets of fifteen and under. Pyramid *e* shows a fairly even balance of males and females in the age range of twenty to fifty which, with the broadest base of all the pyramids, reports large families and relatively low standards of living. Note, also, that the excess of males shown in *c* has disappeared. This suggests that the standard of living is now high enough so that the taking in of roomers and boarders (unattached men of the same ethnic stock) is no longer necessary. The status of "second generation" reports a slight advance in both the economic and social status scale. The process of Americanization is showing interesting results.

Pyramid *g* is similar to pyramid *j*, although with more children and a more even balance of the sexes in the age range of thirty to fifty. Note also that a community of third-generation families has fewer "oldsters" than the apartment house community. This shows that a third generation population is relatively younger in average age than the population of an apartment-house area by reason of relatively fewer "oldsters" and more children. Pyramid *i* conforms more closely to the ideal-type pyramid than any of the others shown. The deviation is chiefly in the male and female brackets from about twenty to fifty years. This suggests, as does the "bulge" in pyramid *j*, some in-migration. In pyramid *i* we assume that the "bulge" is due to the advantage which residence in such a community has by virtue of proximity to industries which draw on it for its labor supply.[19]

19 Population pyramids may be used to show changes in the age and sex distribution of the population of a given community. Such changes are significant indexes to various kinds of social change. Cross-hatching may be used to designate ethnic and racial percentages of a population and thus throw light on certain factors making for cultural homogeneity or heterogeneity. The use of the population pyramid to describe a dust bowl community would show, "before" and "after," significant changes. If pyramids were constructed for mile zone areas along a line drawn from the center to the periphery of a great city or even a city of from 25,000 to 50,000, interesting indexes to the social composition of such areas would be revealed. They would, ideally, show a continuum of pyramids *b*, *d*, *f*, *c*, *g*, *i*, *h*, and *j* in roughly that order. The relation between spatial patterns as revealed in the distribution of typical population patterns and social orders would thus be shown.

The fact that the ecological maps and population pyramids shown here are "dated"

We may now inquire as to what such a way of describing the population of a community is indicative, i.e., of what is it a social index? It gives us a highly accurate statistical perspective on various standards of living, size of families, degree of family solidarity, income, political attitudes, and the like. We would get, in short, what Dr. Robert E. Park called an insight into the "social metabolism" of a community.

Interpretation of symbols.   These observations suggest the symbolic nature of charts, graphs, and maps. Each is an index to the "real" data and, as such, a surrogate for manipulating them *in situ*. The need for care and skill in making and using such representations is thus implied. If the place and position of all manner of physiographic and social phenomena cannot be "trod afoot" through field trips, such devices must be relied on to put our students at least in remote touch with the realities which they symbolize. The accurate making and interpretation of all such devices is one of the major skills which the spatial perspective offers. But their surrogate function should not be relied upon more than is necessary, although the more distant the places and positions the more the physical presence of students there is rendered impossible. The caution which I give in this respect is that the error of reification be avoided, which is mistaking the symbols for the "real" things. To this I add that form and function ought always to be correlated. This is the relation between social morphology and social process.

Maps show various perspectives.   Respecting the plotting of all map data I would enjoin the use of as large-scale maps as is possible, as a "preservative against alarms, panics, and general misunderstanding" of the true relations between human beings. To this advice might well be added the injunction that global maps should be used wherever possible. This principle applies especially to areas large enough to be distorted to some extent by their representation on a two-dimensional plane. The world *is* round and its rotundity has much to do with the student's proper understanding of the several perspectives which it affords. These may be polar, oceanic, hemispheric, or continental. All of them may be had by merely taking a different angle. They constitute related perspectives of the same global entity and each has unique merit. Taken together they may, in a real sense, give the student "his world."

Skill in map making and map reading is basic to "spatial intelligence." Neither size, distance, nor position in any spatial pattern can be accurately

---

does not reduce their value as illustrations of patterns of the spatial distribution of important social phenomena or as tools for demographic analysis. It is spatial and demographic analysis, rather than history, in which we are now interested.

known without skill in the interpretation of maps. New Jersey may appear to the student as the same size or even larger than the subcontinent of Australia unless the maps which represent each are examined for scale. Distances may also be falsely interpreted. Position is always *relative* to climate, rainfall, density of settlement, means of transportation, raw materials, contiguous political jurisdictions, or some other factor which needs to be known. Thus the principle of the *Gestalt* is confirmed in spatial study.

Aids to instruction. For the spatial approach to social phenomena novels as well as maps and field trips are highly appropriate. Among many excellent works I cite the following: Louis Adamic, *The Native's Return*; James Hilton, *Lost Horizon*; Louis Bromfield, *The Farm*; Mari Sandoz, *Old Jules*; Hamlin Garland, *A Son of the Middle Border*; Joseph Conrad, *Typhoon*; Willa Cather, *My Antonia*; and Robert Frost, *New England*. To these might be added such descriptive writings as Stuart Chase, *Rich Land, Poor Land*; Erskine Caldwell and Margaret Bourke-White, *You Have Seen Their Faces*; Willson Whitman, *God's Valley*; and Hans Zinnser, *Rats, Lice and History*. An indispensable resource for the teacher is Isaiah Bowman, *Geography in Relation to the Social Studies*; Cyrill D. Forde, *Habitat, Economy, and Society*, and *The Teaching of Geography*, the 32d Yearbook of the National Society for the Study of Education.

Geo-ecological study an aid to all perspectives on human affairs. Geographic and ecological study is an adjunct to every phase of social study. To the factors making for any given spatial distribution of social phenomena should, of course, be added history. Thus, the perspective which we have discussed here comprehends all the perspectives discussed in the immediately prior chapters. To the question as to the place of spatial study in the curriculum I would reply, "Everywhere." The context in which I have placed it in this discussion suggests that it be an integral phase of all the other major perspectives. If it is to be taught as a separate course it must, likewise, be related to human affairs. *Place* and *position* have little meaning apart from their relation to social activities. They are *basic to* all social study rather than the basic social study.

Generalizations about spatial study. The generalizations which the spatial approach to social phenomena permit might be classified by "place" and "position." The former would deal with the "landscape" as one of the factors conditioning the spatial position of both thing and not-thing values. It is important that students know *where* both thing and not-thing values are; similarly, what the significance of their place is for their *position*. The temptation is simply to "place them" and let it go at that.

Understandings and skills.   Historical study seeks to develop "historical mindedness." The perspective which has been discussed seeks to develop "space mindedness" with all the social implications which attach to it. It also permits a quality of precison which perhaps none of the other perspectives allows. It requires simple statistical skills as well as the skills included in map making and map reading. It allows vicarious journeying to distant and strange places. The magic carpet is the map.

Such study has the potential for the kind of global or at least nonlocal thinking which our time so tragically requires if our students are to understand the significance of place, space, distance, and time-cost in the modern world. But these must always be related to the position which men and their works bear to each other. This is the ultimate concern of all spatial study.[20]

[20] Dan Stiles, "Why Not Teach Geography?" *Harpers Magazine*, May, 1943. See also Lawrence K. Frank, *Nature and Human Nature,* in which he distinguishes between the following environments: geographical (all the noncultural world outside us), internal (the physio-psycho-anatomic environment within us), and the cultural (the human world of man's creation, both public and private).

CHAPTER XXVII

Approaches to an Understanding of the Community

THE PERSISTENT and immediate form in which your students confront the social realities is in their local community. Former chapters have been concerned with it in many ways. We have treated it as part of and counterpart of the Great Society, we have described how it works, and how well it works. We have viewed it from the perspective of the process of growing up, as the place in which the journey of citizenship goes on, and in many other ways.

A new perspective on community study. In this chapter we shall discuss how your students may go out into the local community by means of field trips and how some indexes of it may be brought into the classroom. Among these we shall treat the motion picture, the radio, and the newspaper. We shall also have something to say about the teaching of current events and the analysis of propaganda. We shall look upon the motion picture, the radio, and the newspaper not merely as "aids to instruction" but as cultural objects worthy to be known in their own right. Our major emphasis respecting them will be from the latter point of view.

The field trip. One of the most effective ways by which the community may be known is through study in the field. This may take two main forms: through field trips as organized experiences in exploration and reconnaissance of the local community by an entire class, and as the locale of discrete studies by individual students or committees of them. Plato and Socrates, the pedagogues who taught the children from the households of the citizens of Athens, Jesus of Nazareth, and many great teachers used the out-of-doors as the place of learning. The effectiveness

429

does a roundhouse symbolize? The following meanings come to mind: a place where changing technology can be seen—from steam to diesel power; capital goods in the form of lathes, forges, and the like; obsolescence in the form of locomotives awaiting the scrap heap; the division of labor and the unity of labor; the discipline of work symbolized by the time clock and the timecards arranged in a rack beside it; the difference between casual labor and the skilled trades; and overhead expense and operating costs. These may all be seen, furthermore, in their relation to the process of transportation.

Let us next take the courthouse. Here is a totally different set of symbols. They are those of the service and police state. Everywhere a student turns, he may see, if he has eyes to see, evidences of representative government. He may also see the difference between officials elected by popular will and those who owe their positions to competitive civil service. He may see both occupations and professions. Among the former, the janitor and the grounds-keeper; among the latter the lawyer, the judge, and the sheriff. If a trial is in session he may see the apparatus of justice; trial by jury, the operation of judicial procedures, the citing of the law by his honor, the judge—these and many other things which may be the experiences which confirm what the text gave him only knowledge about, not acquaintance with, which he is now getting.

Let us take one more, the telephone exchange. Here, almost ideally, the advanced role of technology can be seen firsthand. But does this not create unemployment? What is the evidence, pro and con? Maybe, in the short run but not in the long run. But if people eat and grow older in the short run, as they do, what and whom does mechanization profit in the long run? I mean to suggest that the field trip may raise questions, make them more *real*, as well as "settle" them. What is a "telephone girl," and who is she? But there is no simple "what" and "who." Here is an opportunity to study, firsthand, an occupation. "The telephone girl" turns out to be a supervisor, a chief operator, a long-distance operator and many others. Why do some young women become telephone employees, in whatever role? Why do others work in the laundry? Why others in the chain store or the beauty parlor? What is the differential, if such there be, in their education, their career interests, their family obligations? Where do they live? What are their working hours and their pay? What has all this to do with the process of competition for jobs?

Field study in the unit. I am suggesting here that the interpretation of such cultural symbols as a roundhouse, a courthouse, and telephone exchange involves not only looking but searching, inquiring, interviewing, and whatever means are appropriate to know the meaning of a symbol. I am also suggesting that field trips can initiate a unit of study, they can be part of the core of it, or they can give it the finishing touch. They are a means of getting knowledge firsthand, of confirming and supplementing secondhand knowledge, they are a means for sharpening observation, testing principles, and doing everything which social study requires. But no object of field study will ask its own questions and none of them will answer those your students ask. Answers will have to be inferred and tested as best they may. Learning "out-of-doors" is still learning, however more romantic it may be than learning "indoors."

Transitions through field study. I like to think of field study as permitting a kind of transition from more "quiet" and often less-than-adequate knowledge, to knowledge that may come from *all* the senses, even if some of it may be "only sensed," as we say, rather than known. In this view of field experience the following transitions illustrate what I have in mind:

1. *from* knowledge about an assembly line *to* seeing it in operation and sensing the routine and perhaps the tedium which it enforces.
2. *from* knowing in a bookish way "who works here" *to* seeing the different roles involved in various types of work and the co-ordination of those roles.
3. *from* reading about capital equipment *to* seeing it, feeling its weight, and appreciating its precision and cost.
4. *from* using the cliché "the other side of the tracks" *to* going there and observing its standard of living and the way of life it permits.
5. *from* pictures about soil erosion *to* measuring the depth of gullies, and seeing in contrast fields that have been contoured to prevent them.

Through transitions such as these, your students may come to realize the community in ways which bookish learning cannot, by its very nature, allow. Through field experience they may come to know, see, and feel their community as a way of life "aching with vividness." Facts will now take on an operational significance which will clothe them with more practical meaning.

Such a conception of field study is not met by "rubberneck" tours but rather by sober and long-term planning which may readily involve the co-operation of the entire class. Inquiry will find a real and solid ground for its practice and enjoyment. Indeed, inquiry may thus be actually "set afoot," not through extracurricular but through genuine curricular and extramural experience.

Some difficulties in field study. Field study has all the virtues which have been noted. But it also introduces some problems. In permitting your students an immediate reconciliation with "life in the round" it admits the maximum of romance which may, unless you are alert, be little more than romance. Thus it requires a preface and a follow-up. It ought to be connected with and extend classroom study. It may also initiate it. It is much more than "going places and seeing things." It is chiefly, as I view it, a way of confirming what the processes are which go on in various places. Thus it ought to provide the interweaving of theory and that level of practice we know as observation.

You may well encounter some "problems of discipline." The climate is now the real one, the "out-of-doors." The genuine discipline that often inheres in the classroom situation is absent. You are more on your own to make the experience discipline itself as well as those who engage in it. This is the ideal conception of discipline, as I remarked in Chapter II.

Previous reference to community study.   As for community study per se I now refer to former chapters and note their relevance to such an enterprise. Chapter V provided an analysis of both the "great" and the "small" community and suggested their interrelations. Field study can be used to observe the workings implicit in the processes of competition, conflict, accommodation, and assimilation by visiting and studying the institutions which most closely reveal the dominance of each. Such inquiries as the following may be set afoot: identification of some of the natural areas of the community (the various types of residential areas, the business district, and industrial areas), the size, number, and location of parks and playgrounds, and commercial places of amusement; the characteristics of life in various areas in terms of income, standards of living, degrees of freedom and restraint, and social status; what various areas of living and carrying on of business have in common and the ways in which they are different; the density or sparsity of population, the intensity with which land is put to use, that is, the ratio of used to unused land area; the tempo of life which each area reveals; the size of families, the number of persons per room; the degree of privacy enjoyed by members of the family—in short, the community viewed and studied from as many different and related perspectives as its organization allows. (The materials of Chapter XXVI are immediately relevant to community study.)

Such inquiries will require that the knowledge of all the disciplines be drawn upon and the working of all the social processes be put to observational test. These inquiries may be readily disciplined by the logic of the triangular charts given in earlier chapters. The territorial or geo-ecological, the economic, the political, and the cultural ways of viewing human affairs will serve as useful guides to observation and as diagnostic devices. Thus the community which was "out there," chiefly in a physical way may now take on new proportions and meanings. It will become a complex of sights, sounds, and even languages. "Across the tracks" may, as I have suggested, take on social as well as physical meaning. Thus the fallacy that our students know the community merely by virtue of living in it may be revealed for the fallacy which it is.

You might take your cue from the characteristics of modern society given in Chapter V: size, complexity, speed, mechanism, and freedom. These concepts are useful "divining rods" which may lead to many interesting experiences through which such terms, and many others, may take on a quality of reality which merely their word-form is not sufficient to indicate. Furthermore, things which formerly existed only in geographic or areal space may now come to be seen and known in terms of *social* space.

Other concepts such as these may be given more explicit and practical meaning: occupation, social status, cost and price, income, neighborhood, land use, precinct, personality type, and even such a term as public opinion. Current events may be thus "hand-made" rather than taken only from news reports. All the methods of thinking suggested in Chapter XXIII may be employed; students may play the roles of participant observer, spectator, participator, interviewer, and data-gatherer. Honesty and perceptiveness in observation may be tested and improved, case-study and statistical methods may be used as well as the canons of inquiry necessary for the gathering of data for local histories. Indeed, every skill in the entire catalogue of social inquiry may be used and improved.[3]

The "book of life." The whole body of experiences which field study permits may help you, if not your students, realize how cardinal a sin the school has enacted in creating a world in and of itself apart from the world

[3] See again Spencer Brown, *They See for Themselves, op. cit.* See also the "How to Do It Series" published by the National Council for the Social Studies, including practical suggestions on the use of field trips, the utilization of community resources, maps and globes, government publications, oral reports, recordings, how to make public opinion surveys, how to use a bulletin board, a textbook, motion pictures, group discussion, daily newspapers, and many other of the practical aspects of teaching. Such resources as the following contain many useful guides and suggestions as well as basic theory: Sidney and Beatrice Webb, *Methods of Social Study*; Helen Lynd, *Field Work in College Education*; Jean Carol Tripp, *The Uses of Field Work in Teaching Economics*; *A Bibliography on Field Studies in Schools and Colleges*, Revised to January 1, 1947 (Bureau of Field Studies, New Jersey State Teachers College, Upper Montclair, New Jersey); Joanna C. Colcord, *Your Community*; Lloyd A. Cook, *Community Action and the Schools*; Charles R. Henderson, *Catechism for Social Observation*; Gordon W. Blackwell, *Toward Community Understanding*; Edward G. Olsen, *School and Community*; and *The Journal of Educational Sociology*, XIV (September, 1940). The best single source on local history with which I am acquainted is Donald Dean Parker, *Local History: How to Gather It, Write It, and Publish It* (Revised and Edited by Bertha E. Josephson for the Committee on Guide for Study of Local History). (New York: Social Science Research Council, 1944).

of practical human affairs which it ought to be the dedicated concern of
your students to understand. Thus the "imagination which people have
of one another [and] which are the solid facts of society" may be confirmed. By such methods as I have suggested, your students may learn how
to read the "book of life." Like traveling, it gives folks *ideas*, which is one
of the prime functions of social education.

The major mass media. I now wish to deal with such symbols of the
community as the motion picture, the radio, and the newspaper through
which significant expressions of the community may be brought into the
the community. These are representative and powerful types of *mass
media*. But, before I discuss the nature and significance of any of them, I
wish to set forth what I understand they *are*, as mass media. In this
account I shall focus on motion pictures, although what I shall say about
their effect in creating a mass audience applies perhaps quite as well to the
radio and to television which, in essence, permits the "movies" to come
into the home. The relevance of my analysis to the newspaper is perhaps
not quite as direct or accurate, although the newspaper is a mass medium.

Mass media defined. The term "media" is the plural of *medium*. A
medium is an "intermediate," that is, something which stands between
a person and some object of significance in his world. It is something which
connects a person with things which now lie, because of it, within the
range of his senses. Contrariwise, were it not for such media many things
would lie far outside the range of his senses except through his ability to
move through space and go to them. But this ability is always limited by
time-cost factors. Furthermore, motion pictures, the radio, and television
are able to create situations which do not exist "out there" and hence
which cannot be traveled to.

What is a mass audience? Leaving, for the time, the personal and
social effect of mass media I wish now to set forth what is meant by a
mass or a *mass audience*. In doing so, I shall have in mind, particularly,
the phenomenon which motion pictures create.

A mass or a mass audience is not a certain layer in a social structure. It
is not a class in the social-class sense of the meaning and use which we give
that term. Hence mass is not confined to any given social stratum. People
may participate in mass behavior regardless of their class position, their
vocation, their cultural attainments, or their wealth. Manifestations of mass
behavior, as I now use the term, are such as these: war hysteria, the spread
of fashions of various kinds, popular excitement over the kidnaping of a
child or a murder trial, the rise of interest in a sport such as golf, and
a common fear of some foreign ideology. Those who are caught up or who

participate in such behavior cannot be identified with any special layer or layers of the social structure. It is they who "go to the movies," listen to the radio, look at television, and to a large degree read the newspaper. What the people who constitute the mass have in common is activities such as these.

The characteristics of mass behavior.   I now inquire what mass behavior represents, what the nature of the mass is which so behaves, and how the mass behaves.

What mass behavior represents may be known by inquiring who comprise the mass, which is composed of a wide variety of local groups and cultures. These are likely to vary greatly. Thus mass behavior represents a heterogeneous rather than a homogeneous cultural background. This fact also indicates that mass behavior is *exterior* to the realm of local culture. The focus of attention of the mass is on objects and experiences which transcend, or better, lie outside of local cultures. This fact has great significance. It is, in sum, not a folk or local phenomenon. Indeed, it stands in opposition to the way of life and the values of local cultures. From this it follows that, in mass behavior, people are detached in varying degrees from their local cultures. The effect of mass behavior is both destructive and constructive of the values of local cultures. It is destructive in the sense that mass behavior not only "stands on the outside" of local culture but represents an attack on it. The objects on which the mass concentrate are not only innovations but invasions. That is, they create an imagery which is not prescribed or permitted by local cultures: witness the exotic, the strange, and brutal kinds of situations which motion pictures, the radio (and some newspapers) sometimes present. It is these characteristics of the objects presented which detach people from their local cultures.

The area of individual experience in which such influences seem to operate is the area which local life does not satisfy. Thus individuals are responsive to mass appeals chiefly in those areas of their experience in which their dispositions are not organized or served.[4]

The nature of the mass.   The nature of the mass is now my concern. It is made up of detached individuals. This does not deny that they have their local attachments, that they share in convivial associations of many

---

[4] The constructive phase of mass behavior should not be overlooked, even though I shall be less concerned with it than the destructive effects. It may be constructive, depending largely on the quality of the experiences which it affords, by way of permitting individuals to participate in a wider universe of experience than that which their local cultures afford. Those things which their local cultures do not satisfy may thus be served in constructive ways. This is to say that needs which their local cultures do not serve may be served through these experiences.

kinds, that they belong to such primary groups as the family, the church, and the club and that they live and act, to a great extent, in accordance with conventional patterns. But, in so far as persons belong to a mass, they are alienated from these deeply personal relations and become involved in a new area of life which is not covered by local traditions.

One of the chief characteristics of the mass is that it is highly hetero-geneous. The individual components of the mass are essentially alike, are in-dividually indistinguishable, and can be conceived as similar units. Unique individual traits tend to lose their significance. This characteristic may be expressed by saying that the individuals who make up the mass are anony-mous, "without name." This anonymity traces, in part, to the fact that they come from different local groups and hence do not know one another. (It is obvious that I am treating "mass man" in ideal-type terms.)

Furthermore, there is practically no communication between the mem-bers of the mass. Neither do they have any status or accepted position. The mass is, in short, unorganized. It has no "settled framework of life" and no established customs or forms of social relation and no distinct roles are assigned to any of its members. It is inchoate and formless. Its lack of organization follows from the fact that it arises in situations alien to and detached from local culture; is built up from detached [5] individuals with heterogeneous backgrounds and origins and is confronted with cir-cumstances and situations for which there are no established rules for collective, that is, joint behavior. The only thing which its members have in common is the desire to satisfy some need which their local cultures not only do not satisfy but against which most of them probably enforce taboos.

How the mass behaves.   This brings us to inquire how the mass behaves. It behaves, as I have suggested, not in a concerted way but in terms of "merely individual lines of action." This is not the result of consensus or agreement although it may take a surprisingly unanimous direction and thus make mass behavior highly effective. This action is, erroneously, some-times called the expression of public opinion. But it is nothing of the kind for it was not the product of discussion.

The unanimity which the mass may represent in its behavior may be and often is foolish and capricious. The "mobbing" of a movie star by the "bobby-sox" crowd, the "zoot-suit" craze, and "popular" outcries against a kidnaper are instances of the unanimity of which I speak, if not also of foolish and capricious behavior. Other manifestations are unre-strained yelling at an athletic event, a Mardi Gras, milling about in the

[5] "Detached" does not mean "unmarried" but rather "unknown" to each other.

event of a spectacular fire, or even a lynch mob which, happily, is less and less a mode of mass behavior. The effect of such states of tension and excitement is to create an unstable situation or frame of reference. Thus the individual has no moral "landmarks" by which to measure his conduct.

The experience of the mass. Some further comments are in order as to the way mass behavior expresses itself. What is significant is "not the action, but the experience." The objects to which the mass attend (in a movie house or in some other situation in which mass behavior is generated) is foreign to the life of the local culture of the individuals. Thus these objects are both strange and interesting and the experience which they provide is, in however slight or aggravated a degree, "sensational, exciting, and disquieting." Given these characteristics, it is likely that the inner experience of the members of the mass will be in the nature of "awakened disposition, challenged taste, stirred up imagination, or reenforced sentiment." These effects will, I am sure, immediately call to your mind the consequences which many motion pictures, and to varying degrees radio and television experiences, as well as the reading of startling and bizarre accounts in the newspaper, bring about.[6]

The chief way in which the mass behaves is by "making choices, selections, and adoptions." These are the way in which it *acts*. But this is not concerted or planned action; it is merely individual action. Through such action, satisfactions of various kinds are served.

The role and effect of motion pictures and radio. The foregoing provides the framework for a consideration of the role and effect of motion pictures as well as the radio. Movie-goers are Everyman, his wife and children, who come from many different families, communities, local cultures, occupations, and social classes. Such an aggregate of individuals constitutes a mass and exhibits typical mass behavior. It has "no program, no rules,

---

[6] I owe this analysis of the mass to Professor Herbert Blumer of the University of California at Berkeley. See his paper, "Moulding of Mass Behavior Through the Motion Picture," *Human Problems of Social Planning* (Publication of the American Sociological Society, XXIX, No. 3, 1935, Copyright Chicago: The H. G. Adair Printing Company), pp. 115-127. The quotations above and those to follow in this analysis are from this paper. I take full responsibility for interpreting Professor Blumer's remarks when I have not quoted him. For other critiques of motion pictures, some of which are concerned with the industry itself, i.e., with "Hollywood," see: Hortense Powdermaker, *Hollywood the Dream Factory: An Anthropologist Looks at the Movie-Makers* (New York: Little Brown & Co., 1950), and "Celluloid Civilization," *The Saturday Review of Literature*, October 14, 1950; Gilbert Seldes, *The Great Audience* (New York: The Viking Press, Inc., 1950), and "Life on the Tinsel Standard," *The Saturday Review of Literature*, October 28, 1950; Roger Manvell, *Film* (Pelican Books), 1946; James Farrell, *Literature and Morality* (New York: Vanguard Press, 1947), especially the paper, "The Communications Revolution"; and David Riesman, *The Lonely Crowd* (New Haven: Yale University Press, 1952).

no traditions, and no culture." Its individual members have all the characteristics noted earlier: without unique roles, anonymous, no we-feeling, no common loyalties, and no designated functions.

The unique feature of motion pictures lies in their vivid and visual nature. Their appeal is to the senses and, as John Dewey has observed, when we see we also hear and when we hear other senses are aroused. (The sound picture makes the hearing inevitable but even if the sound were not there, we would "add it.") The close-up is a particularly effective aspect of motion pictures. By its use the physical distance between spectators and actors is changed. The theater permits no such effect. Through the close-up the spectators and hearers may become a part of the action and thus increase their sense of participation. Rapport and intimacy are thereby increased.

Another feature of motion pictures is their highly dramatic character. They have "a plot, a development, and a climax." There is also "movement, progressive suspense and sensed participation," all of which aid in the identification of the spectator and hearer with what is being shown. These characteristics are powerful factors which permit the individual to lose himself in the picture. He moves into another world.

Motion pictures reaffirm and undermine.   Here it is significant to note that the appeal of the motion picture is to primary emotions and sentiments which appeal is, of course, inevitable in all drama. Given the nature of the mass, this is the common denominator by which the producer must be guided. If he is to appeal to a heterogeneous audience recruited from all walks of life he must find the level at which a picture may "speak" to everyone in such an audience. From this fact issues the nature of the general influence of the motion picture. It is a *"reaffirmation of basic human values but an undermining of the mores,"* that is, of the values and standards of conduct of local communities and cultures.

The universal appeal of motion pictures.   Since the appeal of motion pictures depends so much on touching the primary emotions, it is easy to understand why they stress the human qualities which are man's universal possessions. Important among these are such qualities as "bravery, loyalty, love, affection, frankness, personal justness, cleverness, heroism, and friendship." The prevailing themes of motion pictures are such as the following: "Conflict between what has our sympathy and what has our antipathy, between the good and bad, between the desirable and the reprehensible." [7]

---

[7] To this Professor Blumer adds: "In motion pictures the sympathetic, the good and the desirable are compounded out of such human qualities as those mentioned above out

This reaffirmation of "basic human values" is, however, often done in contexts which not only run counter to the mores of local cultures but which, because of the nature of the scenes and the action, constitute a threat to them. This is often manifest in scenes and themes which violate the sex taboos of local cultures. Thus, while basic human values and sentiments are reaffirmed, they are often reaffirmed in forms of conduct which are outside the pale of what is considered decent.[8]

The mass audience has no common culture. I have already observed, following Blumer, that movie-goers, as a mass audience, possess no common culture. Thus, they have no basis for interpreting and ordering their cinema experiences, so as to integrate them with the mores of their local cultures. The effect is that the experiences "remain allienated with no scheme to bridge them." On this hangs the concern of many with their moral effect. It is this moral effect which I now wish to discuss.[9]

Motion pictures as forms of art. This brings me to treat, briefly, motion pictures as forms of art. What I shall say applies also to radio and television in so far as they are media for communicating various art forms as well as influencing popular artistic tastes.

First, we need to ask what the generic function of art is. It is, as I understand it, to elicit and accentuate the quality of one's being a "whole" and thus of belonging to the largest, all-inclusive whole, which is the universe in which he lives. In this sense, art carries us out beyond ourselves in order to become better selves.[10] Thus it performs a religious function, with *religious* interpreted in its most exacting etymological sense as that which binds fast, as in the Latin *religare*. This interpretation suggests that art, as symbolism, appeals to universal man.

---

of those already having widespread allegiance, whose value is spontaneously appreciated. The elevation of these qualities to points of virtue and the accompanying re-enforcement of the sentiments for which they stand is what I have in mind in declaring that motion pictures reaffirm basic human values." *Ibid.*, p. 124.

8 My emphasis here is on a certain type of picture. Others which transgress local mores and hence which are considered "bad for young people" depict brutality, coarseness, and many other forms which, judged by the canons of local cultures, are grossly immoral. This emphasis or focus is not to be taken as a blanket attack on or condemnation of all motion pictures. "Some" is not "all," as logic teaches us.

9 With the constructive phases of motion pictures which Professor Blumer discusses I shall not deal here. His remarks on that point are organized not in terms of "good" and "bad" pictures but rather in terms of what the effect of any picture may be by way of making people sensitive of "new areas of life" and preparing them for action in those areas. *Ibid.*, p. 125.

10 As Dewey expresses it, "the work of art operates to deepen and raise to great clarity that sense of an enveloping, undefined whole that accompanies every normal experience." (*Art as Experience*, New York: Minton, Balch & Co., 1934, p. 195). See the chapters "The Common Substance of the Arts" and "The Varied Substance of the Arts." *Ibid.*, pp. 187-244.

However, the art of motion pictures in an advanced and complex society such as ours is not folk art. Hence it does not serve a folk community, nor is it produced by one. It serves a mass audience and is produced, for the most part, according to box-office appeal. This is the appeal to and re-affirmation of basic human values of which Blumer writes, values which, in being human and hence universal, undermine the mores of local cultures.[11]

It is our conviction that, insofar as motion pictures reaffirm basic human values but have the negative effect which Blumer indicates, they do not serve a religious function in the terms in which we have interpreted it.[12]

Implications for the teacher. Now, what does this brief critique of motion pictures as art forms mean for the teacher of the social studies? It is obvious that neither teachers nor the school as a social institution has the power to police or censor the "movies." Indeed I do not choose to discuss censorship by educational, religious, or civil bodies. I choose, rather, to raise the question as to what teachers of the social studies may do to help their students, most or many of whom are regular movie-goers, to understand the forms of art which the "movies" present them. I am concerned with the moral problem of standards of taste in popular art.

The "law of good taste." This concern takes the form of suggesting that teachers seek to educate their students to obey only one law, the *law of good taste* in cinema art. Such an education might, conceivably, help to raise the standards of taste of the whole society a generation hence for it is only through such a process that the school can affect the Great Society in any area of its life.

This is not to suggest that so-called documentary films and a rich variety of other visual aids have no place in social education. My former emphasis on the need for romance and on the affective phases of learning should be sufficient to dispel any such idea. It is, however, to affirm that we have too often used films only as "aids to instruction" rather than as symbols of the informal education which students get outside of the classroom.

The "educative society." I suggest, then, that we need to make a place for the interpretation of the kind of education which students get, with-

[11] Commentary on their undermining effects ranges from James Farrell's remark about the "movies" deluging us with "an ocean of banality" to Sidney Harris' remark that "In the parlance of the movie ads, 'Realistic' means, with all the brutality of life left in and all the beauty of life left out." (See Farrell, *op. cit.*, p. 144: Mr. Harris' remark was made in his column "Strictly Personal," the *Chicago Daily News*, April 21, 1955).

[12] A clear exposition of the nature of the *religious* as used here is to be found in Dewey's *A Common Faith*.

out knowing it, from the "educative society." Motion pictures do, indeed, have a "fun function" which I would not deny to modern youth. But motion pictures have more than a "fun function." They also have, in the terms of Professor Blumer's analysis, a miseducative function. I now mean by miseducation, as I remarked in an earlier chapter, an education which fails to establish relationships.

The mass audience is alienated. I return, in this observation, to two remarks by Blumer. He tells us that the mass audience (of which our students are an integral part) acts by "making choices, selections, and adaptations." He also tells us that "there is no scheme to bridge" or relate these actions of the mass audience with the kinds of experiences which its members have in their local cultures. Herein lies the ground for what I have called "miseducation." This takes the form of continued "alienation" of the experiences or acts which the mass audience has (or engages in) from the norms of local cultures. These "choices, selections, and adaptations" do, however, persist, but chiefly in the form of quite unrealistic reverie and fantasy which, while not always bad or destructive of character organization, tend to encourage escape from the realities with which the lives of the members of the mass audience are bound up. The "movies" are, for them, a window on a completely unreal and often quite inappropriate world.[13]

A unit on leisure. I offer no exhaustive blueprint for a course in "how to look at the 'movies.'" Rather, I suggest a unit on "the uses of leisure" in a course which views human affairs from any one of the contemporary perspectives set forth in Chapters XXII, XXIII and XXIV, for the foregoing analysis reveals social problems and civic and economic aspects of the experience of our students. Such an approach would seek to help them understand what is happening to them, rather than to seek to reform them. This is appropriate to the view, expressed earlier, that the subject matter of a social education be or bear immediately upon the experiences which our students are now having. But they are not only to "wallow" in them. Their task, as I have suggested, is to see them in dimensions and perspectives which are more critical and helpful than those which they

[13] Blumer points out that the play of motion pictures on reverie assumes a different character from that of folk tales. The stimulation of reverie by motion pictures is likely to be destructive and confusing, probably making inner experience more lively but more unsettled and chaotic (*Ibid.*, p. 127). Gilbert Seldes remarks, in criticism of motion pictures, that the function of the popular arts is "to divert, but not to deceive about life." See "Life on the Tinsel Standard," *The Saturday Review of Literature*, October 28, 1950, p. 9.

presently employ. These should relate their "real life situations" to the characteristics of their culture—in this instance, motion pictures, radio, and television.

I am suggesting something closely akin to "If you can't beat 'em, join 'em," by which I mean that preaching against the movies, when and if teachers do it, had better change to studying them. Or, in another metaphor, it seems that we have often done something equivalent to saying "Don't put beans up your nose," which has been as ineffective as legend reports. Much the same attitude is not infrequently taken toward the comics, the newspaper, and various other symbols of community expression.[14]

Teach what is right with the movies. I suggest that it is profitable to undertake sober and systematic study of motion pictures, radio, television, and the comics but not only from the point of view of what is wrong with them but also what is *right* with them. I do not believe that we shall improve the level and quality of tastes in the popular arts by dealing only with their negative and destructive phases. I seek to avoid falling into the pit of silly optimism, but I wonder if Shakespeare's view in *As You Like It* may not have considerable value. He wrote, as you recall,

> Sweet are the uses of adversity,
> Which like the toad, ugly and venomous,
> Wears yet a precious jewel in his head;
> And this our life, exempt from public haunt,
> Finds tongues in trees, books in the running brooks,
> Sermons in stones, and good in everything.

I offer no format for the kind of unit I have suggested other than that the uses of leisure be viewed as a personal and social problem. Its study will, almost certainly, begin from the personal angle. But it should be developed in terms of the social factors which lie behind it. This will take the discussion into the realm of public affairs. Rich and varied aids and suggestions for such a study may be found in such journals as *The Social Studies, Social Education, and Educational Leadership.* Hardly an

[14] I offer no instruction or advice on the comics. No one seems to know what their effect is, although there is some evidence that it is far from contributory to either good or realistic imagery about many phases of human affairs. But the comics, in common with the movies and whatever else has bad effects on youth, can be effectively dealt with only by major changes in our social ideals and institutions. It is much too simple to believe that we can "pluck them out" of the totality of our culture by mere acts of courage or law enforcement. Effective and lasting social change does not come by merely exorcising the "devils" called "the comics," "the movies," or any other symbol. See Dr. Frederick Wertham, *Seduction of the Innocent* (New York: Rinehart & Company, Inc., 1954) and Coulton Waugh, *The Comics* (New York: The Macmillan Co., 1947).

issue of any of them fails to include useful materials on such a task. Note also the 18th Yearbook of the National Council on the Social Studies, *Audio-Visual Materials and Methods in the Social Studies,* as well as every other yearbook of the Council.[15]

The newspaper as a symbol. This brings me to discuss the newspaper as a symbol of the community. It is one of the greatest of the mass media although no one seems able to say, or at least there is little agreement on, just what its effect is on the "mass mind." But the mass audience and the "mass mind" apart, the newspaper has only infrequently been studied as a cultural object worthy to be known in its own right. It is also an "aid to learning" in that materials from it may be used in all the perspectives which I have discussed. But to use it only in that way is, in my view, not enough.

The classic statement on the importance of the newspaper in a free society was made by Thomas Jefferson in his remark, "If left to me to decide whether we shall have a government without newspapers or newspapers without a government, I should not hesitate for a moment to prefer the latter." [16] Fortunately, Jefferson did not have to make that choice, nor do we. But, nevertheless, this statement implies the relation which news and opinion have on the way of life called democratic.

A single test of a general education in social knowledge. Therein lies the need that our students know a great deal more than they do about the newspaper: what it is, what it tries to do, how well it does it, and what they may do about it. If I were asked to name the single test of a student's general education in social knowledge I would say, his ability to read and interpret the news. The school's neglect of it is nothing less than appalling. We teach students to read textbooks, the literature of essayists and poets, and mathematical symbols. We teach them to read a watch, a thermometer, the barometer, and all manner of gauges but we take very little account of, or even ignore, in what seems almost to be a

[15] Other sources in this area are: Leo Rosten, *Hollywood* (New York: Harcourt, Brace & Co., 1941); Edgar Dale (Editor) *Movies and Propaganda,* 7th Yearbook of the National Council for the Social Studies, 1937; Josette Frank, *Comics, Radio, Movies and Children,* Public Affairs Pamphlet, No. 148; Godfrey Elliott, Editor, *Film and Education* (New York: Philosophical Library, 1948); H. S. Busby and Others, *How to Use Radio in the Classroom,* National Association of Broadcasters, 1939; and the Bureau of Educational Research, Ohio State University, Columbus, Ohio. I have found *The Saturday Review* (formerly *The Saturday Review of Literature*) an invaluable resource in trying to keep myself aware in matters relating to education, as well as the whole range of art, drama, and the liberal studies. *The Saturday Review* devotes an entire issue, annually, to matters of education. I have found that the *Bulletin of the National Association of Secondary School Principals* carries one of the most comprehensive book lists to be found in any journal devoted to matters of education.

[16] *Works,* II, p. 55.

446   THEORY AND PRACTICE OF THE SOCIAL STUDIES

studied way, the importance of their knowing how to read a newspaper. It
may be that Professor Robert E. Park has explained the why of this in
his remark that "The middle class, not knowing how to interpret the news,
is disturbed by reading it." Perhaps that is why about all we seem to be
able to do is to quote it, or say what "we saw in it" when, truth to tell,
we *saw* very little in it.

The absence of a structuralized picture. Dr. Erich Fromm has stated the
need for instruction not only in the reading of the newspaper but in our
"reading" of the radio and motion pictures. He writes:[17]

Another way of paralyzing the ability to think critically is the destruction of
any kind of structuralized picture of the world. Facts lose the specific quality
which they can have only as parts of a structuralized whole and retain merely
an abstract, quantitative meaning; each fact is just *another* fact and all that
matters is whether we know more or less. Radio, moving pictures, and newspapers have a devastating effect on this score. The announcement of the bomb-
ing of a city and the death of hundreds of people is shamelessly followed or
interrupted by an advertisement for soap or wine. The same speaker with the
same suggestive, ingratiating voice, which he has just used to impress you with
the seriousness of the political situation impresses now upon his audience the
merits of a particular brand of soap which pays for the news broadcast. News-
reels let pictures of torpedoed ships be followed by those of a fashion show.
Newspapers tell us the trite thoughts or breakfast habits of a debutante with the
same space and seriousness they use for reporting events of scientific or artistic
importance. Because of all this we cease to be excited, our emotions and our
critical judgment become hampered, and eventually our attitude to what is
going on in the world assumes a quality of flatness and indifference. In the name
of "freedom" life loses all structure; it is composed of many little pieces, each
separate from the other and lacking any sense of a whole. The individual is left
alone with these pieces like a child with a puzzle; the difference, however, is
that the child knows what a house is and therefore can recognize the parts of
the house in the little pieces he is playing with, whereas the adult does not see
the meaning of the "whole," the pieces of which come into his hands. He is
bewildered and afraid and just goes on gazing at his little meaningless pieces.

A bridge is lacking. This statement adds another dimension to our
discussion of motion pictures and brings the radio into the focus of our
critical view. But it is about Fromm's reference to the absence of "structure" and our relative inability to create it with all the "little meaningless
pieces" we get from the movies, the radio, and the newspaper that I wish
especially to comment. Professor Blumer's concern over the lack or

[17] *Escape from Freedom* (New York: Rinehart & Company, Inc., Copyright 1941),
pp. 250-251. Dr. Fromm's "another" refers to his previous discussion of a widespread
skepticism about everything that is said or printed and a childish belief in anything we
are told "with authority." You will be richly rewarded by reading the entire book.

absence of a "bridge" relates to the same lack of structure, that is, the absence of pattern or relationship between the experiences had by people as members of a mass audience and as members of local cultures. Many of us find the same "bridge" lacking when we read the newspaper whose "news columns illustrate what is meant by a multitude of diverse unrelated facts." [18] We are unable to create the *Gestalt* which is required to give single news items their meaning, for it is clear that the newspaper's array of them does not constitute a *Gestalt*.

What the news is.   This circumstance suggests the need to say something about what "news" is. News and truth are not the same. Walter Lippmann tells us that the function of news is to "signalize an event"; the function of truth is to "bring to light the hidden facts, to set them in relation . . . and make a picture of reality on which men can act." [19] He has also remarked that "the news columns are common carriers" to which might be added the observation that they succeed only partly in classifying the cargo which their pages carry.[20]

In words almost identical with Lippmann's, John Dewey writes:

"News" signifies something which has just happened, and which is new just because it deviates from the old and regular. But its *meaning* depends upon relation to what it imports, to what its social consequences are. This import cannot be determined unless the news is placed in relation to the old, to what has happened and been integrated into the course of events.[21]

The obligation which the press may or may not have to tell what the news means is not now my concern. It does it, to some extent, on the editorial page where opinion on "what has happened" or "what ought to happen" is set forth within the *Gestalt* of the sociopolitical policy of the paper. But editorials are read by relatively few. It is the front page news which is read widely and avidly by "everybody." The fact is, whether we may like it or not, that we are left pretty much on our own to interpret the front page.[22]

Newspapers report events.   It is chiefly *events* which the newspaper re-

18 John Dewey, *Freedom and Culture* (New York: G. P. Putnam's Sons, 1939), p. 43.
19 *Public Opinion* (New York: Harcourt, Brace & Co., 1922), p. 358. See especially the chapter, "The Nature of News."
20 Walter Lippmann, *Liberty and the News* (New York: Harcourt, Brace & Co., 1920), p. 10. See also Robert E. Park, "News and the Power of the Press," *American Journal of Sociology*, XLVII (July, 1941).
21 *The Public and Its Problems*, pp. 180-181.
22 I use the term "front page" metaphorically to refer to the reporting of a great miscellany of events which may be found on many pages other than the front one, although it carries what the editor believes is the most startling and presumably the most significant news.

ports in the way of news, that is, aside from feature articles by its ace reporters who work on special assignments in the fields of foreign affairs, national legislation, labor-management relations, and the like. Much of this is a report of events but this form of reporting differs from the front page in that it is contextual and has a theme. It may, at times, contain an editorial element. But it is not only the sensational nature of front page events which constitutes the problem for the "average reader" but the fact that they "add up" to nothing but discrete events. They are then sensational "in the degree to which they make a strong impact in isolation from [their] relations to other events that give them significance." [23] This is Fromm's concern in the quotation given above. It is, as I see it, the major problem on which inquiry into the nature of the newspaper through social study ought to focus. Although this requires something more than a reform in the teaching of current events it is that aspect of social study which I should now like to discuss briefly.

Events without meaning are accidents.   Events are saved from being mere events only if students have the skill and understanding necessary to give meaning to them. Without meanings they are accidents and, if they are big enough accidents, they are catastrophes.[24] Since the newspaper does not undertake to indicate their meaning (except through editorials, and these bear only on those events which the editor has selected for comment), students ought to be taught the kind of background which will make the news about current events intelligible. Thus will they get *insight*, which is the ability to interpret the new in terms of the old.

Current events and social processes.   Current events are intelligible only if placed in the processes of which they are the current manifestation. Those processes also indicate the "historical current" of which they are a part. They are always a part of some institutional or organized form of social change. Indeed they are incidents in the life history of such associations. If this fact is not taken into account they are, like the facts we spoke of in Chapter XXII, part of a "glut of occurrences." The student must do what the historian does, which is place events in the context of one or more of the social processes.

Let us suppose that the event which has been reported is a strike. The newspaper may treat such an event as an interference with the reader's comfort. This interpretation (for it is an interpretation) does little more

23 Dewey, *Freedom and Culture*, p. 43.
24 Dewey, "Events and Meanings," *Characters and Events*, Vol. I (New York: Henry Holt & Co., Inc., 1929), pp. 126 and 129.

than catch his interest and perhaps arouse his animosity. This gives the strike a meaning by putting it in the context of a "work stoppage." But this gives it little, if any, continuity. On the contrary, it tends to divorce it from the process or processes of which it is one of the "moving parts." A strike is an instance of a value conflict in the power contest which goes on continuously between management and labor. In this setting it is necessary to know what the value is, what claims and counterclaims have been made, why compromise failed and a strike was called.

This interpretation takes us back to the discussion in Chapter XI in which we discussed sympathetic imagination and introspection. Without these, the strike can mean little and students can do little more than report the newspaper account of it.

Events in contexts. Suppose that the current event is the draining of a swamp. Students ought to know what such an event symbolizes: man's conquest over nature, the work of an administrative authority, or the location of a new industry in a place appropriate to its role in the industrial pattern of a community. Suppose that such a simple thing as the shipment of a cargo of lemons from Spain to England is reported. The English like lemon with their tea. But is that all? How was the exchange paid for? Did English importers have a balance in Spanish pesos or was it a matter of simple barter: so many boxes of lemons for so many boxes of machine tools from Birmingham? It is an international event and, by that token, it connotes a set of relationships far different from those of an intranational event. The Foreign Office in each country may be involved in some way. Or, to offer one more illustration, suppose that the foreign ministers of the NATO powers meet in London for a conference. What is the issue which has brought them together? What sides will each take or to what degree will they find themselves in agreement and on what issue or issues and against whom? Is it "old" or "new" business which brings them together or is it merely a gesture preliminary to another meeting? Through the inquiry which these questions raise the web of old and new is woven to make a meaning.

The place of current events in social study. What is the place of current events? Only in a class in history, or only on Friday, which is "current events day"? To these queries I respond only by saying that current events will have operational meaning only if they are related to something besides themselves and this may be done in many ways. They may be used as illustrations, as citations to contribute to an analogy which will help to contemporize past events, or to begin a unit or a day's work.

If these things seem to imply that "current events day" does not stand high in my preference scale, I offer no rebuttal.[25]

A unit on the newspaper. For a more organized approach to the study of the newspaper I take my cue from W. W. Waymack's article, "America's No. 1 Utility." [26] I suggest that a unit on the newspaper, titled by a caption something like "So you 'Seen It' in the Newspaper," be built on the basis of this article, supplemented by Robert Lasch's paper, "For a Free Press." [27] To these, as an indispensable resource, should be added *Your Newspaper: Blueprint for a Better Press,*[28] and Elmer Davis' *But We Were Born Free.*

Some of the themes which would provoke and direct inquiry might be such as the following:

1. What are the social consequences of the fact that the newspaper is an industry which has become consolidated into fewer and larger units?
2. Our press is "the best in the world"; so what?
3. "You can't believe what you read in the newspaper"—to what does "what" refer?
4. How can we test the objectivity of the news?—the problem of fact and preference or the "news" and the "editorial."
5. What role do the syndicated columnists play? Should not every large city daily have a "battle page" on which the differing views of the columnists are reported?
6. What should be the role of the government, if any, in "policing the news"?
7. With what ethical principles do the major editors agree? Who are those, if any, who would dissent from such a code?
8. What does the newspaper do besides inform? How many "publics" does it address and on what topics?—agriculture, labor-management, sports, fashions, diet, etc.

[25] Weekly journals such as *The Nation, New Republic, Time,* and *U. S. News and World Report* as well as such newspapers as *The New York Times,* the *New York Herald Tribune,* and the *St. Louis Post-Dispatch* are excellent sources of news. Leon Whipple, *How to Understand Current Events* (New York: Harper & Brothers, 1941) and "The Treatment of Current Events" in Henry Johnson, *Teaching of History,* provide excellent ideas for teaching current events. See also the Yearbooks of the National Council for the Social Studies. An excellent article by Howard R. Anderson, "Techniques in Teaching Current Events," *School Life,* November, 1946, is typical of the aids and suggestions to be found in teachers' journals.

[26] *The Saturday Review of Literature,* Nov. 23, 1946.

[27] *The Atlantic Monthly,* July, 1944.

[28] Edited by Leon Svirsky (New York: The Macmillan Co., 1947). This book is by nine Nieman Fellows at Harvard University, 1945-1946. It has no equal as a primer on the newspaper. To these resources should be added readings from the following: Walter Lippmann, *Public Opinion* (New York: Harcourt, Brace & Co., 1922), especially "Part VII, Newspapers"; *A Free and Responsible Press,* Report of the Commission on Freedom of the Press (Chicago: University of Chicago Press, 1947); and William E. Hocking, *Freedom of the Press, A Framework of Principle* (Chicago: University of Chicago Press, 1947). Such a unit would, ideally, fall in a senior year course in social problems or the perspective of the value conflict.

9. To what degree do the great daily newspapers make opinion? To what degree do they only reflect it?

10. How can you account for different news stories in different papers about the "same" event?

11. What is the function of cartoons? Study comparatively those of Burck, Herblock, Fitzpatrick, and include the cartoons by Fisher in *The Saturday Review* and Arno in the *New Yorker* (for reference see Henry Ladd Smith, "The Rise and Fall of the Political Cartoon," *Saturday Review*, May 29, 1954).

12. Do "news" as well as "editorials" "make opinion"? See Walter Lippmann, *Liberty and the News* (New York: Harcourt, Brace & Co., 1920).

13. What is the function of the "human interest story"? See Helen M. Hughes, *News and the Human Interest Story* (Chicago: University of Chicago Press, 1940).

14. Study the structure of headlines. What do they emphasize? Do they ever give false leads?

15. What is the logic or rule which guides the city editor in putting a given news item on a given page or in a particular place on a given page? (See Lippmann, *Public Opinion*, p. 354.)

16. Compare the news and editorials on a given day about a given event in a typical metropolitan daily with that of an issue of "the Negro press" such as the *Pittsburgh Courier* or the *Chicago Defender*. How do you account for the differences? Also examine some issues of the "foreign language press."

17. Plan a field trip to the editorial and press room of a city daily. Do not, however, mistake the mechanics of printing for the selection of the news. Use reporters and editors as resource persons.

18. Compare a city daily with a "country weekly." In what major respects do they differ and what do their differences tell you about the two communities?

These items are suggestive rather than inclusive. They seek to report a conception of a study of the press "not as a bit of supplementary fluff but as an important part of the total educational process." [29] The ideal test of a study of the newspaper would, as I see it, seek to establish the degree to which student opinion respecting the newspaper had changed. By this token, the unit would begin with a brief pretest of their opinion about it.

But opinion is not all. Any metropolitan daily would serve, admirably, as a textbook on many topics. This follows from the fact that it is, for millions of our people, the chief source of their reading. What I would ultimately be concerned with is the impact which study of the newspaper might have on a generation of young people. But this can be tested only by how the American "public" behaves thirty years hence, not the public which your class constitutes at the end of such a unit. But this limitation is not unique to the study of the newspaper; it is universal to all social

[29] Waymack, *The Saturday Review of Literature, op. cit.*

study.[30] I shall not now undertake to discuss the many "faces" which the newspaper presents, each of which suggests useful study. These include the reading and interpretation of charts and graphs, the interpretation of stock market reports, the role of the "funnies," the function of maps, the analysis of editorials by standard criteria of criticism (see below under propaganda analysis), and the problem of bias as it manifests itself in many ways.

A word in conclusion about this phase of social study respecting such an aid to instruction as *The American Observer* and other "newspapers" especially prepared and graded for use in the junior and senior high school. They have their place but do not mistake them or their place for the commercial newspaper. The two are almost as different as night and day. Hence, do not presume that the education which such "pedagogical newspapers" may make possible is the same as that which study of the commercial newspaper may. A study of the ways in which they differ would be appropriate.[31]

I have been discussing symbols of the community, what they are *as such*, and how they may be used to understand the community. The nature of propaganda, which is symbol manipulation par excellence, remains to be treated.

Propaganda is unreasonable persuasion.   I would think of propaganda as unreasonable persuasion.[32] As such, it is an attempt to influence opinion and conduct in such a manner that the person who adopts the opinion or conduct does so without himself making any definite search for reasons. Education, on the other hand, is an attempt to influence opinion and conduct, but in such a way that the person who thinks and acts is stimulated to seek to understand for himself why he does as he does (see Chapter IV).[33]

Why we are susceptible to propaganda.   Centering our interest for the

[30] This is the problem of the "transfer of learning" over a much longer period than most of us usually have in mind. An immediate index of the value of such a unit would lie in the increased reading of the newspaper by your students.

[31] Other excellent resource materials are found in such books as: Edgar Dale, *How to Read a Newspaper*; Lucy M. Salamon, *The Newspaper and the Historian*; Alfred M. Lee, *The Daily Newspaper in America*; Upton Sinclair, *The Brass Check, A Study of American Journalism*; Malcolm Willey, *The Country Newspaper*; and George Seldes, *The People Don't Know: The American Press and the Cold War*.

[32] An excellent reader, suitable to high school use, is Harold F. Graves and John S. Bowman, *Types of Persuasion* (New York: The Cordon Company, distributed by The Dryden Press, Inc., 1938).

[33] Propaganda employs both irrational and nonrational means. See Sidney Hook, *Education for Modern Man* (New York: Dial Press, 1946) for an illuminating discussion of the difference between these two means (pp. 121-124). See also Harold D. Lasswell, *Democracy Through Public Opinion* (Published by George Banta Publishing Co., Menasha, Wisc., 1941). This is a book which senior high school students can read with great profit.

time on propaganda as a form of persuasion, I ask what the social conditions are which make our people so susceptible to persuasion. The factors are many but among them I cite the following:

1. We are a population of 166,000,000 people who constitute, in many ways, a mass audience. With respect to many issues and concerns we are not so much disorganized as unorganized.
2. We are among the most literate people known to history but lack, to a very great extent, the ability to know the meaning of what we read or to reflect critically on it.
3. Almost one half of us live in cities and thus in a relatively impersonal social climate; we are, in many ways, an anonymous people.
4. We are a heterogeneous people of many interests and values which are in varying degrees of conflict. We thus lack a common body of customs and traditions such as is the possession of people in less advanced societies.
5. Our attachments are as varied as the groups which serve our many interests.
6. We are, to a considerable degree, "on the make" and thus often seek our individual advancement at the cost of the general welfare.
7. Our motives and interests are often highly unstable. We frequently change our "social direction." Our social equilibrium is dynamic and often off balance.

This list might be extended further but these observations are enough to identify some of the major preconditions for our being highly susceptible to the appeals of the propagandists for all sorts and kinds of causes. Our "state of mind" is further confused by the enormity of our problems, both individual and collective, and our inability to understand them or our lack of skill or unwillingness to act collectively respecting them (see Chapter VII). In such a cultural setting the propagandist has a field day. He has the "answers" and peddles them with expertness, finesse, and zeal. Furthermore, he has at his command a variety of mass media which no other society in the long sweep of history has ever provided.[34]

Traditional approach to propaganda analysis. I wish now to describe and offer a critique of the technique of propaganda analysis which has prevailed in the teaching of the social studies for about twenty years. This technique has used the following set of devices: (*a*) name calling, (*b*) glittering generalities, (*c*) transfer, (*d*) testimonial, (*e*) plain folks, (*f*) card stacking, and (*g*) band wagon. They have been so widely used that I forego citing illustrations but my critique will, I trust, indicate their limitations.[35]

[34] See John Dewey, "Education as Politics," *Characters and Events*, Vol. II, pp. 776-781, for a profound statement of the school's obligation respecting propaganda and unfounded opinion based on "unreal issues."
[35] *Propaganda Analysis*, Vol. I, No. 2, November, 1937. The author of this set of devices is Clyde Miller. This periodical has been discontinued. Miller's *How to Detect Propaganda* (New York: The Town Hall, Inc., 1930) is still available.

The analysis of propaganda is an exercise in seeking to establish the meaning of the written and spoken word.[36] Two chapters, X and XI, dealt with the problem of meaning. There, and in other chapters, we discussed at considerable length the nature and function of a *Gestalt*, or frame of reference. This is a field or context within which any object gets its meaning. That approach is, however, not even hinted at by the traditional and still prevailing approach to propaganda analysis. Its approach has been in terms of words and phrases and has ignored the document or speech *as a whole*. It has, hence, turned out to be what I would call primarily a hunt for "devilish words." Thus it is "devil-plottish" in its very nature. As such it is based on suspicion and tends, I believe, to engender it.

Propaganda in public affairs may be good or bad. It has, moreover, appeared to define, at least implicitly, all propaganda as bad. I should argue, as I did in Chapter IV, that all propaganda *is* bad as a method of teaching in the schools. But in the affairs of public life which put the use of propaganda in a totally different social frame of reference, it may be good or bad. This depends on the purpose to which it is put. In a time like ours in which problems are often too grave, profound, and complex for the "average citizen" to analyze on his own, there must be some short cuts to their definition, if not their solution. Propaganda is often his only resort.

The propagandist, good or bad, is one who speaks with authority. We observed in Chapter XII that we must sometimes depend on "the method of authority" for the fixing of our beliefs. Hence we must look to the propagandist for our cues. He is then not only necessary but he may be beneficent, depending on the moral quality and factuality of his propaganda. The only way in which many of us can get an opinion is to borrow it; the propagandist is an opinion broker.[37]

A critique of traditional propaganda analysis. But if we wish to put the propagandist's *meaning* to test, the devices listed above will not turn the trick. They focus on what are in substance "magic phrases": their order, their variation and, if spoken, the tone of voice. Their use seems to suppose that if words and phrases can be broken down, analyzed, classified, counted, and tabulated the "secret of secrets, hitherto locked with Merlin in his tree, will emerge, the formula for controlling mankind." [38] But

[36] Ernest Horne, *Methods of Instruction in the Social Studies* (New York: Charles Scribner's Sons, 1937), Chapter IV.

[37] Edward McChesney Sait, *Democracy* (New York: The Century Co., 1921), p. 72.

[38] William Garber, "Propaganda Analysis—To What Ends?" *American Journal of Sociology*, XLVIII (September, 1942), pp. 240-245.

understanding and meaning do not necessarily follow the breakdown of a statement and the examination of each part divorced from the tone and intent of the entire article or statement. Indeed confusion rather than clarity may follow.

It is entirely possible to take the speeches of an Adolf Hitler and a Franklin D. Roosevelt and, by the use of the devices listed, find each equally suspect. This is because these devices do not permit an approach to their speeches as wholes. The basis of genuine criticism is not through rhetorical devices and psychological tricks but rather by an analysis of the total context of the propaganda under investigation. The meaning of a statement is not known by its grammar and inner logic. What students need to learn is relationships, meanings, and the place of parts in a whole. Hitler and Roosevelt might have used many of the same "devices" but they would have used them to portray a different view of life, different approaches to mankind, and a different conception of human dignity.[39] It is one thing to ask, "What does the propagandist say?" It is quite another matter and more appropriate to ask "Why does he say it?" To which might be added, "What does he want me to do?" No writing or statement can be done or made without the use of rhetoric. The issue is, "What is the good or bad of it?" We must ask what the author or speaker's motive is, not only what means he uses.

Historical criticism applied to propaganda analysis. This brings me to suggest a mode of analysis of writings and speeches which I believe more valid than that currently in wide use by teachers of the social studies. It owes its origin to the canons of historical criticism which have been used for no one knows how many years, perhaps several hundred.[40] This analysis takes the form of inquiry into a series of questions, as follows:

1. Is the expression (writing or speech) founded on facts which can be checked, that is, are its facts true or false?
2. Who wrote it or said it and what was his interest in doing so? This implies, as noted above, a concern with what the writer or speaker wants me to do or believe.
3. What emotion does he seek to play on and what "trick words" does he employ to do so?

[39] Garber, *ibid.*, p. 244.
[40] There are many excellent sources on historical criticism among which are these: Louis Gottschalk, *Understanding History, A Primer on Historical Method* (New York: Alfred A. Knopf, Inc., 1950); Langlois and Seignobos, *Introduction to the Study of History*; Edward M. Hulme, *History and Its Neighbors* (New York: Oxford University Press, Inc., 1942) and *Theory and Practice in Historical Study: A Report of the Committee on Historiography* (New York: Social Science Research Council, Bulletin No. 54, 1946).

4. What evidence does he give me? On whose authority does he write or speak?

5. What generalizations does he make and are they supported by his facts?

6. With what organization is the writer or speaker connected, which is to ask, "Whose ax is he grinding?"

7. What idea does he deal with?

Such a series of inquiries is not unconcerned with words but it is concerned with them as means to bring about a given effect. Thus both method and content are identified. If we take account only of means we miss the intent and purpose of the propagandist. This is not to say that language is unimportant, or logic, or the structure of the argument. I remarked in another chapter that "all speech is a trigger for action." To that may now be added the observation that language, in its very origin, is an implement of action. One of the standard methods of the propagandist is the use of ambiguous language, for he wishes to be all things to all men. He thus practices what Dewey has called the "aboriginal logical sin."[41]

Implications for teaching. Given this critique, what are its implications for teaching the analysis of propaganda? I would suggest first that it be approached in the spirit of a game. This will, I feel certain, do much to create the climate in which suspicion and nihilistic skepticism will be discouraged.[42] Propaganda may, thereby, be defined as a quite normal phase of a society in which there is often a clash of opinion. As the teacher, you might say something like this: "We know what this fellow is up to, let's see how he goes at it. I think we can beat him at his own game," or "I believe this man has something worth reading; let's see how he 'works on our minds.' "

Other uses of the methods of historical criticism. But the criteria of criticism which I have noted may be used not only in the analysis of propagandistic writings and speeches. They are the tools for your teaching the analysis of editorials, other sober writings, advertising, and radio speeches. By their use you will practice the use of the secondary school equivalent of the canons of historical criticism. They involve every phase

---

[41] *How We Think* (New York: D. C. Heath & Company, 1933) p. 160. This book should be on your "must list" as a teacher of the social studies.

[42] The classic anecdote which reports the suspicious state of mind which tends to develop in a culture in crisis is the following. Two travelers in a European first-class railroad carriage fell into conversation. Mr. A asked Mr. B, "Where are you going?" To which Mr. B replied, "I am going to Vienna." Thereupon Mr. A said with some annoyance, "Now why don't you tell me the truth? You know that you are going to Vienna so that I'll think you are going to Cracow when you know very well that you're going to Vienna. Why do you lie to me?"

of what we have come to call critical thinking. Former chapters on the several perspectives on human affairs, as well as those dealing with the psychology of teaching-learning and the structure of the teaching-learning act, have given ample illustrations of critical thinking and need not be repeated here. The literature on the teaching of the social studies abounds in excellent references on critical thinking. *Skills in Social Studies*, which is the 24th Yearbook of the National Council for the Social Studies, is one of the best. Some space is devoted in all the Yearbooks of the Council to these skills. They are not, of course, to be used only in propaganda analysis or in the critical study of other forms of writing. They are, as I have emphasized many times, the tools of the method of inquiry and, as such, are part and parcel of social education. It is through their use that belief is fixed by the most reliable method which the human mind has devised.

A caution. Here I would counsel some caution. I wonder if we have not given too much attention to propaganda analysis and thus created the quality of suspicion-mindedness to which I have referred. There is some evidence that students often believe that "it's all propaganda." This is a sad state of mind in a democracy in which propaganda and counter-propaganda are, as I have implied, normal ways of dealing with public issues. We might well teach our students that, rather than try to stop propaganda, they understand how it may be countered and understood.[43]

The aims of the kinds of study discussed in this chapter are those to which I have referred many times: skill and understanding. I would stress, again, that they are mutually related, for the quality of your students' understanding is the function of their skill in analysis.

A special focus. But the materials dealt with here may be said to have a special focus. I would think of it as a focus on the quality of leadership which our society offers. The mass media are the means by which true and false leaders seek their following. Hence skill and understanding concerning the nature and role of mass media may, it is hoped, do much to develop a generation of citizens whom the demagogues cannot fool, as well as to develop a way of life which will produce fewer demagogues. In this observation we confront, again, the problem of good men and good institutions.[44]

[43] Henry S. Commager, "So You Think It's All Propaganda," *The Nation*, April 20, 1945.

[44] Lawrence K. Frank's article, "Dilemma of Leadership," *Society as the Patient*, pp. 308-338, is one of the most perceptive discussions of its kind with which I am acquainted.

CHAPTER XXVIII

The New Disciplines

HERE, AT THE end of many pages, I return to the interest with which I began, the democratic character. I did not view it then as a thing finished and complete, nor do I so view it now.

The direction of change.   I am concerned now, as I have been throughout this book, with process, emergence, becoming, and the direction of change. It is these rather than fixed and final ends which characterize human experience. The Great Oughts of the democratic faith give the democratic character the direction of its growth; the method of intelligence gives it the process by which its growth may be made continuous.

Four disciplines.   I seek now to examine the method of intelligence in the context of four disciplines: *imagination, precision, appreciation,* and *synthesis.*[1] They are not subjects, nor are they only new names for the old and traditional "disciplines." They are drawn from and are basic to all the bodies of knowledge. They are the constituents of the mind and spirit of democratic man, whose nurture is the grand task of a general education.

Just how they are woven together I do not quite know. I only know they are. But, since I cannot treat all of them at once I choose to treat them in the order just noted. This does not deny their altogetherness nor is it meant to affirm that there is a fixed place for any one of them. The logic

---

[1] These four disciplines are implicit in the method of inquiry. I owe their identification to Henry M. Wriston, lately retired as president of Brown University. See his paper, "Nature, Scope and Essential Elements of General Education," *General Education: Its Nature, Scope and Essential Elements, op. cit.,* pp. 1-16. I treat the disciplines in a different order from President Wriston. See a discussion of three disciplines basic to general education in Robert Redfield, *The Redfield Lectures* (Pasadena: The Fund for Adult Education, 1955). Redfield identifies the disciplines of exploration, conversation, and creation.

458

of the ordering which I have given them will, I trust, be implicit in my discussion.

The aims of general education are long-term aims. Hence, what I shall say concerns the image which I hold, not only for this generation of youth but of tomorrow's and tomorrow's and tomorrow's. Nor shall I undertake to deal with that image in terms of fixity or permanence. Rather I shall deal with it in terms of the changing permanence implicit in the Great Oughts of the democratic faith and the method of inquiry by which belief in them may be fixed by the warrant of reason.

The discipline of imagination. I choose first to discuss the discipline of imagination whose other name is the discipline of hypothesis. It finds its dynamics in opinion. But this is not the opinion of egotism; it is the opinion of a mind with fresh and challenging ideas. Nor is it born only of ideas, but of ideas which play upon an abundance of factual knowledge. But it takes its facts not only for what they are but for what they might lead to. Its stuff is hence both fact and fancy.

It is in this sense that the discipline of imagination is also the discipline of hypothesis. In directing us to what might be, it is also the discipline of the tentative. Its symbol is *if*. It is pregnant not only with curiosity, challenge, and discontent but also with dissent. Its task is to *represent*; the task of precision, which follows it, is to *explain*.[2] It is the artistic phase of science.

In being artistic it constitutes both the aesthetic and the ethical phase of the method of inquiry which is the method of intelligence. It is aesthetic in that it is creative; it is ethical in that it sees, with the mind's eye, what might be, what is possible rather than only what now is. These dual virtues are implicit in Shelley's observation that "A man to be greatly good must imagine intensively and comprehensively." Thus imagination must be both free and disciplined. It is, in short, disciplined fantasy.

In being representative, it is "wholly innocent of ideas derived from praise and blame."[3] In that innocence lies its potency. It does not pre-judge what follows it. It is outside of good and evil. It is an expression of curiosity which will not be set at rest without evidence that its representations may lead to new knowledge. It is the child of doubt, the legitimate doubt which initiates all inquiry. Its function is to spur *suppose*. It is the negation of cocksureness. If it is excluded from its rightful place in the realm of knowledge and learning it tends, almost certainly, to

2 Herbert Read, *Education Through Art* (New York: Pantheon Books, Inc., 1945), p. 11.
3 John Dewey, *Art as Experience* (New York: Minton, Balch and Co., 1934), p. 349.

find expression in charlatanism, demagoguery, and in cheap and tawdry forms of art.[4]

We are, I feel, inclined to link imagination with the untrue rather than with what is not now but could be. It is thus suspect. But to suspect or fear it, as I have remarked earlier, is to suspect or fear thought itself. To stifle it is to stifle the creativity of man. To increase the range of it and to set it free is one of the grand purposes of education.

Imagination assigns the question mark to those sentences which, without it, would all speak in the indicative mood. Without it, precision could not assign the decimal point. Through it, new myths are born which in being myths are not untrue, but rather those things by which men live and whose endless pursuit gives direction and purpose to their living. It is this conception of the discipline of imagination of which we now stand in almost tragic need. The myths we need are the myths—or call them ideals if you prefer—which will spur this generation of youth and many generations after it to achieve the knowledge which we still do not have, the knowledge of the genuinely humane way in which human beings may live in dignity, security, and peace. The lack of it is the great source of our remediable trouble.[5] But neither this generation nor the next, nor many more to come, will imagine these new myths unless their power to suppose is born of comprehensive knowledge and a great faith in the potentials of human nature.

I would especially emphasize the fact that the discipline of imagination is not born of sheer unreality. It is born, as I have sought to indicate, of a compound of reality and unreality out of which a still more magnificent reality may come. But whether the "new reality" will be magnificent or mean cannot be prejudged. There is no way of knowing what particular kind of knowledge is "divertible to destruction [and there is] no classifying of knowledge into safe and unsafe."[6] The only way to decrease the destructive consequences and to further the advantageous ones is to teach youth in this generation, and all those which follow, to imagine how we may achieve a more humane knowledge. Such a "representation" will put the discipline of precision to work on the knowledge which we still lack.

In any case, the net of imagination and hypothesis must be cast wide. In being cast wide it must encompass not only what suits the preferences of a given generation but even that which may run counter to its pref-

[4] Hoyt Hudson, *Educating Liberally*, p. 61.
[5] John Dewey, "Philosophy's Future in Our Scientific Age," *Commentary*, October, 1949.
[6] Quoted by John Dewey, *ibid.*, p. 390.

erences. The discipline of imagination involves a great risk. But however great be the risk it carries, the risk which lies in our failure to imagine boldly and along new and untried lanes of thought is the greater. We must teach youth that "Out of this nettle, danger, . . . [they may] pluck this flower, safety."

All that we can be sure of is that, by the use of the discipline of imagination, change will come. For this reason, we ought to teach youth that the chief task of social study is to learn how change may be directed to man's greater goodness and wisdom.

The discipline of precision. The discipline of precision is the hallmark of science. Its task is to forge principles through which, as Ortega y Gasset has expressed it, ideas put truth in checkmate. If youth is to bring to reality that upon which its imagination plays, it must learn to accept the rules of the game imposed by the discipline of precision.

By the discipline of precision, inferences, which are the "great and unavoidable business of life," are drawn according to rules, not according to whims. Through those rules we move from the "if" of imagination to the "then" of knowledge. Through them also, we move from doubt to belief through inquiry, which is the handmaiden of the discipline of precision. Such belief is more than information; it is knowledge. It is the only reliable means of emancipation from chance and fatality.

By the discipline of precision an untidy and chaotic world can be ordered or, paradoxically, one which is ordered on the basis of uninstructed common sense may be reordered on the basis of science. It tells us what is unavoidable and what is modifiable and thus what the limits of both thought and action are. But these limits are not fixed, for the discipline of precision gives us not only new and more reliable knowledge but new and more reliable modes of action.

This discipline can be had at no bargain rates. Its basic operating principle is a search for truth, or objectivity, which presupposes integrity, competence, and humility. It requires a mind trained in the making of accurate and honest observation, a readiness to accept evidence though it run counter to what one would like to believe, it is suspicious of hearsay, willing to go wherever the evidence may lead rather than to the goals of selfish preference, it permits no confusion of fact with preference and employs logic only in the service of clarity in thought. It belongs to no one nation, race, or ethnic group. It harnesses imagination and puts it to work on the facts of reality. It calls for a quality of courage which is unique in the annals of man. No tradition, belief, or practice is excused from the rigors of its method of inquiry.

But I would stress, particularly, the attribute of humility. It requires, in the words of Thomas Huxley, that we "sit down before a fact as a little child, be prepared to give up every preconceived notion, follow humbly wherever and to whatever abysses nature leads, or you shall learn nothing." It is in this sense that the discipline of precision is selfless. The more widely it and its findings are shared and practiced, the greater its achievements. Unless its method and findings are made public they degenerate and die.

The discipline of appreciation. The discipline of appreciation is the means by which youth may lay hold on the Great Oughts. It nurtures all affective learning. Through it, as Edward A. Ross expressed it, is fixed "the generous purpose in the heart." It is the aesthetic arm of education. It is that on which consciousness and ultimately intelligence and knowledge are based. It is, in Lin Yutang's words, "the stuff of human experience."

By the discipline of appreciation youth may have direct contact with sympathy. Reason touches it only indirectly. It is the essence of belief. It pertains to what one would "liefer do"—that is, which he would love to do and that which he believes.

By this discipline comes that of imagination with which inquiry begins and appreciation is the first fruit of it. It is kin to respect. It is being alive to life in all its forms. It is the opposite of indifference. Its expresion is manifold: holding dear, respecting, loving, being responsible, and caring.

I sometimes feel that it is the discipline of which we are apt to be most afraid. Without it, teaching can only be clever, never grand or warm. Without it, learning is uninspired. Without it, there is no profundity. Those who are not schooled in it cannot enjoy or practice sympathetic imagination, which is the means by which we may enter into the experience of others. It is the emotional discipline which fires the imagination and induces the wonder that may lead to true wisdom. It is the indispensable attribute of those who would become leaders. It is the mark of the excellence of the human spirit. It engenders respect without which facts cannot become values.

The discipline of synthesis. Finally there is the discipline of synthesis. It is final in the sense that through it loving and thinking are expressed in the wholeness of self and in good and wise action.

The function of the discipline of synthesis is to perpetuate the type and, wherever possible, to educate beyond the type. These become the true leaders. It is they who achieve success which does not cost another's failure. It is they who constitute the "growth-point of human experience," who, in leading, give back to their fellows more than their debt.[7] The danger, withal, is this: can such select men become efficient without being dangerous and will their greater knowledge insure that they will be trustworthy?

Through this discipline comes discrimination among beliefs. Through it, education persists because interests persist, even to the extent of "learning alone." It reports itself in self-control and in the will, the skill, the knowledge, and the courage to resist the attrition of everyday experience. It engenders faith in the self.

It allows for the mobility of mind and spirit, not for the fixed man for fixed duties of Whitehead's description "who, in older societies was such a godsend, [but who] in the future will be a public danger." [8] It reports itself in a scale of values whose *value*, as well as whose *price*, is known. It produces human beings who know that man not only makes but that he also *believes*. The fullness of its expression is the crown of a truly general education. Its operational presence affirms the wisdom of Emerson's observation that "the only entrance so to know is so to be."

In the measure that your teaching contributes to the shaping of character by these disciplines, your students will, like the great ones of the earth, act out their dreams instead of merely dream of their action. But to do so, they must believe quite as much in longings as in facts. Only then they become

. . . strong in will
To strive, to seek, to find, and not to yield.

[7] C. Delisle Burns, *Modern Civilization on Trial* (New York: The Macmillan Co., 1931), p. 271.

[8] *Science and the Modern World* (Mentor Books, 1954), p. 196.

INDEX OF NAMES

INDEX OF SUBJECTS

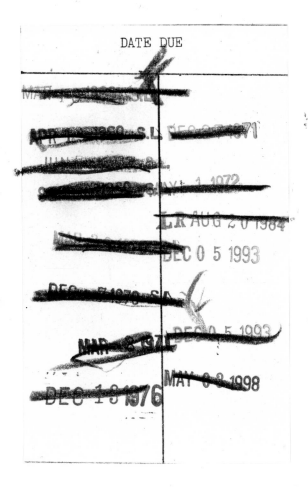